HOFFMANN'S MODERN MAGIC

HOFFMANN'S MODERN MAGIC

by
PROFESSOR HOFFMANN
[Angelo John Lewis]

With a New Introduction by
CHARLES REYNOLDS

Dover Publications, Inc., New York

Published in Canada by General Publishing
Company, Ltd., 30 Lesmill Road, Don Mills,
Toronto, Ontario.
Published in the United Kingdom by Constable and Company, Ltd., 10 Orange Street,
London WC2H 7EG.

This Dover edition, first published in 1978,
is an unabridged republication of the work first
published in its American edition by George
Routledge and Sons, Limited, New York (no
date) under the title *Modern Magic: A Practical Treatise on the Art of Conjuring*. A new
introduction by Charles Reynolds has been prepared especially for this edition.

International Standard Book Number:
0-486-23623-4
Library of Congress Catalog Card Number:
77-99247

Manufactured in the United States of America
Dover Publications, Inc.
180 Varick Street
New York, N.Y. 10014

INTRODUCTION

EVEN after the hundredth anniversary of its first publication in 1876, Professor Hoffmann's classic *Modern Magic* remains a cornerstone of the conjurer's art. Admittedly, some of the trappings of the magician have changed quite a bit since Hoffmann wrote his Victorian magic textbook (though some critics might feel they have not changed enough), and a few methods have become virtually obsolete; but many of the great magical *effects* predate the publication of this textbook by hundreds or, in some cases, even thousands of years. Professor Hoffmann's instructions on how to perform those classics are as valid for the performer of today as they were for the aspiring magician of a century ago. *Populus vult decipi: decipiatur* is the Latin inscription on the original title page of *Modern Magic* and today, as in the time of Professor Hoffmann, the public gives ample evidence of its willingness to be deceived entertainingly, and magicians of their willingness to deceive harmlessly.

Professor Louis Hoffmann, whom Houdini described as "the Brightest Star in the Firmament of Magical Literature," wrote nearly all of his dozens of books and scores of magazine articles under a pseudonym. His real name was Angelo John Lewis and he was, by profession, a barrister. Angelo Lewis was born in London on July 23, 1839, and first became interested in magic at the age of ten, when he witnessed the performance of Professor James Taylor. (It was the custom of magicians in those days to refer to themselves as "Professor," just as some years later, in the era of vaudeville and the music halls, many magicians prefaced their name with the appelation "The Great.") While a schoolboy, Lewis learned some half-dozen tricks which he occasionally performed for his friends. He graduated at Wadham College, Oxford, with degrees of Bachelor and Master of Arts, and went on to study law. It was during his undergraduate days at Oxford that Lewis saw performances by John Henry Anderson, the Wizard of the North, who was the most famous magician of that time, and by several lesser luminaries of the conjuring world as well. During his university days, he was too engrossed in his studies to pursue the performance of magic, and he even dropped the practice of the few tricks he had mastered.

After his graduation, Lewis practiced law until 1876, when a rekindling of interest in magic and the allied arts, along with the success of his part-time journalistic work, led him into what eventually became a career as a full-time writer. In an interview in an early volume of *Sphinx* (at that time the major magazine for magicians), Professor Hoffmann said: "My interest in the subject was revived in the early sixties by seeing a very clever performance by a street conjuror. I began to collect books and apparatus and then to give amateur performances in a small way. Seeing it announced in the newspapers that Messrs. Routledge were bringing out a new series of their *Boy's Magazine*, I wrote them offering to contribute a few articles on conjuring." The publisher's acceptance of that modest offer was to have a profound effect on the course of the magician's art.

It was proposed that Lewis undertake an extended series of articles with the idea of eventually publishing them in collected form. Lewis agreed to do so for a fee of £100 (about $500), most of which he spent on research and on acquiring the magical apparatus that he would write about. At this time Lewis was still a successful barrister with magic as his hobby, and this arrangement, which included none of the royalties that would go to the author of any book today, seemed a fair one. If Lewis had received royalties from the many editions that appeared during the remaining years of his life, his old age might have been a more comfortable one. The diagrams alone cost £320 (about $1,600), or more than three times as much as Lewis received for the writing. In those days, before the invention of photographic halftones, illustration was very expensive, the diagrams being first drawn and then engraved by hand.

Hoffmann's articles ran through some five volumes of the magazine and were subsequently published in book form under the title *Modern Magic* in 1876. Angelo Lewis decided to use the pen name of Professor Hoffmann, because he thought it inadvisable to mix magic with his legal work, thus suggesting to his fellow barristers that he was an expert in the art of trickery.

It is unlikely that Professor Hoffmann or his publishers had any inkling of the impact that the publication of *Modern Magic* would have. Many professional magicians were appalled at the revelations the book contained, for, until that time, the secrets of magic had been closely guarded and passed down over generations, usually by word of mouth, from one magician to another. The book was, by the standards of the time, an immediate success. The first edition of 2,000 copies was priced at seven shillings and sixpence (about $1.90), sold out in a mere six weeks, and was followed by at least seventeen authorized editions of the book, in addition to several unauthorized ones. When the first copies of the book arrived at Martinka and Company, New York City's major magic shop, they were sold out in a few days.

Why was *Modern Magic* such a sensation? Perhaps the key lies in an observation made by Hoffmann in the first chapter: "There is a vast difference between telling how a trick is done and teaching how to do it." *Modern Magic* was the first book in English to really explain how to do the classic effects of magic. H. Adrian Smith, magic historian, collector, and owner of the largest private

magic library in the world, once commented that magic literature, like Gaul, was divided into two parts—books published before *Modern Magic* and those published after.

The earliest books on magic in English (the first was Reginald
Scot's *Discoverie of Witchcraft* in 1584) were written to convince
their readers of the non-existence of witches and other beings
with so-called supernatural powers, and to explain how their
apparently supernatural feats were accomplished. Later books
described the performances of magicians of the day and explained
(with varying degrees of accuracy) how the feats were accomplished, without giving any useful instruction on how the
reader could accomplish the effects himself. *Modern Magic* was
the first real textbook on magic in English and only the second
such book in any language (the first being Robert-Houdin's *Les
Secrets de la Prestidigitation et de la Magie*, published in France
in 1868 and later translated into English by none other than
Professor Hoffmann).

To understand fully the impact of *Modern Magic* on the progress
of the conjurer's art over the past century, we have only to
observe the fundamental changes in magical performance since
the book's publication. In the last quarter of the nineteenth century, magic was still an intimate form of entertainment, being
performed primarily in drawing rooms and small halls. But
although the audience was still a small one, magic had just undergone a major revolution in its presentational style. Influenced by
the great French conjurer Jean Eugene Robert-Houdin, magicians
had thrown aside the pointed hats, flowing robes and cabalistic
trappings of the past and were appearing in the guise of ordinary
mortals who happened to perform miracles. Hoffmann was well
aware of this important change and approvingly commented on it.
He wrote: "The father of modern magic, as we know it, was undoubtedly Robert-Houdin. Up to his time the art of conjuring had
practically stood still for generations. He wore the evening dress
of ordinary life, surrendering apparently, all the advantages which

his immediate predecessors had derived from flowing drapery, and yet, under these more difficult conditions, he produced far more surprising effects than anyone previously attempted." Hoffmann confirmed this by teaching that the most effective magic was that performed with apparently ordinary objects. He believed that "the most successful magician of the future will be one who judiciously combines apparatus and non-apparatus tricks: such apparatus, however, to be of a simple and homely kind, not made admittedly for the purpose of the trick."

While it is obvious that Hoffmann understood this important truism, many of the magicians who were deeply influenced by his writings over the course of the next century forgot it, and the effectiveness of their performances suffered because of it. "The evening dress of ordinary life" in Victorian times was quite different from that of today, yet the image of the magician in inverness cape, top hat and tails still persists. Also, the apparatus "of a simple and homely kind" that would seem quite natural in a Victorian drawing room is, in the magic performance of today, so unusual that it gives the appearance of having been created only to produce the desired effect. Yet today there are still many magicians who present their effects on single-leg tables with black velvet drapes, often with gold fringe, a common piece of furniture in Professor Hoffmann's time but totally unknown—outside of magic performances—in the contemporary world. One can imagine that if the good professor were alive today to see the continued use of the props described in his great textbook, he would thoroughly disapprove.

But, granted that Hoffmann's views on performance style (and, unfortunately, his Victorian trappings) have been basic to the magic of the last century, many other things have changed since he wrote his book. In the introduction to *Modern Magic*, for instance, he describes "two or three appliances, which are of such constant use that they may be said to form the primary stock-in-trade of every conjuror. These are—a short wand, a specially

adapted table, and certain secret pockets in the magician's dress."
He comments that these "are so indispensable that we could hardly
complete the description of half-a-dozen tricks of any pretension
without a reference to one or other of them." It is interesting that
a century later all three of these primary "appliances" have become virtually obsolete, and are used today only in the most specialized circumstances. The wand is still used in the presentation of
some classic effects such as the Cups and Balls, but the tailcoat with
its secret *pochettes* and *profondes*, and the draped table with its
servante and elaborate traps, have been (or should be) relegated
to magic history. It is significant that today's most successful
young magician, Doug Henning, who has starred on Broadway and
in a number of highly successful television specials, has made as
radical a change in the image of the traditional magician in our
time as Robert-Houdin did in his. Instead of the traditional tails
and top hat, Henning has adopted a theatrical version of the dress
of contemporary youth, wearing blue-jeans style pants and skin-
tight T-shirts which offer convincing evidence that nothing he uses
in his amazing effects could be concealed on his body. Thus, when
Henning magically produces a huge owl or a large bowl of fire
(both effects from his repertoire), the amazed response of his audiences is much greater than if he were attired in a tailcoat or a
voluminous opera cape.

Some effects, using props common in the Victorian era but uncommon today, have also disappeared. It is interesting that the
most common image of a magician is a man pulling a live rabbit
from a top hat, yet this feat, almost never seen today, was effective
in the nineteenth century because the magician could borrow a top
hat from any gentleman in his audience. The fact that it was a
borrowed hat made the production of rabbits (and often other unlikely articles such as cannonballs, bird cages and lighted Chinese
lanterns) a truly amazing effect. Today few people, save magicians,
carry top hats, and a contemporary audience might suspect (perhaps correctly) that the hat containing the rabbit is just another
trick magician's prop.

There is another popular area of magic that has been almost completely transformed, in terms of technique, since Professor Hoffmann's time. This is the vast field of card magic. Unquestionably, more technical literature has been published on card magic in the last century than on any other area of magic; the number of books, large and small and in all languages, runs into the thousands.

In Hoffmann's day, the "Pass" *(Sauter la coupe)*, following the dictates of the great Robert-Houdin, was the most important sleight in all card magic. Today, partly because it is extremely difficult to do undetected and because so many effective substitutes (totally unknown in Hoffmann's time) have been invented, it no longer occupies such a central position in card technique. This is not to say that this classic sleight, in the hands of such contemporary card experts as Charles Miller or Derek Dingle, is not powerfully deceptive, but simply that it is no longer the backbone of card conjuring. Through the writings and inventive talents of such men as S. W. Erdnase (whose classic *Expert at the Card Table* was published in 1902), and such contemporary card geniuses as Dai Vernon and Ed Marlo, the entire technique of card magic has changed, with literally hundreds, perhaps thousands, of new sleights and subterfuges invented over the past hundred years. While the techniques have changed radically, however, many of the classic effects remain the same and are still in use today; a great number date back to before the time of Hoffmann to the great Viennese card magician Johann Nepomuk Hofzinser (1806-1875), and perhaps even before.

An interesting inclusion in Hoffmann's chapter on card sleights is instructions on how to throw a card. While not strictly a magic effect, the throwing of playing cards later became a feature in the performances of many major stage magicians like Howard Thurston and Maurice Raymond, who hurled cards from the theater stage to the highest reaches of the top balcony. One of America's cleverest card magicians of today, Ricky Jay, has revived the old feat of card throwing and includes it as a regular feature in his act, and has even written a book on the subject.

Since the publication of *Modern Magic*, two specialized types of magician that were minor figures on the magic stage a century ago have moved into the limelight. One is the illusionist, the magician who specializes in spectacular feats using people and large animals. This type of magician rose to prominence in the era of vaudeville and the music halls, when magicians were required to perform in large theaters where more intimate magic would not be effective. Such master magicians as Herrmann, Kellar, Thurston and Blackstone in America, Maskelyne and Devant in England, and Carter, Raymond, Nicola and Levante touring the globe brought large-scale stage illusions to enthralled theater audiences. The tradition of the grand illusionist remains with us today in the spectacular performances of Doug Henning, Harry Blackstone, Jr., and Siegfried and Roy. The other new breed of magician to rise to prominence has been the mentalist, or mindreader, with such names as Alexander, Annemann and Dunninger prominent. (It was Dunninger who first realized the effectiveness of presenting mental magic on radio and, later, on television.)

Both illusions and mentalism are represented in *Modern Magic*, with explanations of such early illusions as the Sphinx, the Cabinet of Proteus and the Aerial Suspension, as well as an explanation of feats of so-called clairvoyance and second sight. Nevertheless, it is doubtful that Professor Hoffmann realized what prominence they would achieve in the world of magic after the publication of his book. But above all, perhaps, mention should be made of his neglect of the escape, from handcuffs, ropes, boxes and other containers. Houdini, perhaps the best-known magician of all time, made a specialty of this now-classic trick—and the whole subject is never once mentioned in the Professor's treatise.

So a great deal has changed in magic since 1876; but in its exposition of many of the classic effects still being performed, *Modern Magic* continues to be of particular interest to the present-day magic performer. The Egg Bag, the Chinese Rings, the Rising Cards, the Ring on the Stick and, the oldest known magic effect, the Cups and Balls, are all explained in detail. To this last classic effect, described by Professor Hoffmann as "the groundwork of all legerdemain," an entire chapter is devoted. True, there have been some changes in Cups-and-Balls technique over the last century (the use of the *servante* has largely been replaced by the performer working from his coat and pants pockets), but basically the teaching in this chapter remains as solid a grounding in this great effect as one could find. And Hoffmann's strong beliefs on the fundamentals of magic performance are as valid today as when they were first penned: "The ideal entertainment, from the point of view of the spectator, will be one in which feats of dexterity, or supposed dexterity, are worked in conjunction with brilliant stage effects of a more spectacular kind." This prophetic realization describes with uncanny accuracy the approach of most of the major magicians since that time.

After the publication of *Modern Magic*, Professor Hoffmann produced dozens of books on magic and games and wrote scores of magazine articles. Among his most notable books were two sequels to *Modern Magic: More Magic* (1890) and *Later Magic* (1903). He also wrote a novel for juveniles entitled *Conjuror Dick* (1886). In 1885, Professor Hoffmann won a prize of $500 offered by the well-known Boston publication *Youth's Companion* for the best short story for boys. He also revised and edited several editions of *Hoyle's Book on Games*. While never a professional performer, Professor Hoffmann did give occasional magic performances, the proceeds always going to charity. Most of the effects in his repertoire were taken from the pages of *Modern Magic* and its sequels.

In 1903, Professor Hoffmann moved from London to Hastings to live in semi-retirement. There, presumably for financial reasons, he disposed of his original manuscripts and other magic belongings. In a rather pathetic letter to Dr. Samuel C. Hooker, a prominent New York amateur, in May 1913 he wrote: "My magical library was sold (for twenty-five pounds) before your letter came to hand,

and I have long since parted with my collection of apparatus, which at one time was considerable." A few years before his death, he wrote one last "sequel" to his masterpiece. It was titled *Latest Magic*, and was reportedly undertaken at the urging of Houdini. The book, badly written and with very little useful information, completely lacks the flowing, conversational style of his earlier books. Some magic historians believe it was, at least in part, written by someone else; in any case, it certainly did not add to his reputation as the greatest writer on magic of his time. Professor Hoffmann died at the age of eighty on December 23, 1919.

Even today, a century after its publication, *Modern Magic* holds untold riches for the magic enthusiast. Magic historian Henry Ridgely Evans, who once referred to it as "the Old Testament of the conjuring art," summed up well the feelings that many of us have about this charming Victorian textbook. He said, "I never tire of reading *Modern Magic*, though I know all the tricks by heart."

CHARLES REYNOLDS

New York City
November 15, 1977

MODERN MAGIC.

A PRACTICAL TREATISE

ON

THE ART OF CONJURING.

BY

PROFESSOR HOFFMANN.

With 318 Illustrations.

WITH AN APPENDIX CONTAINING EXPLANATIONS OF SOME OF THE BEST
KNOWN SPECIALTIES OF MESSRS. MASKELYNE AND COOKE.

Populus vult decipi: decipiatur.

AMERICAN EDITION.

GEORGE ROUTLEDGE AND SONS, LIMITED
NEW YORK: 9 LAFAYETTE PLACE
LONDON AND MANCHESTER

CONTENTS.

———◆———

CHAPTER 1.

INTRODUCTION.

CHAPTER II.

GENERAL PRINCIPLES OF SLEIGHT-OF-HAND APPLICABLE TO CARD TRICKS.

CHAPTER III.

CARD TRICKS WITH ORDINARY CARDS, AND NOT REQUIRING SLEIGHT-OF-HAND.

CHAPTER IV.

TRICKS INVOLVING SLEIGHT-OF-HAND, OR THE USE OF SPECIALLY PREPARED CARDS.

CHAPTER V.

CARD TRICKS REQUIRING SPECIAL APPARATUS.

CHAPTER VI.

PRINCIPLES OF SLEIGHT-OF-HAND MORE ESPECIALLY APPLICABLE TO COIN TRICKS.

CHAPTER VII.

TRICKS WITH COIN WITHOUT APPARATUS.

CHAPTER VIII.

TRICKS WITH COIN REQUIRING SPECIAL APPARATUS.

CHAPTER IX.

TRICKS WITH WATCHES.

CHAPTER X.

TRICKS WITH RINGS.

CHAPTER XI.

TRICKS WITH HANDKERCHIEFS.

CHAPTER XII.

TRICKS WITH DOMINOES AND DICE.

CHAPTER XVII.

STAGE TRICKS.

CHAPTER XVIII.

CONCLUDING OBSERVATIONS.

APPENDIX.

CHAPTER I.

CHAPTER II.
KEMPELEN.

CHAPTER III.

THEODIN.

CHAPTER IV.

AUTOMATA: PSYCHO.

CHAPTER V.

MARIONETTES.

CHAPTER VI.

CLAIRVOYANCE.

CHAPTER VII.

SPIRITUALISM.

CHAPTER VIII.

PARLOR MAGIC.

MODERN MAGIC.

CHAPTER I.

INTRODUCTION.

CONSIDERING the great antiquity and the un-fading popularity of the magic art, it seems at first sight a matter of wonder that its literature should be so extremely scanty. In England, in particular, is this the case. Until within the last few years it would have been difficult to name a single book worth reading upon this subject, the whole literature of the art consisting of single chapters in books written for the amusement of youth (which were chiefly remarkable for the unanimity with which each copied, without acknowledgment, from its predecessors), and handbooks sold at the entertainments of various public performers, who took care not to reveal therein any trick which they deemed worthy of performance by themselves. Upon a little consideration, however, the scarcity of treatises on "White Magic" is easily accounted for. The more important secrets of the art have been known but to few, and those few have jealously guarded them, knowing that the more closely they concealed the clue to their mysteries, the more would those mysteries be valued. Indeed, the more noted conjurors of fifty years ago strove to keep the secret of their best tricks not only from the outside world, but from their *confrères*. At the present day the secrets of the art are not so well

1

kept; and there is hardly a trick performed upon the stage which the amateur may not, at a sufficient expenditure of shillings or guineas, procure at the conjuring depôts. There being, therefore, no longer the same strict secresy, the literature of magic has improved a little, though it still leaves much to be desired. The general ambition of compilers seems to be to produce books containing nominally some fabulous number of tricks. In order to do this, they occupy two-thirds of their space with chemical and arithmetical recreations, and, as a necessary result, the portion devoted to conjuring tricks, properly so called, is treated so briefly and scantily as to be practically useless.

There is a vast difference between telling how a trick is done and teaching how to do it. The existing treatises, with few exceptions, do the former only. The intention of the present work is to do the latter also; to teach sleight-of-hand generally, as well as particular tricks; and to conduct the neophyte from the very A B C of the magic art gradually up to those marvels which are exhibited on the public stage. The student may rest assured that, if he will diligently follow the instructions here given, he will be able in due time, not merely to astonish his friends *extempore* with a borrowed coin or pack of cards, but to roll two rabbits into one, compel chosen cards to rise spontaneously from the pack, produce lighted lanterns from empty hats, and bowls of gold-fish from empty pocket-handkerchiefs; in a word, to execute all those wonders which he has hitherto deemed the exclusive property of the public performer. There are, of course, different degrees of natural aptitude. " *Non cuivis hominum contingit adire Corinthum.*" It is not every one that can be a Robert-Houdin or a Buatier, but, given the usual number of fingers and thumbs, fair intelligence, and a sufficiency of perseverance, any one who will may become at least a tolerable conjuror. Be it remembered, that we especially stipulate for *perseverance.* A wizard is not to be made in a day, and he who would attain excellence must be content to proceed as he would with music, drawing, or any other accomplishment —viz., begin at the beginning, and practise diligently until he attains the coveted dexterity. The student need not, however, wait the termination of the somewhat formidable course of study we have indicated, before he begins to astonish his friends; on the contrary, there are numerous tricks requiring very little manual dexterity, which are yet, if neatly performed, brilliant in effect. These simpler tricks, for which we shall give full instructions, will supply the beginner, even at the outset, with a fair programme, which he may from time to time enlarge as he feels able to undertake more elaborate illusions.

The first rule to be borne in mind by the aspirant is this: " *Never tell your audience beforehand what you are going to do.*" If you do so, you at once give their vigilance the direction which it is most necessary to avoid, and increase tenfold the chances of detection. We will give an illustration. There is a very good trick (which will be described at length hereafter) in which the performer, after borrowing a handkerchief, gives it to some one to hold. When it is returned, it proves to be torn into small pieces. It is again handed to the holder, who is instructed, in order to restore it, to rub it in a particular manner; but when again unfolded, it is found in a long strip. These effects are produced by successive adroit substitutions, and the whole magic of the trick consists in the concealment of the particular moment at which each substitution is effected. Now, if you were to announce to the audience beforehand that you were about to cause the handkerchief to appear in several pieces, or in a long strip, they would at once conjecture that the trick depended on an exchange, and their whole vigilance being directed to discover the moment of that exchange, you would find it all but impossible to perform the trick without detection. If, on the other hand, you merely roll up the handkerchief, and ask some one to hold it, the audience, not knowing what you are about to do, have no reason to suspect that you have handed him a substitute; and when the transformation is exhibited, the opportunity of detection will have already passed away.

It follows, as a practical consequence of this first rule, that *you should never perform the same trick twice on the same evening.* The best trick loses half its effect on repetition, but besides this, the audience know precisely what is coming, and have all their faculties directed to find out at what point you cheated their eyes on the first occasion. It is sometimes hard to resist an *encore,* but a little tact will get you out of the difficulty, especially if you have studied, as every conjuror should do, the variation and combination of tricks. There are a score of different ways of vanishing a given article, and as many of reproducing it; and either one of the first may be used in conjunction with either of the second. Thus, by varying either the beginning or the end, you make the trick to some extent a new one. The power of doing this readily is very useful, and among other advantages will enable you to meet an *encore* by performing some other trick having some element of similarity to that which you have just completed, but terminating in a different and therefore unexpected manner.

The student must cultivate from the outset the art of "talking," and especially the power of using his eyes and his tongue independently of the movement of his hands. To do this, it will be necessary to prepare beforehand not only what he intends to *do,* but what he intends to *say,* and to rehearse frequently and carefully even the simplest trick before attempting it in public. It is surprising how many little difficulties are discovered on first attempting to carry into effect even the clearest written directions; and nothing but practice will overcome these difficulties. The novice may be encouraged by assuming, as he safely may, that the most finished of popular performers was once as awkward as himself, and were he to attempt any unfamiliar feat, would probably be as awkward still.

Before proceeding to the practice of the magic art, it will be well to give a short description of two or three appliances, which are of such constant use that they may be said to form the primary stock-in-trade of every conjuror. These are—a short wand, a specially adapted table, and certain secret pockets in the magician's dress. There are numerous other appliances of very general use, which will be explained in due course, but those we have named are so indispensable that we could hardly complete the description of half-a-dozen tricks of any pretension without a reference to one or other of them. First in order comes

THE MAGIC WAND.

This is a light rod of twelve to fifteen inches in length, and about three-quarters of an inch in diameter. It may be of any material, and decorated in any manner which the fancy of the owner may dictate. To the uninitiated its use may appear a mere affectation, but such is by no means the case. Apart from the prestige derived from the traditional properties of the wand, and its use by the wizards of all ages, it affords a plausible pretext for many necessary movements, which would otherwise appear awkward and unnatural, and would thereby arouse the vigilance of the audience at possibly the most critical period of the trick. Thus, if the performer desires to hold anything concealed in his hand, by holding the wand in the same hand he is able to keep it closed without exciting suspicion. If it is necessary, as frequently happens, to turn his back upon the audience for an instant, the momentary turn to the table, in order to take up or lay down the wand, affords the required opportunity. We most strongly advise the would-be magician to cultivate from the outset the habitual use of the wand. Even where its employment is not absolutely necessary for the purpose of the trick, its use is in strict accordance with the character he professes to fill, and the dainty touch of the wand, for the supposed purpose of operating a magical transformation, assists materially in leading the audience to believe that such transformation did actually take place at that particular moment, instead of having been (as is really the case) secretly effected at an earlier period.

The next appliance to which we must draw the student's attention is

THE MAGICIAN'S TABLE.

There are plenty of good minor tricks which may be performed anywhere, and with little or no previous preparation, but as soon as the student has outgrown these humbler feats, and aspires to amuse his friends or the public with a pre-arranged *séance*, his first necessity will be a proper table. We do not now refer to the elaborate combination of traps, pistons, etc., which is used for stage performances. This will be duly described in its proper place. The table necessary for an average drawing-room exhibition differs from an ordinary table in two points only—its height, which should be six or eight inches greater than that of an ordinary table—and the addition of a hidden shelf or ledge at the back. Its form and dimensions are very much a matter of fancy and convenience. For most purposes nothing is better than a plain oblong deal table. It should have turned legs of some harder wood, stained and polished, and these, if it is desired to make the table portable, should be *screwed* into the four corners, so as to be readily taken off and put on again as may be required. In length the table may be three to four feet, and in breadth eighteen inches to two feet. Three feet by twenty inches is a very convenient size. At the back should be placed, about six inches below the level of the top of the table, a projecting shelf, six to eight inches in width, and extending nearly from end to end. This shelf, which is technically known as the *servante,* should be covered with thick woollen cloth, in order to deaden the sound of any object falling on it.

Some performers have a rim about half an inch high running along the outer edge of this shelf; while others, in place of the shelf, use a wooden tray, fixed in the same position, and one to two inches in depth. The manner of fixing the shelf is optional. In some tables it is made to slide in and out like a drawer; in others to fold up on hinges against the back of the table, or itself to form the back. This latter is the most convenient mode, as the opening made by the flap when let down gives access to the interior of the table, which forms a convenient receptacle for necessary articles. In this case, the upper part of the table is made box fashion; *i.e.,* is bottomed throughout with wood on a level with the hinges of the *servante,* giving an enclosed space under the whole extent of the table. Over the table should be thrown an ordinary cloth table-cover, of such a size as to hang down about ten or fifteen inches at the front and sides, but not more than an inch or so on the side away from the audience. To prevent its slipping, the cloth may be fastened on this side with a couple of drawing pins. Where traps are used, and the cloth has therefore to be cut, the hanging cloth is dispensed with, and the table is covered with cloth glued on the top, with a margin round it, after the fashion of a card-table, and this may be done, if preferred, even where the table is without mechanism. The adoption of this plan allows of the introduction of gold mouldings, or other ornamentation, on the front and sides. In our own opinion, unless there is some special reason to the contrary in the mechanical arrangements of the table, the plain hanging cover is preferable, as being least suggestive of apparatus or preparation. The precise height of the table is best determined by the stature of the performer. The *servante,* or hidden shelf, should be just so high from the ground as to be level with the knuckles of the performer as his arm hangs by his side; and the top of the table should, as already stated, be about six inches higher than this. It will be found that this height will enable the performer secretly to take up or lay down any article thereon without stooping or bending the arm, either of which movements would suggest to the spectators that his hand was occupied in some manner behind the table. One of the first tasks of the novice should be to acquire the power of readily picking up or laying down any article on the *servante,* without making any corresponding movement of the body, and especially without looking down at his hands. If the performer is uncertain as to the precise whereabouts of a given article, he must ascertain it by a quick glance as he approaches his table, and not after he has placed himself behind it. From this moment he must not again look down, as if once the audience suspect that he has a secret receptacle behind his table, half the magic of his tricks is thenceforth destroyed.

An oblong box, twelve or fourteen inches in length by three in depth, well padded with wadding, and placed on the *servante,* will be found very useful in getting rid of small articles, such as coin, oranges, etc., as such articles may be dropped into the box without causing any sound, and therefore without attracting attention.

In default of a table regularly made for the purpose, the amateur may with little difficulty adapt an ordinary table for use as a makeshift. A common library or kitchen table having a drawer on one side, and raised on four bricks or blocks of wood to the requisite height will answer the purpose very fairly. The table must be covered with a cloth; and should have the drawer pulled out about six inches (the drawer side being, of course, away from the audience) to form the *servante.* A still better extempore conjuring table may be manufactured in a few minutes with the aid of a good-sized folding bagatelle board. Place the shut-up board on a card or writing table (which should be six or eight inches shorter than the board), in such manner that there may be left behind it (on the side which is intended to be farthest from the audience), a strip of table six or seven inches in width. This will form the *servante.* Throw an ordinary cloth table-cover over the bagatelle board, letting it hang down a foot or eighteen inches in front, and tucking its opposite edge under the hinder edge of the board, whose weight will prevent it slipping. If the cloth is too large, it must be folded accordingly before placing it on the table. The table thus extemporized will be of a convenient height, and will answer very fairly for the purposes of an ordinary drawing-room performance.

The conjuror, however, may be called upon to give a sample of his art when neither regular nor extemporized table is available; and even where he is sufficiently provided in this respect, he will frequently have occasion to produce or get rid of a given article without retiring behind his table to do so. The wizards of a century ago met this necessity by wearing openly in front of them a sort of bag or apron, called in the parlance of the French conjurors, a *gibecière,* from its supposed resemblance to a game-bag. This was used not only to carry the cups and balls, and other minor paraphernalia of the art, but for the purpose of procuring, exchanging, or getting rid of any small article at the pleasure of the performer. In fact, this bag supplied the place of the *servante,* which was not then known. It is hardly necessary to observe that the *gibecière* has been long since disused, and a performer who should now appear in a pocketed apron would run much risk of being taken for a hairdresser. Although, however, the *gibecière* is not now, as of old, worn openly, the conjuror of the present day is provided with certain secret substitutes, to explain which it is necessary to say a few words as to

THE MAGICIAN'S DRESS.

It is not very many years since the orthodox dress of the conjuror was a long and flowing robe, embroidered more or less with hieroglyphic characters, and giving ample space for the concealment of any reasonable sized article—say from a warming-pan downwards. The very last specimen of such a garment, to the best of our belief, is, or was, worn by the magician attached to the Crystal Palace. We do not know whether he is compelled by the regulations of the establishment to wear such a robe; but if so, it ought to be liberally considered in his salary. The costume *de rigueur* of the magician of the present day is ordinary "evening dress." The effect of the feats performed is greatly heightened by the close fit and comparative scantiness of such a costume, which appears to allow no space for secret pockets or other place of concealment. In reality, however, the magician is provided with two special pockets, known as *profondes,* placed in the tails of his dress-coat. Each is from four to six inches in depth and seven in width, and the opening, which is across the inside of the coat-tail, slanting slightly downwards from the centre to the side, is, like the *servante,* so placed as to be just level with the knuckles of the performer, as his hand hangs by his side. He can thus, by the mere action of dropping either hand to his side, let fall any article instantly into the *profonde* on that side, or take anything from thence in like manner. The action is so natural, that it may be used under the very eyes of the audience, at very small risk of their observing it; and if the performer at the same moment slightly turns his other side to the spectators, he may be perfectly secure from detection. Some performers have also a couple of *pochettes* (small pockets) made in the trousers, one behind each thigh. These are generally used for purposes of production only, the *profondes* being still employed for getting rid of any article, which, indeed, is their primary purpose, for they were originally made too deep ('*profonde,*' whence their name) to get articles easily out of them. Many professors, in addition to the pockets above mentioned, have also a spacious pocket, opening perpendicularly, inside the breast of the coat, under each arm, for the purpose of what is called "loading," *i.e.,* bringing a rabbit, or other article, into a hat, etc. Other pockets may be added, as the fancy or invention of the performer may dictate; but the above are those generally used.

It will also be found a great convenience to have an elastic band, about an inch in width, stitched around the lower edge of the waistcoat on the inside. When the waistcoat is in wear, the band makes it press tightly round the waist, and any object of moderate size—a card, or pack of cards, a handkerchief, etc.—may be slipped under it without the least risk of falling. Used in conjunction with the pockets before described, this elastic waistband affords a means of instantaneously effecting "changes" of articles too large to be palmed with safety ; one hand dropping the genuine article into the *profonde* on that side, while the other draws the prepared substitute from under the waistband, a very slight turn of the body, towards the table or otherwise, sufficing to cover the movement.

With these few preliminary observations, we proceed to the practice of the art, commencing with the ever-popular class of illusions performed by the aid of playing cards

CHAPTER II.

General Principles of Sleight-of-Hand applicable to Card Tricks.

Among the various branches of the conjuror's art, none will better repay the labour of the student, whether artist or amateur, than the magic of cards. It has the especial advantage of being, in a great measure, independent of time and place. The materials for half its mysteries are procurable at five minutes' notice in every home circle; and, even in the case of those tricks for which specially prepared cards, etc., are requisite, the necessary appliances cost little, and are easily portable—two virtues not too common in magical apparatus. Further, the majority of card tricks are dependent mainly on personal address and dexterity, and, as such, will always be highly esteemed by connoisseurs in the art. Before very large audiences, indeed, the spectators being at a distance from the performer, much of the effect of a card trick is lost; which is probably the reason that, of late years, tricks of this class (with a few exceptions) have been rather neglected by professors; and that many feats which in the times of Conus and Comte were numbered among the sensations of the day, are now almost entirely forgotten. We shall endeavour in the following pages, after explaining the principles of sleight-of-hand applicable to cards, and giving instructions for some of the best of the more commonplace feats, to revive the recollection—and, we hope, the practice—of some of these brilliant performances.

The Cards.—The adept in sleight-of-hand should accustom himself to the use of every description of cards, as frequently none but the ordinary full-sized playing cards may be available. Where, however, the choice is open to him, he should use in the actual performance of tricks, cards of a smaller and thinner make. The common French cards answer the purpose very well. Among cards of English make, some of the best for the purpose are the small cards of the French pattern made by De La Rue & Co. for use in France, and those known as the "Tankerville" cards, both imported by Peck & Snyder, 124 Nassau Street, New York City, which are thin, well made, and of small size, but of the English pattern. In any case, it is well to use only the piquet pack of thirty-two cards (the twos, threes, fours, fives, and sixes being removed), the complete whist pack being inconveniently bulky for sleight-of-hand purposes.

To Make the Pass. (*Sauter la coupe*). — The effect of this sleight, which is the very backbone of card-conjuring, is to reverse the respective positions of the top and bottom halves of the pack, *i.e.*, to make those cards which at first formed the lowe half of the pack, come uppermost, when those cards which at first formed the upper half will of course be undermost. It is used by card-sharpers, immediately after the cards have been cut, to replace them in the position which they

Fig. 1.

occupied before the cut, and from this circumstance derives its French name. There are various methods of producing this effect, some requiring the use of both hands, some of one hand only. These we shall describe in due order.

First Method. (With both hands).—Hold the pack in the left hand, lengthways, with the face downwards, as if about to deal at any game. In this position the thumb will naturally be on the left side of the pack, and the four fingers on the other. Insert the top joint of the little finger immediately above those cards which are to be brought to the top of the pack (and which are now undermost), and let the remaining three fingers close naturally on the remaining cards, which are now uppermost. (*See* Fig. 1.) In this position you will find that the uppermost part of the pack is held between the little finger, which is underneath, and the remaining fingers, which are upon it. Now advance the right hand, and cover the pack with it. Grasp the lower portion of the pack lengthways between the second finger at the upper and the thumb at the lower end, the left thumb lying, slightly bent, across the pack. Press the inner edge of the lower packet into the fork of the left thumb, so that the two packets will be as shown in Fig. 2. Next draw away the upper packet, by slightly extending the fingers of the left hand, at the same time lifting up the *outer* edge of the lower packet, till the edges of the two packets just clear each other (*see* Fig. 3), when by the mere act of closing the left hand they will be brought together as at first, save that they will have changed places. Do this at first very slowly, aiming only at neatness and noiselessness of execution. At the outset the task will be found somewhat difficult, but gradually the hands will be found to acquire a sort of sympathetic

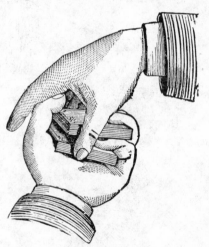

FIG. 2.

action; the different movements which we have above described will melt, as it were, into one, and the two packets will change places with such lightness and rapidity that they will seem to actually pass through each other. A slight momentary depression and elevation of the hands (apparently a mere careless gesture) in the act of making the pass will completely cover the transposition of the cards, which in the hands of an adept is invisible, even to the most watchful spectator.

The above is the most orthodox and the most perfect method of making the pass, and if the student be proficient in this, he need trouble himself very little about the remaining methods, which are inserted chiefly for the sake of completeness, being very inferior in all respects. Wherever in the course of this book the student is directed to make the pass, this first method will be considered to be referred to, unless otherwise specially expressed.

Before quitting the subject of this method, we should mention that it is sometimes necessary to cause the two halves of the pack to 'kiss,' *i.e.*, to bring them face to face. This is effected by turning the original upper packet face upwards in the act of bringing the transposed packets

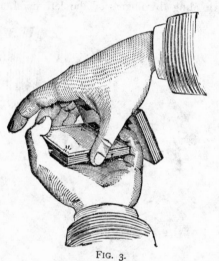

together. When the pass in the ordinary form is fairly mastered, this slight variation will occasion no additional difficulty.

In this, as in all other branches of prestidigitation, the student will find it of the greatest possible advantage to practise before a looking-glass. By this means, better than any other, he will be enabled to judge how far his movements succeed in deceiving the eyes of a spectator. One caution

FIG. 3.

may here be given with advantage : the student of legerdemain must learn to perform all necessary movements *without looking at his hands*, unless for some special reason he desires the spectators to look at them also. In every case, wherever the performer desires his audience to look, his own eyes must take that particular direction ; and wherever he desires his audience not to look, he himself must carefully abstain from looking. Let us suppose, for instance, that a person has drawn a card, and has replaced it in the middle of the pack. The performer desires to bring it to the top, for which purpose it is necessary to introduce the little finger above the card in question, and to make the pass, as above described. When the card is replaced in the pack, the eyes of the drawer are naturally directed towards it; and if the performer were himself to look downward at the cards, it would multiply tenfold the chances of detection. He should pause for a moment, and, looking full at the person who drew the card, ask, "You are certain that you will know that card again?" or make any similar observation. As he speaks, a natural impulse will draw the eyes of the audience to his own face, and he may then make the pass without the slight necessary movement attracting the least attention. It is hard to believe, until tested by actual experience, what apparently obvious movements may be executed under the very noses of an audience, if only their attention is diverted at the right moment by a dexterous use of the eye and voice of the operator.

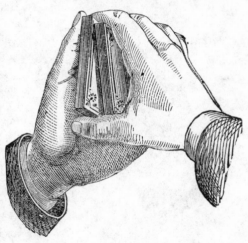

FIG. 4.

Second Method.— (With both hands).— Holding the pack in the left hand, as directed for the first method, grasp as before the lower portion of the pack lengthways between the second finger at the upper end and the thumb at the lower end; move the left thumb, which now takes no part in the operation, a little below the pack to be out of the way. Then slide the lower half of the pack a little to the left, and the upper half to the right till they just clear each other (*see* Fig. 4), when you will be enabled to place what was originally the upper half undermost, and *vice versâ*. This is the theory of the process, but in practice the necessary motions are not nearly so distinct. As you grow more and more expert, the necessary movement from right to left should become gradually smaller and smaller, until at last it is almost imperceptible. You must study to reduce this movement to the very minimum; and in order to do this, endeavour, after you have once seen clearly what it is you have to do, to keep the hands *together* as much as possible. Let the edge of the palm of the right hand rest gently, but firmly, on the first three fingers of the left hand, and let the contact thus made form a kind of hinge or fulcrum for the movement of the hands. When you become expert, you will find that the mere outward movement of the two hands upon this imaginary hinge (the cards being held lightly, and allowed to accommodate themselves to the movement) is sufficient to produce the effect.

We have above recommended you to keep the hands *together* as

much as possible; but there are circumstances under which an ostentatious *separation* of the hands is equally effective. Thus, holding the cards as above directed, you may make the pass by (apparently) merely cutting the cards, lifting, in truth, the under instead of the upper half, the latter making way (by a slight and momentary extension of the left hand) to allow it to pass. You may also, when holding the cards as just cut (*i.e.*, half the pack in each hand),

FIG. 5.

make the pass in the act of bringing them together. To do this you should hold the right hand packet in such manner that the thumb and second finger may project a full inch beyond the face of the cards. At the moment of bringing the two packets together (which should be done with a sidelong motion of the right hand from right to left) this thumb and finger grip the other packet, and slide it out towards the left shoulder, leaving what was originally the right hand packet in the left hand. If this is done neatly, the movement is so subtle that the keenest eye cannot detect that the two packets have changed hands. Having effected the change, you may take your own time as to placing the now uppermost packet on the other. The circumstances of each trick will indicate the cases in which it may be desirable to adopt either of these variations.

Third Method. (With both hands.)—This is very similar to the first method, but much less neat. Take the cards, as in the former case, face downwards in the left hand, but instead of the little finger, insert the second and third fingers immediately above those cards which are to be brought to the top of the pack, and draw the first and fourth fingers below the pack. (*See* Fig. 5.) In this position,

the lower half of the pack is held as in a forceps between the second and third and the first and fourth fingers. Now cover the pack with the right hand as directed for making the pass by the first method, but in this instance grasp therewith (between the first and second fingers at top and the thumb at bottom) the *upper* half of the pack. Raise this upper half slightly, to allow room for the movement of the lower half, and at the same moment slightly extend the fingers of the left hand. (*See* Fig. 6.) This will make the lower packet de-

FIG. 6.

scribe a quarter of a circle. As soon as it is clear of the upper packet, by reversing the motion (*i.e.,* closing the fingers of the left hand, and at the same time lowering the right hand), the two halves of the pack will be again brought together, but that half which was originally undermost will now be uppermost. The movement will be understood more clearly on an inspection of the diagrams *a* and *b* (Fig. 6), *a* representing an end view of the two portions of the pack in their original position, and *b* of the same in their transposed position, the original lower portion being in each case indicated by the darker shade.

Fourth Method. (With the left hand.)—This is almost the same as the method last described, save that the left hand only is used. The upper packet, instead of being held in the right hand, is in this case clipped between the ball of the left thumb and the point where the thumb joins the hand. In other respects the movement is the same.

Fifth Method. (With the left hand.) — Take the cards in the left hand as before. Insert the *third* finger above the cards which are to be brought to the top (and which now form the lower half of the pack), and close the remaining three fingers on the top of the pack. (*See* Fig. 1, but suppose the third finger inserted in place of the fourth.) Now extend the fingers, which will make the upper part of the pack describe a semicircle (*see* Fig. 7), and at the same moment press downward with the thumb the left top corner of the lower packet. This will tilt up the opposite end of the lower packet, and give room, as you again close the fingers, for the upper packet to pass into the lower place. (*See* Fig. 8.) To bring the original upper packet (*i.e.*, the one with the six of hearts at the bottom) from the position indicated in Fig. 7 to that which it occupies in Fig. 8, it is pressed slightly forward with the middle finger, and is thereby made to perform a semi-revolution, the third finger

FIG. 7.

acting as pivot. The packet is by this means turned over endways, *i.e.*, that end of the packet which was originally nearest to the per-former is now farthest from him, and *vice versâ*. The movement is by no means easy to describe, but if followed step by step *with the cards*, will be readily understood.

This method of making the pass has a peculiarity which renders it specially useful in certain cases. When the upper half of the pack describes a semicircle, as above mentioned, the bottom card of such half is in full view of the performer, though the spectators see only the backs of the cards. The per-former thus becomes ac-quainted, unknown to his audience, with that card which, after the pass, be-comes the bottom card of the pack; which know-ledge may occasionally be very useful. The move-ment of the cards in this mode of making the pass is very noticeable; but the circular sweep taken by the upper packet so confuses the eye, that the audience

FIG. 8.

must be extremely keen-sighted to detect the *effect* of the move-ment, which, if neatly executed, has the appearance of a mere flourish. A quick sweep of the arm from left to right as the pass is made will greatly assist in covering the transposition of the cards.

Some perform the pass last described without causing the upper packet to make the semi-revolution above mentioned. The first finger in this case does not participate in the operation, but is left extended beyond the upper end of the pack.

Sixth Method. (With either hand.)—Take the pack in either hand, as if you were about to stand it on end on the table, the backs of the cards being next to the palm. Insert the third finger between the two halves of the pack, and draw the second and fourth

FIG. 9.

fingers behind the pack. In this position, the uppermost half of the pack is held between the third finger and the second and fourth fingers. Clip the lower or front half of the pack at its two top corners between the thumb and the first finger. (*See* Fig. 9.) Now extend the second, third, and fourth fingers, which will carry with them the upper half of the pack. As soon as it is clear of the lower half, again close the fingers, thereby bringing the upper packet to the bottom. (*See* Fig. 10.) This mode of making the pass may be employed as you place the pack on the table, the move-

ment for that purpose serving to cover that by which the cards are transposed. If no table is at hand a quick movement of the hand and arm from right to left, at the moment when the pass is made, will be found to answer equally well.

Seventh Method. (With the right hand.)—This is a mere makeshift for the pass

FIG. 10.

proper, though its effect is the same. It is performed in picking up the cards from the table after they have been cut, and left, as is usual, in two heaps. The performer picks up, as in the ordinary course, the bottom half of the pack (which should properly be placed uppermost after the cut); but, instead of picking them up in the usual way, he picks them up with the second, third, and fourth fingers under, and the first finger above the cards. In placing them apparently upon the upper heap, he tilts up the right hand edge of that heap with the tip of the first finger, and with the remaining fingers slides the heap he already holds under-

FIG. 11.

neath it (*see* Fig. 11), so that the cards are again precisely as they were before the cut. This sham mode of making the pass is rarely used by conjurors, but is said to be frequently employed by card-sharpers.

To "Force" a Card.—By this phrase is signified the compelling a person to draw such card as you desire, though he is apparently allowed absolute freedom of choice. Your first step is to get sight of the bottom card, or, if you want to force a predetermined card, to get that card to the bottom. Having done this, take the pack in the left hand, and insert the little finger halfway down, in readiness to make the pass. Make the pass by the first method, but, before uniting the two halves of the pack in their new position, again slip the little finger of the left hand between them. (The two halves will now be united at the end which is towards the spectators, but divided by the little finger at the end nearest to yourself; and the original bottom card, which is the one you desire to force, is now the bottom of the top heap, resting on the little finger.) Using both hands, with the thumbs above and the fingers below the pack, spread out the cards fanwise from left to right, at the same time offering them to the person who is to draw, and requesting him to select a card. Keep the little finger of the left hand still on the face of the card to be chosen, or you may now use, if more convenient, the same finger of the right hand, both being underneath the cards. As the person advances his hand to draw, move the cards onward with the thumb, so that the particular card shall reach his fingers just at the moment when he closes them in order to draw; and, if you have followed these directions properly, it is ten to one that he will draw the card you wish. It may possibly be imagined that forcing is a very difficult matter, and requires an extraordinary degree of dexterity; but this is by no means the case. The principal thing against which a beginner must guard, is a tendency to offer the particular card a little *too soon*. When the cards are first presented to the drawer, the pack should be barely spread at all, and the card in question should be ten or fifteen cards off. The momentary hesitation of the drawer in making his choice will give time, by moving the cards quicker or slower, as may be necessary, to bring that card opposite his fingers at the right moment. Should the performer, however, miscalculate his time, and the card pass the drawer's fingers before the choice is made, he need not be embarrassed. Still keeping the little finger on the card, he should sharply close the cards, and making some remark as to the drawer being "difficult to please," or the like, again spread them as before, and offer them for the choice.

A moderate degree of practice will make the student so proficient that even a person acquainted with the secret of forcing will have to be very wide-awake in order not to take the desired card. You will, however, sometimes find a person, suspecting your design and wishing to embarrass you, suddenly jerk his hand away from the card which he was apparently about to take, and draw another from a different part of the pack. In the great majority of tricks this is of little consequence, inasmuch as there are numerous ways (which will be hereafter explained) of ascertaining what the drawn card was; out there are some illusions which depend upon the drawer taking a card similar in suit and number to one already prepared elsewhere for the purpose of the trick. In this case it is, of course, absolutely necessary that the card drawn should be the right one; and as even the most accomplished performer cannot always be certain of forcing a single card, another expedient must be used in order to ensure success. This is made absolutely certain by the use of what is called a " forcing pack "—*i.e.*, a pack in which all the cards are alike. Thus, if the knave of hearts is the card to be drawn, the whole pack will consist of knaves of hearts, and the drawer may therefore do his utmost to exercise a free choice, but the card which he draws will certainly be the knave of hearts, and no other. Where more than one card is to be drawn, as, for instance, in the well-known trick of the " rising cards," the pack may consist, instead of similar cards throughout, of groups of two or more particular cards. Thus, one third may be knaves of hearts, one third aces of diamonds, and the remaining third sevens of clubs—the cards of each kind being together. With the aid of such a pack, it will require very little skill to ensure one of each sort being drawn.

To make a " False Shuffle."—False shuffles are of two kinds, according to the object with which they are made. Those of the first kind are designed simply to keep in view a particular card or cards, the remainder of the pack being really shuffled. The second kind are designed to keep the pack in a pre-arranged order, and are shuffles in appearance only, all the cards being brought back to the same relative positions which they occupied before the shuffle.

First Method. (To keep a particular card or cards in view.)— Take the pack in the left hand. If the card to be kept in view is not already on the top of the pack, insert the little finger of the left hand immediately above that card, and make the pass in order to bring it to the top. Transfer this card to the right hand, and slide the remaining cards upon it, by little successive parcels of six or eight cards, one above the other. The known card will now be at the bottom. Return the pack to the left hand. Slide off three or four of the top cards into the right hand, and place the remaining cards, by parcels of six or eight as before, alternately above and below these top cards, till you come to the last card, which is the special one, and which you will place above or below as occasion may require. If there are three or four cards to be kept in view, it makes no difference in the mode of operation, save that you must treat those cards throughout as the single card, and keep them together accordingly.

Second Method. (To keep a particular card in view.)—Bring the card in question, as before directed, to the top of the pack. Take the pack in the left hand, holding it upright on its side, the edges of the cards resting on the palm, the four fingers (which should be slightly moistened) being at the back or top, and the thumb on the face of the pack. Now, with the thumb and middle finger of the right hand (*see* Fig. 12) lift out edgeways that portion of the cards which now forms the middle of the pack, and drop them by packets of five or six at a time upon *the face* of the cards remaining in the left hand, moving aside the left thumb to allow of their passage. The pressure of the fingers will always keep the top card in its place, however many of

the remaining cards you lift out with the right hand; and as you only shuffle on to the face of the pack, however often you repeat the process, this card will still remain at the top.

Third Method.— (To retain the whole pack in a pre-arranged order.)—Take the pack in the left hand, slide off with the left thumb five or

FIG. 12.

six of the top cards into the right hand, and place the remaining cards by parcels of five or six at a time (apparently) alternately above and below these first cards, as in the ordinary mode of shuffling. We say *apparently*, for in reality, although you go through the motion of placing every alternate packet *above* the cards in the right hand, you do not leave it there, but draw it back again with the thumb on to the top of the cards in the left hand, and then place it, by your next movement, *under* the cards in the right hand. The result is, that the cards in the left hand, instead of being placed alternately above and below the cards in the right hand, are really all placed below, and in precisely the same order which they occupied at first.

Some persons are in the habit of making the genuine shuffle, of which the above is an imitation, from the right hand to the left instead of from the left hand to the right, as above described. It may be stated, once for all, that wherever it is found more easy by the student to do with the right hand that which he is here instructed to do with the left, and *vice versâ*, there is not the least objection to his doing so, though the mode here indicated is that which, it is believed, will be found most convenient by the generality of persons.

Fourth Method. (To retain the whole pack in a pre-arranged order.)—Take the upper half of the pack in the right hand and the lower half in the left, the thumb in each case being above and the fingers below the cards. Place the two portions edge to edge, and work in the edges of the cards in the right hand half an inch or so between the edges of those in

FIG. 13.

the left, spreading the cards in the meanwhile to facilitate the introduction; but let the right hand cards project about an inch above the top edges of those in the left hand. (*See* Fig. 13.*) If you were to close up the cards in the relative positions they now occupy, they

---

* The cards of the right-hand packet are darkened in the figure for the better distinguishing of the two packets, though there would, of course, be no such difference of shade in the original.

would be really shuffled. To prevent their being so in fact, as well as in appearance, you clip lengthways between the thumb and second finger of the right hand the cards of the packet on that side, and bend them sharply downwards and outwards. This again disengages them from the other packet, on the top of which you quickly slide them, and press the whole square.

Fifth Method. (To retain the whole pack in a pre-arranged order.)—Make the pass so as to bring the lower half of the pack uppermost. Take the pack in the right hand, keeping the two portions of the pack separated by the little finger of that hand. Hold the cards face downwards a few inches from the table, and let fall, by five or six at a time, those cards which now form the lower half of the pack. You should so arrange that these cards form four little

heaps, falling in the order indicated by the accompanying figure (Fig. 14). Thus the bottom cards must fall at 1, the next lowest at 2, the next (comprising all that

FIG. 14.

remain of the lower packet) at 3, and the remaining cards (being the whole of the upper part) at 4. Now (with the left hand) quickly place packet 1 on packet 4, and (with the right hand) packet 2 on packet 1, and finally (with the left hand) packet 3 on the top of all, when the cards will occupy precisely the same relative positions as at first. The use of the two hands alternately, coupled with the rapidity of the performer, gives to his motions an appearance of carelessness which effectually baffles the spectators, and prevents their suspecting that the heaps are re-arranged in any determinate order.

Sixth Method.—This also retains the cards in their pre-arranged order, with this qualification, that an indefinite number are transferred from the top to the bottom of the pack, the effect being as if the cards had been cut without being shuffled. Holding the cards as directed for the last method, you drop them in four heaps as before, but beginning from the left, and proceeding straight onwards in regular succession. Now place the first heap on the fourth or right hand heap, and the second heap on the first heap, finally placing the third heap either above or below the pile thus made. Where it is necessary, after using this shuffle, to bring back the cards to the precise condition in which they were at first, this object may be effected by the use of the "bridge," hereafter described.

To "Palm" a Card.—Bring the card which you desire to palm (by the pass or otherwise) to the top of the pack. Hold the pack face downwards in the left hand, covering it lengthways with the right. With the left thumb push the top card till it projects about an inch beyond the edge of the pack. With the third finger of the left hand, which is now immediately below the card, press it upwards into the right hand, which should half close over it. You must not mind about bending the card, which will lie curled up against the inside of the hand. You may either let

FIG. 15.

the hand drop negligently to your side, or, still better, take the pack between the fingers and thumb of the same hand (*see* Fig. 15) and offer it to be shuffled. This will give you the opportunity, often very valuable, of seeing what the card in question is. When it becomes necessary to return the card to the pack, the mere motion of taking the pack in the right hand, whether from the left hand or from the table, will effect that object in the most natural manner. If the card retains a curve from its bent position in the hand, you may readily straighten it by ruffling the cards, as described in the next paragraph. If the performer is fortunate enough to have a large hand, a complete pack of cards may be palmed in this manner without difficulty.

To "Ruffle" the Cards.— Hold the pack tightly by its lower end between the fingers and thumb of the left hand, the thumb being above and the fingers below the cards. Cover the pack length-ways with the right hand, and clip the cards between the fingers and thumb as if you were about to make the pass by the first method. Keep the thumb unmoved, but draw the fingers smartly upwards, so as to bend the cards slightly. The springing of the cards as they escape one by one from the pressure of the fingers, and again straighten themselves, causes a peculiar sharp sound.

The ruffle may also be executed with one hand only. Take the pack between the middle finger at top and the thumb at bottom, the first finger resting in a bent position on the back of the cards. Press strongly with the thumb, so as to bend the two ends of the cards smartly outwards, allowing them one by one to escape from the middle finger, and simultaneously straighten the first finger, so as to clip the lower end of the cards between that finger and the thumb.

The ruffle is a mere flourish, but it is by no means without its value. We have indicated in the last paragraph one of its uses, viz., to straighten a card which has been palmed. Apart from this, there are many tricks in which it is desirable to mislead the spectator as to the particular movement by which, or the point of time at which, a particular effect was produced. This may be effected by a judicious use of the ruffle. Suppose, for instance, that the trick con-sists in magically bringing a given card to a particular position in the pack, and that the performer has already, without the knowledge of his audience, placed the card in the required position. If, before showing that it is so placed, he ostentatiously ruffles the cards, nine out of ten of the audience will be persuaded that this noisy movement is in some way the cause of the transposition, and will be proportionately the less likely to discover the true explanation of the feat.

To "Change" a Card. (*Filer la Carte.*)—Some of the most brilliant effects in card-conjuring are produced by the aid of this sleight, by means of which a card, fairly exhibited, is forthwith appa-rently transformed to a different one. There are several modes of producing this effect.

First Method.—Hold the pack in the left hand, as though about to deal the cards. Hold the card to be changed in the right hand, between the first and second fingers. (*See* Fig. 16.) The card into which it is to be changed should have been previously placed (secretly, of course) on the top of the pack. Push this card a little forward with the left thumb, so as to make it project about three-quarters of an inch beyond the remaining cards. Bring the hands close together for an instant, and in that instant place the card held in the right hand *under* the pack, (the second, third, and fourth fingers of the left hand opening to receive it, and the remaining finger making way for it as soon as it reaches the pack). Simultaneously with this movement, the thumb and first finger of the right hand must close upon the card projecting from the top of the pack, and, as the hands separate, carry with them that card in place of the one which the right hand originally held. A half turn of the body to the left or right, a quick down-ward sweep of the right hand, or any other rapid gesture, will assist in cover-ing the momentary bringing together of the hands.

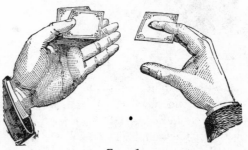

FIG. 16.

In some cases it is better that the right hand alone should move, the left hand being held stationary; in other cases the left hand (the one holding the pack) should make the move-ment, the hand holding the single card being motionless. It will be well to practise both these modes of making the change. The direction in which the performer turns, in order to place the card on his table, or the like, will indicate which is the best mode to use in any given case.

Second Method.—This is a very inferior mode of performing the change, but may be useful as a makeshift while the student is acquiring the greater dexterity required for the former method. Hold the pack upright towards the audience, with the card to be changed at the bottom (and therefore in full view), and the card for which it is to be changed at the top. The pack should be supported by both hands, and the two cards named should project about half an inch to the right beyond the remainder of the pack, the front or

bottom card being between the first and second fingers, and the back or top card between the thumb and first finger of the right hand. (*See* Fig. 17.) Call attention to the bottom card; make a downward sweep with the pack so as to turn the faces of the cards towards the ground, and at the same moment draw

FIG. 17.

off with the right hand the top card, which the audience will imagine to be the one they have just seen at the bottom.

Third Method.—Hold the card to be changed face downwards between the thumb and first and second fingers of the right hand, the thumb being above and the two fingers below the card. Hold the pack in the left hand, as if about to deal the cards, the card for which that first mentioned is to be changed being on the top. Bring the hands rapidly together, pushing the top card with the left thumb about an inch beyond the rest of the pack, and at the same moment place the card held in the right hand with a sliding motion upon the top of the pack. (*See* Fig. 18.) Both this card and the original top card (which is now second) will now be between the two fingers and thumb of the right hand. Press lightly on the top card with the left thumb to keep it back, and quickly draw away the right hand, pressing gently upwards with the two fingers on the face of the second card, which you will thereby draw away in place of the top card. If neatly done, the keenest eyesight cannot detect the substitution of the second card. Your only difficulty will be to find a colourable pretext for placing the card you hold on the top of the pack. This achieved, the rest is easy. The nature of the trick you are performing will frequently suggest a plausible excuse. A very successful plan is to boldly request the company to observe that you do *not* do that which you at the same moment actually do. "You will observe, ladies and gentlemen," you remark, "that I do not, even for one moment, replace the card in the pack, but simply," etc., etc. At the words "replace the card in the pack," the hands are brought together, and make the change. The action, suiting the words, is taken by the audience as an indicative gesture only, and thus the change is effected under their very eyes without exciting the least suspicion. In this mode of making the change, you should aim at being easy and natural, rather than very rapid. The main movement (that which brings the hands together) is undisguised, but at-

FIG. 18.

tributed to a fictitious motive; and the subsidiary movement of the fingers, which actually effects the change, is so slight as to be practically imperceptible.

Fourth Method. (With one hand only.)—Take the pack, face downwards, in the left hand, as if about to deal. Place the card to be changed on the top, and the card for which it is to be changed next below it. With the left thumb push forward the top card to the extent of half its width, letting it rest on the tips of the fingers. This will leave one-half of the second card exposed. By a reverse movement of the thumb, draw back this second card till its outer edge is just clear of the inner edge of the top card. Now press the second card downwards with the thumb so as to bring its opposite edge just above the level of the top card ; then push it back into its place, but this time above instead of below the top card.

Fifth Method. (To change a given card without the aid of the pack.)—A card having been chosen and returned to the pack, make the pass to bring it to the top, and palm it. Give the pack to be shuffled, and when it is returned pick out hap-hazard any card you please, and holding it up between the first finger and thumb cf the right hand (in which is the palmed card), announce boldly that that was the card chosen. You will, of course, be contradicted, whereupon you pretend to be disconcerted, and ask if the person is quite

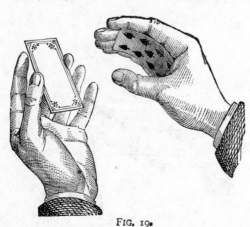

FIG. 19.

certain that that is not the card he drew, and so on. Meanwhile, you take the card, face downwards, between the first finger and thumb of the left hand, whence you immediately take it again in the right hand (*see* Fig. 19), taking it so as to bring the palmed card immediately over it, when the two will at a little distance appear to be only one card. You then say, "Well, if you seriously assure me that it is not the right card, I must endeavour to change it to the right one. May I ask what your card was?" When you are told, you continue, "It is a very simple process. I have merely to lay the card upon my hand, *so*, or if you prefer it, I will change it in your own hands. Oblige me by holding the card face downwards. I think you said your card was"— (say) "the ace of spades? Change!" As you say the words, "lay the card upon my hand," you place the two cards for an instant on the palm of the left hand (*see* Fig. 20), and draw off rapidly the top card, which is the right one, leaving the other palmed in the left hand, which then drops to your side. The audience do not suspect that the change is already effected, or that you have had more than one card in your hand throughout, and if you have performed the

trick neatly, will be utterly nonplussed when the trans- formation is revealed. You may, if you please, conclude by asking what card the audience imagine that they first saw, and, when told, remarking that they must have been mistaken in their impression, as that card has been in Mr. So-and-so's tail- pocket all the evening, as you prove by plunging your left hand (in which the card remains palmed) into the pocket, and producing it ac- cordingly.

FIG. 20.

Sixth Method. (To change several cards at once.)—This sleight is extremely useful in cases where you desire, without the knowledge of the audience, to

FIG. 21.

gain possession of a given number of se- lected cards. Palm in the left hand, face downwards, a num- ber of cards equal to that which you desire to abstract. Take the cards which you desire to gain posses- sion of between the second finger and thumb of the left

hand (after the manner of the single card in Fig. 19). Cover these cards lengthways with the right hand, and palm them in that hand (*see* Fig. 21), at the same moment seizing crossways, with the fingers and thumb of the same hand, the cards already palmed in the left hand (which to the eyes of the spectators will be the same they have just seen), and throw them face downwards on the table.*

To Get Sight of a Drawn Card.—The power of doing this is a *sine quâ non* for the conjuror. As already mentioned, even the most expert operator cannot be absolutely *certain* of "forcing" the card which he desires, and a novice is very likely indeed to find a wrong card occasionally drawn. It is therefore necessary to be provided with a remedy for such a *contretemps*. One mode of meeting the difficulty is to allow the card to be returned to the pack, make the pass to bring it to the top, and palm it, immediately giving the pack to be shuffled, and in so doing to get sight of the card, which remains in your own hand, and can in due time be reproduced in any way you please. (*See* Fig. 15.) For the present purpose, we assume that you do not desire to retain possession of the card, but merely wish to know its suit and value. These may be ascertained as follows :—

FIG. 22.

First Method. — Ask the drawer to return his card to the pack, which you offer for that purpose in the left hand, spreading the pack fanwise, in order that he may insert the card where he pleases. As he replaces the card, slip the little finger of the left hand *below* it, and close the fan. You now have the pack held in the palm of the left hand, but divided just below the chosen card by the little finger, the three remaining fingers being

* The last two very useful and effective sleights are inserted by special permission of the inventor, Professor Hellis, of No. 13, Silver Street, Kensington, one of the cleverest and most genial drawing-room performers of the day.

on the top. Offer the cards to be shuffled, or make any gesture you like with the pack, at the same moment slightly straightening the fingers. The effect of this movement will be to lift the upper packet, and thus open the pack bookwise, the opening being towards yourself, and the lowest card of the top heap, which is the card you desire to ascertain, being for the moment in full view. (*See* Fig. 22.)

Second Method.—Proceed as above, but instead of opening the pack to get sight of the card, bring it secretly to the bottom by the pass, and offer the cards to be shuffled, holding them at the upper end between the thumb and first and second finger of the right hand, and slanting from you at an angle of 45°, as in Fig. 15. As the faces are towards you, you have a full view of the card. Even if it should suggest itself to the audience that you are able to see the bottom card, as they are not aware that the chosen card is now in that position, there is nothing to excite their suspicion.

You may, by way of variety, instead of offering the cards to be shuffled, hold them in the right hand, and make the single-handed " ruffle " above described, at the same time turning their faces slightly towards yourself. You may effect the same object, even more simply, by the mere act of passing the pack from the one hand to the other, keeping the bottom card turned inwards as above.

To " SLIP " A CARD. — Hold the pack in the left hand, having first slightly moistened the fingers, which should rest upon the back of the cards. Open the pack bookwise, at an angle of about 45°, holding the upper

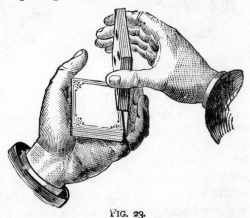

FIG. 23.

packet lengthways between the thumb and second finger of the right hand. Draw this upper packet smartly upwards to a distance of two or three inches from the lower packet. (*See* Fig. 23.) The top card of the upper packet, being held back by the pressure of the fingers upon it, will not move upwards with the rest of the packet; but immediately the remaining cards are clear, will fold itself down on the top of the lower packet. If the top card of the lower packet be examined before and after the slip, the card will appear to have changed, the fact being that the original top card becomes the second after the slip, the slipped card covering it.

To Draw Back a Card. (*Glisser la carte*).—The performer

FIG. 24.　　　　　　　　FIG. 25.

shows the bottom card, then dropping the pack into a horizontal position, face downwards, he draws out, with the thumb and second finger of the other hand, apparently that card, but really the next above it. This is effected as follows:—Hold the pack upright in the left hand between the first finger and thumb, the back of the cards towards the palm, and the thumb and finger about the middle of each side of the pack. Let the third finger, which should be previously moistened, rest on the face of the cards. (*See* Fig. 24.) You will find that in this position, by moving the third finger, you can draw back the bottom card about an inch below the remaining cards, and thereby leave exposed a corresponding portion of the next card. (*See* Fig. 25.) This is the whole mechanism of the operation. You must, of course, take care, after showing the bottom card, to turn the pack downward before you slide back that card in order to draw the next card in its place.

To "TURN OVER" THE PACK.—There are certain tricks (as, for instance, where you have undertaken to produce a given card at a particular number in the pack) for which it is necessary to deal a certain number of cards from the top, and then (without the spectator's knowledge) to continue the deal from the opposite end of the pack. As a necessary preliminary, you must "face" the cards—*i.e.*, bring the upper and lower portions face to face. This you have already been taught to do by means of the pass. Whichever way the pack is turned, it will now, of course, show backs only. Take the pack flat in the left hand, the fingers clipping it rather tightly, but without the aid of the thumb. Pass the thumb underneath, and with the ball of the thumb press the pack smartly upwards (*see* Fig. 26), when it will describe a semi-revolution on its longer axis, the lower face of the pack being thereby brought uppermost. If performed with the hand at rest, the movement is very perceptible; but if you at the same time make a semicircular sweep of the hand and arm from left to right, the smaller movement of the pack in the hand is much less likely to attract notice.

FIG. 26.

To SPRING THE CARDS FROM ONE HAND TO THE OTHER.— This is a mere flourish, and belongs rather to the art of the juggler than to that of the magician; but it is so frequently exhibited by conjurors that a work on magic would hardly be complete without some notice of it. The cards are held in the right hand, between the tips of the second and third finger at the top, and the thumb at the bottom. If the thumb and fingers are now brought slowly nearer together, so as to bend the cards slightly, they will one by one, in quick succession (beginning with the bottom card) spring away from the pack; and if the pressure be continued, the whole of the cards will spring away one after the other in this manner. If the left hand be held at ten or twelve inches distance from the right, with the fingers slightly bent, the released cards will be shot into the left hand, which, as the last cards reach it, should be rapidly brought palm to palm with the right, and square up the pack to repeat the process. By giving the body a quick half turn to the right as the cards are sprung from one hand to the other, you may make the hands (and with them the moving cards) describe an arc of about two feet, and so deceive the eye of the spectator into the belief that the hands are that distance apart, though in reality, as they both move together in the same direction, they retain throughout their original relative distance of ten or twelve inches.

To THROW A CARD.—This sleight also belongs rather to the ornamental than to the practical part of conjuring, but it is by no means

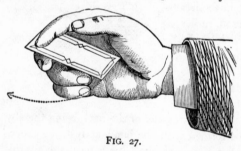

to be despised. It is a decided addition to a card trick for the performer to be able to say, "You observe, ladies and gentlemen, that the cards I use are all of a perfectly ordinary character," and by way of offering them for examination, to send half-a-dozen in succession flying into the remotest corners of the hall or theatre.

FIG. 27.

The card should be held lightly between the first and second fingers, in the position shown in Fig. 27. The hand should be curved inward toward the wrist, and then straightened with a sudden jerk, the arm being at the same time shot sharply forward. The effect of this movement is that the card, as it leaves the hand, revolves in the plane of its surface in the direction indicated by the dotted line, and during the rest of its course maintains such revolution. This spinning motion gives the flight of the card a strength and directness which it would seem impossible to impart to so small and light an object.

A skilled performer will propel cards in this way to a distance of sixty or eighty feet, each card travelling with the precision, and well-nigh the speed, of an arrow shot from a bow. The movement, though perfectly simple in theory, is by no means easy to acquire in practice. Indeed, we know no sleight which, as a rule, gives more trouble at the outset ; but, after a certain amount of labour with little or no result, the student suddenly acquires the desired knack, and thenceforward finds no difficulty in the matter.

THE BRIDGE. — The object of the bridge is to enable the performer, with ease and certainty, to cut or otherwise divide the pack at a given card. It is made as follows : Holding the cards in the left hand, with the thumb across the pack, the performer covers them for an instant with his right hand, as if about to make the pass. Grasping the pack between the thumb and second finger of this hand, he bends the whole of the cards slightly inwards over the first finger of the left hand, immediately afterwards bending the upper or outward portion of the pack backwards in the opposite direction. The effect of the double movement is that the two halves of the pack are bent in a double concave form, *thus* ⌣, though in a much less degree. If the cards be now cut, the concave portions, instead of being, as at first, back to back, will be face to face, *thus* ⌣, leaving in the centre of the pack an elliptical opening, of a maximum width of about an eighth of an inch. This slight hiatus in the middle will generally cause a person who is invited to cut to do so at that particular point, and will in any case enable the performer either to cut or to make the pass at that point with the greatest ease. The cases in which the bridge may be employed with advantage will be more particularly indicated when we come to practically apply the processes already described, but it has a special use which may be at once mentioned. It will be remembered that some of the false shuffles already described leave the cards as if cut, though they in other respects retain their pre-arranged order; and it therefore becomes necessary to again cut them at a particular point, in order to bring them back to their original condition. This point is ascertained by the use of the bridge. The cards are first bent in the manner above described; the false shuffle is then made, leaving the cards in effect cut; but by again cutting or making the pass at the bridge, they are once more precisely as at first.

We have endeavoured to be as explicit as possible in the foregoing description of the different sleight-of-hand processes, so that the reader may, by following our instructions closely, be able to teach himself, unassisted, to perform the various movements described. We have done our best to make our descriptions intelligible, and trust that we have fairly succeeded. We should, however, strongly advise any student who desires to make rapid progress to take, if possible, a few preliminary lessons under the personal guidance of a competent performer, professional or amateur. It is an old saying that an ounce of example is worth a pound of precept, and a reader who has once or twice seen the processes we have described practically illustrated by skilful hands, will not only avoid the difficulties which are sure to be at first found in even the clearest written instructions, but will escape the formation of bad habits, which it may take much time and trouble to eradicate. Should the novice seek such assistance, he must not expect to find that any one performer uses indifferently all the processes we have described. Every Professor has his own favourite methods of procedure, and, generally speaking, pours scorn and contumely upon all others; or, in the words of Byron (a little altered)—

> "Compounds for *sleights* he has a mind to,
> By damning those he's not inclined to."

The student who commences his labours without such assistance must make his own selection. In the "pass" we should recommend him to stick to the first method, the remaining passes being rather curious than useful. Among the false shuffles, the first, third, fifth, and sixth will be found the most effective. For the remaining processes he may be guided by his own taste, and the greater or less facility with which his fingers adapt themselves to one or the other of them.

The various sleights above described will cost the student some time and perseverance before they are fairly mastered, and until they are so it is hopeless to attempt any of the more brilliant feats. For his amusement in the meantime, we subjoin a few tricks for which sleight-of-hand is not necessary, but which, if performed with neatness and tact, will cause considerable astonishment to the uninitiated.

CHAPTER III.

Card Tricks with Ordinary Cards, and not requiring Sleight-of-Hand.

There is a large class of tricks which may be described as consisting of two elements—the discovery of a chosen card by the performer, and the revelation of his knowledge in a more or less striking manner. We propose to give, in the first place, three or four methods of discovering a given card, and then a similar variety of methods of concluding the trick. It must be remembered that for our present purpose we exclude all tricks for which any special dexterity is requisite. There will be little that is absolutely novel in this chapter, but it will be for the student to supply the want of freshness in his materials by the ingenuity of his combinations.

Simple Modes of Discovering a given Card. *First Method.* —Hold the pack face downwards in the left hand, having previously noticed the bottom card. Secretly draw down this card about three-quarters of an inch, and hold the part so drawn down between the thumb and fourth finger of the right hand, the palm of the right hand being above the cards. (*See* Fig. 28.) Now, with the tip of the first or second finger of the right hand, draw down the cards one by one about half an inch (beginning with the top card, and so on), inviting your audience to stop you at any card they may choose. When they do so, draw down all the cards, as far as you have gone, completely away from the remaining cards; but with them draw down at the same time the bottom card. This card, coalescing with the upper portion, will be, to the eyes of the spectators, that at which you were directed to stop. Holding the cards with their backs towards you, request them to observe what the card is. The pack may now be shuffled to any extent, but, being acquainted with the card, you can find or name it at pleasure.

The above may be employed as a means of "forcing," where it is essential to force a given card, and you are not sufficiently proficient to feel certain of effecting that object by the regular method. Thus, suppose that the card which you desire to force is the seven of diamonds, you place that card at the bottom of the pack, and proceed as above direct- ed. When the audience desire you to stop, you draw off the upper packet, and with it the seven of diamonds, which will thereby become the bot-

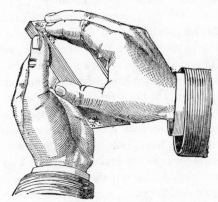

FIG. 28.

tom card of that packet. You request them to note the card, and at once hand the pack to be shuffled. This is a very simple and easy mode of forcing, but it is very generally known, and it would not, therefore, be safe to use it before a large or very acute audience.

Second Method.—Deal the cards into three packs, face upwards, and request a spectator to note a card, and remember in which heap it is. When you have dealt twenty-one cards, throw the rest aside, these not being employed in the trick. Ask in which heap the chosen card is, and place that heap between the other two, and deal again as before. Again ask the question, place the heap indicated in the middle, and deal again a third time. Note particularly the fourth or middle card of each heap, as one or other of those three cards will be the card thought of. Ask, for the last time, in which heap the chosen card now is, when you may be certain that it was the card which you noted as being the middle card of that heap.

This same effect will be produced with any number of cards, so long as such number is odd, and a multiple of three. The process and result will be the same, save that if fifteen cards are used each heap will consist of five cards, and the *third* card of each will be the middle one; if twenty-seven cards, each heap will consist of nine cards, and the *fifth* will be the selected one, and so on.

Third Method.—Take any number of the cards, and deal them face upwards upon the table, noting in your own mind the *first* card dealt. Ask any number of persons each to note a card, and to remember at what number it falls. When you have dealt all the cards you first took in your hand, take them up again, without disturbing their order, and turn them face downwards. In order to show that the trick is not performed by any arithmetical calculation (you should lay great stress upon this, the fact being precisely the reverse), invite the company to take any number they choose of the remaining cards (such number being unknown to you), and place them either above or below the cards you have dealt. Allow the cards to be cut (not shuffled) as many times as the audience please. You now, for the first time, ask each person what was the number of his card, and, on being informed, again deal the cards, turning them face upwards. When the original *first* card appears, count on (silently) from this as number one to the number mentioned, at which number the noted card will again appear. Should the whole of the cards be dealt out without reaching the required number, turn the cards over again, and continue from the top of the pack until that number is reached.

Having indicated how a card may be discovered, we proceed to describe various modes of disclosing the card thus ascertained.

First Method.—Get the card to the top of the pack. Give the pack to some person to hold. The cards should be face upwards, so that the chosen card will be undermost, with the thumb of the holder above and the fingers below the pack. The fingers should extend under the pack for about an inch, but the thumb above not more than half an inch. Request the person to nip the cards tightly, and as he does so give them a smart downward rap with your forefinger, which will knock all the cards out of his hand with the exception of the lowest card, which will be retained by the greater friction of the fingers, and will remain staring him in the face. This is a very old and simple finish, but it appears marvellous to those who witness it for the first time.

You may, if you prefer it, hold the cards yourself as above directed, and allow another person to strike them downwards.   It is well to moisten the fingers (not the thumb) slightly, as you thereby increase the hold on the chosen card.

Second Method.—Get the card to the top of the pack, and hold the pack lightly between the thumb and fingers of the right hand, the thumb being on the face, and the fingers (which should be previously slightly moistened) on the back of the cards. (*See* Fig. 29.)   Give a sharp downward jerk of the hand and arm, when, as

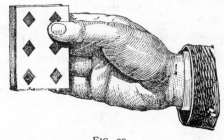

FIG. 29.

in the last case, all the cards will fall save the top card, which is retained by the greater friction of the moistened fingers.

Third Method.—Get the chosen card to the top, and hold the pack in the right hand, lengthways and face downwards, about two feet above the floor or table.   Push the top card a little off the pack sideways, so as to make it project throughout its whole length about an inch beyond the rest of the cards.   Now let fall the pack, when the resistance of the air will cause the top card to turn over in its fall, and to appear face upwards, all the other cards remaining face downwards.

Fourth Method.—Place the card in question and seven other indifferent cards in two rows, face downwards, on the table.   Keep in your own mind which is the chosen card, but do not let the audience see the face of either of the cards.   Ask the drawer if he is sure that he will know his card again.   He will, of course, answer " yes." Now ask either the same or another person to touch four of the eight cards upon the table.   Necessarily, the four which he touches will either include or not include the chosen card.   In either case you take up (whether he touches them or not) the four which do *not* include the chosen card, remarking, " I will return these to the pack." Invite the same person to touch two out of the four which remain. Again take up the two (whether touched or not touched) which do not include the chosen card, saying, " I return these also to the pack."

You have now only two cards left on the table, one of which is the chosen card. Invite one of the spectators to touch one of these cards. As before, whichever he touches, you pick up and return to the pack the non-chosen card, remarking, " We have now only one card left. You have all seen that I dealt out eight cards on the table, and that I have withdrawn seven, you yourselves choosing which I should withdraw. Now, sir, be kind enough to name the card you drew." The card having been named, you turn over the card left on the table, and show that it is the right one.

This trick is based upon a kind of *double entendre,* which, though apparently obvious, is rarely seen through by the audience if performed in a quick and lively manner. The secret lies in the performer interpreting the touching of the cards in two different senses, as may best suit his purpose. If the chosen card is not among the cards touched, he interprets the touching as meaning that the cards touched are rejected, and to be returned to the pack. If the card *is* among those touched, he interprets the touching in the opposite sense,—namely, that the cards touched are to be retained, and the others rejected. If he is lucky in the cards touched, it may happen that he is able to interpret the touching in the same sense throughout the trick, in which case there will be no clue whatever to the secret ; but even in the opposite case, where he is compelled to put aside first the cards touched and then the cards not touched, the difference generally passes unnoticed by the spectators, or, if noticed, is put down as a slip on the part of the performer, rather than as being, as it really is, the key to the trick.

Where the performer is proficient in sleight-of-hand, the above may be worked up into a really brilliant trick. Any indifferent card being drawn and returned, is brought to the top by the pass, palmed, and the pack shuffled. Eight cards are laid out, and the drawn card revealed as above.

Having described these few commencements and terminations, we will next proceed to the discussion of some complete tricks.

To make a Card vanish from the Pack, and be found in a Person's Pocket.—Slightly moisten the back of your left hand. Offer the pack to be shuffled. Place it face downwards on the table, and request one of the company to look at the top card. Request him to place the back of his left hand upon the cards, and press heavily upon it with his right. In order that he may the better comprehend your meaning, place your own hands as described (*see* Fig. 30), and request him to imitate you. When you remove your left hand, the back being moistened, the card will stick to it. Put your hands carelessly behind you, and with the right hand remove the card. All will crowd round to see the trick. Pretend to be very

particular that the person who places his hand on the card shall do so in precisely the right position. This will not only give you time, but draw all eyes to his hands. Meanwhile, watch your opportunity and slip the card into the tail pocket of one or other of the spectators. Now announce that you are about to order the top card, which all have seen, and which Mr. A. is holding down so exceedingly tight, to fly away from the pack and into the pocket of Mr. B., making the choice apparently hap-hazard. On examination

FIG. 30.

your commands will be found to have been fulfilled. It has a good effect, when practicable, to slip the card into the pocket of the same person who is pressing upon the pack.

To place the Four Kings in different parts of the Pack, and to bring them together by a Simple Cut.—Take the four kings (or any other four cards at pleasure), and exhibit them fan-wise (*see* Fig. 31), but secretly place behind the second one (the king of diamonds in the figure) two other court cards of any description, which, being thus hidden behind the king, will not be visible. The audience being satisfied that the four cards are really the four kings, and none other, fold them together, and place them at the top of the pack. Draw attention to the fact that you are about to distribute these four kings in different parts of the pack. Take up the top card, which, being really a king, you may exhibit without apparent intention, and place it at the bottom. Take the next card, which the spectators suppose to be also a king, and place it about half way down the pack, and the next, in like manner, a little higher. Take the fourth card, which, being actually a king, you may show carelessly, and replace it on the top of the pack. You have now really three kings at the top and one at the bottom, though the audience imagine that they have seen them distributed in different parts of the pack, and are proportionately surprised, when the cards are cut, to find that all the kings are again together.

It is best to use knaves or queens for the two extra cards, as being less distinguishable from the kings, should a spectator catch a chance glimpse of their faces.

There are other and better modes of bringing together four apparently separated cards by the aid of sleight-of-hand, which will be explained in due

FIG. 31.

course; but we have thought it well to give also this simpler method, as it is always an advantage to possess two different modes of performing the same feat.

THE FOUR KINGS BEING PLACED UNDER THE HAND OF ONE PERSON, AND THE FOUR SEVENS UNDER THE HAND OF ANOTHER, TO MAKE THEM CHANGE PLACES AT COMMAND.—Exhibit, fanwise, in one hand the four kings, and in the other the four eights. Behind the hindmost of the kings, and so as not to be noticeable by the audience, secretly place beforehand the four sevens. Hold the four eights in the other hand in such manner that the lower of the two centre pips of the foremost is concealed by the first and second fingers. The same pip on each of the other cards will be concealed by the card immediately before it, so that the four cards will to the spectators appear equally like the sevens. Place the pack face downwards on the table. Draw attention to the fact that you hold in one hand the four kings, and in the other the four sevens (really the disguised eights). Fold up the supposed sevens, and place them on the pack Fold up the kings, and place them on the top of the supposed sevens. As the real sevens were behind the last of the kings, they are now on the top, with the kings next, though the audience are persuaded that the kings are uppermost, and the sevens next following. Deal off, slowly and carefully, the four top cards, saying, "I take off these four *kings*," and lay them on the table, requesting one of the spectators to place his hand firmly upon them. Do the same with the next four cards (which are really the kings). Ask if the persons in charge of the cards are quite sure that they are still under their hands, and, upon receiving their assurance to that effect, command the cards they hold to change places, which they will be found to have done.

Four Packets of Cards having been Formed face downwards on the Table, to discover the Total Value of the Undermost Cards.—This trick must be performed with the piquet pack of thirty-two cards. Invite one of the spectators to privately select any four cards, and to place them, separately and face downwards, on the table; then, counting an ace as eleven, a court card as ten, and any other card according to the number of its pips, to place upon each of these four so many cards as, added to its value thus estimated, shall make fifteen. (It must be remembered that *value* is only to be taken into consideration as to the original four cards, those placed on them counting as one each, whatever they may happen to be.) You meanwhile retire. When the four heaps are complete, advance to the table, and observe how many cards are left over and above the four heaps. To this number mentally add thirty-two. The total will give you the aggregate value of the four lowest cards, calculated as above mentioned.

You should not let your audience perceive that you count the remaining cards, or they will readily conjecture that the trick depends on some arithmetical principle. You may say, " You will observe that I do not look even at one single card :" and, so saying, throw down the surplus cards with apparent carelessness upon the table, when they are sure to fall sufficiently scattered to enable you to count them without attracting observation.

To Name all the Cards in the Pack in Succession.— This is an old trick, but a very good one. To perform it, you must arrange the cards of a whist pack beforehand, according to a given formula, which forms a sort of *memoria technica*. There are several used, but all are similar in effect. The following is one of the simplest :—

> " Eight kings threatened to save
> Ninety-five ladies for one sick knave."

These words suggest, as you will readily see, eight, king, three, ten, two, seven, nine, five, queen, four, ace, six, knave. You must also have a determinate order for the suits, which should be red and black alternately, say, diamonds, clubs, hearts, spades. Sort the pack for convenience into the four suits, and then arrange the cards as follows : Take in your left hand, *face upwards*, the eight of diamonds, on this place the king of clubs, on this the three of hearts, then the ten of spades, then the two of diamonds, and so on, till the whole of the cards are exhausted. This arrangement must be made privately beforehand, and you must either make this the first of your series of tricks, or (which is better, as it negatives the idea of arrangement) have two packs of the same pattern, and secretly exchange the prepared pack, at a suitable opportunity, for that with which you have already been performing. Spread the cards (which may previously be cut any number of times), and offer them to a person to draw one. While he is looking at the card, glance quickly at the card next above that which he has drawn, which we will suppose is the five of diamonds. You will remember that in your *memoria technica* " five " is followed by " ladies " (queen). You know then that the next card, the one drawn, was a queen. You know also that clubs follow diamonds : *ergo*, the card drawn is the queen of clubs. Name it, and request the drawer to replace it. Ask some one again to cut the cards, and repeat the trick in the same form with another person, but this time pass all the cards which were above the card drawn, below the remainder of the pack. This is equivalent to cutting the pack at that particular card. After naming the card drawn, ask if the company would like to know any more. Name the cards next following the card already drawn, taking them one by one from the pack and laying them face upwards on the table, to show that you have named them correctly. After a little practice, it will cost you but a very slight effort of memory to name in succession all the cards in the pack.

THE CARDS BEING CUT, TO TELL WHETHER THE NUMBER CUT IS ODD OR EVEN.—This is another trick performed by the aid of the prepared pack last described, and has the advantage of being little known, even to those who are acquainted with other uses of the arranged pack. Notice whether the bottom card for the time being is red or black. Place the pack on the table, and invite any person to cut, announcing that you will tell by the weight of the cards cut whether the number is odd or even. Take the cut cards (*i.e.*, the cards which before the cut were at the top of the pack), and poising them carefully in your hand, as though testing their weight, glance slily at the bottom card. If it is of the same colour as the bottom card of the other or lowest portion, the cards cut are an even number ; if of a different colour, they are odd.

THE WHIST TRICK. TO DEAL YOURSELF ALL THE TRUMPS.— The cards being arranged as above mentioned, you may challenge any of the company to play a hand at whist with you. The cards are cut in the ordinary way (not shuffled). You yourself deal, when, of course, the turn-up card falls to you. On taking up the cards, it will be found that each person has all the cards of one suit, but your own suit being that of the turn-up card, is, of course, trumps ; and having the whole thirteen, you must necessarily win every trick.

The weak point of the feat is, that the cards being regularly sorted into the four suits, the audience can hardly help suspecting that the pack was pre-arranged beforehand. There is another and better mode of performing the trick, by which you still hold all the trumps, but the three remaining players have the ordinary mixed hands. This method, however, involves sleight-of-hand, and would therefore be out of place in the present chapter.

To allow a Person to think of a Card, and to make that Card appear at such Number in the Pack as Another Person shall Name.—Allow the pack to be shuffled and cut as freely as the company please. When they are fully satisfied that the cards are well mixed, offer the pack to any of the spectators, and request him to look over the cards, and think of any one, and to re-member the number at which it stands in the pack, reckoning from the bottom card upwards. You then remark, "Lad es and gentle-men, you will take particular notice that I have not asked a single question, and yet I already know the card; and if anyone will kindly indicate the place in the pack at which you desire it to appear, I will at once cause it to take that position. I must only ask that, by arrangement between yourselves, you will make the number at which the card is to appear higher than that which it originally held." We will suppose that the audience decide that the card shall appear at number 22. Carelessly remark, "It is not even necessary for me to see the cards." So saying, hold the pack under the table, and rapidly count off twenty-two cards from the bottom of the pack, and place them on the top.* You then continue, "Having already placed the card thought of in the desired position, I may now, without suspicion, ask for the original number of the card, as I shall commence my counting with that number." We will suppose you are told the card was originally number 10. You begin to count from the top of the pack, calling the first card 10, the next 11, and so on. When you come to 22, the number appointed, you say, "If I have kept my promise, this should be the card you thought of. To avoid the sus-

---

* When the number named is more than half the total number of the pack, *i.e.*, more than 16 in a piquet pack, or more than 26 in a whist pack, it is quicker, and has precisely the same effect, to count off the difference between that and the total number from the top, and place them at the bottom. Thus, in a piquet pack, if the number called be 12, you would count off 12 from the bottom, and place them on the top; but if the number called were 24, you would achieve the same object by counting 8 from the top, and passing them to the bottom.

picion of confederacy, will you please say, before I turn it over, what your card was." The card being named, you turn it up, and show that it is the right one.

In all tricks which depend on the naming of a card drawn or thought of, it adds greatly to the effect to have the card named before you turn it up.

This trick, unlike most, will bear repetition ; but it is well on a second performance to vary it a little. Thus you may on the second occasion say, when the card has been thought of, "I will choose for myself this time ; your card will appear at number 30." It is desirable to name a number very near the total number of the pack (which we are now supposing to be a piquet pack), as the difference between that and the total number being very small, it is easy to see at a glance the number of cards representing such difference, and pass them to the bottom of the pack. You take in this instance two cards only, that being the difference between 30 and 32, and pass them to the bottom, when the card will, as you have announced, be the thirtieth.

If you are able to make the pass, you will, of course, avail yourself of it to transfer the requisite number of cards to the top or bottom of the pack.

THE CARDS REVEALED BY THE LOOKING-GLASS.—This is rather a joke than a feat of magic, but it will create some fun, and may often be kept up for some time without being discovered. Take up your position on one side of the room, facing a good-sized mirror or chimney-glass. Make your audience stand or sit facing you, when they will, of course, have their backs to the glass. Offer the cards to be shuffled and cut. Take the top card and hold it high up, with its back to you and its face to the audience. As it will be reflected in the mirror opposite you, you will have no difficulty in naming it, or any other card in like manner, till your audience either find you out, or have had enough of the trick.

TO GUESS FOUR CARDS THOUGHT OF BY DIFFERENT PERSONS. —Offer the pack to be shuffled. Place it on the table, and taking off the four top cards with the right hand, offer them to any person, and ask him to notice one of them, shuffle them, and return them to you. When they are returned, place them. face downwards, in your left hand. Take the next four cards, and offer them to another person in like manner. Proceed in like manner with a third and fourth group of four. When all the sixteen cards are returned, deal them out in four heaps, face upwards. Ask each person in which heap his card now is. That of the first person will be the uppermost of his heap, that of the second person second in his heap, and so on. It will sometimes occur that two of the cards chosen are in the same heap, but the rule will still apply. Should there be three persons only to choose, you should give them three cards each; and deal in three heaps.

THE PAIRS RE-PAIRED.—After performing the last trick, you may continue, " As you have not yet found me out, I will repeat the experiment, but in a slightly altered form. This time I will invite you to think of two cards each, and all present may join if they please." After giving the pack to be shuffled, you deal out twenty cards, face upwards, but placing them in couples. Invite as many of the company as please to note any particular couple they think fit, and to remember those two cards. When they have done so, gather up the cards, picking them up here and there in any order you please, taking care, however, that none of the pairs are separated. You now deal them out again, face upwards, in rows of five, according to the following formula : *Mutus dedit nomen Cocis*, which, being interpreted, signifies, " Mutus gave a name to the Coci," a people as yet undiscovered. On examining the sentence closely, you will observe that it consists of ten letters only, m, u, t, s, d, e, i, n, o, c, each twice repeated. This gives you the clue to the arrangement of the cards. which will be as follows

M	U	T	U	S
1	2	3	2	4
D	E	D	I	T
5	6	5	7	3
N	O	M	E	N
8	9	1	6	8
C	O	C	I	S
10	9	10	7	4

You must imagine the four words printed as above upon your table. You must deal your first card upon the imaginary M in MUTUS, and the second on the imaginary M in NOMEN, the two next cards on the two imaginary U's, the two next on the two T's, and so on. You have now only to ask each person in which row his two cards now appear, and you will at once know which they are. Thus, if a person says his two cards are now in the second and fourth rows, you will know that they must be the two cards representing the two I's, that being the only letter common to those two rows. If a person indicates the first and fourth rows, you will know that his cards are those representing the two S's, and so on.

THE MAGIC TRIPLETS.—This trick is precisely similar in principle to the last, but twenty-four (instead of twenty) cards are used, and they are dealt in triplets, instead of pairs. After the spectators have made their selection, you take up the cards as directed for the last trick, taking care to keep the respective triplets together. You then deal them in rows of six, the formula in this case being:

L	I	V	I	N	I
L	A	N	A	T	A
L	E	V	E	T	E
N	O	V	O	T	O

ANOTHER MODE OF DISCOVERING A CARD THOUGHT OF.—Have the pack well shuffled. Then deal twenty-five cards, in five rows of five cards each, face upwards. Invite a person to think of a card, and to tell you in which row it is. Note in your own mind the first or left-hand card of that row. Now pick up the cards in vertical rows, *i.e.*, beginning at the last card of the last row, placing that card face upwards on the last of the next row, those two on the last of the next row, and so on. When you have picked up all the cards in this manner, deal them out again in the same way as at first. You will observe that those cards which at first formed the first cards of each row, now themselves form the first row. Ask the person in which row his card now is. When he has told you, look to the top row for the first card of the original row, when the card thought of will be found in a direct line below it. As you have just been told in which lateral row it is, you will not have the least difficulty in discovering it, and by a slight effort of memory you may even allow several persons each to think of a card, and name it. A comparison of the subjoined tables, showing the original and subsequent order of the cards, will explain the principle of the trick.

First Order.

1	2	3	4	5
6	7	8	9	10
11	12	13	14	15
16	17	18	19	20
21	22	23	24	25

Second Order.

1	6	11	16	21
2	7	12	17	22
3	8	13	18	23
4	9	14	19	24
5	10	15	20	25

Thus we will suppose you are told that the card thought of is originally in the third line. Remember the first or key-card of that line, designated in the table as 11. If the card is in the fourth line after the second deal, you look to the top line for the key-card, and on finding it you have only to observe which card in the fourth row is immediately beneath it, to be sure that that card (in this instance designated by the number 14) is the card thought of.

You may perform the trick with either sixteen, twenty-five, thirty-six, or forty-nine cards, either of those being a square number, and thus making the number of cards in a row equal to the number of rows, which is essential to the success of the trick.

To Guess, by the aid of a Passage of Poetry or Prose, such one of Sixteen Cards as, in the Performer's Absence, has been Touched or Selected by the Company.—This feat is performed by confederacy, the assistance of the confederate being open and avowed, but the mode in which the clue is given constituting the mystery. You allow the pack to be shuffled, and then deal sixteen cards, the first that come to hand, either face upwards or face downwards, in four rows on the table. The sole preparation on the part of yourself and your confederate is to commit to memory the following simple formula—*animal, vegetable, mineral, verb,* signifying respectively one, two, three and four. You retire from the room while the card is chosen, your confederate remaining. Upon your return your confederate selects and hands for your perusal a passage in any book which the audience may select, only taking care that the first word in such passage which comes within either of the four categories above mentioned, shall be such as to represent the number of the row in which the card is, and that the second word which comes within either of those categories shall represent the number at which the card stands in that row. We will suppose, for instance, that the passage handed to the performer is that portion of Hamlet's soliloquy commencing, "Oh, that this too too solid *flesh* would *melt.*" Here the first word which comes within either of the four categories is "flesh," which, being clearly animal (1), indicates that the chosen card is in the first row. The second word coming within either of the categories is "melt," which, being a verb (4), indicates that the chosen card is the *fourth* of its row. Had the passage been "*To be,* or not *to be,* that is the question," the two verbs would have indicated that the card was the fourth of the fourth row. "How *doth* the little busy *bee,*" etc., would have indicated the first of the fourth row, and so on. With a little tact and ingenuity on the part of the operators, this may be made an admirable trick, and, unlike most others, will bear being repeated, the mystery becoming deeper as passages of varying character and different length are employed.

To Detect, without Confederacy, which of Four Cards has been Turned Round in your Absence.—It will be found upon examining a pack of cards, that the white margin round the court cards almost invariably differs in width at the opposite ends. The difference is frequently very trifling, but is still sufficiently noticeable when pointed out, and may be made available for a trick which, though absurdly simple, has puzzled many. You place four court cards of the same rank, say four queens, in a row, face upwards, taking care that the wider margins of the cards are all one way. You then leave the room, and invite the company to turn round lengthways during your absence any one or more of the four cards. On your return you can readily distinguish which card has been so turned, as the wider margin of such card will now be where the narrower margin was originally, and *vice versâ.*

There is so little chance of the trick being discovered, that you may, contrary to the general rule, repeat it if desired. Should you do so, it is better not to replace the cards already turned, as this might give a clue to the secret, but carefully note in your own mind their present position, by remembering which you can discover any card turned just as easily as at first.

To Arrange Twelve Cards in Rows, in such a manner that they will Count Four in every Direction.—This is rather a puzzle than a conjuring trick, but may sometimes serve as an interlude to occupy the minds of your audience while you are preparing for some other feat. The secret is to place nine of the twelve cards in three rows, so as to form a square; then place the remaining three cards as follows: the first on the first card of the first row, the second on the second card of the second row, and the last on the third card of the last row.

To Place the Aces and Court Cards in Four Rows, in such a manner that neither Horizontally nor Perpendicularly shall there be in either Row two Cards alike either in Suit or Value.—This also is a puzzle, and a very good one. The key to it is to begin by placing four cards of like value (say four kings) in a diagonal line from corner to corner of the intended square, then four other cards of like value (say the four aces) to form the opposite diagonal. It must be borne in mind, that of whatever suit the two centre kings are, the two aces must be of the opposite suits. Thus, if the two centre kings are those of diamonds and hearts, the two centre aces must be those of clubs and spades; and in adding the two end aces, you must be careful not to place at either end of the line an ace of the same suit as the king at the corresponding end of the opposite diagonal. Having got so far, you will find it a very easy matter to fill in the remaining cards in accordance with the conditions of the puzzle. The sixteen cards when complete will be as in Fig. 32, subject, of course, to variation according to the particular cards with which you commence your task.

THE CONGRESS OF COURT CARDS. —Take the kings, queens, and knaves from the pack, and place them face upwards on the table in three rows of four each, avoiding as much as possible the appearance of arrangement, but really taking care to place them in the following order: In the first row you have only to remember not to have two of the same suit.

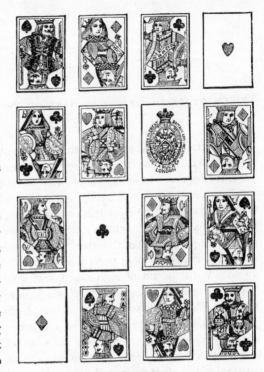

FIG. 32.

Begin the second row with a card of the same suit with which you ended the first, let the second card be of the same suit as the first of the first row, the third of the same suit as the second of the first row, and so on. The third row will begin with the suit with which the second left off, the second card will be of the same suit as the first of the second row, and so on. Now pick up the cards in vertical rows, beginning with the last card of the bottom row. The cards may now be cut (not shuffled) any number of times, but, if dealt in four heaps, the king, queen, and knave of each suit will come together.

CHAPTER IV.

TRICKS INVOLVING SLEIGHT-OF-HAND OR THE USE OF SPECIALLY PREPARED CARDS.

WE have already explained the nature and use of the " forcing" pack of cards. It may be well, before we go further, to give a short account of one or two other species of prepared cards.

THE LONG CARD.—This is the technical name for a card longer or wider, by about the thickness of a sixpence, than the rest of the pack. This card will naturally project to that extent beyond the general length or width of the other cards, and the performer is thereby enabled to cut the pack at that particular card whenever he chooses to do so. With the aid of such a card, and a tolerable proficiency in " forcing " and " making the pass," many excellent tricks can be performed. Packs with a long card can be obtained at any of the conjuring depôts. The best plan, however, is to purchase two ordinary packs, precisely alike, and to have the edges of one of them shaved down by a bookbinder to the requisite extent, when you can insert any card of the other pack at pleasure to form your long card, and thus avoid the suspicion which would naturally arise from the performance of several tricks with the same card. A still greater improvement upon the ordinary long-card pack is the *biseauté* or tapering pack, in which, though only one pack is used, any card may in turn become the long card. A *biseauté* pack consists of cards all of which are a shade wider (say the thickness of a shilling) at one end than the other. (*See* Fig. 33, in which, however, the actual difference of width is exaggerated, in order to make the shape of the card clear to the eye.)

When two cards shaped as above are placed one upon another, but in opposite directions, the effect is as in Fig. 34. If the whole pack is at the outset placed with all the cards alike (*i.e.,* their ends tapering in the same direction), by reversing any card and returning it to the pack, its wide end is made to correspond with the narrow ends of the remaining cards, thereby making it for the time being a "long" card. By offering the pack for a person to draw a card, and turning the pack round before the card is replaced, the position of that card will thus be reversed, and you will be able to find it again in an instant, however thoroughly the cards may be shuffled. By pre-arranging the pack beforehand, with the narrow ends of all the red cards in one direction, and those of the black cards in the other direction, you may, by grasping the pack between the finger and thumb at each end (*see* Fig. 35), and, drawing the hands apart, separate the black cards from the red at a single stroke, or, by preparing the pack accordingly, you may divide the court cards from the plain cards in like manner. Many

FIG. 33.   FIG. 34.

other recreations may be performed with a pack of this kind, which will be noticed in due course. The long card and the *biseauté* pack have each their special advantages and disadvantages. The long card is the more reliable, as it can always be distinguished with certainty from the rest of

FIG. 35.

the pack; but it is very generally known, and after having made use of it for one trick, it is clear that you cannot immediately venture upon another with the same card. It is further comparatively useless unless you are proficient in "forcing." The *biseauté* pack may be used without any knowledge of "forcing," and has the advantage that any card may in turn become the key card, but it is treacherous.

The necessary turning of the pack is likely to attract observation, and any little mistake, such as allowing the card to be replaced in its original direction, or a few of the cards getting turned round in shuffling, will cause a breakdown. Notwithstanding these disadvantages, both the long card and the *biseauté* pack will be found very useful to the amateur; but it should be borne in mind that both these appliances are in reality only makeshifts or substitutes for sleight-of-hand. Professionals of the highest class discard them altogether, and rely wholly on the more subtle magic of their own fingers.

We subjoin a few of the best of the feats which specially depend upon the use of a long card or the *biseauté* pack.

A CARD HAVING BEEN CHOSEN AND RETURNED, AND THE PACK SHUFFLED, TO PRODUCE THE CHOSEN CARD INSTANTLY IN VARIOUS WAYS.—Request some person to draw a card, spreading them before him for that purpose. If you use a long-card pack you must force the long card; if you are using a *biseauté* pack any card may be drawn, the pack being reversed before the card is replaced. The card being returned, the pack may be shuffled to any extent, but you will always be able to cut by feel at the card chosen.

You may vary the trick by taking the cards upright between the second finger and thumb of the right hand, and requesting some one to say, "One, two, three!" at the word "three" drop all the cards save the card chosen, which its projecting edge will enable you to retain when you relax the pressure upon the other cards.

Another mode of finishing the trick is to request any one present to put the pack (previously well shuffled) in his pocket, when you proceed, with his permission, to pick his pocket of the chosen card. This is an effective trick, and, if you are proficient in sleight-of-hand, may be also performed with an unprepared pack of cards. In the latter case, when the chosen card is returned to the pack, you make the pass to bring it to the top, palm it, and immediately offer the cards to be shuffled. (*See* Fig. 15.) The pack being returned, you replace the chosen card on the top, and when the pack is placed in the pocket you have only to draw out the top card. The feat of cutting at the chosen card may also by similar means be performed with an ordinary pack. For this purpose you must follow the directions last above given up to the time when, the pack having been shuffled, you replace the palmed card on the top. Then transfer the pack to the left hand, and apparently cut with the right. We say *apparently*, for though to the eye of the spectator you merely cut the cards, you really make the pass by sliding the lower half of the pack to the left, the fingers of the left hand at the same moment opening a little to lift the upper packet, and so give room for the upward passage of the lower packet. The cards remaining after the pass in the left hand, which the spectators take to be the bottom half of the pack, are in reality the original upper half; and on the uppermost of such cards being turned up, it is found to be the one which was chosen.

Another good mode of finishing the trick is to fling the pack in the air, and catch the chosen card. For this purpose, after forcing the long card, and after giving the pack to be shuffled, you cut the pack at the long card as before, but without showing it, and place the original lower half of the pack on the top. The chosen card will now be at the bottom. Take the pack face downwards upon the right hand, and quickly transfer it to the left, at the same time palming (with the right hand) the bottom card. Spread the cards a little, and fling them into the air, clutching at them with the right hand as they descend, and at the same moment bring the chosen card to the tips of the fingers. The effect to the spectators will be as if you actually caught it among the falling cards.

This feat also may be performed without the aid of a long card, and without the necessity of forcing a card. In this case, as in the pocket-picking trick, you make the pass as soon as the card is returned to the pack, in order to bring it to the top, and palm it; then offer the pack to be shuffled. When the cards are handed back, place the chosen card for a moment on the top of the pack, and endeavour to call attention—indirectly, if possible—to the fact that you have no card concealed in your hand. Then again palming the card, you may either yourself fling up the cards or request some other person to do so, and terminate the trick as before.

A still more effective form of this trick, in which the chosen card is caught upon the point of a sword, will be found among the card tricks performed by the aid of special apparatus.

The following is a good long-card trick, but demands considerable proficiency in sleight-of-hand. You "force" the long card, allowing it to be returned to any part of the pack, and the whole to be well shuffled. You then say, "You must be by this time pretty certain that, even if I knew your card in the first instance, I must have quite lost sight of it now. If you do not feel quite certain, please shuffle the cards once more." Every one being fully satisfied that the card is completely lost in the pack, you continue, "Let me assure you that I do not know, any more than yourselves, where-abouts in the pack your card is at this moment. You can all see that I have no duplicate card concealed in my hands. I will now take the top card, whatever it may be, or, if you prefer it, any one may draw a card from any part of the pack, and I will at once change it to the card originally chosen." The audience will probably prefer to draw a card, which, when they have done, you continue, "I presume the card you have just drawn is not the one originally chosen. Will the gentleman who drew the first card look at it and see if it is his card?" The reply is pretty certain to be in the negative. During the discussion you have taken the opportunity to slip the little finger of the left hand immediately *above* the long card (which, it will be remembered, was that first drawn), and to make the pass, thereby bringing it to the top, and enabling you to palm it. You now ask the person holding the second card to place it on the top of the pack, which you immediately transfer to the right hand, thus bringing the palmed card upon it. You then say, "To show you that this trick is not performed by sleight-of-hand, or by any manipulation of the cards, I will not even touch them, but will place them here on the table in sight of all. Will the gentleman who drew the first card please to say what his card was?" The card being named, you slowly and deliberately turn over the top card, which will be found to be transformed into that first chosen. The other card is now the next card on the top of the pack, and, as somebody may suspect this, and by examining the pack gain a partial clue to the trick, it will be well to take an early opportunity of removing this card, either by shuffling, or by making the pass to bring it to the centre of the pack.

If you make use of a *biseauté* pack, there is, of course, no necessity for forcing the card in the first instance.

You may also reveal a chosen card with very good effect in the following manner: A card having been freely drawn, open the pack in such manner that it may be placed, when returned, immediately under the long card, which, by the way, should in this instance really be a *wide* card, though the term " long card " applies, as already mentioned, to both kinds of card. The pack may be moderately shuffled, with very little risk of the two cards being separated, the greater width of the long card tending to shelter the card beneath it, and making it very unlikely that that card will be displaced. If after the shuffle the long card does not happen to be tolerably high up in the pack, you should cut the cards in such manner as to make it so. Holding the cards in a horizontal position, face downwards, above the table, the thumb being on one side and the fingers on the other side of the pack, you say, " Ladies and gentlemen, I am now about to drop the cards, a few at a time, in a number of little heaps upon the table, stopping when you tell me to do so. It will be equally open to you to stop me when I have made one or two heaps only, or not until I have made seven or eight, but, whenever it is, the card at the top of the heap last made will be the identical card which was just now drawn, and which has since, as you have seen, been thoroughly shuffled in the pack." You now drop the cards, four or five at a time, on various parts of the table. When the word " stop " is pronounced you let go all the remaining cards below the long card, which, from its greater width, a very slight pressure suffices to retain. The card chosen having been next below the long card, is now at the top of the last heap. You ask the person who drew to name his card, and, touching the back of the top card with your wand, turn it over to show that it is the right one.

If you are tolerably expert in sleight-of-hand you may repeat the trick in a yet more striking manner. Proceed as before up to the moment when the word " stop " is pronounced. Having let fall as before all the cards below the long card, lay down the remainder of the pack, and take in the left hand the heap which you last dealt. Cover it with the right hand for an instant, and, sliding away the hand gently to the right, palm the top card, and immediately take by one corner the next card, holding it face downwards until the drawer has named his card, which was, we will suppose, the queen of hearts. As soon as the card is named, you turn towards the audience the face of the card you hold, saying, " Here is the card, as before." **Do not** look at it yourself, but at once replace it on the pack, and, covering the pack with the right hand, leave the palmed card upon it. You are by this time made aware by a murmur, if not by a more decided manifestation on the part of the audience, that something is wrong. You ask what is the matter, and are told that, so far from showing the queen of hearts, the card you produced was a totally different one, say, the seven of spades. You pretend to look embarrassed, and ask if they are quite sure. "It is very strange," you remark, " I never failed in this trick before. Will you allow me to try again ? " Then, appearing to recollect yourself, " Oh, of course ! " you exclaim, " I forgot to touch the card with the magic wand." You do so. " Will some one be kind enough to look at the card now ? " The card is examined, and proves to be, as it ought to have been originally, the queen of hearts.

To teach the Company a Trick which they Learn with-out Difficulty ; then to allow them to Succeed or to cause them to Fail at your Pleasure.—This surprising trick is per-formed with the piquet pack of thirty-two cards, from which you must beforehand take away, and secretly pocket, one card of each suit, the spectators, however, believing that you use the whole thirty-two cards.

You announce to the company that you will teach them a trick. You deal the cards face upwards in rows of four, according to the rules set forth in the trick already described under the title of " The Congress of Court Cards," *i.e.*, you place a card of each suit in the top row ; you commence each row with a card of the suit with which the row above ended ; you make the second of each row the same suit as the first of the row above, and the third the same suit as the second of the row above, and so on. Thus, if your top row be club, diamond, heart, spade, your second will be spade, club, diamond, heart ; your third, heart, spade, club, diamond ; your fourth, diamond, heart, spade, club ; your fifth, club, diamond, heart, spade ; your sixth, spade, club, diamond, heart ; and your seventh, heart, spade, club, diamond. You now gather up the cards as directed in the trick already mentioned, *i.e.*, in vertical rows, from the bottom up-wards, commencing at the right-hand bottom corner. The pack thus arranged may be cut any number of times, but, if dealt in four heaps, all the cards of each suit will be found to be together.

So far, the trick is ingenious rather than astonishing, although, the arrangement of the cards having reference only to the suits, and not to individual cards, the cards do not at first sight appear to be specially arranged; and if you are rapid and apparently careless in placing them, the spectators will in all probability believe that they are placed hap-hazard. If you can induce this belief, you will greatly heighten their surprise at finding the different suits regularly sorted after the deal. But the trick is not yet finished. You again place the cards as before, remarking that the trick is simplicity itself when once the principle is known, and on this occasion you draw special attention to the necessary arrangement of the cards. Having completed the trick for the second time, you invite some of the audience to try their hands, which they do, and of course succeed, there being really no difficulty in the matter. When one or two have tried and succeeded, they will probably disparage the trick, as being absurdly easy. "Pardon me," you say, "you have succeeded so far, because it was my will and pleasure that you should do so. You seem incredulous, but I am perfectly serious. To prove that I am so, I give you warning that the next person who attempts the trick will fail. Come, who accepts the challenge?" Some one is sure to respond, and in all probability to offer you a bet that he will succeed. "Sir," you reply, "I never bet on certainties, or your money would be already lost. I have said that you shall fail, and you cannot, therefore, possibly succeed." You have, meanwhile, secretly palmed the four cards which you pocketed before beginning the trick, and have watched your opportunity to replace them on the table with the rest of the pack.

Your opponent may now try as much as he pleases, but he cannot possibly succeed, the fact being that the process above described produces the desired effect with twenty-eight cards, but will not do so with thirty-two. The first thought of your audience is sure to be that you have abstracted some of the cards in order to make the trick fail, but on counting they find the number correct. Not one in a hundred will suspect that the reverse is the case, and that when you performed the trick the pack was incomplete.

By the time three or four of the company have tried and failed, you will probably have found an opportunity of again pocketing a card of each suit; and you may then announce that, having sufficiently proved your power, you will now graciously condescend to remove the prohibition, and allow the next person who tries to succeed This, of course, he will do; and the trick may very well end here, with the satisfaction on your part that you have kept your secret, and that, even when removed from the sphere of your adverse influence, your pupils will fail in performing the trick, making the attempt, as they naturally will, with the full piquet pack. But it is just possible that a *contretemps* may arise, for which it will be well to be prepared. Some one of the audience, more acute than the generality, may suggest again counting the cards, to see if all are there when the trick succeeds. Even in this case you need not be discomfitted. At once offer yourself to count the cards, and, gathering them up for that purpose, add to them the four which you removed, which you should again have palmed in readiness. Count them deliberately on to the table, and, when every one is satisfied that the pack is complete, announce that you will once more perform the trick, in order to let every one see that you actually use no more and no less than thirty-two cards. Place the cards as before, counting aloud as you do so, till the whole thirty-two cards are placed. So far you have not varied your method of proceeding, but to succeed with the whole thirty-two cards you must secretly make a slight variation in the manner of picking up. You will remember that the cards were picked up *face upwards*, beginning from the bottom of the right hand row, placing the cards of that row on those of the next row, and so on. Now, to perform the trick with thirty-two cards, the bottom cards of each row must be gathered up all together, and placed on the face of the pack. Thus, if the bottom card of the first or left hand row be the knave of spades, that of the second row the ten of diamonds, that of the third row the ace of hearts, and that of the fourth row the seven of clubs, those four cards must be picked up as follows : The knave of spades must be placed (face upwards) on the ten of diamonds, the ten of diamonds on the ace of hearts, and the ace of hearts on the seven of clubs, which will occupy its own place on the face of the cards of the last or right-hand row. For convenience of picking up, it will be well to place the four rows very near together, slightly converging at the bottom, when it will be tolerably easy, by a bold, quick sweep of the left hand from left to right, to slide the three other cards in due order, on to the bottom card of the last row ; while the performer, looking not at the cards but at his audience, diverts their attention by any observations which may occur to him. The trick in this form requires considerable address, and the performer should not, therefore, venture upon it until, by frequent practice, he can be certain of placing the four cards neatly with his left hand, and without looking at his hands, which woul ' infallibly draw the eyes of the audience in the same direction, and thereby spoil the trick.

To Distinguish the Court Cards by Touch.—This trick is performed by means of a preliminary preparation of the court cards, to be made as follows : Take each court card separately, edge upwards, and draw a tolerably sharp knife, the blade held sloping backwards at an angle of about 45°, once or twice along the edge from left to right. This will be found to turn the edge of the card, so to speak, and to leave on each side a minute ridge, not noticeable by the eye, but immediately perceptible, if sought for, to the touch. Prepare the opposite edge of the card in the same way, and again mix the court cards with the pack, which is now ready for use.

Offer the prepared pack to be shuffled. When the pack is returned to you, you may either hold it above your head, and, showing the cards in succession, call "court card" or "plain card," as the case may be, or you may offer to deal the cards into two heaps, consisting of court cards in one heap and plain cards in the other, every now and then offering the cards to be again shuffled. You can, of course, perform the trick blindfold with equal facility.

You should endeavour to conceal, as much as possible, the fact that you distinguish the court cards by the sense of touch, and rather seek to make your audience believe that the trick is performed by means of some mathematical principle, or by any other means remote from the true explanation. This advice, indeed, applies more or less to all tricks. Thus your knowledge of a forced card depends, of course, on sleight-of-hand ; but you should by no means let this be suspected, but rather claim credit for some clairvoyant faculty ; and *vice versâ*, when you perform a trick depending on a mathematical combination, endeavour to lead your audience to believe that it is performed by means of some impossible piece of sleight-of-hand. Further, endeavour to vary your *modus operandi*. If you have just performed a trick depending purely on sleight-of-hand, do not let the next be of the same character, but rather one based on a mathematical principle, or on the use of special apparatus.

To NAME ANY NUMBER OF CARDS IN SUCCESSION WITHOUT SEEING THEM.—*First Method.*—This trick, in its original form, is so well known that it is really not worth performing ; but we describe it for the sake of completeness, and for the better comprehension of the improved method. The performer takes the pack, and secretly notices the bottom card. He then announces that he will name all the cards of the pack in succession without seeing them. Holding the pack behind him for an instant, he turns the top card face outwards on the top of the pack ; then holding the pack with the bottom card towards the audience, he names that card. From the position in which he holds the pack, the top card, which he has turned, is towards him, and in full view. Again placing his hands behind him, he transfers the last named to the bottom, and turns the next, and so on in like manner. Even in an audience of half-a-dozen only, it is very likely that there will be some one acquainted with this form of the trick, who will proclaim aloud his knowledge of "how it is done." We will suppose that you have performed the trick with this result. Passing your hands again behind you, but this time merely passing the top card to the bottom, without turning any other card, you reply that you doubt his pretended knowledge, and name the card as before. He will naturally justify his assertion by explaining the mode of performing the trick. You reply, " According to your theory, there should be an exposed card at each end of the pack. Pray observe that there is nothing of the kind in this case " (here you show the opposite side of the pack), " but, to give a still more conclusive proof, I will for the future keep the whole of the pack behind me, and name each card *before* I bring it forward. Perhaps, to preclude any idea of arrangement of the cards, some one will kindly shuffle them." When the cards are returned, you give them a slight additional shuffle yourself, and remarking, " They are pretty well shuffled now, I think," continue the trick by the

Second Method.—Glance, as before, at the bottom card. Place the cards behind you, and name the card you have just seen. Passing the right hand behind you, palm the top card, and then taking hold of the bottom card (the one you have just named) face outwards, with the two first fingers and thumb of the same hand, bring it forward and throw it on the table. Pause for a moment before you throw it down, as if asking the company to verify the correctness of your assertion, and glance secretly at the card which is curled up in your palm. Again place your hands behind you, call the name of the card you last palmed, and palm another. You can, of course, continue the trick as long as you please, each time naming the card which you palmed at the last call. You should take care to have a tolerably wide space between yourself and your audience, in which case, with a very little management on your part, there is little fear of their discovering the secret of the palmed card.

You should not be in too great a hurry to name the card you have just seen, or the audience may suspect that you gained your knowledge in the act of bringing forward the card you last named. To negative this idea, you should take care first to bring forward again the right hand, manifestly empty, and do your best to simulate thought and mental exertion before naming the next card.

To make Four Cards change from Eights to Twos, from Black to Red, etc.—For this trick you require three specially-prepared cards. The backs should be similar to those of the pack which you have in ordinary use, the faces being as depicted in Fig. 36. They may be purchased at any of the conjuring depôts.

You place these three cards privately at the bottom of the pack. You begin by remarking

FIG. 36.

that you will show the company a good trick with the four eights and the two of diamonds. (If you use a piquet pack, you must provide yourself with a special two of diamonds, of similar pattern to the rest of the pack.) You take the pack, and picking out the four genuine eights, hand them for examination. While they are being inspected,

FIG. 37.

you insert the little finger of your left hand between the three bottom cards (the prepared cards) and the rest of the pack. When the eights are returned, you place them with apparent careless-ness on the top of the pack (taking care, however, to have the eight of clubs uppermost), and hand the two of dia-monds for examination. While this card is being examined, you make the pass to bring the three pre-pared cards on the top. The two of diamonds being returned, you lay it on the table, and taking off the four top cards, which are now the three prepared cards and the eight of clubs, you spread them fanwise, when they will appear to be the four eights, as in Fig. 37. The eight of clubs is alone completely visible, one half of each of the other cards being covered by the card next preceding it. The spectators

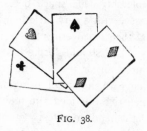

FIG. 38.

naturally take the four cards to be the four ordinary eights which they have just examined. Insert the two of diamonds behind the

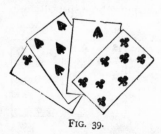

FIG. 39.

eight of clubs, and lay that card in turn on the table. Close the cards and again spread them, but this time with the opposite ends outward, when they will appear to be the four twos, as in Fig. 38. Again take in the eight of clubs in place of the two of diamonds, and *turn round* the supposed two of hearts. This you may do easily and naturally

by remarking, "I must now touch something black ; my coat-sleeve will do. I gently pass either card along it, thus, and replace it as before. The cards are now all black cards," which they actually appear to be. (*See* Fig. 39.) Again substitute the two of diamonds for the eight of clubs, touch any red object, and again turn and spread out the cards, when they will appear to be all red cards, as in Fig. 40. Once more take in the eight of clubs in place of the two of diamonds, and replace the four cards on the pack, again making the pass in order to bring the three prepared cards to the bottom, and to leave the genuine eights on the top.

There is a more elaborate form of this trick procurable at the conjuring depôts, in which several groups of cards are used in succession, and the changes are proportionately multiplied, various colours and patterns being produced in the place of the ordinary figures on the cards. In our own opinion, the trick loses rather than gains by this greater elaboration, as the more fanciful changes have the dis-

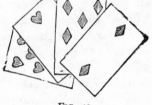

advantage of showing clearly (which the simpler form of the trick does not) that the cards used are not ordinary cards; and this being once understood, the magic of the trick is destroyed.

We have had occasion more than once to direct you to turn round the cards, and it will be well for you to know how to do this neatly and without

FIG. 40.

exciting suspicion. Hold the four cards fanwise in the left hand, the fingers behind and the thumb in front of the cards. Having exhibited them, turn their faces towards yourself, and with the thumb and finger of the right hand close the fan, and taking them by their upper ends lay them face downwards on the table. Their lower ends will now be away from you, and when you desire again to exhibit the cards (in a transformed condition), you have only to turn them over *sideways*, and pick them up by the ends which are now directed towards you. This little artifice (which is simplicity itself in practice, though a little difficult to describe) must be carefully studied, as upon neat manipulation in this respect the illusion of the trick mainly depends.

A Card having been Drawn and Returned, and the Pack shuffled, to make it Appear at such Number as the Com-

PANY CHOOSE.*—Invite a person to draw a card. Spread out the pack that he may replace it, and slip your little finger above it. Make the pass in order to bring the chosen card to the top; palm it, and offer the pack to be shuffled. When the pack is returned to you, replace the chosen card on the top, and make the first of the false shuffles above described, but commence by sliding off into the right hand the *two* top cards (instead of the top card only), so that the chosen card may, after the shuffle, be last but one from the bottom. Take the pack face downwards in the left hand, and carelessly move about the pack so that the bottom card may be full in view of the audience. Inquire at what number the company would like the card to appear; and when they have made their decision, hold the pack face downwards, and with the first and second fingers of the right hand draw away the cards from the bottom one by one, throwing each on the table face upwards, and counting aloud " one," " two," " three," and so on. The first card which you draw is naturally the bottom one, and the chosen card, which is second, would in the ordinary course come next; but you " draw back " this card with the third finger of the left hand (*see* page 36) and take the next instead, continuing in like manner until you have reached one short of the number at which the card is to appear. You now pause, and say, " The next card should be the card you drew. To avoid any mistake, will you kindly say beforehand what it was?" at the same time placing the card face downwards on the table. When the card is named, you request the drawer or some other person to turn it up, when it is found to be the right one.

Another Method.—The card having been drawn and replaced, bring it to the top by the pass, palm it, have the pack shuffled, and replace it on the top. Invite the audience to choose at what number it shall appear. They choose, we will suppose, fifth. " Very good," you reply; "permit me, in the first place, to show you that it is not there already." Deal out the first five cards, face downwards, and show that the fifth is not the chosen card. Replace the five cards, in their present order on the pack, when the card will be at the number named.

---

* Another form of this trick, in which sleight-of-hand is not needed, has been given at page 52.

SEVERAL PERSONS HAVING EACH DRAWN AND RETURNED A
CARD, TO MAKE EACH CARD APPEAR AT SUCH NUMBER IN THE
PACK AS THE DRAWER CHOOSES.—Allow three or four persons each
to draw a card. When all have drawn, make the pass in such manner
as to bring the two halves of the pack face to face. The pack should
not, however, be equally divided. The upper portion should only
consist of about half-a-dozen cards, and therefore in making the pass
you should insert the finger only at that number of cards from the
bottom. Receive back the drawn cards on the top of the pack,
" ruffling " the cards (*see* page 27), and saying " Pass ! " as each card
is replaced. You may casually remark, " Your card has vanished ;
did you see it go ? " When all are returned, you quickly " turn over "
the pack (*see* page 37), and, taking off the top card, say, addressing
yourself to the person who last returned a card, " You see your card
has vanished, as I told you. At what number in the pack, say from
the first to the tenth, would you like it to re-appear ? " We will
suppose the answer to be " the sixth." You deal five cards from the
end of the pack that is now uppermost, then pretending a momentary
hesitation, say, " I fancy I dealt two cards for one ; allow me to count
them again." This draws the general attention to the cards on the
table, and gives you the opportunity to again turn over the pack.
You continue, after counting, " We have five, this makes six ; then
this should be your card. Will you say what the card was ? " You
place the card on the table, face downwards, and do not turn it till it
is named, this giving you the opportunity to again turn over the pack,
to be ready to repeat the operation with the next card. You must be
careful to invite the different persons to call for their cards in the
reverse order to that in which they are replaced in the pack. Thus,
you first address the person who last returned his card, and then the
last but one, and so on. You must tax your ingenuity for devices to
take off the attention of the spectators from the pack at the moment
when it is necessary to turn it over ; and as each repetition of the
process increases the chance of detection, it is well not to allow more
than three or four cards to be drawn.

If you have reason to fear that the cards left undealt will run
short, you may always replace any number of those already dealt
upon the reverse end of the pack to that at which the chosen cards are.

The "Three Card" Trick.—This well-known trick has long been banished from the *répertoire* of the conjuror, and is now used only by the itinerant sharpers who infest race-courses and country fairs. We insert the explanation of it in this place as exemplifying one form of sleight-of-hand, and also as a useful warning to the unwary.

In its primary form, the trick is only an illustration of the well-known fact that the hand can move quicker than the eye can follow. It is performed with three cards—a court card and two plain cards. The operator holds them, face downwards, one between the second finger and thumb of the left hand, and the other two (of which the court card is one) one between the first finger and thumb, and the other between the second finger and thumb of the right hand, the latter being the outermost. Bringing the hands quickly together and then quickly apart, he drops the three cards in succession, and challenges the bystanders to say which is the court card. If the movement is quickly made, it is almost impossible, even for the keenest eye, to decide with certainty whether the upper or lower card falls first from the hand, and consequently which of the three cards, as they lie, is the court card. This is the whole of the trick, if fairly performed, and so far it would be a fair subject for betting, though the chances would be much against the person guessing; but another element is introduced by the swindling fraternity, which ensures the discomfiture of the unwary speculator. The operator is aided by three or four confederates, or "bonnets," whose business it is to start the betting, and who, of course, are allowed to win. After this has gone on for a little time, and a sufficient ring of spectators has been got together, the operator makes use of some plausible pretext to look aside from the cards for a moment. While he does so one of the confederates, with a wink at the bystanders, slily bends up one corner of the court card, ostensibly as a means of recognition. The performer takes up the cards without apparently noticing the trick that has been played upon him, but secretly (that corner of the card being concealed by the third and fourth fingers of the right hand) straightens the bent corner, and at the same moment bends in like manner the corresponding corner of the other card in the same hand. He then throws down the cards as before. The bent corner is plainly visible, and the spectators, who do not suspect the change that has just been made, are fully persuaded that the card so bent, and no other, is the court card. Speculating, as they imagine, on a certainty, they are easily induced to bet that they will discover the court card, and they naturally name the one with the bent corner. When the card is turned, they find, to their disgust, that they have been duped, and that the dishonest advantage which they imagined they had obtained over the dealer was in reality a device for their confusion.

To Nail a Chosen Card to the Wall.—Procure a sharp drawing pin, and place it point upwards on the table, mantelpiece, or any other place where it will not attract the notice of the spectators, and yet be so close to you that you can cover it with your hand without exciting suspicion. Ask any person to draw a card. When he returns it to the pack, make the pass to bring it to the top, palm it, and immediately offer the pack to be shuffled. While this is being done, place your right hand carelessly over the pin, so as to bring the centre of the card as near as possible over it, and then press gently on the card, so as to make the point of the pin just penetrate it.

When the pack is returned, place the palmed card upon the top, and thus press home the pin, which will project about a quarter of an inch through the back of the card. Request the audience to indicate any point upon the woodwork of the apartment at which they would like the chosen card to appear; and when the spot is selected, stand at two or three feet distance, and fling the cards, backs foremost, heavily against it, doing your best to make them strike as flat as possible, when the other cards will fall to the ground, but the selected one will remain firmly pinned to the woodwork. Some little practice will be necessary before you can make certain of throwing the pack so as to strike in the right position. Until you can be quite sure of doing this, it is better to be content with merely *striking* the pack against the selected spot. The result is the same, though the effect is less surprising than when the cards are actually thrown from the hand.

The Inseparable Sevens.—Place secretly beforehand three of the four eights at the bottom of the pack, the fourth eight, which is not wanted for the trick, being left in whatever position it may happen to occupy. (The suit of this fourth eight must be borne in mind, for a reason which will presently appear.) Now select openly the four sevens from the pack, and spread them on the table. While the company are examining them, privately slip the little finger of the left hand immediately above the three eights at the bottom, so as to be in readiness to make the pass. Gather up the four sevens, and place them on the top of the pack, taking care that the seven *of the same suit as the fourth eight* is uppermost. Make a few remarks as to the affectionate disposition of the four sevens, which, however far apart they are placed in the pack, will always come together; and watch your opportunity to make the pass, so as to bring the three eights, originally at the bottom, to the top. If you are sufficiently expert, you may make the pass at the very instant that you place the four sevens on the top of the pack; but, unless you are very adroit, it is better to bide your time and make it an instant later, when the attention of the audience is less attracted to your hands. You then continue, "I shall now take these sevens (you can see for yourselves that I have not removed them), and place them in different parts of the pack." At the words, "You can see for yourselves," etc., you take off the four top cards, and show them fanwise. In reality, three of them are eights, but the fourth and foremost card being actually a seven, and the eighth pip of each of the other cards being concealed by the card before it, and the audience having, as they imagine, already seen the same cards spread out fairly upon the table, there is nothing to suggest a doubt that they are actually the sevens. (You will now see the reason why it is necessary to place uppermost the seven of the same suit as the *absent* eight. If you had not done so the seven in question would have been of the same suit as one or other of the three sham sevens, and the audience, knowing that there could not be two sevens of the same suit, would at once see through the trick.) Again folding up the four cards, you insert the top one a little above the bottom of the pack, the second a little higher, the third a little higher still, and the fourth (which is a genuine seven) upon the top of the pack. The four sevens, which are apparently so well distributed throughout the pack, are really together on the top, and you have only to make the pass, or, if you prefer it, simply cut the cards, to cause them to be found together in the centre of the pack.

THE INSEPARABLE ACES.—This is really only another form of the last trick, though it differs a good deal in effect. You first pick out and exhibit on the table the four aces, and request some one to replace them on the pack, when you place three other cards secretly upon them. This you may either do by bringing three cards from the bottom by the pass, or you may, while the company's attention is occupied in examining the aces, palm three cards from the top in the right hand, and, after the aces are replaced on the top, simply cover them with that hand, thereby bringing the three palmed cards upon them. You now say, " I am about to distribute these aces in different parts of the pack ; pray observe that I do so fairly." As you say this, you take off and hold up to the audience the four top cards, being the three indifferent cards with an ace at the bottom. You cannot, of course, exhibit them fanwise, as in the last trick, or the deception would be at once detected ; but the spectators, seeing an ace at the bottom, and having no particular reason for suspecting otherwise, naturally believe that the cards you hold are really the four aces. Laying the four cards on the table, you distribute them, as in the last trick, in different parts of the pack ; taking care, however, that the last card (which is the genuine ace), is placed among the three already at the top.

You now invite some one to cut. When he has done so, you take up the two halves, in their transposed position, in the left hand, at the same time slipping the little finger of that hand between them. The four aces are now, of course, upon the top of the lower packet. You then announce, " I am now about to order the four aces, which you have seen so well divided, to come together again. Would you like them to appear on the top, at the bottom, or in the middle of the pack ? I should tell you that I know perfectly well beforehand which you will choose, and indeed I have already placed them at that particular spot." If the answer is, " In the middle," you have only to withdraw the little finger, and invite the company to examine the pack to see that they are already so placed. If the answer is, " On the top," you make the pass to bring them there. To produce them at the bottom is rather more difficult, and unless you are pretty confident as to your neatness of manipulation, it will be well to limit the choice to "top" or "middle." In order to be able to bring the four aces to the bottom, you must, in picking up the cards after the cut, push forward a little with the left thumb the four top cards of the lower packet, and slip the little finger below and the third finger above them, so as to be able to make the pass above or below those four cards as occasion may require. If you are required to bring those four cards to the top, you must withdraw the little finger (thereby joining those cards to the upper cards of the lower packet) and make the pass with the aid of the third finger instead of the fourth. If, on the contrary, you desire to produce the four aces at the bottom, you simply withdraw the third finger, thereby leaving the aces at the bottom of the upper packet, when the pass will bring them to the bottom of the pack.

We have described the trick as performed with the aces, but the effect will, of course, be the same with four kings, four queens, or any other four similar cards.

HAVING PLACED THE FOUR ACES IN DIFFERENT POSITIONS IN THE PACK, TO MAKE THE TWO BLACK CHANGE PLACES WITH THE TWO RED ONES, AND FINALLY TO BRING ALL FOUR TOGETHER IN THE MIDDLE OF THE PACK.—This trick may immediately follow that last described. Again selecting the four aces (or such other four cards as you used for the last trick), and placing them on the table, take the two red ones, and opening the pack bookwise in the left hand, ostentatiously place them in the middle, at the same time secretly slipping your little finger between them. Ask the audience to particularly notice which of the aces are placed in the middle, and which at top and bottom. Next place one of the black aces on the top, and then turning over the pack by extending your left hand, place the remaining black ace at the bottom. As you again turn over the pack to its former position, make the pass, which the movement of the pack in turning over in the hand will be found to facilitate. The two halves of the pack having now changed places, the aces will, naturally, have changed their positions also, the two black ones now being in the middle, and the two red ones at top and bottom;

but it would be very indiscreet to allow the audience to know that this is already the case. As has been already mentioned, when a given change has taken or is about to take place, you should always seek to mislead the spectators as to the *time* of the change, as they are thereby the less likely to detect the mode in which it is effected. In accordance with this principle, you should endeavour in the present case to impress firmly upon the minds of your audience that the cards are as they have seen you place them; and for that purpose it is well to ask some one to say over again, for the general satisfaction, in what parts of the pack the four aces are.

At this point a *contretemps* may arise, for which it is well to be prepared. The person interrogated may possibly forget the relative position of the two colours, and may, therefore, ask to see again how the cards are placed; or some person may have seen or suspected that you have already displaced them, and may make a similar request for the purpose of embarrassing you. In order to be prepared for such a contingency, it is desirable, after you make the pass as above mentioned, not to allow the two halves of the pack to immediately coalesce, but to keep them still separated by the little finger. If you have done this, and for any reason it becomes necessary to show the cards a second time in their original condition, you have only to again make the pass, in order to bring them back to the same position which they occupied at first, making it a third time in order to effect the change.

We will suppose that the audience are at length fully satisfied that the two red aces are in the middle, and the two black ones at the opposite ends of the pack. You then say, "Ladies and gentlemen, I am about to command these aces to change places. Pray observe by what a very simple movement the transposition is effected." Making a quick upward movement with the right hand, you ruffle the cards, at the same moment saying, "Pass!" Turning the faces of the card to the audience, you show them that the red aces are now at top and bottom, and the black ones in the middle. While exhibiting them, take an opportunity to slip the little finger between these latter, and in closing the cards (while they are still face upwards), again make the pass, and place the pack face downwards on the table. You then say, "I have now, as you see, made the aces change places. I don't know whether you saw how I did it. Perhaps I was a little too quick for you. This time I will do it as slowly as you please, or, if you prefer it, I will not even touch the cards with my hands, but merely place my wand upon the pack, so. Pass! Will you please to examine the pack for yourselves, when you will find that the aces have again changed places, and have returned to their original positions." This is found to be the case. You continue, "You have not found me out yet? Well, to reward your attention, as this really is a very good trick, I will show you how to do it for yourselves." Pick out the four aces, and hand the two red ones to one person, and the two black ones to another person. Then, taking the pack in your left hand, and addressing yourself first to the person on your right, request him to place the two aces which he holds respectively at the top and bottom of the pack. Then, turning to the other person, request him to place the two other aces in the middle of the pack, which you (apparently) open midway with the right hand for the purpose. In reality, instead of merely lifting up, as you appear to do, the top half of the pack, you make the pass by sliding out the bottom half of the pack to the left. This movement is completely lost in your quick half turn to the left as you address the second person, which so covers the smaller movement of the cards as to make it absolutely imperceptible; and it is in order to create the excuse for this useful half turn, that we have recommended you to place the aces in the hands of two different persons, and to begin with the person on your right. When the second pair of aces are thus replaced in the middle of the pack they are in reality placed between the two others, which the audience believe to be still at top and bottom. You now hand the pack to a person to hold, placing it face downwards in his palm, and requesting him to hold it very tightly, thus preventing any premature discovery of the top or bottom card. You then say, "I have promised to show you how to perform this trick. To make it still more striking, we will have this time a little variation. Instead of merely changing places, we will make all the four aces come together." Then, addressing the person who holds the cards, you continue, "The manner of performing this trick is simplicity itself, though it looks so surprising. Will you take my wand in your right hand? Hold the cards very tightly, and touch

the back with this end of the wand.   Quite right.   Now say ' Pass !'
It is very simple, you see.   Let us see whether you have succeeded.
Look over the pack for yourself.   Yes, there are the aces all together,
as well as I could have done it myself.   You can try it again by yourself at your leisure, but please don't tell any one else the secret, or you
will ruin my business."

The above delusive offer to show "how it's done" can be equally
well adapted to many other tricks, and never fails to create amusement.

A Card having been thought of, to make such Card
Vanish from the Pack, and be Discovered wherever the
Performer pleases.—This trick should be performed with twenty-
seven cards only.   You deal the cards, face upwards, in three packs,
requesting one of the company to note a card, and to remember in
which heap it is.   When you have dealt the three heaps, you inquire
in which heap the chosen card is, and place the other two heaps, face
upwards as they lie, upon that heap, then turn over the cards, and
deal again in like manner.   You again inquire which heap the chosen
card is now in, place that heap undermost as before, and deal again
for the third time, when the card thought of will be the first card
dealt of one or other of the three heaps.   You have, therefore, only
to bear in mind the first card of each heap to know, when the proper
heap is pointed out, what the card is.   You do not, however, disclose
your knowledge, but gather up the cards as before, with the designated
heap undermost ; when the cards are turned over, that heap naturally
becomes uppermost, and the chosen card, being the first card of that
heap, is now the top card of the pack.   You palm this card, and hand
the remaining cards to be shuffled.   Having now gained not only the
knowledge, but the actual possession, of the chosen card, you can
finish the trick in a variety of ways.   You may, when the pack is
returned replace the card on the top, and giving the pack, face upwards, to a person to hold, strike out of his hand all but the chosen
card (*see* page 44) ; or you may, if you prefer it, name the chosen
card, and announce that it will now leave the pack, and fly into a
person's pocket, or any other place you choose to name, where, it
being already in your hand, you can very easily find it.   A very

effective finish is produced by taking haphazard any caid from the pack, and announcing that to be the chosen card, and on being told that it is the wrong card, apologizing for your mistake, and forthwith "changing" it by the fifth method (*see* page 32) to the right one.

Some fun may also be created as follows :—You name, in the first instance, a wrong card—say the seven of hearts. On being told that that was not the card thought of, you affect surprise, and inquire what the card thought of was. You are told, let us say, the king of hearts. "Ah," you remark, "that settles it ; I felt sure you were mistaken. You could not possibly have seen the king of hearts, for you have been sitting on that card all the evening. Will you oblige me by standing up for a moment," and, on the request being complied with, you apparently take the card (which you have already palmed) from off the chair on which the person has been sitting. The more shrewd of the company may conjecture that you intentionally named a wrong card in order to heighten the effect of the trick ; but a fair proportion will always be found to credit your assertion, and will believe that the victim had really, by some glamour on your part, been induced to imagine he saw a card which he was actually sitting on.

This trick is frequently performed with the whole thirty-two cards of the piquet pack. The process and result are the same, save that the card thought of must be one of the twenty-seven cards first dealt. The chances are greatly against one of the last five cards being the card thought of, but in such an event the trick would break down, as it would in that case require four deals instead of three to bring the chosen card to the top of the pack.

It is a good plan to deal the five surplus cards in a row by themselves, and after each deal, turn up one of them, and gravely study it, as if these cards were in some way connected with the trick.

To cause a Number of Cards to Multiply invisibly in a Person's keeping.—Secretly count any number, say a dozen, of the top cards, and slip the little finger of the left hand between those cards and the rest of the pack. Invite a person to take as many cards as he pleases, at the same time putting into his hands all, or nearly all, of the separated cards. If he does not take all, you will be able to see at a glance, by the number that remains above your little finger, how many he has actually taken. Pretend to weigh in your hand the remaining cards, and say (we assume that you are using a piquet pack), " I should say by the weight that I have exactly twenty-two cards here, so you must have taken ten. Will you see if I am right?" While he is counting the cards he has taken, count off secretly from the pack, and palm in the right hand, four more. When he has finished his counting, you say, " Now will you please gather these cards together, and place your hand firmly upon them?" As you say this, you push them towards him with your right hand. This enables you to add to them, without attracting notice, the four cards in that hand. Continue, " Now how many cards shall I add to those in your hand? You must not be too extravagant, say three or four." The person addressed will probably select one or other of the numbers named, but you must be prepared for the possibility of his naming a smaller number. If he says " Four," you have only to ruffle the cards in your hand, or make any other gesture which may ostensibly effect the transposition; and he will find on examination that the cards under his hand are increased by four, according to his desire. If he says " Three," you say, " Please give me back one card, to show the others the way." This makes the number right. If "two" are asked for, you may ask for *two* cards to show the way; or you may say, " Two, very good! Shall I send a couple more for anybody else?" when some one or other is pretty sure to accept your offer. If one only is asked for, you must get two or three persons to take one each, taking care always by one or the other expedient to make the number correspond with the number you have secretly added. While the attention of the company is attracted by the counting of the cards, to see if you have performed your undertaking, again palm the same number of cards as was last selected (suppose three), and, after the cards are counted, gather them up, and give them to some other person to hold, adding to them the three just palmed; then taking that number of cards from the top of the pack, and again replacing them, say, " I will now send these three cards into your hands in the same manner." Ruffle the cards, as before, and, upon examination, the number of cards in the person's hands will again be found to be increased by three.

THE PACK BEING DIVIDED INTO TWO PORTIONS, PLACED IN THE KEEPING OF TWO DIFFERENT PERSONS, TO MAKE THREE CARDS PASS INVISIBLY FROM THE ONE TO THE OTHER.—This trick is identical in principle with the one last described, but the *mise m scène* is more elaborate, and several circumstances concur to give it a surprising effect. It was a special favourite with the late M. Robert-Houdin, and we shall proceed to describe it as nearly as possible in the form in which it was presented by him.

The performer brings forward a pack of cards, still in the official envelope. These he hands to a spectator, with a request that he will open and count them. He does so, and finds that they have the full complement (of thirty-two or fifty-two, as the case may be). He is next requested to cut the pack into two portions, pretty nearly equal, and to choose one of the packets. Having made his selection, he is further asked to count the cards in the packet chosen. The general attention being, meanwhile, drawn away from the performer, he has ample opportunity to get ready in his right hand, duly palmed, three cards of another pack, but of similar pattern to those of the pack in use. (These may previously be placed either on the *servante* or in the performer's right-hand *pochette*; or he may, if he prefers it, have them ready palmed in his right hand when he comes upon the stage to commence the trick.) The spectator, having duly counted the chosen pack, declares it to consist, say, of seventeen cards. "A capital number for the trick," remarks the performer. "Now, sir, will you be kind enough to take these seventeen cards in your own hands" (here he pushes them carelessly towards him, and joins the three palmed cards to them), "and hold them well up above your head, that every one may see them. Thank you. Now, as your packet contains seventeen cards, this other" (we are supposing a piquet pack to be used) "should contain fifteen. Let us see whether you have counted right." The performer himself audibly counts the remaining packet, card by card, on the table; immediately afterwards taking the heap in his left hand, and squaring the cards together, thus obtaining the opportunity to separate and palm in his right hand the three top cards. He continues, "Fifteen cards here—and—how many did you say, sir?—yes, seventeen, which the gentleman holds, make thirty-two. Quite right. Now will some one else oblige me by taking charge of these fifteen cards." He hands the cards with the left hand, and at the same moment drops the three palmed cards into the *profonde* on the right side, immediately bringing up the hand, that it may be seen empty. " Now, ladies and gentlemen, I will show you a very curious phenomenon, all the more astonishing because you will bear me witness that, from the time the cards were counted, they have not been even one moment in my possession, but have remained in independent custody. Will you, sir " (addressing the person who holds the second packet), " hold up the cards in such a manner that I can touch them with my wand. I have but to strike the cards with my wand once, twice, thrice, and at each touch a card will fly from the packet which you are now holding, and go to join the seventeen cards in the other packet. As this trick is performed by sheer force of will, without the aid of apparatus or dexterity, I shall be glad if you will all assist me by adding the force of your will to mine, which will greatly lighten my labour. At each touch of the wand, then, please, all present, mentally to command a card to pass in the manner I have mentioned. Are you all ready! Then we will make the experiment. One, two, THREE! Did you see the cards pass? I saw them distinctly, but possibly my eyes are quicker than yours. Will each of the gentlemen who hold the cards be good enough to count his packet ?" This is done, and it is found that the one holds twenty cards, and the other twelve only.

It is obvious that the two packets now collectively contain duplicates of three cards, while three others are missing; but it is extremely unlikely that any one will suspect this, or seek to verify the constitution of the pack.

TO ALLOW SEVERAL PERSONS EACH TO DRAW A CARD, AND THE PACK HAVING BEEN SHUFFLED, TO MAKE ANOTHER CARD DRAWN HAPHAZARD CHANGE SUCCESSIVELY INTO EACH OF THOSE FIRST CHOSEN.—Invite a person to draw a card. This first card need not be forced, as it is not essential for you to know what card it is, so long as you afterward keep it in sight. When the card is returned to the pack, insert the little finger under it, and make the pass in order to bring it to the bottom Make the first of the false shuffles (*see* page 23), and leave it at the bottom. Again make the pass to bring it to the middle of the pack, and force the same card on a second and again on a third person, each time making a false shuffle, and leaving the chosen card, which we will call *a,* ultimately in the hands of the last person who drew.* When you have concluded the last shuffle, which (the card not now being in the pack) may be a genuine one, you offer the pack to some person who has not yet drawn, and allow him to draw any card he pleases, which second card we will call *b.* You open the pack, and ask the persons holding the two cards to replace them one on the other; that first chosen, *a,* being placed last—*i.e.,* uppermost. You make the pass to bring them to the top, and palm them, and then immediately hand the pack to be shuffled by one of the company. This being done, you replace them on the top of the pack, and, spreading the cards, and appearing to reflect a moment, pick out by the backs as many cards as there have been persons who drew (*i.e.,* four) including among them the two cards *a* and *b.* Exhibiting the four cards, you ask each drawer to say, without naming his card, whether his card is among them. The reply is, of course, in the affirmative. Each person who drew, seeing his own card among those shown, naturally assumes that the remaining cards are those of the other drawers; and the remainder of the audience, finding the drawers satisfied, are fully convinced that the cards shown are the four which were drawn. You now replace the cards in different parts of the pack, placing the two actually drawn in the middle, and secretly make the pass to bring them to the top. Then, spreading the cards, you invite another person to draw, which you allow him to do wherever he chooses. When he has done so, you request him to name aloud his card, which we will call *c.* Holding the card aloft, you ask each of the former drawers in succession, " Is this your card?" To which each answers, " No." After having received this answer for the last time, you " change " the card by the first method (*see* page 28) for the top card. You now have the card *a* (the one drawn several times) in your hand, while *b* has become the top card, and *c,* which you have just exhibited, is at the bottom. You continue, before showing *a,* " You are all agreed that this is not your

---

* The different drawers should be persons tolerably far apart, as it is essential that they should not discover that they have all drawn the same card.

card ; you had better not be too sure. I will ask you one by one.
You, sir," addressing the first drawer, " are you quite sure this is not
your card ? " He is obliged to own that it now is his card. " Pardon
me," you say, breathing gently on the back of the card, " it may have
been so a moment ago, but now it is this lady's," exhibiting it to the
second drawer, who also acknowledges it as her card. To the third
person you say, " I think you drew a card, did you not ? May I ask
you to blow upon the back of this card ! It has changed again, you
see, for now it is your card." The card having been again recognized, you continue, " There was no one else, I think," at the same
moment again making the change by the first method, so that *a* is
now at bottom and *b* in your hand. The person who drew *b* will,
no doubt, remind you that you have not yet shown him his card.
You profess to have quite forgotten him, and, feigning to be a little
embarrassed, ask what his card was. He names it accordingly, upon
which you ask him to blow upon the card you hold, and, turning it
over, show that it has now turned into that card. Then again making
the change, you remark, "Everybody has certainly had his card now."
Then, yourself blowing upon the card you hold, which is now an
indifferent one, you show it, and remark, " You observe that now it
is nobody's card."

In this trick, as in every other which mainly depends upon forcing a given card, there is always the possibility that some person
may, either by accident or from a malicious desire to embarrass you,
insist upon drawing some other card. This, however, must not discourage you. In the first place, when you have once thoroughly
acquired the knack of forcing, the victim will, nine times out of ten,
draw the card you desire, even though doing his utmost to exercise,
as he supposes, an absolutely free choice; and the risk may be still
further diminished by offering the cards to persons whose physiog-
nomy designates them as likely to be good-naturedly easy in their
selection. But if such a *contretemps* should occur in the trick we have
just described, it is very easily met. You will remember that the first
card drawn is not forced, but freely chosen. It is well to make the
most of this fact, and for that purpose, before beginning the trick, to
offer the cards to be shuffled by several persons in succession, and
specially to draw the attention of the audience to the fact that you

cannot possibly have any card in view. When the card is chosen, offer to allow the drawer, if he has the slightest suspicion that you know what it is, to return it, and take another. He may or may not accept the offer, but your evident indifference as to the card chosen will make the audience the less likely to suspect you afterwards of desiring to put forward any particular card. If, notwithstanding, a wrong card is drawn the second time, leave it in the hand of the drawer, and at once offer the cards to another person, and again endeavour to force the proper card, *a*, and let the wrong card take the place of *b* in the foregoing description. In the very unlikely event of a second wrong card being drawn, leave that also for the moment in the hands of the drawer, and let that card take the place of *c* in the finish of the trick.

To make Four Aces change to Four Kings, and Four Kings to Four Aces.—This very effective trick is performed by the aid of four cards, which are so prepared as to appear aces on the one side and kings on the other. To make them, take four ordinary aces and four ordinary kings, and peel off half the thickness of each card. This may be easily done by splitting one corner of the card with a sharp penknife, when the remainder can be pulled apart without difficulty. The cards being thus reduced in thickness, paste back to back the king and ace of each suit, placing them in a press or under a heavy weight, that they may dry perfectly smooth and flat. Better still, entrust the process to some person who is accustomed to mounting photographs, when, at a trifling cost, you will have your double-faced cards thoroughly well made.

Place these four cards beforehand in different parts of the pack, the " ace " side downwards, *i.e.*, in the same direction as the faces of the other cards. Place the genuine aces face downwards on the top of the pack, which being thus disposed, you are ready to begin the trick.

Take the pack in your hand, face uppermost. Remark, " For this trick I want the aces and kings," and pick out, one by one, the real kings and the sham aces. Lay these cards on the table, the kings face upwards, and the prepared cards with the " ace " side uppermost. Draw the attention of the audience to these cards, and meanwhile make the pass so as to bring the two halves of the pack face to face, when the four genuine aces will (unknown to the audience) be at the lower end of the pack. Place the four kings ostentatiously upon the opposite end of the pack, *i.e.*, that which is for the time being uppermost.

You now borrow a hat. Placing the pack for a moment on the table, and taking the four false aces in one hand and the hat in the other, place the aces on the table, and cover them with the hat, at the same moment turning them over. Then taking the pack in your hand, once more show the kings, and replacing them, say, "I shall now order these four kings to pass under the hat, and the four aces to return to the pack. I have only to touch the cards with my wand, and say, 'Pass,' and the change is accomplished." As you touch the cards with the wand, turn over the pack (*see* page 37), the bringing together of the hands and the gentle tap with the wand effectually covering the slight movement of the hand. If you do not use the wand, a semi-circular sweep of the hand which holds the cards in the direction of the hat, as you say " Pass," will answer the same purpose.

Having shown that the cards have changed according to command, you may, by repeating the process, cause the cards to return to their original positions. It is better not to carry the trick further than this, or some of the audience may possibly ask to be allowed to examine the cards, which would be embarrassing.

After the trick is over, make the pass to bring the pack right again, and then get the double-faced cards out of the way as soon as possible. The best way to do this, without exciting suspicion, is to take them up in the right hand, and apparently turn them over and leave them on the top of the pack, but in reality palm them, and slip them into your pocket, or elsewhere out of sight. After having done this, you may safely leave the pack within reach of the audience, who, if they examine it, finding none but ordinary cards, will be more than ever puzzled as to your *modus operandi*.

HAVING MADE FOUR PACKETS OF CARDS WITH AN ACE AT THE BOTTOM OF EACH, TO BRING ALL FOUR ACES INTO WHICHEVER PACKET THE COMPANY MAY CHOOSE.—Take the four aces, or any

other four cards of equal value, from the pack, and throw them face upwards on the table. While the company's attention is being drawn to
them, make the pass, as in the last trick, so as to bring the two halves
of the pack face to face. The company, having satisfied themselves
that the four cards shown are really the four aces, and are without
preparation, take them up, and replace them face downwards upon
the top of the pack, which you hold in the left hand, remarking, " I
am going to show you a trick with these four aces. I shall first place
them on the table, and put three indifferent cards on each of them."
Meanwhile, get the thumb of the left hand in position for the
"turn over," and the instant that you have drawn off the top card
with the right hand, turn over the pack, which the movement of
the hands in removing the top card will enable you to do without
attracting notice. This top card is really an ace, and you may therefore show it, as if by accident, while placing it on the table. Lay
it face downwards, and then place three cards from the end you have
just brought uppermost (which the audience will believe to be the
other three aces), in a line with it on the table. Next place three
more cards, taken from the same end of the pack, upon each of the
three cards last dealt. When you come to that first dealt (the genuine
ace), before dealing the three cards upon it, you must again turn
over the pack, thereby bringing the three aces on the top. You thus
have upon the table four packets of four cards each, one packet consisting of aces only, and the remaining three packets of indifferent
cards; but the audience imagine that the aces are divided, and that
there is one at the foot of each packet. You now ask any one to
touch two out of the four packets. The two packets which he
touches may include, or may not include, the one containing the four
aces. Whichever be the case, take up and put aside the two which
do *not* include the packet of aces, and remark, " We will place these
aside," an observation which will be equally appropriate whether
those were the two touched or not. Next ask the same or another person to touch one of the two remaining packets, and in like
manner add that one which does not contain the aces to the two
already set aside. Placing these three packets on the table, request
some one of the company to place his hand upon them, and hold
them tightly; then, taking the remaining packet yourself, observe.

"You have three aces, and I have only one; but by virtue of my magic power I shall compel those three aces to leave your hand, and come to mine, I just touch the back of your hand, so" (touching it with the cards you hold), "and say, 'Pass.' The change is already accomplished. Here are all four aces. Please to examine your own cards, when you will find you have not a single ace left. Let me remind you that the audience chose, and not I, which of the four packets you should take, and which one I should retain." *

There is another method of performing this trick, which dispenses with the necessity of "turning over" the pack. In this case, as you place the four aces on the top of the pack, you insert the little finger of the left hand under the three uppermost, and make the pass to bring these three to the bottom, still, however, keeping the finger between them and the rest of the pack. You deal out the four top cards (supposed to be the four aces), as above, and three others on each of the three non-aces. You next ask some person to draw any three cards (taking care not to let him draw one of the three at the bottom), and place them at the top of the pack. The moment he has done so, you again make the pass, thus bringing the three aces upon them. You then say, taking off (without showing) the three top cards, "Now I will take these three cards, freely drawn from the middle of the pack, and place them here on this last ace." From this point the course of the trick is the same as already described.

To CHANGE THE FOUR ACES, HELD TIGHTLY BY A PERSON, INTO FOUR INDIFFERENT CARDS.—This is a most brilliant trick, and puzzles even adepts in card-conjuring. In combination with the "Shower of Aces," which next follows, it was one of the principal feats of the Elder Conus, and subsequently of the celebrated Comte.

The trick is performed as follows:—You begin by announcing that you require the assistance of some gentleman who never believes anything that he is told. The audience generally take this as a joke,

---

* It will be observed that this trick is terminated after the manner described at page 45, to which the reader is recommended to refer, as the above description will be more clearly intelligible by the aid of the further explanations there given.

but for the purpose of this trick it is really rather an advantage to have the assistance of a person who will take nothing for granted, and will be satisfied with nothing short of ocular demonstration of any fact which you desire him to concede. Some little fun may be made in the selection, but a volunteer having at last been approved of, you request him to step forward to your table. Selecting from the pack the four aces, you ask him to say aloud what cards those are, at the same time holding them up that all may see them. Then laying the aces face upwards on the table, you hand him the remainder of the cards, and ask him to ascertain and state to the company, whether there is any peculiarity about the cards, and whether, in particular, there are any other aces in the pack. His reply is in the negative. You then ask whether any other person would like to examine the pack. All being satisfied, you take the pack, face downwards, in your left hand, and picking up the four aces with the right, place them on the top, at the same moment slightly ruffling the cards. Then taking the aces one by one (without showing them) you place them face downwards on the table. Addressing the person assisting you, you say, "I place these four aces on the table. You admit that they are the four aces." Your victim, not having seen the faces of the cards since they were replaced on the pack, and having noticed the slight sound produced by your ruffling the cards, will, in all probability, say that he does not admit anything of the sort. "Why," you reply, "you have only just seen them; but I'll show them to you again, if you like." Turning them face upwards, you show that the four cards really are the aces, and again replace them on the pack, ruffle the cards, and deal out the four aces face downwards as before. You again ask your assistant whether he is certain this time that the four cards on the table are the aces. He may possibly be still incredulous, but if he professes himself satisfied, you ask him what he will bet that these cards are really the aces, and that you have not conjured them away already. He will naturally be afraid to bet, and you remark, "Ah, I could tell by the expression of your countenance that you were not quite satisfied. I'm afraid you are sadly wanting in faith, but as I can't perform the trick, for the sake of my own reputation, until you are thoroughly convinced, I will show you the cards once more." This you do, and again replace them on the pack, but before doing so, slip the little finger of the left hand under the top card of the pack. Again take off the aces with the finger and thumb of the right hand, carrying with them at the same time this top card. Then with a careless gesture of the right hand toward the audience, so as to show them the face of the undermost card (the one you have just added), you continue, "I really can't imagine what makes you so incredulous. Here are the aces" (you replace the five cards on the pack)—"I take them one by one, so, and place them on the table. Surely there is no possibility of sleight-of-hand here. Are you all satisfied that these are really the aces *now?*" The audience having noted, as you intended them to do, that the fifth or bottom card was not an ace, naturally conclude that other cards have been by some means substituted for the aces, and when you ask the question for the last time, you are met by a general shout of "No!" You say, with an injured expression, "Really, ladies and gentlemen, if you are all such unbelievers, I may as well retire at once. I should hope that, at least, you will have the grace to apologize for your unfounded suspicions." Then, turning to the person assisting you, you continue, "Sir, as every act of mine appears to be an object of suspicion, perhaps *you* will kindly show the company that those are the aces, and replace them yourself on the top of the pack."

This he does. But during the course of the above little discussion, you have taken the opportunity to count off, and palm in your right hand, the five top cards of the pack. It is hardly necessary to observe that while doing this, you must scrupulously refrain from looking at your hands. The mode of counting is to push forward the cards one by one with the thumb, and to check them with the third finger, of the left hand. A very little practice will enable you to count off any number of cards by feel, in this manner, with the greatest ease. When the aces are replaced on the top of the pack, you transfer the pack from the left to the right hand, thus bringing the palmed cards above them, then placing the whole pack on the table, face downwards, inquire, "Will you be good enough to tell me where the aces are *now?*" The answer is generally very confident, "On the top of the pack." Without taking the pack in your hand, you take off, one by one, the four top cards, and lay them face downwards on the table, as before; then taking up the fifth card and exhibiting it to the company, observe, "You see there are no more aces left, but if you like you can look through the pack." So saying, you take up the cards, and run them rapidly over with their faces towards the spectators, taking care, however, not to expose either of the five at the top, four of which are the genuine aces. Then, addressing your assistant, you say, "The company being at last satisfied, perhaps you will be good enough to place your hand on those four cards, and hold them as tightly as possible." Then, holding the pack in the left hand, you take between the first finger and thumb of the right hand the top card of the pack, being the only one left of the five you palmed and placed over the aces, and say, "Now I am going to take four indifferent cards one after the other, and exchange them for the four aces in this gentleman's hand. Observe the simplicity of the process. I take the card that first comes to hand" (here you show the face of the card that you hold, which we will suppose to be the seven of diamonds), "I don't return it to the pack, even for a moment, but merely touch the hand with it, and it becomes the ace of (say) spades" (which you show it to be). At the words "return it to the pack," you move the card with what is taken to be merely an indicative gesture, towards the pack, and at the same instant "change" it by the third method (*see* page 30) for the top card of the pack, which is one of the aces.

You now have the seven of diamonds at the top of the pack, with the remaining three aces immediately following it. You must not show this seven of diamonds a second time, and it is therefore necessary to get it out of the way. The neatest way of doing this is as follows:— You remark, "To show you that I take the cards just as they come, I will give them a shuffle," which you do as indicated for the *first* of the "false shuffles" (*see* page 23), subject to the modification following. Pass into the right hand first the top card (the seven of diamonds) alone, and upon this card pass the next three, which are the three aces, then the rest of the cards indifferently. When all the cards are thus passed into the right hand, shuffle them again anyhow, but take care to conclude by bringing the four lowest cards to the top; you will now have the three aces uppermost, and the seven of diamonds in the fourth place. Taking off the top card, and drawing it sharply over the hand of the person assisting, you show that it also is an ace, and in like manner with the next card, making, if you choose, a false shuffle between. After the third ace has been shown, make a false shuffle, and finally leave at the top the last ace, with one card above it. This may be effected by bringing up from the bottom in concluding the shuffle the two bottom cards, instead of the last (the ace) only. Taking the top card between the thumb and first finger of the right hand, and showing it with apparent carelessness, so as to give the company the opportunity of remarking that it is not an ace, you replace it on the pack for an instant, saying, "We have had three aces, I think. Which is it that is wanting?" Here you glance down at the aces on the table. "Oh! the ace of diamonds. Then the card that I hold must change to the ace of diamonds." You have meanwhile effected the change, and turning up the card you hold, you show that it is the ace of diamonds.

You may, if you please, use the first instead of the third method of making the "change" in performing this trick, but the first method demands a higher degree of dexterity to make it equally deceptive; and the movement used in the third method has in this instance the advantage of appearing to be the natural accompaniment of the words of the performer.

THE SHOWER OF ACES.—This trick forms a very effective sequel to that last described, or may with equal facility be made to follow many other card tricks. To perform it, the first essential is the possession of a pack of cards similar in size and pattern to that you have in general use, but consisting of aces only. You can purchase such a pack at most of the conjuring depôts, or you may, without much difficulty, manufacture one for yourself. If you decide upon the latter course, you must first procure thirty or forty blank cards backed with the requisite pattern. These you can transform into aces in two ways. The first is, to split three or four ordinary cards of each suit, and, after peeling off, as thin as possible, the face of each, carefully cut out the pips, and paste one in the centre of each of your blank cards. This process, however, takes a considerable time; and, when the sham aces are collected in a pack, the extra thickness of the paper in the centre of each produces an objectionable bulge. The better plan is to procure a stencil-plate representing the figures of a club, heart, and diamond, which will enable you to produce any number of the aces of those suits, using Indian ink for the clubs, and vermilion, mixed with a little size, for the hearts and diamonds. The ace of spades you must dispense with, but this is of little consequence to the effect of the trick.

You must have these cards close at hand, in such a position as to enable you to add them instantly, and without attracting observation, to the pack you have been using. If you use the regular conjuror's table, before described, you may place your pack of aces on the *servante.* If you do not use such a table, you may place them in one of your *pochettes.* In either case, you will have little difficulty in reaching them at the right moment, and placing them on the top of the ordinary pack, holding the whole in your left hand, but keeping the little finger between. Having done this, you say to the person who has been assisting you (in continuation of the trick you have just performed), "You appear to be fond of aces, sir. How many would you like?" He is fully convinced, having previously examined the pack, that you have only the ordinary four; but, from a desire to put your powers to an extreme test, he may possibly name a larger number—say, seven. "Seven!" you reply; "that is rather unreasonable, seeing there are only four in the pack. However, we will make some more. Do you know how to make aces? No? Then I will show you. Like all these things, it's simplicity itself, when you once know it. Will you oblige me by blowing upon the pack?" which you hold just under his nose for that purpose. He does so, and you deliberately count off and give to him the seven top cards, which all prove to be aces. You then say, "Perhaps you would like some more. You have only to blow again. Come, how many will you have?" He again blows on the pack, and you give him the number desired. While he is examining them, you cover the pack for a moment with your right hand, and palm a dozen or so of the remaining aces. Then remarking, "You blew a little too strongly that time. You blew a lot of aces into your waistcoat," you thrust your hand into the breast of his waistcoat, and bring out three or four of the palmed cards, leaving the remainder inside; then pull out two or three more, dropping them on the floor, so as to scatter them about and make them appear as numerous as possible. You then say, "There seem to be a good many more there yet. Perhaps you will take them out yourself." While he is doing so, you palm in the right hand all the remaining aces. When he professes to have taken out all, you say, " Are you quite sure that you have no more aces about you? You blew very hard, you know. I really think you must have some more. Will you allow me?" Then, standing on his right, you place your right hand just below his eyes, and spring the remaining aces from it, in the manner indicated for springing the cards from hand to hand (*see* page 37), the effect being exactly as if a shower of cards flew from his nose.

SEVERAL PERSONS HAVING EACH DRAWN TWO CARDS, WHICH HAVE BEEN RETURNED AND SHUFFLED, TO MAKE EACH COUPLE APPEAR IN SUCCESSION, ONE AT THE TOP AND THE OTHER AT THE BOTTOM OF THE PACK.—This capital trick was also a great favourite with Comte, who christened it, for reasons best known to himself, by the poetical name of " The Ladies' Looking-glass."

The cards having been freely shuffled, you invite a person to draw two cards, allowing him free choice. Opening the pack in the middle, you ask him to place his cards together in the opening. You bring them to the top by the pass, make the first of the false shuffles, and conclude by leaving them on the top. Offer the cards to a second person to draw a couple, but in opening the cards for him to return them, make the pass, so that they may be placed upon the pair already drawn, which are thereby brought to the middle of the pack. Again make the pass, so as to bring all four to the top Make another false shuffle, leaving those four on the top, and offer the cards to a third and fourth person, each time repeating the process. Make the false shuffle for the last time, so as to leave all the drawn cards in a body on the top of the pack, with one indifferent card above them. The audience believe that they are thoroughly dispersed, and your first care must be to strengthen that impression. If you are expert in card-palming, you may palm the nine cards, and give the pack to be shuffled by one of the spectators; but this is not absolutely necessary, and there is some risk of the company noticing the absence of part of the pack. You remark, "You have all seen the drawn cards placed in different parts of the pack, and the whole have been since thoroughly shuffled. The drawn cards are therefore at this moment scattered in different parts of the pack. I can assure you that I do not myself know what the cards are " (this is the only item of *fact* in the whole sentence) ; " but yet, by a very slight, simple movement, I shall make them appear, in couples as they were drawn, at top and bottom of the pack." Then, showing the bottom card, you ask, " Is this anybody's card ? " The reply is in the negative. You next show the top card, and make the same inquiry. While you do so, you slip the little finger under the next card, and as you replace the card you have just shown, make the pass, thus bringing both cards to the bottom of the pack. Meanwhile, you ask the *last* person who drew what his cards were. When he names them, you " ruffle " the cards, and show him first the bottom and then the top card, which will be the two he drew. While exhibiting the top card, take the opportunity to slip the little finger of the left hand immediately under the card next below it, and as you replace the top one make the pass at that point. You now have the third couple placed top and bottom. Make the drawer name them, ruffle the cards, and show them as before, again making the pass to bring the card just shown at top, with that next following, to the bottom of the pack, which will enable you to exhibit the second couple in like manner. These directions sound a little complicated, but if followed with the cards will be found simple enough.

You may, by way of variation, pretend to forget that a fourth person drew two cards, and, after making the pass as before, appear to be about to proceed to another trick. You will naturally be re-minded that So-and-so drew two cards. Apologizing for the over-sight, you beg him to say what his cards were. When he does so, you say, "To tell you the truth I have quite lost sight of them ; but it is of no consequence, I can easily find them again." Then nipping the upper end of the cards between the thumb and second finger of the right hand, which should be slightly moistened, you make the pack swing, pendulum fashion, a few inches backwards and forwards, when the whole of the intermediate cards will fall out, leaving the top and bottom card alone in your hand. These you hand to the drawer, who is compelled to acknowledge them as the cards he drew.

To MAKE TWO CARDS, EACH FIRMLY HELD BY A DIFFERENT PERSON, CHANGE PLACES.—For the purpose of this trick you must have a duplicate of some one of the cards, say the knave of spades, and you must arrange your pack beforehand as follows: The bottom card must be a knave of spades; the next to it an indifferent card, say the nine of diamonds: and next above that, the second knave of spades. You come forward carelessly shuffling the cards (which you may do as freely as you please as to all above the three mentioned), and finish by placing the undermost knave of spades on the top. The bottom card will now be the nine of diamonds, with a knave of spades next above it. Holding up the pack in your left hand, in such a position as to be ready to "draw back" the bottom card (*see* page 36), you say, "Will you all be kind enough to notice and remember the bottom card, which I will place on the table here, so as to be in sight of everybody." So saying, you drop the pack to the horizontal position, and draw out with the middle finger of the right hand apparently the bottom card, but really slide back that card, and take the one next to it (the knave of spades), which you lay face downwards on the table, and ask some one to cover with his hand. You then (by the slip or pass) bring the remaining knave of spades from the top to the bottom, and shuffle again as before, taking care not to displace the two bottom cards. Again ask the company to note the bottom card (which is now the knave of spades), and draw out, as before, apparently that card, but really the nine of diamonds. Place that also face downwards on the table, and request another person to cover it with his hand. The company are persuaded that the first card thus drawn was the nine of diamonds, and the second the knave of spades. You now announce that you will compel the two cards to change places, and after touching them with your wand, or performing any other mystical ceremony which may serve to account for the transformation, you request the person holding each to show his card, when they will be found to have obeyed your commands. The attention of the audience being naturally attracted to the two cards on the table, you will have little difficulty in palming and pocketing the second knave of spades, which is still at the bottom of the pack, and which, if discovered, would spoil the effect of the trick.

To Change Four Cards, drawn haphazard, and placed on the table, into Cards of the same Value as a Single Card subsequently chosen by one of the Spectators.—This trick is on the same principle as that last above described, but is much more brilliant in effect. To perform it, it is necessary, or at least desirable, to possess a forcing pack consisting of one card several times repeated. We will suppose your forcing pack to consist of queens of diamonds. Before commencing the trick, you must secretly prepare your ordinary pack in the following manner:—Place at the bottom any indifferent card, and on this a queen; then another indifferent card, then another queen; another indifferent card, then another queen; another indifferent card, and on it the fourth and last queen. You thus have at the bottom the four queens, each with an ordinary card next below it. Each indifferent card should be of the same suit as the queen next above it, so that all of the four suits may be represented. Shuffle the cards, taking care however, not to disturb the eight cards above mentioned. Then say, "I am about to take four cards from the bottom, and place them on t' e table. Will you please to remember what they are?" Show the bottom card, then, dropping the pack to the horizontal position, "draw back" that card, and take the next, which is one of the queens, and, without showing it, lay it face downwards on the table. You now want to get rid of the card you have already shown, which is still at the bottom. To effect this without arousing suspicion, the best and easiest plan is to shuffle each time after drawing a card, not disturbing the arranged cards at the bottom, but concluding the shuffle by placing the bottom card, which is the one you desire to get rid of, on the top of the pack. Thus after each shuffle you are enabled to show a fresh bottom card, which, however, you slide back, and draw the next card (a queen) instead. Repeat this four times, when you will have all four queens on the table, though the audience imagine them to be the four cards they have just seen. In order to impress this more fully upon them, ask some one to repeat the names of the four cards. While the attention of the audience is thus occupied, you secretly exchange the pack you have been using for your forcing pack, and advancing to the audience say, "Now I shall ask some one to draw a card; and whatever card is drawn, I will, without even touching them, transform the four cards on the table to cards of the same value. Thus, if you draw a king they shall all become kings; if you draw a ten, they shall become tens, and so on. Now, choose your card, as deliberately as you please." You spread the cards before the drawer, allowing him perfect freedom of choice, as, of course, whatever card he draws must necessarily be a queen of diamonds. You ask him to be good enough to say what the card he has drawn is, and on being told that it is a queen, you say, "Then, by virtue of my magic power, I order that the four cards now on the table change to queens. Pray observe that I do not meddle with them in any way. I merely touch each with my wand, so! Will some one kindly step forward, and bear witness that the change has really taken place."

If you do not possess a forcing pack, but rely upon your own skill in forcing with an ordinary pack, it is well to prepare this second beforehand by placing the four queens (supposing that you desire a queen to be drawn) at the bottom. Making the pass as you advance to the company, you bring these to the middle and present the pack. It is comparatively easy to insure one or other of four cards placed together being drawn.

TWO HEAPS OF CARDS, UNEQUAL IN NUMBER, BEING PLACED UPON THE TABLE, TO PREDICT BEFOREHAND WHICH OF THE TWO THE COMPANY WILL CHOOSE.—There is an old schoolboy trick, which consists in placing on the table two heaps of cards, one consisting of seven indifferent cards, and the other of the four sevens. The performer announces that he will predict beforehand (either verbally or in writing) which of the two heaps the company will choose; and fulfils his undertaking by declaring that they will choose "the seven heap." This description will suit either heap, being in the one case understood to apply to the number of cards in the heap, in the other case to denote the value of the individual cards.

The trick in this form would not be worth noticing, save as a prelude to a newer and really good method of performing the same feat. You place on the table two heaps of cards, each containing the same number, say six cards, which may be the first that come to hand, the value of the cards being in this case of no consequence.

You announce that, of the two heaps, one contains an odd and the other an even number. This is, of course, untrue; but it is one of the postulates of a conjuror's performance that he may tell professionally as many fibs as he likes, and that his most solemn asseverations are only to be taken in a Pickwickian sense. You continue, "I do not tell you which heap is odd and which is even, but I will predict to you, as many times as you like, which heap you will choose. Observe, I do not influence your choice in any way. I may tell you that you will this time choose the heap containing the odd number." While delivering this harangue, you take the opportunity of palming in your right hand a single card from the top of the pack, and place the remainder of the cards apart on the table. When the audience have made their choice, you pick up the chosen heap with the right hand, thereby adding the palmed card to that heap, and, coming forward, ask some one to verify your prediction. The number is, naturally, found to be odd. You then bring forward the second heap, which is found to be even. Join the two heaps together, and again separate them, palming the top card of the odd heap, replace the two heaps on the table, and this time predict that the audience will choose the heap containing the even number. When they have made their selection, you have only to pick up the non-chosen heap with the hand containing the palmed card, and the chosen heap with the empty hand.

You may with truth assure the audience that you could go on all the evening predicting their choice with equal certainty, but it is best not to repeat the trick too often. You will do wisely to pass on at once to the next trick, which will enable you to display your powers of divination in a yet more surprising form.

A Row of Cards being placed Face Downwards on the Table, to indicate, by turning up one of them, how many of such Cards have during your absence been transferred from one end of the Row to the other.—This trick is somewhat out of place in this chapter, inasmuch as it involves no sleight-of-hand, but we insert it here as forming an appropriate sequel to that last described. It is thus performed :—You deal from the top of the pack, face downwards on the table, a row of fifteen cards. To all appearance, you are quite indifferent what cards you take, but, in reality, you have pre-arranged the first ten cards in the following manner :—First a ten, then a nine, then an eight, and so on down to the ace inclusive. The suits are of no consequence. The eleventh card should be a blank card, if you have one of the same pattern as the pack ; if not, a knave will do. This card, in the process which follows, will stand for o. When the fifteen cards are dealt, their arrangement will therefore be as follows :—

10, 9, 8, 7, 6, 5, 4, 3, 2, 1, o, *, *, *, *,—

the four asterisks representing any four indifferent cards. This special arrangement is, of course, unknown to the audience. You now offer to leave the room, and invite the audience, during your absence, to remove any number of the cards (not exceeding ten) from the right hand end of the row, and place them, in the same order, at the other end of the row. On your return, you have only to turn up the eleventh card, counting from the beginning or left hand end, which will indicate by its points the number of cards removed. A few examples will illustrate this fact. Thus, suppose that two cards only have been removed from the right to the left hand end, the row thus altered will be as follows :—

*, *, 10, 9, 8, 7, 6, 5, 4, 3, [2], 1, o, *, *.

The eleventh card from the left will be a two, being the number moved. Suppose that seven cards have been removed, the new arrangement will be—

2, 1, o, *, *, *, *, 10, 9, 8 [7], 6, 5, 4, 3,

and the card in the eleventh place will be a seven. Suppose the audience avail themselves of your permission to the fullest extent, and remove ten cards, the same result follows.

5, 4, 3, 2, 1, o, *, *, *, *, [10], 9, 8, 7, 6.

If no card is moved, the o will remain the eleventh card, as it was at first. If you repeat the trick a second time, you must replace the cards moved in their original positions. Do not, if you can possibly help it, allow the audience to perceive that you count the cards.

You are not necessarily restricted to fifteen cards, but may increase the number up to twenty if you please, making up the complement by increasing the number of the indifferent cards at the right hand of the original row.

The trick may be equally well performed with dominoes, or with numbered pieces of paper, as with playing cards.

SEVERAL CARDS HAVING BEEN FREELY CHOSEN BY THE COMPANY, RETURNED AND SHUFFLED, AND THE PACK PLACED IN A PERSON'S POCKET, TO MAKE SUCH PERSON DRAW OUT ONE BY ONE THE CHOSEN CARDS.—This trick is an especial favourite of the well-known Herrmann, in whose hands it never fails to produce a brilliant effect. The performer hands the pack to one of the company, who is requested to shuffle it well, and then to invite any four persons each to draw a card. This having been done, the pack is returned to the performer, who then requests the same person to collect the chosen cards face downwards on his open palm. The cards so collected are placed in the middle of the pack, which is then handed to the person who collected them, with a request that he will shuffle them thoroughly. After he has done so, the pack is placed by the performer in the volunteer assistant's breast pocket. The performer now asks one of the four persons who drew to name his card. He next requests the person assisting him to touch the end of his wand, and then as quickly as possible (that the mystic influence may not have time to evaporate) to put his hand in his pocket, and draw out the card named. He takes out one card accordingly, which proves to be the very one called for. A second and third card are named and drawn in the same manner, to the astonishment of all, and not least of the innocent assistant. The fourth and last card, which is, say, the ten of spades, he is requested to look for in the pack, but it proves to be missing, and the performer thereupon offers to show him how to *make* a ten of spades. To do so, he requests him to blow into his pocket, where the missing card is immediately found. But he has, unfortunately, blown too strongly, and has made not only a ten of spades, but a host of other cards, which the performer pulls out in quantities, not only from his pocket, but from the inside of his waistcoat—ultimately producing a final shower from his nose.

This trick, which appears marvellous in execution, is really very simple, and depends for its effect, not so much on any extraordinary degree of dexterity, as on the manner and address of the performer. When the four cards are replaced in the middle of the pack, the performer makes the pass to bring them to the top, and palms them. He then hands the pack to be shuffled. When it is returned, he replaces them on the top, and, placing the person assisting him on his left hand, and facing the audience, places the pack in the left breast pocket of such person, taking care to place the top of the pack (on which are the chosen cards) outwards. In asking the names of the drawn cards, he puts the question first to the person who *last* replaced his card (and whose card is therefore on the top), and so on. He is particular in impressing upon the person assisting him that he must draw out the card as quickly as possible, thus giving him no time to select a card, but compelling him, so to speak, to take that which is readiest to his hand, which will always be the outermost, or top card.

Should he notwithstanding, by accident or finesse, draw out a card from the middle of the pack, the performer at once says, "Oh, you were not half quick enough! You must pull out the card as quick as thought, or the magic influence will go off. Allow *me!*" then pulling out the outer card himself, he shows that it is the right one. When three cards have been thus produced, he himself plunges his hand into the pocket, and takes out the whole pack, with the exception of the then top card, which is the fourth of the cards drawn; then, pretending to recollect himself, he says, "Stay; we had four cards drawn. Will you say what your card was, madam?" We have supposed that it was the ten of spades. He hands the pack to the person assisting him, saying, "Will you find the ten of spades, and return it to the lady?" Being in his pocket, of course it cannot be found in the pack, and on blowing into the pocket it is naturally discovered there. The performer meanwhile has palmed about a third of the pack, which he introduces into the pocket at the same moment that he places his hand therein to take out the supposed superfluous cards. From this stage to the close the trick is merely a repetition of that already given under the title of the "Shower of Aces" (*see* page 97), to which the reader is referred.

THE CARDS HAVING BEEN FREELY SHUFFLED, AND CUT INTO THREE OR FOUR HEAPS, TO NAME THE TOP CARD OF EACH HEAP.— Note the bottom card of the pack, which we will suppose to be the nine of diamonds. Shuffle the cards, so as to bring this card to the top, and palm it. Then remark, "But perhaps you would rather shuffle for yourselves," and hand the pack to some one of the company for that purpose. When the pack is returned, replace the card on the top, and continue, placing the pack on the table, "You observe that I do not meddle with the cards in any way. Now will some one be good enough to cut them into two, three, or four parts, when I will at once name the top card of each." To do this you must take especial notice where the upper part of the pack is placed, as you know that the top card of this particular heap is the nine of diamonds. Placing your finger gravely, not on this, but on one of the other heaps, you say, appearing to reflect, "This is the nine of diamonds." We will suppose that it is in reality the queen of spades. You take it in your hand without allowing the audience to see it, and, noticing what it is, at once touch the top card of another heap, saying, "And this is the queen of spades." Glancing in like manner at this card, which is, say, the seven of clubs, you touch another card, and say, "This is the seven of clubs." We will suppose that this third card is really the ace of hearts. You conclude, taking up the card you have all along known (the real nine of diamonds), "And this last is the ace of hearts." Then, throwing all four on the table, show that you have named them correctly.

This trick should be performed with considerable quickness and vivacity, so as not to give the audience much time for thought as you name the cards. It is further necessary that the spectators be well in front of you, and so placed that they cannot see the faces of the cards as you pick them up.

TO ALLOW A PERSON SECRETLY TO THINK OF A CARD, AND, DIVIDING THE PACK INTO THREE HEAPS, TO CAUSE THE CARD THOUGHT OF TO APPEAR IN WHICHEVER HEAP THE COMPANY MAY CHOOSE.—Hand the pack to the company, with a request that they will well shuffle it. When it is returned, cut the pack into three heaps on the table, and invite some one to secretly think of a card.

When he has done so, say boldly, " The card you have thought of is in *this* heap," touching one of them—say the middle one. " Will you be kind enough to name it ? " The person names, say, the queen of spades. You continue, " Your card, as I have already told you, is in this centre heap. To satisfy you that it is so, and that I do not now place it there by means of any sleight-of-hand, I will, in the first place, show you that it is not in either of the other heaps." Gathering together the two heaps in question, and turning them face upwards, you come forward to the audience, rapidly spreading and running over the cards the while in order to ascertain whether the queen of spades is among them. If it is not, the trick has so far succeeded without any trouble on your part ; and, after showing that the card is not among those you hold, you bring forward the remaining packet, and show that you were correct in your assertion. You then say, " I do not generally repeat a trick, but on this occasion, as you may possibly imagine that my success was a mere result of accident, I will perform the trick once more, and, if you please, you shall your-selves name beforehand the packet in which the card thought of shall appear." The packet having been chosen, you join the other two in your left hand, and invite some one to think of a card. When he has done so, you come forward, as before, to show that it is not among the cards you hold. Luck may again favour you ; but if not, and you see the card chosen among those you hold in your hand, you quickly draw it, by a rapid movement of the second finger of the right hand, behind the rest of the pack, and, continuing your examin-ation, show the company, to all appearance, that the card is not there. Having done this, you again turn the pack over (when the card thought of will be on the top), and, covering the pack for a moment with the right hand, palm that card. Then, picking up with the same hand the heap remaining on the table, you place the palmed card on the top, and, transferring the cards to the left hand, you say, " You are welcome to watch me as closely as you please. You will find that I shall cut these cards at the precise card you thought of." To all appearance you merely cut the cards, but really at the same moment make the pass (by lifting away the lower instead of the upper half of the packet). The upper part of the packet, with the card on the top, remains in the left hand. You request some one to look at the top card, which is found to be the card thought of.

Should the card in the first instance prove to be among the *non*-designated cards, you will proceed as last directed; but do not in this case repeat the trick.

To allow a Person secretly to think of a Card, and, even before such Card is named, to select it from the Pack, and place it singly upon the Table.—This trick is on the same principle, and performed in a great measure by the same means, as that last described. You invite a person to think of a card (without naming it). When he has done so, you offer the pack to another person to shuffle, and finally to a third person to cut. Then, selecting any one card from the pack, you walk to your table, and, without showing what it is, place it face downwards on the table, retaining the rest of the pack in your left hand. Then, addressing the person who was requested to think of a card, you say, "The card which I have just placed on the table is the one you thought of. Will you be good enough to name it?" We will suppose that the card thought of was the ace of spades. You say, as in the last trick, "Allow me to show you, in the first place, that the ace of spades is no longer in the pack." Coming forward to the audience, and rapidly running over the cards, you catch sight of the ace of spades, and slip it behind the rest. Having shown that it is, apparently, not in the pack, you turn the cards over (when the ace will, of course, be on the top), and palm it. Leaving the pack with the audience, you advance to your table, and pick up the card on the table with the same hand in which the ace of spades is already palmed. Draw away the card towards the back of the table, and, as it reaches the edge, drop it on the *servante*, and produce the ace of spades as being the card just picked up. The trick requires a little practice, but, if well executed, the illusion is perfect.

The above directions are framed upon the assumption that you are performing with a proper conjuror's table, which, as already stated, has a *servante*, or hidden shelf, at the back for the reception of objects which the performer may require to pick up or lay down without the knowledge of his audience. The trick may, however, be performed without the aid of such a table, but will, in such case, require some little variation.

If you are using an ordinary table, the most effective mode of finishing the trick is as follows :— Walk boldly to the table, and pick up with the right hand (in which the card actually thought of is palmed) the card lying on the table, and, without looking at it yourself, hold it towards your audience, remarking, " Here it is, you see, the ace of spades." The card being, in truth, a totally different one (say the seven of diamonds), the audience naturally imagine that the trick has broken down, and a derisive murmur apprises you of the fact. You thereupon glance at the card, and affect some little surprise and embarrassment on finding that it is a wrong one. However, after a moment's pause, you say, taking the card face downwards between the thumb and second finger of the left hand, "Well, I really don't know how the mistake could have occurred. However, I can easily correct it." Change the card by the fifth method (*see* page 32), and, after a little byplay to heighten the effect of the trans formation, again show the card, which this time proves to be the right one. The audience will readily conclude that the supposed mistake was really a feint, designed to heighten the effect of the trick.

A Card having been Secretly Thought of by one of the Audience, to place two Indifferent Cards upon the Table, and to Change such one of them as the Audience may select into the Card thought of.—Arrange your pack beforehand in such manner that among the fifteen or sixteen undermost cards there may be only one court card, and note at what number from the bottom this card is. Advance to the company, offering the cards face downwards in the ordinary way, and requesting some person to draw a card. Then, as if upon a second thought, say, before he has time to draw, " Or, if you prefer it, you need not even touch the cards, but merely think of one as I spread them before you." So saying, spread the cards one by one, with their faces to the company, beginning at the bottom. The single court card being conspicuous among so many plain cards, and there being nothing apparently to create a suspicion of design about the arrangement it is ten to one that the person will note that particular card, which we will suppose to be the knave of hearts. When you have run over twelve or fourteen cards in this way, ask, still moving on the cards, "Have you thought of a card?" On receiving an answer in the affirmative, you make the pass two cards belo.. the court card (which you know by the number at which it stands), and forthwith make a false shuffle, leaving the last three cards undisturbed, so that the court card remains third from the bottom. Turning to the audience, you remark, "I will now take the two bottom cards, whatever they may happen to be, and lay them on the table." Then, holding up the pack in the left hand, with the bottom card towards the audience, you inquire, "That is not your card, sir, I suppose? not that?" each time lowering the cards in order to draw away with the moistened finger of the right hand, and place face downwards on the table, the card just shown. The second time, however, you do not really draw the card you have shown, but draw back that card and take the one next to it—viz., the knave of hearts. You then, standing behind your table and facing the audience, again repeat the question, "You are quite sure, sir, that neither of these two cards is the card you thought of? Which of them would you like me to transform into your card, the right or the left?" Whichever the answer is, it may be taken in two ways, and you interpret it as may best suit your purpose. Thus, if you have placed the knave of hearts on your own right, and the choice falls on the right-hand card, you interpret it to mean the one on *your own* right hand. If, on the contrary, the person chooses the card on the left, you interpret him to mean the card on *his* left, and therefore on *your* right; so that in either case you make the choice fall on the knave of hearts.* Taking up the other card, and holding it, without apparent design, so that the audience can see what it is, you return it to the pack. Then say boldly, "This card upon the table will forthwith change to the card you thought of. Will you be good enough to name it?" If he names the knave of hearts, you have nothing to do but to turn up, or request some other person to turn up, the card on the table, and show that it is the right one.

---

* The reader should specially note this expedient, as it is of constant use in conjuring.

It is, however, quite possible that the person, by accident or design, may have thought, not of the knave of hearts, but of some other card, say the nine of diamonds. Even in this case you need not be at a loss, although the card on the table is a wrong one. When the card is named, you say, "The nine of diamonds. Quite right! Let me show you, in the first place, that it is not here in the pack." Advancing to the audience, and at the same time running over the cards, as in the last trick, you draw the nine of diamonds behind the other cards, and show that, apparently, it is not among them. On turning the pack over it will be at the top. Taking the pack in the left hand, and, returning to your table, pick up (with the right hand) the knave of hearts, and without looking at it yourself, say, " Here it is, you see, the nine of diamonds." Then, with a careless gesture, and making a half turn to the right or left to cover the movement, " change " the card by the third method (*see* page 30), taking care not to show the card after the change. The audience will naturally exclaim that the card you have just shown them is not the nine of diamonds. You affect great surprise, and ask, " Indeed, what card was it then?" They reply, "The knave of hearts." "The knave of hearts; surely not!" you exclaim, again showing the card in your hand, which is now found to be the nine of diamonds. "Indeed," you continue, "you could not possibly have seen the knave of hearts, for that gentleman in the front row has had it in his pocket all the evening." The knave of hearts was, in truth, left after the change on the top of the pack. As you advance to the audience, you palm it, and are thereby enabled to find it without difficulty in the pocket of a spectator, or in any other place which you may choose to designate.

It will be observed that the mode here indicated of changing a wrong card into a right one differs from that described in the last trick. Either method will be equally available, but it will be well to practise both, as it is a great desideratum to be able to vary the *dénouement* of a trick.

The course of action above directed in the event of an unexpected card being thought of, may be made available as a means of escape from a break-down in many other cases. Thus, for instance, if you are using a *biseauté* pack, and a chosen card has been replaced without the pack having been previously reversed, or if you have from any other cause accidentally lost the means of discovering a card drawn, you may still bring the trick to an effective termination as follows:— Give the pack to some one to shuffle, and then, drawing a card haphazard, and placing it face downwards on the table, announce boldly that the card drawn is now upon the table. Ask the person to name his card, show apparently that it is not in the pack, and finish the trick in one or other of the modes above described.

A CARD HAVING BEEN DRAWN AND RETURNED, AND THE PACK SHUFFLED, TO DIVIDE THE PACK INTO SEVERAL HEAPS ON THE TABLE, AND TO CAUSE THE DRAWN CARD TO APPEAR IN SUCH HEAP AS THE COMPANY MAY CHOOSE.—Invite a person to draw a card. When it is returned, make the pass to bring it to the top. Make a false shuffle, and leave it still at the top. If any of the audience requests to be allowed to shuffle, palm the card, and hand him the pack. When it is returned, again place the card on the top.

Taking the cards in the right hand, face downwards, drop them, in packets of four or five cards each, on the table, noting particularly where you place the *last* packet (on the top of which is the chosen card). Ask the audience in which of the heaps they would like the chosen card to appear, and when they have made their choice, pick up all the other packets and place them in the left hand, placing the packet on which is the chosen card at the top. Divide the chosen packet into two, and bid the audience again choose between these, placing the cards of the non-chosen packet below the pack in the left hand. If the packet still remaining will admit of it, divide it into two again, but endeavour so to arrange matters that the packet ultimately chosen shall consist of two cards only, concealing however from the audience the precise number of cards in the packet. When you have reached this stage of the trick, palm the drawn card, which we will suppose to have been the ace of diamonds, and picking up with the same hand the chosen packet, secretly place that card on the top. Place the three cards face downwards side by side, the ace of diamonds in the middle, and ask the audience which of the three they desire to become the card originally drawn. If they choose the middle card, the trick is already done, and after asking the person to name his card, and showing that neither of the two outside ones is the card in question, you turn up the ace of diamonds.

If the choice falls on either of the outside cards, gather together all three, without showing them (the ace still being in the middle) and ask some one to blow on them. Then deal them out again in apparently the same order as before, but really deal the second for the first, so as to bring that card into the place of the card indicated. Then, after showing the two other cards as above directed, finally turn up the ace of diamonds, and show that it is the card originally chosen.

To change a drawn Card into the Portraits of several of the Company in succession.—For the purpose of this trick you will require a forcing pack of similar pattern to your ordinary pack, but consisting throughout of a single card, say the seven of clubs. You must also have half-a-dozen or more sevens of clubs of the same pattern, on the faces of which you must either draw or paste small caricature portraits, after the manner of Twelfth Night characters; which should be of such a kind as to excite laughter without causing offence. You arrange your pack beforehand as follows:—On the top place a fancy portrait, say of a young lady; then a seven of clubs, then a fancy portrait of a gentleman, then a seven of clubs; another fancy portrait of a lady, another seven of clubs, and so on; so that the first eight or ten cards of the pack shall consist of alternate portraits and sevens of clubs (the top card of all being a lady's portrait), and the rest of the pack of sevens of clubs only.

Secretly exchange the prepared pack for that which you have been using. Invite a young lady to draw, taking care to offer that part of the pack which consists of sevens of clubs only, so that the card she draws will, of necessity, be a seven of clubs. You then say, when she has looked at the card, "Will you now be kind enough to return that card to the pack, when I will paint your portrait on it." You open the cards bookwise, about the middle of the pack, for her to return the card, and when she has done so, request her to breathe on it. As she does so, you "slip" (*see* page 35) the top card of the pack on to that which she has just replaced, and on examining that card (which she takes to be the one she has just seen) she is surprised to find that it is still a seven of clubs, but adorned with a more or less flattering likeness of herself. You continue, after the portrait has been handed round and replaced, "I would willingly give you this portrait to take home, but, unfortunately, being only a magical picture, the likeness fades very quickly. Will you oblige me by breathing on it once more, when you will find that the likeness will vanish, and the card will again be as it was at first." On her doing so, you again slip the top card (which is now an ordinary seven), on to the portrait, and on again examining, the lady is compelled to admit that the card is again as she first drew it. You then offer to paint on the same card a gentleman's likeness, and proceed as before, each time after taking a likeness changing it back again to an ordinary seven, which adds greatly to the effect of the trick.

You may, if you please, use allegorical instead of caricature portraits; *e.g.*, for a young lady, a rosebud; for a conceited young man, a poppy or dandelion, or a donkey's head. It is hardly necessary to observe that nothing short of very close intimacy would excuse the use of any portrait of a disparaging or satirical nature.

A CARD HAVING BEEN DRAWN AND RETURNED, AND THE PACK SHUFFLED, TO PLACE ON THE TABLE SIX ROWS OF SIX CARDS EACH, AND TO DISCOVER THE CHOSEN CARD BY A THROW OF THE DICE.— The effect of this surprising trick is as follows :—You invite a person to draw a card, allowing him the utmost freedom of selection. You allow the drawer to replace his card in any part of the pack he pleases, and you thoroughly shuffle the cards, finally inviting him to "cut." Then dealing out six rows of six cards each, face downwards on the table, you offer the drawer a dice-box and a pair of dice, and after he has thrown any number of times to satisfy himself that the dice are fair and unprepared, you invite him to throw each singly, the first to ascertain the row in which his card is, and the second to discover at what number it stands in the row. He throws, say, "six" first, and "three" afterwards, and on examination the card he drew proves to be the third card of the sixth row.

The whole mystery consists in the use of a forcing pack, all the cards of which are alike, and which must not consist of a less number than thirty-six cards. The dice are perfectly fair, but as each card of each row is the same, it is a matter of perfect indifference what numbers are thrown. It is advisable to gather up all the other cards, and to request the person to name his card, before allowing the one designated by the dice to be turned up. This will draw the attention of the company to the card on the table, and will give you the opportunity to re-exchange the cards you have used for an ordinary pack (from which, by the way, the card answering to the forced card should have been withdrawn). This pack you may carelessly leave on the table; so that in the event of suspicion attaching to the cards, it will be at once negatived by an examination of the pack.

The trick may be varied by using a teetotum, numbered from one to six, instead of the dice; or you may, if you prefer it, make the trick an illustration of second sight, by pretending to mesmerize some person in the company, and ordering him to write down beforehand, while under the supposed mesmeric influence, the row and number at which the drawn card shall be found. The mode of conducting the trick will be in either case the same.

A Card having been withdrawn and replaced, to call it from the Pack, and to make it come to you of its own accord.—This is a very simple trick, but, if neatly executed, will create a good deal of wonderment. It is performed as follows :— You must procure beforehand a long hair from a lady's head. One end of this must be fastened by means of a bent pin, or in any other way you find most convenient, to the front of your waistcoat, which should be a dark one. At the other end of the hair fix a little round ball (about half the size of a pepper-corn) of bees'-wax. Press this little ball lightly against the lowest button of your waistcoat, to which it will adhere. You will thus always be able to find it at a moment's notice, without groping or looking down for it, which would be likely to draw the eyes of the spectator in the same direction.

Request the audience to examine the cards, that they may be sure that there is no preparation about them, and as a further proof get two or three persons to shuffle them in succession. When the cards are returned to you, invite some person to draw one, and, while he is examining it, drop your right hand carelessly to your waistband, and remove the little ball of wax to the tip of your right thumb, to which it will adhere without interfering with the movements of the hand. When the card is returned, make the pass to bring it to the top of the pack, and press the little ball of wax upon the back of the card, as near the edge as possible. Then shuffle the cards. The shuffle may be a genuine one, but you must take care to keep the lower edge of the chosen card half an inch or so below the remaining cards, that the little ball of wax may not be disturbed. The chosen card will, after the shuffle, be in the middle of the pack, but attached to your waistcoat by the hair. Spread the cards *face upwards* on the table (by which means the wax, being on the back of the card, will be out of sight), taking care not to detach the hair. You then address your audience to the following or some similar effect :—" In the old style of conjuring, I should merely have picked out your card, and handed it to you ; and there was a time when people would have thought that a very good trick, but nowadays we should regard that as a very lame conclusion. I can assure you that I have not the smallest idea what your card was. How do you suppose I intend to find out?" Various guesses are hazarded, but you shake your head at each. "No," you continue, "my process is much simpler than any you have suggested. I shall merely order the card you chose to walk out of the pack, and come to me." Pronounce any magic formula you like, at the same time beckoning to the cards, and gradually withdrawing yourself away from the table, when the card must needs follow you. As it reaches the edge of the table, receive it in the left hand, and then take it in the right, drawing off with the first finger and thumb of the left hand the wax at the back. Ask the person who drew whether that was his card, and again hand the card and the rest of the pack for examination. This little trick, though simple, will require a good deal of practice to enable you to perform it neatly, but the effect produced by it will well repay your trouble.

It may be well to mention, once for all, as bees'-wax is an article of frequent use in magical operations, that if, as sometimes happens, the pure wax is found too hard, or not sufficiently adhesive, the addition of a small quantity (say an eighth part) of Venice turpentine, mixed with it in a melted condition, will make it all that can be desired.

The Whist-Trick.* Improved Method. To deal your-self all the Trumps, the three other Players holding the usual mixed Hands.—Having decided which suit (suppose dia-monds) is to be the trump suit, arrange the pack in such manner that every fourth card shall be of that suit, the intervening cards being taken haphazard. When about to perform the trick, secretly exchange the pack you have hitherto been using for the prepared pack. Make the bridge (*see* page 39), and then a false shuffle by the third method (*see* page 24). Invite some one to cut, and make the pass at the bridge, thus restoring the cards to their original condition. Deal in the usual manner, when you will be found to hold all the trumps, the remaining suits being distributed in the ordinary way among the other three players.

Where in this or any other trick it is found necessary to change one pack for another, the following will be found the neatest way of effecting that object. Have the prepared pack in the *pochette* on the left side. Hold the ordinary pack in the right hand, and in mov-ing from the audience to your table, drop the left hand to the *pochette,* seize the prepared pack, bring the hands together, and make the pass with the two packs, when they will have changed hands. Drop the left hand, and get rid of the ordinary pack into the *profonde,* the prepared pack being left in the right hand. Any little clumsi-ness in making the pass is of small consequence, the hands being covered by the body. If, however, you find it impossible to make the pass with so large a bulk of cards, the prepared pack may be placed under the waistband, held in position by a strap of half-inch-wide elastic, stitched to the inside of the vest; the right hand in this case, at the moment of the turn to the table, transferring the ordinary pack to the left, and immediately drawing down the prepared pack, while the left hand, as in the former case, drops the ordinary pack into the *profonde.*

* For an inferior form of this trick, in which sleight-of-hand is not employed, see page 51.

CHAPTER V.

Card Tricks Requiring Special Apparatus.

We propose to describe in this chapter such card tricks as require the aid of some mechanical appliance or apparatus, but are still appropriate for a drawing-room performance. There are some few tricks performed with cards (such as the Fairy Star, the Demon's Head, and the like) which necessitate the use of a mechanical table, or other apparatus of an elaborate and costly character. These will not be here noticed, but will be given, at the close of the work, in the portion devoted to Stage Tricks.

We may here anticipate a not unlikely question on the part of the student—viz., "How can I best obtain the necessary apparatus?" In some instances, an amateur with a mechanical turn may be able to manufacture his appliances for himself; and where this is the case, we would by no means discourage his doing so, as he will thereby derive a double amusement from his study of the magic art. But where the student has not the ability or inclination to do this, we should strongly advise him not to attempt to have his apparatus made to order by persons unaccustomed to this class of work, but to go direct to one or other of the regular depôts. Magical apparatus requires so much precision in its details, and so much attention to apparent trifles, that the first attempt of any workman, however skilful, is almost sure to be a failure; and by the time the defects are rectified, the purchaser will find that he has paid more for a clumsy makeshift than he would have done for a thoroughly good article had he gone to the right quarter. Experience will quickly prove that inferior apparatus is dear at any price.

Peck & Snyder, 124 Nassau Street, New York City, are the largest manufacturers, importers, and dealers in sports, pastimes, and trick materials. They will forward illustrated catalogues on application, giving details of an infinite variety of Optical, Chemical, Mechanical, Magnetical, and Magical Experiments, and ingenious deceptions. Supplementary sheets are issued from time to time, giving descriptions of new novelties. One peculiarity of their business is that every purchaser is taught, by the very explicit instructions that accompany each article and by correspondence, to perform whatever Tricks he may buy, so that he may exhibit them with ease and without fear of detection, and no trouble is spared in order to make him perfect in what he purchases. Prices are generally low : where a seemingly high price occurs the professor or skilled amateur will readily realize that it is occasioned by the elaborateness of the mechanism of the particular apparatus desired, and the cost that such precision in manipulative manufacture involves. The purchaser—we speak from personal experience—can always depend on receiving uniform courtesy, good value, and sound practical instruction.

The novice must be warned against imagining that, when he has got into the region of apparatus, the necessity for personal address and dexterity will be diminished. On the contrary, there is hardly a trick among those we are about to describe which does not demand more or less practical knowledge of sleight-of-hand. We shall assume, in the following pages, that the reader has carefully followed and studied the directions already given, in which case he will find little difficulty in this portion of the work.

THE MAGIC SWORD. A CARD BEING DRAWN AND REPLACED, AND THE PACK FLUNG IN THE AIR, TO CATCH THE CHOSEN CARD ON THE POINT OF THE SWORD.—We have already described a trick somewhat similar in effect, in which, the pack being flung in the air, the chosen card is caught in the hand of the performer. The trick in this form makes a very good prelude to the still more surprising one which we are about to describe.

It will be remembered, that, in the trick above mentioned, an ordinary pack is used, and the spectator is allowed to draw whatever card he pleases. The card, when returned, is brought to the top by the pass, and palmed; and, though supposed to be caught amid the falling shower, in reality never leaves the hand of the performer. The audience may possibly have a suspicion of this, and you may hear a faint murmur to the effect that " he had the card in his hand! " and so on.   When this occurs, it serves as a very natural introduction to the trick with the sword. You say, " Ah! you fancy I had the card in my hand? I will repeat the trick, in order to show you that you are mistaken. Will some one be kind enough to draw another card ? Thank you. Don't return the card to me, but put it back in the pack yourself. Now be kind enough to shuffle thoroughly. You cannot say I have the card in my hand this time, at all events. Excuse me one instant, while I fetch my magic sword." You go behind your screen, and return, holding in your hand a drawn sword. You place yourself in fencing attitude, and, addressing the person who holds the cards, say, " I am going to give you the words, one ! two ! three !   At the word ' three ! ' will you please throw the cards in the air, so as to fall lightly on the point of my sword, when I will pick out with the point the identical card you drew. Spread the cards a little in a fan shape before you throw them, so that I may get a fair

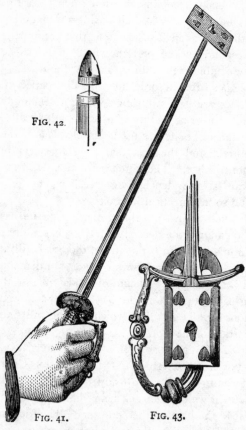

FIG. 42.

FIG. 41.   FIG. 43.

sight of them. Are you ready? One, two, THREE!" At the word three, the cards are thrown, the performer makes a lunge among them, and a card is instantly seen fluttering on the point of the sword, and, on examination, is found to be the very card which was drawn.

The secret of this surprising feat lies mainly in the sword. This is an ordinary small-sword (*see* Fig. 41), with a three-sided rapier blade, but altered in a particular way for the purpose of the trick. The tip of the blade (*see* Fig. 42) is cut off at about a third of an inch distance from the extreme point, and across the concave side of this tip, and also across the corresponding part of the shortened blade, are soldered minute cross-pieces of brass, each bent outwards in the middle, so as to form, with the concavity of the blade, a kind of eye just large enough to admit freely a piece of thin black elastic cord, the other end of which is passed through a similar small hole in the guard of the hilt. The elastic thus lies along the hollow side of the blade, passing through the two "eyes" already mentioned, and is kept in position by a knot at each end. The tension of the elastic holds the moveable tip in its natural position at the end of the blade. It may, however, be drawn away from it in any direction as far as the elastic will permit, but, when released, immediately flies back to its old position. On the same side of the hilt—viz., the side farthest away from the palm of the hand when grasping the sword (*see* Fig. 43)—is fixed a flat, oblong piece of tin, painted black, with its longer edges folded over about half an inch on each side, in such manner as to form a receptacle for a card.

Unless you are tolerably expert in forcing, you will also require some forcing cards of the same pattern as the ordinary pack you have in use. These, however, need not be a full pack, a dozen cards alike being amply sufficient for your purpose. You commence your preparations by taking one of the cards of the forcing pack, cut a small slit in its centre with a penknife, and thrust completely through it the moveable tip of the sword (taking care not to enlarge the hole more than absolutely necessary), and place the sword thus prepared out of sight of the audience, but so as to be easily got at when you want it. Have your forcing cards in your pocket, or somewhere where you can lay your hand on them without attracting observation, and your ordinary pack on the table. You may begin by remarking, " Let me ask you to take particular notice that I perform this trick with whatever card you choose, not influencing your choice in any way. To show you that I don't compel you to take any particular card, I will just take a handful of cards from the top of the pack " (as you say this you place your forcing cards, which you have previously palmed, for an instant on the top of the ordinary pack, immediately taking them off again, as if they had formed part of it, and were the handful of cards you referred to, and offer them to some one to draw). " Take whichever you please—first card, last card, middle card, it is precisely the same to me. Observe that I don't attempt to press upon you any particular card, but hold the cards perfectly motionless while you make your choice." As soon as a card is drawn, without waiting for it to be replaced, return to your table, holding the remaining forcing cards in your left hand. Pick up the pack with your right hand. Place it on the cards in your left hand, at the same moment making the pass to bring these cards to the top. Palm these (with the right hand), and, dropping them into your *profonde*, or elsewhere out of sight, advance with the pack to the person who drew, and request him to replace his card, and shuffle thoroughly. While he does so, you retire to fetch your sword, as before mentioned. Before returning to the audience, you prepare it as follows :—Taking it in your right hand in the ordinary manner, you draw down with the other hand the pierced card, and slide the card endways into the receptacle on the hilt. The elastic, which is now stretched to double its ordinary length, will pull at the card pretty tightly ; but you retain it in position by pressing on the face of the card with the second and third fingers of the hand that grasps the hilt. Having done this, you return to the audience, taking care so to stand that the back of the hand that holds the sword shall be towards them. When the cards are flung in the air, as already described, you make a lunge among them, and at the same moment relax the pressure of the fingers on the pierced card. The elastic, being thus released, flies rapidly back to its original position, and carries the moveable tip, and with it the card, to the end of the blade, by which the card appears to be trans-fixed, as in Fig. 41. The movement of the sword in the lunge, coupled with that of the falling cards, completely covers the rapid flight of the pierced card from hilt to point. To get the card off the sword, pull it down the blade, and tear it roughly off. When you have taken off the card, drop the point of the sword, and hand the card at once to the drawer for examination. This serves to divert attention, not only from the sword itself, but also from the cards scattered on the ground, among which the one actually drawn still remains.

This trick is sometimes performed with three cards instead of one The working of the trick is the same, save that you use a forcing pack consisting of three cards repeated, and that in preparing the sword the two first cards which are threaded on the elastic are perforated with holes of such a size, as to allow them, when released, to slide partially down the blade, the first nearly to the hilt, and the second about half way.

THE RISING CARDS *(La Houlette).*—SEVERAL CARDS HAVING BEEN DRAWN, RETURNED, AND SHUFFLED, TO MAKE THEM RISE SPONTANEOUSLY FROM THE PACK.—This is one of the best of card tricks. The performer advances, pack in hand, to the company. He invites three persons each to draw a card. The cards having been drawn, they are replaced in different parts of the pack, which is thoroughly shuffled. The performer then places the pack in a tin box or case, just large enough to hold it in an upright position. This case is generally in the form of a lyre, open in front and at the top, and supported on a shaft or pillar, twelve or fifteen inches high (*see* Fig. 44). He then asks each person in succession to call for his card, which is forthwith seen to rise slowly from the pack, without any visible assistance, the performer standing quite apart.

The ingenuity of different professors has added little embellishments of a humorous character. For instance, the performer may remark, addressing one of the persons who drew, " I will not even ask the name of your card, sir. You have only to say, ' I command the card I drew to appear,' and you will be obeyed." He does so, but no effect is produced; the cards remain obstinately motionless. The command is repeated, but with the same result The performer feigns embarrassment, and says, " I must really apolo- gize for the disobedience of the cards. I cannot tell how it is; they never behaved in this way before. I am afraid I must ask you to name the card, after all, when I will try my own authority." The card proves to have been a queen, say the queen of spades. "Oh," the performer says, "that quite explains it. Queens are not accustomed to be ordered about in such a peremptory manner. If we try again in becoming language, I dare say we shall be more successful. Let us try the experiment. Say, 'Will your Majesty oblige the company by appearing?'" Thus propitiated, the card rises instantly. Occasionally a knave is one of the cards drawn, and, when summoned, scandalizes the performer by appearing feet foremost. He is appropriately rebuked, and thrust down again by the professor, upon which he immediately reappears in a proper attitude. Sometimes a card, after coming up half way, begins to retire again, but at the command of the performer starts afresh, and rises completely out of the pack.

These apparently surprising effects are produced by very simple means. In the first place, the cards which rise from the pack are not those actually drawn, but duplicates of them, arranged beforehand. The performer ensures the corresponding cards being drawn by using a forcing pack, made up of repetitions of the three cards in question, which we will suppose to be the queen of spades, the ten of hearts, and the seven of diamonds, with some other single card at the bottom. The tin case, in the original form of the trick, has two compartments—the one to the front being large enough to hold a complete pack, but the hinder one adapted to contain six or eight cards only. In this hinder compartment are placed six cards, three of them being those which are intended to rise, and the other three indifferent cards. A black silk thread is fastened to the upper edge of the partition between the two compartments, and is thence brought under the foremost card (which is, say, the queen of spades), over the next (an indifferent card), under the third (the ten of hearts), over the fourth (an indifferent card), under the fifth (the seven of diamonds), over the sixth (an indifferent card), finally passing out through a minute hole at the bottom of the hinder compartment. If the thread be pulled, the three cards named will rise in succession, beginning with the hindmost—viz., the seven of diamonds. The three indifferent cards are put in as partitions, or fulcrums, for the thread to run over. If these partitions were omitted, the three chosen cards would rise all together.

The thread may be drawn in various ways. Sometimes this is

done by the performer himself, standing behind or beside the table. Another plan is to have the thread attached to a small cylindrical weight within the pillar, which is made hollow, and filled with sand. The weight rests on the sand until the operator desires the cards to rise, when, by moving a trigger at the foot of the pillar, he opens a valve, which allows the sand to trickle slowly down into a cavity at the base; and the weight, being thus deprived of its support, gradually sinks down, and pulls the thread. (The pillar in this case is made about two feet high, as the weight must necessarily travel six times the length of a card.) Others, again, draw the thread by means of a clockwork arrangement in the table, or in the pillar itself, answering the same purpose as the sand and weights. The arrangement which we ourselves prefer, where practicable, is to have the thread drawn by an assistant, who may either be placed behind a screen, or may even stand in full view of the audience, so long as he is at some little distance from the table. The silk thread is quite invisible, if only you have a tolerably dark background. The only portion as to which you need feel any anxiety is that immediately connected with the cards. To conceal this it is well, if you use a special table, to have a small hole bored in the top, through which the thread may pass. The card-stand being placed immediately in front of the hole,

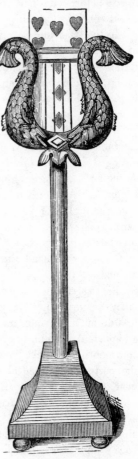

FIG. 44.

the thread will pass perpendicularly downward for the first portion of its length, and will thus be concealed behind the pillar. In default of a hole, a ring of bent wire attached to the table will answer the same purpose. The great advantage of having the thread pulled by a living person instead of a mechanical power is, that you can take your own time in the performance of the trick; whereas, if you use a weight or clockwork, there is always a danger of a card beginning to rise before you have called for it, or possibly not rising at all— either contingency being rather embarrassing.

In the latest and best form of the trick, the second compartment of the case is dispensed with, and the apparatus may be handed round for examination both before and after it is used. In this case three cards are forced and returned as already mentioned; but the performer, as he reaches his table, adroitly exchanges the forcing pack for another already prepared, and placed on the *servante* if a regular conjuring-table is used, or, if not, concealed behind some object on the table. This pack is prepared as follows:—The last six cards are arranged with the thread travelling in and out between them, just as the six cards in the hinder compartment were in the older form of the trick. A knot is made in the silk thread, which is hitched into a notch an eighth of an inch deep, made in the lower edge of the *sixth* card. The knot prevents the thread from slipping, but does not interfere with its being instantaneously detached when, the trick being over, you hand the whole apparatus, cards and all, to be examined.

Some performers use no stand or pillar for the card-case, but fix it by a short plug projecting for that purpose on its under side, in a decanter of water on the table. Some, again, in order to exclude all apparent possibility of mechanical aid, fasten it on the top of a common broomstick, fixed in the floor of the stage, and broken over the performer's knee at the conclusion of the trick. To our own taste, the trick is best performed without any special card-case whatever, the pack being placed in an ordinary glass goblet with upright sides, first handed round to the audience for inspection. It is here absolutely self-evident that the glass can give no mechanical assistance; and as the audience know nothing of the exchange of the packs, the immediate rising of the cards at the word of command appears little short of miraculous.

It only remains to explain the *modus operandi* of the little variations before alluded to. The offended dignity of the queen, declining to appear when summoned in too cavalier a manner, is accounted for by the fact that the performer or his assistant refrains from pulling the thread until the offender has adopted a more respectful tone. The phenomenon of the knave first appearing feet foremost, and then invisibly turning himself right end uppermost, is produced by the use of two knaves, the first (*i.e.*, hindmost) being placed upside down, and the second (with an indifferent card between) in its proper position. When the performer pushes the first knave down again, with a request that it will rise in a more becoming attitude, he thrusts it down, not as he appears to do, in the same place which it originally occupied, but among the loose cards forming the front portion of the pack, thus getting it out of the way, and allowing the thread to act on the second knave. It is hardly necessary to observe that, for producing this particular effect, the cards must be of the old-fashioned single-headed pattern. The alternate ascent and descent of a given card is produced by using a card at whose lower edge, between the back and front of the card, is inserted a slip of lead-foil. The card, so weighted, sinks down of itself as soon as the pull of the thread is relaxed, and may be thus made to rise and fall alternately, as often as the operator chooses, and finally, by a quick, sharp jerk, to jump right out of the pack.

Another very telling incident is the transformation of an eight to a seven, or a seven to a six. A seven of spades, say, has been one of the drawn cards, but when it is summoned an eight of spades appears. The performer apologizes for the mistake, and, giving the card a touch of his wand, shows it instantly transformed to a seven. This is effected by sticking (with a little bees'-wax) a loose spade pip in the appropriate position on an ordinary seven of spades. The performer takes out the supposed eight with one hand, and thence transfers it to the other. In so doing he draws off, with the hand which first held the card, the loose pip, and, holding the card face downwards, touches it with the wand, and shows that it has apparently changed to the card drawn.

There is a mode of performing the trick of the rising cards entirely without apparatus, and without the necessity of forcing particular cards. The performer in this case invites a person to draw a card, and when it is returned makes the pass to bring it to the top of the pack. He then makes a false shuffle, leaving it on the top, and offers the pack to a second person to draw. When he has done so, and before he replaces the card, the performer makes the pass to bring

the card first drawn to the middle, so that the second card is placed upon it, and then again makes the pass to bring both together to the top. The process may be repeated with a third card. The three cards are thus left at the top of the pack, that last drawn being the outermost. The performer now asks each person, beginning with the last who drew, to name his card, and, holding the pack upright in his right hand, the thumb on one side, and the third and fourth fingers on the other, with the face of the pack to the audience (*see* Fig. 45), he causes the cards to rise one by one by pushing them up from the back by an alternate movement of the first and second fingers (which should previously be slightly moistened). If the face of the cards is held fairly to the spectators, it will be impossible for them to discover that the cards do not rise from the middle of the pack.

FIG. 45.

We have been more prolix than we could have desired in the description of this trick, but minute details are the very soul of conjuring. The experience of Horace, " *Brevis esse laboro, obscurus fio,*" applies with peculiar force to the magic art ; and if we occasionally irritate the reader of quick apprehension by too great minuteness, he must remember that we have, as far as we can, to anticipate every possible question, and that a single point left unexplained may render useless an otherwise careful description.

THE JUMPING CARDS.—TWO OR THREE CARDS HAVING BEEN DRAWN, RETURNED, AND SHUFFLED, TO MAKE THEM JUMP OUT OF THE PACK.—This trick is somewhat similar in working to that of the rising cards as performed in the hand, which we have just described. The course of the two tricks is precisely the same up to the point when, the two or three cards having been drawn and returned, you have got them all to the top of the pack. Here, however, the resemblance ceases. In the present case you drop the whole pack into an open-mouthed box, made for that purpose, and announce that, although the chosen cards have been replaced in different parts of the pack, and the whole have since been thoroughly shuffled, you have only to blow upon them in order to separate them visibly from the rest of the pack. You blow upon the box accordingly, when the chosen cards instantly fly out of the pack, rising to a height of three or four feet, and fall on the table.

The secret of the trick, apart from the sleight-of-hand necessary to bring the chosen cards together at the top of the pack, lies in the box. It is in general appearance something like a miniature pedestal for a statue, but hollow, and open at the top, the cavity being rather more than large enough to hold a pack of cards. (*See* Fig 46.) It is divided longitudinally into two compartments, the foremost being large enough to hold a whole pack, the hindmost to hold only three or four cards, the partition between the two coming about half way up the box. The bottom of the larger compartment is level with the top of the plinth, but the smaller is

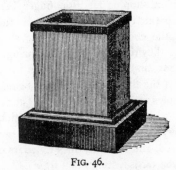

FIG. 46.

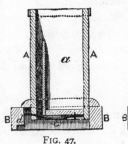

FIG. 47.   FIG. 48.

open to the whole depth, save that across it is a steel spring about half an inch in width. Fig. 47 represents a section of the apparatus, A being the upper part, of which *a* is the larger or front compartment, and *b* the smaller compartment at the back. B is the plinth. A is so constructed as to slide forwards on, or rather in, B, to the extent of about an eighth of an inch, but is prevented doing so, in the normal condition of the apparatus, by the spring c, which is screwed to the bottom of A, its free end pressing against the side of the plinth. If, however, the spring be pressed down from above, so as to be below the level of the shoulder d (for which purpose a thin slip of wood is supplied with the apparatus), and A be at the same time pushed towards d, it will slide forward to the position indicated in Fig. 48, and the spring c will be held down beneath the shoulder d. This is the condition in which the apparatus is first exhibited to the audience. After turning it over, to show that there are no cards already concealed in it, the performer places in it the pack, first, however, slipping his little finger between the chosen cards (which are on the top) and the rest of the pack, so as to enable him to drop the chosen cards into the smaller compartment at the back, where they rest upon the bent spring. (*See* Fig. 48.) Standing behind the box, and placing his hands around the plinth, as if to hold it steady, the fingers of each hand being in front, and the thumb behind, he blows smartly upon the box, at the same moment pushing A forward with the thumbs to the position which it occupies in Fig. 47. The spring c, being drawn back with it beyond the shoulder d, is released, and instantly flies up to its old position, shooting out of the box the cards resting upon it.

This trick is sometimes, like that of the rising cards, worked with a forcing pack, duplicates of the forced cards being placed beforehand in the hinder compartment. This method, however, is very inferior to that above described, and would hardly be adopted by any performer who had acquired a competent mastery of sleight-of-hand.

To make a Card stand upright by itself on the Table.—This is a little trick of hardly sufficient importance to be performed by itself; but as an incident introduced in the course of some more pretentious illusion, produces a very good effect. A great deal of the sparkle of a conjuring entertainment depends upon the performer's readiness in what may be called "by-play," consisting of a number of minor tricks not supposed to form part of the settled programme, but merely introduced incidentally, and used, as it were, as a garnish to the more important feats. Thus, when a coin, an egg, or other small article, is required for the purpose of a trick, the performer may fetch it openly from behind the scenes, or have it handed to him by his servant; but this is a commonplace proceeding. The higher class of performers prefer in such cases to produce the article from the hair, whiskers, or pocket of one of the audience; and in like manner, when the article has served its purpose, to make it vanish by some magical process, rather than by the prosaic methods of every-day life. These little incidents serve to keep the audience on the *qui vive*, and they further assist materially in keeping up the *continuity* of an entertainment. In a thoroughly good performance the audience should have no time to think, but should be led direct from one surprise to the contemplation of another.

The trick we are about to describe is of the class above alluded to. In the course of one or other of your card tricks, you have or make occasion to ask some person to go and place a given card on the table, or to examine a card already placed there. He does so, and is about to return to his place; but you check him. " No, sir, that won't do. I want everybody to see what card it is. Will you be good enough to stand it up on end, with its face to the company, so that everybody can see it." He looks foolish, and finally says that he can't do it. " Not do it ? " you reply. " My dear sir, it's the simplest thing in the world. Allow *me !* " and taking the card from him, you place it upright on the table, and leave it standing without any visible support. Taking it up again, you hand it round, to show that there is no preparation about it, and on receiving it back, again stand it upright, but with the other end upwards; or, if challenged, allow the audience themselves to choose a card, which you cause to stand alone with equal facility.

The secret lies in the use of a very small and simple piece of apparatus, being, in fact, merely a strip of tin or sheet brass, an inch and a half in length, and five-eighths of an inch in width, bent at a shade less than a right angle—say $85°$; its shorter arm being one-third of its length. On the outer surface of the long arm is spread a thin layer of bees'-wax (made more adhesive by the addition of a small portion of Venice turpentine), and to the inner surface of the shorter arm is soldered a small piece of lead, about an eighth of an inch thick. When you desire to perform the trick, you have this little appliance concealed in your right hand, the longer arm between the first and second fingers, and the shorter arm pointing towards the little finger. Picking up the card with the left hand, you transfer it

to the right, taking hold of it in such manner that the fingers shall be behind and the thumb in front of the card. As you place the card on the table (which, by the way, must be covered with a cloth), you press against it (*see* Fig. 49) the waxed side of the slip of tin, which will slightly adhere to it, and thus form a prop or foot, the little lump of lead acting as a counterpoise to the weight of the card. You pick it up with the same hand, and as you transfer it to the other, you will find no difficulty in removing and secreting between the fingers the little prop.

FIG. 49.

If the wax is properly amalgamated, it should leave no mark on the card.

CHANGING CARD-BOXES, AND TRICKS PERFORMED WITH THEM. —The changing card-box in its simplest form is a small flat box in walnut or mahogany. (*See* Fig. 49.) Its outside measurement is four inches by three, and not quite an inch deep. Inside it is just large enough to admit an ordinary-sized playing card. The upper and lower portions of the box, which are connected by hinges, are exactly alike in depth, and each is polished externally, so that the box, which, when open, lies flat like a book, may be closed either way up; **and** either portion will, according as it is placed, become box or lid in turn. Thus, by using a card which, unknown to the audience, has two faces—*e.g.*, is an ace of hearts on the one side, and an ace of spades on the other—and placing such card in one side of the open box, you have only to close the box with that side uppermost, or to turn over the box as you place it on the table, to transform the card just shown into a different one. There is nothing in the appearance of the box itself to indicate that it has been turned, so to speak, wrong side up, and a very little practice will enable you to turn it over, as you place it on the table, without attracting observation.

There is a further appliance in connection with the box in question, which, however, may be used with or without it, as may best suit the trick in hand. This is a loose slab, *a*, of the same wood of which the interior of the box is made, of the thickness of cardboard, and of such a size as to fit closely, though not tightly, in either half of the box. When so placed, it has the appearance of the inside top or bottom of the box. When the box is closed in such manner that the part in which this slab is placed is uppermost, the slab falls into the lower portion, thus forming a false bottom on whichever side happens to be undermost. If a card (say the ace of hearts) be secretly

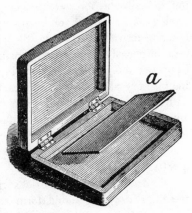

FIG. 50.

placed in either side of the box, and this slab placed on it, the box will appear empty. If now another card (say the knave of spades) be openly placed in either side, and the box closed in such manner that the portion containing the false bottom is undermost, no change will take place ; but if, either in closing the box or subsequently, it is so placed that the side containing the false bottom becomes uppermost, the false bottom will at once drop into the opposite division, and on re-opening the box the ace of hearts will be revealed, and the knave of spades will in its turn be concealed. The effect to the spectators is as if the knave of spades had changed into the ace of hearts.

These card-boxes are frequently worked in pairs, as follows:—
The boxes are prepared by placing a different card secretly in each,
say an ace of hearts in the one, and a knave of spades in the other.
The performer brings them forward to the company, each hanging
wide open, and held by one corner only, with the first and second
finger inside, and the thumb outside the box, taking care, however, to
hold each by the side containing the false bottom, which is thus kept
in position by the pressure of the fingers. So held, the boxes appear
absolutely empty. Having drawn attention to the entire absence of
any preparation, the performer lays them open upon the table, and,
taking up a pack of cards, requests two of the company each to draw
one. They, of course, imagine that they are making a free choice,
but in reality he forces (either by sleight-of-hand, or by means of a
forcing pack) the ace of hearts and the knave of spades. Again
bringing forward the two boxes, he requests each person to place his
card in one of them, taking care so to arrange that the person who
has drawn the ace of hearts shall place it in the box already containing the concealed knave of spades, and *vice versâ.* Closing each box
with the portion containing the false bottom uppermost, he now
announces that at his command the cards will change places, which,
on re-opening the boxes, they appear to have done. By again turning over the boxes, they may be made to return to their original
quarters.

Numerous other good tricks may be performed with the aid of
these boxes, which should form part of the collection of every conjuror. By placing a given card beforehand beneath the false bottom,
and forcing a like card, you may allow the card drawn to be torn into
twenty pieces, and yet, by placing the fragments in the box, or firing
them at it from a pistol, restore the card instantly, as at first. In
like manner, you may cause a given card to be found in the apparently empty box, or may cause a card openly placed therein to vanish
altogether. The changing-box is also sometimes employed by those
who are not proficient in sleight-of-hand, as a substitute for forcing,
in the following manner:—The performer requests some person to
draw a card, and, without looking at it, to place it face downwards in
the box for supposed safe keeping. The box is presently opened by
the same or some other person, who is requested to note what the

card is.   He does so, believing the card to be that which was drawn, and which he had just before seen placed in the box; whereas the card he now examines is, in reality, one concealed beforehand in the box by the performer to suit his purpose, the card actually drawn being now hidden by the false bottom.

THE MECHANICAL CARD-BOX.—This also is a piece of apparatus for changing a chosen card to another.   It is somewhat the same in principle as the card-boxes last described, but differs from them a good deal in detail.   It is an oblong wooden box, in external measurement about four and a half inches by three and a half, and four inches high.   Internally, the measurement is so arranged that, putting the lid out of the question, the front of the box is of exactly equal area with the bottom.

Against this front (*see* Fig. 51) lies a slab of tin or zinc, working on a cloth hinge along its lower edge, thus rendering it capable of either lying flat on the bottom of the box (which it exactly covers), or of being folded up against the front, the upper edge

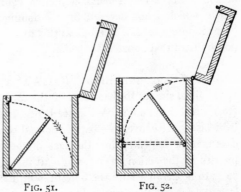

FIG. 51.   FIG. 52.

of which projects slightly inwards, so as to aid in concealing it. This flap, like the whole inside of the box, is painted black.   On one point of its upper surface is a little stud, which, when the flap is raised, fits into a hole prepared for it in the lock, across which passes the hinder end or tail of the bolt.   The box is prepared for use as follows :—The key is turned, as if locking the box (which, however, is held open), thus pushing forward the bolt of the lock, and the flap is lifted up against the front, the stud passing into the little hole before-mentioned.   The key is then again turned as if unlocking the box, when the tail of the bolt catches the stud, and secures the flap. The box will in this condition bear any amount of examination, but as soon as it is closed, and the key turned to lock it, the tail of the bolt, being again shot forward, no longer retains the stud, and the flap falls. When in actual use, a card (say the ace of spades) is placed upon the flap, and folded up with it against the front of the box. The card to be changed (suppose the nine of diamonds) is in due course openly placed in the box, which is then handed to some one with a request that he will himself lock it, that there may be no possibility of deception. The trick proceeds, and when the box is again opened, the card placed therein is found transformed to the ace of spades.

Some card-boxes are so made, that the flap, instead of falling actually *upon* the bottom of the box, falls parallel to it, but at a dis-tance of an inch or so above it, leaving a hollow space beneath capable of containing a lady's handkerchief, a canary, or any other small article, which, being covered by the falling flap, is thus apparently changed into a card. The box in this case is somewhat taller in pro-portion than that above described.

THE "CARD AND BIRD" BOX.—This is, in form and general appearance, similar to that form of the card-box last above described (that which has an enclosed space beneath the flap), but its working is precisely the converse—*i.e.*, the normal condition of the flap in this case is to lie folded against the back of the box, against which it is pressed by the action of a spring. It may, however, be folded down so as to lie parallel with the bottom, a little catch projecting from the inner surface of the front, holding it in that position. (*See* Fig. 52.) The lock is in this case a mere sham, having neither key nor keyhole, but a little stud projecting from the lower edge of the lid, and repre-senting the "staple" of the lock, presses, when the box is closed, upon an upright pin passing through the thickness of the wood up the front of the box, and thereby withdraws the catch, when the flap flies up, concealing the card which has just been placed upon it, and reveal-ing the bird or other object which had previously been concealed beneath it.

The same principle is sometimes applied to the "card-box," the flap when "set" lying flat on the bottom of the box, leaving no hollow space below.

THE CARD TRIPOD.—This is a miniature table, standing five or six inches high. It has a round top of about the same diameter, supported on a tripod foot. It is provided with an ornamental cover of tin or pasteboard, shaped somewhat like the top of a coffee-pot, just large enough to fit neatly over the top of the table, and about an inch deep. The table has a false top, made of tin, but japanned to match the real top, and of such a size as to fit tightly within the cover. If the false top be laid upon the true one, and the cover placed over both, the cover will, on being again removed, carry with it the false top, and leave exposed the real one, which, however, the audience take to be that which they have already seen.

The reader will already have perceived that the card-tripod is, in effect, very similar to the changing card-box. Like the card-box, it may be used either singly or in pairs, and the tricks performed by its aid will be nearly the same. Thus two forced cards drawn by the audience may be made to change places from one tripod to another, a card drawn and destroyed may be reproduced from its own ashes, or a card drawn and placed on the tripod may be made to vanish altogether, the drawn card being in each case laid upon the false top, that to which it is to be apparently transformed having been previously placed under the false and upon the true top. A card once changed, however, cannot be restored to its original condition, and the card-tripod is, therefore, in this respect inferior to the card-box.

THE "TORN CARD."—This is a very effective trick. The performer requests some one of the company to draw a card, and, having done so, to tear it up into any number of fragments. He does so, and hands them to the operator, who returns one corner to him, with a request that he will take particular care of it. The performer announces that out of the torn fragments he will restore the card anew, for which purpose he first burns the fragments on a plate or otherwise, carefully preserving the ashes. He then brings forward one of the changing card-boxes already described, and, after, showing that it is empty, closes it, and places it on the table in view of all present. He next takes the ashes of the torn card, and, loading a pistol with them, fires at the box. (If he has not a pistol at hand, placing the ashes on the box, rubbing them on the lid, or any other act which gets rid of them will answer the same purpose.) When the box is opened, the card is found whole as at first, with the exception of one corner, being (ostensibly) that which was retained by the drawer. Taking this piece in his right hand, and holding the card by one corner between the thumb and first finger of his left hand (*see* Fig. 53), the performer makes a motion as if throwing the small piece towards it.' The small piece instantly vanishes from his hand, and at the same moment the card is seen to be completely restored, the torn corner being in its proper

place. Some performers, instead of giving the drawer the torn corner to take charge of in the first instance, burn ostensibly the whole of the pieces, and pretend surprise on finding that there is a corner missing when the card is restored. Directly afterwards, however, they pick up the missing fragment from the floor, where they have just previously dropped it, and the trick proceeds as already described.

FIG. 53.   FIG. 54.

The reader will, no doubt, already have conjectured that the card drawn is a forced one, and that the supposed restored card was concealed beforehand under the false bottom of the card-box. This pretended restored card is, in reality, an ingenious though simple piece of apparatus, constructed as follows :—A piece of tin is cut to the exact size and shape of a card ; out of this, at one of the corners, is cut an oblong piece, measuring about one inch by five-eighths. This piece is attached by a spring hinge, *a a*, on one side of it, to the larger piece of tin, in such manner that it can be folded back (*see* Fig. 54) flat against it ; the action of the spring, however, bringing it back again, when released, to its original position. To this piece of tin is soldered lengthways a narrow tail-piece, of such a length as to extend nearly to the opposite end of the larger piece of tin. This tail-piece forms a kind of handle wherewith to bend back the smaller piece of tin on its hinge, and at the same time acts as a check to prevent the action of the spring pressing the smaller piece beyond the plane of the larger one. A playing card is split in two in order to reduce its thickness, and the face of the card thus reduced is pasted on the front of the larger piece of tin. Previously, however, a piece, somewhat smaller than the little moveable flap, is torn out of one corner, and pasted on the flap in such a manner that, when the latter is released, the torn piece will occupy its proper position with respect to the remainder of the card. which will thus appear complete. When, however, the moveable flap is folded back, and so held by the pressure of the forefinger upon the tail-piece, the torn portion of the card will be folded back with it, as in Fig. 54. When the mechanical card is placed in the box, it should be thus folded back, and kept in position by a little bit of thin wire, half an inch long, and bent into a miniature staple or clip, which, slipped over the end of the tail-piece and the adjoining edge of tin, will effectually hold the flap back, and yet may be got rid of in an instant, when the forefinger is ready to take its place. You must take care so to place the card in the box as to be face uppermost when the box is opened, as the audience must not, of course, see the back. When you desire to make the card complete, you have only to slip aside the forefinger, and thus release the moveable flap.

There are torn cards now made entirely of pasteboard, dispensing with the tin plate at the back. This is a decided improvement.

As to the disappearance of the loose corner from your hand, you will find little difficulty when you have learnt the art of coin-palming, to be hereafter explained. Assuming that you have at present no knowledge on this subject, you may proceed as follows :—Take the bit of card between the forefinger and thumb of your right hand, and as you make the motion of throwing it towards the mechanical card, push it with the ball of the thumb between the first or second joints of the first and middle fingers. This releases the thumb, and the inside of your hand being turned away from your audience, you run little risk of discovery, particularly as the same piece, apparently, is now seen in its proper place as part of the restored card.

We must not omit to mention that there is a mode of performing the "torn card" trick in which the use of the mechanical card is dispensed with. In this case the performer secretly takes an ordinary card, say the knave of spades, and tears off one corner, which he carefully preserves. The card thus mutilated he places in a card-box, or other similar piece of apparatus. Pack in hand, he advances to the company, and "forces" the knave of spades, having, meanwhile, the little corner piece of the concealed card hidden between the second and third fingers of his right hand. The card having been drawn, he requests the drawer to tear it up, and place the pieces on a plate, which he hands him for that purpose. Having received the pieces, he says carelessly, "You had better keep one piece for the purpose of identification;" and, so saying, hands him apparently one of the fragments of the card just torn, but really the concealed corner piece, which he drops from his hand on the plate for that purpose in the very act of picking up. The trick then proceeds as already described up to the finding of the card partially restored, in which condition it is handed to the drawer, and its identity proved by showing that the torn edge exactly corresponds with the corner retained. The trick may either end here, or, by using a second card-box, card-tripod, or the like, the card and corner may be again changed for a complete card.

MECHANICAL CHANGING CARDS.—These are of two or three kinds, but all have the same object—viz., the apparent transformation of the card to a different one. In some cases the change is from a court card of one suit to the same card of another suit—*e.g.*, a king of spades to a king of hearts, involving merely the alteration of the pip in the corner. This is effected by having the card made double, that portion of the front card on which the pip should be being cut out. The hindmost card, which is pasted only round the extreme edge to the front one, is a plain white card, but with the appropriate pip, say a spade, neatly painted in the proper position, to allow of its showing through the opening in the front card, which thus has the appearance of an ordinary king of spades. Between the two cards is a moveable slip, worked by a pin through a slip in the back, on which is painted a heart pip. By moving this slip, the heart is in turn brought opposite the opening, covering the spade pip, so that the card now appears to be the king of hearts. The card as above described is of the old single-headed pattern, but the same principle may be applied to double-headed cards. In this case both of the " pip " portions of the front card are cut away as in Fig. 55, while on the upper corresponding portion of the hinder card is painted (say) a spade, and on the lower a heart, as in Fig. 56. The moveable slip is of such a shape and size as to cover the one or the other, according as it

FIG. 55.   FIG. 56.   FIG. 57.

is drawn up or down; and on the upper part of this (*see* Fig. 57) is painted a heart, and on the lower a spade. When, therefore, the slip is pushed *up*, the heart pip on the slip and the heart pip on the hindmost card are shown, so that the card appears to be a king of hearts. When, on the other hand, the slip is drawn *down*, the spade pip of the hinder card is revealed, and at the same time the slip covers over the heart pip of this latter, and exhibits its own spade pip, giving the card the appearance of a king of spades.

These mechanical cards are used in various ways. Such a card may be introduced with good effect in the trick of the "rising cards," before described. The king of spades, we will suppose, is one of the cards drawn. The changing card is made one of those which rise from the pack, but is so arranged as to appear as the king of hearts. When the king of spades is called for, this card rises. The performer feigns to be taken by surprise, and asks the person who drew the card whether he is sure he is not mistaken, and that the card he drew was not the king of hearts. The drawer naturally maintains the correctness of his own recollection, while the performer as stoutly insists that the cards never deceive him, and that, if the king of spades had been drawn, the king of spades would infallibly have risen when called. At last, as if tired of the dispute, he says, " Well, I still maintain you were mistaken ; but as you insist that your card was the king of spades, why, we will make this into a king of spades." So saying, and holding up the card between his middle finger and thumb, he touches its face with his wand, and at the same moment with the first finger moves the slide, when the card changes to the king of spades. The little dispute as to the supposed mistake, which the audience have hitherto believed to be genuine, gives to the transformation an impromptu air which is very effective. The performer may go on to say, still holding up the card, "You are quite satisfied now, I presume." The drawer assents. "Then if so, as it would spoil my pack to have *two* kings of spades in it, you will allow me, before proceeding further, to change the card back again. Change!" Again he touches the card with his wand, and it is seen to change back again to the king of hearts.

Another mode of using the mechanical card is in conjunction with the changing card-boxes, above described. In this case the changing cards are used in pairs. One of them, arranged as the king of spades, is secretly placed in the one box, and the other, arranged as the king of hearts, in the other. Two of the spectators are requested each to draw a card, and two genuine kings of the same respective suits are forced upon them. Taking the cards so drawn, and showing the card boxes apparently empty, the performer places one of the cards in each, taking care to place the king of hearts in the box containing the ostensible king of spades, and *vice versâ*. He now commands the two cards to change places, and, opening the boxes, shows that his commands are obeyed. He then remarks, "Now, I dare say you all think that the trick depends on the boxes. To show you that it is not so, I will again order the cards to change; and this time I will not place them in the boxes, but will merely take one in each hand, so. If your eyes are quick enough, you will see the cards fly across from the one hand to the other. Observe, the king of spades is in my right hand, and the king of hearts in my left. One, two, three—Change!" (with a stamp and a slight flourish of the cards). "Did you see them fly? Here is the king of hearts in my right hand, and the king of spades has passed to my left. I will put them in the boxes once more." You put each in the box which it before occupied, in doing so again making the change, but without closing the boxes. You continue, "Please to notice which

I put in each box—the king of hearts in the right hand box, and the king of spades in the left hand box. Is that right?" The audience reply in the affirmative. "Excuse me," you say, "I fear you are mistaken. You did not notice, perhaps, that the cards had changed again." You show that this is so, and then close the boxes so as to bring the cards originally drawn uppermost. Opening them once more, you show that the cards have again changed, and then remark, "I have shown you that the secret does not lie in the boxes, perhaps you would like to satisfy yourselves that there is no preparation about the cards," which you accordingly hand for examination.

Another form of changing card is known as a "flap card." This is a card across whose centre is fixed a moveable flap of exactly half its size. When the flap is folded one way, it covers the upper half, and when it is folded the other way the lower half of the card, in each case revealing a different surface. (*See* Fig. 58.) On one of such surfaces is pasted, say, a queen of clubs (made thin by peeling off the back), and on the other surface, say, a nine of diamonds, prepared in like manner. Thus the card will appear, according as the flap is folded, alternately a queen of clubs or nine of diamonds. An indiarubber spring

FIG. 58

tends to draw the flap down, so that the normal condition of the card is to appear as, say, the nine of diamonds. When exhibited to the company, the flap is forced over in the opposite direction, so that the card appears to be the queen of clubs. The thumb and finger hold the flap down until the right moment, when they relax their pressure, and the flap flying up, the card is instantly transformed to the nine of diamonds.

CHAPTER VI.

Principles of Sleight-of-Hand more especially applicable to Coin Tricks.

Before attempting tricks with coin, it will be necessary for the student to practise certain sleights and passes which more especially belong to this particular branch of the magic art, though the sleight-of-hand used in "coin tricks" is more or less applicable to most other small objects. The principles which we have given

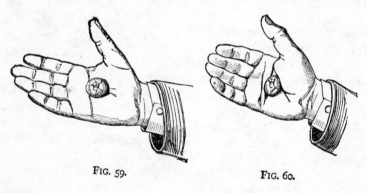

Fig. 59.   Fig. 60.

for card tricks will not here be of any direct assistance to the student; but the readiness of hand and eye which he will have acquired, if he has diligently put in practice the instructions already given, will be of great value to him as a preliminary training, and it may safely be predicted that any person who is a first-rate performer with cards will find little difficulty in any other branch of the art.

The first faculty which the novice must seek to acquire is that of " palming "—*i.e.*, secretly holding an object in the open hand by the contraction of the palm. To acquire this power, take a half-crown, florin, or penny (these being the most convenient in point of size), and lay it on the palm of the open hand. (*See* Fig. 59.) Now close the hand very slightly, and if you have placed the coin on the right spot (which a few trials will quickly indicate), the contraction of the palm around its edges will hold it securely (*see* Fig. 60), and you may move the hand and arm in any direction without fear of dropping it. You should next accustom yourself to use the hand and fingers easily and naturally, while still holding the coin as described. A very little practice will enable you to do this. You must bear in mind while practising always to keep the inside of the palm either downwards or towards your own body, as any reverse movement would expose the concealed coin. When you are able to hold the coin comfortably in the right hand, practise in like manner with the left, after which you may substitute for the coin a watch, an egg, or a small lemon—all these being articles of frequent use in conjuring.

Being thoroughly master of this first lesson, you may proceed to the study of the various " passes." All of the passes have the same object—viz., the apparent transfer of an article from one hand to the other, though such article really remains in the hand which it has apparently just quitted. As the same movement frequently repeated would cause suspicion, and possibly detection, it is desirable to acquire different ways of effecting this object. For facility of subsequent reference, we shall denote the different passes described by numbers.*

PASS 1.—Take the coin in the right hand, between the second and

---

* It should be here mentioned that the term "palming," which we have so far used as meaning simply the act of *holding* any article, is also employed to signify the act of *placing* any article in the palm by one or other of the various passes. The context will readily indicate in which of the two senses the term is used in any given passage.

It is hardly necessary to remark that the diagrams, save where the letterpress indicates the contrary, represent the hands of the performer *as seen by himself.*

third fingers and the thumb (*see* Fig. 61), letting it, however, really be supported by the fingers, and only steadied by the thumb. Now move the thumb out of the way, and close the second and third fingers, with the coin balanced on them, into the palm. (*See* Fig. 62.) If the coin was placed right in the first instance, you

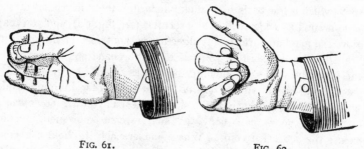

FIG. 61. FIG. 62.

will find that this motion puts it precisely in the position above described as the proper one for palming ; and on again extending the fingers, the coin is left palmed, as in Fig. 60. When you can do this easily with the hand at rest, you must practise doing the same thing with the right hand in motion toward the left, which should meet it open, but should close the moment that the fingers of the right hand touch its palm, as though upon the coin, which you have by this movement feigned to transfer to it. The left hand must thenceforward remain closed, as if holding the coin, and the right hand hang loosely open, as if empty.

In the case of an article of larger size than a coin—as, for instance, a watch or an egg—you need not take the article with the fingers, but may let it simply lie on the palm of the right hand, slightly closing that hand as you move it towards the left. The greater extent of surface in this case will give you plenty of hold, without the necessity of pressing the article into the palm. Remember that, in any case, the two hands must work in harmony, as in the genuine act of passing an article from the one hand to the other. The left hand must therefore rise to meet the right, but should not begin its journey until the right hand begins its own. Nothing looks more awkward or unnatural than to see the left hand extended with open palm, before the right hand has begun to move towards it.

After the pass is made, a judicious use of the wand will materially assist in concealing the fact that the object still remains in the right hand. For this purpose the performer should, before commencing the pass, carelessly place the wand under either arm, as though merely to leave his hands free. Immediately that the pass is made the right hand should, with a sort of back-handed movement, which under the circumstances is perfectly natural, grasp the wand, draw it from under the arm, and thenceforth retain it till an opportunity occurs of disposing of the coin as may be necessary. The position of the fingers in the act of holding the wand is such as to effectually mask the concealed coin, while yet the hand appears perfectly easy and natural. The same expedient may be employed with equal advantage in the remaining passes.

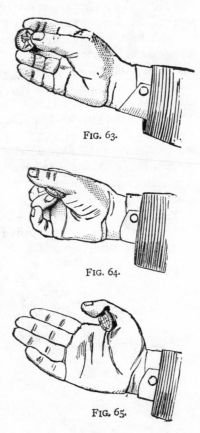

FIG. 63.

FIG. 64.

FIG. 65.

PASS 2.—This is somewhat easier than Pass 1, and may sometimes be usefully substituted for it. Take the coin edgeways between the first and third fingers of the right hand, the sides of those fingers pressing against the edges of the coin, and the middle finger steadying it from behind. (*See* Fig. 63.) Carry the right hand towards the left, and at the same time move the thumb swiftly over the face of the coin till the top joint just passes its outer edge (*see* Fig. 64) ; then bend the thumb, and the coin will be found to be securely nipped between that joint and the junction of the thumb with the hand. (*See* Fig. 65.) As in the last case, the left hand must be closed the moment the right hand touches it; and the right must thenceforth be held with the thumb bent slightly inwards towards the palm, so that the coin may be shielded from the view of the spectators. This is an especially quick mode of palming, and if properly executed the illusion is perfect. It is said to be a special favourite of the elder Frikell.

Pass 3.—Hold the left hand palm upwards, with the coin in the position indicated in Fig. 59. Move the right hand towards the left, and let the fingers simulate the motion of picking up the coin, and instantly close. At the same moment slightly close the left hand, so as to contract the palm around the coin, as in Fig. 60, and drop the hand, letting it hang loosely by your side.

Pass 4. (*Le Tourniquet*).—This (sometimes known as the "French drop") is an easy and yet most effective pass. Hold the left hand palm upwards, with the coin as shown in Fig. 66.

Now move the right hand towards the left, passing the thumb of the right hand under, and the fingers over the coin, closing them just as they pass it. The effect is the same to the eye of the spectator as if you seized the coin with thumb and fingers, but, in reality, at the moment when the coin is covered by the fingers of the right hand, you let it drop quietly (*see* Fig. 67) into the palm of the left.

Fig. 66.

The right hand you should carry upwards and forwards after it leaves the left hand, following it with your eyes, and thereby drawing away the attention of the audience from the other hand. (*See* Fig 68.) Do not be in too great a hurry to drop the left hand, but turn the palm slightly towards you, with the fingers a little bent, and, after a moment's pause, let it fall gently to your side. The hollow made by the bent fingers will be sufficient to hold the coin.

This pass is available even for a sixpence or threepenny piece, which from their small size, cannot readily be palmed by the ordinary means. It is also very useful for "ball" conjuring.

PASS 5. (*La Pincette*).—This is a modification of the pass last described. The coin is held as in Fig. 69, between the thumb and first and second fingers of the left hand. You then make the

FIG. 67.

movement of taking it between the same fingers of the other hand, which for that purpose makes a kind of "swoop" down

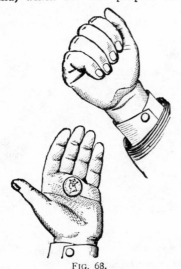

upon it, the back of the hand being kept towards the spectators. At the moment when the coin is covered by the fingers of the right hand, it is allowed to slip gently down into the palm of the left, and the right is instantly elevated as if containing it.

PASS 6.—This pass is best adapted for use with three or four coins, as the chink of the coins against one another materially assists the illusion. Having to get rid of, say, four pence or florins, you take them in the right hand, as indicated

FIG. 68.

in Fig. 70, viz., well back towards the wrist. Move the right hand sharply towards the left, with the fingers foremost, so that the finger-tips of the right hand may come smartly, at about right angles, against the palm of the left, at the same time slightly bending the fingers. The coins, instead of being shot forward (as to the eye and ear of the spectators they appear to be) into the left hand, are, in

reality, retained in the hollow formed by the fingers of the right, as in Fig. 71. They are turned completely over as the hands come in contact, producing a loud chink. The left hand is, of course, closed, and the thumb of the right is allowed to sink gently on the coins, so that when the hand falls by your side, they may not make a second chink, and so betray their presence in the wrong hand.

FIG. 69.

PASS 7. (*La Coulée*).—This pass is best adapted for a coin of large diameter, like the French five-franc piece, and is but little used by English conjurors. If, however, the student has a very small hand (a serious disadvantage in conjuring generally), he may find it con-

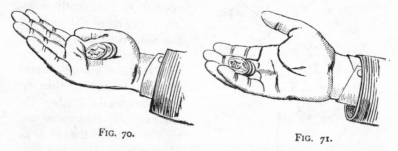

FIG. 70.   FIG. 71.

venient to use the pass in question with a half-crown or penny. Take the coin in the right hand between the first and second fingers and the thumb, and in the act of apparently transferring it to the left hand, gently slide it with the ball of the thumb into the position shown in

Fig. 72, where it is held by the pressure of the first and fourth fingers against its opposite edges, the hand remaining completely open.

PASS 8.—The peculiarity of this pass is, that it is made while holding the wand in the hand, a case in which none of the other passes are available. Holding the wand and coin in the right hand, as indicated in Fig. 73, you strike the edge of the coin sharply against the palm of the left hand, and instantly close that hand. The effect of the movement is to drive back

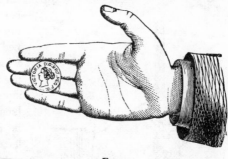

FIG. 72.

the coin (which should be held very lightly) into the position shown in Fig. 74, in which, being behind the first three fingers, it is completely hidden. You should lose no time in relaxing the fingers of the right hand, and gently closing them around the coin, as their straightened position, if continued, might arouse suspicion. You must, however, be careful that, in doing so, you do not allow the coin to chink against the wand, as the sound would naturally draw attention to its whereabouts.

FIG. 73.

It must not be imagined that all of the passes above given are in turn used by every performer. Almost every conjuror has his favourite pass or passes, either selected from those above described, or invented by himself. Any mode by which a coin can be held in the hand without indicating its presence may be worked up into a pass. Thus, some performers will hold a coin by its edges between two of the fingers, or between the thumb and the side of the hand. Others, again, hold the coin flat against the first or second joint of the second or third finger, retaining it by slightly bending the finger. The novice should experiment till he ascertains which method best suits the conformation of his own hand. We have speci-fied the hand to and from which each pass is generally used; but if the student de-sires to attain special excel-lence, he should practise until he is able to use each from left to right, as well as from right to left. In performing before a company of spectators, and standing with the left side towards them, it is well to use a pass which apparently trans-fers the coin from the right hand to the left, and *vice versâ.* The coin is thus left in the hand farthest away from the spectators, and the performer has the benefit of the cover of the body in dropping it into the *pochette,* or otherwise disposing of it.

Fig. 74.

The student will here, as in card conjuring, find great advan-tage in practising before a looking-glass, before which he should, in the first place, actually *do* that which he afterwards pretends to do, and carefully notice the positions and motions of his hands in the first case, which he should then do his best to simulate, that there may be as little difference as possible between the pretence and the reality. He should further accustom himself *always to follow with his eyes the hand in which the object is supposed to be,* this being the most certain means of leading the eyes and the minds of his audience in the same direction. When he is able to perform the passes neatly with a single florin or penny, he should then practise with coins of smaller size, with two coins at once, and afterwards with three or four.

A word of caution may here be desirable. These passes must by no means be regarded as being themselves tricks, but only as processes to be used in the performance of tricks. If the operator, after pretending to pass the coin, say, from the right hand to the left, and showing that it had vanished from the left hand, were to allow his audience to discover that it had all along remained in his right hand, they might admire the dexterity with which he had in this instance deceived their eyes, but they would henceforth guess half the secret of any trick in which palming was employed. If it is necessary immediately to reproduce the coin, the performer should do so by appearing to find it in the hair or whiskers of a spectator, or in any other place that may suit his purpose, remembering always to indicate beforehand that it has passed to such a place, thereby diverting the general attention from himself. As the coin is already in his hand, he has only to drop it to his finger-tips as the hand reaches the place he has named, in order, to all appearance, to take it from thence.

Having given this little piece of advice as to the hand in which the coin actually is, we must add a few words more as to the hand in which it is *not*. Whenever you have (apparently) placed any article either in the closed hand, or in some piece of apparatus from which it is afterwards to disappear, you should not, as a rule, show that the article has departed from the spot where you have apparently placed it, without interposing some magical process, however slight, which may colourably account for its disappearance. A mere nothing will suffice—a touch of the wand, the pronouncing of a magic formula, the pressure of a finger; but in some form or other the ceremony should never be omitted. Thus, to take a very simple example, we will suppose that by means of Pass 1 you have apparently placed in the left hand a coin, which really remains in the palm of the right. If you at once open the left hand, and show that the coin is not there, the spectators will naturally jump to the correct explanation, viz., that you did not, in reality, put the coin there at all. If, however, you delay opening the left hand for a minute or two, so as to let the audience get accustomed to the idea that the coin is therein, and then, before opening it, touch the hand mysteriously with your wand, or even simply, as you slowly open the left hand, rub the ball of the wrist with the second and third fingers of the hand which holds the coin (*see* Fig. 75), you not only give that hand an occupation apparently inconsistent with the fact of anything remaining concealed in it, but you suggest to the audience that the gesture in question is the cause of the disappearance of the coin. It is surprising what an effect even such a trifle as this has in misleading the judgment of a spectator.

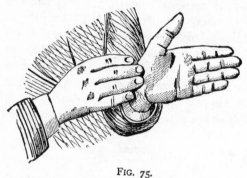

FIG. 75.

He knows perfectly well, in the abstract, that touching the closed hand with the wand, or rubbing it with a finger of the opposite hand, is not an adequate cause for the disappearance of the coin; but the fact being indisputable that the coin *has* disappeared, the mind unconsciously accepts the explanation which is thus indirectly offered. The advice here given becomes less important where, before the hand is opened, you are able to get rid of the object from that in which it originally appeared. Here the spectator is precluded from imagining that you retained it in the hand in which he first saw it, as that hand also is shown to be empty, and the absolute disappearance of the coin being a self-evident fact, you may leave the spectator to account for it in his own manner.

The various passes may be employed not only to cause the disappearance of an article, as above described, but to secretly exchange it for a substitute of similar appearance. These exchanges are of continual use in conjuring; indeed, we may almost say that three parts of its marvels depend on them. Such an exchange having been made, the substitute is left in sight of the audience, while the performer, having thus secretly gained possession of the original, disposes of it as may be necessary for the purpose of the trick. We proceed to describe various forms of changes, denoting them, as in the case of the passes, by numbers.

Change 1.—You desire, we will suppose, to exchange—or, in conjuror's parlance, to "ring"—a florin, marked by the audience, for another. You have the latter, which we will call the "substitute," ready palmed in your left hand, of course taking care to keep the palm turned away from the audience. Taking the marked florin in the right hand, you palm it in that hand by Pass 1, but instead of closing the left hand as the fingers of the right touch it, keep that hand loosely open, and show lying on its palm the substitute, which the audience take to be the original just placed there by your right hand.

Change 2.—This is the same as Change 1, save that you use with the right hand Pass 2 instead of Pass 1.

Change 3.—Here also you use Pass 2, but you have the substitute palmed in the right hand instead of the left. Taking up the marked florin with the same hand, you make with it Pass 2, at the same instant dropping the substitute from its palm into the left hand. This is a very neat and effective change. Some performers are expert enough to make this change by means of Pass 1 instead of Pass 2, the genuine coin taking the place of the substitute in the palm; but this demands dexterity of a more than average order.

Change 4.—For this change you must have the substitute palmed in the right hand, and take the marked coin between the thumb and second finger of the left. Then by Pass 4 appear to take it in the right hand, and at the proper moment exhibit the substitute, which you have already in that hand.

Change 5.—Have the substitute palmed in your right hand, and hold the marked coin openly on the palm of the left. Pick up the genuine coin with the right hand, at the same moment releasing the palmed substitute, which will accordingly fall into the left hand, the fingers of which should be held slightly hollowed, the better to conceal it. Show the marked coin in the right hand, and say, "You have seen me take up this coin visibly, I will make it return invisibly," or make some other appropriate observation. Close the left hand, make Pass 1 or 2 with the right hand, with a motion towards the left, but without bringing the hands near together. The marked coin will, after the pass, be concealed in your right palm. Immediately opening your left hand, you show the substitute, which the audience believe to be the original which they have just seen.

There are many other changes; indeed, they are almost too numerous to describe. If you are able to palm and to make the various passes neatly, you will readily invent methods of "ringing" for yourself; in the meantime, you will find that the above will answer every necessary purpose, so far as coin tricks are concerned.

CHAPTER VII.

Tricks with Coin without Apparatus.

(For Florin read Quarter.)

There is an immense variety of tricks with coin—some with apparatus, some without; some demanding a thorough mastery of sleight-
of-hand; some so simple as to be within the compass of the merest
tyro. The only classification which we shall attempt will be to
divide them into such as do and such as do not require special
apparatus.

A Florin being spun upon the Table, to tell blindfold
whether it falls head or tail upwards.—You borrow a
florin, and spin it, or invite some other person to spin it, on the table
(which must be without a cloth). You allow it to spin itself out,
and immediately announce, without seeing it, whether it has fallen
head or tail upwards. This may be repeated any number of times
with the same result, though you may be blindfolded, and placed at
the further end of the apartment.

The secret lies in the use of·a florin of your own, on one face of
which (say on the "tail" side) you have cut at the extreme edge a
little notch, thereby causing a minute point or tooth of metal to project from that side of the coin. If a coin so prepared be spun on the
table, and should chance to go down with the notched side upwards,
it will run down like an ordinary coin, with a long continuous
"whirr," the sound growing fainter and fainter till it finally ceases;
but if it should run down with the notched side downwards, the friction of the point against the table will reduce this final whirr to half
its ordinary length, and the coin will finally go down with a sort of
"flop." The difference of sound is not sufficiently marked to attract
the notice of the spectators, but is perfectly distinguishable by an

attentive ear. If, therefore, you have notched the coin on the "tail" side, and it runs down slowly, you will cry "tail;" if quickly, "head."

If you professedly use a borrowed florin, you must adroitly change it for your own, under pretence of showing how to spin it, or the like.

You should not allow your audience to imagine that you are guided by the sound of the coin, as, if once they have the clue, they will easily learn to distinguish the two sounds. They are not, however, likely to discover the secret of the notch, and if any one professes to have found out the trick, you may, by again substituting an unprepared florin, safely challenge him to perform it.

ODD OR EVEN, OR THE MYSTERIOUS ADDITION.—This is a trick of almost childish simplicity, depending upon an elementary arithmetical principle. We have, however, known it to occasion great perplexity, even to more than ordinarily acute persons.

You take a handful of coins or counters, and invite another person to do the same, and to ascertain privately whether the number he has taken is odd or even. You request the company to observe that you have not asked him a single question, but that you are able, notwithstanding, to divine and counteract his most secret intentions, and that you will in proof of this, yourself take a number of coins, and add them to those he has taken, when, if his number was odd, the total shall be even; if his number was even, the total shall be odd. Requesting him to drop the coins he holds into a hat, held on high by one of the company, you drop in a certain number on your own account. He is now asked whether his number was odd or even; and, the coins being counted, the total number proves to be, as you stated, exactly the reverse. The experiment is tried again and again, with different numbers, but the result is the same.

The secret lies in the simple arithmetical fact, that if you add an odd number to an even number the result will be odd; if you add an odd number to an odd number the result will be even. You have only to take care, therefore, that the number you yourself add, whether large or small, shall always be odd.

To change a Florin into a Penny, back again, and then to pass the same invisibly into the pocket of the owner. —This is a trick of genuine sleight-of-hand, and will test your expertness in two or three different passes. Having beforehand palmed a penny in your right hand, you borrow from one of the company a florin (or half-crown), requesting the owner to mark it in such manner that he may be able to identify it. Make him stand up facing you, your own right side and his left being towards the audience. Taking the marked florin between the fingers and thumb of the right hand (the back of which, from your position, will be toward the spectators), you ask him whether he is nervous, whether he can hold fast, and so on. On receiving satisfactory replies, you state that you are about to put him to the test, and request him to hold out his right hand, telling him that you are about to count three, and that at the word "three" you will drop the florin into his hand, which he is to close tightly upon it. You accordingly count, "One! two! three!" each time making a motion as of dropping the florin into his hand, and at the word "three" actually do drop it, when he closes his hand upon it, as directed; but you are not satisfied. "That won't do, my dear sir," you exclaim; "you are not half quick enough—you allow all the electric fluid to escape. We'll try once more, and pray be a little quicker in your movements. Oblige me with the coin again. Now, then, are you ready?—One! *two!!* three!!!" giving the words with great energy. As you say "three" you stamp your foot, and apparently again drop the florin, but really drop the penny instead, by Change 3. He is sure this time to close his hand very quickly, and, having no reason to the contrary, naturally believes that it is the florin which he holds, your previous feint, when you did actually drop the florin, being specially designed to lead him to that conclusion. You next request him to hold the closed hand high, that all may see it. This draws the general attention to him, and away from yourself, and enables you to place in your palm the florin, which was left, after the change, in the bend of your right thumb. You continue, "You did better that time, sir. Now, what will you bet me that I cannot take that two-shilling-piece out of your hand without your knowing it?" Whether he admits or defies your power, the course of the trick is the same.

" Well," you say at last, "you seem so determined that I am almost afraid to take the whole of the two-shilling piece away from you, I think I must be content with one-and-elevenpence. Allow me to touch your hand with my wand." You do so, and on opening his hand he discovers that the two-shilling piece has changed into a penny.

You thank him for his assistance, hand him the penny, and dismiss him to his seat. Naturally enough, he objects to accept the penny in place of his florin. You pretend at first not to understand him, but, as if suddenly enlightened, you exclaim, " Oh, the florin, you want the florin ? My dear sir," indicating the penny, " that *is* the florin. At present it is under an electric influence, but you have only to wait till that goes off (it won't take more than three weeks or so), when it will resume its former appearance. You don't believe me, I see ; but I can easily convince you by discharging the electric fluid, when the change will take place at once. Observe ! " You take the penny between the thumb and second finger of the left hand (after the manner indicated in Fig. 66), and make Change 4, making a gentle rubbing movement with the fingers and thumb of the right hand before you open that hand and disclose the restored florin, at the same time carelessly dropping your left hand to your side, and letting fall the penny into your *pochette* on that side. Bring up the left hand again, showing, but without apparent design, that it is empty ; and still holding the coin in the right hand, make Pass 1, as if you transferred it to the left hand. Make a motion with the left hand, as if handing the coin, and say to the owner, " Will you be good enough to examine the florin, and see that it is the same you marked." He naturally holds out his hand for the coin, which he believes to be in your left hand, and which you pretend to give him ; but it has vanished. " Well," you say, " is it the same florin ? " Looking, probably, rather foolish, he replies that he has not got it. " Not got it ! " you say ; " why I have just given it to you. I passed it into your pocket. Look for yourself." He forthwith begins to search his pockets. " You are trying the wrong one," you say ; " this is the pocket." As if desiring merely to assist his search, you plunge into any pocket which he has not yet tried your right hand (in the palm of which the coin was left after the pass), and letting the coin drop to the finger ends, take it out as if it were already in the pocket, as nine-tenths of the audience will believe it to have been.

To make a marked Florin and Penny, wrapped in separate Handkerchiefs, change places at command.—Borrow a florin (or half-crown) and a penny, requesting the owners to mark them, that they may be sure of knowing them again. Also borrow two pocket handkerchiefs.

It may be well to mention, once for all, that it is generally desirable to borrow from the audience, when you can, any indifferent article used in a trick (*e.g.,* a hat, a watch, or a handkerchief), as you thereby seem to give a guarantee for the absence of preparation. Articles so borrowed are taken upon trust, so to speak, and by making a secret exchange you may still use a prepared substitute, which will escape the close scrutiny to which any article confessedly provided by yourself would be subjected.

While the articles above mentioned are being collected from the audience, you secretly palm in your left hand a penny of your own. Receiving the borrowed coins in your right hand, apparently transfer them to the left, but really only transfer the florin, the marked penny remaining in your right hand. This may be effected by making Pass 2 with the marked penny, at the same time allowing the marked florin to drop from the palm as directed in Change 3. Take the earliest opportunity of transferring the marked penny to the palm of the right hand, and showing the marked florin and the substitute penny (which the spectators take to be the genuine one) on the open left hand, place them on your table, begging the audience to observe that they do not for one moment leave their sight. Then picking up with the right hand the florin, on which you may casually show the mark, and throwing one of the borrowed handkerchiefs over the hand, take hold (through the handkerchief) of apparently the florin which you have just shown, but really of the marked penny, and transfer the marked florin to the palm. The shape of the coin, which the audience take to be the florin, will be distinctly seen through the handkerchief, whose folds will fall down around it. Give the handkerchief containing the coin to some person, requesting him to hold it tightly just below the coin, and well above his head, that all may see it.* Now take up the substitute penny, and apparently wrap it, in like manner, in the second handkerchief, really substituting as before the coin concealed in your palm. The substitute penny, which remains in your right hand, you must drop into your *pochette* or *profonde* at the first available opportunity. Give the second handkerchief to another person to hold. The first handkerchief now, to all appearance, contains the florin, and the second the penny. Invite the two persons to stand face to face, the hands holding the handkerchiefs just touching, and after gravely cautioning them to hold very tight, etc., etc., give their hands a gentle rap with your wand, saying, " Change ! " Upon examination, the coins are found to have obeyed your commands.

Managed with neatness and address, this is an admirable drawing-room trick ; the previous marking of the coins apparently precluding any possibility of using substitutes, and allowing the spectator no alternative but to admit that by some mysterious means the identical coins have changed places.

A similar trick may be performed without the use of the handkerchief. As before, you borrow a marked florin and penny, exchanging the latter for one of your own, and palm the genuine one. Taking up the marked florin from the table, you hand it to some one to hold, substituting for it as you do so the genuine penny by Change 3, as indicated in the trick last described. The florin is thus left in your right hand. Palm it, and take up the substitute penny between the second finger and thumb of the left hand, and pretend by Pass 4 to transfer it to the right, which you immediately close. Drop the penny into your *pochette* on the left side, and announce that by your magic power you will compel the penny which you hold to change places with the florin held by the spectator. When the hands are opened, the supposed change is found to be accomplished.

To make two marked Coins, wrapped in separate Handker-chiefs, come together in one of them.—The coins and handkerchiefs borrowed for the purpose of the last trick will again serve in this one. Palm in your right hand a penny of your own, and throw over the

---

* This takes it out of the range of his eyes, and prevents his indulging any desire for a premature examination of the contents.

same hand one of the borrowed handkerchiefs. This will effectually conceal the substitute penny, which you may now take between the finger and thumb. Holding the handkerchief spread out upon the open hand, you take up with the left hand the marked penny and place it on the handkerchief, as if to wrap it therein, but at the same time with the third finger push a fold of the handkerchief under the substitute penny in your right hand. You now invert the handkerchief over your left hand for a minute, allowing the marked penny to drop back into that hand, and at the same time twist the fold already mentioned around the substitute. The audience see the shape of a coin wrapped up in the handkerchief, and naturally believe

that it is that of the marked penny which you have apparently placed inside it. In reality, it is that of your own penny, wrapped merely in an outside fold. You now hand the handkerchief to some one to hold, requesting him to grasp the coin, and hold tightly.

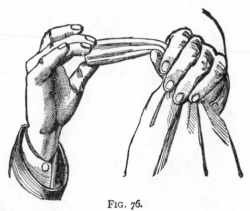

FIG. 76.

The marked penny, it will be remembered, remains in your left hand, and the marked florin on the table. As you go to take up the latter, you transfer the penny to your right hand, and palm it; then pick up the florin, holding it at the tips of the fingers. Spread the second handkerchief on the open palm of the left hand. Bring the florin down smartly upon it, and by the same movement let the penny fall from the palm on to the handkerchief. The two coins will now be lying (covered by the right hand) on the handkerchief, a couple of inches apart. Close the left hand on both coins, and turn the hand over, so that the edges of the handkerchief hang down. With the right hand grasp the handkerchief five or six inches below the coins. Take one of these through the handkerchief between the finger and thumb of the left hand, letting the other fall loose inside the handkerchief, which you then invite some one to hold in like manner, but in a horizontal position. (*See* Fig. 76.) This position is adopted in order that the two coins may not, by any accidental chink, prematurely disclose the fact that both are already in the handkerchief.

You now announce that you are about to make both coins pass into one handkerchief. Advancing to the person who holds the first handkerchief, you request him, still maintaining his hold, to remove his hand four or five inches below the coin, to give you room to operate. First showing that your hand is empty, you gently rub the

FIG. 77.

substitute penny through the handkerchief between your finger and thumb, when, being only wrapped within a fold, it quickly falls into your hand. No one ever thinks of inquiring at this point whether it is the marked one or not. Taking it in the left hand, in position for Pass 4, you say to the person holding the second handkerchief " Having extracted this penny from the one handkerchief, I will now pass it into the other. I won't even touch the handkerchief, but will simply take the coin in my hand, and say, ' Pass!' Will you be good enough, at the word ' pass,' to let go of the coin you are holding, but still keep hold of the handkerchief with the other hand." Appearing, by Pass 4, to take the penny in the right hand, you open that hand with a quick motion towards the handkerchief, saying, " Pass ! " The person holding the handkerchief looses his hold, as directed, when the two coins are heard to chink together, as though the second coin had just arrived in the handkerchief, and on examination they are, of course, found to be those marked.

We may here describe another and still neater mode (the invention, we believe, of M. Robert-Houdin) of apparently wrapping a coin securely in a handkerchief, though really only covered by an outer fold.

Holding the coin upright between the fingers and thumb of the left hand, throw the handkerchief fairly over it. Having shown that it is fairly covered, remark, " But perhaps you may fancy I have changed the coin. Allow me to show you that I have not." With the right hand, palm upwards, take the coin through the handkerchief, (as shown in Fig. 77), between the first and second fingers of that hand. For a moment let go with the left hand (but without removing it from under the handkerchief). Turn over the right hand towards yourself, and again seize the coin with the left hand ; but this time nip the opposite edge of the coin to that which it first held, and through the double thickness of the hand-

FIG. 78.

kerchief. Remove the right hand from the coin, and with it raise the outer edge of the handkerchief and show the coin, as in Fig. 78. Then let the edges of the handkerchief fall. Apparently the coin is underneath, and in the centre of the handkerchief ; but in reality it is outside, lying in a slight fold on the side away from the spectators.

The above description sounds intricate, but, if carefully followed with the coin and handkerchief will be found perfectly simple in practice. It is worth while taking some pains to acquire this sleight, as it is of great value in coin tricks.

To Pull Four Florins or Half-crowns through a Hand-kerchief.—You begin by borrowing four marked half-crowns, florins, or penny-pieces, and a silk or cambric handkerchief. You then request the assistance of a very strong man. This gives an opportunity for a little fun in the selection. Having at last found a volunteer to your liking, you seat him on a chair facing the company. Spreading the handkerchief on your left palm, and placing the four coins upon it, you close your hand upon them through the hand-kerchief, and hand them to him, requesting him to hold them firmly. Then, as if suddenly recollecting yourself, you say, " Pardon me, I have omitted one little detail which is rather important. Oblige me with the handkerchief again for one moment, if you please. I ought to have shown the company that there are no holes in it." (The last sentence should not be pronounced until you have gained possession of the handkerchief, as the company might possibly declare them-selves satisfied of the fact without examination, which would not answer your purpose.) The handkerchief being returned to you, you spread it out to show that it is free from holes, coming among the audience to do so, and appearing to lay great stress upon the fact. Again spreading it over your left hand, you count the coins one by one upon it; then giving a glance round at the company, you say, as you quickly return to your platform, " You have all seen that the four coins are fairly wrapped in the handkerchief," or make any other remark in order to draw the general attention, as a sharp, quick remark almost always will, to your face and away from your hands. At the same moment you move the left thumb over the face of the coins, thereby covering them with a fold of the handkerchief, and seize them, through the fold thus made, between the thumb and fingers of the right hand, as indicated in Fig. 79, immediately withdrawing the left hand. The coins will now be held in the right hand, the hand-kerchief hanging down loosely around them. To any one who has not watched your movements with more than ordinary vigilance, it will appear that the coins are within and under the handkerchief, though they are, in reality, wrapped in an external fold. Giving them a twist round in the handkerchief, you hand it to the person assisting you, asking him to say whether the money is still there, to which he naturally replies in the affirmative. You then tell him to grasp the handkerchief with both hands three or four inches below the coins, and to hold as tightly as he possibly can. Placing your wand under your right arm, and taking hold of the coins (through the handkerchief) with both hands, the right hand undermost, you begin to pull against him, making a show of pulling with great force, and remarking that you are very glad it is not *your* handkerchief, that you

should not have thought he was so strong, etc. Meanwhile, and while the company are enjoying the discomfiture of the owner of the handkerchief, you untwist the latter, and secretly get the money out of the fold into your right hand, and palm it therein. Give one last pull with your left hand, and let go smartly, observing that you fear you must give it up, and own yourself conquered. Take your wand in your right hand; this will make it seem natural for you to keep that hand closed, and will materially aid in concealing the fact that the money is therein. Your an-

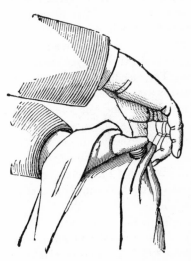

FIG. 79.

tagonist, or the spectators for him, will by this time have discovered that the money has vanished; but you pretend to be unconscious of the fact, and request him to give it back, that you may return it to the owners. He naturally declares that he has not got it. With all the seriousness that you can command, you insist that he has it, and that he must restore it. On his continued denial you suggest that he should search his pockets, which you tap, one after another, with your wand, each giving a metallic sound as if containing money; but the coins are still not to be found. At last, after all his pockets have been tried in vain, you, as if upon a sudden thought, tap the leg of his trousers, the metallic chink still following every tap of the wand till you have nearly reached his feet, when you exclaim, " Yes, there it is. Will you have the kindness to put your foot on that chair ? " He does so, and quickly transferring your wand to the left hand, with the fingers of the right you turn up the edge of the trouser, giving at the same time a slight shake, when the four coins are seen to fall out, to the great surprise of the victim.

This effect is produced as follows : The coins being in your right hand, you introduce them with the second, third, and fourth fingers under the edge of the trouser ; then, with the first finger and thumb which are left outside, you nip them through the cloth, and hold them an instant till you have withdrawn the remaining fingers, when with a slight shake you let them fall.

The metallic chink on tapping the pockets may be produced in two ways. One method is to use a hollow metal wand, japanned to match the one you ordinarily use, and containing throughout its length a loose piece of thick wire, which, striking against the sides of the tube, exactly imitates the chink of money. The other mode is to use merely the ordinary wand, allowing the end which you hold to chink against the money held in the same hand. With a little prac· tice the effect is equally deceptive as with the special wand.

To pass a Marked Florin (or Half-crown) into the Centre of two Oranges in Succession.—For this excellent trick a little previous preparation is necessary. A slit, an inch and a half deep, and just large enough to admit a florin, is made in each of two oranges, and in one of them a florin (which for distinction we will call No. 1) is placed. These must be put in readiness behind the scenes, or so placed as to be out of sight of the audience.

The performer palms in either hand a second florin (No. 2), and advancing to his audience, borrows from one of them a florin, first marked by the owner. (This last we will call No. 3). He invites special attention to the fact that throughout the experiment he is about to perform, the coin is never removed from their sight, and he accordingly places it (really substituting, by one or other of the changes, florin No. 2) in full view on his table. He then goes out to fetch an orange, and takes the opportunity of slipping the marked florin (No. 3) into the vacant one. He brings forward *this* orange publicly, and places it on his table at his *right* hand. (The other orange he has meanwhile placed in his secret pocket on the right side, ready for palming at a moment's notice.) He then says, "I think, by the way, it would be as well to have *two* oranges. Can any gentleman oblige me with one?" No one responding, he looks about him, and presently stepping up to one of his audience, pretends to take from his hair, hat, or handkerchief this second orange (which contains, it will be remembered, florin No. 1), and places it on the *left* hand side of the table. He now (standing behind his table) asks into which orange, the right or the left, he shall pass the florin. As the right of the audience is his left, he is at liberty to interpret the answer in whichever way he thinks proper, and he does so in such manner as to designate the orange containing the non-marked florin, No. 1. Thus, if the audience say "the left," he answers, "On my left? Very good!" If they choose "the right," he says, "On your right? Very good!" Not one person in a thousand will detect the equivoque.

Taking up florin No. 2 from the table, and holding it in his left hand, he pretends by the *tourniquet* to take it in his right, and thence to pass it into the orange, meanwhile dropping it from his left hand on to the *servante*, or into the *profonde*. Showing his hands empty, he cuts open the orange, and exhibits the florin (No. 1) therein contained. Before giving the audience time to examine it for the mark, he hears, or pretends to hear, a murmur among them to the effect that that was not the orange chosen. "Pardon me," he says, "some of you seem to think that I had a special reason for preferring this particular orange. I gave you absolute liberty to choose which you liked, and I understood you to say that you chose this one. However, in order to satisfy everyone, I will repeat the trick with the other orange." Taking up the second orange, he thrusts the knife through it, in the slit already made, and gives the knife thus loaded to some one to hold. Then, standing at some distance from it, he takes up florin No. 1, and, getting rid of it by one or other of the "passes" previously described, he makes a motion as of throwing it towards the orange. He now requests the person holding the orange himself to cut it open ; when the genuine florin, No. 3, is found therein, and duly identified.

The finding of the second orange in the possession of the company may, if preferred, be omitted, and both oranges be brought forward openly in the first instance.

Occasionally a refractory spectator may insist upon the wrong orange (*i.e.*, that containing the genuine coin) being cut open first. As you have offered the audience the choice, you cannot well resist this; but it makes very little difference. In accordance with the general desire, you cut open the orange, and show the coin (No. 3), drawing particular attention to the mark. Its identity being fully established, you offer, for the general satisfaction, to pass the same coin into the second orange. Being satisfied that it was the genuine coin in the first case, the audience will the more readily believe that it is so in the second ; but in this case you should cut open the second orange yourself, as it will be necessary to again substitute the genuine florin before you hand the coin to be examined.

THE FLYING MONEY.—TO MAKE A COIN PASS INVISIBLY FROM THE ONE HAND TO THE OTHER, AND FINALLY THROUGH THE TABLE. —Have ready beforehand a florin or half-crown, with a little wax on one side of it, and take an opportunity of secretly sticking it, by means of the wax, against the under side of the table (any ordinary table) with which you intend to perform the trick. Have also a similar coin of your own palmed in your right hand. Borrow a marked florin from one of the company, and lay it carelessly upon the table, but in so doing exchange it for the one previously palmed. You now have the substitute on the table, and the marked coin palmed in its place. Turn up your sleeves, to show that they have nothing to do with the trick, and make a few introductory remarks about the extraordinary power of the mesmeric influence as applied to metallic substances ; then, taking up the coin from the table between the fingers and thumb of the left hand, which you hold with the palm towards the company, so as to show incidentally that it is otherwise empty, continue to the following effect :—" Here, ladies and gentlemen, is an ordinary coin, a mere inert piece of silver. If you take it in your hand, there it will remain till you lay it down. But let a person possessing the mesmeric gift only breathe upon it " (you suit the action to the word), "and it is at once endowed with hearing, sense, and motion, and will fly from hand to hand at the mere word of command, and that so rapidly, that its flight is absolutely invisible. See, I take it *so* " (taking it in the right hand). "One, two, three! Pass! and it flies back into my left hand again. In order to show that there has been no substitution, perhaps the owner will kindly verify the mark." The coin is examined, and found to be the same.

This illusion is produced as follows :—When you breathe upon the substitute coin, you naturally turn the left hand palm upwards. In the act of taking that coin in the right hand, which you do with the hands in the position depicted in Fig. 69, you drop the genuine coin, which was previously palmed in the right hand, into the left, the position of the hand concealing it from the audience. After a momentary pause, you close the left hand, and hold it extended about level with your eyes. At each of the words, " One, two, three," you make a slight motion of the right hand towards it, and at the word " Pass," palm the coin by means of Pass 1, at the same time making a half turn of your body to the left, opening the left hand, and pointing with the index finger of the right hand to the coin lying therein. While it is being examined for the mark, you drop the substitute, which remains palmed in your right hand, into the *pochette* on that side, and bring up your hand empty.

Having proceeded thus far, borrow a second florin, but without in this case suggesting that it should be marked, breathe upon it, and lay it with that first used upon the table. Now with your right hand take up one of the coins, and by Pass 1 pretend to transfer it to the left, really retaining it in the palm of the right hand. Then take up the second coin between the fingers and thumb of the right hand, and announce that you are about to make the coins, which you now hold in each hand, come together. Holding your arms well apart, you make a motion with the left hand as if throwing something towards the right, at the same moment saying as before, " One, two, three! Pass ! " and making the two coins in the right hand come together with an audible chink. You then open the hand, and show that the left is empty, and that both of the coins are together in the right hand.

You continue, "You all think you know how that was done, I dare say. You imagine, no doubt, that the money was merely thrown from one hand to the other with extreme rapidity. 'The quickness of the hand deceives the eye,' as Shakspeare (or somebody else) says. I will therefore show you the same experiment in another form in which you will find that no such solution is admissible. I will pass the money right through this table, which is, as you see, pretty solid. The quickness of the hand would not be of much use in this case. I take one of the coins in the left hand, as before."

Here, however, you introduce a feint. Taking up the coin in the right hand, you transfer it to the left, but purposely do it with a pretended awkwardness, and hold the right hand afterwards rather stiffly, so as to lead the spectators to believe that you have really retained the coin in the right hand. To do this cleverly will require considerable practice, but it will by no means be labour lost, as feints of this kind are of frequent use.

The spectators, delighted to have, as they imagine, caught you tripping, are sure to exclaim that the coin is still in your right hand. "Surely, ladies and gentlemen," you say, with an injured air, "you don't think that I would avail myself of such a transparent artifice. See for yourselves!" opening your hands. "I won't ask you to apologize, but pray give me a little more credit for the future. Come, we will have no mistake about it this time." Take the florin between the finger and thumb of the left hand, and, by means of the *tourniquet* or *pincette*, appear to transfer it to the right. Pick up the second coin with the left hand, and place that hand under the table, holding the closed right hand above it. Say "Pass!" open the right hand, show it empty, and at the same moment chink the two florins together in the left hand, and bring them up for inspection.

Looking around you, you continue, "I am afraid you are only half convinced; some of you look incredulous still. Come, we will try the experiment once more, and we will see whether you can find me out this time. As before, I take one coin in each hand." This time you actually do so. You again pass your left hand under the table, detaching in its passage the third florin, which you had previously stuck to the under side of the table, but taking care that the two do not prematurely jingle together. Then, holding the other florin with the fingers of the right hand, which should be held palm downwards about a foot above the table, make Pass 1 with that hand, thus bringing the coin into its palm, and at the same time chink the other two coins in the left hand, and bring them up for examination. One of them, in this instance, is a substitute, and therefore, in the unlikely event of the audience insisting that the trick should be performed with marked coins, this last act must be omitted.

With a regular conjuring-table, the trick might be made even more surprising, from the facilities which the *servante* would afford for getting rid of and regaining the coin. But even if you habitually use such a table, it is better not to avail yourself of it for this purpose. The trick is, in any shape, too minute for stage performance, and in a drawing-room it is apt to draw special attention to the table, which in the case of a trick-table is a little embarrassing.

To RUB ONE SIXPENCE INTO THREE.—This is a simple little parlour trick, but will sometimes occasion great wonderment. Procure three sixpences of the same issue, and privately stick two of them (as directed for the florin in the last trick) with wax to the under side of a table, at about half an inch from the edge, and eight or ten inches apart. Announce to the company that you are about to teach them how to make money. Turn up your sleeves, and take the third sixpence in your right hand, drawing particular attention to its date and general appearance, and indirectly to the fact that you have no other coin concealed in your hands. Turning back the table-cover, rub the sixpence with the ball of the thumb backwards and forwards on the edge of the table. In this position your fingers will naturally be below the edge. After rubbing for a few seconds, say, " It is nearly done, for the sixpence is getting hot ;" and, after rubbing a moment or two longer with increased rapidity, draw the hand away sharply, carrying away with it one of the concealed sixpences, which you exhibit as produced by the friction. Pocketing the waxed sixpence, and again showing that you have but one coin in your hands, repeat the operation with the remaining sixpence.

THE MULTIPLICATION OF MONEY.—This is an old and favourite trick. It may be performed with shillings, pence, or florins, as may best suit your convenience. Whichever you use (we will suppose florins), you prepare for the trick by secretly palming in the right hand such number (say three) as you intend to magically add. Advancing to the audience, you beg the loan of ten or a dozen florins (the precise number is immaterial), at the same time requesting some one of the company to collect them, and bring them to you. He collects, we will suppose, twelve. You request him to count them openly upon the table, that all may be able to verify their number. This being done, you invite a second person also to step forward and assist. Picking up from the table the same number of coins as you have concealed in your palm, you give them to one of the two persons (whom we will call *A*) to hold. Then, taking up the remaining coins, you request the second person (whom we will call *B*) to take charge of them. When he holds out his hand to receive them, you let fall with them the palmed coins, so that he really receives twelve, though he believes that he has only nine. You make him close his hand, and hold it high above his head. You then ask *A* for the coins you entrusted to him. On his returning them to you, you take them between the second finger and thumb of the left hand, and pretend by the *tourniquet* to transfer them to the right, really getting rid of them at the earliest opportunity on the *servante*, or into one of your *pochettes*. The audience believe that the three coins are in your closed right hand. You announce that you are about to pass them invisibly into the hand of *B*, and after the necessary amount of magical gesture, you open your hand, and show that they have vanished; and *B*, on examining his stock, finds that the supposed nine have increased to twelve.

It is a very good plan, in performing this trick, for the performer himself to collect the coins from the company in a plate, the coins to be added being held in the same hand which carries the plate, when, the thumb being naturally above and the fingers below, the coins are effectually concealed. After the coins have been counted, the performer, taking the plate in the other hand, pours them from it into the hand which already holds the concealed coins, thus bringing them together easily and naturally.

A further improvement may be made in the trick by using, in place of an ordinary plate, a special plate or salver, generally made of tin japanned, but sometimes of crockery or china. The speciality of this plate (which is known as the "money plate," or "multiplying salver") consists in a flat space running along its bottom, between its upper and under surface, just wide enough and deep enough to hold concealed a row of coins (florins or shillings, as the case may be), and closed at the one end, but open at the other, the opening being concealed by the edge of the plate. (*See* Fig. 80.) You prepare the plate beforehand by placing in the concealed space three, four,

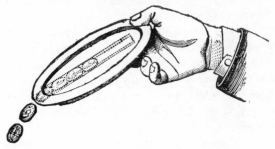

FIG. 80.

or six coins, and place it on your table. When you first take it up, you take hold of it *near the opening*, when you may, of course, handle it as freely as you please, as, the mouth of the passage being upwards, the coins cannot possibly fall out. Letting the plate hang downwards in a perpendicular position, and passing it carelessly from hand to hand, the audience cannot help observing that you have nothing concealed in your hands. Then collect (or count out, if already collected) the money ·in the plate, and, after taking away and handing to *A* a number equal to the coins concealed, pour the remainder direct from the plate into the hands of *B*, first, however, so reversing the position of the plate (which you may do by merely transferring it from the one hand to the other) as to turn the opening of the passage away from you. When you now slope the plate to pour the remaining coins into his hands, the money in the concealed passage will naturally pour out with them (*see* Fig. 80), thus making the required addition with hardly a possibility of detection.

It is a good plan to perform the trick first without, and then to repeat it with, the aid of the money plate, making a great point in the second instance of the fact that you do not even touch the money, and accounting for the use of the plate as designed to preclude all possibility of the use of sleight-of-hand, or any other mechanical mode of deception. The spectators, having already seen you perform the trick without the aid of the plate, are precluded from supposing that this latter has any special connection with the secret; and seeing clearly that you have in this instance no coins concealed in your hands, naturally conclude that the same was the case on the former occasion. Thus the repetition of the trick, instead of assisting them to a solution, rather increases the mystery.

The trick may be varied at pleasure so far as regards the manner of the disappearance of the coins which are supposed to be passed invisibly into the hands of the person holding the larger number. One mode is to ask one of the company to wrap them up in a piece of stiff paper, for which you forthwith secretly substitute a piece of similar paper, in which a like number of coins have been wrapped, but have been removed, the paper, however, retaining the form of the coins. Taking this in the left hand, you pretend to take from it, invisibly, with the finger and thumb of the right hand, each coin in succession, and to pass it in the same manner into the hand of the person holding the remaining coins, finally tearing the paper in half to show that they have really passed away from it. Or you may, if you prefer it, place the coins in question on the "vanishing plate," to be hereafter described, whence they mysteriously disappear as you take them off one by one. This is a very effective mode. Or you may place them in the "plug-box," the "Davenport cabinet," or any other of the various appliances after-mentioned for vanishing money.

To make a Marked Sixpence vanish from a Handkerchief, and be found in the Centre of an Apple or Orange previously examined.—Have ready, concealed in either hand, a sixpence of your own, with a little wax smeared on one side of it. Roll another minute portion of wax into a round ball half the size of a peppercorn, and press it lightly upon the lowest button of your waistcoat, so that you may be able to find it instantly when wanted. You must also have at hand an ordinary full-sized table-knife and a plate of oranges.

You begin by borrowing a sixpence (requesting the owner to mark it) and a handkerchief. You spread the handkerchief flat on the table, with its sides square with those of the table. Then standing behind your table, you place ostensibly the borrowed sixpence, but really your own (with the waxed side up), in the centre of the handkerchief, then fold over the corners, one by one, beginning with one of those nearest to yourself, in such manner that each shall overlap the sixpence by about an inch, gently pressing each corner as you fold it down. Ask some one to come for-ward, and ascertain by feeling the hand-kerchief, that the six-pence is really there. Then offer the knife for inspection, and after all are satisfied that it is without pre-paration, hand the plate of oranges to be examined in like manner, requesting the audience to choose

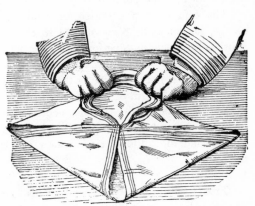

FIG. 8L.

one for the purpose of the trick. While they do so, your fingers go in search of the little ball of wax, and press it against one side of the marked sixpence, which still remains in your hand. Press the six-pence against one side of the blade of the knife, at about the middle of its length, and lay the knife on the table, the sixpence adhering to its under side. Then taking hold of the handkerchief, as represented in Fig. 81, and blowing on its centre, draw the hands quickly apart. The two corners of the side next to you will thus be brought one into each hand, and adhering to one of them (the one which you first folded down), will be the substitute sixpence, which will thus appear to have vanished. Hand the handkerchief for examination, that it may be seen that the coin has really disappeared, and meanwhile get rid of the substitute into your pocket or elsewhere. Turn up your sleeves, and show that your hands are empty. Then take up the knife (taking care to keep the side on which the sixpence is away from the spectators), and cut open the orange. Cut about half way down with the *point*, and then finish the cut by drawing the whole length of the blade through the opening thus made. This will detach the sixpence, which will fall between the two halves of the orange, as though it had all along been contained therein. Wipe it with the handkerchief to remove the juice of the orange from it, and at the same time rub off any wax which may still adhere to it, and hand it for identification.

The coin may, if preferred, be found in an egg instead of the orange, the audience being invited to choose which shall be used. This trick is sometimes performed by the aid of a knife made for this special purpose, with a small spring lever, after the manner of a flute key, soldered against one side of the blade. The coin is held in position by the short arm of the lever, which answers the same purpose as the wax in the form of the trick above described. The disadvantage of using this, which is known as the "fruit knife," is, that you cannot hand the knife for examination, and this, to our mind, spoils the trick.

THE TRAVELLING COUNTERS.—This is a very similar trick to that already described under the title of the "Multiplication of Money." It is performed with twelve metal counters. The performer begins by counting the twelve counters on the table; then, taking up four of them, he hands them to a spectator to hold, and taking the remainder in his own hand, commands them to change places. On examination, his commands are found to be obeyed. The spectator has eight, while the performer has only four. The spectator is now requested to take charge of the eight, when the operator commands the four which he himself holds to rejoin them. This, also, is found to be accomplished. The operator now hands the twelve to a second spectator, requesting him to hold them tightly. After a moment's interval, he is requested again to count them, but finds that he has grasped them too tightly, for they are now welded

together into a solid mass.   The performer again takes them, and by
merely breathing on them, restores them to their original state.

The student, with the experience which he has by this time
gained, will naturally conjecture that the trick is in reality performed
with sixteen loose counters, and twelve soldered together; that the
performer commenced the trick with four counters palmed in his
right hand, which he secretly added to the four which he handed to
the spectator; that, taking up the remaining eight, and apparently
transferring them from his right hand to his left, he really transferred
four only, leaving the remainder in the right hand; and that when he
again handed the eight counters to the spectator, he added these last
to them.   That in apparently transferring the remaining four from
hand to hand he palmed them, forthwith dropping them into one of his
pochettes, and taking from the same place, or from under his waistband,
the solid twelve, which he finally handed to the second spectator in
place of the twelve loose counters ; again substituting the loose ones,
as before, when by breathing on them he professed to restore them to
their primitive state.

As the student has so successfully guessed all this, it would be an
impertinence on our part to further explain the trick.

THE WANDERING SIXPENCE.—Have ready two sixpences, each
slightly waxed on one side.   Borrow a sixpence, and secretly exchange
it for one of the waxed ones, laying the latter, waxed side uppermost,
on the table.   Let any one draw two cards from any ordinary pack.
Take them in the left hand, and, transferring them to the right, press
the second waxed sixpence against the centre of the undermost, to
which it will adhere.   Lay this card (which we will call *a*) on the
table, about eighteen inches from the sixpence which is already there,
and cover that sixpence with the other card, *b*.   Lift both cards a
little way from the table, to show that the sixpence is under card *a*,
and that there is apparently nothing under card *b*.   As you replace
them, press lightly on the centre of card *a*.   You may now make the
sixpence appear under whichever card you like, remembering that, if
you wish the sixpence *not* to adhere, you must bend the card slightly
upwards in taking it from the table; if otherwise, take it up without
bending.

CHAPTER VIII.

Tricks with Coin requiring Special Apparatus.

The "Heads and Tails" Trick.—This is a pretty little trick, of an unpretending nature, but of very good effect, especially if introduced in a casual and apparently *extempore* manner. The performer borrows, or produces from his own pocket, four penny-pieces. Placing them upon the table, he requests some one to make a pile of them, all one way, say "tail" upwards. He next requests the same or another person to turn over the pile so made, without disturbing the relative position of the coins, and announces with an air of supernatural knowledge that they will now all be found "head" upwards. This appears so ridiculously obvious, that the audience naturally observe (with more or less straightforwardness of expression) that "any fool could tell that." "Pardon me," says the performer, "it is not quite such a simple matter as you think. I very much doubt whether any of you could do as much. I will place the coins again; watch me as closely as you please. I will place them as before— Tail, tail, tail, tail. Is that fairly done? Now I will turn them over." He does so, letting the tips of his fingers rest upon them. "What are they now?" A general chorus replies, "All heads, of course!" But on examination it is found that only three are "heads," and one a "tail." Again he arranges them, placing them this time alternately—head, tail, head, tail. He turns them over. The natural order (beginning from below) would again be head, tail, head, tail; but they are found to be head, tail, tail, tail. Again he places them, tail, tail, tail, head. When turned over they should be tail, head, head, head, but are found to be tail, head, alternately.

The secret lies in the use of a prepared penny, consisting of similar halves (in the case above described two "tails") soldered together, so as to be " tail " on either side. This the performer palms in his right hand. After first going through the operation with the genuine coins, as above, he picks them up with his left hand, and apparently transferring them to the right, really transfers three of them only. He then performs the trick with these and the prepared coin, when the apparently miraculous result above described becomes a matter of course.

It is best not to repeat the trick too often, and a little practice is necessary in order to be able to return the three genuine coins neatly to the left hand (in which the fourth borrowed coin must be retained throughout the trick), at the same time secretly retaining your own. It is a frequent occurrence for one or other of the company, imagining that the seeming wonder is, in some unexplained way, a result of some natural principle, to request to be allowed to try for himself. It is obvious that, under such circumstances, it would not do to hand him the prepared coin, and hence the necessity for ome quick and natural method of again getting the four genuine coins together.

The trick may be brought to an effective conclusion as follows : After you have got rid of the double-faced penny, you may continue, " Perhaps it is a little too complicated for you with four coins ; suppose we try it with one only, and I won't even turn it over." Placing one of the genuine pence on the middle of the right palm, which you hold out horizontally before you, you draw special attention to the fact that the coin is (say) " tail " upwards. Quickly covering it with the other hand, you say, " What is it now ? " " Tail," is the reply. " Wrong again ! " you say, and, lifting up the hand, show that the coin has this time vanished altogether. This mysterious disappearance is effected as follows : When you apparently cover the coin with the left hand, you bring the hands together with a quick lateral motion as though sliding the one across the other. This shoots the coin from the palm down the opposite sleeve, the motion being so quick that the keenest eye cannot detect it. This little sleight is by no means difficult, and is well worthy of acquirement, as it may be introduced with equal effect in many tricks.

THE MAGIC COVER AND VANISHING HALFPENCE.—This is a very old trick, but is still very popular with a juvenile audience.

The principal apparatus consists of half-a-dozen halfpence, of which the centre portion has been cut out, leaving each a mere rim of metal. Upon these is placed a complete halfpenny, and the whole are connected together by a rivet running through the whole thickness of the pile. When placed upon the table, with the complete coin upwards, they have all the appearance of a pile of ordinary halfpence, the slight lateral play allowed by the rivet aiding the illusion. A little leather cap (shaped something like a fez, with a little button on the top, and of such a size as to fit loosely over the pile of halfpence), with an ordinary die, such as backgammon is played with, complete the necessary requirements.

You begin by drawing attention to your magic cap and die, late the property of the king of the fairies. In order to exhibit their mystic powers, you request the loan of half-a-dozen halfpence (the number must, of course, correspond with that of your own pile), and, while they are being collected, you take the opportunity to slip the little cap over your prepared pile, which should be placed ready to hand behind some small object on the table, so as to be unseen by the spectators. Pressing the side of the cap, you lift the pile with it, and place the whole together in full view, in close proximity to the die. The required halfpence having been now collected, you beg all to observe that you place the leather cap (which the spectators suppose to be empty) fairly over the die. Taking the genuine coins in either hand, you pretend, by one or other of the passes, to transfer them to the other. Holding the hand which is now supposed to contain the coins immediately above the cap, you announce that they will at your command pass under the cap, from which the die will disappear to make room for them. Saying, "One, two, three! Pass!" you open your hand, and show that the coins have vanished. If you use a regular table, you may place them on the *servante*, and show both hands empty; and then, lifting up the cap by the button, you show the hollow pile, covering the die, and appearing to be the genuine coins. Once more covering the pile with the cap, you announce that you will again extract the coins, and replace the die; and to make the trick still more extraordinary, you will this time pass the coins right through the table. Placing the hand which holds the genuine coins beneath the table, and once more saying, "One, two, three!

Pass!" you chink the coins, and, bringing them up, place them on the table. Again picking up the cap, but this time pressing its sides, you lift up the hollow pile with it, and disclose the die. Quickly transfer the cap, without the pile, to the other hand, and place it on the table, to bear the brunt of examination, while you get rid of the prepared coins.

The trick may be varied in many ways, according to the ingenuity of the performer, but it belongs at best to the "juvenile" school of conjuring, and we have not thought it worth while to waste space in elaborating it.

THE ANIMATED COIN, WHICH ANSWERS QUESTIONS, ETC.— This trick is performed in a variety of different ways, some with apparatus, some without. The effect produced is as follows :—The performer borrows a coin, and, after making a few mesmeric passes over it, drops it into a glass upon the table, where it immediately begins to jump about as if alive. The performer then announces that the coin thus mesmerized has the power of fortune-telling, naming chosen cards, predicting the number that will be thrown by a pair of dice, etc. The coin answers "Yes" by jumping three times, "No" by jumping once—according to the approved spiritualistic code of signals. We shall not stay to discuss the questions asked, which are of the same class as those which are generally put to the Magic Bell or Drum, but proceed at once to explain the various modes of producing the movement of the coin.

One plan is for the performer to have a coin of his own, to which is attached a long black silk thread, the other end of which is in the hand of an assistant behind the scenes, or elsewhere out of sight of the audience. This coin is placed on the table in readiness, but concealed from the spectators by some larger object in front of it. When the performer advances to the table with the borrowed coin, he secretly picks up the prepared one, and drops the latter into the glass as being that which he has borrowed. A short, quick jerk of the thread by the assistant will make the coin spring up and fall back again, producing the required chink. It is only necessary to be careful not to jerk the thread so violently as to make the coin fly out of the glass. It is desirable, where practicable, to make the thread pass either through a hole in the top of the table, or a ring fixed to its surface and placed immediately behind the glass. This will keep that portion of the thread nearest to the glass perpendicular behind it, in which position it will be completely hidden by the glass, and so be invisible.

Some performers prefer to use the actual coin borrowed. The arrangements in this case are the same as above described, save that the silk thread, instead of having a substitute coin attached to it, has merely a pellet of wax at its end. The performer having handed round the glass for inspection, and standing in front of the table with his left side turned towards the audience, picks up a pellet of wax with his right hand at the same moment that, holding the borrowed coin in his left hand, he begs the spectators to take especial notice that he really uses the borrowed coin, and no other. Having said this, he transfers the coin, by a perfectly natural movement, to his right hand, and pressing against it the waxen pellet, drops it into the glass.

FIG. 82.

The third and last mode of performing the trick is by means of a special glass, with a hole drilled through its foot. This is placed on a suitable pedestal (*see* Fig. 82), in which works up and down a steel needle, forming the upper portion of a kind of loose piston, *a*. The top of the pedestal is covered with green baize, allowing free passage to the needle, which when pushed upward strikes the coin from below, with much the same effect as the thread pulling it from above. This pedestal is only available with one of the mechanical tables which will be described in connection with "stage tricks." Such tables contain, among other contrivances, what are called "pistons," being small metal rods, which, by pulling a string, are made to rise vertically an inch or so above the surface of the table, sinking down again as soon as the cord is released. The pedestal is placed immediately above one of these, whose movement is in turn communicated to the loose piston in the pedestal, and thence to the coin.

It only remains to be stated how the necessary knowledge for the answers is communicated to the person who controls the movements of the piece. With respect to chosen cards, the cards are either indicated by the wording of the questions, or are agreed on beforehand, the performer taking care to "force" the right ones. The assistant is enabled to predict the throw of the dice by the simple expedient of using a small boxwood vase, in which there are two compartments, in one of which a pair of dice (apparently the same which have just been dropped in haphazard from the top) have been arranged beforehand for the purpose of the trick. The ordinary fortune-telling questions, as to "Which young lady will be married first?" "Which spends most time at her looking-glass?" "Which has most sweethearts?" and so on, are either answered in accordance with previous arrangement, or according to the fancy of the moment. Of course, where a question of this kind is asked, the performer takes care to follow up the question by designating a number of persons in succession, so that a mere "Yes" or "No" may be a sufficient answer.

We shall next proceed to describe three or four pieces of apparatus designed to cause a piece of money to disappear, and therefore well adapted for commencing a coin trick. There are other appliances, more particularly adapted for re-producing a coin. Any of these will be available for the conclusion; the particular combination being at the option of the performer.

The Vanishing Halfpenny Box. To make a Halfpenny vanish from the Box, and again return to it.—This is a little round box, made of boxwood, about an inch deep, and of such diameter that its internal measurement exactly admits a halfpenny; in other words, that if a halfpenny be placed in it, it exactly covers the bottom. The top and bottom of the box are lined with some bright-coloured paper, and with it is used a halfpenny, one side of which is covered with similar paper. If therefore this halfpenny be placed in the box with the papered side upwards, the halfpenny is naturally taken to be the bottom of the box, which thus appears empty.

The performer begins by tendering the box for examination, keeping the while the prepared halfpenny palmed in his right hand. When the box has been sufficiently inspected, he borrows a half-penny from the audience, and secretly exchanges it for his own, taking care that the spectators only see the unprepared side of the latter. He then announces that this box, apparently so simple, has the singular faculty of causing the disappearance of any money entrusted to its keeping, as they will perceive when he places in it the halfpenny he has just borrowed. He places the halfpenny in it accordingly, holding it with the uncovered side towards the audience, but letting it so fall that it shall lie in the box with the papered side upwards. He now puts the lid on, and shakes the box *up and down,* to show by the rattling of the coin that it is still there. He desires the audience to say when they would wish the coin to leave the box, and on receiving their commands, touches the lid with his wand, and again shakes the box. This time, however, he shakes it laterally, and as in this direction the coin exactly fits the box, it has no room to rattle, and is therefore silent. He boldly asserts that the coin is gone, and opening the box, shows the inside to the spectators, who seeing, as they suppose, the papered bottom, are constrained to admit that it is empty. Once again he closes the box, and touches it with the wand, announcing that he will compel the coin to return. Shaking the box up and down, it is again heard to rattle. Taking off the lid, he turns the box upside down, and drops the coin into his hand. This brings it out with the papered side undermost, and so hidden. Again handing the box to be examined, he exchanges the prepared halfpenny for the one which was lent to him, and which he now returns to the owner with thanks.

A variation may be introduced by causing the borrowed halfpenny to re-appear in some other apparatus, after it has vanished from the box in question. The borrowed coin may, if desired, be marked, in order to heighten the effect of the trick.

The Rattle Box. To make a Coin vanish from the Box, though still heard to rattle within it.—This is a useful and ingenious little piece of apparatus. It is an oblong mahogany box, with a sliding lid. Its dimensions are about three inches by two, and one inch in depth externally; internally, it is only half that depth, and the end piece of the lid is of such a depth as to be flush with the bottom. Thus, if a coin be placed in the box, and the box held in such a position as to slant downwards to the opening, the coin will of its own weight fall into the hand that holds the box (*see* Fig. 83), thus giving the performer possession of it without the knowledge of the audience.

Between the true and the false bottom of the box is placed a slip of zinc, which, when the box is shaken laterally, moves from side to side, exactly simulating the sound of a coin shaken in the box. In its normal condition, however, this slip of zinc is held fast (and therefore kept silent) by the action of a spring also placed between the two bottoms, but is released for the time being by a pressure on a particular part of the outer bottom (the part in contact with the fingers in Fig. 83).

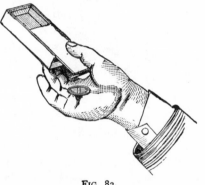

FIG. 83.

A casual inspection of the box suggests nothing, save, perhaps, that its internal space is somewhat shallow in proportion to its external measurement.

The mode of using it is as follows: The performer invites any person to mark a coin, and to place it in the box, which he holds for that purpose as represented in the figure; and the coin is thus no sooner placed in the box than it falls into his hand. Transferring the box to the other hand, and pressing the spring, he shakes it to show by the sound that the coin is still there; then, leaving the box on the table, he prepares for the next phase of the trick by secretly placing the coin, which the audience believe to be still in the box, in any other apparatus in which he desires it to be found, or makes such other disposition of it as may be necessary. Having done this, and having indicated the direction in which he is about to command the coin to pass, he once more shakes the box to show that it is still *in statu quo.* Then, with the mystic word " Pass ! " he opens the box, which is found empty, and shows that his commands have been obeyed.

THE PEPPER-BOX, for vanishing money.—This is a small tin box, of the pepper-box or flour-dredger shape, standing three to four inches high. (*See* Fig. 84.) The box portion (as distinguished from the lid), is made double, consisting of two tin tubes sliding the one within the other, the bottom being soldered to

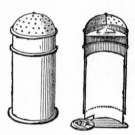

the inner one only. By pulling the bottom downwards, therefore, you draw down with it the inner tube, telescope fashion. By so doing you bring into view a slit or opening at one side of the inner tube, level with the bottom, and of such a size as to let a coin, say a two-shilling piece, pass through it easily. (*See* Fig. 85.) The lid is also specially prepared. It has an inner or false top, and between the true and false top a loose bit of tin is in-

FIG. 84.   FIG. 85.

troduced, which rattles when the box is shaken, unless you at the same time press a little point of wire projecting from one of the holes at the top, and so render it, for the time being, silent.

The box is first exhibited with the inner tube pushed up into its place, and the opening thereby concealed. A marked coin is borrowed, but either before or after the coin is placed therein, as may best suit his purpose, the performer secretly draws out the inner tube a quarter of an inch or so, thus allowing the coin to slip through into his hand. As he places the box on the table, a very slight pressure suffices to force the tube up again into its original position, and close the opening. Having made the necessary disposition of the coin, the performer takes up the box, and shakes it, to show (apparently) that the coin is still there, pressing on the little point above mentioned

when he desires it to appear that it has departed, and immediately opening the box to show that it is empty. The pepper-box will not bear
minute inspection, and is in this particular inferior to the rattle-box.

The Brass Money-box, for the same purpose.—This is on a
similar principle to that of the pepper-box, but has no rattle movement, and is not adapted for
any coin of larger size than a
shilling. Its shape will be
best understood from an examination of the diagrams.
(*See* Figs. 86, 87.) It has no
moveable lid, but merely a slit
in the top, just large enough to
admit the coin, which, when
once dropped in, cannot be got
out again without a knowledge
of the secret.

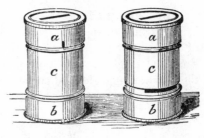

FIG. 86.   FIG. 87.

This, like the pepper-box, consists of two tubes one within the
other; but the inner tube is firmly soldered to the two end pieces,
a and *b*, which are solid. The only moveable portion is the outer
tube *c*, which is so arranged as to slide upwards (within *a*) for about
an eighth of an inch, thereby disclosing the opening of the inner
tube, and allowing the coin to slip through. Fig. 87 represents the
box with the slit open, and Fig. 86 with it closed.

Some little practice is required to use the money-box with dexterity. The performer should hold it tightly by the middle between
the finger and thumb of his right hand, taking care that the side on
which the secret opening is shall lie toward the inside of his hand.
As he drops the coin through the slit, he should press lightly on the
top with the fingers of the left hand, and at the same time push *c*
upwards with the right hand. The coin will now slip through into
his hand, while a slight downward pressure as he replaces the box on
the table will again push down *c*, and make all close as before. If
the performer prefers to use one hand only, he should press downwards on the top with the first finger, at the same time pressing
upwards with the second finger and thumb.

There are various ways of using this little apparatus. It may either be used as above, as a means of surreptitiously gaining possession of a coin, to be afterwards produced in some other apparatus, or it may be used by itself singly, the coin being made apparently to fall through the bottom at the will of the performer. It may also be used as a puzzle, its secret being so well concealed that it will bear a very minute examination without discovery.

THE BRASS BOX FOR MONEY, KNOWN AS THE "PLUG-BOX."—
This is a piece of apparatus so ingenious in construction, and capable of being used in so many different ways, that we should recommend the student of magic to make it one of his first investments. It is about three inches in height, and one and a half in diameter, and is composed of four separate parts. *See* Fig. 88, in which *a* represents the

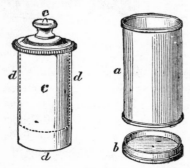

FIG. 88.

outside or body of the box, being in reality a mere brass tube open at both ends, with a moveable bottom, *b*, which fits tightly in the end of *a*, appearing when in its place to be a fixture, and to form with *a* one complete whole; *a* has no lid, properly so called, but is closed by inserting in it what appears to be a solid brass plug or piston. This plug, however, though in appearance solid, also consists of two parts—the plug proper, *c*, which is really solid, and a brass sheath, *d*, exactly fitting it as to its diameter, but a quarter of an inch longer, thus leaving, when *c* is placed in *d*, and pushed home, a hollow space at the bottom of *d* capable of containing a florin or half-crown. The sheath *d* is of precisely the same length as *a*, and is so made as to fit easily upon *c*, but tightly within *a*. When the plug-box is exhibited to the audience, the bottom, *b*, is in its proper place, and *c*, which is shown apart from *a*, is covered with its sheath, *d*. There being nothing in its appearance to point to any other conclusion, the spectators naturally believe that the apparatus consists of those two parts only. If now the plug be placed within the box, and pushed home, the moveable bottom, b, will be pressed out, and fall into the hand of the performer. On again withdrawing the plug, the sheath d, which, as already mentioned, fits more tightly within a than upon c, is left within a; the bottom of d, which comes exactly flush with the lower edge of a, now appearing to be the bottom of the latter. To the eyes of the audience, the box is exactly as they saw it at first, and it may even be examined pretty freely, with little risk of its secret being discovered by any one.

The plug-box may be used in a variety of different ways—to vanish, reproduce, or exchange. For the first purpose, the coin to be got rid of is dropped into a. When the plug is inserted, and pressed home, the coin falls, with b, into the hand of the performer; and on the plug being again withdrawn, nothing is seen but the interior of d, which is of course empty. Where it is desired to use the box for the purpose of reproducing a coin, such coin is placed beforehand within d. The box is first shown empty, but has only to be closed and re-opened, and the coin is found within it. For exchanges, the substitute is placed in d, and the genuine coin in a. This latter falls out with the bottom, and the substitute is in due course discovered. A half-crown may thus be changed to a penny, or a sovereign to a shilling.

But the chief use of the plug-box is as an auxiliary in those more important tricks in which the coin, apparently remaining up to the last moment in the spectator's own possession, is suddenly made to appear in some quarter to which (if it had really so remained) it could not possibly have been transported by natural means. The performer in this case places a similar coin beforehand in d. Dropping, or allowing the owner to drop, the marked coin into a, he closes the box, which he shakes to prove that the coin is really there. Giving the box to some one to hold, he is then enabled, without exciting the smallest suspicion, to retire, and make what disposition he pleases of the marked coin, which he has thus got into his own possession. When he has completed his arrangements, he again takes the box, and, opening it, takes out the substitute, which the audience naturally believe to be the genuine coin; and getting rid of this by sleight-of-hand or otherwise, passes the coin (at that very moment, so far as the audience can judge) to the place where it is ultimately destined to be found.

A favourite mode of using the plug-box is as follows:—A coin (say a florin) is wrapped in a small piece of paper, after which the coin is taken out and the paper again folded in such a manner as to retain the impression of the coin, and so to look, as far as possible, as if still containing it. The paper thus folded is placed beforehand in *d*, and the performer, borrowing a florin, requests the owner to wrap it carefully in a piece of paper, which he hands him for the purpose, and which is similar in size and general appearance to the folded piece. The florin, thus wrapped up, is placed in *a*, and the box closed, the performer thus gaining possession of paper and coin. The box is then handed to the owner of the money, who is asked to open it and see for himself that his money is still there. Seeing the folded paper, which he takes to be the same in which his money was wrapped, he answers in the affirmative. The box is again closed, the coin, meanwhile, being disposed of according to the pleasure of the operator—the owner finding on a closer examination that his money has departed from the box, though the paper in which it was wrapped (as he imagines) still remains.

THE HANDKERCHIEF FOR VANISHING MONEY.—This is another appliance for vanishing a coin. It is an ordinary handkerchief of silk or cotton, in one corner of which, in a little pocket, is sewn a coin, say a florin or a penny, or any substitute which, felt through the substance of the handkerchief, shall appear to be such a coin. The mode of using it is very simple. Holding the handkerchief by the corner in which is the coin, and letting it hang loosely down, the performer borrows a similar coin, and, after carelessly shaking out the handkerchief, to show that all is fair, he places, to all appearance, the borrowed coin in the centre (underneath), and gives the handkerchief to some one to hold. In reality, he has only wrapped up the corner containing the substitute coin, and retains the genuine one for his own purposes. When it is desirable to make it appear that the coin has left the handkerchief, he simply takes it from the person holding it, and gives it a shake, at the same moment rapidly running the edges of the handkerchief through his hands, till the corner containing the coin comes into one or the other of them.

The Demon Handkerchief (*Le Mouchoir du Diable*).—This is a recent improvement on the above, and possesses a much wider range of utility, inasmuch as it really does cause the disappearance of any article placed under it, and is available to vanish not only coin, but a card, an egg, a watch, or any other article of moderate size. It consists of *two* handkerchiefs, of the same pattern, stitched together all round the edges, and with a slit of about four inches in length cut in the middle of one of them. The whole space between the two handkerchiefs thus forms a kind of pocket, of which the slit above mentioned is the only opening. In shaking or otherwise manipulating the handkerchief, the performer takes care always to keep the side with the slit away from the spectators, to whom the handkerchief appears to be merely the ordinary article of everyday use. When he desires by its means to cause the disappearance of anything, he carelessly throws the handkerchief over the article, at the same time secretly passing the latter through the slit in the under side, and hands it thus covered to some one to hold. Then, taking the handkerchief by one corner, he requests him to let go, when the object is retained in the space between the two handkerchiefs, appearing to have vanished into empty air.

This, like the plug-box, is an appliance which no conjuror should be without. It may be purchased ready-made at any of the *depôts* for magical apparatus, or may be of home-manufacture, which in this case (contrary to the general rule) is not unlikely to produce the better article.

The Davenport Cabinet.—This little cabinet must by no means be confounded with the wardrobe in which the notorious Brothers performed their mystic evolutions. The cabinet now in question is but four inches high and two and a half square, and consists of two parts, an outer case, or body, covered at the top, but otherwise open throughout, and a drawer, occupying the upper portion of its interior space. (*See* Fig. 89.) When the drawer is removed, the case, which has no bottom, may be examined throughout, and will be found to be perfectly plain and unsophisticated ; save that a keen examiner might observe a little brass pin, a quarter of an inch long, projecting from the back of the cabinet on the inside, just on a level with the bottom of the drawer when replaced in its proper position. The drawer

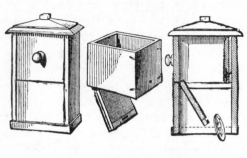

FIG. 89.　　　FIG. 90.　　　FIG. 91.

may also be examined, and will be found to be perfectly plain, with the bottom (which is so thin as to preclude any suspicion of a concealed space), covered within and without with black cloth. On turning the drawer round, and examining the back, a minute hole may be discovered, corresponding in situation with the brass pin already mentioned. If a pin be thrust into this hole, the purpose of the two is immediately manifest ; for the pressure of the pin releases a tiny catch, and allows the bottom of the drawer, which is in reality only supported by this catch at the back and a cloth hinge in the front, to drop into the position indicated in Fig. 90. This is precisely what takes place when the drawer, being restored to its proper position in the cabinet, is duly closed. The pressure of the brass pin at the back releases the catch, and the bottom of the drawer falls as just described, and allows any article which may have been placed therein to drop into the hand of the person holding the cabinet. (*See* Fig. 91.) The act of pulling out the drawer again presses the bottom up to its proper place, where it is secured by the catch until once more released by the pressure of the pin. The strong point of this ingenious little apparatus is that it is absolutely self-acting, and its secret can only be detected by examining the cabinet from below at the moment when the drawer is pushed home ; and this it is easy to prevent by the simple expedient of handing each portion *separately* for inspection.

The performer begins by handing first the cabinet and then the drawer for examination. Then, placing the cabinet on the palm of his hand, he invites any one of the audience to deposit any small article, a coin, a ring, a watch, etc., in the drawer, and to replace the drawer in the cabinet. As soon as the drawer is closed, the article drops through into his hand. Taking hold of the cabinet with the other hand (lifting it by the top only, and with the very tips of his fingers, so as to preclude all apparent possibility of deception), he places it on the table or elsewhere, in full view. Having thus gained possession of the borrowed article, he concludes the trick by reproducing it in any manner he thinks proper.

We have thus far discussed pieces of apparatus more especially designed to cause the *disappearance* of a coin, and thus adapted for use in the first stage of a trick. We shall next consider such as are intended to reproduce, under more or less surprising circumstances, the coin thus got rid of, such reproduction forming the second stage, or *dénouement.*

THE NEST OF BOXES.—This consists of a number, generally six, but sometimes more, of circular wooden boxes, one within the other, the largest or outer box having much the appearance, but being nearly double the size, of an ordinary tooth-powder box, and the smallest being just large enough to contain a shilling. The series is so accurately made, that by arranging the boxes in due order one within the other, and the lids in like manner, you may, by simply putting on all the lids together, close all the boxes at once, though they can only be opened one by one.

These are placed, the boxes together and the lids together, anywhere so as to be just out of sight of the audience. If on your table, they may be hidden by any more bulky article. Having secretly obtained possession, by either of the means before described, of a coin which is ostensibly deposited in some other piece of apparatus, *e.g.*, the Davenport Cabinet, you seize your opportunity to drop it into the innermost box, and to put on the united lids. You then bring forward the nest of boxes (which the spectators naturally take to be one box only), and announce that the shilling will at your command pass from the place in which it has been deposited into the box which you hold in your hand, and which you forthwith deliver to one of the audience for safe keeping. Touching both articles with the mystic wand, you invite inspection of the first to show that the money has departed, and then of the box, wherein it is to be found. The holder opens the box, and finds another, and then another, and in the innermost of all the marked coin. Seeing how long the several boxes have taken to open, the spectators naturally infer that they must take as long to close, and (apart from the other mysteries of the trick), are utterly at a loss to imagine how, with the mere moment of time at your command, you could have managed to insert the coin, and close so many boxes.

If you desire to use the nest for a coin larger than a shilling, you can make it available for that purpose by removing beforehand the smallest box. Nests of square boxes, with hinged lids and self-closing locks, are made, both in wood and in tin, on the same principle. These are designed for larger articles, and greatly vary in size and price.

THE BALL OF BERLIN WOOL.—An easy and effective mode of terminating a money trick is to pass the marked coin into the centre of a large ball of Berlin wool or worsted, the whole of which has to be unwound before the coin can be reached. The *modus operandi*, though perplexing to the uninitiated, is absurdly simple when the secret is revealed. The only apparatus necessary over and above the wool (of which you must have enough for a good-sized ball), is a flat tin tube, three to four inches in length, and just large enough to allow a florin or shilling (whichever you intend to use for the trick) to slip through it easily. You prepare for the trick by winding the wool on one end of the tube, in such manner that when the whole is wound in a ball, an inch or so of the tube may project from it. This you place in your pocket, or anywhere out of sight of the audience. You commence the trick by requesting some one to mark a coin, which you forthwith exchange, by one or other of the means already described, for a substitute of your own, and leave the latter in the possession or in view of the spectators, while you retire to fetch your ball of wool, or simply take it from your pocket. Before producing it, you drop the genuine coin down the tube into the centre of the ball, and withdraw the tube, giving the ball a squeeze to remove all trace of an opening. You then bring it forward, and place it in a glass goblet or tumbler, which you hand to a spectator to hold. Taking the substitute coin, you announce that you will make it pass invisibly into the very centre of the ball of wool, which you accordingly pretend to do, getting rid of it by means of one or other of the Passes described in Chapter VI. You then request a second spectator to take the loose end of the wool, and to unwind the ball, which, when he has done, the coin falls out into the goblet.

The only drawback to the trick is the tediousness of the process of unwinding. To obviate this, some performers use a wheel made for the purpose, which materially shortens the length of the operation.

THE GLASS GOBLET AND COVER.—This apparatus consists of an ordinary glass goblet, of rather large size, with a japanned tin cover, in shape not unlike the lid of a coffee-pot, but of sufficient height to contain, in an upright position, a couple of florins or half-crowns. These are placed side by side in a flat tube, just large enough to admit them, fixed in a slightly sloping position in the upper part of the cover, and divided in two by a tin partition. Across the lower end of this tube is a tin slide, which, in its normal condition, is kept closed by the action of a spring, but is drawn back whenever a knob on the top of the cover is pressed down. If a slight pressure be applied, one coin only is released; but if the knob be still further pressed down, the second also falls. The mechanism of the cover is concealed by a flat plate or lining, also of tin, soldered just within it, with an oblong opening just large enough to admit of the passage of the coins. The inside of the cover is japanned black, the outside according to the taste of the maker.

You take care not to bring on the goblet and cover until you have, by substitution, gained possession of the two marked coins which you have borrowed for the purpose of the trick. Retiring to fetch the glass and cover, you prepare the latter by inserting the marked coins. This you do by holding the cover upside down, pressing the knob (thus drawing back the spring slide), and dropping the coins into their receptacle. On removing the pressure on the knob, the slide returns to its normal position. You then bring forward the goblet and cover, and place them on the table. Holding the goblet upside down, to show that it is empty, you place the cover over it, ostensibly to prevent anything being secretly passed into it, and, for still greater security, throw a handkerchief, borrowed for that purpose, over the whole. You now announce that, notwithstanding the difficulties which you have voluntarily placed in the way, you will pass the two marked coins through the handkerchief, and through the metal cover into the glass. Taking in your right hand one of the substitutes, which have all along remained in sight, and which the audience take to be the genuine coins, you pretend by Pass 1 to transfer it to your left, and pressing gently on the knob with the last-mentioned hand, cause one of the marked coins to drop from the cover, at the same moment opening the hand to show that the coin has left it. The audience hear, though they do not see, the fall of the coin. With the second coin it is well to introduce an element of variety, and you may therefore offer to dispense with the handkerchief, that all may see as well as hear the coin arrive. As a further variation, you may use your wand as the conducting medium. Taking the substitute coin in the left hand, you apparently, by Pass 4, transfer it to your right. Then taking the wand in the left hand, you hold it perpendicularly, with its lower end resting upon the knob of the cover. Holding it with the thumb and second finger of the right hand, one on each side of it, you draw them smartly downwards, at the same time pressing with the wand on the knob, when the second coin will be seen and heard to fall into the glass. Taking off the cover, and leaving it on the table, you bring forward the glass, and allow the owners to take out and identify the coins.

It is a great addition to have a second cover, similar in appearance to the first, but hollow throughout, and without any mechanism. You are thus enabled to hand both goblet and cover for examination before performing the trick. As you return to your table, your back being towards the spectators, you have ample opportunity for substituting the mechanical cover, the plain one being dropped either into one of your *profondes,* or on to the *servante* of your table.

THE GLASS WITHOUT COVER, FOR MONEY. — This is of tumbler shape, without foot, and of green or other dark-coloured glass, so that it is semi-opaque. In this instance no cover is used, and the borrowed coins are not seen, but merely heard, to drop into the glass, where they are found in due course.

The secret of the glass lies in a false bottom of tin, working on a hinge, and held down by a catch worked by a pin through the bottom of the glass, and flying up with a spring when released. The performer, having gained possession of three or four borrowed coins by either of the means before mentioned, retires to fetch the glass, and takes the opportunity to place the coins beneath the false bottom. He then comes forward, glass in hand. He does not offer the glass for examination, but turns it upside down, and rattles his wand inside it, showing, ostensibly, that it is empty. Having done this, he places it on his table, as near the back of the stage as possible, at the same time moving the catch, and so releasing the false bottom, which naturally flies up, and uncovers the concealed coins. Standing at a considerable distance from the glass, he takes one by one the substitutes, which to the eyes of the audience represent the genuine coins, and gets rid of them by one or other of the various passes, saying as each one apparently vanishes from his hand, " One, two, three—Pass ! " At the same moment the sound of a falling coin is heard, proceeding apparently from the glass, but really from behind the scenes, or any other available spot out of sight, where an assistant, placed as near to the glass as circumstances will admit, drops *another* coin into *another* glass. If the position of the assistant, with reference to the audience, is pretty nearly in a straight line with the glass which they see, the illusion will be perfect. When all the coins are supposed to have passed in this manner, the performer, advancing to the glass, pours out, either upon a tray or upon his open palm, the borrowed coins, and leaving the glass upon the table, comes forward, and requests the owners to identify them.

We have thus far described eight different contrivances for vanishing money, and (including the " plug-box," which may be used in both ways) five for reproducing it. It is obvious that either of the first may be used in combination with either of the second, producing some fifty different effects. By the use of sleight-of-hand in place of apparatus at either stage of the trick, still more numerous variations may be produced, and these may be still further multiplied by the use of other appliances to be hereafter described, which, though of less general utility, may be occasionally introduced with excellent effect. The apparatus which we shall next describe is one which is very frequently used in combination with that last mentioned. It is known as

THE MIRACULOUS CASKET.—This is a neat leather- or velvet-covered box, about three inches by two, and two and a half high. When opened, it is seen to be filled with a velvet cushion or stuffing, after the manner of a ring-case, with four slits, each just large enough to admit a half-crown or florin. (*See* Fig. 92.) By an ingenious mechanical arrangement in the interior, which it would take too much space to describe at length, each time the box is closed one of the coins is made to drop down into the lower part, and on the box being reopened is found to have vanished.

The casket may be used in many tricks with good effect. In combination with the magic glass, last above described, it is employed

FIG. 92.

as follows:—The four coins which have been substituted for the genuine ones are placed, in sight of all, in the magic casket, which is then closed, and handed to one of the audience to hold. The performer then states that he is about to order the four coins now in the casket to pass one by one into the glass upon the table. "One!" he exclaims. A coin is heard to fall into the glass. The person who holds the casket is requested to open it; three coins only are left. It is again closed, and the performer says, "Two!" Again the chink of the falling coin is heard, and another coin is found to have disappeared from the casket. The operation is repeated till all have vanished, and the operator pours forth from the glass four coins, which, on examination, are found to be the same which were originally borrowed, and which the audience believe that they saw placed in the casket.

The casket may also be used with capital effect in conjunction with

THE HALF-CROWN (OR FLORIN) WAND.—This is a wand, apparently of ebony, but really of brass, japanned black. It is about twelve inches in length, and five-eighths of an inch in diameter. On one side of it, and so placed as to be just under the ball of the thumb when the wand is held in the hand, is a little stud, which moves backwards and forwards for a short distance (about an inch and a quarter), like the sliding ring of a pencil-case. When this stud is pressed forward, a half-crown or florin, as the case may be, appears on the opposite end of the wand (*see* Fig. 93), retiring within it when the stud is again drawn back. The half-crown is a genuine one, but is cut into

FIG. 94.

FIG. 95.

FIG. 93.

three portions, as indicated in Fig. 94, which represents a transverse section of it at right angles to the actual cuts. Each of the three segments is attached to a piece of watch-spring, and from the direction of the cuts it is obvious that, when these pieces of watch-spring are pressed together (as they naturally are when drawn back into the wand), *c* will be drawn behind, and *a* in front of *b*. (*See* Fig. 95.)

The wand is used as follows :—The performer palms in his left hand as many half-crowns as he intends to produce. Then, taking the wand in the right hand, and lightly touching with it the spot whence he desires to (apparently) produce a half-crown, he pushes forward the stud, and the split coin appears on the opposite end of the wand. He now draws the upper part of the wand through the left hand, at the same moment pressing back the stud, and causing the split coin to retire within the wand, immediately handing for examination with the left hand one of the half-crowns already placed there, and which by this gesture he appears to have just taken from the top of the wand. This is again repeated, and another half-crown exhibited, till the stock in the left hand is exhausted.

It is desirable, on each occasion of pressing forward or withdrawing the stud, to place the opposite end of the wand in such a situation as to be a little shielded from the eyes of the spectators, so that they may not see the actual appearance or disappearance of the coin. A very slight " cover " will be sufficient. The end of the wand may be placed within a person's open mouth (and withdrawn with the half-crown thereon), within a pocket, or the like. Where no such cover is available, a quick semi-circular sweep should be made with the wand as the coin is protruded or withdrawn.

With the aid of this wand the passage of the four half-crowns from the casket to the glass, just described, becomes still more effective. The four substitute half-crowns having been placed in the casket, and the latter closed, the performer announces that he will withdraw them visibly, one by one, and will then invisibly pass them into the glass. Further, to prove that the trick is not performed by any mechanical or physical means, he will not even take the casket in his hand, but will withdraw the coins one by one with his wand, and thence pass them direct into the glass. Touching the casket with the wand, he presses the stud, and shows the half-crown on the end. Apparently taking off the coin with his left hand, as before described (the hand, however, being in this case empty), he makes the motion of throwing the coin from the hand to the glass, saying, " Pass ! " The sound of a falling coin is heard (as already explained), and he shows that his hand is empty, the same process being repeated as to the remaining coins.

The wand may also be effectively introduced in the trick of the Shower of Money, which next follows. After having caught in the ordinary manner such number of coins as he thinks fit, the performer perceives, or pretends to perceive, that the audience suspect that the coins are in some manner concealed in his right hand. To show that this is not the case, he offers to catch a few coins on the top of his wand instead of in his hand, and finishes the trick by producing two or three on the wand accordingly. Wherever you can, as in this instance, produce the same result by two wholly different methods the effect on the audience is most bewildering. Their conjectures as to the explanation of the first method being inadmissible as to the second, and *vice versâ*, the more they puzzle over the matter, the further are they likely to be from a correct solution.

THE SHOWER OF MONEY.—The magical phenomenon known under this name surpasses the philosopher's stone, in the pursuit of which so many of the wise men of old expended their lives and fortunes. The alchemist's secret aimed only at producing the raw material, but the magician's quick eye and ready hand gather from space money ready coined. Unfortunately, the experiment is subject to the same drawback as the more ancient process—viz., that each twenty shillings produced cost precisely twenty shillings, leaving hardly sufficient profit to make this form of money-making remunerative as a commercial undertaking.

The effect of the trick is as follows :—The performer borrows a hat, which he holds in his left hand. Turning up his sleeves, he announces that he requires a certain number, say ten, of florins or half-crowns. The spectators put their hands in their pockets with the idea of contributing to the supposed loan ; but the professor, anticipating their intention, says, " No, thank you ; I won't trouble you this time. There seems to be a good deal of money about to-night ; I think I will help myself. See, here is a half-crown hanging to the gaselier. Here is another climbing up the wall. Here is another just settling on this lady's hair. Excuse me, sir, but you have a half-crown in your whiskers. Permit me, madam ; you have just placed your foot on another," and so on. At each supposed new discovery the performer takes with his right hand, from some place where there clearly was nothing an instant before, a half-crown, which he drops into the hat held in his left hand, finally turning over the hat, and pouring the coins from it, to show that there has been " no deception."

The explanation is very simple, the trick being merely a practical application of the art of " palming," though its effect depends on the manner and address of the operator even more than on his skill in sleight-of-hand. The performer provides himself beforehand with ten half-crowns. Of these he palms two in his right hand, and the remainder in his left. When he takes the hat, he holds it in the left hand, with the fingers inside and the thumb outside, in which position it is comparatively easy to drop the coins one by one from the hand into the hat. When he pretends to see the first half-crown floating in the air, he lets one of the coins in his right hand drop to his finger-tips, and, making a clutch at the air, produces it as if just caught. This first coin he really does drop into the hat, taking care that all shall see clearly that he does so. He then goes through a similar process with the second; but when the time comes to drop it into the hat, he merely pretends to do so, palming the coin quickly in the right hand, and at the same moment letting fall into the hat one of the coins concealed in his left hand. The audience, hearing the sound, naturally believe it to be occasioned by the fall of the coin they have just seen. The process is repeated until the coins in the left hand are exhausted. Once more the performer appears to clutch a coin from space, and showing for the last time that which has all along been in his right hand, tosses it into the air, and catches it visibly in the hat. Pouring out the coins on a tray, or into the lap of one of the company, he requests that they may be counted, when they are found to correspond with the number which he has apparently collected from the surrounding atmosphere.

Some performers, by way of bringing the trick to a smart conclusion, after they have dropped in all the coins, remark, "The hat begins to get heavy," or make some similar observation, at the same time dipping the right hand into the hat, as if to gauge the quantity obtained; and, giving the money a shake, bring up the hand with four or five of the coins clipped breadthwise against the lowest joints of the second and third fingers. Then pretend to catch in quick succession that number of coins, each time sliding one of the coins with the thumb to the finger-tips, and tossing it into the hat.

It is by no means uncommon to see a performer, after having apparently dropped two or three coins into the hat in the ordinary way, pretend to pass in one or more through the side or crown. This produces a momentary effect, but it is an effect purchased at the cost of enabling an acute spectator to infer, with logical certainty, that the coin seen in the right hand was not the same that was, the moment afterwards, heard to chink within the hat; and this furnishes a distinct clue to the secret of the trick.

It is obvious that, in the above form of the trick (which so far should be classed among " tricks without apparatus "), the performer cannot show the inside of his hands; and it is not uncommon to find an acute observer (particularly where the performer is guilty of the indiscretion we have just noted) so far hit upon the true explanation, as to express audibly a conjecture that the money which the performer catches is really the same coin over and over again. There is, however, a mechanical appliance known as the " money-slide," which is designed to meet this difficulty, and to enable the performer still to catch the coin, though he has but a moment before shown that his hand is empty.

The money-slide is a flat tin tube, about eight inches in length, an inch and a quarter in width, and of just such depth as to allow a half-crown or florin (whichever coin may be used) to slip through it freely, edgeways. It is open at the top, but is closed at the lower end by a lever, acting like the lever of a shot-pouch. (*See* Fig. 96, which

shows the external appearance of the tube, and Fig. 97, which represents, on a somewhat larger scale, a section of its essential portion.) The normal position of the lever (which works on a pivot, *a*) is as shown in Fig. 97, being maintained in that position by a small spring. Under such circumstances, the passage of the tube is barred by the pin *d* (which works through a small hole in the face of the tube) ; but if *ac,* the longer arm of the lever, be pressed down, the pin *d* is withdrawn, but the extreme lower end of the tube is for the moment barred by the bent end of *ac.* The pressure being withdrawn, the lever returns to its former condition. When required for use, four or five half-crowns are dropped into the tube from the upper end, and the tube is fas-

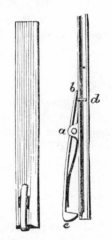

FIGS. 96, 97.

tened, by a hook affixed to it for that purpose, inside the waistcoat of the performer, so that its lower end hangs just above the waistband, the lever side of the tube being next the body. If the tube be lightly pressed through the waistcoat, the longer arm of the lever is thereby pressed down. The pin *d* is lifted, and the row of half-crowns slide down to the bottom of the tube, where, however, they are arrested by the bent end of *ac*. As soon as the pressure is removed, the lever returns to its position. The mouth of the tube is left open, and the first of the half-crowns drops out, and would be followed by the others, but the pin, *d*, which at the same moment returns to its position across the tube, stops their further progress. Thus each time the lever is pressed and again released, one half-crown, and one only, drops out at the mouth of the tube.

The use of this appliance in the trick we have just described will be obvious. The performer, having turned up his sleeves to prove that they have no part in the matter, shows that his right hand is absolutely empty. Continuing his observations, his hand rests for a moment with a careless gesture against his waistcoat, the ball of the wrist being above and the fingers below the waistband. A momentary pressure causes a half-crown to fall into his hand. This he palms, and in due course proceeds to catch, as already described.

As the capacity of the slide is limited, and the same gestures frequently repeated would be likely to excite suspicion, it is best to begin the trick in the ordinary manner, and after having produced three or four coins in this way, to overhear, or pretend to overhear, a suggestion that the coin is all the while in your hand. Ostentatiously throwing the coin with which you have so far worked, into the hat, you draw special attention (not in words, but by gesture) to your empty hand (the left hand is never suspected), and then have recourse to the slide. You throw the coin thus obtained into the hat, and again show your hand empty. You produce another coin from the slide, and make this serve you for the next two or three catches, and so on, as circumstances may dictate.

The money magically caught as above may be used for the trick of the Multiplication of Money, described at page 176, the two forming a natural and effective sequence.

THE VANISHING PLATE, OR SALVER.—This is a most useful and ingenious piece of apparatus. In appearance it is an ordinary japanned tin tray, of about ten inches in diameter; but it has the faculty of causing money placed upon it to disappear in a most surprising manner. A number of coins, collected from the company, are placed upon the salver. The performer, standing but a few feet from the spectators, openly takes them off one by one, but each, as his fingers grasp it, vanishes utterly. His sleeves (which in conjuring come in for a vast amount of undeserved suspicion) may be rigorously examined ; but even though, as a concession to popular prejudice, he should bare his arm to the shoulder, the result would still be the same.

A closer inspection of the salver (which the performer takes good care not to permit) would reveal the fact, that though apparently consisting, like any other, of only one thickness of metal, it is in reality made double, allowing sufficient space between its upper and under surface for the concealment of any number of coins laid singly. The centre portion of the upper surface, though apparently of a piece with the rest, is in reality moveable, though pressed upwards and kept in its place by the action of four small springs. When the performer apparently picks up a coin (which he takes care shall be on this centre portion), he presses smartly upon it, at the same moment drawing it sharply towards the outer rim. The moveable portion of the salver yielding to the pressure, the effect is as shown in the figure (Fig. 98), and the coin is shot under the outer rim, between the upper and under surface of the salver, the moveable portion rising

FIG. 98.

again to its place as soon as the momentary pressure is removed. The tray is japanned in such manner that the circular lines of the pattern correspond with the outline of the moveable portion, and will bear any amount of mere ocular inspection, so long as it is not permitted to be handled.

The vanishing salver may be introduced with good effect in many tricks, as, for instance, that of the Multiplication of Money, above referred to, the coins to be magically added being placed upon the salver, whence they are taken off one by one, and commanded to pass into the hands of the person who holds the money. It may also be advantageously used in conjunction with the glass described at page 201, each coin, as it vanishes from the salver, being heard to drop into the glass.

THE " CHANGING " PLATE.—The student has already been made acquainted with various methods of exchanging a marked coin, etc., for a substitute. There are still one or two appliances for this purpose remaining to be described, all taking the form of metal plates or trays, but greatly varying in their construction.

The first, which we only mention for the sake of completeness, as it is now superseded by later and better inventions, consists of a small circular tin tray, with a round hole or well in the centre, of about an inch and a half in diameter and a quarter of an inch in depth. The lines of the pattern are so arranged as to make this cavity as little noticeable as possible. The well is moveable, forming, in fact, a portion of a sliding piece below the tray, in which sliding piece *two* such wells are excavated, the one or the other in turn corresponding to the opening in the tray, according as the sliding piece is pushed backwards or forwards. When the tray is required for use, the substitute coin is placed beforehand in one of the two wells, which is then pushed out of sight, and the other brought below the opening. The borrowed coin is received on the plate, and allowed to drop into the empty well. As soon as this is done, the operator, with his forefinger, which is naturally beneath the plate, draws back the slide, and brings the other coin in sight, while the genuine one drops into his hand. The construction of the plate, though simple enough in itself, is a little difficult to explain; but as we only allude to it in order to counsel the student to avoid it, any obscurity in our description is of little importance.

The instrument now used for the same purpose is known as the French changing-plate, and may be described as a combination of the vanishing salver (page 209) and the multiplying money-plate (page 177). It is round, and has beneath it a flat tube similar to that of the multiplying plate; and it is in this tube that the substitute coins are placed. The upper surface of the plate is similar in appearance to that of the vanishing plate; but in this case the centre portion is divided across the middle, and one half only is moveable, sinking downwards to the depth of a quarter of an inch all along the dividing line, whenever pressure is applied to a particular portion of the under surface of the plate. The coins to be changed are received by the operator on this moveable portion, and immediately handed to some person to hold, the performer sloping the plate, and (apparently) pouring the coins into the hands or hat held out to receive them. In reality, in the act of sloping the plate, he depresses the moveable portion of the surface, and, as a natural consequence, the coins, instead of sliding, as they appear to do, right off the plate, slip between the upper and under surface, while the substitutes fall from the tube below into the hands of the person who is to take charge of them. The whole movement is so rapid, and the fall of the substituted coins coincides so exactly with the disappearance of the genuine ones, that the eye is completely deceived. The tray, having apparently served its purpose, is carried off by the magician or his servant, with ample opportunity to make any necessary disposition of the genuine coins.

A still later improvement is that which is known as

THE TRAY OF PROTEUS.—The tray to which the inventors (Messrs. Hiam & Lane) have given the above high-sounding title, is the latest, and not the least ingenious, of the series of magical trays.

The tray in question will not only change, but add, subtract, or vanish coins, under the very eyes of the spectators. In form it is an oblong octagon, measuring eight inches by six, and standing about three-quarters of an inch high. (*See* Fig. 99.) It is divided across the centre, and one half of the centre portion is moveable in the same manner as in the case of the tray last described, save that in this instance the depth between the upper and under surface of the tray being greater, this moveable portion is depressible to a proportionately greater depth. The opposite or fixed side of the tray is divided horizontally (*see* Fig. 100, representing a longitudinal section) into two levels or platforms, *a* and *b*, the lower, *b*, having a raised edge. Where the tray is to be used for the purpose of "changing," the coins to be substituted are placed in a row on the upper platform, a. The genuine coins are placed by the performer, holding the tray as indicated in Fig. 99, on the moveable flap, c. Slightly lowering the opposite end of the tray, he presses the button d, thus sloping the flap c, and the coins naturally slide into b. Still keeping the flap open, he now tilts up the opposite end of the tray. The genuine coins cannot return, by reason of the raised edge of b; but the substitute coins in their turn slide out upon c, which is then allowed to return to its original position. The necessary movement, though comparatively tedious in description, is in skilful hands so rapid in execution that, where coins of the same kind are substituted

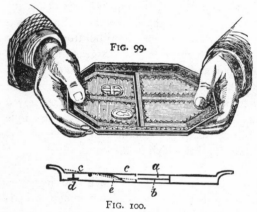

FIG. 99.

FIG. 100.

— *e.g.*, half-crowns for half-crowns—the most acute spectator cannot detect that any change has taken place. A most startling effect is produced by substituting coins of a different kind, as pence for half-crowns, the coins appearing to be transformed by a mere shake into a different metal. The change involving a double process—viz., the disappearance of certain coins and the appearance of others—it is obvious that the tray will be equally available for either process singly. Thus coins placed upon the tray may be made to instantly vanish, or, by reversing the process, coins may be made to appear where there was nothing a moment previously. In like manner, a given number of coins may be increased to a larger, or decreased (in this case really *changed*) to a smaller number.

This tray has not, like that last described, any additional flat tube beneath the tray, but one end of a and b is closed by a little slide, hidden beneath the edge of the tray, to allow of the money therein being extracted when necessary.

CHAPTER IX.

Tricks with Watches.

To indicate on the Dial of a Watch the Hour secretly thought of by any of the Company.—The performer, taking a watch in the one hand, and a pencil in the other, proposes to give a specimen of his powers of divination. For this purpose he requests any one present to write down, or, if preferred, merely to think of, any hour he pleases. This having been done, the performer, without asking any questions, proceeds to tap with the pencil different hours on the dial of the watch, requesting the person who has thought of the hour to mentally count the taps, *beginning from the number of the hour he thought of.* (Thus, if the hour he thought of were "nine," he must count the first tap as "ten," the second as "eleven," and so on.) When, according to this mode of counting, he reaches the number "twenty," he is to say "Stop," when the pencil of the performer will be found resting precisely upon that hour of the dial which he thought of.

This capital little trick depends upon a simple arithmetical principle; but the secret is so well disguised that it is very rarely discovered. All that the performer has to do is to count in his own mind the taps he gives, calling the first "one," the second "two," and so on. The first-seven taps may be given upon any figures of the dial indifferently; indeed, they might equally well be given on the back of the watch, or anywhere else, without prejudice to the ultimate result. But the eighth tap must be given invariably on the figure "twelve" of the dial, and thenceforward the pencil must travel through the figures *seriatim*, but in reverse order, "eleven," "ten," "nine," and so on. By following this process it will be found that at the tap which, counting from the number the spectator thought of, will make twenty, the pencil will have travelled back to that very number. A few illustrations will make this clear. Let us suppose, for instance, that the hour the spectator thought of was twelve. In this case he will count the first tap of the pencil as thirteen, the second as fourteen, and so on. The eighth tap in this case will complete the twenty, and the reader will remember that, according to the directions we have given, he is at the eighth tap always to let his pencil fall on the number twelve; so that when the spectator, having mentally reached the number twenty, cries, "Stop," the pencil will be pointing to that number. Suppose, again, the number thought of was "eleven." Here the first tap will be counted as "twelve," and the ninth (at which, according to the rule, the pencil will be resting on eleven) will make the twenty. Taking again the smallest number that can be thought of, "one," here the first tap will be counted by the spectator as "two," and the eighth," at which the pencil reaches twelve, will count as "nine." Henceforth the pencil will travel regularly backward round the dial, and at the nineteenth tap (completing the twenty, as counted by the spectator) will have just reached the figure "one."

The arithmetical reason for this curious result, though simple enough in itself, is somewhat difficult to explain on paper, and we shall therefore leave it as an exercise for the ingenuity of our readers.

To Bend a Borrowed Watch Backwards and Forwards. —This little deception is hardly to be called a conjuring trick, but it may be introduced with good effect in the course of any trick for which a watch has been borrowed. Looking intently at the watch, as though you noticed something peculiar about it, you remark to the owner, "This is a very curious watch, sir; it is quite soft." Then taking it (as shown in Fig. 101), with the dial inwards towards your own body, and holding it between two fingers of each hand on the back, and the thumb of each hand on the face, you bend the hands outwards, at the same time bringing the points of the fingers nearer together, immediately bringing them back to their former position. The motion may be repeated any number of times. By a curious optical illusion, which we are not able to explain, but which we assume to be produced in some way by the varying shadow of the fingers on the polished surface of the metal, the watch appears, to a spectator at a little distance, to be bent nearly double by each outward movement of the hands. The illusion is so perfect, that great amuse-

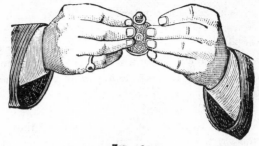

FIG. 101.

ment is occasionally produced by the consternation of the owner, who fancies that irreparable injury is being done to his favourite "Waltham" If, however, his faith in your supernatural powers is so great as to resist this ordeal, you may test it even more severely by means of

THE WATCH-MORTAR AND THE MAGIC PISTOL.—The watch-mortar is an apparatus in the form of an ordinary mortar, with a pestle to match. Suggesting to the owner of the borrowed time-keeper that it wants regulating, you offer to undertake that duty for him. He probably declines, but you take no notice of his remonstrances, and, placing his watch in the mortar, bring down the pestle with a heavy thump upon it. A smash, as of broken glass, is heard, and, after sufficient pounding, you empty the fragments of the watch into your hand, to the horror of the owner. You offer to return the fragments, but he naturally objects to receive them, and insists that you restore the watch in the same condition as when it was handed to you. After a little discussion, you agree to do so, premising that you can only effect the object through the agency of fire. Fetching a loaf of bread, you place it on the table in view of the company. Then wrapping the fragments of the watch in paper, you place them in a pistol, and, aiming at the loaf, request the owner of the watch to give the signal to fire. The word is given, "One, two, three—Bang!" Stepping up to the loaf, you bring it forward to the spectators, and tearing it asunder, exhibit in its very centre the borrowed watch, completely restored, and bright as when it first left the maker's hands.

The seeming mystery is easily explained. The mortar has a moveable bottom, which allows the watch at the performer's pleasure to fall through into his hand. There is a hollow space in the thick end of the pestle, closed by a round piece of wood lightly screwed in, which, fitting tightly in the bottom part of the mortar, is easily unscrewed by the performer, or rather unscrews itself, as he apparently grinds away at the ill-fated chronometer. In the cavity are placed beforehand the fragments of a watch, which, thus released, fall into the mortar, and are poured out by the performer into his hand, in order to show that there has been "no deception." When the performer goes to fetch the loaf, he has already obtained possession of the watch, which, after giving it a rub upon his coat-sleeve or a bit of leather to increase its brightness, he pushes into a slit already made in the side of the loaf. When the loaf is torn asunder (which the performer takes care to do from the side opposite to that in which the opening has been made), the watch is naturally found imbedded therein.

If a regular conjuring-table is used, the loaf may be placed in readiness on the *servante.* The performer in this case, having got possession of the watch, and holding it secretly palmed, borrows a hat. Walking carelessly behind his table, he asks, as if in doubt, "Who lent me this hat?" holding it up with one hand, that the spectators may see that it is empty. While all eyes are thus drawn to the hat, he with the other hand forces the watch into the loaf, and then, in bringing the hat down on the table, introduces the loaf into it, after the manner of the well-known "cannon-ball" trick, to be described hereafter. The hat is then placed on the table as if empty, and the pistol fired at the hat. This little addition heightens the effect of the trick, but demands somewhat greater address on the part of the performer.

The pistol employed, being of constant use in magical perform‑ ances, will demand a special explanation. It consists of two parts, viz., an ordinary pocket-pistol, and a conical tin funnel, measuring about five inches across its widest diameter, and tapering down to a

tube of such a size as to fit easily over the barrel of the pistol
This tube is continued inside the cone, and affords a free passage for
the charge, which consists of powder only. Any object which
is apparently to be fired from the pistol is pressed down be
tween the outside of this tube and the inside of the tin cone, where
it remains wholly unaffected by the explosion. The outside of the
cone is japanned accorning to taste, the tube and the rest of the
interior being always black.

There are numerous other ways of finishing the trick, with or
without the use of the pistol. The watch-mortar has discharged
its duty when it has apparently reduced the borrowed watch to
fragments, and has placed it in reality in the hands of the performer. The sequel of the trick, with which the mortar has nothing
to do, will depend on the ingenuity of the performer and his command
of other apparatus.

There is another form of watch-mortar, which is frequently used,
though to our own taste it is very inferior to that above described.
It consists of a cylindrical tin box or case, about four inches high
and three in diameter, open at the top, standing on a broad flat foot.
Within this fits loosely another similar cylinder, of about an inch less
in depth. The upper edge of this latter is turned over all round,
giving the two the appearance of being both of a piece. The whole
is closed by an ornamental cardboard cover, also cylindrical. If this
cover be lifted lightly—*i.e.,* without pressure—it will come off alone;
but if its sides are pressed, they will clip the turned-over edge of the
upper or moveable compartment, and lift this with it. In this form
of the trick the borrowed watch is placed in a little bag, and the two
together deposited in the upper compartment. In the mortar proper
—*i.e.,* the space between the two compartments—is placed beforehand a similar little bag, containing the broken fragments of a watch.
The cover being under some pretext put on, the upper compartment
is lifted off with it, and the pounding consequently falls on the prepared fragments.

THE SNUFF-BOX VASE.—This is an apparatus of frequent use in
Watch Tricks, and it may be also made available with many
other articles. It is made of various sizes, from five to eight inches

in height, and of the shape shown in Fig. 102. It consists of three parts, the cover *a*, the vase proper *c*, and a moveable portion *b*, the latter being made with double sides, so that it fits at once in and upon *c*. If *a* is raised without pressing its sides, it comes off alone; but if its sides are pressed in removing it, it lifts off *b* with it. In this compartment *b* is placed a small round box of tin or cardboard (from which the vase derives its name), and another box, exactly similar in appearance, is placed underneath *b*, inside the vase proper *c*. Whether, therefore, the cover is removed with or without *b*, the audience see apparently the same box within. The only circumstance that could possibly excite suspicion would be the greater depth of *c* as compared with *b*; and this is obviated by making the bottom of *c* moveable, resting on a spiral spring passing

through the foot of the apparatus. When *b* is in the vase, the bottom of *c* sinks down to make way for it, but again rises by the pressure of the spring as soon as *b* is removed. To the eye of the spectator, therefore, the interior of the vase appears always of the same depth.

Some vases are made with a "clip" action in the lid, so that by slightly turning round the knob on the top three projecting teeth of metal are made to tighten upon *b*, and thus attach it to *a*, a reverse movement of the knob again releasing it. In this form of the apparatus the cover may be lifted by the knob only, without the necessity of pressing on the sides—a very decided improvement.

The snuff-box vase may be used to cause the appearance, disappearance, or transformation of any article small enough to be contained in one of the boxes within. Thus, in the case of the last trick, the performer, having

FIG. 102.

secretly obtained possession of the borrowed watch, may, instead of using the loaf, conclude the trick with good effect as follows :— Retiring for an instant in order to fetch the vase, he places the watch in the small box contained in *c*. Returning, he removes the cover only, thus exposing the interior of *b*, and requests one of the audience to examine and replace the small box therein contained. The box is seen by all to be empty, and, being replaced, the vase is again covered. The operator now fires at the vase. Having done so, he again brings it forward, but this time removes *b* along with the cover. The other box, which the audience take to be the same, is now exposed, and, on being examined, is found to contain the restored watch.

If you do not happen to possess the watch-mortar or the magic pistol, you may make the trick equally effective without them, by using in their place the " Demon Handkerchief," described at page 195. Having borrowed the watch, you place a substitute (which you must have ready palmed) under the handkerchief, and give it to some one to hold. Then fetching the snuff-box vase (and concealing the watch in *c*), you exhibit and replace the empty box in *b*, as above, and place the vase on the table. Taking a corner of the handkerchief, you request the person holding it to drop it when you count "three." Then saying, " One, two, three. Pass ! " you wave the handkerchief, which appears to be empty, and advancing to the table and uncovering the vase, show that the watch is now in the box.

It is obvious that the snuff-box vase may equally well be used to produce the opposite effect—*i.e.*, after having openly placed a watch or other article in either of the boxes, you may, by exposing in turn the other box, cause it to apparently disappear, or in like manner make it apparently change to any article previously placed in the second box.

THE WATCH BOX.—This is an oblong mahogany box—size, four inches by three, and two and a half deep. To the eye of the uninitiated, it is a simple wooden box, with lock and key, and padded within at top and bottom. In reality, however, one of its sides is moveable, working on a pivot. (*See* Figs. 103, 104.) In its normal position, the side in question is held fast by a catch projecting from the corresponding edge of the bottom of the box. To release it, pressure in two places is required—a pressure on the bottom of the box so as to lift the catch, and a simultaneous pressure on the upper part of the moveable side of the box, thus forcing the lower part outwards, and allowing the watch or other article placed in the box, to fall into the hand of the performer. For this purpose the box is held as shown in Fig. 103.

The manner of using the box is as follows: A borrowed watch is placed in it, the owner being requested, in order to ensure its safe

FIG. 103.

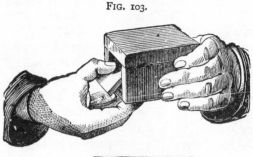

keeping, himself to lock it up and keep the key. The performer places the box on his table, in full view, but avails himself of the moment during which his back is turned to the audience to extract the watch, as shown in Fig. 103, and to again close the secret opening. Having thus gained possession of the watch, he can conclude the trick by causing it to re-appear in the snuff-box vase, or in any other way that he thinks proper.

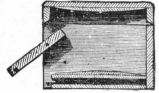

FIG. 104.

There is an improved watch-box, the invention of the late M. Robert-Houdin, which contains, concealed in the lid, a mechanical arrangement producing a ticking sound, which may be set in motion and again stopped at the pleasure of the performer. By using this box, the watch may be heard apparently ticking inside until the very moment when it is commanded by the operator to pass to some other apparatus.

THE WATCH TARGET.—This is in appearance an ordinary-looking round target, of about twelve inches in diameter, and supported on an upright pillar. It is painted in concentric circles, and on the bull's-eye is fixed a little hook. Its use is as follows: A watch having been borrowed, and smashed to pieces or made to disappear altogether, as before explained, the performer brings forward the target, which is either held by the assistant or placed upon the magician's table. Producing the magic pistol, the performer proceeds to load it (visibly or invisibly, according to the circumstances of the trick) with the borrowed watch or the fragments thereof. Then, taking careful aim, he fires at the target, when the borrowed watch is seen to alight on the little hook already mentioned, whence it is removed and handed to the owner.

A closer inspection of the target, which is sometimes of wood, but more often of tin, japanned, would disclose the fact that the bull's-eye is moveable, revolving perpendicularly on its own axis. It is coloured alike on both sides, and each side is provided with such a hook as already mentioned, so that whichever side of the bull's-eye is for the time being level with the face of the target, no difference is perceptible to the spectator. There is a little projecting pin, or stop, at one point of the diameter of the bull's eye, which prevents its making more than a half revolution, and a little spiral spring, attached to one of the two pivots on which it moves, compels it to turn, when at liberty, always in one particular direction until stopped by the pin, so that its normal condition is to have one particular side, which we will call, for greater clearness, side *a*, always turned towards the face of the target. The bull's-eye may, however, be turned round, so that the opposite side, *b*, is towards the face of the target, and there is a little catch which retains it as so turned; but the instant the catch is withdrawn, the action of the spring makes it fly round again to its old position. The catch is released by means of a stiff wire passing through the pillar on which the target rests, and terminating in a round disc of metal in the foot. The mode of connection between the wire and the catch varies according to the fancy of the maker; but, whatever this may be, the catch is invariably released by an *upward* pressure of the disc from below. If the target is held in the hand of the assistant, this is effected by the direct pressure of the fingers; but in stage performances, where the target is placed on a table, this, as indeed almost every other mechanical piece, is set in motion by the upward movement of a wire rod (known as a piston), made, by the pulling of a string, to rise through the upper surface of the table.

When the target is required for use, the bull's-eye is twisted round, so that the side *a* is turned towards the back, and in this position it is fixed by the catch. The borrowed watch is then hooked on the same side of the bull's-eye. The assistant, in bringing forward the target, takes care to keep the face turned towards the spectators, so that the watch, being behind, is unseen. At the moment of firing the pistol the disc is pressed upwards, and the catch being thus withdrawn, the bull's-eye instantly spins round, and the side *a*, on which is the watch, takes the place of side *b* on the face of the target. The movement is so instantaneous that the quickest eye cannot follow it, and the explosion of the pistol at the same moment aids still further to baffle the vigilance of the spectators, to whom it appears as if the borrowed watch had really passed from the pistol to the face of the target.

This forms an effective conclusion to the Watch-Mortar Trick, the fragments (supposed to be those of the borrowed watch) being placed in the pistol, and remaining there. Where the watch-box, above described, is used, you merely go through the motion of taking the watch out, invisibly, through the top of the box, and in like manner placing it in the pistol.

THE MESMERISED WATCH. TO MAKE ANY WATCH A REPEATER.—This is a trick which may be incidentally introduced with advantage in the course of any illusion in which a borrowed watch is employed. The performer, addressing the owner, asks carelessly, " Is this watch a repeater ? " The answer is in the negative, and the performer resumes, " Would you like it to become a repeater ? I have only to mesmerise it a little." So saying, he makes pretended mesmeric passes over the watch, every now and then holding it to his ear. At last he says, " I think it will do now. Let us try." Taking the chain between his finger and thumb, he lets the watch hang down at full length in front of him. " Come, watch, oblige me by telling us the hour that last struck. (We will suppose that the time is twenty minutes to nine.) To the astonishment of all, the watch chimes eight successive strokes, with a clear bell-like tone. " Now the last quarter." The watch chimes " two " and stops. " You see, sir, that under the mesmeric influence your watch becomes a capital repeater. Let us test its intelligence still further. Here is a pack of cards; will you oblige me by drawing one. Now, watch, tell me what card this gentleman has taken; and answer in the proper spiritualistic fashion, by three strokes for 'yes,' and one for 'no.' Do you know the card?" The watch chimes thrice. "Very good. Is it a club?" The watch chimes once. "Is it a spade?" The watch again strikes once. "Is it a heart?" The watch chimes three times. "The card is a heart, is it? Now, will you tell us what heart?" The watch chimes seven, and stops. "The watch declares that your card was the seven of hearts, sir. Is that so?" The card is turned, and shown to have been correctly named. Another card (say the queen of hearts) is now drawn. The watch names the suit as before, but when ordered to name the particular card, remains silent, and the performer therefore puts further questions. "Is the card a plain card?" Answer, "No." "It is a court card, is it? Well, is it the knave?" Answer, "No." "Is it the queen?" "Yes." Other questions may in like manner be put, *e.g.*, as to the number thrown by a pair of dice. The watch is at any moment handed for inspection, and if any suggestion of special mechanism be made, a second watch is borrowed, and mesmerised with the like result.

The secret lies in the use of an ingenious little piece of apparatus, which is placed in the waistcoat pocket of the performer, and from which the sound proceeds. This apparatus, which is represented in Fig. 105, consists of a short brass cylinder (about an inch and a quarter in depth, and two inches in diameter), containing a small clock-bell, with the necessary striking mechanism, which is wound up beforehand with a key, after the manner of a watch. This mechanism is set in motion by pressure on the button *a*, the hammer continuing to strike as long as the pressure is continued, but ceasing as soon as the pressure is removed. The cylinder, which is perforated all round, in order to give free passage to the sound, is placed upright in the left pocket of the performer's waistcoat, which should be just so tight

FIG. 105.

around the ribs that the mere expansion of the chest shall cause the necessary pressure against the button *a*, the pressure ceasing when the chest is again contracted. (The placing of a playing-card in the pocket for *a* to rest against will be found to facilitate the arrangement.) This is the whole of the secret. In working the trick the performer has only to take care to hold the watch in a tolerably straight line between the pocket and the audience, when, the line in which the sound travels being the same as if it actually came from the watch, it will be almost impossible to detect the deception.

Some performers, instead of placing the apparatus in the pocket, as above described, hold it in the right hand (the wand being held in the same hand) and cause it to strike by the pressure of the fingers. This is in one sense less effective, inasmuch as you cannot show the hands empty, but it is a very much more easy and certain method, so far as the striking is concerned.

The striking apparatus is generally made to give from fifty to sixty strokes. The performer must be careful not to prolong the trick until the whole are expended, or the unexpected silence of the watch may place him in an embarrassing position.

It is hardly necessary to remark that the drawn cards are forced. Where the watch is made to disclose the numbers thrown by a pair of dice, the dice are either loaded, and thus bound to indicate certain given numbers, or a box is used in which a pair of previously-arranged dice take the place, to the eyes of the audience, of the pair just thrown.

CHAPTER X.

TRICKS WITH RINGS.

THE FLYING RING.—The majority of ring tricks depend upon the substitution at some period of the trick of a dummy ring for a borrowed one, which must be so nearly alike as not to be distinguishable by the eye of the spectator. This desideratum is secured by using wedding-rings, which, being always made plain, are all sufficiently alike for this purpose. You may account for your preference of wedding-rings by remarking that they are found to be imbued with a mesmeric virtue which renders them peculiarly suitable for magical experiments; or give any other reason, however absurd, so long as it is sufficiently remote from the true one. As, however, many ladies have a sort of superstitious objection to remove their wedding-rings, even for a temporary purpose, it will be well to provide yourself with an extra one of your own, so as to meet a possible failure in borrowing.

There is a little appliance, exceedingly simple in its character, which may be used with advantage in many ring tricks. It consists of a plain gold or gilt ring, attached to a short piece of white or grey sewing-silk. This again is attached to a piece of cord elastic, fastened to the inside of the coat sleeve of the performer, in such manner that, when the arm is allowed to hang down, the ring falls about a couple of inches short of the edge of the cuff. Some, in place of the elastic, use a watch barrel, attached in like manner; but the cheaper apparatus, if properly arranged, is equally effective. It is obvious that if a ring so prepared be taken in the fingers of the hand to whose sleeve it is attached, it will, on being released, instantly fly up the sleeve. This renders it a useful auxiliary in any trick in which the sudden disappearance of such a ring is an element, and a little ingenuity will discover numerous modes of making it so available.

One of the simplest modes of using it is as follows : Producing a small piece of paper, to which you direct particular attention, you state that a wedding-ring wrapped up therein cannot be again extracted without your permission. A wedding-ring is borrowed in order to test your assertion, and you meanwhile get in readiness the flying ring, which is attached, we will suppose, to your left sleeve. Receiving the borrowed ring in your right hand, you apparently transfer it to the other hand (really palming it between the second and third fingers, and at the same moment exhibiting your own ring), and immediately afterwards drop the borrowed ring into the *pochette* on that side. You must take care so to stand that the back of your left hand may be towards the spectators, that the thread, lying along the inside of your hand, may not be seen. Spreading the paper on the table, and placing the ring upon it, you fold the paper over it, beginning with the side away from you, and pressing it so as to show the shape of the ring through it. As you fold down a second angle of the paper you release the ring, which forthwith flies up your sleeve. You continue to fold the paper, and repeating your assertion that no one can take the ring out without your permission, hand it to a spectator, in order that he may make the attempt. On opening the paper he finds that you were very safe in asserting that he could not take the ring out of it, inasmuch as the ring is no longer in it.

Having gained possession of the borrowed ring, you may reproduce it in a variety of different ways, according to your own fancy and invention. For instance, you may, retiring for a moment, bring forward the " snuff-box vase " described at page 217, meanwhile wrapping the ring in a piece of paper similar to that you have already used, and placing it in one of the boxes contained in the vase. Bringing the vase forward to the audience, you open it in such manner as to exhibit the other box, in which, after it has been duly examined, you request one of the audience to place the empty paper. Closing the vase, and placing it on the table, you fire your pistol at it, or merely touch it with your wand, and order the ring to return to the paper. You now open the vase at the compartment containing the first box. Drawing particular attention to the fact that you have not even touched the box, you again offer it for inspection. The folded paper, which the audience take to be the same, is duly found therein, and, on being opened, is shown to contain the borrowed ring.

A similar effect, on a smaller scale, may be produced by privately placing the paper containing the ring in the inner compartment of the "plug-box" (described at page 192), and requesting one of the audience to place the original folded paper in the outer compartment.

To Pass a Ring from the one Hand to either Finger of the other Hand.—This is a very old and simple trick, but it has puzzled many, and comes in appropriately in this place, as affording another illustration of the use of the "flying ring." The only additional preparation consists of a little hook, such as is used to fasten ladies' dresses, sewn to the trouser of the performer just level with the fingers of his right hand when hanging by his side, but a little behind the thigh, so as to be covered by the coat-tail. Borrowing a wedding-ring, the performer receives it in his right hand, immediately transferring it in appearance (as in the last trick) to his left hand. Showing in place of it the flying ring, which is already in his left hand, he drops the right hand to his side, and slips the borrowed ring on the little hook. Then remarking, "You all see this ring, which I have just borrowed. I will make it invisibly pass to my right hand, and on to whichever finger of that hand you may please to select." Here he waves his right hand with an indicative gesture, thus indirectly showing that he has nothing therein, and again lets the hand fall carelessly by his side. As soon as the finger is chosen, he slips the borrowed ring upon the end of that particular finger, immediately closing the hand so as to conceal it, and holds out the hand at arm's length in front of him. Then saying, "One, two, three! Pass!" he releases the flying ring, and, opening both hands, shows that the left is empty, and that the borrowed ring has passed to the selected finger of the right hand.

The hook may, if preferred, be dispensed with, the ring being simply dropped into the *pochette* on the right side, and again taken from thence when required.

To Pass a Ring through a Pocket-handkerchief.—This is but a juvenile trick, but we insert it for the sake of completeness. It is performed by the aid of a piece of wire, sharpened to a point at each end, and bent into the form of a ring. The performer, having this palmed in his right hand, borrows a wedding-ring and a handkerchief (silk for preference). Holding the borrowed ring between the fingers of his right hand, he throws the handkerchief over it, and immediately seizes with the left hand, through the handkerchief, apparently the borrowed ring, but really the sham ring, which he adroitly substitutes. He now requests one of the spectators to take hold of the ring in like manner, taking care to make him hold it in such a way that he may not be able to feel the opening between the points, which would betray the secret. The ring being thus held, and the handkerchief hanging down around it, a second spectator is requested, for greater security, to tie a piece of tape or string tightly round the handkerchief an inch or two below the ring. The performer then takes the handkerchief into his own hand, and, throwing the loose part of the handkerchief over his right hand, so as to conceal his mode of operation, slightly straightens the sham ring, and works one of the points through the handkerchief, so getting it out, and rubbing the handkerchief with his finger and thumb in order to obliterate the hole made by the wire in its passage. He now palms the sham ring, and produces the real one, which has all along remained in his right hand, requesting the person who tied the knot to ascertain for himself that it has not been tampered with.

To Pass a Ring through the Table.—This also is a juvenile trick, but a very good one. The necessary apparatus consists of an ordinary glass tumbler, and a handkerchief to the middle of which is attached, by means of a piece of sewing-silk about four inches in length, a substitute ring of your own. Borrowing a ring from one of the company, you announce that it will at your command pass through the table ; but as the process, being magical, is necessarily invisible, you must first cover it over. Holding the handkerchief by two of the corners, you carelessly shake it out (taking care to keep the side on which is the suspended ring towards yourself), and wrapping in it apparently the borrowed, but really the suspended ring, you hand it to one of the company, requesting him to grasp the ring through the handkerchief, and to hold it securely.

A word of caution may here be given, which will be found more :r less applicable to all magical performances. Have the room in which you perform as brilliantly lighted as you please, but take care so to arrange the lights, or so to place yourself, that all the lights may be in front of you, and none behind you. The trick we are now describing affords a practical illustration of the necessity for this. If you have any light behind you, the handkerchief, as you shake it to show that it is not prepared, will appear semi-transparent, and the spectators will be able to see the suspended ring dangling behind it. For a similar reason, you should always endeavour to have a dark background for your performances, as any thread, or the like, which you may have occasion to secretly use will then be invisible at a short distance, while against a light background —*e.g.*, a muslin curtain or white wall-paper—it would be instantly noticeable.

But to return to our trick : we left one of the spectators tightly holding the suspended ring, covered by the folds of the handkerchief. Your next step is to request the audience to choose at what particular spot in the table the ring shall pass through it. When they have made the selection, you place the tumbler upon the spot chosen, and request the person having charge of the ring to hold his hand immediately over the glass, around which you drape the folds of the handkerchief. "Now," you say, "will you be kind enough, sir, to drop the ring in the glass." He lets go, and the ring falls with an audible "ting" into the glass. "Are you all satisfied," you ask, "that the ring is now in the glass ? " The reply will generally be in the affirmative ; but, if any one is sceptical, you invite him to shake the glass, still covered by the handkerchief, when the ring is heard to rattle within it.

Your next step is to borrow a hat, which you take in the hand which still retains the genuine ring, holding it in such manner that the tips of the fingers are just inside the hat, the ring being concealed beneath them. In this condition you can freely exhibit the inside of the hat, which is seen to be perfectly empty. You now place the hat under the table, mouth upwards, relaxing as you do so the pressure of the fingers, and allowing the coin to slide gently down into the crown. Leaving the hat under the table, which should be so placed that the spectators cannot, as they stand or sit, see quite into the crown, you take hold of the extreme edge of the handkerchief, and saying, "One, two, three! Pass!" jerk it away, and request some one to pick up the hat, and return the borrowed ring to the owner.

We have given the trick in its simplest form, but it is obvious that it is capable of any amount of variation as regards the circumstances under which the vanished ring is again found. The "plug-box" (page 192) or the "nest of boxes" (page 197) may be here made available, the performer placing the ring where it is to be afterwards found, during his momentary absence in search of the necessary apparatus.

To Pass a Ring invisibly upon the Middle of a Wooden Wand, the Ends being held by two of the Spectators.—In this trick, the handkerchief prepared (with the ring attached) for the purpose of the last illusion may be again employed, though some use for the present purpose a handkerchief with a ring stitched in one corner. In our own opinion, the suspended ring is preferable, and we shall describe the trick accordingly. The only other requisite will be the magic wand, or any short stick or rod of such diameter that a finger-ring may slip easily upon it. Having borrowed a ring, you proceed to wrap it (in reality the substitute) in the handkerchief, and hand it to some one to hold. The borrowed ring, of course, remains in your hand. Picking up with your other hand your wand, you transfer it to the hand containing the ring. Taking hold of it by the extreme end, you pass the ring over it, which a very little practice will enable you to do without the smallest difficulty. You then say, "I am about to order the ring which Mr. So-and-so is holding, to leave the handkerchief, and pass on to this wand. For greater security, I will ask two of the gentlemen present to hold the ends. Will some one volunteer for the purpose?" Two candidates having come forward, you place yourself facing the person who is holding the ring in the handkerchief, at the same time sliding your hand with the ring to the centre of the wand, and holding the latter in a horizontal position across your body. You now invite the two volunteers each to take hold of one end, pretending to be very particular that the wand should be perfectly horizontal, this giving you an excuse for keeping your hand upon it, sliding it backwards and forwards, and raising now one end, now the other, till the level is such as to satisfy your correct eye. When at last you are satisfied, you ask the person in charge of the ring to step forward, so as to bring it immediately above the wand, over which you immediately spread the pocket-handkerchief, letting the edges fall on either side of the wand. As soon as the wand is covered, you can of course remove your hand. Then, taking hold of one corner of the handkerchief, you request the holder of the ring to let go at the word " Three," and saying, " One, two, three—Pass ! " draw away the handkerchief sharply, which, brushing against the genuine ring, will set it revolving rapidly, as though it had just passed on to the wand.

Some professors introduce the " flying ring " in the performance of this trick, thus dispensing altogether with the handkerchief. The slight variations in working thereby rendered necessary will readily suggest themselves without further explanation.

THE MAGIC BALL AND RINGS.—This is a recent improvement on the trick last described. The performer borrows three rings, which in this instance, as the trick does not depend upon a substitution, may be of any pattern. They should not, however, be too large, for which reason ladies' rings are preferable. These he places, or requests the owners to place, in the " Davenport cabinet" (*see* page 195), the " watch-box " (*see* page 219), or any other apparatus which will enable him secretly to get possession of them. He then brings in and hands for inspection an ebony ball, an inch and a half to two inches in diameter (through which is bored a hole of three-eighths of an inch in diameter), and a brass rod about two feet in length, with a knob at each end, and of such a thickness as to pass freely through the ball. Both are closely scrutinized, and admitted to be fair and solid. In sight of all he unscrews one of the knobs, and places the ball upon the rod, throwing a handkerchief over it, and requesting two of the audience to hold the ends. Passing his hand under the handkerchief, he orders the ball to drop into his hand, when his command is instantly obeyed.

He next orders the rings to pass from the cabinet, and to take the place of the ball on the brass rod. On removing the handkerchief, the rings are seen on the rod, and the cabinet, on examination, is found empty.

The secret consists in the use of *two* balls, one of which (that handed round for inspection) has no speciality. The other is divided into two parts, the section being vertically through the bore. (*See* Fig. 106.) These two parts fit closely together, and being (as is

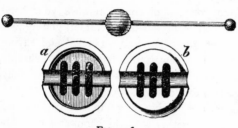

FIG. 106.

also the solid ball) carved in concentric circles parallel to the opening, the division is not readily noticeable. The two halves, *a* and *b*, are hollowed out to contain the rings, each having three slots or mortices cut at right angles to the direction of the hole through the ball. When the performer retires to fetch the ball and rod, he places the borrowed rings in these slots. When the two halves of the ball are brought together, the rings will encircle the hole through the centre, and the rod, when passed through the ball, will pass through the rings also. The performer places the trick ball, thus prepared, under his waistband, or in one of his *pochettes,* and, returning, hands for inspection the brass rod and the solid ball. While these are being examined, he palms the trick ball, and in passing over the rod apparently the ball which has just been examined, adroitly substitutes that which contains the rings. After having thrown the handkerchief over the rod, he passes under it his hand, still containing the solid ball. It is an easy matter to pull asunder the hollow ball, and this in turn is palmed, and the solid ball passed to the end of the fingers, before the performer, again uncovering his hand, which he brings out palm downward, carelessly throws down the solid ball, as being that which he has just taken off the rod. This is the only part of the trick which requires any special dexterity, and any difficulty which may be at first found will quickly disappear with a little practice.

When the ball comes apart, the rings are, of course, left on the rod.

A further improvement may be made in the trick by using a sword with a rapier blade in place of the brass rod. The trick is not only more effective in appearance, as the sword appears to cut through the ball, but the tapering shape of the blade makes the trick much easier to perform, as you have only to draw the ball down towards the hilt, when the swell of the blade will force the two halves of the ball apart, leaving them naturally in your hand. It is best in this case simultaneously to let the solid ball drop from your palm to the floor. This draws all eyes downwards, and gives you ample opportunity to drop the halves of the trick ball into your secret pocket. In this form of the trick you, of course, hold the sword yourself in the ordinary manner, and you may, if you prefer it, dispense with the handkerchief, using your hand only to mask the operation, at once stepping forward, as the ball drops to the ground, and saying, " Will the owners be kind enough to identify their rings ? "

To Pass a Borrowed Ring into an Egg.—This is an effective conclusion to a ring trick. The necessary apparatus consists of two wooden egg-cups, inside one of which, at the bottom, is cut a mortice or slot just large enough to receive one-half the circumference of a lady's ring, and to hold it in an upright position. The second egg-cup has no speciality, being, in fact, merely a dummy, designed be handed to the audience for inspection. An ordinary button-hook, or a piece of wire bent into the shape of a button-hook, completes the preparations.

We will assume that the performer has, in the course of one or other of the tricks already described, secretly obtained possession of a borrowed ring, which the audience believe still to remain in some place or apparatus in which they have seen it deposited. The operator, retiring for an instant, returns with a plate of eggs in one hand, and the dummy egg-cup in the other. The special egg-cup, with the ring already in the mortice, is meanwhile placed either under his waistband, or in one or other of his *pochettes*, so as to be instantly get-at-able when required. Placing the eggs on the table, he hands round the egg-cup for inspection. that all may observe that it is wholly without preparation, and in turning to place the egg-cup on the table, he substitutes for it the one which contains the ring, but which the audience naturally believe to be that which they have just examined.

Bringing forward the plate of eggs, the performer requests the company to choose whichever they please. While they are making their selection, he carefully turns back his sleeves, showing indirectly that his hands are empty. Taking the chosen egg with the tips of his fingers, and showing it on all sides, to prove that there is no pre-paration about it, he says, "Now, ladies and gentlemen, you have seen me place the ring which this lady has kindly lent me in 'so-and-so'" (according to the place where it is supposed to be). "You have selected, of your own free choice, this particular egg among half-a-dozen others. I am about to command the ring to leave the place where it now is, and to pass into the very centre of this egg. If you think the egg is prepared in any way, it is open to you even now to choose another. You are all satisfied that the egg has not been tampered with? Well, then, just observe still that I have nothing in my hands. I have merely to say, 'One, two, three! Pass!' The ring is now in the egg." At the word, "Pass," the performer taps one end of the egg with his wand, just hard enough to crack it slightly. "Dear me," he says; "I did not intend to hit quite so hard; but it is of no consequence." Stepping to the table, he places the egg, *with the cracked end downwards,* in the prepared egg-cup, using just sufficient pressure to force the egg well down upon the ring, the projecting portion of which is thereby forced into the egg. The egg being already cracked, a very slight pressure is sufficient. Bringing forward the egg in the cup, the hook already mentioned, and a table-napkin, he taps the top of the egg smartly with his wand, so as to crack it, and offering the hook to the owner of the ring, requests her to see whether her property is not in the egg. The ring is immediately fished out, and being wiped upon the napkin, is recognized as that which was borrowed. The apparatus in which it was originally placed is, on being examined, found empty.

THE MAGIC ROSE.—This little apparatus affords the means for a graceful termination of a ring trick. A ring having been made to disappear in any of the modes before described, the operator, retiring for a moment, returns with a rose-bud in his hand. Advancing to the owner of the ring, he requests her to breathe on the flower. As she does so, the bud is seen slowly to open, and in the centre of the new-blown flower is found the missing article.

The idea of the flower, warmed into bloom under a fair lady's breath, is so poetical that it seems quite a pity to be obliged to confess that the rose is an artificial one, made chiefly of tin, and that its petals, normally held open by the action of a spring, are, when the flower is first brought on, kept closed by a sliding ring or collar upon the stalk, again re-opening as this collar is drawn back by the magician's fingers.

CHAPTER XI.

Tricks with Handkerchiefs.

We have already discussed a good many tricks in which handkerchiefs are employed in one way or another. The present chapter will be devoted to those feats in which the handkerchief forms the sole or principal object of the illusion. Where practicable, the handkerchief used should always be a borrowed one (so as to exclude the idea of preparation); and in borrowing it will occasionally be necessary to use a little tact in order to make certain of getting the right article for your purpose, without admitting, by asking specially for any particular kind of handkerchief, the limited extent of your powers. Thus, whenever the trick depends upon the substitution of a handkerchief of your own, it is necessary that the borrowed handkerchief should be of a plain white, so as not to have too marked an individuality, and of a small size, so as to be easily palmed or otherwise concealed. These desiderata you may secure, without disclosing that they are desiderata, by asking if a *lady* will oblige you with a handkerchief, ladies' handkerchiefs being invariably white, and of small size. If a lace handkerchief (which would be inconveniently distinguishable from your substitute) is offered, you may pretend to fear the risk of injuring the lace, and on that account to prefer a less valuable article. In "knot" tricks, on the contrary, you should, if possible, use a silk handkerchief, which, from its softer nature, will be found more tractable than cambric.

We will begin by describing a couple of little "flourishes," which may be incidentally introduced in the performance of more ambitious tricks, and which will sometimes be found useful in occupying the attention of the audience for a moment or two while some necessary arrangement is being made behind the scenes for the purpose of the principal illusion. The first we will call—

THE HANDKERCHIEF THAT CANNOT BE TIED IN A KNOT.— The performer, having borrowed a handkerchief, pulls it this way and that, as if to ascertain its fitness for the purpose of the trick. Finally twisting the handkerchief into a sort of loose rope, he throws the two ends one over the other, as in the ordinary mode of tying, and pulls smartly; but instead of a knot appearing, as would naturally be expected, in the middle of the handkerchief, it is pulled out quite straight. "This is a very curious handkerchief," he remarks; "I can't make a knot in it." The process is again and again repeated, but always with the same result.

The secret is as follows: — The performer, before pulling the knot tight, slips his left thumb, as

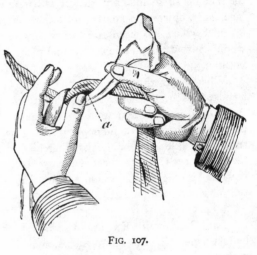

FIG. 107.

shown in Fig. 107, beneath such portion of the "tie" as is a continuation of the end held in the same hand. The necessary arrangement of the hands and handkerchief, though difficult to explain in writing, will be found quite clear upon a careful examination of the figure.

THE HANDKERCHIEF THAT WILL NOT BURN.—This may be used either separately or in conjunction with the foregoing. The performer, taking the handkerchief, asks if it will burn. The owner naturally answers that she has no doubt it will. "Suppose we try," says the performer; and taking the handkerchief by two of its corners, he draws it three or four times obliquely upwards across the flame of a lighted candle, without its receiving the slightest injury.

There is really no mystery whatever about this, although, to those who have never tried it, it appears very surprising, and the spectators are generally persuaded that you have somehow substituted another handkerchief, made incombustible by chemical means. The performer has only to take care not to allow the handkerchief to rest motionless while in contact with the flame. In the act of drawing the handkerchief over the candle, the contact of any given part with the flame is so momentary, that it is barely warmed in its passage. You must, however, take care not to attempt this trick with a handkerchief which has been scented, as any remains of spirit about it would cause it to ignite instantly, and place you in a rather awkward position.

Where a substitute handkerchief has to be burnt in the course of a trick, it is by no means a bad plan to exhibit with the substitute (which the audience take to be the original) this phenomenon of supposed incombustibility, and appearing to grow careless from repeated success, at last to allow the handkerchief to catch fire. If you can by such means induce the audience to believe, for the time being, that the burning was an accident, you will the more astonish them by the subsequent restoration.

The Vanishing Knots.—For this trick you must use a silk handkerchief. Twisting it rope-fashion, and grasping it by the middle with both hands, you request one of the spectators to tie the two ends together. He does so, but you tell him that he has not tied them half tight enough, and you yourself pull them still tighter. A second and a third knot are made in the same way, the handkerchief being drawn tighter by yourself after each knot is made. Finally, taking the handkerchief, and covering the knots with the loose part, you hand it to some one to hold. Breathing on it, you request him to shake out the handkerchief, when all the knots are found to have disappeared.

When the performer apparently tightens the knot, he in reality only strains one end of the handkerchief, grasping it above and below the knot. This pulls that end of the handkerchief out of its twisted condition in the knot into a straight line, round which the other end of the handkerchief remains twisted; in other words, converts the knot into a slip-knot. After each successive knot he still straightens this same end of the handkerchief. This end, being thus made straight, would naturally be left longer than the other which is twisted round and round it. This tendency the performer counteracts by drawing it partially back through the slip-knot at each pretended tightening. When he finally covers over the knots, which he does with the left hand, he holds the straightened portion of the handkerchief, immediately behind the knots, between the first finger and thumb of the right hand, and therewith, in the act of covering over the knots, draws this straightened portion completely out of the slip-knot.

Some performers (among whom we may mention Herrmann) make this feat still more effective by borrowing half-a-dozen handkerchiefs, and allowing them all to be tied end to end by the spectators. After each knot the professor pretends to examine it, asking, "What kind of a knot do you call this, sir?" and meanwhile pulls it into the required condition. The joined handkerchiefs are then placed one upon the other on a chair or in a hat, and are immediately afterwards shown to be separate.

The student must be on his guard against one particular kind of knot, which cannot be pulled into the condition above-named. We allude to the very common mode of tying, in which the two ends to be tied are placed side by side, and tied simultaneously in a single knot. The employment of this kind of knot may generally be avoided by holding the two ends to be tied at a tolerably wide angle, so that they cannot very well be drawn parallel. If, however, a spectator appears determined to tie this particular knot, it is better to allow him to do so, and then remark, "As the knots are tied by yourselves, ladies and gentlemen, you can have little doubt that they are all fair. However, for the greater satisfaction of all present, I will ask some gentleman to be good enough to untie one of them, which will give a fair criterion of the time it would take, in a natural way, to get rid of the remainder." So saying, you hand the knot in question to be untied, and in subsequently giving the ends to be again joined, select a more accommodating person to tie them.

As the tricks which follow mainly depend upon the substitution of a second handkerchief, we shall in the first place describe two or three modes of effecting the necessary exchange, with and without the aid of apparatus.

To Exchange a borrowed Handkerchief for a Substitute.—Have the substitute handkerchief tucked under your waistcoat, at the left side, so as to be out of sight, but within easy reach of your hand. Receive the borrowed handkerchief in your right hand, and as you 'left wheel' to your table to place it thereon, tuck it under your waistband on the right side, and at the same moment pull out with the other hand the substitute, and throw the latter on the table. The substitute handkerchief (which the audience take to be the real one) being thus left in full view, you may, without exciting any suspicion, retire with the genuine one, and dispose of it as may be necessary for the purpose of your trick.

You may, however, sometimes desire merely to gain possession of a borrowed handkerchief, or to place it within reach of your assistant, without yourself leaving the apartment. In this case the substitute may be placed as before, but on your *right* side. Receiving the borrowed handkerchief in your right hand, you hold it loosely hanging down between the second and third, or third and fourth fingers. This leaves the thumb and first finger free, and with these you quickly pull down, as you turn to go to your table, the substitute. You thus have both handkerchiefs held openly in the same hand; but both being of like appearance, the audience take them to be one only. Passing behind your table, you let fall the borrowed handkerchief upon the *servante*, and throw the substitute upon the table.

A very audacious and generally successful mode of effecting the change is as follows : Taking the handkerchief, and pressing it into a moderately small compass, the performer says, "Now I am going to make this handkerchief disappear. There are plenty of ways of doing it. I'll show you one or two. This is Professor De Jones's method. He just turns round, *so*, to put the handkerchief on the table" (performer turns accordingly), "but meanwhile the handkerchief is gone. Ah, you were too sharp for me! You saw me poke it up my sleeve? Quite right, here it is. I see Professor De

Jones's method wouldn't have any chance with *you*. This is Professor De Smith's method." He turns as before. "The handkerchief is gone again. Not far, though, for here it is" (turning back breast of coat and showing handkerchief). "Professor De Robinson does it like this." (He turns away for an instant, and tucks handkerchief under waistband.) "Here it is, you see, under the waistcoat." (Pulls it out again.) "Now, you may very well imagine that, if I had intended to have used any of these methods myself, I shouldn't have explained them. You will find that my plan is quite a different one. When I want to get rid of a handkerchief, I just take it to the candle, and set it on fire, so" (holds handkerchief over candle, and sets light to it) ; or, "I place it in such and such a piece of apparatus," etc., etc.

On the first two occasions of showing where the handkerchief is placed, the performer really does exhibit the genuine article ; but at the third pretended feint, though he really does tuck it under his waistband, he pulls out again, not the same handkerchief, but a substitute, placed there beforehand. The action is so natural, and so much in harmony with his previous acts, that not one in a hundred will suspect that he has thereby really changed the handkerchief.

The mode of exchange last described, ingenious as it is, has one serious drawback—viz., that it gives the audience a clue which it is better that they should not have, and suggests suspicions and conjectures which, but for such a clue, they would never have thought of. To an acute mind, even such a slight hint as this will suggest enough to destroy half the effect of any subsequent trick in which a similar process of disappearance or exchange is employed, and even in the case of less intelligent spectators it will tend to diminish the *prestige* of the performer, by showing by what shallow artifices an illusion may be produced.

There are two or three pieces of apparatus for effecting the exchange of a handkerchief by mechanical means. A very good one is that known as "The Washerwoman's Bottle," in conjunction with which we will take the opportunity of describing the very effective trick known as

THE LOCKED AND CORDED BOX.—The "Washerwoman's

Bottle " is a simple and inexpensive piece of apparatus, of frequent use in handkerchief tricks. In appearance it is an ordinary black bottle, save that it has a rather shorter neck and wider mouth than the generality of such vessels. In reality it is made of tin, japanned black, and is divided by a vertical partition, commencing just below the mouth, into two compartments. One of these has a bottom, but the other has none, forming, in fact, a mere passage *through* the bottle. In the bottomed compartment is placed beforehand a piece of cambric, or dummy handkerchief, also about a glassful of port wine, or some other liquor of similar colour.

The performer borrows a lady's handkerchief. Pretending that he is obliged to fetch some other article for the purpose of the trick, he says, as if struck by a sudden thought, " But I mustn't run away with the handkerchief, or you might fancy that I had tampered with it in some way. Where shall I put it? Ah! the very thing. Here's a bottle belonging to my washerwoman, which she left behind her the last time she came. It's sure to be clean, for she is a most particular old lady. We often hear of a lady carrying a bottle in her handkerchief, why not a handkerchief in a bottle? First, madam, please see that I have not exchanged the handkerchief. Right, is it? Well, then, here goes for the bottle." Standing behind his table, in full view of the spectators, he stuffs the borrowed handkerchief into the bottle, ramming it down with his wand. In so doing, he grasps the bottle with his left hand around its base, which he rests on the edge of the table nearest to himself, in such manner that about half the bottom projects over the edge. When he places the handkerchief in the bottle, he places it in the open compartment, and pushes it with his wand right through the bottle into his left hand, if he desires to obtain personal possession of it, or lets it fall on the *servante,* if it is to be carried off by his assistant. We will assume, for our present purpose, that he simply pushes it into his left hand, whence it is easy to get rid of it into the *pochette* on the same side. He now places the bottle in the centre of the table, but in doing so hears, or pretends to hear, a sound of liquid therein. " I hope the bottle was empty," he remarks, " I never thought about that." He shakes the bottle. and the liquid therein is distinctly audible. " Good gracious! " he exclaims, " I'm afraid I have ruined the handkerchief." He now pours the liquid into a glass, and then, putting his fingers inside the bottle, he pulls out the prepared piece of cambric, which, of course, is wet and stained. Leaving it hanging from the neck of the bottle, he advances to the owner, and expresses his regret at the accident; but the audience, who begin to suspect that the pretended mistake is really a part of the trick, insist that the handkerchief shall be restored in its original condition. The performer feigns embarrassment, but at last says, "Well, ladies and gentlemen, I cannot dispute the justice of your observations. The handkerchief certainly ought to be returned clean as at first, and as my washerwoman has been the cause of the mischief, she is the proper person to repair it. Will you excuse my stopping the entertainment for an hour or two, while I go to fetch her? You object to the delay? Well, then, I will bring her here by spiritualistic means, *à la* Mrs. Guppy. Pardon me one moment." He retires, and returns with a square box and the magic pistol. Placing the box on the table, and making a few mysterious passes over it with his wand, he says, in his deepest tones, "Spirit of Mrs. Tubbs, I command you to pass into this box, there to remain until you have repaired the damage which your carelessness has caused." Then taking the saturated cambric from the bottle, he crams it into the pistol, and, retiring to the farthest portion of the stage, fires at the box. Laying down the pistol, and taking p the box, he advances to the owner of the handkerchief, and, offering her the key, begs her to unlock it. She does so, expecting to find her handkerchief, but finds instead a second box. This, and four or five others in succession, are opened, and in the innermost is found the handkerchief, folded and ironed, as if newly returned from the wash.

With the reader's present knowledge, it would be almost superfluous to tell him that the operator avails himself of his momentary absence to damp and fold the handkerchief, and to press it with a cold iron. (If a hot one can be obtained, so much the better, but there is no absolute necessity for it.) Having done this, he places it in the square nest of boxes (see page 197), and closing them returns to the audience. The magic pistol has already been described (page 216). Where an assistant is employed, the performer merely pushes the handkerchief through the bottle on to the *servante,* as already mentioned, and the assistant, passing behind the table on some pretext or other, carries it off, and places it in the nest of boxes, while the audience are occupied by the pretended discovery of wine in the bottle. The trick in this form appears even more surprising, inasmuch as the performer does not leave the stage at all, and the box is brought in and placed on the table by a person who, to all appearance, has never had the handkerchief, even for a moment, in his possession.

In order still further to heighten the effect of the trick, the handkerchief is sometimes caused to reappear in the innermost of a nest of boxes which has throughout the entertainment been hung up in full view of the audience, and the outermost of which is carefully corded and sealed. The performer in this case, after firing at the supposed box (for the audience are, of course, ignorant that there are more than one), directs his assistant to take it down from its elevated position, and to place it on the table. Cutting the cords, and opening the box, he produces from it another, corded like the first. From this second box, he produces another smaller box, of an ornamental character (the square nest of boxes above mentioned). This he hands to the owner of the handkerchief, with a request that she will open it, and the result is as already described.

The trick in this form is one of the very best exhibited on the stage, and yet, as indeed are most of the best feats, it is performed by the simplest possible means. The outer box is an ordinary deal box, *bonâ fide* sealed and corded, but the second, though equally genuine in appearance, has no bottom, and the cord, though apparently quite complete, does not cross beneath the box, which is, in fact, nothing more than a wooden shell, or cover, with a lid to it. When the performer takes out this second box and places it on the table, he tilts it forward for a moment, and in that moment slips the nest of boxes (which is placed in readiness on the *servante*), underneath it, immediately afterwards raising the lid, and taking out the nest, as if it had all along been contained therein.

It only remains to explain the mode by which the nest of boxes, with the handkerchief therein, is placed upon the *servante*. Some performers employ the rather too transparent expedient of making the assistant bring in, then and there, a small round table, behind which, on a *servante* of its own, is placed the closed nest of boxes. A better plan, where the size of the nest permits, is to have it placed open, before the performance commences, on the *servante* of the centre table. It is then an easy matter for the performer or his assistant (as the case may be) to slip in the folded handkerchief, and close the boxes, the remainder of the trick proceeding as already described.

Some performers use for the purpose of this trick a special mechanical table, which, by means of a lifting apparatus, itself introduces the nest of boxes through a trap into the bottomless box, without the necessity of tilting the latter.

THE REVERSIBLE CANISTER.—This is another piece of apparatus more particularly designed for changing a handkerchief, though equally available for many other exchanges. In appearance it is an ordinary cylindrical canister, closed with a cap, and similar in shape to those in which tea is kept, but of smaller size, being only five to six inches in height. In reality, however, that which appears to be the body of the canister is a mere tube, within which slides up and down an inner can-

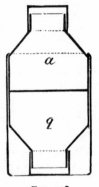

FIG. 108.

ister, which is made double-headed, *i.e.*, like two shallow canisters placed bottom to bottom. (*See* Fig. 108.) The pattern of the outer tube is alike at top and bottom, so that whether the combined canister is as shown in the figure, with compartment *a* uppermost, or turned upside down, with compartment *b* pushed into view, the appearance to the eye of the spectator is the same. The canister is prepared by placing beforehand in one or other of the compartments, say *b*, a piece of cambric, as much like a lady's handkerchief as possible. Compartment *a* is then pushed upwards, as shown in the figure. Borrowing a handkerchief, the performer requests the owner to place it for safe keeping in the canister, which he brings forward for that purpose. As he turns to replace it on the table, he takes advantage of the moment during which his back is towards the spectators to push down *a* (thus pushing out *b* at the opposite end of the tube), and at the same time to turn over the canister, which, when placed on the table, will still look as shown in the figure, but will have, in reality, *b* uppermost. Presently taking out the prepared cambric, which the spectators take to be the handkerchief, he burns or otherwise disposes of it, to be subsequently reproduced by the simple process of again reversing the canister.

This is a simple and inexpensive piece of apparatus, but it will not bear examination, and the process of reversing is a little awkward. For these reasons it is rarely employed by professional performers, who for the same purpose more generally use what is known as

THE BURNING GLOBE.—This is a hollow brass globe of four to six inches in diameter, mounted on a foot of about the same height, and surmounted by a cap or lid, so that it forms, in fact, a spherical canister. A raised band, also of brass, passes horizontally round the globe; and this, which is apparently a mere ornament, is really designed to conceal the fact that the globe is divided into two separate hemispheres, revolving one upon the other. Within this external globe is an inner one, divided into two compartments, each having a separate opening, and so contrived that each of these openings in turn is made to correspond with the opening of the external globe, according as the upper hemisphere of the latter is moved round from right to left, or *vice versâ*. The globe is, like the canister, prepared by placing a substitute handkerchief, or piece of cambric, in one or other of the inner compartments, and then bringing the other compartment into correspondence with the external opening. A borrowed handkerchief being openly placed in the empty compartment, the performer, by merely giving a half turn to the foot of the apparatus, brings the compartment containing the substitute uppermost, the action being so little noticeable that it may be used with impunity before the very eyes of the audience.

THE TRANSFORMED HANDKERCHIEF.—This is one of Herrmann's favourite tricks, and affords a very good example of his style of working. The performer comes forward, requesting the loan of a lady's handkerchief. While it is being procured, he produces from the hair or whiskers of one of the spectators a lemon, which he carelessly thrusts under somebody's nose in order to prove its genuineness,

(This lemon, which, of course, was palmed, is a prepared one, from which the pulp has been scooped out, and which contains a substitute handkerchief, so cannot be handed for examination.) Turning for an instant towards the stage, he tosses the lemon to his assistant, who catches it, and places it on the table. The momentary turn from the audience enables him to get from under his waistband, and to palm, a little bundle of pieces of cambric, each about four inches square. Taking the borrowed handkerchief, h rolls it into a ball between his hands, and hands it (apparently) to some one to hold, in reality substituting the torn pieces of cambric. He then turns, and takes a few paces towards his table, meanwhile tucking the handkerchief under his waistcoat, and taking therefrom in place of it a strip of cambric, about four or five feet long and four inches wide, rolled up into a small compass. This he palms. Suddenly turning back, he exclaims, " My dear sir, what *are* you doing with that handkerchief? I never told you to do that!" The innocent holder looks up in astonishment, but the performer continues, "Will you have the kindness to open the handkerchief?" He does so, and finds it in pieces. After a little chaff about making him pay for the damage, the performer says, " Well, I suppose I must show you how to restore it." Here he again takes the pieces, and folds them together, saying, " See, you must take them as I do, and rub them very gently with the left hand." Substituting the prepared slip, he hands it to him; but, when he begins to rub, exclaims again, "Dear me, dear me! what are you doing now? I told you the *left* hand. You are making matters worse than ever." The handkerchief is now found in a long strip. The performer endeavours to induce the owner to accept it in this shape, which he assures her is the newest style; but she naturally objects, and begs that it may be restored to its original condition. For that purpose, the performer, rolling the slip into a ball, places it in his magic pistol (*see* page 215), and rams it down with his wand. Appearing to reflect for a moment, he says, " Where shall I fire it? Ah! suppose I aim at that lemon on the table?" " Bang ! " goes the pistol, and the performer, taking a knife, cuts the lemon all round (flinging the rind carelessly on the stage), and produces the substitute handkerchief (professedly the original). He comes forward to the audience with it, and, after thanking the owner, makes a gesture of returning it; but, as if struck by a sudden thought, checks himself, and says, "I'm afraid it smells rather strong of the lemon. Will you allow me to scent it for you? I have some capital Eau de Cologne here." Going back to his table, he places the handkerchief on a plate, and pours scent on it, turning as he does so to the owner, and saying, "Please tell me when you think there is enough." While his back is turned, the attendant, who has been standing by holding a lighted candle, with a mischievous wink at the company, tilts the candle, and sets the handkerchief on fire. The performer apologizes for his assistant's stupidity, but appeals to the company to bear witness that it was no fault of his, and bringing forward the plate, with the handkerchief still blazing, offers it to the owner. She, of course, declines to take it, and the performer, remarking, "You don't like it in this condition; well, then, suppose I put it in paper for you," places the plate on the floor, telling the assistant to put it on the table, and runs off to get the paper. The attendant tries to lift off the plate, but finds that it burns his fingers. However, after several attempts, getting the plate a little nearer to the table at each, he manages to place it on the table. This little by-play amuses the audience, and gives the performer the few moments which he requires for his preparations behind the scenes. Coming forward with a sheet of clean white paper, he wraps therein the still blazing handkerchief, crushing it together so as to extinguish the flames. He offers the packet so made to the lady, who, believing that it contains nothing but ashes, declines to receive it, when the professor, tearing the paper apart, pulls out the handkerchief perfectly restored, while the burnt fragments have vanished.

The effect last mentioned is produced by the use of a double paper, pasted together round three of its sides, and thus forming a kind of bag in the centre. In this bag the performer, during his momentary absence from the stage, places the genuine handkerchief, folded so as to occupy as little space as possible. The handkerchief, therefore, lies between the two thicknesses of the paper, and when the rolled up packet is torn open from outside, may be removed without disturbing the burnt fragments, which still remain inside the paper.

Where it is necessary, as for the purpose of this trick, to introduce some article into a lemon, the necessary preparation should be made as follows :—A lemon with a thick hard rind should be selected, and a plug-shaped piece, about an inch and a half in diameter, should be scooped with a sharp knife out of one end. The pulp may now be removed, leaving the rind a mere shell, while the piece originally cut out will form a kind of stopper, which may be secured in its place by thrusting a hair-pin or piece of wire through the fruit and plug from side to side, and nipping off the ends flush with the outer surface. When the performer exhibits the lemon, he takes care to have the cut end inwards towards his palm; so that the circular mark is concealed by the fingers, and when he desires to produce the handkerchief he cuts the opposite end.

THE HANDKERCHIEF CUT UP, BURNT, AND FINALLY FOUND IN A CANDLE.—We have already described one or two modes in which a handkerchief, after being apparently cut up, or burnt, may be reproduced in its original condition. This is another and very effective form of the same trick.

Having borrowed a white handkerchief, you exchange it, by one or other of the means already described, for a substitute of similar appearance, and place the latter on the table. You then remember that, as you are about to burn the handkerchief, you will want a candle. You call to your attendant, but he, previously instructed, does not answer, and after a momentary pause you determine to fetch it yourself. You have, however, no sooner left the stage, than you meet the defaulter, and angrily remarking, in a stage whisper, so that the audience may hear, that he is never at hand when you want him, or making some similar observation, you order him to bring a lighted candle. Your absence is only momentary, but it has enabled you to throw him the real handkerchief, which he forthwith rolls up, and places inside a candle made hollow for the purpose; which he then places in a candlestick, lights, and brings on the stage. You have meanwhile taken up the substitute handkerchief, and advanced to the audience, getting ready the while in your palm a small piece of cambric, about six inches in diameter. Taking the handkerchief by the centre, in the same hand, you pull out between the first finger and thumb a portion of the piece of cambric, which is naturally taken to be a part of the handkerchief. Handing to one of the spectators a pair of scissors, you request him to cut off a small portion of the handkerchief. He cuts off a piece of the cambric. Holding this piece in the one hand, and taking the remainder, with the substitute handkerchief hanging down below it, in the other, you offer to teach the company your patent method of mending handkerchiefs, requiring neither thimble, needle, nor thread. Applying the cut edges to the candle, you set them on fire, rubbing them together. Finally, blowing out the flame, and throwing the handkerchief over the hand that holds the pieces, you palm them, and immediately afterwards show the handkerchief (*i.e.*, the substitute) completely restored.

The mode of procedure so far is pretty well known, and it is highly probable that one or more of the audience will be acquainted with it. Accordingly, you may safely expect to perceive in some quarter or other, knowing glances, or confidential communications as to "how it's done." Noticing, or pretending to notice this, you say, "Ah, I see there is a gentleman there who thinks he has found me out. You fancy, no doubt, sir, that I have performed this trick in the old fashion, by cutting a piece of cambric which does not form part of the handkerchief. Why, my dear sir, the trick in that form is as old as—your grandmother. But it is my own fault; I quite forgot to show you that the handkerchief was really cut. It is my rule never to perform the same trick twice over, but I feel so hurt at your unkind suspicion that I must break my rule for once, and this time you shall cut the handkerchief yourself." You offer him the scissors, and holding up the handkerchief (which the audience naturally believe to be the genuine one) by the middle, you allow him to cut a piece fairly out of it, immediately afterwards spreading it out, and showing that a large hole is made in the centre. Again, you hold the edges to the candle, but this time, as if by accident, you let the flames fairly catch hold of the handkerchief, which you are compelled to drop upon a plate or tray, and to let it burn itself out. For a moment, you feign to be embarrassed, and the audience are half inclined to believe that you have made a mistake, and your trick has failed; but you quickly recover your confidence, and remark, "This is not precisely what I intended, ladies and gentlemen. I am afraid I have made a little mistake, but fortunately it is easily remedied. The fact is, I forgot to pronounce the magic word at the right moment, and the handkerchief has in consequence stopped short at the first stage of transmigration. To make it pass into the second stage, that of renewed existence, I must again employ the agency of fire. See, I place the ashes in my magic pistol, and ram them down with the mystic wand. Now what shall I aim at? Ah! the candle on the table! A capital mark, and as it has been before you throughout the trick, you know that it cannot have undergone any preparation." (You fire, aiming at the candle.) "Did you see it pass? No. It has done so, nevertheless; but I must have put in a little too much powder, for it has gone right into the candle." (You bring the candle forward.) "Will some one oblige me by seeing if it is really in the candle." The candle is broken in half, and the handkerchief is found embedded therein.

The candle used for the purpose of the above trick is sometimes a genuine wax or composite candle, but more often a mere pasteboard tube, previously cut half asunder in the middle (so as to break without difficulty), and then covered with glazed white paper, in imitation of a candle, a genuine candle-end being inserted at the top. If a candle of this latter description is used, the performer must himself break it, as a spectator doing so would at once discover that it was a prepared article.

Before quitting the subject of handkerchiefs burnt and restored, we may mention a little appliance called the "handkerchief table," which is designed for this purpose. It is precisely the same in make and operation as the table or tripod, described at page 139, for burning and restoring a card, but a little larger. To those acquainted with the card tripod, the use and effect of the handkerchief table will be sufficiently obvious, without any special explanation.

THE SHOWER OF SWEETS.—This is a trick which is sure to be well received by a juvenile audience. The performer comes forward with an ordinary plate or salver, which he hands for examination, and then places on the table. He next borrows a handkerchief. Laying it flat over the plate, he lifts it up by nipping the middle with his finger and thumb, letting the four corners hang down. He then strokes down the handkerchief with the other hand, under the pretence of mesmerising it, when a shower of burnt almonds, chocolate creams, acidulated drops, etc., pours down upon the plate. Again he strokes the handkerchief, and again the shower pours down ; and the plate, being by this time full, is handed round to the company to prove that in the quality of the sweets, at any rate, there is " no deception."

The secret lies in the use of a small bag, of cambric or fine calico, shaped like an inverted letter V. The edges are turned in at the mouth, and through each hem is passed a straight piece of watch-spring or whalebone, one a little longer than the other. The natural tendency of these is to lie side by side, keeping the mouth of the bag closed ; but if pressure be simultaneously applied to both ends of the springs, the longer one assumes the shape of a semicircle, thereby opening the bag. Through the opposite end of the bag is passed a pointed wire hook. The bag is beforehand filled with nuts or bon-bons, and hung by the hook to the edge of the table on the side away from the spectators. Though the bag is mouth downwards, the action of the spring keeps it closed, and nothing can fall out. When the operator, standing behind the table, draws the handkerchief over the plate, he allows a portion of the hinder edge to hang over the edge of the table nearest to himself. When he picks up the handkerchief, which he does with his finger and thumb, he takes hold, through the handkerchief, of the upper part of the bag. The bag is thus lifted up within the handkerchief, but is concealed by the folds of the latter hanging down around it. The movement of the hand in stroking down the handkerchief presses the springs, and the bag opens, again closing as soon as the pressure is relaxed. When all the contents have fallen, the performer drops the handkerchief, bag and all, on the table, while he advances to the audience with the results of the trick, and, on again picking up the handkerchief, lets fall the empty bag upon the *servante*, or slips it into his pocket.

It will be observed that, in the form of the trick above described, the use of both hands is necessary—one to hold the handkerchief, while the other, stroking it down, presses the springs, and causes the bag to open. There is an improved form of the bag, used, and, we believe, invented by Robert-Houdin, which enables the performer, holding the handkerchief at arm's length, to perform the trick by mere word of command, without using the left hand at all. The bag is in this case of the form shown in Fig. 109. No springs are used, but the bag, when filled, is closed by folding down the flap, and hooking the little ring over the hook, the bag thereby assuming the appearance shown in Fig. 110. It is picked up within the handkerchief as described in the case of the spring bag; but when it is desired to produce the sweets, a slight inclination of the hook to the left (effected by a barely perceptible movement of the thumb and finger) causes the ring to slip off and the flap to fall down, as in Fig. 109, releasing the whole contents of the bag.

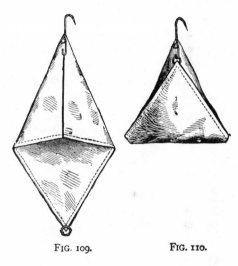

FIG. 109.   FIG. 110.

The trick may be still further improved by having two similar bags stitched back to back, each with its own ring and hook. In this case an inclination to the left releases one hook, and an inclination to the right the other. The two bags may be filled with bonbons of different colours or descriptions, or the one may be fi'led with bonbons and the other with grey peas. In this case you may introduce the trick by some observations upon the singular effects of the human breath, and how greatly such effects vary in different persons. A handkerchief is borrowed, and a lady and gentleman are requested each to hold a plate. The lady is requested to breathe on the handkerchief, and a shower of bonbons falls on her plate. The gentleman breathes in his turn, and retires, amid derisive applause, with a plate of peas.

While upon the subject of the mysterious production of sweets, we may incidentally mention another piece of apparatus designed for this purpose. This is a wand, made to correspond in general appearance with that habitually used by the performer. Internally, it is a hollow tube, with a stiff wire running throughout its whole length. One end of this wire is fixed to a moveable cap, which covers the upper end of the wand, while the other terminates in a sort of little wooden plug, which closes the opening at the other end. A spiral spring within the upper end of the wand tends to force the cap upwards, and so to keep the opposite end closed ; but if pressure be applied to the cap, the plug is forced outwards, and the tube thereby opened. *See* Fig. 111, in which *a* represents the wand in its normal condition (*i.e.*, closed), while *b* represents it with the cap pressed downwards, and the opposite end consequently open.

FIG. 111.

To prepare the wand for use, the cap is pressed and the valve opened. The wand is then filled with very minute sweetmeats, of the description known among juveniles as "hundreds and thousands;" after which the pressure on the cap is removed, and the plug allowed to retire into its place. The wand, thus prepared, is at the proper moment brought forward in place of the ordinary wand, which in its present condition it exactly resembles. The performer then declares his intention of passing a shower of sweets into the pocket of a spectator, and, having first shown it empty, touches the inside with the wand, at the same moment pressing the cap, when the sweets within escape into the pocket.

THE FEATHERS FROM AN EMPTY HANDKERCHIEF.—This is a very simple illusion, but has nevertheless been a favourite with many noted *prestidigitateurs*. Its effect is as follows :—The performer comes forward with a large handkerchief, or small shawl, which he shakes about in all directions, to show that it is empty. Throwing it over the left hand, he with the other grasps it by the middle, and removing the hand over which it was thrown, lets it hang perpendicularly down. To all appearance it is still empty ; but on being shaken it is seen to contain some solid object. With a twist of the wrist, the performer turns the handkerchief and its contents upwards.

The handkerchief naturally falls down over the coat-sleeve, leaving exposed a handsome military plume. The performer grasps, with the left hand, the stem of this plume and the centre of the handkerchief, immediately drawing away the right arm from beneath it. Again the handkerchief on being waved about is seen to contain something, which being held upright, the handkerchief falls down as before, and a second plume is revealed. The operation is again and again repeated with a like result, till fifteen or twenty plumes have been produced ; the handkerchief being at any moment handed for examination.

The explanation lies in the fact that the plumes, which may be compressed into a very small compass, are laid beforehand along the arms of the performer, who puts on his coat over them. The stems of the plumes are nearest to the hands. When the handkerchief is thrown over either hand, the other hand catches hold through it of the stem of one of the feathers. This hand now remains stationary, while the other arm is drawn from under the handkerchief. The fact that the plumes come out of the sleeves is thus much less patent than if the opposite hand made the motion and drew the feather out. The plumes on being drawn out expand considerably ; so much so, indeed, that it is hard to believe that the quantity with which the stage is strewn could possibly have been concealed about the person of the performer.

Some performers have in addition a bundle of plumes fastened together by a thread, and laid along the inside of the trousers and waistcoat, in such manner that the stems are just within the breast of the latter. After having exhausted his sleeves, the operator, holding the handkerchief (by two of its corners) across his chest, to show that it is quite empty, catches hold, with the second and third fingers, of the stem of the bundle within the waistcoat, and moving the handkerchief with a quick sidelong motion from left to right, or *vice versâ*, draws out the feathers behind it, and immediately breaking the thread, shakes them out in a shower on the stage.

There is another form of the same trick, in which the handkerchief plays only a secondary part, but, from its near relation to that last described, we insert it in this place. It is generally called

THE FLYING PLUME.—For this trick you require two plumes, as nearly as possible alike in appearance. To the stem of each should be attached a loop of string or ribbon, two or three inches in length. You must also have a japanned tin tube, of about twenty inches long, and three in diameter. On either end is fitted a cap, of about two inches in depth. One of these caps is perfectly plain, but within the other is an inner cap, made after the fashion of the middle compartment of the snuff-box vase (*see* page 217). The relative tightness of the inner and outer caps is such that, if in removing the outer one with the finger and thumb some slight degree of lateral pressure is exerted, it nips the inner cap, which comes off with it ; but if the outer cap is removed without pressure, the inner cap remains on the tube, forming a false top to it. Within this inner cap, which is internally about an inch and a half deep, is glued a short end of a third plume, similar in colour and appearance to the two others. The interior of the tube is divided into two parts by a longitudinal division, also of tin, running diagonally nearly from end to end. The tube is thus divided into two wedge-shaped compartments, the cap at one end giving access to the one, and the cap at the other end to the other ; each being large enough to contain a plume. (*See* Fig. 112, representing a section of the entire tube, and Fig. 113, giving a slightly enlarged view of the ends.) The tube is prepared beforehand by filling the compartment which is closed by the double cap with bonbons of various kinds ; the other compartment being left empty. One of the plumes is concealed in the left sleeve of the performer, as in the last trick.

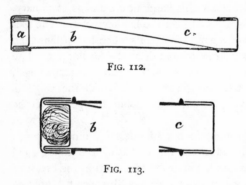

FIG. 112.

FIG. 113.

These preparations having been duly made beforehand, you come forward with a small shawl, or large handkerchief, the tube, and the second plume. Laying the tube and plume upon the table, you request the audience to satisfy themselves that the shawl contains nothing. You then ask some one to step forward and take care of the shawl, which you meanwhile carelessly throw over your left hand, immediately after taking hold of its centre with your right, as before described, and drawing the left arm away. It is needless to remark, to those who have followed the explanation of the last trick, that the hidden plume is thereby brought under the shawl, though, being held by the loop of ribbon, there is nothing to betray its presence. You hand the shawl in this condition to the person who has volunteered to hold it, requesting him to keep it at arm's length, still hanging down. Next taking up the tube, you open it at the plain or unprepared end, and holding it mouth downwards, show that it is (apparently) empty; then ostentatiously place the plume therein, and put the cap on.

In returning to your table you take the opportunity to reverse the tube, and to lay it down in such a manner that the opposite end (*i.e.,* that with the false top) may be turned towards the audience. Some performers do this by letting the tube fall, as if by accident, but this is, in our opinion, a clumsy and inartistic proceeding. By gesticulating a little with the tube, in announcing what you are about to do, so that the audience may, little by little, become less certain as to which end you have just opened, and by carelessly transferring the tube from the one hand to the other just as you lay it on the table, you may make the change with scarcely a chance of detection, even by the keenest observer. You then say, "I shall now, ladies and gentlemen, make the plume which you have just seen me place in this tube travel into the shawl which that gentleman is holding, while the tube will be completely filled with objects of interest for the juvenile spectators." Here you may possibly hear, or if not, you pretend to hear, a murmur to the effect that the feather has already left the tube. "Pardon me," you say, "the plume has not yet left the tube, neither will it do so until I give the command," and so saying, you take off the cap, leaving on the false top. The audience see the little bit of feather within, which they naturally take to be the end of the genuine plume. Again you replace the cap; and after going through some appropriate magical ceremony, again remove it, but this time carrying off the false top with it. (It should have been mentioned that the tube is japanned in such manner that the eye cannot detect any difference whether the false top is on or off.) Placing the cap, with the false top within it, on the table, you come forward and pour the sweets from the tube, while the shawl is on examination found to contain the plume.

Some performers, for the purpose of this trick, use a tube with a false top, as above described, but open from end to end, without the diagonal partition above mentioned. Before placing the plume in the tube, which they do standing behind the table, they secretly remove the cap at the lower end, and allow the plume to fall through on the *servante,* where it remains. In this case, there is no production of sweets, but the plume having been produced from the shawl, the performer removes both caps, and hands the empty tube for examination.

THE MAGIC LAUNDRY.—There is very little brilliancy, either of invention or of manipulation, in this trick, but it is nevertheless generally very well received.

The performer requests the loan of half-a-dozen handkerchiefs, taking care to accept white handkerchiefs only. These he collects in a wooden box, having somewhat the appearance of a good-sized tea caddy. Having got the required number, he places the box upon his table, and invites the attention of the audience to an ordinary tin or wooden pail. This he fills with water, and placing it in front of the stage, takes the handkerchiefs out of the box, and drops them in, stirring them about with his wand ; and making as much fun as he can by his pretended anxiety that they shall be thoroughly washed. Having kept this up as long as the audience appear to be amused thereby, he wrings out the handkerchiefs one by one, and throws them into a little shallow metal tub or pan (japanned, and about four inches in depth), which his assistant at this moment brings forward for that purpose, together with a cover after the manner of a saucepan-lid, and a pistol, both of which he places carelessly on the table. Having placed the handkerchiefs in this little tub, the performer announces that having washed them, he will now proceed to dry them, for which purpose he pours over them a little spirits of wine, to which he sets fire. After letting them blaze for a moment or two he claps on the cover. "Your handkerchiefs are now dried, ladies and gentlemen," he says, "but I have still to fold and iron them. It does not take very long, as you will see." Taking up the pistol, he fires at the tub, and immediately removing the cover, comes forward to the audience, and requests them to identify their handkerchiefs, which are seen neatly folded, and apparently just washed and ironed, within it.

The intelligent reader will have already guessed that the trick depends upon a substitution of handkerchiefs. The box in which the genuine handkerchiefs are received has within it a moveable flap, between which and the back of the box the substitutes are placed. When the required number has been collected, this flap is let fall, releasing the substitute handkerchiefs, and at the same time covering the genuine ones. The substitutes having been dropped into the pail of water, the assistant carries off the box, and behind the scenes damps and folds the borrowed handkerchiefs, pressing them flat with a hot iron, if available; if not, with a cold one. The tub or pan which is used for the conclusion of the trick has an inner lining of such a size as to fit tightly within it, but about an inch less in depth. The lid again fits within this after the manner of a saucepan lid, but not quite so tightly as the lining itself fits within the outer pan. The folded handkerchiefs are placed within this lining, and the lid placed on, or rather in it—the two together as brought forward having the appearance of a lid only. When the performer claps the lid on the pan, the lining is thereby introduced, but when he again removes it, the lining is left in, exposing the folded handkerchiefs, while the substitutes remain concealed between the true and false bottoms of the pan.

The performer, of necessity, accepts white handkerchiefs only, as a coloured one would betray the secret, from the absence of its "double" among the substitutes. Some performers, in order to obviate the suspicion which might be suggested by an evident preference of white handkerchiefs, arrange that a coloured one, of which they possess a duplicate, shall be offered by a confederate among the audience. This certainly heightens the effect of the trick, as it seems to negative the idea of substitution, and though in general we deprecate, as belonging to a low class of art, the employment of confederates, this is just the case in which the use of such an expedient may for once be deemed admissible.

The Egg and the Handkerchief.—For this capital feat, which is generally identified with the name of Colonel Stodare, the following are the requirements :—A glass goblet, two small handkerchiefs (generally of plain crimson silk, and about sixteen inches square), a larger silk handkerchief—to which is attached, by a silk thread of about four inches in length, a blown egg-shell—and a hollow metal egg made of zinc, enamelled white, with an oval opening on one side of it measuring about an inch and a half by one inch, or a little more.

The performer comes forward, having in his right hand the goblet and one of the red silk handkerchiefs. The larger silk handkerchief is thrown with apparent carelessness over the other hand, and upon it rests the blown egg, so placed that the thread may be out of sight, while beneath the egg, concealed in a fold of the handkerchief, lies the second red handkerchief, rolled up into as small a compass as possible. The metal egg is, meanwhile, placed in the left-hand secret pocket of the performer, who introduces the trick as follows : "I have here, ladies and gentlemen, a drinking-glass, a couple of silk handkerchiefs, and an egg, all, as you will perceive, of the most ordinary description." He passes quickly in front of the audience, as though tendering the articles for examination (taking care, however, to keep his right arm advanced towards the spectators, so that the glass and small silk handkerchief may bear the brunt of inspection), and finally places the glass and small handkerchief on a table or chair in full view. "Pray observe," he continues, "that not one of the articles is removed from your sight, even for one moment. Now, please follow me closely. I will place the egg in the glass, and cover it over with this handkerchief." This he does by one movement, for as the egg is already lying on the handkerchief, a mere turn of the wrist places the egg in the glass, and at the same time lets fall the handkerchief over it; and at the same time the smaller handkerchief, which was concealed in the larger, is released, and falls into the glass with the egg. "You have all seen me place the egg in the glass" (at the same time shaking the glass, to show by the sound that the egg is still there), "which I will not again touch. I shall now take this small handkerchief" (the one which has remained on the table), "and standing as far as possible away, I shall command the handkerchief to dissolve and pass into the glass, and the egg which is now in the glass to come into my hands." So saying, he holds up the handkerchief, in such manner as to show indirectly that he has nothing else in his hands. Taking a few steps, as though merely to get further from the glass, and holding the handkerchief hanging down between the finger and thumb of the right hand, he drops the other hand to his side, and secretly takes from his pocket the hollow egg, which he palms, keeping the opening outwards. He then, standing with his left side towards the spectators, joins his open hands, as in Fig. 114, the handkerchief hanging down between them. Requesting the audience to watch him narrowly, that they may be quite sure that there is no deception, he begins to wave his joined hands slowly up and down, the second and third fingers of the right hand (which, it will be remembered,

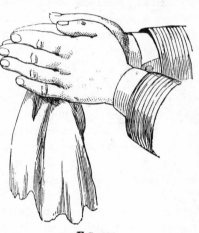

FIG. 114.

is away from the audience) meanwhile gradually working the handkerchief into the hollow of the egg. He every now and then pauses to show that the handkerchief is gradually diminishing, an l at last when it is wholly worked into the egg, opens his hands, and shows the egg lying in his palm, taking care, of course, that the opening is undermost. To all appearance, the handkerchief has changed into an egg. "Here is the egg," he remarks; "let us see if the handkerchief also has obeyed my bidding." So saying, he lays the egg, still with the opening downwards, upon the table, and taking hold with the finger and thumb of the handkerchief which covers the glass, lifts it daintily up, carrying with it, concealed in its folds, the egg-shell attached thereto, and leaving the duplicate red handkerchief lying in the glass.

It may sometimes, though not very often, occur that one or other of the spectators, suspecting some peculiarity about the egg, may ask to be permitted to examine it. This, of course, you cannot permit, while to refuse would destroy half the prestige of the illusion. Fortunately, there is a way out of the difficulty which absolutely enhances the effect of the trick. " You would like to see the egg," you reply ; "by all means. It is a special feature of my entertainment that all articles used therein will bear the strictest examination. Here is the egg. During these few words, you have taken up the sham egg with the fingers of your right hand, taking care, of course, to keep the opening away from the audience, and have thence apparently transferred it to your left, with which hand you offer it to the too curious spectator. It is hardly necessary to remark, that in the apparent transfer of the egg to the left hand, you have really palmed it in your right; and as you extend the left hand to the spectator, you quietly drop it from the right into the *pochette* on that side. The inquirer holds out his hand to receive it. " Pray examine it closely," you say, opening your empty hand over his own. " What ! you have not got it ? Ah, that is *your* fault; you were not quick enough. I always find that this experiment makes the egg excessively volatile." This unexpected *dénouement* never fails to raise a laugh against the individual who has sought to embarrass you, while the impromptu disappearance of the egg will be regarded by many as the most marvellous portion of the trick. The same expedient will be equally available to prevent the examination, at an awkward moment, of other small articles.

There is another method, in which the trick is performed with handkerchiefs borrowed from the audience. In this case, *two* metal eggs, like that above described, are used, the blown egg being dispensed with. The performer commences the trick by borrowing two handkerchiefs, a lady's handkerchief, and a larger one, preferably of silk. These he places on his table, secretly exchanging the smaller one for a substitute of his own, and retires for a moment to fetch a glass. He takes advantage of his momentary absence to insert the handkerchief of which he has gained possession into one of the hollow eggs, and returns with this egg lying (the opening downwards) on his left palm, the other hand holding the glass, while the second hollow egg is concealed in his left *pochette.* Coming forward to the audience, he picks up, in passing, the larger handkerchief from the table, and handing the glass, as forming the principal portion of the apparatus, for examination, throws the handkerchief over the hand which holds the egg, showing by its outline beneath the silk that it has not been removed, and meanwhile drawing out with the finger and thumb of the concealed hand the handkerchief hidden therein ; which is thus ready to be placed in the glass along with the egg, under cover of the larger handkerchief. The rest of the trick proceeds as already described, save that in this instance, the egg not being attached to the outer handkerchief, it is necessary to clip it with the fingers through the handkerchief when the latter is removed. To do this easily and effectually, it is well, in placing the egg in the glass, to place it with the opening upwards, the edges of the opening giving a readier hold than the unbroken surface of the opposite side.

THE HAND BOX, FOR VANISHING A HANDKERCHIEF.—While discussing the subject of handkerchief tricks, we must not omit to mention the " hand box," a clever little contrivance for causing the disappearance of a handkerchief. It consists of a little tin box, of the size and shape of the heel of a gentleman's boot, closed on all sides, save that which answers to the front portion of the heel, which is left open. (*See* Fig. 115.) To one of its sides is

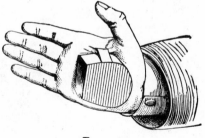

FIG. 115.

riveted or soldered a steel spring, about an inch in length. The free end of this spring forms with the side of the box a sort of clip, by means of which the box can be attached (as shown in the Figure) to the fleshy part of the hand, the opening being towards the fingers. Being within the hand, it is of course unseen by the audience. The manner of its use is much the same as that of the hollow egg described in the last trick, save that the hand box is never exhibited. As soon as the handkerchief is fairly worked in, the left hand is closed, as if containing it ; the effect being to the audience as if the handkerchief was merely rolled up and placed in the left hand. On opening the hand, the handkerchief is found to have disappeared, the performer having meanwhile plenty of opportunity to drop the concealed handkerchief, box and all, into the *pochette* on his right-hand side.

The hand box may be made available in a variety of ways, as follows: The performer having borrowed a handkerchief, secretly changes it for a substitute, which he leaves in full view on the table. Having made what disposition he pleases of the original, he returns, meanwhile placing the hand box in position, and causing by its means the disappearance of the substitute, orders the borrowed article to be found in such place as he may think proper.

CHAPTER XII.

TRICKS WITH DOMINOES AND DICE.

TO ARRANGE A ROW OF DOMINOES FACE DOWNWARDS ON THE TABLE, AND ON RETURNING TO THE ROOM TO TURN UP A DOMINO WHOSE POINTS SHALL INDICATE HOW MANY HAVE BEEN MOVED IN YOUR ABSENCE.—This is a capital drawing-room feat. You place a row of twenty dominoes face downwards upon the table, avoiding as far as possible the appearance of any special arrangement, but nevertheless taking care that the points of the first domino (commencing from the left) shall amount to twelve, the points of the second to eleven, and so on, each decreasing by one point till you reach the thirteenth, which will be the double-blank. The points of the remaining seven are a matter of indifference. You now propose to give the company a specimen of your powers of clairvoyance, and for that purpose leave the room, first requesting the company to remove during your absence any number of dominoes (not exceeding twelve) from the right to the left hand of the row, in other respects retaining their order. On your return you advance to the table, and address the company to the following effect: " Ladies and gentlemen, as I have already told you, I have the privilege of possessing the clairvoyant faculty, and I am about to give you a specimen of my powers. Now it would seem at first sight sufficiently surprising that I should be able merely to tell you the number of dominoes which have been moved in my absence, but that might be easily effected by confederacy, or many other very simple expedients. I propose to do much more than this, and to show you not only that I know the number that you have just displaced, but that I can read the dominoes before you as readily in their present position as though they were lying face upwards. For instance, this domino " (touching one of the row with your finger or wand) " represents the number which have been moved in my absence. Will some one please to say what that number was? " The answer is, we will suppose, " Seven." " Seven," you repeat, turning over the domino you have touched. " You see that I was right. Would you like me to name some more? They are all equally easy. This, let me see—yes, this is a two; this is a nine; this is a double-six; this is a double-blank;" turning over each domino to show that you have named it right.

This feat, which appears perfectly miraculous to the uninitiated, is performed by the simplest possible means. All that you have to do is to count secretly the row of dominoes as far as the thirteenth from the left-hand end, or (which is the same thing) the eighth from the right hand end, the points of which will invariably be the same as the number moved from the right to the left of the row. You do not know, until the domino is turned up, what that number actually was, but you must by no means let the audience suspect this. You must boldly assume to know the number, and from that knowledge, aided by some clairvoyant faculty, to have selected a domino whose points shall represent that number. Thus, having selected the proper domino, you call upon the audience to state the number moved, after which the turning up of the selected domino is regarded by the audience merely as a proof that you were correct in the previous knowledge for which they, without the smallest foundation, give you credit. After this domino has been turned up, it is easy, knowing the original order of the thirteen of which it forms one, to name two or three on either side of it. In most instances you will only know the total figure of a given domino, as two or three different combination of points will give the same total. (Thus a total of seven may be represented by either six and one, five and two, or four and three.) But there are two or three dominoes of which, if you know the total, you know the points also. Thus a total " twelve " must be always " double-six," a " blank " always " double-blank," a " one " always " blank one." By naming one or two of these, as if hap-hazard, you will prevent the audience suspecting, as they otherwise might, that your knowledge is limited to the *total* of each domino.

It is obvious that this is a trick which cannot be repeated, as the necessary rearrangement of the dominoes would at once attract attention. You may, however, volunteer to repeat it in a still more surprising form, really performing in its place the trick next following, one of the best, though also one of the simplest, in the whole range of the magic art.

To allow any Person in your absence to arrange the Dominoes in a Row, face downwards, and on your return to name blindfold, or without entering the Room, the end numbers of the Row.—You invite the audience to select any one of their number to arrange the whole of the dominoes face downwards upon the table. This he may do in any manner he pleases, the only restriction being that he is to arrange them after the fashion of the *game* of dominoes—viz., so that a six shall be coupled with a six, and a four with a four, and so on. While he does this, you leave the room, and, on being recalled, you at once pronounce, either blindfold, or (if the audience prefer it) without even entering the room, that the extreme end numbers of the row are six and five, five and two, etc., as the case may be.

This seeming marvel depends upon a very simple principle. It will be found by experiment that a complete set of dominoes, arranged in a row according to domino rules (*i.e.*, like numbers together), will invariably have the same number at each end. Thus if the final number at one end of the row be five, that at the opposite end will be five also, and so on; so that the twenty-eight dominoes, arranged as above, form numerically an endless chain, or circle. If this circle be broken by the removal of any domino, the numbers on either side of the gap thus made will be the same as those of the missing domino. Thus, if you take away a "five-three," the chain thus broken will terminate at one end with a five, and at the other with a three. This is the whole secret of the trick: the performer secretly abstracts one domino, say the "five-three;" this renders it a matter of certainty that the row to be formed with the remaining dominoes will terminate with a five at the one end and a three at the other, and so on with any other domino of two unequal numbers.

The domino abstracted must not be a "double," or the trick

will fail. A little consideration will show why this is the case. The removal of a double from the endless chain we have mentioned produces no break in the chain, as the numbers on each side of the gap, being alike, will coalesce; and a row formed with the remaining dominoes under such conditions may be made to terminate in any number, such number being, however, alike at either end. A domino of two different numbers, on the other hand, being removed, " forces," so to speak, the series made with the remainder to terminate with those particular numbers.

To Change, invisibly, the Numbers shown on either Face of a Pair of Dice.—Take a pair of ordinary dice, and so place them between the first finger and thumb of the right hand (*see* Fig. 116), that the uppermost shall show the " one," and the lowermost the " three " point, while the " one " point of the latter and the " three " point of the former are at right angles to those first named, and concealed by the ball of the thumb. (The enlargement at *a* in the figure shows clearly the proper position.) Ask some one to name

FIG. 116.

aloud the points which are in sight, and to state particularly, for the information of the company, which point is uppermost. This having been satisfactorily ascertained, you announce that you are able, by simply passing a finger over the faces of the dice, to make the points change places. So saying, gently rub the exposed faces of the dice with the forefinger of the left hand, and, on again removing the finger, the points are found to have changed places, the " three " being now uppermost, and the " one " undermost. This effect is produced by a slight movement of the thumb and finger of the right hand in the act of bringing the hands together, the thumb being moved slightly forward, and the finger slightly back. This causes the two dice to make a quarter-turn vertically on their own axis, bringing into view the side which has hitherto been concealed by the ball of the thumb, while the side previously in sight is in turn hidden by the middle finger. A reverse movement, of course, replaces the dice in their original position. The action of bringing the hands together, for the supposed purpose of rubbing the dice with the opposite fore-finger, completely covers the smaller movement of the thumb and finger.

After having exhibited the trick in this form once or twice, you may vary your mode of operation. For this purpose take the dice (still retaining their relative position) horizontally between the thumb and second finger, in the manner depicted in Fig. 117, showing "three-one" on their upper face; the corresponding "three-one," or rather "one-three," being now covered by the forefinger. As the points on the opposite faces of a die invariably to-gether amount to seven, it is obvious that the points on the under side will now be "four-six," while the points next to the ball of the thumb will be "six-four." You show, alternately raising and lowering the hand, that the

FIG. 117.

points above are "three-one," and those below "six-four." Again going through the motion of rubbing the dice with the opposite fore-finger, you slightly raise the thumb and depress the middle finger, which will bring the "six-four" uppermost, and the "three-one" or "one-three" undermost. This may be repeated any number of times; or you may, by moving the thumb and finger accordingly, produce either "three-one" or "six-four" apparently both above and below the dice.

The trick may, of course, be varied as regards the particular points, but the dice must, in any case, be so placed as to have similar points on two adjoining faces.

To Name, without seeing them, the Points of a Pair of Dice.—This is a mere arithmetical recreation, but it is so good that we cannot forbear to notice it. You ask the person who threw the dice to choose which of them he likes, multiply its points by two, add five to the product, multiply the sum so obtained by five, and add the points of the remaining die. On his telling you the result, you mentally subtract twenty-five from it, when the remainder will be a number of two figures, each representing the points of one of the dice.

Thus, suppose the throws to be five, two. Five multiplied by two are ten; add five, fifteen, which, multiplied by five, is seventy-five, to which two (the points of the remaining die) being added, the total is seventy-seven. If from this you mentally deduct twenty-five, the remainder is fifty-two, giving the points of the two dice—five and two. But, you will say, suppose the person who threw had reversed the arithmetical process, and had taken the points of the second die (two) as his multiplicand, the result must have been different. Let us try the experiment. Twice two are four, five added make nine, which, multiplied by five, is forty-five, and five (the points of the other die) being added to it, bring the total up to fifty. From this subtract twenty-five as before. The remainder, twenty-five, again gives the points of the two dice, but in the reverse order; and the same result will follow, whatever the throws may be.

CHAPTER XIII.

THE CUPS AND BALLS.

THE subject of the present chapter may be said to be the groundwork of all legerdemain, being, we believe, the very earliest form in which sleight-of-hand was exhibited. At the present day it is not very often seen, save in the bastard form known as "thimble-rig," and used as a means of fleecing the unwary upon race-courses and at country fairs. It is, however, well worthy the attention of the student of modern magic, not only as affording an excellent course of training in digital dexterity, but as being, in the hands of an adept, most striking in effect. It is by no means uncommon to find spectators who have received more elaborate feats with comparative indifference, become interested, and even enthusiastic, over a brilliant manipulation of the cups and balls.

The prestige of the illusion is heightened by the simplicity of the appliances used, consisting merely of three tin cups about three inches high, each in the form of a truncated cone, with a rim or shoulder round the base (*see* Fig. 118), the ordinary wand, four little cork balls, three-quarters of an inch or a little less in diameter, and blackened in the flame of a candle, three larger balls of about an inch and a quarter in diameter, and four more of such a size as to just fill the goblet. These last are generally stuffed with hair, and covered with cloth. The number of balls may vary according to the particular "passes" which the performer desires to exhibit, but the above will be found sufficient for most purposes. The performers of the olden time were accustomed to use the *gibecière*, or apron with pockets, already mentioned, and to perform at a table having no speciality, save that it was a little higher than those in ordinary use; but at the present day the *gibecière* is entirely discarded, the *servante* of the table answering the same purpose. The arrangement of the table and apparatus is shown in Fig. 118.

The whole art of cup-and-ball conjuring resolves itself into two elements—(1), the exhibition of a ball under a cup where a moment previously there was nothing; and (2) the disappearance of a ball from beneath a cup under which the audience have just seen it (or believe that they have seen it) placed. The routine is as follows:—

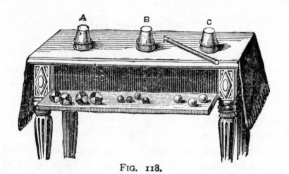

FIG. 118.

A cup is lifted, to show that there is nothing beneath it, and again replaced, mouth downwards, on the table. A ball is taken in the right hand, transferred to the left, and thence ordered to pass under the cup. The hand is opened, the ball has vanished, and, on the cup being lifted, is found beneath it. Again, the ball, first exhibited in the right hand, is thence openly transferred, either directly under the cup, or first to the left hand, and thence to the cup. All having seen it placed beneath the cup, it is now commanded to depart, and on again lifting the cup, it is found to have vanished. It will hardly be believed, until proved by experiment, of what numerous and surprising combinations these simple elements are capable.

The sleight-of-hand requisite for the cups and balls is technically divisible into four different acts or movements, viz.—1. To "palm" the ball. 2. To reproduce the palmed ball at the end of the fingers. 3. To secretly introduce the palmed ball under the cup. 4. To simulate the action of placing the ball under the cup. The modes of effecting these objects will be discussed in due order.

1. To Palm the Ball. *First Method.*—We use the generic term "palm" for the sake of convenience, though in this first method, which is that most generally used, the ball is really concealed between the second and third fingers, and not in the palm. Take the ball be tween the first finger and thumb of the right hand; slightly bend the fingers (*see* Fig. 119), and at the same moment roll the ball with the

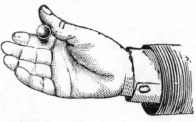

FIG. 119.

thumb across the first and second fingers, till it rests between the second and third fingers (*see* Fig. 120), which should slightly separate

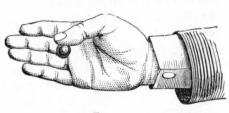

FIG. 120.

to receive it, again clos ing as soon as it is safely lodged. The ball will now be as shown in Fig. 121, and it will be found that the hand can be opened or closed with perfect freedom, and, indeed, be used in any manner, without being in the least hampered by its presence. The student should practise palming the ball in this manner both in the act of (apparently) trans ferring the ball to the left hand, and in that of (appa rently) placing it under a cup lifted by the left hand for that purpose.

Second Method.—The second method is to ac tually "palm" the ball, in the same manner as a coin.

FIG. 121.

For this purpose the ball is, as before, taken between the first finger and thumb of the right hand, but is thence made by the thumb to roll between the tips of the third and fourth fingers, which immediately close into the palm, and, again opening, leave the ball behind them. With a little practice, two balls in succession may be palmed in this way, and then a third by the first method.

FIG. 122.

Third Method.—The third method is that which was adopted by the celebrated Bosco, a most accomplished performer with the cup and balls. Being accustomed to use balls of a larger size than those above described, and therefore too bulky to palm by the first method, he used to hold them by means of a slight contraction of the little finger. (*See* Fig. 122.) The necessary movement of the fingers to place the ball in position is nearly the same as by the first method.

2. To Reproduce the Palmed Ball at the End of the Fingers.—The mode of doing this will vary according to the method by which the ball is palmed. If according to the first or third method, the ball is simply rolled back to the finger-tips with the ball of the thumb, exactly reversing the process by which it was palmed. But if the ball was palmed

FIG. 123.

by the second method, it is, for the time being, not get-at-able by the ball of the thumb. In this case the first step is to close the third and fourth fingers upon the ball (*see* Fig. 123), and therewith roll it to the position shown in Fig. 122, when the thumb is enabled to reach it, and to roll it to the finger-tips in the manner just described.

3. To Secretly Introduce the Palmed Ball under the Cup.—This is always done in the act of raising the cup (with the right hand), for the ostensible purpose of showing that there is nothing underneath it. The chief thing to be attended to is the position of the right hand (in which we are supposing a ball to be palmed by one or other of the methods above mentioned) in raising the cup. This should be done with the hand spread almost flat upon the table, and grasping the cup, as low down as possible, between the thumb and the lowest joint of the forefinger. In the act of raising the cup, the fingers naturally assume the position shown in Fig. 124,

whereby the ball is brought in close proximity to, and slightly under, the edge of the cup. If the ball be palmed by the first method, all that is necessary in order to release it is a slight back-ward movement of the se-cond, and a forward move-ment of the third finger, made just before the cup

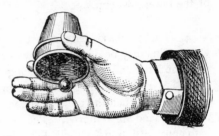

FIG. 124.

again touches the table. This will be found to drop the ball imm $\cdot$ diately under the cup. If the ball be palmed by the third method, its introduction under the cup is a still easier matter, as by the act of raising the cup it is brought directly underneath it, and is released by the mere act of straightening the third and fourth fingers. If the ball is palmed by the second method, it becomes necessary, before taking hold of the cup, to close the third and fourth fingers slightly (*see* Fig. 123), and bring the ball to the position shown in Fig. 122. From this point the operation is the same as if the ball had been originally palmed by the third method.

It is sometimes necessary to introduce a ball between two cups. It will be remembered that each cup is made with a cylindrical rim or shoulder. The purpose of this shoulder is that, when two cups are placed one upon the other (*see* Fig. 125), there may be a space between them sufficient to receive a ball or balls. To further facili-tate the introduction of the ball, the top of each cup is made, not flat, but concave.   When it is desired to introduce a ball between two cups, that object is effected as follows:—Having the ball ready palmed in the right hand, the performer takes up a cup in the same hand, and with it covers the second cup, at the same moment introducing the ball beneath it in the ordinary manner, but with the addition of a little upward jerk, rather difficult to describe, but easily acquired with a little practice.   The ball is thereby thrown to the top of the uppermost cup, and, in again falling, is received by the concave top of the lowermost cup.

FIG. 125.

4. To Simulate the Action of Placing a Ball under a Cup.—This may be done in two ways.   The first is to raise the cup with the left hand, apparently placing the ball underneath it with the right, but really palming it.   Care must be taken that the edge of the cup shall touch the table at the very moment that the fingers of the right hand are removed.   The second and more common method is to apparently transfer the ball to the left hand, palming it in the transit, and then bringing the closed left hand close to the cup on the table, raise the cup with the other hand, and immediately replace it with a sort of scraping movement across the fingers of the now opening left hand.

When the student has thoroughly mastered the various operations above described, he will have little to learn save the combination of the various Passes, a matter of memory only.   There are, however, one or two subordinate sleights with which he should make himself acquainted before proceeding publicly to exhibit his dexterity.

To Produce a Ball from the Wand.—The wand is supposed to be the reservoir whence the magician produces his store of balls, and into which they vanish when no longer needed.   The mode of production is as follows:—The performer, holding the wand in his left hand, and drawing attention to it by some remark as to its mysterious power of production and absorption, secretly takes with his right hand, from the *servante* or elsewhere, a ball, which he immediately palms (preferably by the first method).   Daintily holding the wand by either end with the left hand, in such manner as to show that the hand is otherwise empty, he slides the thumb and fingers of the right hand (the back of which is naturally towards the audience) lightly to the opposite end, at the same moment rolling the ball with the thumb to the ends of the fingers, as already described. (*See* Fig. 126.) The ball thus comes in sight just as the hand leaves the wand, the effect to the eyes of the spectators being that the ball is, by some mysterious process, squeezed out of the wand.

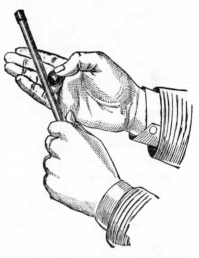

FIG. 126.

To Return a Ball into the Wand.—This is the converse of the process last described. Taking the wand in the left hand, as before, and the ball between the thumb and second joint of the forefinger of the opposite hand, the performer lays the end of the wand across the tips of the fingers, and draws the hand gently downwards along it, at the same time palming the ball by the first method.

To Pass one Cup through another.—This is an effective sleight, and by no means difficult of acquirement. Taking one of the cups, mouth upwards, in the left hand, and holding another in a similar position in the right hand, about a foot above it, the performer drops the right hand cup smartly into that in the left hand (which latter should be held very lightly). If this is neatly done, the lower cup will be knocked out of the hand by the concussion, while the upper one will be caught and held in its place; the effect to the eye of the spectator being as if the upper cup had passed through the other. The lower cup may either be allowed to fall on the ground or table, or may be caught by the right hand in its fall.

The successive appearances and disappearances of the balls under-neath the cups are known by the name of "Passes;" the particular combination of such passes being governed by the taste and invention of the performer. The series most generally in use is derived from a work dating from the last century, the *Récréations Mathématiques et Physiques* of Guyot; and Guyot, we believe, borrowed it from a German source. The series given below, which will be found very effective, is derived mainly from that of Guyot, as improved by Ponsin, a later and very ingenious writer on the art of presti-digitation.

The cups and balls require, even more than conjuring generally, a running accompaniment of *talk*. Each Pass should have its own "*boniment*," or "patter," carefully prepared and frequently rehearsed. It would be impossible to give, within any reasonable limits, appro-priate patter for each of the Passes. This each performer must arrange for himself, so as to suit the style and character in which he performs; as it is obvious that the low comedy style of a mounte-bank at a country fair would be utterly unsuitable in an aristocratic drawing-room, and *vice versâ*. We shall, however, give a specimen or two in the course of the various Passes. The burlesque introduc-tion next following is a paraphrase of a similar address quoted by Robert-Houdin :—

Introductory Address.—"Ladies and Gentlemen,—In an age so enlightened as our own, it is really surprising to see how many popular fallacies spring up from day to day, and are accepted by the public mind as unchangeable laws of nature.

"Among these fallacies there is one which I propose at once to point out to you, and which I flatter myself I shall very easily dispose of. Many people have asserted, and, among others, the celebrated Erasmus of Rotterdam, that a material object can only be in one place at one time. Now I maintain, on the contrary, that any object may be in several places at the same moment, and that it is equally possible that it may be nowhere at all.

"I must beg you to observe, in the first place, that I have nothing in my hands—except my fingers; and that between my fingers there is nothing save a few atoms of the mysterious fluid which we call the atmosphere, and through which our jolly old Earth spins so merrily along. But we must leave the common-place regions of astronomy, and return to the mysteries of hermetic science.

" I have before me, as you will have noticed, three little cups or goblets. The metal of which these are composed is an amalgam of costly minerals, unknown even to the most profound philosophers. This mysterious composition, which resembles silver in its solidity, its colour, and the clearness of its ring, has over silver this great advantage, that it will at pleasure become impalpable as air, so that solid bodies pass through these goblets as easily as they would through empty space. I will give you a curious illustration of this by making one goblet pass through another." (This the performer does in the manner already described, and after a moment's pause, continues, taking up his wand in his left hand, and secretly palming a ball in his right.) "This little wand, you are possibly aware, ladies and gentlemen, goes by the name of Jacob's Rod. Why it is so called I really don't know; I only know that this simple-looking wand has the faculty of producing various articles at pleasure. For instance, I require for the purpose of my experiment a little ball. My wand at once supplies me." (He produces a ball from the wand, and lays it on the table.)

With this or some similar introduction, the performer proceeds to exhibit

PASS I. HAVING PLACED A BALL UNDER EACH CUP, TO DRAW IT OUT AGAIN WITHOUT LIFTING THE CUP.—Having produced a ball from the wand as last described, and having laid it on the table, the operator continues,—" Allow me to show you once more that all the cups are empty " (he raises them one by one, and replaces them), " and that I have nothing in either of my hands. I take this little ball " (he picks it up with the right hand, and apparently transfers it to the left, really palming it in the right), " and place it under one of the cups." Here he raises the cup with the right hand, and simulates the action of placing the ball under it with the left. "I draw another ball from my wand " (this is really the same ball, which remained palmed in the right hand), " and place it in like manner under the second cup." He goes through the motion of transferring it to the left hand and thence to the cup, as before, but this time actually does what on the former occasion he only pretended to do, and leaves the ball under the middle cup. " I produce another ball " —(he half draws the wand through his fingers, but checks himself half-way). "I think I heard some one assert that I have a ball already in my hand. Pray satisfy yourselves " (showing the palms of his hands, the fingers carelessly apart) "that such is not the case. A lady suggested just now, by the way—it was only said in a whisper, but I heard it—that I didn't really put the balls under the cup. It was rather sharp on the part of the lady, but you see she was wrong. Here are the balls." * So saying, the performer lifts up the middle cup with his left hand, and picking up the ball with his right, holds it up that all may see, immediately replacing it under the same cup. The last movement is simulated only, the ball being in reality palmed in the supposed act of placing it under the cup. " We have now a ball under each of these two cups. We only want one more, and— here it is "—apparently producing a third ball (really the same again) from the wand. "We will place it under this last cup." He actually does so. "Now, ladies and gentlemen, we have three cups and three balls, one under each cup. So far, I admit that I have not shown you anything very surprising, but now comes the puzzle, to take the balls from under the cups. Perhaps some of you sharp gentlemen will say there isn't much difficulty in that. Lift the cup, and pick up the ball ! " He suits the action to the word, lifting up the third goblet with the left hand, and picking up the ball with the right. " A very good solution, but it doesn't happen to be the right one. The problem is to draw out the balls without lifting the cups." Here he replaces the cup, apparently placing the ball beneath it, but really palming it, as already described in the case of the middle cup, and then returns to the first or furthest cup ; touching the top of the

---

* The reader will understand that nobody has in fact made any such observation, but the overhearing of an imaginary objection is often of great use, as enabling the performer to do some necessary act, which he could not well have done without such pretext. Thus in this instance, the performer wants a plausible excuse—first, for altering his apparent intention of immediately producing a second ball from the wand ; and, secondly, for lifting the middle cup, and so regaining possession of the ball. A conjuror thus addressing an imaginary objector is said in French "*parler à la can- tonade,*" but the phrase has no precise equivalent among English performers.

goblet, he lets the palmed ball drop to his finger tips, and immediately exhibits it, saying—" This is the way *I* take the balls out of the cups. The ball being no longer needed, I return it into the wand." This he does as described at page 277, immediately afterwards, if desired, handing the wand for examination. " In like manner I draw out the second ball " (he repeats the same process with the middle goblet), "and pass that also into my wand. I need not even handle the goblets. See, I merely touch this third goblet with my wand, and the ball instantly appears on the top." The company, of course, cannot see any ball on the end of the wand, but a ball is nevertheless taken thence by the process already described, of letting the palmed ball drop to the tips of the fingers, as they come in contact with the wand. " I pass this also into my wand. Stay, though, on second thoughts, I shall want a ball for my next experiment, so I will leave it here on the table."

We have given a somewhat elaborate description of this first Pass, in order to give the reader some idea of the various feints and artifices employed in relation to the cups and balls. It would be impossible, from considerations of space, to do this as to each of the Passes, and the reader must therefore remember that the descriptions following give merely the essential outlines, which must be worked up to dramatic effectiveness by the ingenuity of the individual performer. Where practicable, we shall allow the few words put into the mouth of the performer to indicate the actions accompanying them, only giving special " stage directions " in cases where the performer does *not* suit the action to the words. For the sake of distinctness, we shall indicate the goblets (reckoning from the left hand of the performer) as A, B, and C. (*See* Fig. 118.)

Pass II. To make a Ball Travel invisibly from Cup to Cup.—" Now, ladies and gentlemen, if you watch very closely, you will be able to see the ball travel from one cup to another. I take the ball " (transfers it apparently to left hand) " and place it under this cup (C). You all see that there is nothing under this one " (B). In raising B with the right hand he introduces under it the palmed ball. " I shall now command the ball which I have just placed under the first cup (C) to travel under this one (B). Attention !

and you will see it pass." He makes a motion of the wand from the one cup to the other. "There it goes! This cup (C), as you see, is empty, and under this one (B) is the ball. I will replace it under this same cup" (B). He in reality palms it. "There is nothing under this cup" (A). He secretly introduces the ball under A. "Now observe again. Pass! Did you see it? No? well, I don't much wonder at it, for I can't always see it myself. Here it is, however" (lifts A), "and this cup (B) is empty." He replaces the cups on the table, and lays the ball beside them.

Pass III. Having placed a Ball under each of the end Cups, to make them pass successively under the Middle Cup.—Before commencing this Pass, the performer, while placing the goblets in line, or otherwise engaging the attention of the audience with his left hand, takes from the *servante* with his right, and palms, a second ball. He continues, "For my next experiment, ladies and gentlemen, I shall require two balls. I need hardly remark that I could instantly supply myself from the wand; but there is a curious faculty about the balls themselves; they have a constant tendency to increase and multiply. For instance, without having recourse to the wand, I can instantly make this one ball into two" (he takes up the ball on the table in his left hand, taking care so to hold it that all may see that there is nothing else in his hand), "and the most curious part of the matter is, that though mathematicians insist that the whole is always greater than its part, in this case each of the parts will be found precisely equal to the whole." As he speaks, he takes the ball from the left hand with the fingers of the right, at the same time dropping the palmed ball into the left hand, and now taking care to so hold his *right* hand as to show that it contains the one ball only. He then again replaces this ball in the palm of the left hand, where it lies side by side with the second ball. Rubbing the left palm with the second and third fingers of the right, with a circular motion, he gradually lifts the fingers, and shows the single ball apparently transformed into two, both of which he places on the table.

"You will observe that there is nothing under this cup (C). I will place under it this ball ' (he really palms it) ; "neither is there anything under either of these two cups " (B and A). He lifts the cups one with each hand, and secretly introduces the palmed ball under B. " I take this second ball, and place it under this cup " (A). He really palms it. " We now have a ball under each of these two cups " (A and C). " I draw the ball out of this one " (C). He touches the top of the cup, and produces the ball last palmed at his finger-tips. " I order it to pass under this middle cup " (B). He apparently transfers it to the left hand, really palming it, and then makes a motion with the left hand, as if passing it into B. " It has passed, you see ! " He raises B with his right hand, showing the ball under it, and in replacing it secretly introduces the second palmed ball. " Now I order the ball in this cup (A) to pass in like manner." He waves his wand from A to B, and then lifts B. " Here it is, and these two outer cups " (turning them over with the wand) " are per-fectly empty."

PASS IV. HAVING PLACED TWO BALLS UNDER THE MIDDLE CUP, TO MAKE THEM PASS UNDER THE TWO OUTER ONES.—" You have just seen these two balls pass under the middle cup ; now, by way of variety, we will make them pass out of it. I will take the two balls, and place them under the middle cup." He really so places one only, palming the other. " You observe that there is nothing either under this (A), nor under this (C)." Here he secretly introduces the palmed ball beneath C. " Now I order one of the balls under the middle cup to pass under one of the outer cups. Let us see if it has done so " (lifts middle cup with left hand). " Yes, here is only one left." He takes it up and shows it with right hand, then makes the gesture of replacing, but really palms it. " Let us see where it has gone to " (lifts A with right hand, and in replacing it secretly intro-duces the palmed ball under it). " It is not under this one. Then it must be under this." He lifts C. " Yes, here it is. Now I com-mand the other ball in like manner to leave the middle cup, and pass under the other (A). Pass ! Here it is, you see, and this one (B) is entirely empty."

PASS V. TO PASS THREE BALLS IN SUCCESSION UNDER ONE CUP.—" So far, ladies and gentlemen, what I have shown you has been mere child's play." He drops the right hand carelessly to the *servante,* and picks up two more balls, one of which he holds between the fingers, and the other in the palm. "The real difficulty only begins when we begin to work with three balls. Now which of these two balls" (taking up the two balls from the table) "is the largest? This one, I fancy, has the advantage, so I will pinch a little piece off to make a third ball." He goes through the motion of pinching the ball with the fingers of both hands, at the same moment letting fall the ball in the palm to the tips of the fingers of the right hand. "Yes, this will do. It isn't quite round, but that is easily rectified." He rolls it between the fingers. "That is better. Now watch me closely, ladies and gentlemen." He places the balls upon the table, with the exception of the fourth, which remains concealed between the fingers. "You see that there is nothing under either of the cups." He raises all three, and introduces the fourth ball under the middle one (B). He then picks up one of the balls on the table, and apparently transfers it to his left hand, really palming it. "I command this ball to pass into the middle cup. It has passed, you see" (raising the cup with the right hand, and in replacing it, introducing the ball now palmed). The operation is repeated in like manner, until three balls have been shown under the cup, the fourth finally remaining palmed in the right hand.

PASS VI. TO PLACE THREE BALLS ONE AFTER THE OTHER UPON THE TOP OF ONE OF THE CUPS, AND TO MAKE THEM FALL THROUGH THE CUP ON TO THE TABLE.—At the conclusion of the last Pass the performer had brought three balls under the centre cup B, a fourth remaining concealed in his hand. In lifting B to exhibit the three balls, and in replacing it beside them, he takes the opportunity of introducing beneath it this fourth ball. He next takes one of the three balls thus exposed, and placing it on the top of this same goblet (B), covering it with a second goblet (A). Making any appropriate gesture he pleases, he commands the ball to fall through the lower goblet on to the table. He then overturns (without separating) the two goblets, their mouths being towards the spectators, when the ball which he had secretly introduced will be discovered, and will appear to be that which the spectators have just seen placed on the top of the goblet (and which really still remains between the two goblets), and picks up the two goblets together, mouth upwards, with the left hand, and with the right hand takes out that which is now uppermost (B). He turns both the goblets down upon the table, placing A over the ball which he has just shown. If this is neatly done, the other ball, which has remained in A, will not be discovered, but will as it falls be covered by A, which will now have beneath it two balls. The performer now places one of the remaining balls on the top of A, covering it with either of the other goblets, and again goes through the same process till he has shown first two, and then three balls under the cup, the fourth remaining, at the close of the Pass, between the two cups last used.

PASS VII. TO PASS THREE BALLS IN SUCCESSION UPWARDS THROUGH THE TABLE INTO ONE OF THE CUPS.—You concluded the last Pass (we will suppose the reader to represent for the time being the performer) by lifting two cups together to show three balls beneath the undermost. Holding two cups in the left hand, you turn them over, mouth upwards. Taking with the right hand that which is now uppermost, you place it on the table in the ordinary position, still retaining the other, in which, unknown to the spectators, a fourth ball still remains. You continue, "Ladies and gentlemen, you may possibly imagine that there is some trick or sleight-of-hand in what I have shown you, but I am now about to perform an experiment in which that solution is clearly inadmissible. I propose to pass these three balls, one after the other, through the solid table into this empty goblet. Pray watch me carefully. I take away one of the balls " (you take in the right hand one of the three on the table), "and hold it beneath the table, thus. My left hand, as you will observe, is perfectly empty. I have only to say, ' Pass ! ' " (You palm the ball in the right hand, at the same time giving a gentle tap with one finger against the under surface of the table, and immediately bring up the hand, taking care, of course, to keep its outer side towards the spectators ; then gently shake the cup which you hold in the left hand, and turn the ball out upon the table.) "Here it is, you see. Now I will put it back in the cup" (you pick up the ball with the right hand, and drop it into the cup, secretly letting fall with it the palmed ball),

" and take another ball." You repeat the process, and show two balls in the cup ; then again (each time dropping in the palmed ball), and show three, retaining the fourth ball, still palmed, in your right hand.

PASS VIII. TO PASS TWO BALLS IN SUCCESSION FROM ONE CUP TO ANOTHER WITHOUT TOUCHING THEM.—You again place the three cups in a row on the table, secretly introducing under the right hand cup (C) the ball which remained in your right hand at the close of the last Pass, and then openly place the three other balls on the tops of the three cups. You then proceed, " I will take this ball " (that which is on B), " and place it under this same cup " (B). You really palm it. " I take this other ball " (that which is upon A), " and place it under this cup " (A). You secretly introduce with it the ball which you have just palmed. " I take this last " (that upon C), " and place it under this goblet (A) ; or, stay, I will pass it invisibly to this one " (C)—really palming it. " It has passed, you see." You lift C, and show the ball which is already there ; and in again covering the ball with the cup, you secretly introduce that which you last palmed. You now have in reality two balls under each of the end cups, and none under the centre one ; but the spectators are persuaded that there is one ball under each cup. " We now have one ball under each cup. Now I shall command the ball that is under the centre cup to pass into either of the end ones at your pleasure. Which shall it be ? " Whichever is chosen, suppose C, you raise and show the two balls under it. You then ostensibly replace the two balls under C, but really replace the one only, palming the other. You then raise the middle cup (B), to show that it is empty, and, in replacing it, introduce the ball you have just palmed under it. " Now I shall next order one of the two balls you have just seen under this cup (C) to go and join the one which is already under this other (A). Pass ! Here it is, you observe." You raise A to show that there are two balls under it. You also raise C to show that it now only contains one ball, and leave all three balls exposed on the table.

PASS IX. TO MAKE THREE BALLS IN SUCCESSION PASS UNDER THE MIDDLE CUP.—At the conclusion of the last Pass, three balls were left in view, while a fourth, unknown to the audience, was hidden under the middle cup. You proceed, picking up a ball with the right hand, " I take this ball, and place it under this cup " (C) ; (in reality palming it). " I now order it to pass under the middle cup. Presto ! Here it is, you see." You raise the middle cup to show that the ball has obeyed your command, and, in again covering the ball, secretly introduce with it that which you have just palmed. " I take this one " (you pick up another), " and place it under this cup " (A)—here you palm it as before—" and order it also to pass under the middle cup." You raise the middle cup, and show that there are now two balls under it, and, in again covering them, introduce the ball which you last palmed. " I take this last ball, and place it under this cup " (C)—palming it—" whence I shall command it to again depart, and join its companions under the middle cup. This time it shall make the journey visibly." You take your wand in the left hand, and with it touch the cup C. " Here it is, you see, on the end of my wand. You don't see it ? Why, surely it is visible enough. Look." You pretend to produce the palmed ball from the wand, and exhibit it to the company. " You can all see it *now*." You lay down the wand, and go through the motion of transferring the ball to the left hand, really palming it in its passage. " Now, then, pray watch me closely, and you will see it pass under the cup. One, two, three !" You make the gesture of throwing it through the middle cup, and open the hand to show it empty, immediately turning over the goblets to show that there are three balls under the middle and none under the outer ones.

Pass X. The "Multiplication" Pass.—For the purpose of this Pass it is necessary to borrow a hat, which you hold in the left hand. You then place the three balls in a row upon the table, and cover each with one of the cups. It will be remembered that a fourth ball remains palmed in your right hand. You now lift up the right hand goblet (C), and place it on the table close beside the ball which it lately covered, and as you do so, secretly introduce beneath it the palmed ball. You pick up with the right hand the ball which you have thus uncovered, and go through the motion of dropping it into the hat, really palming it in the moment during which the hand is concealed inside the hat, and at the same moment simulating, by gentle tap against the inside, the sound which the ball would make if actually dropped into the hat. You next lift B in like manner, introducing the ball just palmed beneath it, and go through the motion of placing the second ball, which is thereby left exposed, in the hat. You do the same with the third cup, then return to the first (which the spectators believe to be now empty, and from which they are astonished to see you produce another ball), continuing till you have raised each cup in succession eight or ten times, and, on each occasion of lifting a cup to uncover a ball, introducing beneath it the ball which you had just previously palmed. To the eyes of the spectators, who believe that the balls are really dropped into the hat, the effect will be exactly as if new balls, by some mysterious process of reproduction, came under the cups at each time of raising them. When you think your audience are sufficiently astonished, you remark, " I think we have about enough now ; the hat is getting rather heavy. Will some one hold a handkerchief to receive the balls ? " When the handkerchief is spread out, you carefully turn over the hat, and the general astonishment will be intensified at discovering that it contains nothing.

There is, of course, a ball left under each of the cups, and a fourth palmed in your right hand. This latter will not again be wanted, and you should therefore, while attention is drawn to the hat, drop it upon the *servante*, or into one of your *pochettes*.

PASS XI. TO TRANSFORM THE SMALL BALLS TO LARGER ONES.—While the attention of the spectators is still occupied by the unexpected *dénouement* of the last Pass, you should prepare for this one by secretly taking with your right hand from the *servante*, and palming (by either the second or third method, the first being only available for the small balls) one of the larger balls. You then address the spectators to the following effect :—" Ladies and gentlemen, you see that I have little difficulty in increasing the number of the balls to an unlimited extent. I will now repeat the experiment in another form, and show you that it is equally easy to make them increase in size. You will observe that, notwithstanding the number of balls which I have just produced from the cups, there are still plenty more to come." Here you raise C, and show that there is a ball still under it. You replace it on the table at a few inches' dis-tance, and as you do so, secretly introduce under it the larger ball which you have just palmed. Taking up the small ball in your right hand, you say, " To make the experiment still more surprising, I will pass the ball upwards through the table into the cup." So saying, you place the right hand under the table, dropping as you do so the little ball which you hold on the *servante,* and taking in its place another of the larger balls. " Pass ! " you exclaim, at the same time giving a gentle rap on the under surface of the table. You bring the hand up again as if empty. You do not touch the first cup, but repeat the operation with the second, B, and again with A ; on each occasion of passing the hand under the table exchanging a small ball for a larger one, and immediately afterwards introducing the latter under the cup next in order. The last time, however, you merely drop the small ball on the *servante,* without bringing up any other in exchange. You now have, unknown to the audience, one of the larger, or medium-sized balls under each of the cups ; and if you were about to end with this Pass, you would merely lift the cups and show the balls, thus apparently increased in size, underneath. We will assume, however, that you propose to exhibit the Pass next following (one of the most effective), in which case the necessary preparation must be made in the act of raising the cups ; and we shall therefore proceed at once, while the balls still remain covered, to describe

PASS XII. TO AGAIN TRANSFORM THE BALLS TO STILL LARGER ONES.—The last Pass having reached the stage we have just described, *i.e.,* a large ball being under each cup, but not yet ex-hibited to the audience, you secretly take in your *left* hand from the *servante* one of the still larger balls. These balls should be soft and elastic, and of such a size that, if pressed lightly into the cup, they shall require a slight tap of the cup on the table to dislodge them.

Having taken the ball in the left hand, you hold it at the ends of the fingers behind the table, as near the top as possible consistently with its being out of sight of the spectators. Then saying, " Now, ladies and gentlemen, I must ask for your very closest attention," you raise C with the right hand, and with the same movement lower it for a moment behind the table, and over the ball in the left hand, which remains in the cup of its own accord.   All eyes go instinc‑ tively to the ball on the table, whose increased size is a new phenomenon, and not one in a hundred will, in this first moment of surprise, think of watching the cup, which is naturally supposed to have, for the moment, concluded its share of the trick.   You re‑ place the cup on the table lightly, so as not to loosen the ball, mean‑ while getting ready another ball in the left hand, and repeat the operation with B.   With A you make a slight variation in your mode of procedure.   Taking a third ball in your left hand, you hold it as before, but, as if through carelessness or clumsiness, allow it to be seen for a moment above the edge of the table.   When you raise the third cup, you move it behind the table as before, and make a feint of introducing the ball which the spectators have just seen, but really let it drop on the *servante,* and replace the cup empty.   A murmur from the audience will quickly apprise you that they have, as they imagine, found you out.   Looking as innocent as you can, you inquire what is the matter, and are informed that you were seen to introduce a ball into the cup.   "I beg your pardon," you reply, lifting up, however, not A, which you have just replaced, but C, which is the farthest remote from it.   There is really a ball in this cup, but having been pressed in, and fitting tightly, it does not fall. The audience, seeing you raise the wrong cup, are more and more confirmed in their suspicion.   "Not that one, the other," they ex‑ claim.   You next raise B, the ball in which also does not fall, for the reason already stated.   "No, no," the audience shout, "the other cup, the end one."   "You are really very obstinate, gentlemen," you reply, "but pray satisfy yourselves," turning over A as you speak, and showing the inside, which is manifestly empty, and your critics rapidly subside.   Meanwhile, you drop your left hand to the *ser‑ vante,* and secretly take from it *two* similar balls.   Then, addressing the audience, you say, "Surely, gentlemen, you don't imagine that, if I wanted to place a ball under a cup, I should set about it after such a clumsy fashion as this!"   As you say this, you place your left hand in your left pocket, as if taking a ball from thence (as it obviously would not do to give the audience cause to suspect the existence of a secret receptacle behind the table), and bring out again the two balls, but allow one only to be seen, keeping the other concealed in the palm. Bringing the cup over the hand, you squeeze in *both* balls as far as you can, when the innermost will remain, but the outermost not having sufficient space, will drop out again on the table. The audience, not knowing that there are *two* balls, believe the cup, which you now replace on the table, to be empty. You continue, " No, gentlemen ; when I pass a ball under a cup, you may be sure that I don't let anybody see me do so." As you speak, you take the ball on the table in your right hand, and make the movement of transferring it to your left, really palming it by the second method, and holding the left hand closed and high, as if containing it, and keeping your eyes fixed thereon, you carelessly drop your right hand till the finger-tips rest on the table, when you are able to let fall the ball upon the *servante.* You continue, " I will now pass this ball under either of the cups which you like to name. Indeed, I will do more ; I will cause this ball invisibly to multiply itself into three, one of which shall pass under each of the cups. First, however, let me show you that there is nothing under the cups at present." You raise each in turn— " Nothing here, nothing here, and nothing here! " The balls still adhere to the sides of the cups, which, therefore, appear to be empty, but you replace each with a slight rap on the table, and thereby loosen the ball within it. " Now, then ! " You bring the two hands together, and gently rub them over each cup in turn ; finally parting them and showing that both are empty, and then lifting the cups, show the three large balls underneath.

Some performers, in lifting each cup with the right hand, introduce a fresh ball, held in the left hand, as already explained. The effect is the same as in the " Multiplication " Pass, already described, with this difference, that on each occasion of uncovering a ball, the ball remains on the table, which thus becomes gradually covered with an ever-increasing number of balls. Some, again, conclude by apparently producing from the cups objects much larger than they could naturally contain, *e.g.*, large apples, Spanish onions, etc. This is effected in the same manner as the introduction of the large balls just described, save that in this case the object, which cannot really go into the cup, is merely held against its mouth with the third finger of the right hand, and dropped with a slight shake, as if there was a difficulty in getting it out.

There are many other cup-and-ball Passes, but the series above given will be found as effective as any. If any reader desires to follow the subject further, we would refer him to the *Récréations Mathématiques et Physiques* of Guyot, already quoted, or another old work, under the same title, by Ozanam, in which this branch of prestidigitation is treated at considerable length.

CHAPTER XIV.

BALL TRICKS REQUIRING SPECIAL APPARATUS.

BEFORE proceeding to the description of the tricks which form the subject of this Chapter, it may be well to mention one or two principles of sleight-of-hand, not yet noticed, which have a special application to ball tricks, and are also useful with regard to oranges, apples, eggs, etc. The Pass called the *tourniquet,* or " French drop," described already in relation to coin, will be found equally applicable to balls up to a couple of inches in diameter, but is not available for objects of larger size. Balls of larger diameter are best palmed by one or other of the methods following.

First Method.—Taking the ball in either hand, the performer tosses the ball from palm to palm (at a few inches' distance) four or five times, finally making the motion of tossing it from the right hand to the left, but really retaining it in the right by a slight contraction of the palm, and at the same time closing and elevating the left hand, and following it with the eyes, as though it contained the ball. It is obvious that a ball of the size now under consideration (say of two to three inches in diameter) would not admit of the hand containing it being perfectly closed ; and this must be borne in mind in the position of the left hand, the fingers of which must not be tightly closed, as they would if apparently containing a coin or other very small article, but merely curved inward, the palm, of course, being turned toward the performer's own body, so as not to disclose the secret of its emptiness. Where the hand of the performer is small, or the ball is of such a size as not to be readily retained in the right hand by the contraction of the palm, the thumb may be used to assist in supporting it.

Second Method.—Taking the ball between his open hands, the performer rolls it round and round between his palms, as though it were a lump of clay which he was moulding into a spherical form; and in so doing gradually turns his hands till the back of his right hand is undermost, when, with an inward movement of that hand towards himself, he palms the ball therein, at the same time closing and elevating the left hand, as described for the last method.

To Vanish a Large Ball with the aid of the Table.—*First Method.* Standing behind his table, the ball being some six or eight inches from its hinder edge, the performer places both hands round it, apparently picking it up and bringing it forward between his two hands, from which, however, the ball is, on examination, found to have vanished. Its disappearance is effected as follows :— At the moment when the performer encircles the ball with his hands, he gives, with the little finger of the hand which is inner-most—and therefore unseen by the audience—a quick jerk to the ball, which is thereby made to roll towards the hinder edge of the table, and drop upon the *servante*, on which there should be a padded box or basket to receive it. The action is wholly concealed from the spectators by the hands, which, with the exception of the finger which does the work, should remain motionless.

Second Method.—Standing behind his table, as in the last case, the performer tosses up the ball, and catches it again three or four times, keeping the hands low, so as to be near the edge of the table. The hands naturally sink in the act of catching the ball; and after having caught it once or twice, the performer, as he lowers them, drops it on the *servante*, immediately raising them again with the action of throwing up the ball, taking care to follow it with the eyes in its imaginary flight. If this is done neatly, the eyes of the spectators will instinctively travel in the same direction, and the effect to them will be as if the ball vanished at the highest point of its upward flight, instead of disappearing, as it really does, at the moment of reaching the hands in its fall. This method may also be employed for objects other than of spherical shape.

Third Method.—The performer, standing behind his table as before, and placing the ball thereon, covers it with the right hand,

and rolls it round and round in circles, each time bringing it nearer and nearer to the hinder edge of the table, till it finally rolls over, and drops upon the *servante*. He continues the motion of the hand for two or three turns, as though the ball was still under it, gradually working back towards the centre of the table, the effect to the spectator being as if the ball melted away under the operator's fingers.

Fourth Method.—This is generally employed to apparently pass one object into another—say a small ball into a large one. The performer, standing a little behind his table, with his right side slightly turned to the spectators, takes in his right hand the small ball, and in his left the large one. The latter he holds about shoulder high, keeping his eyes fixed upon it, and remarking, " I shall now pass this small ball into this large one," he draws back and lowers the right arm, as though to give it impetus, as one naturally does in the act of throwing. This brings the right hand just over the padded box or basket on the *servante,* and allows him to drop the small ball therein. Without any pause, he brings the right hand smartly up to the left, describing a tolerably wide arc in its transit, and then, separating his hands, shows that the smaller ball has vanished, having apparently passed into the large one. This sleight is not confined to objects of spherical form, but may be used with any article of convenient size.

With this introduction, we shall now proceed to describe a few of the most popular " ball tricks."

THE BALL BOX.—The leading idea of most of the tricks which we are about to describe is the magical appearance or disappearance of a ball. So far, they resemble the cup-and-ball tricks described in the last Chapter, but with this difference, that, in the case of the present series, the main effect is produced by mechanical means, any sleight-of-hand employed being rather an accessory than the leading feature. The oldest and simplest of the mechanical appliances for this purpose is that known as the " ball-box," consisting of a box two to six inches in height, of the shape shown in Fig. 127, and containing a ball which just fills it. The box consists of three portions—the lower portion, or box proper *a,* the lid *c,* and an intermediate portion *b*, being a hollow hemisphere coloured externally in imitation of the ball, and so fitted with reference to the box and lid, that it may be either lifted off with the lid, leaving the box apparently empty, or may be left upon the box when the lid is removed, the effect to the eye being as if the ball had returned to the box. The ball-box is generally of turned boxwood, and is scored with concentric circles, which serve to disguise its double opening. Simply stated, its effect is as follows:—The solid ball is first shown in the

box, and then openly taken from it, and the box covered with the lid. The ball is then got rid of in one or other of the modes before described, and a pretence is made of passing it invisibly into the box. The lid is removed without the intermediate portion *b*, and the ball appears to have returned to the box. Again the lid is replaced, and again removed; but this time *b* is removed with it, and the box again appears empty. The trick in this form is to be found in every toy-shop, and is so well known as to produce scarcely any illusion, but its transparency

FIG. 127.

may be considerably diminished by previously palming (in the right hand) the moveable shell *b*, the convex side being inwards, and then handing round the remaining portions and the solid ball for inspection. When they are returned, the performer apparently places the ball in the box, but really makes a secret exchange, and places *b* in the box instead. Upon again removing the lid, and with it *b*, the ball has disappeared; and as the audience have, as they believe, inspected the whole apparatus, the mode of its disappearance is not quite so obvious as in the first case. At best, however, the ball-box, in this its pristine form, is a clumsy and inartistic contrivance, and has long been relegated to the juvenile and country-fair school of conjuring. There is, however, an improved apparatus for producing a similar effect, which is generally worked in couples, under the name of

THE RED-AND-BLACK-BALL VASES.—The receptacle for the ball is in this case made in the form of a neat vase, and without any of those tell-tale grooves which disfigure the older ball-box. (*See* Fig. 128.) Like its prototype, it is in three parts, which we will distinguish as before by the letters *a, b,* and *c*. The portion *b,* however, in this case goes completely within the lid *c,* within which it fits just tightly enough to be lifted off with it. When, however, the performer desires to leave *b* upon *a,* he presses down, in the act of lifting off the cover, a moveable button or stud at the top. This pushes out the shell *b* from the cover, and, when the latter is lifted, leaves it upon *a.* When used in pairs, the ball-vases are usually made with one red and one black ball, the shells *b* of each vase being also one black and one red. The balls are first offered for examination, after which the red ball is placed in the vase containing the black shell, and the black ball in that which contains the red shell. The vases are then covered, and on the covers being again removed, leaving the hollow shells upon the vases, the red ball being covered by the black shell, and the black ball by the red shell, the effect to the spectator is as if the two balls had changed places. By leaving alternately the one or the other shell over its respective vase, the ball in the opposite vase being left uncovered, the vases may be made to appear as if both containing red balls or both black balls, the genuine balls being finally again exhibited as at first.

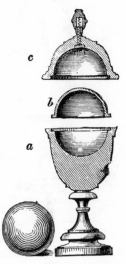

FIG. 128.

There is yet another form of ball-box, also frequently worked in pairs, and designed to simulate the apparent passage of a ball from the one box to the other. The vase in this case consists of two parts only, the vase proper *a,* and the cover *b,* but the latter is of such a height as to completely contain the ball, and of such a size internally, that, if the ball be jerked up into the cover, it will not again fall, unless a slight shake be used to displace it. (*See* Fig. 129.) Each vase has its own ball, and the mode of use is as follows:—One of the vases is prepared beforehand by jerking up the ball into the cover, which may then be removed, showing the vase apparently empty ; or both may be first shown empty, and the ball then introduced secretly

under the cover, after the manner of the cups and balls. The remaining vase and ball are offered for inspection, and when they are returned, the ball is placed within and covered over, after which the closed vase is placed upon the table; but in the act of doing this the performer gives the apparatus a slight upward jerk, thereby causing the ball therein to rise into the cover, where it remains. The second vase is once more shown empty ; but in replacing it on the table, the performer puts it down sharply, thereby causing the ball to drop from the cover into the cup. He now orders the ball, which the company have seen placed in the first vase, to pass invisibly into the second ; and on again opening the two, this transposition will appear to have taken place, and by a repetition of the process the

FIG. 129.

ball may be made to travel backwards and forwards from one vase to the other.

Morison's Pill-box.—In this trick (called by French conjurors *La Pilule du Diable*) the device of the " shell " is carried still further. The box in this case is spherical, standing upon a thin stem (*see* Fig. 130), and each part (box proper and lid) contains a half shell, the edge of one having a rebate or shoulder, so as to fit into the other, the two conjoined having the appearance of a solid ball. The genuine ball is of such a size as just to fill the hollow shells when thus joined. The lower shell fits loosely in the box, the upper one a little more tightly, so as not to fall out unless pressed down by the button on the top of the lid, which not only loosens it from the lid, but presses it into union with the lower shell.

The mode of using the apparatus is as follows :—It is first brought forward with the one half shell in the box, and the other in the lid, the true ball, which is of the same colour as the shell (generally black) being placed within the lower shell. The ball is ostentatiously removed, and the box closed. The ball is then either placed in some piece of apparatus adapted to cause its disappearance, or is made to vanish by sleight-of-hand in one or other of the modes already described. The ball is now ordered to return to the box, which, for greater certainty, is once more shown empty. The performer again closes it, pressing as he does so the button on the top of the lid, thus compelling the two half shells to coalesce; and on again re-opening the box, the ball has, to all appearance, returned as commanded.

The ball-box now under consideration has this great advantage over the single-shell vases, that the sham ball can be completely removed from the box, and shown on all sides, thus (apparently) negativing the possibility of its being a shell only.

The trick may be also worked very effectively by using a genuine ball of a different colour to the shell, with the addition of a duplicate of each. Thus, if the shell be black, you must be provided with a solid ball of the same colour, and two red balls. One of the latter, as also the solid black ball, should be of such a size as to go inside the shell, the remaining red ball being of the same size as the shell in its complete condition. The half shells being in their place in the box, the performer brings it forward, together with the smaller red and

FIG. 130.

black ball, keeping the remaining red ball concealed in his palm. Borrowing a handkerchief, he wraps (apparently) the black ball therein, and gives it to some one to hold (really substituting the palmed red ball, and getting rid of the black ball as soon as he can into one of his secret pockets). He then places the remaining red ball in the box, and having covered it over, commands the black ball in the handkerchief to change places with the red one in the box. Upon examination, the change has apparently taken place, the red ball in the box being now enclosed within the hollow shell, and thus having all the appearance of the solid black ball.

The Ball which changes to a Rose. — This is little more than an enlarged edition of the apparatus just described, the ball in Morison's pill-box being generally of about an inch and a half in diameter, while in the present case the ball is nearly double that size. (*See* Fig. 131.) The only other difference is the addition of a short pin, about a sixteenth of an inch in length, projecting from the bottom of the cup, and fitting into a corresponding hole in the lower shell. The addition of this pin enables the performer, after having pressed the stud at top, and thus caused the ball to appear in the previously empty box, to again cause its disappearance. This is effected by opening the box with a slight lateral pressure, when the pin acts as a stop or check to hold back the lower shell ; and the shells which are in this instance made to fit rather more loosely together, are thus forced to separate again, the lower being left in the cup and the upper in the lid, as before.

This apparatus is generally used with a solid black ball and a couple of artificial rose-buds, as nearly alike as possible. The

apparatus is brought forward empty, and with the solid ball and one of the rose-buds, is handed to the audience for inspection. The two half shells, joined together so as to form a hollow ball, with the second rose-bud within, are placed ready to hand in one of the *pochettes* of the performer. The audience having duly examined the apparatus, the performer returns to his table, secretly exchanging as he does so the solid for the hollow ball. This latter he places openly in the cup, taking care that the hole in the lower shell duly corresponds with the pin at bottom,

Fig. 131.

and puts on the cover. He now announces that the ball which he has just placed in the cup will at command fly away, and that the rose-bud which he holds shall take its place. The disappearance of the visible rose-bud is effected in any way that the invention or the appliances at command of the performer may suggest ; and on the box being opened, so as to part the two shells, the ball has apparently disappeared, and the rose has taken its place. By again closing the box, and this time pressing the stud on the top, the flower may again be made to vanish, and the ball to reappear in its original position.

The popular trick of the " flower in the button-hole," which will be described under the head of Miscellaneous Tricks, may be used in conjunction with this apparatus, the ball being found in the place of the flower, while the latter is made to appear in the button-hole.

A similar apparatus to the above is sometimes made in metal, and of a size sufficient to enclose a cannon-ball, which being made to disappear, its place is supplied by a variety of articles which have been otherwise disposed of at an earlier period.

THE OBEDIENT BALL.—This trick is of Japanese origin, and from that circumstance is sometimes known as the Japanese Ball. It is performed with a large black wooden ball, about five inches in diameter, with a hole bored through it from side to side. A piece of stout rope, four or five feet in length, with a knot at one end, completes the apparatus. The performer commences by passing the rope through the ball, and hands both for examination. The ball is found to run loosely upon the rope, and both are manifestly quite free from mechanism or preparation. The articles being returned, the performer places his foot upon the knotted end of the rope, and taking the other end in his right hand, holds it in a perpendicular position. The ball is raised as far as the length of the rope will admit, and, on being again released, immediately runs down again, as would naturally be expected. The performer now announces that, in obedience to his will, the laws of gravity will be in this particular instance suspended. Accordingly, on his again raising the ball to any portion of the rope, it remains stationary at that height until released by his command, when it instantly runs down. Other persons are invited to come forward, and to place the ball at any height they please, the ball again remaining stationary until released by the word of the operator, when it slowly descends, stopping, however, in its course, and remaining fixed whenever commanded by the performer to do so

The secret lies in the fact that the hole in the ball is not made straight from end to end, but curved, with an angle or break in the middle. (*See* Fig. 132.) So long as the rope is slack, it runs through easily enough, but as soon as it is drawn taut, and thus forced into a straight line, it is clipped by the opposite angles *a*, *b*, and *c*, creating an amount of friction which would support a much greater weight than that of the ball. The performer has, therefore, only to draw the rope taut when he desires the ball to remain stationary, and to slacken when he desires it to run down.

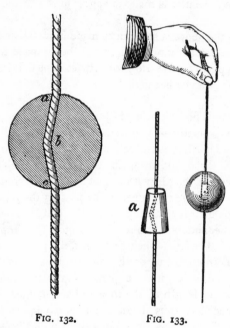

FIG. 132.   FIG. 133.

There is another form of the Obedient Ball, designed for drawing-room use. The ball in this case is about two and a half inches in diameter, and the bore is straight, but tapering from a quarter of an inch at the one opening to about half an inch at the other. The cord used is a thin piece of whipcord, and the ball therefore runs quite loosely upon it. There is, however, in this case an additional element in the apparatus, consisting of a little black wooden plug, about an inch in length, and tapering so as to fit midway in the bore of the ball. (*See* Fig. 133, in which *a* represents a nearly full-sized view of the plug in question.) The plug is bored after the manner of the large ball, the hole being of such a size as to just allow the cord to run through it. This plug is secretly threaded upon the cord before commencing the trick; the cord, which in this case has a tassel instead of a knot at one end, being passed through it from the larger end. This plug is kept concealed in the hand of the performer, the string being allowed to dangle down on each side of it. The ball is handed round for examination, and, when returned, the cord is passed through it from the side which has the larger opening. The ball is then allowed to drop quickly to the full extent of the cord. As it runs down, it encounters the plug, which is thereby placed in position within the ball, and both run down together until stopped by the tassel. From this point the working of the trick is the same as with the larger ball.

CHAPTER XV.

Hat Tricks.

The present Chapter will be devoted to those tricks in which a hat plays a special or prominent part. Borrowed hats have been used in the course of many of the tricks already described, but the part played by the hat has been of an incidental and subordinate character. In the tricks next following the hat is the principal article employed.

The majority of hat tricks are different modifications of the same broad idea, viz., the production from a borrowed and apparently empty hat of various articles, in size and number much exceeding what any hat could in the natural way contain. One of the best is that of

The Cannon-balls in the Hat.—The earliest and simplest form of this trick is limited to the production of a solid wooden globe, blacked to resemble a cannon-ball. The introduction of the ball into the hat is effected as follows:—The ball, which has a hole of about two inches in depth by one in diameter bored in it towards its centre, is placed on the *servante* of the performer's table in such manner that the hole above-mentioned shall slant upwards and outwards, at an angle of about 45°. To keep the ball steady, and to prevent its rolling off, some performers have a slight circular hollow scooped in the surface of the *servante* itself. A more convenient plan, however, is to use an india-rubber ring (such as is given to infants teething). This may be placed on any part of the *servante*, and makes a capital rest or bed for the ball. A bit of half-inch rope, with the ends joined so as to form a ring, will answer the same purpose.

When the performer desires to introduce the ball into the hat, which we will suppose to have been borrowed for the purpose of some previous trick just completed, he takes the hat with his thumb outside and his fingers inside the brim, and holds it up with its mouth towards the spectators, so as to show indirectly that it is empty (*see* Fig. 134). Carelessly lowering his hand, he brings the hat mouth downwards on the table, and, drawing it towards him, slips the second finger into the hole in the ball (*see* Fig. 135), when the mere action of crooking the finger brings the ball into the hat. He then, still holding the ball supported by the finger, walks away

FIG. 134.

from the table towards the owner of the hat, with the apparent intention of returning it. Just before reaching him, however, he pretends to notice that it is somewhat heavy, and looking into it, says, "Dear me, sir, there is something rather peculiar about this hat. Are you aware that there is something in it?" The owner naturally professes ignorance of the fact; and the performer, after keeping the audience in suspense for a moment or

FIG. 135.

two, turns the hat over, and lets the ball fall out upon the stage.

The performer may in some degree heighten the effect of the trick by making it appear that the ball is wedged very tightly in the hat, as the difficulty of introducing it becomes thereby presumably the greater. This is managed by holding the hat with both hands, as shown in Fig. 136, when the extended finger-tips will prevent the ball from falling as long as may be desired, however much the hat may be shaken.

The trick, as above described, is of very short duration. In order to lengthen, and at the same time to diversify it, a second ball is sometimes employed, of similar appearance, but of different construction.

FIG. 136

This second ball (*see* Figs. 137, 138, the latter representing a section of the ball) is a strongly made hollow sphere of tin or zinc, with a circular opening of about three and a half inches across, closed by a sort of sliding door, *a*, also circular, working on two curved arms, *b b*, which move on two pivots, *c c*, at opposite sides of the ball on the inside. In this door is a hole an inch in diameter, answering the same purpose as the hole bored in the solid ball.

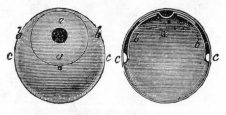

FIGS. 137, 138.

The ball is filled beforehand with bonbons, small toys, or any other articles suitable for production. Thus "loaded," it is placed upon the *servante*, and introduced into the hat as above described. The performer goes through the ceremony of pretending to discover something in the hat, but does not, as in the last case, at once produce the ball. Slipping back the sliding door, he brings out, one by one, the articles contained in the ball, not hurriedly, but with deliberation, as he thereby produces the effect of greater quantity. Having emptied the ball, he again closes the circular slide, remarking that the hat is now quite empty. As a proof that it is so, he turns the hat mouth downwards as above directed, preventing the ball from falling with the tips of his fingers. Again he moves towards the owner, as if to return the hat, and again pretends to find something in it. This time, however, he does not allow the ball to fall on the ground, as, being hollow, it will not bear rough usage, but lifts it out with his left hand, taking care that the " door " side shall be downwards, next his palm. Observing that

he will have the ball packed up for the owner of the hat to take home with him, he returns to his table, and places it thereon. As the ball was in his left hand, the right is still holding the hat, and this gives him the opportunity to introduce the second (*i.e.*, the

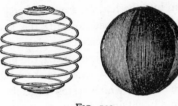

FIG. 139.

solid) cannon-ball, which should be placed in readiness at the opposite corner of the *servante*. This also is produced in due course, and, being manifestly solid, naturally leads the audience to infer that the other was so also.

What are known as " multiplying balls " are frequently used in conjunction with the cannon-balls. These are cloth-covered balls of about two and a half inches in diameter. In appearance they are solid, but in reality are mere outer coverings of cloth, kept distended by spiral skeletons of wire (*see* Fig. 139), and may be pressed quite flat, in which condition they occupy an exceedingly small space, though they immediately regain their shape on being released. A large number of these may be packed in the hollow cannon-ball, and when taken out, produce a pile extending far above the mouth of the hat, the cannon-ball lying hidden beneath them.

The hollow ball may also be filled with soft feathers, of which what will seem an incredible quantity when spread out may be compressed into a very small space. Feathers are, however, objectionable in a drawing-room, from the difficulty of collecting them from the carpet.

THE "HUNDRED GOBLETS" FROM A HAT.--The goblets used for this purpose are of polished tin, about four inches in depth, and made without ornament or projection of any kind. Being all of the same size, and slightly tapering, a large number of them may be fitted one within the other, and yet occupy little more space than a single one. The goblets thus packed are placed in a bag of black alpaca, just large enough to receive them, and concealed on the *servante*, or in one of the *profondes* of the performer. When it is desired to introduce them into the hat, they are grasped in either hand, the back of the hand being turned towards the audience, and thus covering them. The hand is now carelessly placed in the hat, as though to take something out. Once introduced, the goblets are produced one by one, and placed mouth downward on the table, their number giving an appearance of bulk which seems to exclude the possibility of their having been all contained within so small a space. Two or three parcels of goblets may be introduced successively, and brought out one by one, with little difficulty.

We may here mention a little expedient which will be found of great assistance where the performer desires to introduce into a hat a bundle of goblets (or any similar article) from either of his secret pockets. We will suppose that the article in question is in the right-hand *profonde*. Taking the empty hat in the opposite hand (the left), he stoops a little, and holding it down near the floor, with its mouth toward the company, gently moves it round and round in circles, gazing at it intently, as though anticipating some important result. This draws all eyes to the hat, and enables him to drop his right hand to the *profonde*, and bring out, under cover of the hand and wrist, the article to be introduced. Continuing the motion, he gradually brings the mouth of the hat upwards, so that the company can no longer see into it, and suddenly plunges his right hand into it, as though merely to take out the article or articles which he, in fact, thereby introduces. This may be repeated from the *profonde* on the opposite side; and thus two successive packets of articles may be produced without even going near the table.

A Dozen Babies from a Hat.—Among the various objects available for production, may be enumerated dolls, of which a dozen, each eight or nine inches in height, may be produced from a borrowed hat. The dolls for this purpose are of coloured muslin, stretched over a framework or skeleton of spiral wire, after the fashion of the multiplying balls (*see* Fig. 140), and may be compressed vertically to a thickness of about three-quarters of an inch. A dozen of them may be packed within the hollow cannon-ball, described above, resuming their shape as soon as they are released.

FIG. 140.

The Magic Reticules.—This is one of the most modern hat tricks. The reticules, which are of cardboard covered with leather, are, when expanded, as shown in Fig. 141. They are, however, constructed so as to fold into a very small compass, in manner following. The ends, *a a*, are only attached to the reticule at their lower edges (which form a kind of leather hinge), and may be folded inwards flat upon the bottom of the reticule. (*See* Fig. 142.) The ends of the ribbon *b*, which forms the sling or handle of the reticule, run freely through two holes *c c* in the upper side of the reticule, and are attached to the ends *a a* at the points *d d*. The ends being folded down, as in Fig. 142, the reticule becomes a hollow oblong, open from end to end, as in Fig. 143. The angles, being made of soft leather, are flexible, and by pressing the sides in the direction indicated by the dotted lines (*see* Fig. 143), the

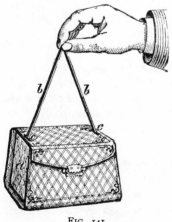

FIG. 141.

reticule is brought into the condition shown in Fig. 144, and, on being again folded, into that shown in Fig. 145, in which condition

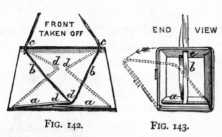

FIG. 142.

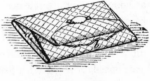

FIG. 143.

it is little larger than a pocket-book. Half-a-dozen reticules thus folded, and packed in a bag of black alpaca, or held together by an india-rubber ring, form a small and compact parcel, and are easily introduced into the hat. The performer having got them out of the bag, has only to unfold each, so as to bring it into the condition shown in Fig. 144, when the mere act of lifting

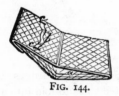

FIG. 144.

FIG. 145.

the reticule out of the bag by the ribbon *b* raises the sides and ends, and restores it to the shape shown in Fig. 141.

THE DRUMS FROM THE HAT.—In this trick the performer generally begins by producing from the hat a number of the multiplying balls described at page 307. He next produces a miniature drum, prettily ornamented, then another, then a third and a fourth, each being a shade larger than its predecessor, and the last of such a size as barely to be containable within the hat.

With the reader's present knowledge, he will readily conjecture that the drums are so constructed as to fit one within the other, the multiplying balls being packed within the smallest of the four. One end of each drum is loose, and falls inwards upon the opposite end, upon which it lies flat, thus giving space for the introduction of another drum, a size smaller. Across the loose end, and parallel to it, is fixed a wire, forming a handle whereby the performer may lift the drum out of the hat, the act of doing so raising the end into its proper position, and a wire rim round the inside of each drum preventing the loose end being drawn out altogether. Each drum is taken out with the loose end upwards ; but the performer, in placing it on the table, turns it over, thus bringing the solid end up. In default of this precaution, the loose end would fall back again to its old position, and so betray the secret. The drums are usually made oval, rather than round, as they are thus better suited to the shape of a hat.

THE BIRDCAGES FROM THE HAT.—Not content with cannonballs, drums, and ladies' reticules, the public of the present day requires that birdcages and living birds should be produced from an empty hat.

The birdcages used vary in their construction. Some are made to fit one within the other, after the fashion of the drums

FIG. 146.   FIG. 147.

just described, save that the birdcages, unlike the drums, are lifted out by the solid and not the loose ends, which fall down of their own accord. Those in most general use, however, are of the shape shown in Fig. 146, and are alike in size, measuring about six inches in height, by five in breadth and depth. The bottom is made to slide upwards on the upright wires which form the sides. When it is desired to prepare the cage for use, a canary is first placed therein, and the bottom is then pushed up as far as it will go (*see* Fig. 147),

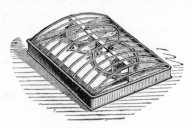

the sides, which work on hinges at *a a a a*, being folded one by one upon the bottom, the cage finally assuming the shape shown in Fig. 148. It is in this condition that the cages, generally three in number, are introduced into the hat, either from the *servante* or from inside the vest of the performer ; and in the act of lifting

FIG. 148.

out (which is done by the wire loop at top), the sides and bottom falling down, the cage again becomes as in Fig. 146.

THE CAKE (OR PUDDING) IN THE HAT.—This is an old and favourite hat trick. The necessary apparatus consists of two parts— first, a round tin pan *a* (*see* Fig. 149), four inches in depth, and tapering from five inches at its greatest to four and a half inches at its smallest diameter. It is open at each end, but is divided into two parts by a horizontal partition at about two-thirds of its depth. Second, a larger tin *b*, japanned to taste, five and a half inches in depth, and so shaped as to fit somewhat tightly over the smaller tin. In the larger end of the latter is placed a hot cake or pudding, and in this condition it is placed on the *servante* of the table, projecting a little over the edge. The performer borrows a hat, and in passing behind his table, tips cake and tin together into it. The chances are that the tin will fall small end upwards. (the opposite end being the heaviest) ; but if not, the performer turns the tin, so as to bring it into that position. Placing the hat mouth upwards upon the table, he announces

FIG. 149.

his intention of making a cake in it; for which purpose he takes, one by one, and mixes in the tin *b*, a quantity of flour, raisins, eggs, sugar, and the other ingredients for a cake, adding water enough to make the mixture into a thick batter. This he pours into the hat, holding the tin with both hands, at first high above it, but gradually bringing it lower and lower, till at last, as if draining the last drop of the mixture, he lowers the mouth of the tin right into the hat, and brings it well down over the smaller tin. On being again raised, it brings away within it the smaller tin and its liquid contents, the cake being left in the hat. He next proceeds to bake the cake, by moving the hat backwards and forwards at a short distance over the flame of a candle, and, after a sufficient interval, exhibits the result, which is cut up and handed round to the company for their approval.

As the batter round the sides of b is apt to cause a to stick pretty tightly into it, a folding ring is generally fixed inside a, in order to facilitate its removal after the close of the trick.

THE WELSH RABBIT.—This is a trick of a comic character, and in the hands of a spirited performer is sure to be received with applause, particularly by the younger members of the audience. Its effect is as follows:—The performer brings in in one hand a sauce-pan, fancifully decorated, and in the other a plate, with bread, cheese, pepper, etc. With these ingredients he proposes to make a Welsh Rabbit, and to give the audience, without extra charge, a lesson in cookery. Chopping the bread and cheese together in a burlesque fashion, and seasoning with pepper and salt to a degree which no palate short of a salamander's could possibly stand, he shovels all into the saucepan, and claps the lid on. For a moment he is at a loss for a fire, but this difficulty is quickly conquered. Borrowing a gentle-man's hat, and a lady's pocket-handkerchief, he requests permission to use them for the purpose of the experiment. This is readily accorded, but the respective owners look on with consternation when the performer proceeds to set fire to the handkerchief, and, dropping it still blazing into the hat, to cook the Welsh Rabbit by moving the saucepan to and fro over the flames. Having done this for a minute or two, he extinguishes the flames by lowering the saucepan for a moment into the hat. Then again removing it, and taking off the lid, he brings it forward to the company, and exhibits, not the expected Welsh Rabbit, or " rare-bit," but a genuine live rabbit, every vestige of the cheese and other ingredients having disappeared.

The secret of this ingenious trick lies mainly in the construction of the saucepan, which consists of four parts, designated in the diagram (Fig. 150) by the letters *a, b, c,* and *d; a* is the lid, which has no speciality, save that the rim round it is rather deeper than usual; *b* is a shallow tray or lining, of the same depth as the lid, fitting easily within the top of the saucepan; *a*, on the contrary, fits tightly within *b* ; *c* is the body of the saucepan, and has no speciality ; *d* is an outer sheet or covering, loosely fitting the lower part of the saucepan, and, like it, is japanned plain black, the upper part and lid being generally of an ornamental pattern. (For our own part, we much

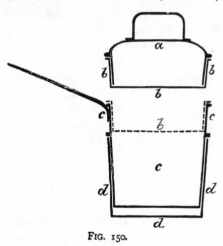

FIG. 150.

prefer either plain black or polished tin throughout, as savouring less of mechanism or preparation.) The presence or absence of *d* does not alter the general appearance of the saucepan, and cannot, therefore, be detected by the eye. It should be mentioned that *d* is so made, that between its bottom and the bottom of the saucepan is a space of about half an inch in depth, and in this space, before the apparatus is brought forward, is placed a substitute handkerchief, sprinkled with a few drops of spirits of wine or eau de Cologne, to render it more inflammable; within the saucepan is placed a small live rabbit, after which *b* is put in its place, and pressed down.

The performer is now ready to begin the trick. He brings forward the saucepan, holding it as in Fig. 151, in which position the pressure of the first and second fingers on *d* prevents it falling off, as, being loose, it would otherwise do. Placing it on the table, he mixes the bread, cheese, etc., on the plate, and then pours all into the saucepan, where, of course, they fall into *b*. As *b* is comparatively shallow, it is well to place the saucepan in some tolerably elevated situation, so that the audience may not be able to see into it, or they may perceive that the bread, etc., do not fall to the bottom. The lid is next placed on the saucepan. The hat and handkerchief are borrowed, the latter, which is to serve as fuel, being dropped into the hat.

The performer, as if bethinking himself of a possible difficulty, carelessly remarks, "We mustn't have the stove too small for the saucepan;" and so saying, lifts the latter, as shown in Fig. 151, and lowers it for a moment into the hat, as though testing their relative sizes. In that moment, however, he relaxes the pressure of his fingers on *d*, and so

FIG. 151.

leaves it within the hat, placing the saucepan on the table beside it. When he again takes out the (supposed) handkerchief, and sets light to it, it is, of course, the substitute that is actually burnt, the genuine handkerchief meanwhile remaining hidden beneath *d* in the crown. The effect of the flames rising from the hat, in which the audience cannot suppose any preparation, is very startling, and yet, unless the substitute handkerchief is unusually large, or the spirit has been applied with a too liberal hand, there is no real danger of injuring the hat. The performer moves about the saucepan above the blaze at such a distance as not to inconvenience the animal within, and, after a moment or two, brings the saucepan sharply down into the hat, for the ostensible purpose of extinguishing the flames, but in again lifting it out he brings with it *d*, and places all together on the table. Nothing is now left in the hat but the borrowed handkerchief, which may be restored in any manner which the performer's fancy may suggest. When the lid of the saucepan is removed, as it fits more tightly within *b* than the latter fits within the saucepan, it naturally carries *b* with it, thus causing the disappearance of the bread, cheese, etc., and revealing in its place the live rabbit.

Some fun may be created by selecting beforehand an assistant from the juvenile portion of the audience, and dressing him up with a pocket-handkerchief round his head, and another by way of apron, to act as assistant cook.

A guinea-pig or small kitten may be substituted for the rabbit, the performer accounting for the wrong animal being produced by supposing that he must have made some mistake in mixing the ingredients.

CHAPTER XVI.

MISCELLANEOUS TRICKS.

UNDER this head we propose to describe such tricks as do not come within either of the preceding categories. We shall make no attempt at classifying them, save that we shall, as far as practicable, describe the best known and simplest feats first, and thence proceed to the more complicated. Stage tricks, *i.e.*, tricks adapted to the stage only, will be treated in the Chapter next following. We will begin with

THE CUT STRING RESTORED.—This is a trick of such venerable antiquity, that we should not have ventured to allude to it, were it not that the mode of working which we are about to describe, though old in principle, is new in detail, and much superior in neatness to the generally known methods.

After having offered the string, which should be about four feet in length, for examination, the performer takes the ends (pointing upwards) between the first and second finger and thumb of the left hand, and the first finger and thumb of the right hand, letting the remainder of the string hang down in a loop between them. Now bringing the right hand close to the left, he draws that portion of the string which is held in the right hand towards himself between the first and second fingers of the left hand (thus crossing at right angles that end of the cord which is held in the left hand), continuing to pull until half the length of the string has passed the left hand, and at the same time slipping the third finger of the left hand between the two parts of the string, which will thus be as shown in Fig. 152, in which, for convenience of reference, the three lines in which the

string now hangs are marked *a*, *b*, and *c*, and one-half of the string
is shown black, and the other half white, though of course there
would be no such difference of colour in the original.* The

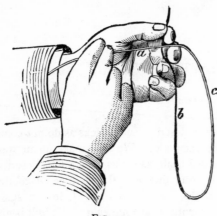

FIG. 152.

first finger and thumb of
the right hand, still re-
taining the end which
they already hold, seize
the portion *b* at the point
marked with that letter,
the third finger of the
left hand at the same
time drawing back the
portion *a* towards the
palm of the hand. The
string will thus be
brought into the position
shown in Figs. 153 and
154, (in the latter of
which, for the sake of clearness, the thumbs are made transparent),
the part now held horizontally between the two hands, which appears
to be the middle of the string, really being only the immediate continuation of the end
held in the left hand.
The whole operation
of arranging the string
in proper position,
though tedious to de-
scribe, does not tale
half a second in prac-
tice.

The performer next
requests some person
to cut the string, thus

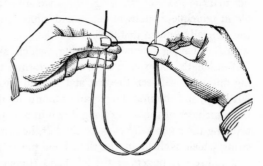

FIG. 153.

arranged, in half, and this being (apparently) done, he transfers the

---

* It should be mentioned that, in order to economize space in the diagrams, the
actual length of the string is represented as much shortened.

string altogether to the right hand, keeping the point of junction of the crossed pieces hidden between the finger and thumb. (*See* Fig. 155.) He now gives either end to some one to hold, and, placing his open left hand near to the end thus held, winds the string rapidly round it, sliding off as he does so the short piece, which, as soon as it is clear of the longer portion, he presses with his thumb between the second and third fingers of the same hand. On again unwinding the string from the left hand, it is found apparently whole as at first.

The principle of the trick being very generally known, you will frequently find some one of the audience proclaim his acquaintance with it, and declare that you have merely cut a short piece off the end of the string. "Pardon me," you reply, "my dear sir; that method of performing the trick has long since been exploded.

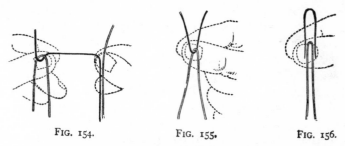

FIG. 154.   FIG. 155.   FIG. 156.

I will at once show you that I do not make use of any such shabby expedient. Of course, if a piece was, as you suggest, cut off the end, the string would be that much shorter after the operation. Will some one be kind enough to measure it?" While this is being done, you secretly double in a loop the little piece which was cut off on the former occasion, and which has still remained in your right hand. When the string is returned to you, you double it in half, and allow it to hang down between the first finger and thumb of the right hand, drawing up immediately above it the little loop you have just formed. (*See* Fig. 156.) You now ask some one again to cut the string, which he apparently does, in reality merely dividing the little loop. You go through any magical gesticulations you please, and ultimately again conceal the cut ends between the fingers, and produce the string once more restored. On being measured, it is found to have lost nothing of its length.

The trick in this second form being performed by wholly different means, the repetition will puzzle even those who knew, or believed they knew, the *modus operandi* in the first case.

My Grandmother's Necklace.—The trick which bears this title is also a very old one, but is little known in the improved form we are about to describe. In its older shape it is performed with three perforated wooden balls or beads, threaded on a couple of tapes, whose ends are held securely by two of the spectators. The problem is to detach the beads without breaking the tapes, and this is effected as follows:—The tapes, which should be from four to six feet in length, are beforehand doubled in the middle, and slightly joined at the bend of each with fine cotton or silk of the same colour. The tapes are thus really middle to middle, though to a casual observer they appear to be merely laid side by side. The performer comes forward with the tapes, thus prepared, thrown over his left arm (taking care that the point of junction shall be on the side towards his body, and therefore concealed), and with the beads in his hands. These latter, which are mere wooden balls, from one to two inches in diameter, perforated so as to freely admit the tapes, he hands for examination. When they are returned, he threads them one after another upon the tapes, holding the latter in a loop, so that the balls may sink down to the middle, and so cover the point of junction.

FIG. 157.

He next requests two of the company to come forward and hold the tapes, and hands two ends to the one and two to the other. Each person believes that he holds one end of each tape, though, in reality, each has both ends of the same tape. The performer now takes from each one of the ends which he holds, and crossing the tapes in the manner shown in Fig. 157, gives to each the end which the other previously held. Holding a hat below the balls, he requests each person to pull smartly at the word "three." The word of command is given, "One, two, Three!" and the thread breaking, the balls fall into the hat, though the ends of the tapes still remain in the hands of the holders.

The improvement to which we have alluded consists in the use of *six* balls, three red and three black. The red balls having been first threaded on the tapes, and the two ends having been crossed and returned to the holders in manner already described, the black balls are in turn threaded on the tapes at either end, and the performer, holding the hat beneath, and addressing one of the persons who hold the tapes, says, "Which will you have, sir, the red balls or the black?" Whichever the answer, the result is the same, for the red balls only can come off the tapes, the black remaining still upon them; but in either case the performer is able to satisfy the choice which has been made. If the red balls have been chosen, he says on their falling, "You chose the red, I think. You see that your commands are at once obeyed." If, on the other hand, the black are chosen, the performer says, "You prefer the black? Then *I* will take the red," which he does accordingly. The audience, having heard the choice freely offered, and not being aware of the subterfuge by which the implied undertaking is fulfilled, naturally believe that the performer was able to take off or leave on the tape whichever group of balls he pleased.

THE "BONUS GENIUS," OR VANISHING DOLL.—While upon the subject of old-fashioned tricks, we may briefly notice that known under the name of the Bonus Genius, which has puzzled many generations of our forefathers, and, though now rarely exhibited by professional performers, is still a great favourite with juvenile audiences. The Bonus Genius is a little wooden figure of a man, four to six inches in height, and more or less grotesque in colour and design. A little cloak, made small above and full below, like the skirt of a doll's dress, and with no opening save where the head of the figure passes through, completes the apparatus. There are, however, two points about the doll and his cloak which are unknown to the spectators. First, the head of the doll is moveable, a wooden peg forming the neck, and fitting, somewhat tightly, into a corresponding hole in the body; secondly, there is stitched on the inside of the cloak, just below the opening for the neck, a little pocket, of the description known among tailors as a "patch" pocket, and of such a size as to contain the head easily. The performer, holding up the figure, and introducing it to the company as his flying messenger, warranted to outstrip the electric telegraph, covers it with the cloak, so that nothing but the head is seen. Grasping the figure under the cloak with his right hand, the performer holds a burlesque conversation with him, finally entrusting him with a message to be immediately delivered to the President of the United States, the Shah, or any other individual at a distance. The figure does not move. "Well, sir, are you not going?" asks the performer. The figure shakes his head from side to side, an effect easily produced by turning the body backwards and forwards under the cloak. "You won't, eh? Why not, I should like to know? Oh! I see what you mean. I haven't given you your travelling expenses." As he says the last words, he grasps the figure and cloak from the outside round the neck with the left hand, and draws away the right from beneath the cloak, secretly carrying with it the body, and putting his hand in his pocket, as though in search of money. He leaves the body of the figure in his pocket, and brings out the hand again empty, but in the position of holding a coin between the finger and thumb. "There, sir," he says, "there is a shilling for you," making the gesture of giving it. "You don't see the coin, ladies and gentlemen; but the fact is, what I have just given him is fairy money; the weight of the ordinary coinage would interfere with the rapidity of his flight. Now, sir, make haste; you have nothing to wait for now."

The performer has, meanwhile, again put the right hand under the cloak, and with two fingers holds the little pocket open for the reception of the head. As he says the last words, he gives the head a sharp downward rap with the fingers of the left hand, and lets it fall into the little pocket, the effect being as if the figure had suddenly vanished. The performer shakes the cloak, and turns it inside out to show that it is empty, taking care always to grasp it by that part which contains the head, when all other portions of the cloak may be shown freely; and as the audience are not aware that the figure is divisible, and supposing it to be indivisible, it would be clearly much too large to be concealed in the closed hand, there is nothing to lead them to guess the secret. If it is desired to make the doll reappear, the head is pushed up again through the opening of the cloak, the hand beneath supporting it by the peg which forms the neck, and it may thus be made to vanish and return any number of times.

With tolerable skill in " palming," the little pocket may be dispensed with, the head being simply held in the hand. This mode of working is, in our own opinion, to be preferred, as the cloak may then be handed for examination without giving even the infinitesimal clue which the pocket might suggest. Some performers, to still further hoodwink the spectators, make use of two figures—the first, which is handed round for inspection, being solid, and being afterwards secretly changed for its counterpart with the moveable head. Others again use only one figure, which is solid throughout, but are provided with a separate head (whose existence is, of course, not suspected by the spectators), and having handed round the solid figure for examination, conceal this, and work the trick with the head only.

THE DANCING SAILOR.—The Dancing Sailor is a figure cut out of cardboard, eight or nine inches in height, and with its arms and legs cut out separately, and attached to the trunk with thread in such a manner as to hang perfectly free. The mode of exhibiting it is as follows :—The performer, taking a seat facing the company, with his legs slightly apart, places the figure on the ground between them. As might be expected, it falls flat and lifeless, but after a few mesmeric passes it is induced to stand upright, though without visible support, and on a lively piece of music being played, dances to it, keeping time, and ceasing as soon as the music ceases.

The secret lies in the fact that, from leg to leg of the performer, at about the height of the figure from the ground, is fixed (generally by means of a couple of bent pins), a fine black silk thread, of eighteen or twenty inches in length. This allows him to move about without any hindrance. On each side of the head of the figure is a little slanting cut, tending in a perpendicular direction, and about half an inch in length. The divided portions of the card-board are bent back a little, thus forming two " hooks," so to speak, at the sides of the head. When the performer takes his seat as before mentioned, the separation of his legs draws the silk comparatively taut, though, against

FIG. 158.

a moderately dark background, it remains wholly invisible. When he first places the figure on the ground, he does so simply, and the figure naturally falls. He makes a few sham mesmeric passes over it, but still it falls. At the third or fourth attempt, however, he places it so that the little hooks already mentioned just catch the thread (*see* Fig. 158, showing the arrangement of the head), and the figure is thus kept upright. When the music commences, the smallest motion, or pretence of keeping time with the feet, is enough to start the sailor in a vigorous hornpipe.

THE BOTTLE IMPS.—These are miniature black bottles, about two inches in height, with rounded bottoms, and so weighted that, like "tumbler" dolls, they rise of their own accord to the perpendicular, and will not rest in any other position. The proprietor, however, has a charm by which he is able to conquer their obstinate uprightness. For him, and for him only, they will consent to be laid down, and even to stand at an angle of 45°, though they again rebel if any other person attempts to make them do the same.

The little bottles are made of *papier maché*, or some other very light material, varnished black, the bottom of each being a half bullet, spherical side downwards. The centre of gravity is therefore at the bottom of the bottle, which is thus compelled always to stand upright. The performer, however, is provided with one or two little pieces of iron wire, of such a size and length as just to slip easily into the bottle. One of these being held concealed between the finger and thumb, it is a very easy matter, in picking up the bottle, to slip it in, and this slight additional weight neutralizing the effect of the half bullet at the foot, causes the bottle to lie still in any position. Having shown that the bottle is obedient to the word of command, the performer again picks it up with the neck between the first and second fingers and thumb, carelessly turning it bottom upwards, and thus allowing the bit of wire to slip out again into the palm of his hand, when he is able to again tender the bottle for experiment. Partaking of the nature of a puzzle as well as a conjuring trick, this little toy has amused thousands, and if neatly manipulated, may be repeatedly exhibited, even before the same spectators, with little fear of detection.

The Vanishing Gloves.—This is a capital trick with which to commence an entertainment ; when coming, as it should do, unannounced, and before the performance proper has commenced, it has an air of improvisation which greatly enhances its effect, and at once awakens the attention of the audience.

The performer comes forward in full evening dress. While saying a few words by way of introduction to his entertainment, he begins to take off his gloves, commencing with that on his right hand. As soon as it is fairly off, he takes it in the right hand, waves the hand with a careless gesture, and the glove is gone. He begins to take off the other, walking as he does so behind his table, whereon his wand is laid. The left hand glove being removed, is rolled up into a ball, and transferred from the right hand to the left, which is immediately closed. The right hand picks up the wand, and with it touches the left, which being slowly opened, the second glove is found to have also disappeared.

The disappearance of the first glove is effected by means of a piece of cord elastic, attached to the back of the waistcoat, and thence passing down the sleeve. This should be of such a length as to allow the glove to be drawn down and put on the hand, and yet to pull it smartly up the sleeve and out of sight when released. It is desirable to have a hem round the wrist of the glove, and to pass the elastic through this like the cord of a bag, as it thereby draws the wrist portion of the glove together, and causes it to offer less hindrance to its passage up the sleeve. Upon taking off the glove, the performer retains it in his hand, and lets it go when he pleases. He must, however, take care to straighten his arm before letting it slip, as otherwise the elastic will remain comparatively slack, and the glove will, instead of disappearing with a flash, dangle ignominiously from the coat-cuff.

The left hand glove is got **rid** of by palming. The performer, standing behind his table as already mentioned, rolling the glove between his hands, and quickly twisting the fingers inside, so as to bring it into more manageable form, pretends to place it in his left hand, but really palms it in his right. He now lowers the right hand to pick up his wand, and as the hand reaches the table, drops the glove on the *servante*. He now touches the left hand with the wand, in due course opening the hand and showing that the glove has departed.

Some performers vanish both gloves by means of elastic, one up the right sleeve, the other up the left, but in doing so they offend against one of the cardinal precepts of the art, viz., never to perform the same trick twice in succession by the same means. The audience having seen the manner of the first disappearance, are all on the alert, and are not unlikely on the second occasion to guess the means employed. If, on the other hand, the performer adopts the plan indicated above, the two modes of producing the effect being different, each renders it more difficult to discover the secret of the other.

THE EGG-BAG.—This is a very old-fashioned trick, but, if performed with address, is by no means ineffective. It was exhibited in a modified form by the Japanese jugglers who visited London a few years ago. We shall first describe it in the simple form adopted by them, and shall then proceed to explain the older and more elaborate version.

The Japanese egg-bag is about eight inches in depth and six in breadth, and made of alpaca, tammy, or some similar opaque material. Its only peculiarity is that one of its sides is double, the stuff being folded down inwards from the mouth of the bag to about two-thirds of its depth, and stitched at the sides, but left open at its lower edge. The effect of this arrangement is to make a sort of pocket, mouth downwards, inside the bag. If any small article, such as an egg, be placed within the bag, and the bag be turned upside down, the article will not fall out, but will fall into the pocket, which, in the reversed position of the bag, will be mouth upwards. This will enable you to conceal the presence of any article in the bag, as you may turn it upside down, and even inside out, without any fear of the article falling; and so long as you take care to keep the "pocket" side of the bag towards yourself, the spectators have not the least reason for suspecting that the bag is otherwise than empty. The uses to which this little bag may be put are various. Amongst others, it is available either to produce or cause the disappearance of an egg, and may thus, in combination with other apparatus, be made useful for many tricks. We shall content ourselves with describing one only of the modes of using it.

The performer comes forward, having in his hand the bag, in which is beforehand placed a small egg. He turns the bag upside down and inside out, thus proving, to all appearance, that it is perfectly empty. Holding the bag for a moment with his teeth, he pulls back his coat cuffs, to prove that he has nothing concealed in that quarter, taking care as he does so to show clearly that his hands are empty. Taking the bag in his left hand, and imitating (if he can) the clucking of a hen, he dips his right hand into it, and produces an egg (or rather *the* egg). This he places in his mouth, letting all see that he does so, then making a gesture of swallowing, he again dips his hand in the bag, and produces a second egg, of which he disposes in the same way, repeating the operation until a dozen or more have been apparently produced and swallowed. With the reader's present knowledge, it is hardly necessary to suggest to him that the egg, though fairly placed in the mouth, is, under cover of the hand, instantly pushed out again with the tongue, and palmed, rendering it a very simple matter to produce (apparently) another egg from the bag. Although so absurdly simple, the trick is effective, and if neatly performed, produces a complete illusion.

The bag which is more generally known as the "egg-bag" is a much larger affair, measuring eighteen to twenty inches in width, by fourteen or fifteen in depth. In its most approved form, one side of the bag is made double, the double side being stitched all round, save for about four inches at one corner of the bottom of the bag. The little opening thus left affords therefore the sole access to the space between the double sides. Between these double sides, and immediately below their upper edge, is stitched a broad band, with a row of a dozen or more little pockets, each capable of holding an egg, end upwards. Each pocket covers about two-thirds of the egg, which is prevented from falling out spontaneously by a little piece of elastic round the edge of the pocket, though it will slip out and fall into the space between the double sides on the slightest pressure being applied to it.

The bag is prepared for use by placing an egg in each of the little pockets we have mentioned. The eggs used are either blown shells or imitation eggs of wood or tin, with one real one for the performer to break as a specimen, and so lead the audience to the belief that all are equally genuine. The bag being brought forward is turned upside down—of course nothing falling from it. The performer then, thrusting his arms down to the bottom, and seizing the bag by the corners inside, turns it inside out, taking care, however, to keep the double side towards himself. Having thus conclusively proved its emptiness, he again brings back the bag to its normal condition, and in the act of doing so, squeezes with his finger and thumb (through the stuff) the genuine egg out of its pocket. It falls into the space between the double sides, and by gently sloping the bag downwards in the direction of the opening at the corner, he brings the egg into the outer bag, whence he produces it, and breaks it to show its genuineness, as already mentioned. Again he turns the bag inside out, shaking and twisting it, and again produces an egg from it as before, repeating the operation until the supply of eggs is exhausted. Sometimes he varies his proceedings by trampling or jumping on the bag, which he lays for that purpose on the floor, with its lower edge towards the audience. The eggs are thus on the side remote from the spectators, and in trampling on the bag it is very easy for the performer to avoid the particular line in which he knows them to be.

It was formerly the fashion, after bringing out a number of eggs as above described, to finish by producing the hen which is supposed to have laid them. This was done by an adroit exchange of the bag just used for another containing a hen, hung in readiness behind a chair, or some other convenient cover. This latter bag having no double side, or other preparation, might safely be abandoned to the inspection of the most curious spectator. Where it is not intended to produce the bird, it will still be well to have the second bag, so as to be able to make an exchange, and to hand the bag for inspection.

It is a great improvement to the egg-bag to have the lower portion, say the last three inches of its depth, made of network, so that the spectators can at once see each egg as it falls to the bottom of the bag. It is hardly necessary to observe that in this case the inner lining of the double side must terminate where the network commences.

To Produce Eggs from a Person's Mouth.—While upon the subject of eggs, we may notice this, though it has always appeared to us a rather disagreeable trick. It is rarely exhibited as a separate feat, but generally as a prelude to some other illusion, for the performance of which three or four eggs are necessary.

The performer, requiring eggs, sends his assistant to fetch a plate. On his return, he places him, holding the plate with both hands in front of him, facing the company. The performer standing beside him, and gently patting him on the head, an egg is seen to appear between his lips. This is taken from him, and placed on the plate. The performer, passing behind him, now stands on his other side, and again patting his head, another egg is produced in like manner. This is repeated until the requisite number of eggs is procure , the assistant, as each fresh one is produced, simulating increasing difficulty, as though the eggs were forced up from the stomach by a powerful muscular effort.

This effect is produced as follows : We will suppose that five eggs are to be produced. One is placed beforehand in the mouth of the assistant, and four more are placed in the *pochettes*, or tucked under the waistband of the performer, two on each side. Having placed his assistant in position, the performer secretly takes one of these latter into his right hand, and palms it. Patting the assistant on the head with his left hand, he waits until the egg appears between the teeth, and immediately on its appearance, raises his right hand as if to receive it, thus bringing up the palmed egg opposite the mouth, while the egg that is already in the mouth slips back, under cover of the hand, out of sight. The palmed egg is laid on the plate, and the performer, in the act of passing behind his assistant, palms a second egg in his left hand. The same pantomime is again gone through, save that in this case the right hand pats the head, and the left hand is held to the mouth to receive the egg. After four eggs have been produced in this manner, the fifth, which has been all along in the mouth, is produced apparently in like manner, but the performer takes care that in this instance it shall be seen beyond a doubt that the egg really does come from the mouth ; which being manifestly the case in this instance, the audience are pretty sure to jump to the conclusion that all were produced in an equally *bonâ fide* manner.

THE PILLARS OF SOLOMON, AND THE MAGIC BRADAWL.— There is a very old-fashioned apparatus, sometimes called the Pillars of Solomon, for apparently uniting a piece of cut string. It consists of two slips of wood, each about four inches in length by five-eighths

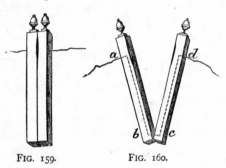

FIG. 159.　　　FIG. 160.

of an inch square, laid side by side. At about an inch from one end of each, a transverse hole is bored, and through this, passing through both slips, a string is passed, and may be drawn backwards and forwards from side to side. (*See* Fig. 159.) The apparatus having been shown in this condition, the performer passes a knife between the two slips, thus apparently dividing the string ; but the string is notwithstanding still drawn backward and forwards through the holes, as sound as ever.

The secret lies in the fact that the string does not, in reality, go straight through the two slips of wood from side to side. A glance at Fig. 160 will enlighten the reader as to its real course. Instead of passing straight through from *a* to *d*, as it appears to do when the two pillars are laid side by side (which is the condition in which they are first exhibited to the spectators), it passes down the length of the first pillar from *a* to *b*, out at *b*, and into the second pillar at *c*, whence it passes upwards, and emerges at *d*. The passing of the knife between the two points *a* and *d* does not therefore affect the string in the least.

It is obvious that in this form of the apparatus the two pillars, being joined by the cords at the points *b c*, cannot be completely separated, and the fact of their always being kept close together at the lower end is quite sufficient to betray to an acute observer the principle of the trick. There is, however, an improved form of the same apparatus, in which, after the apparent cutting of the cord, the two pillars are held wide apart, one in each hand of the performer, and yet, when they are again placed side by side, the string runs backwards and forwards merrily as ever. The pillars are, in this instance, of the form shown in Fig. 161. They are about six inches in length, of light and elegant shape, having at each end a ball or knob of about an inch and a quarter in diameter, flattened on one face to allow of the pillars being laid closely side by side. The cord, as in the former case, passes down the first pillar from *a* to *b*, but instead of passing out at *b*, it is rolled round a little pulley working in the lower knob of that pillar. (*See* Fig. 162, which gives a sectional view of the lower portion of each pillar.) A similar

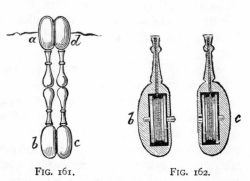

FIG. 161. FIG. 162.

cord is passed down from *d* in the second pillar to *c*, and is there rolled round a second pulley, but in the opposite direction to that of the first cord; so that, if both pulleys move in the same direction, the cord on the one will be wound, and the cord on the other unwound. Each pulley is of one piece with its axis, the axis of the one terminating in a little square tenon or nut, and that of the other in a corresponding mortice or hollow, so that when the two pillars are placed side by side, their axes fit the one into the other, and whichever of the two pulleys is set in motion, the like movement is communicated to the other. The effect of this is as follows: If the cord at *a* be pulled, it unwinds that portion of the cord which is wound on the pulley at *b*, and by the same movement winds up the cord on the other pulley; and *vice versâ.* We have omitted to mention that there is glued into a little hole on the flat side of each of the upper knobs, exactly opposite the points a and b, a very minute piece, say an eighth of an inch in length, of similar cord; these greatly heightening the appearance of reality upon the apparent cutting of the cord.

The pillars are brought forward side by side, the nut of the one pulley fitting strictly into the hollow of the other. The performer shows, by drawing the cord backwards and forwards, that it fairly traverses the two pillars from side to side. Taking a knife, he passes it between the two pillars, and to all appearance cuts the cord, immediately taking the pillars one in each hand, and showing the cut ends (really the short bits on the inside) to prove that it is fairly cut through. Again bringing the pillars together, taking care that the mortice and the nut correspond as before, he commands the cord to be restored, and again pulls it backwards and forwards as at first.

Some little fun may be created by placing the upper knobs of the pillars pincer-fashion, one on each side of a person's nose, the cord being thus apparently made to run right through the nose. An air of greater probability may be given to this curious effect by first piercing the nose with the magic bradawl. This is in appearance an ordinary bradawl, but the blade is so arranged as to recede into the handle on the slightest pressure, again reappearing (being, in fact, forced forward by a spiral spring in the handle) as soon as the pressure is removed. A duplicate bradawl of ordinary make is first handed round for examination, and the trick bradawl being adroitly substituted, the performer proceeds therewith to bore a hole through the nose of any juvenile volunteer who will submit to the operation. Holding a piece of cork on one side of the nose, he apparently thrusts the awl through the nose, the sinking of the blade into the handle exactly simulating the effect of a genuine perforation. (Some performers make use of a sponge moistened with some liquid resembling blood, which by a little pressure is made to trickle down from the imaginary wound; but this is a piece of realism which we think is better omitted.) The nose being thus apparently pierced, the imagination of the spectators is in a measure prepared to accept the

phenomenon of the restored cord running through it as already
described.

THE MAGIC COFFERS.—These are round tin boxes, japanned to
taste, and made generally about five inches in depth by three in diameter, though they are sometimes larger. (*See* Fig. 163.) The only
speciality about them is a moveable portion *a*, which may either be
removed with the lid or left upon the box, according as the lid is
lifted with or without lateral pressure. This moveable portion is
bottomed with a grating of parallel wires, an eighth of an inch apart.
The coffers are generally worked in pairs, the effect produced by them
being the apparent transmission of the contents of the one to the
other, and *vice versâ*. They may be worked with various articles.
For our present purpose we will suppose that the performer desires to
change white haricot beans to coffee-berries, both of which suit
the apparatus very well. He beforehand fills the one coffer with
beans, and the moveable compartment belonging to it with coffee-
berries, doing exactly the reverse as to the
second coffer. The coffers are now brought
forward, and the performer, removing the
lids (*with* the moveable compartments), allows
the spectators to satisfy themselves that
each coffer is full to the bottom, and that
the contents are nothing more or less than
what they appear to be. This being established, he returns to his table, and again puts
the lids on the coffers, taking care that that
which contains the beans shall be placed on
the coffer containing the coffee-berries, and
vice versâ. He now requests two of the
younger spectators to step forward, and assist
him with the trick. A couple of volunteers

FIG. 163.

having been procured, they are made to salute the audience, and are
then seated upon chairs at each side of the stage, each being entrusted
with one of the coffers, which, that all may see, they are requested to
hold with both hands above their heads. The performer, standing
between them, says, " Now, young gentlemen, I must caution you to

hold tight, or the electrical forces which are rapidly generating in these magic coffers will carry them clean away, and possibly you along with them. Now, first please tell me, just to start fair, which coffer is it that you have got, sir, the one with the beans, or the one with the coffee-berries?" The chances are ten to one against the *extempore* assistants remembering which was which, and the majority of the audience will be equally uncertain. The professor pretends surprise and disappointment. "Ladies and gentlemen, you cannot possibly appreciate the beauty of these philosophical experiments unless you follow them carefully from the commencement. I will open the coffers once more." So saying, he opens first the one coffer and then the other, taking care, however, to lift the lids only, so that the one which really contains the coffee-berries shows the layer of beans, and that which contains the beans the layer of coffee-berries. In each case he takes up a handful, and lets them flow back from his hand into the coffer, the better to impress upon the audience the con- tents of each, finally placing a bean in the hands of the youth who holds the supposed coffer of beans, and a berry in the hands of the holder of the supposed coffee-berries. Again closing the lids, he requests the person holding the bean to throw it into the closed coffer held by the other. The juvenile, looking foolish, replies that it can't be done; and a similar reply is received from the youth holding the other coffer. The performer, addressing the company, asks some one else to make the attempt, but equally without success. He continues, " Gentlemen, among this large and brilliant audience not one person can be found who will undertake to throw this little bean into one of those coffers. Imagine, then, the difficulty of passing the whole of the beans which this coffer contains into the other, not dropping even one on the way, and at the same moment transferring the whole of the berries in this coffer into that which, a moment before, was full to the brim with the beans. But it must be done. Young gentlemen, will you be kind enough to repeat with me, One, two, three! At the word "three," by the way, you had better close your eyes, or they might possibly be injured by the shower of beans and berries. Are you ready, Mr. Beans? Are you ready, Mr. Berries? Now, then, One! two! *three! ! !* Did you feel them pass? I hope they did not hurt you. Now let us once more open the coffers. I have kept my word, you see—Mr. Beans has the coffee-berries, and Mr. Berries has the beans. Will you please step forward, and show the company that the coffers are, as at first, full to the very bottom." The lids, containing the moveable compartments, he meanwhile places care-lessly upon his table.

Some performers make the change more than once, and it is obvious that the contents of the coffers may be made to apparently change places any number of times. If this is done, however, the secret of the false tops is apt to be suspected ; whereas, in the method above described, the audience have, as they believe, proved the coffers full to the bottom, both before and after the trick ; and this greatly increases the difficulty of accounting for the transposition.

The object of having the false tops bottomed with open wirework, instead of with tin, is to be prepared for the expression of a suspicion on the part of the audience as to the existence of a false top. In such case the performer, borrowing a penknife, passes it well down through the upper layer of beans, etc., and through the wirework, thus proving (apparently) that the coffer is open to the bottom. In the trick as above described, however, the expression of such a sus-picion is a very remote contingency.

The trick is sometimes performed with sweetmeats in one or both of the coffers, and in this form has an added charm for a juvenile audience, who complete the trick by swallowing that portion of the apparatus.

THE BRAN AND ORANGE TRICK.—This trick is performed with a single coffer, in appearance very similar to those used in the last trick, but slightly different in construction. The false top is, in this case, bottomed with plain tin. The bottom of the coffer is moveable, being soldered to a circular rim or shoulder of tin about a quarter of an inch in depth, over which the coffer fits pretty tightly, though the projecting edge of the bottom enables the performer to remove it without difficulty. The performer must also be provided with an ordinary oblong wooden box. Its precise dimensions are unimpor-tant, save that it should be a good deal larger than the coffer, but about an inch or so less in height. This box is filled with bran, as also is the false top of the coffer. A couple of oranges, as much alike as possible, must also be provided. One only of these is produced to the audience, the other being beforehand placed on the *servante* of the table.

The performer begins by placing upon the table the coffer and the box of bran. Removing the lid (with the false top), he brings forward the coffer, and shows that it is perfectly empty. In returning to his table, he loosens (though without removing) the moveable bottom, and replaces the coffer on the table. He next brings forward the box of bran, showing that there is no preparation about it, and in replacing it on the table, places it in front of the coffer, which, however, being the taller, remains visible behind it. He next introduces the orange, either palming it (from one of his *pochettes*), and magically producing it from some person's nose or whiskers, or by the more prosaic method of having it brought in by his assistant. He now returns to his table, and, standing behind it, proceeds to fill the coffer with bran. This he does by placing the coffer upright in the box, holding it with one hand and ostentatiously pouring in bran with the other until it is full. In placing the coffer in the box, however, he takes it up quite *without* the bottom, so that he is, in reality, only filling an open tube. Meanwhile, he secretly picks up, with his disengaged hand, the second orange from the *servante*, and places it upon the bottom, which remains behind the box. Having filled the coffer, and remarking, "Pray observe that it is quite full," he (before removing it from the box) covers it with the lid, and then lifting it out, again places it behind the box in such manner as to go neatly over the bottom and the orange upon it. (Of course, in the act of lifting the coffer, all the contents run back again into the box.) Having now got the second orange within the coffer, and having, by a gentle pressure, again settled the bottom in its place, the performer places the coffer on a second table or a chair close in front of the audience. He then says, " I am about to order the bran with which this coffer is filled " (here he raises the lid without the false top, and the coffer therefore appears full of bran) " to pass back again into the box from which it was taken, and this orange " (here he passes behind his table, and holding up the orange, replaces it six or eight inches from the hinder edge) "to pass into the coffer in place of it. Now, first for the bran. One, two, three ! Pass ! Did you see it fly from the coffer into the box ? You didn't ? Well, at any rate, you shall see the orange pass. I take it up *so*" (here he places his two hands round it, and rolls it on to the *servante* in manner described at page 294, coming forward with the hands together, as though still containing it, and holding them over the coffer at a few inches' distance), "and squeeze it smaller and smaller, in this manner, till it becomes small enough to pass right into the coffer, as you see." Here he separates his hands, showing them empty, and immediately taking off the cover *with* the false top, rolls out the orange, and shows that the coffer is otherwise empty.

The trick as above described is susceptible of a good many variations. If the performer uses a trap-table, the orange may be made to pass through a trap instead of being rolled off at the back of the table, though the latter method, if neatly executed, can hardly be surpassed in illusive effect. A more substantial improvement may be made by causing the bran, instead of simply disappearing as above mentioned, to reappear in some other quarter. There are many pieces of apparatus which may be used for this purpose, perhaps as good as any being the improved sweet-bag (*see* page 248). This should be previously filled with bran, and hooked to the back of the table. The performer in this case borrows a handkerchief, which he carelessly spreads on the table, and a gentleman's hat, which he places mouth upwards beside it. Instead of announcing that the bran will return from the coffer to the box from whence it was taken, he states that it will, at command, pass into the handkerchief which he holds, and which as he speaks he picks up, with the bag beneath it, holding it, without apparent intention, just above the hat. At the word "Pass!" he slightly turns his wrist, thereby releasing the flap of the bag, and a shower of bran is instantly seen to pour down into the hat. This little addition greatly enhances the effect of the trick.

THE RICE AND ORANGE TRICK.—In this feat rice and an orange are made to change places, but by wholly different means from those last above described.

The apparatus in this case consists of three japanned tin cones, about ten inches in height by five at the base, and each having a brass knob at the top—and an ornamental vase of tin or zinc, standing about the same height as the cones, and having a simple metal cover, or top. Of the cones (all of which are open at the bottom), two are hollow throughout, but the third has a flap or moveable partition half-way down, inclosing the upper half of the internal space. This flap works on a hinge, and is kept shut by a little catch, which is withdrawn by pressure on a little button outside the cone, when the flap drops down, and lets fall whatever has been placed in the enclosed space. (*See* Fig. 164.) The cone is prepared for the trick by filling this space with rice, and closing the flap; and the three cones are then placed in a row on the performer's table, the prepared one being in the middle. The vase (*see* Fig. 165) is constructed as follows :— Its depth inside is less by about an inch than its depth outside, leaving, therefore, between its true

FIG. 164.

and false bottoms, an empty space, *a*. A circular hole is cut in the inner or false bottom, but this hole, in the normal condition of the vase, is kept closed by a circular disc of metal, *b*, exactly fitting it. This disc is soldered upon an upright wire rod, passing through

FIG. 165.

the foot of the apparatus, and terminating in another disc, *c*, somewhat smaller in size. Round this rod is a spiral spring, whose action tends to press it down, and thereby to keep the disc or valve normally closed, though it rises, and thereby opens the valve (as shown by the dotted lines in the figure), whenever upward pressure is applied to *c*. The face of the upper disc, *b*, is slightly concave, corresponding with the rest of the interior of the vase. The vase is prepared for the trick by placing an orange in it, and in this condition it is brought forward and placed on the table by the performer or his assistant. A small paper bag full of rice is brought in at the same time, and completes the preparations.

With this introduction, we proceed to describe the trick as worked by Herrman.

The performer begins by borrowing two hats, and places them one on the other, the mouths together, on a chair or table. He then (by palming) produces an orange from the hair or whiskers of a spectator, and places this on another table. He next brings forward and exhibits the vase, filling it as he advances with rice from the paper bag, and thus concealing the orange which is already placed therein. He calls attention to the genuineness of the rice and the simplicity of the cover, and finally putting on the latter, places the vase on the ground, or elsewhere, in view of the audience. He pretends a momentary hesitation as to where to place it, and in the slight interval during which he is making up his mind he presses up the button within the foot. This opens the valve, allowing the rice to escape into the space *a*, and leaving the orange again uncovered. The audience is, of course, unaware that such a change has taken place.

Leaving the vase for the moment, he requests the audience to choose one or other of the three cones on the table. The choice almost always falls on the middle one (which, it will be remembered, contains the concealed rice). This he places on the top of the upper hat. He next asks the audience to select one or other of the remaining cones, and places this over the orange upon the table, showing by rattling his wand within it that it is hollow throughout, and, if desired, handing round the remaining one for inspection.

At this point we hasten to anticipate an objection which will probably occur to the reader. We have said that the audience, when called upon to choose one of the three cones, *almost* always select the middle one, and we have proceeded on the assumption that they do so. " But suppose," says the acute reader, " that they *don't* choose the middle one, but select one of the end ones; the trick is spoilt, as neither of the others will produce the rice." By no means, O acute reader! If we had requested the audience to choose which of the cones should be placed upon the hat, there might have been a little difficulty, no doubt; but we did nothing of the kind. We merely asked them to choose one of the cones. If their first choice falls on one of the end ones, we hand it round for examination, and finally place it *over the orange*. Then, standing behind the table, we ask the audience to make their choice between the two remaining cones, right or left. Which-ever is chosen, we are safe; for as we have already had occasion to explain in connection with the trick of the half-crown in the orange (*see* page 171), the right of the audience is our left, and *vice versâ*, so that by taking their reply in the sense which suits our purpose we are certain to be right. We therefore, in any case, take the cone containing the rice as being the one designated, and place this on the hat, sending round the other for inspection. As the audience have, to all appearance, been allowed perfect freedom of choice, and have actually examined two out of the three cones, they are very unlikely to suspect any preparation about the remaining one.

The trick is now all but complete. Once more the performer raises the cone placed on the hat, to show that there is nothing underneath it ; and as he replaces it presses the button, thereby letting the flap fall, and the rice pour out upon the hat, though it remains still concealed by the cone. He next lifts up the cone under which is the orange, and holding the latter up, replaces it, but in again covering it with the cone, makes a feint of removing and slipping it into his pocket. Then noticing, or pretending to notice, a murmur on the part of the company, he says, "Oh, you think I took away the orange, but I assure you I did not." The company being still incredulous, he again lifts the cone and shows the orange. " Here it is, you see, but as you are so suspicious, I won't use the cover at all, but leave the orange here in full view on the table." He again lays the orange on the table, but this time on what is called a " wrist trap." Leaving it for the moment, he advances to the vase, and holding his hands together cup-fashion over it, but without touching it, he says, "I take out the rice, so, and pass it under this cover" (walking towards the cone on the hat, and making a motion of passing something into it). " Let us see whether it has passed." He raises the cover, and the rice is seen. " Perhaps you think, as you did not see it, that I did not actually pass the rice from the vase to the cover. At any rate, you will not be able to say the same about the orange. I take it up, before your eyes, so ! " He places his hands round it on the table, and at the same moment presses the lever of the trap, which opens, and lets it fall through into the table, closing again instantly. Keep-ing his hands together, as though containing the orange, he advances to the vase, and holding his hands over it, says, " Here is the orange which has not left your sight even for a single moment. I gently press it, so " (bringing the hands closer and closer together) " and make it smaller and smaller, till it is reduced to an invisible powder, in which state it passes into the vase." He separates his hands, and shows them empty, and then opening the vase, rolls out the orange, and shows the vase empty, all the rice having disappeared.

The mechanism of the Wrist Trap will be explained in the next Chapter. If the performer does not possess a trap table, he can cause the orange to disappear in the manner referred to at page 337.

THE MAGIC WHISTLE.—The student will not have proceeded far in his magical experience before he meets with an often-recurring nuisance, in the person of some individual, old or young, who knows, or pretends to know, the secret of all his tricks, and whose greatest delight it is, by some *mal-à-propos* question or suggestion, to cause the performer embarrassment. The magic whistle is specially designed to punish, and, if possible, to silence, an individual of this kind. It is of turned boxwood, and of the shape shown in Fig. 166, and yields a shrill and piercing note. The performer, bringing it forward and blowing through it, announces that this little

FIG. 166.

whistle, so simple in appearance, has the singular faculty of obeying his will, and of sounding or not sounding at his command alone. The loquacious gentleman is pretty sure to question the fact, or is on some pretence selected to make trial of its truth. The performer places him directly facing the audience, and after himself once more sounding the whistle, hands it to him in order to try his skill. He blows vigorously, but in vain ; not a sound can he produce, but his mouth and lips gradually become obscured with a white or black dust. He finally retires to his seat amid the laughter of the audience, and generally much less disposed to make himself prominent during the remainder of the evening.

The secret lies in the fact that there are two whistles—one is a perfectly ordinary instrument, but the other, though similar in appearance, does not sound, but is perforated round the inner side of the head (*see* the Figure) with a number of small holes. The head unscrews, and is beforehand filled with finely powdered chalk or charcoal, which, when the whistle is blown, is forced through the holes, and settles round the mouth of the victim.

With the present knowledge of the reader, the necessary exchange of the two whistles will not be regarded as offering any difficulty.

There is a larger appliance for the same purpose in the shape of a flageolet. Another apparatus of like effect, though differing a little in detail, is called

THE MAGIC MILL.—This is a little Mill of the form shown in Fig. 167, and five or six inches in height. It is made of zinc or tin, and consists of two portions—the upper part Λ, and the base B (*see* Fig. 168), the former sliding over the latter (as shown by the dotted lines in Fig. 167), and fitting easily upon it. A is hollow throughout; *a* and *b b* are hollow tubes open at each end, a third little tube *c* springing at right angles from *a*. The base, B, is a hollow chamber, closed on all sides save at the openings *d* and *e e*. This chamber is beforehand fitted with powdered chalk or charcoal; after which A is placed in position over it. If, under these circumstances, any person blows smartly through the tube *a*, the effect will vary according to the position of B within A. If B be so turned that the three holes *d* and *e e* correspond with the tubes *a* and *b b*, the breath entering at *d* will force out the contents of B through the tubes *b b*, and powder the lips of the person blowing, as in the case of the magic whistle. But if, on the contrary, B be turned ever so little to the right or left, the three openings in B no

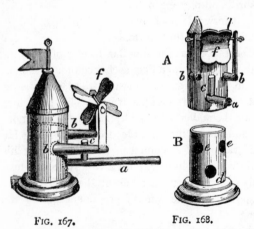

FIG. 167. FIG. 168.

longer corresponding with the tubes, the latter will be closed, and the breath having no other outlet, will be forced upwards through the upright tube *c*, thereby setting the little vane *f* in rapid motion. The latter is the condition in which the apparatus is brought forward by the performer. Blowing through *a*, he sets the mill in motion, and invites others to do likewise, in which, of course, they succeed without difficulty; but when the turn of the intended victim arrives, the performer gives A a slight twist round, in such manner as to bring the openings of B in correspondence with the three tubes, with the result already explained. We have omitted to mention that there is on the under surface of B a little raised point, corresponding in position with the opening *d*, so that the performer is able to tell instantly by feel whether B is or is not in the required position.

As a matter of convenience, we shall, before proceeding further with the explanation of individual tricks, describe two or three pieces of apparatus of general utility, to one or other of which we shall have frequent occasion to subsequently refer.

THE DRAWER-BOX.—This is a piece of apparatus of very frequent use in the magic art. In appearance it is an ordinary drawer, with

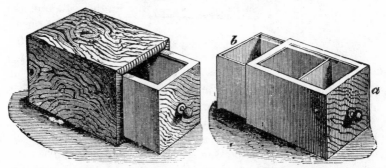

FIG. 169.   FIG. 170.

an outer box or case of walnut or mahogany (*see* Fig. 169), and is made of various dimensions, according to the size of the articles with which it is intended to be used, and which may range from a pack of cards to a live rabbit. Its use is to produce or to cause the disappearance of a given article; the drawer having the faculty of appearing full or empty at pleasure.

The first step towards the comprehension of the apparatus will be to completely take out the drawer, which, however, even when removed, does not at first sight indicate any speciality. On a closer examination, it will be found that the drawer is in reality double (*see* Fig. 170), consisting of two parts, *a* and *b*, the latter sliding backwards and forwards freely within the former, which is, in fact, a mere case or shell, open at one end. If any object, suppose an orange, be placed in *b*, and *a* and *b* together be placed in the outer case, it is obvious that, upon drawing out *a*, *b* will come with it, and the orange will be seen; but if *b* be held back, *a* will be drawn out alone, and the apparatus will be apparently empty. For the means of retaining *a* at pleasure, it will be necessary to examine the outer case, which will be found to have a groove or mortice cut in its under surface (*see* Fig. 171), along which lies a spring or tongue of wood, fixed by a screw

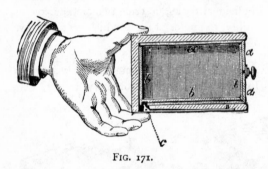

at one end, the other, or free end, being provided with a catch or stud *c*, which, upon pressure, is forced through an opening in the bottom of the outer case, and made to sink into a little hole or notch in the bottom of *b*, being

FIG. 171.

again withdrawn by the action of the spring as soon as the pressure is removed. The bottom of the outer case is covered with velvet, ostensibly as a finish, but really to conceal the wooden tongue. When it is desired to draw out *a* without *b*, the apparatus is held as shown in Fig. 171, and a gentle pressure applied by the finger through the velvet upon the free end of the wooden tongue, thus forcing the catch upwards, and keeping *b* back. If *a* be drawn out without this pressure, *b* will come with it. The upper edge of *a* is turned over all round, so that a casual observer is not likely to detect any difference in the thickness of the sides of the drawer, whether it is drawn out with or without its inner casing.

Some drawer-boxes have a different arrangement for holding back the inner drawer, consisting of a little wire bolt lying loosely in a cylindrical cavity in the hinder end of *b*, corresponding with a similar cavity in the side of the outer case. As long as the drawer-box is kept in its normal position, this pin offers no obstacle to the withdrawal of *b* with *a*; but if the box be turned over on the side in which is the bolt, the latter drops partially into the hole in the outer case, thus bolting *b* to it, until, by again turning over the apparatus, the bolt is made to drop back again into its original position. The arrangement is rather difficult to explain in writing, but will become

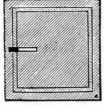

FIG. 172.

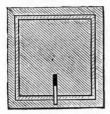

FIG. 173.

quite clear upon an examination of Figs. 172 and 173, both representing a section of the hinder end of the drawer-box, the one in its upright and the one in its turned-over position. The necessary turning over of the box is plausibly accounted for by the performer's desire that the audience shall, for greater fairness, have a full view of the top of the apparatus.

There is an ingenious addition sometimes found in drawer-boxes of French make, whereby *b* may be at pleasure bolted to *a*, and the two may thus be handed for examination, with little chance of their secret being detected. The bolting and unbolting is effected by a slight movement up or down of the knob in front, thereby raising or depressing a kind of hook of bent tin, working in the thickness of the front of *a*. Fig. 174 shows this hook in its raised or unhooked, and Fig. 175 in its depressed or hooked condition.

FIG. 174. FIG. 175.

The drawer-box, as above described, is available to produce or dis-

appear, but not to change articles. With a slight modification, however, it may be made available for changing also. The inner drawer
b is in this case made only half the depth of *a*, or even less; and thus,
when closed, there is left between the bottom of *b* and that of *a* a
considerable space, so that *a* and *b* may in this case each be made to
hold a given object, and an apparent transformation be effected.
Thus, for instance, *b* may be filled with bran, and any small article,
such as a borrowed pocket-handkerchief, be placed in *a*. The drawer
is first pulled out with *b*, and shown filled to the brim with bran;
but on being closed and again opened (without *b*), the bran is
apparently transformed into the handkerchief.

Another modification of the drawer-box is known as

THE DISSECTING DRAWER-BOX.—This is, in general appearance,
not unlike the ordinary drawer-box already described, but with this

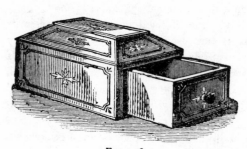

difference, that the
outer case has a raised
top, somewhat of a
sarcophagus shape.
(*See* Fig. 176). The
drawer is partially
drawn out to show
that it is empty, is
again closed, and on
being once more
drawn out, proves to

FIG. 176.

be full to the brim with flowers. These having been distributed, the
performer, to prove the perfect emptiness of the apparatus, not only
takes the drawer completely out, but takes the outer case (which is
constructed accordingly, the sides, top, and bottom being hinged
to the back) apart, as shown in Fig. 177. Notwithstanding this,
upon again reconstructing the case, and replacing and reopening the
drawer, it is once more found filled with flowers.

The reader, being acquainted with the ordinary drawer-box, will
have no difficulty in accounting for the first harvest of flowers, but
the second may possibly puzzle him a little. The secret lies in the
top of the outer case, which, as we have already mentioned, is slightly

pyramidal in form, allowing a considerable space between its inner and outer surface, and in this space is packed the second supply of flowers. This space is closed on its under side by a flat wooden slab *a*, of the same area as the inside of the drawer, held in position by a thin wooden slip or bead at either end. The hindmost of these beads, *b*, is so arranged as to yield to pressure, and, when the drawer is pushed slightly in, gives way just enough to release

FIG. 177.

the slab before mentioned, which thereupon falls flat upon the bottom of the drawer, and upon it the hitherto concealed flowers, which, spreading as they fall, completely fill the drawer.

THE CHANGING CARD-DRAWER.—This is a smaller variety of the drawer-box, designed specially for use in card tricks. The inner drawer is just large enough to contain a pack of cards, which may thus be produced or vanished by its means. Between the bottoms of the true and false or outer drawer, is a space of about an eighth of an inch. This makes the apparatus available not only to produce or vanish as above mentioned, but to transform one card into another. The card to be changed is for this purpose placed in the outer drawer, which, when closed, carries it under the bottom of the inner drawer, and in this latter is placed the card for which it is to be changed, or *vice versâ.*

There is an improved form of the card-drawer, with a double change, effected on the principle of the dissecting drawer-box. This is just as above described, with the addition that when the two drawers are pressed smartly home, the action releases a thin slab of wood forming apparently part of the inner surface of the case, and exactly equal in area to the bottom of the inner drawer, into which it falls. When required for use, a card is placed above this slab, which, falling when required, covers the card already in the box, and exhibits instead that which had been concealed above it, as in the case of the changing card-boxes, described in the chapter devoted to card tricks. The uses of such an apparatus will be obvious; but we will describe, by way of illustration, one very good trick which may be performed with it.

The apparatus is prepared beforehand by placing a given card (say the knave of spades) above the moveable slab, and another (say the eight of diamonds) in the outer drawer. The performer invites two persons to each draw a card, and "forces" upon them the knave of spades and eight of diamonds. The cards being replaced in the pack, he, if he has used an ordinary pack, brings them to the top by the "pass," and palms them, or if he has used a forcing pack, exchanges that pack for an ordinary one from which those two cards have been removed. Leaving the pack on the table, he exhibits the card-drawer, taking out both drawers together, and showing, apparently, that case and drawer are absolutely empty. Closing the drawer, he announces that he will make the drawn cards leave the pack, and pass into the drawer. One of the cards (the eight of diamonds) is named, and pulling out this time the outer drawer only, he shows that it contains that card, which is taken out, and handed to the person who drew it. Again the drawer is closed, being this time pushed sharply home. The second card, the knave, being now named, the drawer is again opened, and this card shown; the drawer being again taken wholly out, and the drawer and case turned in all directions for inspection, as before, the operator only taking care to hold the drawer with one finger inside, that the moveable slab may not, by falling out, betray its presence.

CHANGING CADDIES.—These are of various kinds. We will begin with the simplest, thence proceeding to the more complicated. The conjuror's caddy, in its most elementary form, is an oblong box, about six inches in length by five in height and four in width. (*See* Fig. 178.) One-half of its interior, which is divided into two compartments by a transverse bar across the top, is occupied by a drawer, or moveable compartment, so arranged as to slide freely backwards and forwards from end to end, according as the caddy is allowed to slope in the one direction or the other. (*See* Figs. 179 and 180.)

Each compartment has its own lid, the caddy sometimes, but not always, having an outer lid in addition.

We will suppose that it is desired to produce any article from the caddy, first shown empty. The article in question (say an egg, hard-boiled for safety) is beforehand placed in the moveable compartment, which we will suppose to occupy for the time being the space under lid *a*, as shown in Fig. 179. The performer takes off

FIG. 178.

the opposite lid *b*, and shows the space beneath empty. Before removing the second lid, he slopes the caddy in the opposite direction, so as to bring the moveable compartment under lid *b* (*see* Fig. 180), and thus is enabled to show the space under *a* also empty. He then

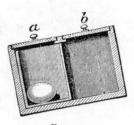

FIG. 179.

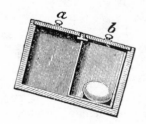

FIG. 180.

proceeds with the trick, and at the right moment produces the article from the caddy.

It is obvious that the caddy above described is only available for appearances and disappearances, and not for transformations. To

obviate this defect, the majority of caddies are now made with *three*
compartments (*see* Fig. 181), with a sliding drawer occupying two of
them.   The caddy in this form may be used to "change" objects in

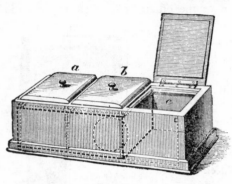

FIG. 181.

manner following:—
The sliding drawer
being as shown in
Fig. 181, the article
to be ultimately pro-
duced (say an orange)
is placed in *b*.   The
three compartments
are now shown empty,
beginning with *c*, and
allowing the sliding
drawer to assume the
position shown in
Fig. 182, before in turn uncovering *a* and *b*.   The article to be
changed (say a watch) is now placed openly in compartment *b*.   The
performer closes the lid, and, after a moment's interval, reopens it,
but in that interval slopes the caddy so as to again bring the sliding

drawer into the posi-
tion shown in Fig.
181, when the orange
is again brought un-
der *b*, and, on re-
moving the lid, is dis-
closed.   To show that
the watch has really
disappeared, the caddy
may again be shown
(apparently) empty,
in the same manner
as at first.

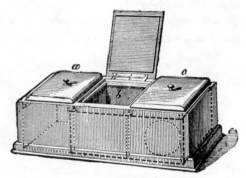

FIG. 182.

There are a good many varieties of caddies made.   One is known
as the "skeleton" caddy, from the fact that the bottom is made to
take out, so that the company can look through all three compartments.   The sliding drawer in this case is bottomless, and is so

arranged as only to slide when the performer releases it by pressing upon a particular spot in the ornamental moulding round the bottom of the caddy. This pressure withdraws a little pin, which normally rests in a little hole in the side of the sliding drawer, and thus renders it for the time being a fixture. In some caddies, again, the sliding drawer does not run up and down by its own weight, but is moved backwards and forwards from below by means of a projecting pin passing through a slit in the bottom of the caddy. The caddy in this case does not require to be inclined one way or the other, and is on this account preferred by many to the other make.

The trick next described will introduce to the reader a changing caddy of another and special construction.

THE MAGIC VASE AND CADDY. (To make peas change places with a handkerchief.) — For this trick two special pieces of apparatus are necessary. The first is a tin vase, of the shape shown in Fig. 183, and generally of about ten inches in height. It consists of three parts, the vase proper *a*, the cover *b*, and a moveable compartment or well, *c*, which is constructed upon a principle which we have had frequent occasion to notice, the cylindrical portion of *a* passing between the inner and outer wall of this moveable compartment. It is coloured exactly similar to that portion of *a*

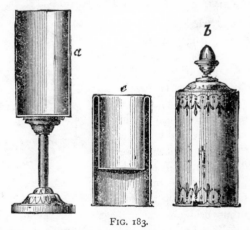

FIG. 183.

which it covers, which therefore looks exactly the same to the ordinary spectator, whether *c* be in its place or removed. The internal depth, however, of *c* is little more than half as deep as that of the actual vase, *a*. The cover *b* exactly fits over *c*, and by means of a little appliance called a "bayonet-catch," will either lift *c* with it when removed, or release *c* and leave it upon *a*.

As this "bayonet-catch" is of constant use in magical apparatus, it will be desirable to describe it somewhat minutely. A rectangular cut or slit (*see* the enlarged view in Fig. 184) is made in the lower

FIG. 184.

edge of the cover *b*. Its perpendicular arm is about a quarter of an inch in length, and its width about an eighth of an inch. A small pin or stud, about an eighth of an inch in length, projects perpendicularly from the lower edge of *c*, at such a height that when *b* is placed over *c*, the upper or horizontal arm of the slit shall be just level with it. If the upright arm of the slit be brought immediately over this pin, the latter will, as the cover sinks down, travel upward along the opening as far as the junction with the transverse portion of the slit. If the cover be now again lifted, the pin will, of course, offer no obstruction to its removal ; but

if the cover be first slightly turned to the right, the pin will become engaged in the transverse portion of the slit, and upon then lifting the cover, it will carry with it the pin, and all connected with it. When it is desired to lift off the cover *alone*, it will only be necessary to turn the cover a little to the left,

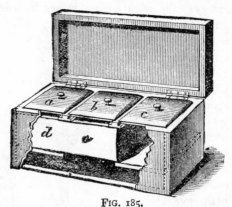

FIG. 185.

thus bringing the pin again over the upright portion of the slit.

The second piece of apparatus is a caddy (Fig. 185), in appearance not unlike an ordinary tea caddy, with three equal-sized compartments, each having its own lid. Upon close inspection it will be discovered that the internal depth of these compartments is somewhat shallow in comparison with the external measurement of the caddy, leaving a space about an inch deep between the inner and outer bottoms. A sliding drawer, working from end to end of the caddy, as already explained, occupies the space of two compartments. Supposing this for the moment removed, it would be found that the external caddy, in the space occupied by the *two* end compartments, *a* and *c*, has a false bottom covering the hollow space we have already mentioned, but that the space occupied by the middle compartment *b* has none. Of the two moveable

FIG. 186.

compartments, which together constitute the sliding tray already mentioned (*see* Fig. 186), the one *d* has a bottom, the other *e* has not.

When the sliding drawer is in its proper position in the caddy, and is pushed as far as it will go towards the one or the other end, the result is as follows :—If it is pushed to the right, the bottomless compartment *e* occupies the space at that end, under lid *c*, while the opening in the false bottom of the caddy is, for the time being, closed by the bottom of *d*, which now occupies the middle space. If the sliding tray is pushed to the opposite end (*i.e.*, to the left), *d* will occupy the space *a* at that end, while the bottomless compartment *e*, being over the opening, gives access to the space beneath.

The caddy is prepared for the purpose of the trick by placing in the space between the true and false bottoms a white handkerchief, and the sliding tray is then pushed to the right, so as to bring compartment *d* to the middle, and thus close the opening. The vase is prepared by filling both divisions with peas. The two pieces of apparatus having been placed on the table by the assistant, the performer opens the caddy, and taking off the lids of the three divisions, and holding it with his fingers inside the right hand end (thereby preventing any possibility of the tray shifting), brings it forward to the audience, and passing rapidly in front of them, begs to introduce to their notice an old tea caddy, in which he has accidentally discovered some curious magical properties. In the present condition of the caddy all three compartments appear exactly alike, and of equal depth ; and the interior being of a dead black, the spectators are not likely to notice that they are somewhat shallow. Again closing the

lids, and replacing the caddy on the table, he next draws attention to
the vase.   Taking off the cover without the moveable compartment,
and holding it upside down, he pours the peas contained in the upper
compartment (which should not be *quite* full) into the cover, and back
again two or three times, finally offering a handful for inspection.
He then borrows a lady's handkerchief, which should as nearly as
possible resemble the substitute hidden in the caddy.   He asks permission to place it, for the purpose of the trick, in the vase.   This
is, of course, readily granted, but the peas are in the way.   After a
moment's pretended hesitation, he says, " Well, I will put them in
the caddy.   Pray observe that I really do so." So saying, he pours
them into *d* (which, it will be remembered, is for the time being the
centre compartment), leaving that compartment uncovered, so that
they may remain visible to all.   He then places the handkerchief
in the apparently empty vase, which he closes and places on the
table.   He continues, " You have all seen me place the handkerchief
in the vase, and the peas in the caddy.   Now I will show you a very
curious experiment.   Perhaps some scientific gentleman among the
audience will explain how the effect is produced; for I confess that
though I have performed this trick some scores of times, I am not
quite certain myself as to the reason of the phenomenon.   Let me
beg you once more to assure yourselves that these are genuine peas,
real common-place peas at twopence a pint, with no nonsense about
them." As he says this, he passes along the front rank of the spectators, exhibiting the peas in the caddy, and occasionally taking out a
handful, and offering them for closer inspection.   As he reaches the
end of the line, he says, " You are all thoroughly satisfied that these
are genuine peas, and that the lady's handkerchief is in the vase upon
the table.   Quite right.   Now observe, I don't even touch the vase,
and yet, at the word of command, the handkerchief will pass into
the caddy which I hold in my hand.   Pass ! " During the last few
words, and holding the caddy for an instant with the lid towards the
audience, so as to screen his hand, he has pushed the sliding tray to
the left, so that *d*, containing the peas, now occupies the end space,
while the bottomless compartment *e* has taken its place in the middle.
Dipping down through this compartment into the hollow space beneath, he takes out the substitute handkerchief.   " My commands

are obeyed. Here is the handkerchief. But where are the peas? Probably, as the handkerchief has taken the place of the peas, the peas have taken the place of the handkerchief. Let us see." He uncovers the vase, lifting this time with the cover the moveable compartment containing the real handkerchief. " Yes, here are the peas, right enough," shaking the vase, and taking them up by handfuls to show them. He continues, " Now I dare say this seems very surprising to you, but in truth it is comparatively simple. The real difficulty begins when you try to make the handkerchief and the peas travel back again to their original situation. This part of the experiment is so difficult, that I always feel a little nervous over it, but I must make the attempt." Pushing the substitute handkerchief openly down to the position it originally occupied, he takes the opportunity, in carrying the caddy back to the table, to slide back the tray as at first, and, after a little more talk, shows that the peas have returned to the caddy, and lifting the cover alone from the vase, produces therefrom the genuine handkerchief.

THE COVER, TO PICK UP ANY ARTICLE.—This (called in French "*ramasse-tout*") is a brass cover of six to ten inches in height, and of the shape shown in Fig. 187. Within it works backwards and forwards on a spring hinge, a kind of scoop, pressing, when at rest, against the side of the cover, as in Fig. 188, but moving into the position shown in Fig. 189 whenever pressure is applied to the button *a*, again returning to its original position when such pressure is removed. The manner of using it is as follows :—The performer, we will suppose, desires to cause the disappearance of an orange, in order that it (or a counterpart) may be subsequently produced in some other quarter. Placing the orange upon the table, he places the cover over it, pressing, as he

FIG. 187.

does so, the button *a*, so as to draw back the scoop. As his hand quits the cover, the pressure being removed, the return of the spring causes the scoop to clip the orange tightly against the side of the cover; and if the cover be now lifted without pressing the button, it will carry the orange with it. If it is desired again to produce the orange, the button is pressed in the act of lifting the cover, which then leaves the orange on the table.

It is hardly necessary to observe that the cover is always lifted perpendicularly, so that the spectator cannot see the interior.

It is well to be provided with a second cover similar in external

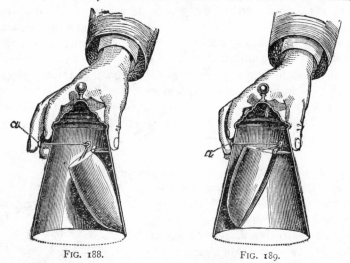

FIG. 188.   FIG. 189.

appearance, but without any mechanism. This may be handed round for inspection, and afterwards secretly exchanged for the mechanical cover.

THE CHANGING COVER.—This cover is available not only, as in the last case, to produce or vanish, but also to change one article for another. It is somewhat of the pattern of an ordinary round dish cover, with a metal knob on the top. (*See* Fig. 190.) It is divided by a vertical tin partition *a* (*see* Fig. 191), into two equal compartments, *b* and *c*. The lower, or open side of each of these compartments is of course semicircular. A flat tin plate, *d*, also semicircular, works on an upright axis, *e*, passing upwards through the centre of the cover, and terminating in the knob on the top. By turning, therefore, this knob halfway round to the right or left, the performer is enabled to close whichever of the compartments happens for the time being to be open, at the same time opening that which was previously shut. There is a little point or stop on the upper side of the semi-circular plate, which meeting resistance from the vertical partition, prevents the plate making more than the necessary half-turn either way.

The apparatus is prepared by placing the article representing the result of the supposed transformation (say an apple) in either compartment, and turning the knob so as to close that compartment, and open the other. The article to be changed (say an orange) is placed upon the table, and the performer places the cover upon it, taking care that the open compartment for the time being shall come fairly over it. He then gives a half turn to the knob, thereby closing the compartment which has hitherto been open, and securing the orange within it, and at the same time releasing the apple, into which, on the

FIG. 190.

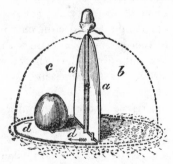

FIG. 191.

cover being again raised, the orange appears to be transformed. In this case, as in the last, it is well to have a plain counterpart cover to hand round for inspection if necessary.

The uses to which the changing cover may be put are very numerous. The following is an instance of a rather original application of it, which produces a capital effect. We will suppose that the performer has executed a trick in which he has availed himself of the assistance of some juvenile member of the audience, and that an apple has been one of the " properties " of the trick. The trick being concluded, the professor asks his temporary assistant whether he would like to have the apple, and is of course eagerly answered in the affirmative. "Very well," says the professor, "you shall have it; but you must first earn it by a little display of dexterity. I will put it under this cover." He suits the action to the word. "Now I am going to say, One, two, three! At the word 'Three' I shall raise the cover, and you must try to snatch the apple before I replace it. If you can catch the apple in this manner three times in succession, it is yours; but on one further condition, that you eat it at once here upon the stage." The conditions are readily accepted. "One, two, three!" cries the professor, raising the cover and disclosing the apple, which is instantly snatched up. A second time the process is gone through, with a like result. "You mean to win, I can see," remarks the performer. "Now, once more, and the apple will be yours; but I warn you I shall be rather quicker this time. One! two!! three!!!" The eager boy springs forward, and clutches—not the apple, but a Spanish onion, which had been placed in the second compartment of the cover. "You have won, sir," says the professor, pretending not to notice the change; "but don't forget the second part of your bargain. You are to eat it at once, before leaving the stage." We will leave to the imagination of the reader the discomfiture of the victim, and the amusement of the spectators; also the subsequent magical processes by which the transformed apple may be restored to its original and more fragrant condition.

THE CHANGING LADLE.—This is a piece of apparatus designed for secretly obtaining possession of a chosen card or piece of writing. The bowl, so to speak, of the ladle is in the form of a segment of a cylinder (*see* Fig. 192), the size of its opening being about four inches by two and a half, and its depth three inches. It is made of tin, with a thin, cylindrical handle. The edges of the bowl are turned inwards all round to the extent of about a sixteenth of an inch, thereby serving to disguise a moveable slab of tin, *a*, which moves backwards and forwards like the leaf of a book within the ladle, working upon a hinge at its lower edge. This is made to work backwards and forwards by a wire rod passing through the whole length of the handle, and terminating in a little knob or cap at its outer end. The normal position of *a* is to lie against the inner or handle side of the bowl (*see*

Fig. 193), being retained in that position by the effect of a spiral spring in the handle, which draws the wire back. If, however, pressure be applied to the knob or cap at the end of the handle, the wire is forced downwards, thereby bringing the móveable leaf *a* against the outer side of the bowl, as shown in Fig. 194.

There are various modes in which the changing ladle may be made useful. For example, it may be used to burn and restore a card. For this purpose, the ladle is prepared by placing in it beforehand any indifferent card of similar pattern to the pack in use, and is in this condition placed on the performer's table, in such manner that the spectators may not observe that there is already a card in it. The performer then comes forward and hands to one of the company a pack of cards, with a request that he will select any one he pleases. While he is making his selection, the performer or his assistant places on the table and sets fire to some spirits of wine on a bowl or plate. A card having been chosen, the performer requests the drawer to return it to him, and, in order to exclude the possibility of any exchange or sleight-of-hand, volunteers to receive it at arm's length in the ladle, which he brings

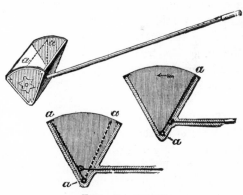

FIGS. 192, 193, 194.

forward for that purpose, holding it by the extreme end of the handle, and pressing with his palm the knob at the top, thereby bringing the moveable leaf into the position shown in Fig. 194, with the card already in it pressed flat against the outer side of the bowl, and thus completely hidden. The chosen card being placed in the ladle, the performer, in returning to his table, relaxes the pressure of his palm, thereby bringing the moveable leaf back into the position of Fig. 193, releasing the dummy card, and concealing that chosen against the inner side of the bowl. He then drops apparently the chosen, but really the substitute, card into the flames, taking care as he does so not to turn the face of the card toward the audience. The ladle, with the genuine card in it, is carried off by the assistant as having served its purpose, and the chosen card is subsequently restored after any fashion which the fancy of the operator may dictate.

The ladle may also be used to apparently burn and restore a paper on which one of the company has written any words or figures. In this case a blank half-sheet of note-paper, folded in four, is beforehand placed in the ladle, and a piece of paper folded in the same way is handed to one of the audience, with a request that he will write what he pleases upon it, again fold it, and place it in the ladle. It is then either apparently burnt (as in the case of the card), or placed in some other apparatus, the operator making a great point of the fact that he does not touch the paper. As the genuine paper remains in the ladle, it is, of course, very easy for the performer to ascertain what is written upon it, and having displayed his knowledge, to ultimately reproduce the paper under any circumstance which he thinks fit. Sometimes the trick is varied by requesting a spectator to write a question upon the paper, which is subsequently reproduced with an appropriate answer written beneath the question.

THE CONE, OR SKITTLE. (*La quille*).—This is a block of polished box-wood, of the shape shown in Fig. 195, with a thin shell of the same material exactly covering it, and so closely resembling it in appearance, that the solid block and the hollow shell, seen apart, cannot be dis-

tinguished the one from the other. The cone is made in various sizes, from three inches in height by one and a half at the base, to seven inches in height by three at the base. It is worked with a paper cover, consisting of an open tube of cartridge paper about double the height of the cone, and tapering in such manner that its larger end shall fit loosely over the cone. The performer brings forward this paper tube in his right hand, and the cone (with the hollow shell upon it) in his left, taking care to hold his fingers beneath it in such manner that the solid cone cannot fall out. He first calls attention to the paper tube, which the audi-

FIG. 195.

ence are allowed to examine at pleasure. When it is returned to him, he says, "You are now quite satisfied that there is no preparation about this tube, which is, in fact, simply a cover for this block of wood." As if merely suiting the action to the word, he covers the block with the tube, immediately removing it again, and carelessly laying the cover on the table. In removing it, however, he grasps

it with a gentle pressure, and so takes off with it the hollow shell (*see* Fig. 196), of whose existence the audience have no suspicion. He continues, " Perhaps you would also like to examine the block, which you will find to be a plain, solid piece of wood, without mechanism or preparation of any kind." The block having been duly examined, the supposed empty cover is placed upright upon the table ; and the solid block having been disposed

FIG. 196.

of by any means in the performer's power, is ordered to pass invisibly under the cover, which being raised, the hollow shell is seen, appearing to the eye of the audience to be the block itself, and to have found its way there in obedience to the performer's command.

The above is the working of the "cone" in its simplest and barest form ; but no skilled performer would dream of presenting the illusion in such a common-place way. To make the trick effective, it should be so arranged as to make the cone apparently change places with some other article. There are many combinations which might be suggested, but we shall content ourselves with describing one or two of those in most general use. The smaller sized cones may be worked in conjunction with a goblet and ball (the same as those used for the Cups and Balls), in manner following :—Having tendered for inspection the cone and cover as already described, and placed them on the table, the performer offers the goblet and ball in like manner for inspection. When they are returned, he places them also upon the table, a little distance apart, and meanwhile palms a second ball, which should be in readiness either on the *servante,* or in one of his *pochettes.* He now places the paper cover (which, it will be remembered, contains the hollow shell) over the first ball on the table. " Pray observe." he remarks, " that I have fairly covered over the ball " (here he raises and replaces the cover, pressing so as to lift the shell with it, and showing that the ball is still there). " The goblet, as you have seen, is perfectly empty." (Here he raises the goblet, and, in replacing it, introduces the second ball under it, as described in the chapter devoted to the Cups and Balls.) " I shall now order the ball to pass from the cover under the goblet." He waves his wand from the one to the other. " Presto ! Prestissimo ! Pass ! " (He raises the goblet, and shows that the ball has (apparently) passed under it.) The first ball still remaining under the paper tube, he cannot at present raise it, so proceeds rapidly to the next stage of the trick, that the omission may not be noticed. " So far," he remarks, " the trick is mere child's play. The real difficulty is to pass the cone under the cover in place of the ball. However, I will make the attempt." So saying, he picks up the cone with his right hand, and apparently transfers it to his left, really palming it, and immediately afterwards dropping his right hand to his side, and getting rid of the cone into the *profonde.* Then, taking two or three steps away from the table, still holding the left hand as if containing the cone, and looking towards the cover, he says, " One, two, three, Pass ! " with a motion of the hand as if throwing something; immediately showing the hands empty, and lifting up the cover (but this time by the top, so as not to exert any pressure against its sides), and show- ing the hollow shell, which now conceals the ball, and is taken by the spectators to be the genuine cone. " We have succeeded pretty well so far, ladies and gentlemen," he remarks ; " it remains to be seen whether I shall be equally successful in bringing back the cone and ball to their original positions. I dare say you would all like to know how the trick is done, and therefore this time I will vary the mode of operation, and make the transposition visibly." (Here he drops his right hand to the *profonde,* and secretly palms the solid cone.) " First the cone " (he passes his right hand, keeping the back towards the audience, upwards along the cover, and, as it reaches the top, brings the cone into view). " Pray once more assure yourselves that it is fair and solid. Now for the ball." He picks up the ball with the left hand, and holding it between the finger and thumb, apparently transfers it, by the pass called the *tourniquet* (*see* page 150), to the right, forthwith getting rid of it into the *profonde* on the left side. " Pray observe that it does not leave your sight even for a moment." Then holding his hand high above the paper cover, he makes a "crumbling" movement with it, immediately showing it empty, and lifting the cover with a slight pressure, so as to carry the shell with it, shows the ball beneath. The attention of the spectators being naturally attracted to the ball, it is an easy matter to let the hollow shell slip out of the paper cover upon the *servante,* and again to hand the cover for examination.

Some performers, instead of using the goblet, work the small cone with the " ball-box " (*see* page 296).

It is obvious that the directions above given will apply only where the cone is of a size so small as to be readily palmed, in which case it is hardly conspicuous enough to be used before a large audience. Where a cone of larger dimensions is employed, it is necessary to vary the mode of operation. We shall therefore proceed to describe the trick in its stage form, as worked by Herrmann and other public performers.

The cone in this case is about seven inches high, and is worked in conjunction with a "drawer-box" of such a size as to contain it easily. Having handed round for inspection the cover and cone, as already described, the performer suddenly remembers that he requires an orange, which he forthwith produces from his wand. (It is hardly necessary to observe that the orange is beforehand placed in readiness in one of the *pochettes,* and is produced from the wand in the manner described for producing a ball. *See* page 276). Laying down the orange on the table, he next exhibits the drawer-box, taking the drawer completely out, and, after showing it on all sides, replacing it. He then covers the orange on the table with the paper cover (containing the hollow shell), and places the solid cone in the drawer-box, which being of the kind described at page 345, he turns upon its side, with its top toward the audience. He meanwhile palms in his right hand, from his pocket or the *servante,* a second orange. He now announces that he is about to take the orange back again, which he does by passing his wand up the side of the cover, and immediately producing therefrom the second orange. He places this upon another table at a little distance, and covers it with a borrowed hat, making as he does so a feint of removing it, and slipping it into his tail pocket. He hears, or pretends to hear, some one remark that he took away the orange, and answers accordingly. " Oh! you think I took away the orange. Allow me to assure you that I did nothing of the kind." (He lifts up the hat, and shows the orange in its place.) " I will cover it again ; or, still better, to prove that I do not take it away, I won't cover it at all, but leave it here in full view on the table." He replaces it on the table, but this time places it on what is called a " wrist-trap," in readiness for a subsequent disappearance. " Having taken the orange from under the cover," he continues, " I have now to make the solid block vanish from the drawer, and take its place ; but I shall do it this time invisibly. See, I have only to wave my wand from the one to the other, and the thing is done. The drawer is empty " (pulling out the false drawer only), " and here is the block " (he lifts the paper cover, and shows the hollow shell). " Now I come to the most difficult part of the trick, which is to bring both articles back to their original position. First, I will take the block of wood." He covers the shell with the paper tube, and makes a move-ment of his wand from the cover to the drawer. " Pass! Let us see whether it has obeyed." He this time pulls the drawer completely out, and lets the block fall heavily on the stage. " Now for the orange." He places both hands round it, as if picking it up between them, and presses as he does so the spring of the trap, which opening, lets the orange fall through into the table. Bringing the hands, still together, immediately above the paper cover, he rubs them together as if compressing the orange, finally separating them and showing them empty, and immediately afterwards lifting the cover with the hollow shell, and showing the first orange beneath it.

It will be observed that the trick above described is, in some of its parts, very similar to that described at page 337. The mechanism of the wrist-trap will be found explained in the next chapter. In the meantime the student may produce the same effect without using a trap at all, by means of the sleight described at page 294.

THE CONE AND BOUQUET.—This is another form of the cone

trick, involving the use of rather more elaborate apparatus. The cone in this case is about five inches in height by three at the base, and tapers very slightly. It may be either of boxwood, as in the

trick last described, or the block may be of any hard wood, and the hollow shell of tin to fit, each blacked and polished, so as to look exactly alike. It is used in conjunction with a paper cover as before, and two little bunches of flowers, exactly alike, and of such a size as to be just covered by the hollow shell. Each of these little bouquets is made upon a tin framework, consisting of a wire arch springing from a flat saucer-like base. (*See* Fig. 197.) A pedestal and cover complete the apparatus.

FIG. 197.

The pedestal *a* (*see* Fig. 198) is cylindrical; and about six inches in height, by four across the top. Its upper surface consists of a circular plate of tin, working up and down piston-wise in the pedestal. This is forced upwards by a spiral spring, but yields to pressure, sinking vertically to a depth of four or five inches when necessary. The upper edge of the pedestal is slightly turned in all round, so that the top may not be pressed out altogether by the force of the spring. An outer casing of tin, *b*, fits over *a*, just so tightly as to resist the upward pressure of the spring when forced down by any object between the pedestal and this casing. The

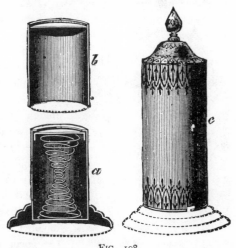

FIG. 198.

cover, *c*, is about double the height of *a*, and by means of a bayonet catch (*see* page 352) may be lifted off either with or without *b* at pleasure.

The pedestal is prepared for use by removing *b*, and placing one of the little bouquets on the top of *a*; then again putting on *b*, and forcing it down into its place, when the condition of the apparatus will be as shown (in section) in Fig. 199. The wire arch prevents the flowers being crushed out of shape by the pressure of the spring. The pedestal and cover are now brought forward and placed on the table; also the cone (with the shell on), the paper tube to cover it, and the remaining bunch of flowers. The paper tube is first exhibited, placed over the cone, and removed with the hollow cone within it, as in the last trick. The solid cone is then offered for examination, and having been duly inspected, is placed upon the pedestal. The per-

FIG. 199.

former makes a movement as if about to place over it the cover *c*, but checks himself in the act, and shows that this cover is empty and hollow throughout. He then puts on the cover, and reverting to the bunch of flowers on the table, covers it with the paper tube. He next announces that in obedience to his command, the block and the bunch of flowers will change places. He raises the paper tube, holding it by the top, and thus leaves behind the hollow shell, covering and concealing the bunch of flowers. He next takes off the cover of the pedestal, first, however, turning the bayonet catch, so as to lift off with the cover the casing *b*. The solid cone is carried off between the casing

FIG. 200.

and the cover (*see* Fig. 200), while the action of the spring, the casing being removed, brings the concealed bunch of flowers to the top of the pedestal, in the position lately occupied by the cone. Having shown that the cone and the flowers have changed places, the performer next undertakes to bring them back to their original situation, which, by reversing the process, he does without difficulty.

The pedestal above described is a very useful piece of apparatus, being available either to produce, change, or vanish any article of appropriate size. A very effective trick may be performed therewith by causing an empty tumbler to appear full, or *vice versâ*. In this case, however, it should by no means be admitted that an *exchange* takes place, as the supposed filling of an empty glass with water by covering it with an evidently unsophisticated cover, is rather the more surprising phenomenon.

THE FLYING GLASS OF WATER. — This capital trick was, we believe, first introduced to the public by Colonel Stodare, to whom the profession is indebted for many first-class illusions. The necessary apparatus consists of a couple of ordinary glass tumblers, exactly alike, with an india-rubber cover just fitting the mouth of one of them, and a coloured handkerchief of silk or cotton made double (*i.e.*, consisting of two similar handkerchiefs sewn together at the edges), with a wire ring (of the size of the rim of one of the tumblers, or a fraction larger) stitched loosely between them, in such manner that when the handkerchief is spread out the ring shall be in the middle.

FIG. 201.

The performer, beforehand, nearly fills one of the tumblers with water, and then puts on the india-rubber cover, which, fitting closely all round the edge, effectually prevents the water escaping (*see* Fig. 201). The glass, thus prepared, he places in the *profonde* on his right side. He then brings forward the other glass and a decanter of water, and the prepared handkerchief, and in full view of the audience fills the glass with water up to the same height as he has already filled the one in his pocket, and hands round glass and water for inspection. When they are returned, he places the glass upon the table, a few inches from its hinder edge, and standing behind it, covers it with the handkerchief, first spreading out and showing both sides of the latter, proving, to all appearance, that there is no preparation about it. In placing the handkerchief over the glass, he draws it across in such manner as to bring the hidden ring as exactly as possible over the top of the glass. Then placing the left hand over the handkerchief, as shown in Fig. 202, he raises, apparently, the glass within the handkerchief, but really the empty handkerchief only, which is kept distended by the ring, and, at the same time, under cover of the handkerchief, gently lowers the glass of water with the other hand on to the *servante.* This is by no means difficult, as the pretended carefulness of the operator not to spill the water allows him to make the upward movement of the left hand as deliberate as he pleases. All that is really necessary is to take care *to follow with his eyes the movement of the left hand,* which will infallibly draw the eyes and the minds of the audience in the same direction. Having raised the supposed tumbler to a height of about two feet from the table, the performer brings it forward to the audience, and requests that some gentleman with a steady hand will favour him with his assistance. A volunteer having been found, and having given satisfactory replies as to the steadiness of his nerves, and the strength of his constitution generally, is requested to place his hand under the handkerchief and take the glass. As he proceeds to obey, the performer lets go of the handkerchief with the left hand, still retaining one corner with the right, and lets the right arm with the handkerchief drop to his side. Pretending to believe that the gentleman has taken the glass, and not to notice its disappearance, he turns carelessly aside, and brings forward a small table or chair, saying, " Put it here, please." Looking, generally, somewhat foolish, the victim replies

FIG. 202.

that he has not got it. If the performer is a good actor, he may here make some fun by pretending to believe that the victim has concealed the glass, and pressing him to return it. At last he says, "Well, if you won't give it to me, I must find it for myself," and he proceeds to tap with his wand the sleeves and pockets of the unfortunate individual, but without success, till, on touching him between the shoulders, he pretends to tell by the sound that the glass is there. "Yes, here it is," he remarks. "I am sorry to be obliged to ask you to turn your back on the company, but to show them that there is no deception on my part, I am compelled to do so. Will you please turn round for one minute." On his doing so, the performer, again shaking out the handkerchief, and showing both sides of it to prove it empty, spreads it over the back of the victim. Again he taps with his wand, which, striking the ring through the handkerchief, causes an unmistakeable hard sound to be heard; and then grasping the ring as before through the handkerchief, he deliberately raises it up in a horizontal position, the effect being as if the glass had again returned to the handkerchief. He then says, "I don't think I will trouble this gentleman again; he is too much of a conjuror himself;" then turning rapidly to the audience, he says, "Catch, ladies and gentlemen," and "flicks" the handkerchief quickly towards the spectators, who duck their heads in expectation of a shower. "Pardon me, ladies, I fear I alarmed you; but you need not have been afraid; I never miss my aim. That gentleman has the glass" (designating any one he pleases). "May I trouble you to step forward one moment, sir?" On the person indicated doing so, the performer places him facing the audience, and under cover of his body takes the second glass out of the *profonde*, and throws the handkerchief over it, remarking, "Yes, ladies and gentlemen, here it is, in this gentleman's tail pocket." Then taking hold of the glass with the left hand beneath the handkerchief, he clips with the first finger and thumb, through the handkerchief, the edge of the india-rubber cover, and thus drawing off the cover inside the handkerchief, hands round the glass and water for inspection.

Two improvements have recently been made in this trick, which, though trifles in themselves, greatly heighten the effect. Upon a performance of the trick as already described, it is not uncommon to find some person, more acute than the average, guess that there is a ring in the handkerchief. The first of the improvements we have mentioned is designed to make the ring no longer a fixture, and yet to insure bringing it into the right position when necessary. This is

FIG. 203.

effected by stitching the two handkerchiefs together, not only round the edge, as already explained, but also as shown by the dotted line in Fig. 203. This confines the ring to the triangular enclosure, *a e d,* within which, however, it is allowed to move freely, not being attached to the handkerchief in any way. If the handkerchief is held by the two corners *a d* (which should be distinguished by a mark of coloured silk or worsted, so as to be readily identified by the performer) the ring will take its proper place in the middle, as shown in the figure. If, on the other hand, the handkerchief be held by either the corners *a b* or *c d,* the ring will forthwith run into the angle *a d e* or *d a e,* as the case may be, and the handkerchief, if grasped a little below this particular corner, may be twisted or pulled through the hands ropewise, proving, with apparent conclusiveness, that there is no ring or shape concealed in it.

The second improvement is to have ready on the *servante* a small piece of sponge, recently dipped in water. This is picked up by the right hand of the performer as he places the genuine glass on the *servante.* When he has moved away from his table, at the moment of requesting his volunteer assistant to take the glass, he places the right hand for a moment under cover of the handkerchief, and squeezes the sponge, the water that immediately pours from it being, apparently, accidentally spilt, and so negativing any possible doubt on the part of the spectators that the glass is really in the handkerchief. With these two additions the trick is one of the most effective that can possibly be performed, whether in a drawing-room or on the public stage.

THE BOWLS OF WATER AND BOWLS OF FIRE PRODUCED FROM A SHAWL.—After the explanation of the last trick, the reader will form a tolerably good guess at the means of performing this, which has puzzled thousands, and is still one of the most popular feats in the *répertoire* of the conjuror.

The performer comes forward with a shawl in his hand, which he spreads out and exhibits on both sides, to show (as is really the fact) that there is no preparation about it. The spectators being satisfied on this point, and the orchestra playing the "Ghost Melody" or other appropriate accompaniment, he swings the shawl about in time to the music, finally throwing it over his left shoulder and arm, the arm being held square before him. The arm now gradually sinks down, and the form of some solid object is seen defined beneath the shawl, which, being removed, reveals a glass bowl brimming with water, and with gold fish swimming about in it. This is repeated a second and a third time, the performer sometimes discarding the shawl, and borrowing a pocket-handkerchief among the audience for the production of the last bowl.

The bowls used are saucer-shaped, measuring six to eight inches in diameter, and one and a half to two inches in depth. Each is closed by an india-rubber cover, after the manner of the tumbler in the last trick. Thus secured, they are concealed about the person of the performer. The precise mode of concealment varies a little. Where three bowls are to be produced, one is generally carried beneath the coat-tails, in a sort of bag open at the sides, suspended from the waist, and the other two in pockets, opening perpendicularly, inside the breast of the coat or waistcoat, one on each side.

Sometimes, by way of variation, bowls of fire are produced. The bowls are in this case of thin brass. They have no covers, but the inflammable material (tow moistened with spirits of wine) is kept in position by wires crossing the bowl at about half its depth, and is ignited by a wax match, struck against the inside of the bowl under cover of the shawl and immediately dropped into the bowl, when the contents instantly burst into a blaze. Some bowls have a mechanical arrangement for igniting the tow, but we ourselves much prefer the simple bowls above described.

It was originally the practice to throw the shawl over a small round table, immediately removing it, and exhibiting the bowl upon the table. Modern performers discard the table, and produce the bowls in the midst of the audience.

THE BOWL OF INK CHANGED TO CLEAR WATER, WITH GOLD FISH SWIMMING IN IT.—The performer brings forward a goblet-shaped glass vase, six or eight inches in height, nearly full of ink. To prove that the ink is genuine, he dips a playing-card into it, and brings it up with the lower half stained a deep black. Next, taking a ladle, he ladles out a portion of the liquid, and pours it on a plate, which is handed round for inspection. He next borrows a handkerchief from one of the audience, and covering the vase with it, announces that, by the exercise of his magic power, he will transform the ink in the vase to water. On removing the handkerchief, this transformation is found to be accomplished, while a couple of gold fish, placidly swimming about in the bowl, sufficiently prove that the trick is not performed, as might be imagined, by means of some chemical reagent.

The explanation, though by no means obvious, is very simple. The liquid in the vase is plain water; but a bottomless black silk lining, fitting the vase, and kept in shape by a wire ring round its upper edge, gives it the appearance of ink to a spectator at a little distance. In removing the handkerchief, the performer clips with it the wire ring, bringing away the lining within the handkerchief, and revealing the clear water in the glass.

But the reader will naturally inquire, " How, then, are the black-ened card and the genuine ink ladled out on the plate accounted for ? "

The blackened card, though apparently an ordinary one, has the same figure, say a knave of diamonds, on both its sides; but the lower half of the one side is beforehand stained with ink. The performer dips it in with the unsoiled side toward the audience; but giving it a half-turn as he removes it, thereby brings the blackened side in front. The ink poured on the plate is accounted for with equal simplicity. The ladle (*see* Fig. 204) is of tin, having a hollow handle of the same metal, with a minute hole opening therefrom into the bowl. There is a similar small hole near to the top of the handle. The bowl is beforehand filled with

FIG. 204.

ink, which is thence allowed to run into the handle ; after which the upper hole is stopped with a little pellet of wax, or a small piece of paper is pasted over it. By reason of a well-known natural law, the liquid will not run out of the lower hole until the upper one is opened. As the performer dips the ladle apparently into the ink in the bowl, he scrapes off with his nail the wax or paper with which the upper hole is stopped, and the ink immediately runs into the bowl, whence it is poured upon the plate.

THE INEXHAUSTIBLE BOTTLE.—The same natural principle which prevents the ink from flowing into the bowl of the ladle until the upper hole is opened, is the basis of this old but still popular trick. The inexhaustible bottle, though in appearance an ordinary glass bottle, is in reality of tin, japanned black. Internally it is divided into three, four, or five separate compartments, ranged round a central space, and each tapering to a narrow-mouthed tube, which terminates about an

FIG. 205.

inch within the neck of the bottle. A small pinhole is drilled through the outer surface of the bottle into each compartment, the holes being so placed that when the bottle is grasped by the hand in the ordinary way (*see* Fig. 205), each hole may be covered by one or other of the fingers or thumb. The central space is left empty, but the surrounding compartments are filled, by means of a funnel with a very tapering nozzle, with the wines or liquids expected to be most in demand, or to which it is intended to limit the spectators' choice. A tray full of glasses, made specially of very thick glass, so as to contain in reality much less than they appear to do, completes the apparatus.

The performer comes forward with the magic bottle, followed by an attendant bearing the tray of glasses. He commences by openly pouring water into the bottle, and out again, so as indirectly to raise the inference that the bottle must be perfectly empty. The water, in truth, really passes into the centre space only, and thence runs out again as soon as the bottle is tilted. The fingers, meanwhile, are tightly pressed on the different holes, and thus excluding the air, effectually prevent any premature flow of wine from the various compartments. The performer, still holding the bottle mouth downwards, says, " You observe, ladies and gentlemen, that the bottle is now perfectly empty, and yet, by my magic art, I shall compel it to refill itself for your benefit." He then, addressing various individuals, asks each whether he prefers port, sherry, gin, etc., and when the answer is given, has only to raise the finger stopping the air-hole of that particular compartment to cause the liquid named to flow from the bottle, stopping as soon as the finger is again pressed on the hole. It is a good plan, in order to prevent confusion, to place the liquors in the bottle in alphabetical order, commencing from the hole stopped by the thumb. Some performers increase the variety of the liquors produced, by placing beforehand in certain of the glasses a few drops of various flavouring essences. By this means a compartment filled with plain spirits of wine may be made to do duty for brandy, whiskey, etc., at pleasure, according to the glass into which the liquid is poured.

The trick is sometimes elaborated by the performer, by way of conclusion, apparently breaking the bottle, and producing therefrom a borrowed handkerchief or other article which has been made to disappear in some previous trick. This is effected by means of an additional speciality in the construction of the bottle. The compartments containing the liquids in this case terminate a couple of inches above the bottom of the bottle, and the part below this, which has a wavy edge, like fractured glass, is made to slip on and off. (*See* Fig. 206.) The performer, having produced the wines, pretends to crack the bottle all round by rapping it with his wand, and, having apparently cracked it, pulls the bottom off, and exhibits the handkerchief, which was beforehand placed in readiness therein. The two parts of the bottle joining with great nicety, there is little fear that the pretended crack will prematurely attract attention.

FIG. 206.

Where the trick is performed before a very large audience, a single bottle would not contain sufficient liquor to answer all the demands upon it. In this case it is necessary to change the bottle, sometimes more than once in the course of the trick. This is most frequently done under cover of a chair or table; but where the trick is performed on the stage, a more elaborate expedient is sometimes employed. The bottle used has in this case an outer shell or casing of tin, open at the bottom, the actual receptacle for the liquids being within this. When the bottle is exhausted, the performer with apparent carelessness places it upon a small table, standing against the side scene, pending the arrival of more glasses, or under any other convenient pretext. The bottle is, in truth, placed immediately over a small round trap, the performer being guided as to its proper position by a couple of small pins projecting upwards from the surface of the table, against which pins he pushes the bottle. The moment it is so placed, the assistant behind the scenes, who has his eye to a hole in the partition, and his arm extended within the table, opens the trap, pulls down the empty interior of the bottle, and instantly replaces it with a full one, which he holds in readiness, and at the moment when the performer again grasps the bottle to continue the trick (and thereby furnishes the necessary resistance), pushes it sharply up into its place.

THE BOTTLE AND RIBBONS.—This is another favourite bottle trick. The bottle is in this case also of tin, with an enclosed space round the sides to contain wine, commencing about an inch and a half from the lower end, and terminating just within the mouth.

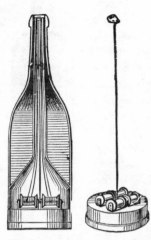

(*See* Fig. 207.) The bottle has no bottom, and there is thus a passage, in the shape of an inverted funnel, extending through its whole length. A cylindrical base or stopper (*see* Fig. 208) just fits into the space at the bottom of the bottle, and on this are fixed six or eight small reels or bobbins. On each of these is wound a yard or so of ribbon, each of a different colour. An upright wire rod springs from the centre of this base, terminating just within the neck of the bottle in a little flat piece of metal, perforated with as many holes as there are ribbons; and one end of each of the ribbons is brought up through one of these holes, and a little knot made upon it to prevent its slipping back again.

FIG. 207.   FIG. 208.

The ribbons being in position, and the space in the bottle duly filled with wine, the performer brings it forward, and, after pouring out a glass or two, asks some lady present which is her favourite colour, and on receiving an answer, gently taps the bottle with his wand, and immediately draws out with the tip of his forefinger from the neck, and presents to her, a ribbon of the desired colour. More wine is produced, alternately with fresh ribbons, until all are exhausted.

The above is the drawing-room form of the trick. Upon the stage, it is slightly varied. The same kind of bottle is used, but the internal provision of reels and ribbons is removed, so that the bottle remains a simple tin bottle, open at the bottom, with the funnel-shaped passage already mentioned extending through its entire length. The performer, having poured out a glass or two of wine, places the bottle on a stool or table, through the pillar of which is a hole or passage communicating with a corresponding hole in the stage. Beneath this is stationed the performer's assistant, who is provided with a large number of various coloured ribbons, and a thin rod of three or four feet in length, with a small point or blunt pin at the top. The performer takes care always to repeat in an audible voice the name of the colour called for. This is a signal to the assistant to hitch one end of the ribbon in question on the top of the rod, and hold it in readiness beneath the stage. He does not, however, push it up through the bottle until warned by the sound of the tap of the wand on the bottle that the performer is ready to receive it. The performer, on his part, takes care, before tapping the bottle, to place his thumb upon the mouth, so as to prevent the rod passing too far. Sometimes a combination of colours is asked for, as, for instance, the tricolour, or any other national group of colours.

After having produced a reasonable number of ribbons, an effective finish may be made as follows :—A last colour or combination of colours having been demanded, the performer does not draw the ribbons, as hitherto, completely out of the bottle, but leaves them hanging down loosely on each side of it. He now announces that, at the word of command, the ribbons shall, of their own accord, return into the bottle. The assistant takes his cue accordingly, and at the third tap of the wand draws the ribbons smartly down again ; their instantaneous disappearance within the bottle being exceedingly effective.

THE NEW PYRAMIDS OF EGYPT, OR THE WINE AND WATER TRICK.—This trick may be very well worked in conjunction with either of the bottle tricks already described, and we therefore notice it in this place. Its effect is as follows :—The performer pours out a glass of wine and a glass of water, finally transferring both to a small decanter. Placing the decanter on a small round stand, and the empty glasses on similar stands on either side of it, he covers each with a pyramidal cover, and announces that at his command the mixed wine and water will again separate, and pass into the empty glasses, the spectators being allowed to choose into which of the glasses each element shall pass. The choice having been made, he fastens a tape or ribbon to the centre pyramid, and thence to each of the side ones, giving the audience to understand that, by a mysterious kind of capillary attraction, the wine and water will travel along this ribbon to their respective destinations. A few moments having elapsed, the ribbons are untied and the covers removed. The decanter is found to be empty, and the wine and water to have respectively returned to the glasses designated by the audience.

The glasses used have no speciality, but the decanter has a small hole in its under side. This is plugged with a pellet of wax, which, however, is instantly removeable at pleasure. Of the three stands, two (those on which the glasses stand) have no preparation, being mere raised shapes of tin. The third is similar in appearance, but is, in fact, a hollow box, with three or four little holes drilled in its upper side, for a purpose that will presently appear. Of the three covers, the centre one is hollow throughout, but the other two have each its upper portion occupied by a hollow chamber or reservoir, divided in two by a vertical partition, and tapering down to a tube with a very small opening. Each

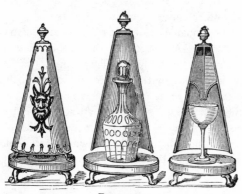

FIG. 209.

of these compartments has an air-hole at the top. (*See* Fig. 209.)

These two covers are beforehand prepared for the trick by filling the two compartments of each, one with wine and the other with water. The air-holes are stopped with pellets of wax, but for the sake of distinction the " wine " compartment of each is plugged with red wax, and the " water " compartment with white wax. Any other distinguishing mark is, of course, equally good. So long as the air-holes are thus stopped, there is no fear of the liquid running out. The performer, having filled the glasses as already described, mixes the contents in the decanter, and in placing the latter on the stand, removes the wax plug from the bottom, thus allowing the wine to run out, and to percolate through the above-mentioned holes into the stand, where it remains. He next places the empty glasses on their respective stands, and places the covers over them. He then asks the audience into which of the glasses they desire that the wine shall travel, and into which the water. When they have made their decision, he has only to remove the red pellet from the cover which is over the glass into which the wine is to pass, and the white pellet from the opposite cover. The tying of the tape from cover to cover is merely designed to give time for the liquids to reach their respective destinations, and is, indeed, altogether dispensed with by many performers. The air-holes may be stopped by means of tinfoil pasted over them, instead of the wax, if preferred. The foil is instantly removeable by scraping with the nail.

THE MYSTERIOUS FUNNEL.—This is a little appliance on the same principle, which may be incidentally introduced with good effect in the course of a wine trick. It is a tin funnel, made double throughout, with a space of half-an-inch or so between its inner and outer sides. It is, in fact, a funnel within a funnel, joined at the upper edges. (*See* Fig. 210.) It has an air-hole, *a*, generally on the under side of the handle. When required for use, the hidden space is filled with wine. The simplest way of doing this is to stop the spout of the funnel with the finger, and then to fill it with wine, which, seeking its own level, will gradually rise to the same height in the outer space as it stands at inside the funnel. This must, of course, be done with the air-hole open. When the space is filled, the air-hole is stopped, and the wine remaining inside the funnel allowed

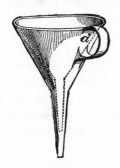

FIG. 210.

to run out. The funnel will now appear perfectly empty, and may be used as a funnel in the ordinary way.

The mode of using the funnel is somewhat after the following manner, subject, of course, to variation, according to the taste and invention of the performer :—

A juvenile is invited to take a glass of wine, the produce of either of the preceding tricks. When he has imbibed it, the performer asks a second juvenile whether he would like a glass also. The reply is pretty sure to be in the affirmative, but the performer pretends to find, when about to oblige him, that his store is exhausted. He begins to apologize for the supposed disappointment, but as if suddenly bethinking himself, says, "However, you shan't be disappointed. If I can't supply you in the natural way, I must do so in a supernatural way. Suppose we take back the wine this young gentleman has just drunk. I don't suppose it will be any the worse. Let me see, where is my magic funnel. Oh, here it is. Let us make sure first that it is quite clean." He pours water through it, and then holds it up to the light in such a manner that the audience can see right through, thus indirectly showing them that it is empty. "Now, sir" (addressing the youngster who has drunk the glass of wine), "I am going to take back that glass of wine. Be kind enough to bend your elbow, and hold it over the mouth of the funnel, so. And you, sir" (addressing the expectant), "perhaps you will be kind enough to take this young gentleman's other arm, and work it gently up and down. In fact, we are going to transform him into a pump. Now, sir." The performer holds the glass under the funnel, and as soon as the pretended pumping begins, opens the air-hole, when the wine runs into the glass, and is handed to the second young gentleman as a reward for his exertions.

Acted with spirit, this little interlude is sure of an uproarious reception from the juvenile portion of the audience, particularly if the operator possesses the magic bradawl described at page 332, and makes use of it to bore a small hole in the victim's elbow before beginning to pump the wine from it.

THE BOX OF BRAN TRANSFORMED TO A BOTTLE OF WINE.— While upon the subject of wine tricks we may mention this, which is by no means the least surprising of the illusions to which "the bottle" gives birth. The necessary apparatus consists of four pieces. First, a plain cylindrical tin box A (*see* Fig. 211), japanned to taste, and about six inches high by three in diameter. Secondly, B, a similar box, so far as external appearance is concerned, but materially different in its internal construction. This latter is bottomless, but has a horizontal tin partition at about three-quarters of an inch from

the top. These two boxes have but one lid, which fits either indifferently. The third article is a cylindrical pasteboard cover (Fig.
212), closed at the top, and of such
a size as to fit loosely over B, but an
inch or two taller. The fourth item is
a bottle, made of tin, japanned black,
and of somewhat peculiar construction. (*See* Fig. 213.) As a measure
of capacity, it terminates just below
the shoulder, the remainder, or body
of the bottle, being, in fact, merely a
tube closed at the bottom, in which
this upper portion works. A spiral
spring within the body presses the
neck portion upward into its proper

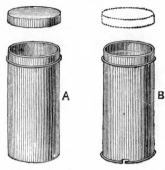

FIG. 211.

position ; but if pressure be applied, the neck portion will sink downward into the body, as shown in Fig. 214, in which condition it just
fits into B. A small point projects from the lower part of the bottle,
and corresponds with a bayonet catch at the bottom of B, which is in
fact designed as a case or cover for the bottle.

For the performance of the trick the operator will require, in addition to the apparatus above mentioned, an
oblong deal box, half full of bran. (Rice is
sometimes used, but is not so good.) Any
box will answer the purpose, so long as it is
not less than fifteen inches or so in length,
and nine in breadth and depth. In preparing
for the trick, the first step is to fill the bottle,
or the "fillable" portion thereof, with wine
or some other liquid. The bottle is then
corked ; B is placed over it and pressed down,
an l the bayonet-catch fastened. In this condition, but without a lid, B is placed in the
deal box, and buried in the bran. The box
of bran being now brought forward and placed
on the table, the performer is ready to begin the trick. He first
draws attention to A, which he hands round for inspection, as also

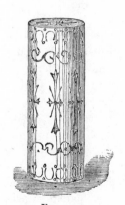

FIG. 212.

the pasteboard cover. When they are returned, he brings forward the box of bran, moving his hand backwards and forwards in it, and distributing a few handfuls to show its genuineness.

FIG. 213.

Replacing the box on the table, he proceeds to fill A with bran. This he does by dipping A completely in the box, and scooping up the necessary quantity. As if to show all fair, he pours the bran out again into the box, and then makes a second dip to refill it. This time, however, he makes an exchange, and instead of bringing up A, brings up B, filling as he does so the shallow space at the top of the latter, which thus appears to be full to the brim. Placing it on the table, and putting the lid on, he places the pasteboard cover over it, and, addressing the company, volunteers to teach them how to extract wine from bran, and wine bottles from tin boxes. After a moment's pause, and the orthodox touch with the wand, he removes the cover, giving it at the same time a slight twist, thus releasing the catch, and removing B within the cover. The spring within the bottle now meeting no resistance, presses the neck portion upwards into its proper position, with all the appearance of a genuine bottle; and as it, in its present condition, is considerably taller than B, it can hardly be suspected that it was a moment ago concealed in the latter, particularly as the performer immediately proceeds to give a further proof of its genuineness by pouring a glass of wine from it.

FIG. 214.

In connection with the above trick we may describe another useful piece of apparatus, known as

THE BRAN BOTTLE.—This is a bottle, which, being covered over for an instant, vanishes, leaving in its place a heap of bran. The bottle is, like that last described, of tin, with a false bottom or partition, about an inch below the shoulder, so that it holds about a glassful of wine. The place of the ordinary bottom is supplied by a disc of tin, with a raised shoulder round it, fitting loosely within the bottle, so as to drop out by its own weight, unless kept in place by some external pressure. The cover is a mere cylinder of pasteboard, closed at the top. The bottle is prepared for use by filling the lower portion with bran, and putting the bottom in place (where it is retained by the pressure of the fingers), then filling the upper part with wine. The performer first pours wine from the bottle, and then places it on a plate, ostensibly to show that it does not pass through any opening in the table, but really for a reason which will presently appear. He now places the cover over the bottle, and on again lifting it presses the sides slightly, and so lifts the bottle with it. The loose bottom, having no longer anything to hold it, remains on the plate, concealed by the bran which pours from the bottle, and into which the bottle is apparently transformed. Meanwhile, all eyes being drawn to the heap of bran, the performer lowers his hand, containing the cover, for an instant behind the table, and relaxing the pressure of his fingers, lets the bottle slip out on the *servante*, immediately coming forward with the cover, and carelessly showing that it is empty.

In combination with the Bran Bottle, the trick last above described is greatly heightened in effect, the bottle appearing under the cover which has just been placed over the tin box—the bran from the latter óeing found under the cover which a moment previously concealed the bottle, and the tin box being found to have passed into the large box of bran. The Bran Bottle may also be worked with great effect in combination with the trick of the "Bran and Orange," described at page *335.*

THE BRAN GLASS.—This is an ingenious and very useful piece of apparatus. It is made in all sizes, from that of an ordinary wine-glass to a goblet large enough to hold a rabbit. Its effect is as follows:—The glass is brought forward apparently filled with bran to the brim. The performer proves its genuineness by taking up a handful of it, and scattering it over the stage. A brass cover is now placed over the glass, and instantly removed, when every particle of bran is found to have disappeared, and in place of it is found some article which had been conjured away at some earlier period of the trick. The explanation is very simple. The glass is shaped as shown in Fig. 215, with straight sides, tapering outwards. The supposed bran is really a hollow shape of tin, *a*, closed at the top,

FIG. 215.

but open at the bottom, with bran gummed all over it, and a handful of loose bran spread on the top. At each side of its upper edge is a little wire point, just overpassing the edge of the glass. The cover (*see* Fig. 216), which is of such a size as to cover the glass as far as the upper part of its stem, has no speciality about it, save a shallow groove running round its upper edge on the inside, as shown by the dotted line. When the cover is placed on the glass, and pressed smartly down, the two points already mentioned are forced into this groove, which thus grips the tin shape, and when again removed, lifts it out of the glass, leaving behind whatever article may have been beforehand placed within.

Where the bran glass is of large size, the metal cover is indispensable; but for glasses not exceeding the ordinary tumbler size, it is preferable to cover the glass with a borrowed handkerchief only, the hollow shape being in this case made, not of tin, but of thin cardboard. The two points are dispensed with, but in place of them there should be a piece of thread, in length about double the diameter of the glass, fastened from side to side of the shape. This, hanging down on the side of the glass which is toward the performer, is caught hold of through

FIG. 216.

the handkerchief, and thus handkerchief and shape are lifted together.

The Bran Glass may be made available in a variety of ways; the trick next following will afford a good practical illustration of its use.

To Fire Borrowed Rings from a Pistol, and make them

Pass into a Goblet filled with Bran and covered with a Handkerchief, the Bran Disappearing, and being found elsewhere.—The glass used in this instance is of ordinary tumbler size. It is not brought forward as above, with the bran shape already in place, but empty, and may therefore be freely offered for inspection. With it is brought forward a wooden box, of any size and shape, filled with bran, and in this, ready to hand, is concealed the bran shape. We have already had occasion to describe the magic pistol, or rather pistol tube; but the tube used in this instance (*see* Fig. 217) has an additional peculiarity. It is of comparatively small size, being about two inches wide at the mouth. Within this mouth fits easily a tin cup, *a*, about an inch and three quarters in depth, and having its

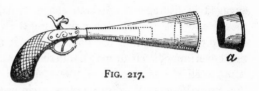

FIG. 217.

edge turned over outwards all round, so as to afford a ready grip to the palm when it may be necessary to remove it. The pistol is beforehand loaded with powder, and the cup above described is placed in the mouth of the tube.

The performer begins by asking the loan of three rings, to be fired from his magic pistol. To preclude the possibility of their being exchanged, he requests the owners to drop them into the pistol themselves. First, however, by way of wad, he takes a small piece of white paper, and presses its centre portion into the mouth of the pistol tube, its edges projecting all round, and forming a sort of cup to receive the rings. Three rings having been offered, and dropped into the pistol, the performer closes over the edges of the paper, and presses them down with his wand, the effect being as if the rings were fairly rammed down into the pistol, though they really remain in the cup, just within the mouth. He now hands the pistol to one of the spectators, requesting him to hold it muzzle upwards above his head. In handing it to him, he places for a moment his own right hand over the mouth of the tube, his palm being flat upon it, and in again removing the hand lifts out and palms the cup (which the projecting edge enables him to do with perfect ease). He has thus obtained possession of the rings. (As the holder of the pistol has been instructed to hold it above his head, he is not very likely to look into it; but lest he should do so, and discover that the rings are already removed, it is well to place in the tube beforehand a piece of crumpled white paper, to represent that which contained the rings.)

The performer now hands round the glass for examination, and subsequently draws attention to the box of bran. While doing this he has little difficulty in getting the rings out of the cup and paper into his right hand. He then, holding the glass in his left hand, dips it into the box, and fills it with bran, which he forthwith pours slowly back again to prove its genuineness. Meanwhile, his right hand is engaged in fishing up the bran shape among the bran, placing it mouth upwards in the box, and dropping the rings into it. When he again dips the glass into the box, he slips it mouth downwards over the shape, immediately turning it into the natural position, and bringing it up, to all appearance, full of bran As the rings were in the shape, they are, of course, now in the glass. He brushes the loose bran off the top, and then covers the glass with a borrowed handkerchief, taking particular notice on which side hangs the loop of thread. The person holding the pistol is now requested to take good aim, and fire at the glass. He does so, and the performer, lifting the handkerchief with the shape within it, lets the latter drop on the *servante,* and advancing with the glass, requests the owners to identify their rings.

The trick may either end here, upon the supposition that the bran has been blown away altogether by the explosion, or the bran may be shown to have passed to some other place. There are numerous methods of effecting this latter transposition For instance, the pea vase (*see* page 351), first shown empty, may be used, or the bran may be made to fall out of a second borrowed handkerchief, by means of the bag shown at page 248, or may be found in the apparatus next described.

THE "DOMINO-BOX" (SOMETIMES CALLED THE "GLOVE-BOX"). —This is a little oblong box of walnut or rosewood, measuring about four inches in length by two inches in width, and an inch and a quarter in depth. It has a sliding lid, drawing out in the ordinary manner, but the whole box has a tightly-fitting inner lining, which may be pulled out, drawer fashion, with the lid. (*See* Fig. 218.) It

is used as follows :—Any small article, say a glove or a lady's handkerchief, is secretly placed inside this inner lining. The performer
exhibits the box to the company, and to show that it is empty, turns
it over towards them, and draws
the lid nearly out, drawing out
with it at the same time the inner
lining or drawer also. (*See* Fig.
219.) From the position of the
box, the drawer is, at a very short
distance, completely hidden by the
lid. The box is, of course, seen

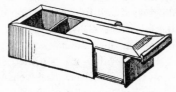

FIG. 218.

to be perfectly empty. The performer now closes it, and turning its
right side upwards, places it on the table. He then proceeds with
the next stage of the trick, and at the right moment again opens the

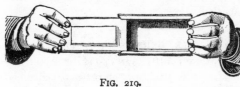

FIG. 219.

box, or invites some
one else to do so.
This time the lid alone
is drawn out, and the
hidden article is found
in the box.

There is another
speciality about the Domino-box, which renders it available to cause
the disappearance of a coin placed in it; though, as in the case of the
" Rattle-box," described in the chapter devoted to coin tricks, the
coin is heard to rattle within it till the very
moment of its disappearance. This is effected
as follows :—Between the bottom of the
drawer and that of the box proper is a very
small space, just large enough to allow a
shilling to lie between the true and false bottom. On the under side of the drawer, how-

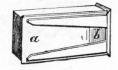

FIG. 220.

ever (*see* Fig. 220, showing the under side of the drawer portion), are
glued two thin slips of wood, gradually approaching each other, and
thereby narrowing this space to a width of about half an inch. If
when the lid is withdrawn *with* the drawer, as already explained, a
shilling or sovereign is dropped into the box, and the box again closed,
the coin will have plenty of room to rattle about as long as it remains

at the end *a*, but if shaken down with a sharp jerk in the direction of the end *b*, it will become caught in the narrower portion of the opening, and will thenceforth be silent, unless it may suit the purpose of the performer to release it again, which he can do by a sharp downward jerk in the direction of *a*. Of course, as the coin is below the false bottom, it will appear to have vanished when the box is opened in the ordinary way.

The Domino-box is sometimes used to change a sovereign to its equivalent in silver, the "change" being b, forehand wrapped in paper, and concealed in the drawer. It is sometimes also caused to fill itself with bonbons, in place of a coin deposited in it.

These boxes are usually made in pairs, alike in appearance, but the one is a simple box without any speciality, and may therefore be handed round for examination, the mechanical box being adroitly substituted at the right moment. The fact that *two* boxes are used is, of course, carefully concealed.

The Coffee Trick. (Coffee Berries changed to Hot Coffee, White Beans to Sugar, and Bran to Hot Milk).— The pieces of apparatus used in this trick are of brass or japanned

FIG. 221.

tin, and are three in number, two being tall cylindrical vases, standing eighteen to twenty inches in height, the third a goblet-shaped vase, of about half that height. The latter is made upon the principle of the "bran glass," above described, consisting of three portions (*see* Fig 221), the goblet *a*, the cover *c*, and a shallow tray *b*, which fits into the goblet, and which, if the cover is pressed down smartly, and again removed, is lifted off with it. It differs, however, from the "bran shape" in the fact that *b* is open at top instead of at bottom, and is only about one-fifth the depth of the goblet, leaving therefore considerable space below it. This portion of the apparatus is prepared for use by placing in the goblet a quantity of hot milk, putting *b* in position above it, and finally filling *b* with loose bran.

The construction of the other two vases will be quickly understood upon an inspection of Figs. 222, 223. *a* is the vase, and *c* the cover fitting loose-ly over it, but between these two is a well, *b*, made double, so as to fit at once into and outside of *a*, after a mode of construction which we have more than once had occasion to notice. There is a bayonet-catch at the lower edge of *c*, corresponding with a pin or stud at the lower edge of *b*, so that *c* may

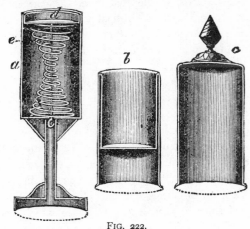

FIG. 222.

be lifted off either with or without *b*. There is a similar catch at the lower edge of *b*, corresponding with a stud at the bottom of *a*, but cut in the opposite direction to the other catch, so that the action of unlocking *a* from *b* locks *b* to *c*, and *vice versâ*.

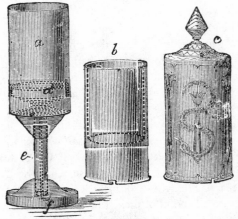

FIG. 223.

The vase *a* requires a special description. A shallow saucer of tin, *d*, just fits the interior of the vase, working up and down therein piston-fashion, but prevented from coming out alto-gether by the fact that the upper edge of *a* is slightly turned inwards all round. Below *d* is a spiral spring, whose action tends to force *d* to the top of the vase, as shown in Fig. 222. From the centre of *d*, however, there extends downwards through the spiral spring a piece of stiff wire *e*, with a crook, *f*, at the end. The foot of the vase is hollow throughout. If the saucer *d* is forced down by pressure from within, this wire, as soon as it reaches the position shown in Fig. 223, will hook itself within the foot of the vase, and so keep down *d*, until the crook is again released, when the whole will instantly return to the condition shown in Fig. 222. The bottom of the foot is open, so that the fingers can without difficulty find and release the crook when necessary.

The vases are prepared by pressing down *d* in each as shown by the dotted lines in Fig. 223, and filling the well of the one with hot coffee, and that of the other with loaf-sugar. Their respective covers are then placed over them. The attention of the audience is first directed to a couple of wooden boxes, each about half as long again as the vases, and ten or twelve inches in depth, one of which is filled with coffee-berries, and the other with white haricot beans. The performer now uncovers the vase which contains the coffee, first turning the bayonet-catch so as to lift off the well *b* with the cover, and shows, by holding the vase upside down and rattling his wand within it, that it is perfectly empty. He now fills it with coffee-berries, laying it down in the box to do so, and holding it by the foot with one hand while he shovels the berries into it with the other. Having completely filled it with the berries, he holds it aloft, and, to show that there is "no deception," tilts it, and lets them run back again into the box. Again he dips it into the box, but, as he does so, releases the crook (which the fingers of the hand holding the vase are just in position to do), and thus lets *d* fly up to the top of the vase. Again he brings up the vase, apparently full as before, but really having only a mere layer of berries, of the depth of *d*, at the top. He now puts on the cover, the well in which again forces *d* and the superposed layer of coffee-berries down to make way for it, and causes the crook again to catch beneath the hollow of the foot. The same operation is now gone through with the vase whose well contains the sugar, and the box of white beans. The performer lastly takes from the third vase a handful of bran, which he scatters to show its genuineness, and then places the cover over it. The trick is now really completed. On removing the respective covers (taking care, of course, first to turn the bayonet-catches in the right direction), the wells are released from the covers and locked to the vases, which are thus found full respectively of hot coffee and sugar, and, on removing the cover of the third vase, the bran is lifted off with it, and the milk is revealed.

Some coffee vases, and more particularly those of French make, dispense with the bayonet-catch, replacing it by a peculiar arrangement inside the top of the cover. The upper edge of the well is slightly turned in all round, and the turning of the knob at the top of the cover causes three flat bolts or catches to shoot out circularly from the edges of a hollow disc, soldered to the top of the cover inside, and insert themselves under this projecting edge. (*See* Figs. 224, 225.) The mechanical arrangement by which this is effected is almost impossible to explain in writing, though it becomes readily

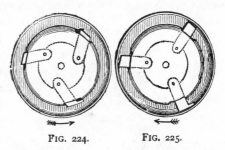

FIG. 224.   FIG. 225.

intelligible upon an actual inspection of the apparatus, and will be understood without much difficulty after a slight study of the above diagrams, the arrow in each case indicating the direction in which the knob must be turned, in order to bring the bolts into the condition shown in the opposite diagram.

THE INEXHAUSTIBLE BOX.—The inexhaustible box is, to all outward appearance, a plain wooden box, of walnut, mahogany, or rosewood, in length from twelve to twenty inches, and in depth and width from nine to fifteen inches. Whatever its dimensions, its width and depth, exclusive of the lid, must be alike. To prove that it is without preparation within, the performer turns it over on the table towards the spectators, and, lifting the lid, shows that it is perfectly empty. Again he closes it, and, turning it right side upwards, opens it once more, and instantly proceeds to take from it a variety of different articles. At any moment the box is again turned over towards the audience, and shown to be empty ; but it is no sooner replaced, than the performer recommences taking from it toys, bonbons, etc., the supply being many times larger than could possibly be contained at one time in the box.

The bottom *a b* of the box (*see* Fig. 226) is moveable, working on a hinge *b* extending along its front. When the box is turned over to the front, this bottom piece does not turn over with it, but remains flat upon the table as before. A piece of wood *b c*, of exactly similar size and shape, is glued to *a b* at right angles. When the box stands right side upwards, this piece lies flat against the front of the box, whose upper edge is made with a slight "return," so as to conceal it. When the box is turned over to the front, this piece, like the bottom, retains its position, while any object which had previously been placed in the box remains undisturbed, but hidden by this latter piece. (*See* Figs. 226, 227.) It is, of course, necessary that such object should be of such a size as not to overpass the arc which the edge of the box describes in its change of position, and the length from *b* to *c* must be exactly the same as that from *a* to *b*.

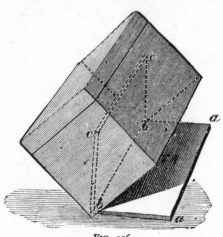

FIG. 226.

The mode of using the box will require little explanation. Any number of objects, not overpassing the limits we have mentioned, may be placed in the box, which, being then turned over, can be shown apparently empty. The box being replaced in its normal position, the articles are again within it, and can be produced at pleasure. The effect of "inexhaustibility" is produced as follows:—Each time that the performer turns over the box to show that it is empty, he takes from the *servante*, or from his pockets, and places upon *a b*, a fresh supply of articles, to be produced as soon as the box is again right side upwards.

It should be mentioned that the hinge at *b* is made to act freely, so that the bottom may by its own weight retain its position when the box is turned over, and not turn over with the box. Some boxes are made with a catch or pin at some part of *a*, so as to prevent *a b* falling prematurely while the box is being placed on the table, or while the performer carries round the box, and shows that, inside and out, it is without preparation. This, however, the performer may safely do, even without the use of any catch or fastening, by taking care to grasp the box, when carrying it, by its front edge, with his fingers inside it. The fingers will thus press *b c* closely against the front of the box, and will thereby effectually prevent *a b* from shifting its position. The box is, of course, in the case supposed, really empty. The performer has therefore to make an opportunity for introducing what may be needful into it; this he may do by remarking as he

FIG. 227.

replaces it on his table, "You are by this time, ladies and gentlemen, tolerably well satisfied that there is nothing in this box; but for the greater satisfaction of those who may not have been able to see the interior as I carried it round, I will once more show you that it is absolutely empty." So saying, he turns it over, and once more shows the interior, at the same time placing on *a b* whatever article he designs to produce.

THE JAPANESE INEXHAUSTIBLE BOXES.—This is a form of the same apparatus, in which an additional element of mystery is produced by the use of a box within a box. The inner box is an ordinary inexhaustible box, as last described, but made with a flat wooden lid, instead of the hollow or "box" lid used in the older form of the trick.

The outer box just fits over the inner, and is, in fact, a mere cover for it, being an ordinary wooden box, save that it has no front. The two are brought on one within the other. The performer begins by taking the smaller box (which is ready filled with the objects to be produced) completely out of the larger, and shows that the latter is absolutely empty. He then places the two boxes together, as shown in Fig. 228 turning over the smaller box to show its interior,

as already described. After this has been done, the smaller box is tilted back to its normal position within the larger, the lid of the latter being slightly lifted to allow it to pass, and then both lids being opened together, the production of the contents commences. The function of the larger box is, in fact, merely to act as a screen to the hinder part of the

FIG. 228.

smaller, when turned over towards the audience. The only advantage of the Japanese over the ordinary box is that it may be worked on any table, and with spectators on all sides, but this advantage is counterbalanced by the drawback that nothing can be produced save what was originally in the box, neither can the smaller box be carried round, and shown empty. This, however, may be met by beginning the trick with the two boxes together, and then, after having brought to light the whole of the original contents, offering (for the pretended purpose of heightening the effect) to continue the trick without the aid of the outer box. The inner box may thenceforth be replenished from behind in the same way as the ordinary Inexhaustible Box.

The Inexhaustible Box is frequently made the vehicle for those distributions of bonbons, toys, etc., which to the juvenile mind form by no means the least attractive feature of a magical performance. It is also available for the production of flowers, multiplying balls (*see* page 307), goblets, bird-cages, and the miscellaneous assortment of articles generally associated with "hat" tricks. One of the most effective modes of using it is in connection with the very pretty trick next following.

THE FEAST OF LANTERNS.—The performer, having exhibited the box empty, as already described, turns it over again, and instantly produces from it a paper lantern of many colours, with a lighted candle in it. This he hands to his assistant or one of the company to hang up at some convenient part of the stage or room, and returning to the box produces another, and yet another, till ten or twelve, or even a larger number, have been produced,

FIG. 230.

the box being every now and then turned over to prove it empty. The effect of a number of lanterns thus mysteriously produced from an empty box, and hung about the stage in all directions, is most brilliant. As the candles do not burn very long, and there may be some risk of the lanterns catching fire, it is well to make this trick the *finale* of the entertainment, and to allow the curtain to fall before the illumination has had time to lose its effect.

FIG. 229.

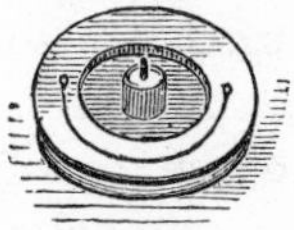

A great part of the effect of the trick lies in the very considerable bulk of the lanterns, three or four of which would apparently be more than sufficient to fill a box from which a dozen or so are produced. This arises from the construction of the lanterns themselves, which are of the kind used for Christmas-trees and illuminations, and when open offer a considerable cylindrical surface (*see* Fig. 229), though when closed they are little more than flat discs (*see* Fig. 230). They are placed in the box in the condition shown in the last-mentioned figure; but when lifted out by the wire at top, at once expand, concertina-fashion, and assume the shape shown in Fig. 229. They are lighted in sundry ways, one method being as follows :—Each lantern contains about three-quarters of an inch of candle, from which the wick has been removed, and a wax match inserted in its stead. Against the front of the box, or rather against the wooden flap *b c* (*see* Fig. 227), is glued a tablet *d* of sand-paper upon which to strike the match, and a gentle rub against this instantly lights the candle, when the lantern is immediately lifted out, as already explained. There is, however, an improvement whereby the lanterns are not only made to occupy much less space, but may be lighted simultaneously. In this case the little cylinder which forms the socket for the candle, and which should be about half an inch in diameter, instead of occupying the middle of the space at the bottom of the lantern, is placed at one side of such space. One of the lanterns, viz., that which is to be undermost when they are grouped together, has no further preparation; but the second, by the side of its own socket, has a round hole in the bottom, just large enough to give room for the socket of the first. The next, or third lantern, has two holes, allowing the passage of the sockets of the first and second. The fourth has three holes, the fifth four, the sixth five, the seventh six, and the eighth seven, so that when the lanterns are placed one upon another in proper order, the sockets of the lower lanterns come up in a circle through the holes in the bottom of the uppermost one. The tops and bottoms are made of tin, which is not only safe from catching fire, but occupies very little space. In this case the original wicks of the candles are retained, but are slightly moistened with turpentine to render them instantly inflammable, and are lighted by a lucifer or wax match struck in the ordinary way, the merest touch sufficing to ignite them. They may then be lifted out in rapid succession with great effect. A group of six or eight lanterns thus prepared may be produced from a borrowed hat, being previously con-cealed in the breast or tail-pocket of the performer, and "loaded" into the hat at any convenient opportunity. It is desirable in this case to have a friction tablet glued upon the top of the uppermost lantern to strike the match upon, as the hat lining is hardly adapted for that purpose.

The lanterns above described are the most generally used, and are by much the easiest to manipulate. There is, however, a spherical lantern also obtainable at the toy-shops, which has a decidedly prettier effect. This form of lantern is, when shut up, as shown in Fig. 231.

To develop it, the wires *a* and *b* are each made to describe a semi-circle, as shown by the dotted line, bringing the whole into the condition shown in Fig. 232, in which condition it is maintained by slipping the loop of *a* under *b*. The best plan for lighting in this case is to have a separate small piece of candle, prepared with a match wick, as above-mentioned, placed in readiness on the *servante*, and a small pin or sharp nail projecting upwards from the bottom of the box to act as a candlestick. The candles in the lantern

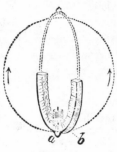

FIG. 231.

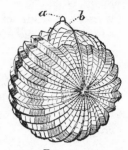

FIG. 232.

will in this case need no special preparation. The performer first lights the prepared candle by rubbing it against the tablet, and then presses it down upon the upright pin we have mentioned. The other candles are in turn lighted from this, each lantern being put into shape before being lifted out of the box, which must in this case be of tolerable size, in order to admit of their ready development.

THE BUTTERFLY TRICK.—This is a trick of Japanese origin, which became very popular two or three years since. In effect it is as follows :—The performer brings forward an ordinary fan, and a couple of bits of tissue-paper, each torn into a fanciful likeness of a butterfly. Taking these upon his hand, he gently fans them, the motion of the air speedily causing them to rise above his head. Still gently fanning them, he causes them to hover, now high, now low, now fluttering along the wall, now descending into a gentleman's hat, whence they presently emerge to again flutter hither and thither at his pleasure.

The point that most strikes an attentive observer is the fact that, whether they fly high or low, the butterflies always keep *together*. Sometimes they may be a couple of feet apart, sometimes only a few inches, but they never exceed the above limit; and the spectator naturally concludes that an extraordinary degree of dexterity must be necessary to enable the performer to keep them from diverging more widely. Here, however, in truth lies the secret of the trick, which is, that the so-called butterflies are connected by a piece of very fine silk a couple of feet in length, which, when the butterflies are in motion, is absolutely invisible to the spectators. The remainder of the trick is a matter of practice, though it is less difficult than would be imagined by any one who had never attempted it.

Some performers have the silk thread attached to one of the buttons of the coat. This arrangement will be found greatly to facilitate the working of the trick.

The paper for the butterflies is better torn than cut, and should be as nearly as possible of the shape of a St. George's cross, and about two inches square.

The Wizard's Omelet. (Borrowed Rings and Live Doves produced from an Omelet.)—This is a trick which always produces a great sensation, whether performed upon the stage or in the drawing-room. Its effect is as follows: The performer produces either naturally or magically (*e.g.*, from the egg-bag, or from the mouth of his assistant, as described at page 329) three eggs, which he hands round for examination. His assistant next borrows from the audience three ladies' rings, receiving them, in order to prove that he does not tamper with them in any way, on the performer's wand instead of in his hands. The wand, with the rings still upon it, is laid upon the table. The assistant next brings in an omelet pan, and places it, with its lid beside it, on the table. The performer breaks the eggs into it, dropping in shells and all—then pours some spirits over it, to which he sets fire, and while it is still blazing drops the rings from the wand into it. He brings it forward to show that the rings are really in the flames; and on returning to his table, claps the cover on the pan, and fires a pistol (any ordinary pistol) over it. Without a moment's interval, he again removes the cover. All traces of the omelet and egg-shells have vanished, but in their* place are found three live doves, each with a ribbon round its neck, to which is attached one of the borrowed rings.

The explanation of this surprising result is simplicity itself. The reader, with his present knowledge, will readily conjecture that, as to the rings, a subsitution is effected; but he may not so easily guess the manner of such substitution. It will be remembered that the rings were collected by the assistant on the performer's wand. This arrangement, which is ostensibly adopted to prevent, in reality facilitates an exchange. The assistant makes his collection with three dummy rings placed beforehand on the lower end of the wand, and concealed by the hand in which he holds it; which, we will suppose, is the right hand. In returning to the stage, he takes hold with the left hand of the opposite end of the wand, and allows the borrowed rings to run down into that hand, at the same moment releasing the dummy rings from the right hand, and allowing them to run upon the middle of the wand in place of the others. He now has the borrowed rings in his left hand, and (laying the wand with the substitutes on the table) carries them off with him to prepare for the *dénouement* of the trick.

FIG. 233.

The only other matter which will require explanation is the construction of the omelet pan. This is a shallow pan of brass or tin, about ten inches in diameter, by two and a half in depth. Within this is an inner pan, also of brass or tin, fitting tightly within it, but about half an inch less in depth. The lid is made with a very deep rim or shoulder all round, and just fits within the lining, though less tightly than the latter fits within the pan. (*See* Fig. 233, in which *a* represents the pan, *b* the lining, and *c* the lid.) The assistant, as soon as he gets behind the scenes, loops the borrowed rings to the ribbons, which are already tied round the necks of the three doves, and places the latter in *b*, immediately putting on *c* (the two together having the appearance of a simple cover), and brings forward the pan and cover. The performer now makes his omelet, and drops the substitute rings into it. In bringing forward the pan to show that the rings are really there, he takes care to avoid the owners of them, who would alone be likely to detect the substitution. When he claps on the cover, the trick is really done, the firing of the pistol being merely for effect. When the cover is again removed, the lining remains in the pan, concealing the omelet beneath it, and revealing the doves, with the rings attached to their necks.

THE ROSE IN THE GLASS VASE.—The ingenious piece of apparatus which we are about to describe was, we believe, the invention

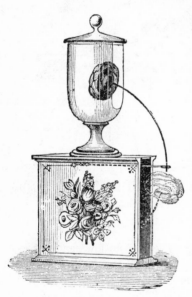

of Robert-Houdin. It consists of a glass vase, on a foot, and with a glass lid, standing altogether eight to ten inches in height. This is placed on a square box-like plinth or pedestal, of wood covered with morocco, and measuring about eight inches square by six in height. The lid is placed upon the vase, which, being transparent, is clearly seen to be empty. A borrowed handkerchief is for a moment thrown over the whole, and again removed, when a handsome rose (natural or artificial) is seen to have mysteriously found its way into the vase; whence it is removed, and handed to the company for inspection.

FIG. 234.

The secret of this mysterious appearance is twofold, lying partly in the vase and partly in the pedestal. The vase, which at a little distance appears as simple and commonplace as any in a confectioner's window, has a segment cut off one side, leaving an opening of about five inches in height by three and a half in width. (*See* Fig. 234.) This opening is kept turned away from the audience. The pedestal, like the vase, is closed on every side except the side remote from the spectators, which is open. A curved wire arm, with a "clip" at the end to receive the stalk of the rose, works up and down, describing a quarter of a circle, in this open space. A spring hinge, on which this arm works, impels it to assume the position shown in the figure, thus lifting the rose through the opening into the vase. The apparatus is set by forcing down the arm with the rose into the position indicated by the dotted lines, in which position it is retained by a little catch, until the performer, in the act of covering the vase with the handkerchief, presses a stud at the upper side of the pedestal. This withdraws the catch, and allows the rose to rise into the vase. Of course, the performer in taking out the flower does so from the top, and with proper precautions not to disclose the existence of the opening at the back of the vase.

The ingenuity of the reader will probably suggest to him combinations to make the trick more effective. To those who have not such ready invention, we may remark that the trick may be very effectively combined with that of the ball that changes to a rose, and *vice versâ* (*see* page 300), or a duplicate rose may be placed in the *mouchoir du diable* (described at page 195), and thence ordered to pass to the vase.

THE CHINESE RINGS.—These are rings of brass or steel, in diameter from five to nine inches, and in thickness varying from a quarter to three-eighths of an inch. The effect of the trick to the spectator is as follows:— The rings are given for examination, and found to be solid and separate; but at the will of the operator they are linked together in chains of two, three, or more, becoming connected and disconnected in a moment, and being continually offered for examination. Finally, after the rings have become involved in an apparently inextricable mass, a slight shake suffices to disentangle them, and to cause them to fall singly upon the stage.

FIG. 235.

The sets of rings sold at the conjuring depôts vary in number, ranging from six to twelve. The set of eight, which is perhaps the most usual number, consists of one "key" ring, two single rings, a

set of two linked together, and a set of three linked together. The "key" ring (*see* Fig. 235), in which lies the secret of the trick, is simply a ring with a cut or opening, *a,* in it. For use upon a public stage, where the performer is at a considerable

FIG. 236.

distance from his audience, there may be a gap of an eighth of an inch between the ends, but for drawing-room use, they should just touch each other. Some rings are made to "clip" like an ear-ring, and some have the opening cut diagonally instead of square, but the simple square cut is, in our own opinion, the best.

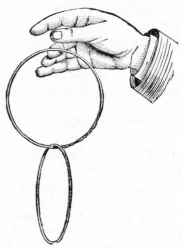

We shall, in the first place, describe the trick as performed with the set of eight rings above mentioned, afterwards noticing the more elaborate performance with twelve. We must premise, however, that the manipulation of the rings admits of almost infinite variation, and that the practice of performers differs greatly as to the mode of working them.

FIG. 237.

The performer comes forward holding the eight rings in his left hand, arranged as follows. First (*i.e.*, innermost), comes the set of three; then the "key" ring (the opening uppermost in the hand), then the set of two; and, lastly, the two single rings. Taking the first of these, he hands it to a spectator for examination; passing it when returned to another person, and carelessly handing a second ring to be examined in like manner. This should be done without any appearance of haste, and with an air of being perfectly indifferent as to how many of the rings are examined. The two "singles" having been duly inspected, the performer request sone of the spectators to take them both in his right hand, at the same time taking in his own right hand the next two rings, which, it will be remembered, are the set of two, though the audience naturally believe them to be, like the first, separate.

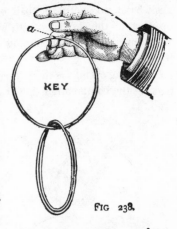

FIG 238.

"Now, sir," the professor continues, "will you be good enough to link one of the rings which you hold into the other." The person addressed looks more or less foolish, and finally "gives it up." "You can't?" says the performer, in pretended surprise. "My dear sir, nothing is easier. You have only to do as I do. See!" Laying down the rest of the rings, he holds the two as in Fig. 236, and makes a gentle rubbing motion with the thumb upon the rings, and then lets fall one of them, which naturally drops to the position shown in Fig. 237. He now

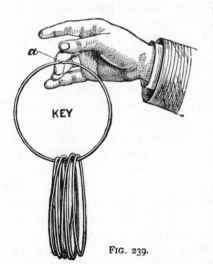

FIG. 239.

hands these two rings for examination. The spectators seek for some joint or opening, but none is found; and meanwhile the performer transfers the next ring (the "key") to his right hand, keeping the opening under the thumb. He now takes back with the left hand the two single rings, immediately transferring one of them to the right hand, and with the ball of the thumb presses it through the opening in the key ring, into which it falls, with exactly the same effect as the apparent joining of the two linked rings a moment before. Again he separates and again joins the two rings. The second single ring is now made to pass through in like manner, making the combination shown in Fig. 238. The performer remarks,

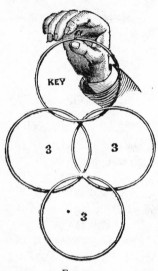

"We now have three joined together. Here are three more, as you see (shaking those in the left hand), all solid and separate, and yet at my will they will join like the others." Making a rubbing motion with the thumb as before, he drops two of the three, one by one, from the hand, when they will appear as a chain of three. These he hands for examination, taking back the set of two, and linking them one after the other into the key ring, to which now four rings are attached. Again taking back the set of three, he links these also one by one into the key ring, which thus has seven rings inserted

FIG. 240.

in it. (*See* Fig. 239.) Using both hands, but always keeping the opening of the key ring under one or the other thumb, he now takes off these seven rings, commencing with the two single ones, and again offering them for examination ; then taking off the set of two. Last of all, he unlinks the set of three, and then, holding them at length in his left hand, joins the upper one to the key ring, thus making a chain of four, of which the key ring is the uppermost. He next takes the lowermost ring of the four, and links that into the key ring, bringing the four rings into a diamond shape, as shown in Fig. 240. Again unlinking the lower ring, he takes up the set of two, and connects them with the key ring, holding them up above it, thus making a chain of six, the key ring being third from the top. (*See* Fig. 241.) Taking the upper ring between his teeth, he links the two single rings into the key ring on either side, making the figure of a cross, as shown in Fig. 242. As the hands are now occupied in holding the

single rings forming the arms of the cross, he can no longer keep the opening of the key ring concealed by the thumb, but it is extremely un-likely that among so many rings, so slight a mark in one of them will attract notice. Regaining possession of the key ring, he links all one by one into it, so as again to bring them into the condition depicted in Fig. 239. Then, holding the key ring with both hands, and with the open-ing downwards, about a couple of feet from the floor (*see* Fig. 243), he shakes the rings violently, at the same time gently straining open the key ring, when the seven rings will all in succession drop through the slit, and scatter themselves about the floor, the general impression being that they all fall separate, though the grouped sets, of course, remain still united.

It is not an uncommon thing to see a performer commit the *gaucherie* of handing *all* the rings, save only

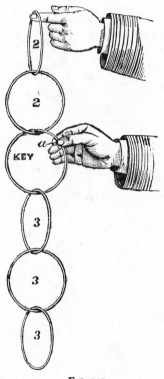

FIG. 241.

the key ring, to be examined in the first instance ; the key ring being hidden under the breast or under the tail of the coat, and being added to the set in returning to the table. The spectators are thus needlessly made acquainted with the fact that certain of the rings are already linked together, and this once admitted, the trick loses nine-tenths of its effect.

The set of twelve rings is less frequently seen, and is rather more complicated to manage, though in good hands it is capable of much more brilliant effects than the smaller number. The set consists of five single rings, a group of two, a group of three, and two key rings. These are held in the hands of the performer in the following order. First (*i.e.*, innermost) a key ring, then the group of three, then the

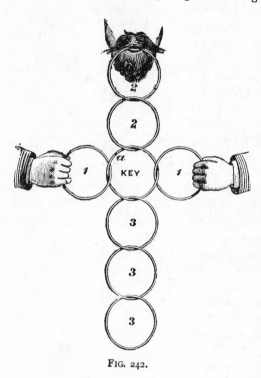

FIG. 242.

second key ring, then the group of two, and lastly the five single rings. The latter are distributed for examination. While they are still in the possession of the audience, the performer requests one of the spectators to link two of them together, and himself taking in his right hand the group of two, pretends to link the latter, as already described, and hands them for examination. The performer meanwhile takes in his right hand one of the key rings, and collects the single rings in his left. As soon as the group of two are handed back, he links one of them to the key ring in his right hand, thus forming a chain of three, with the key ring uppermost. Next linking the lowest ring into the key ring, he forms Fig. 238, which, by holding the two lower rings apart, assumes the shape of a triangle. Again disengaging the lower ring, passing one of the single rings from the left hand to the right, and laying down on the table all the rings remaining in that hand (the group of three uppermost) he joins the single ring to the key ring, thus making a chain of four, of which the key ring is second from the top. These he lays, still linked, upon the table, and takes up from the heap already lying there the three uppermost (which, it will be remembered, are the group of three), and holding them for a moment together in the hand, lets them fall one by one to form a second chain of three. Taking the next ring of the heap (the second key ring) in his disengaged hand, he steps forward, and requests some one to take hold of either of the three rings, and to pull against him, in order to prove their solidity. This ascertained, he passes the upper ring of the three into the hand which already holds the key ring, and links it into the key ring, thus forming a second chain of four, of which in this case the key is the uppermost. Linking the lowermost into the key ring, he shows the rings as in Fig. 240. Once more unlinking the lower ring, so that the four again

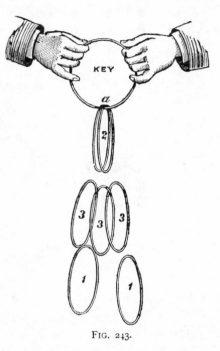

FIG. 243.

appear as a single chain, he proceeds (apparently) to link all the twelve together. This is effected as follows :—

Taking two of the single rings, the performer links them into the key ring of the chain which he holds, He next links one of these same single rings into the key ring of the other chain, thus linking the two chains together at a distance of one ring from the end of the chain. He thus has ten rings joined. He now takes the two chains one in each hand by the ends remotest from the point of juncture, immediately after picking up and holding (one in each hand) the two remaining single rings. These, of course, he does not and cannot link with the rings adjoining them, but the audience seeing that all the rest are linked together, readily believe that these also form part of the chain. The precise arrangement of the rings will be readily understood from an inspection of Fig. 244.*

The feat may either end here, the rings, still linked, being gathered together and carried off by the assistant, or the performer may link all

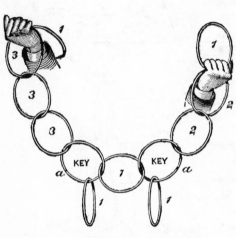

FIG. 244.

one by one into either of the key rings, and then shake them out and scatter them on the floor in the manner already described as to the eight rings. The performance may be elaborated to any extent, the two key rings giving a wonderful facility of combination, but whatever be the passes adopted they should not be too numerous, as the trick, however skilfully worked, consists only of repetitions of the same primary elements, and the interest of the spectators will quickly diminish.

The performer should, in manipulating the rings, study neatness and lightness, rather than rapidity. The effect should be as though the rings *melted* into and out of one another, and the smallest appearance of force or exertion should be avoided. It has a very good effect in disengaging the rings one from another, to hold them together for a moment or two after they are actually disconnected, and then holding them parallel to each other, to draw them very slowly apart.

---

* The numbers 1, 2, 3, in the centre of the various rings in Figs. 240—244, indicate whether the ring in question is a " single " or forms part of the group of two or of three, as the case may be.

The precise moment of their separation is thus left uncertain, the illusion being thereby materially heightened. A single ring may in this way be drawn along a chain of three or four, the effect being as if the disengaged ring passed *through* the whole length of the chain.

THE CHARMED BULLET.—As a rule, people object to being shot at, and the least nervous person might fairly demur at facing the muzzle of a loaded pistol at six paces' distance; but the magician is superior to such weakness, and will face a bullet with as little compunction as he would stop a ball at cricket. Neither must it be imagined that there is any " deception," at any rate in the quality of the articles employed. The pistol is a real pistol, the powder is genuine powder, and the bullet—an ordinary leaden bullet—is chosen and marked by one of the audience, fairly placed in the pistol, and fairly rammed home. The pistol is fired with deliberate aim by a dis-

interested spectator; but no sooner has the smoke cleared away than the performer is seen standing unharmed, with the marked bullet caught between his teeth.

So much for the effect of the trick; now for the

FIG. 245.

explanation. The pistol (*see* Fig. 245) is, as already stated, an ordinary weapon, and the only speciality of the bullets is that they are a size or two smaller than the bore of the pistol. The ramrod, *b*, is a plain cylinder of wood or metal, tapering very slightly at each end. The secret lies in the use of a little metal tube *a*, about two inches in length, open at one end, but closed at the other. This tube, which is of such a size as to fit loosely within the barrel of the pistol, but tightly upon either end of the ramrod, is placed in the right-hand *pochette* of the performer, and a small bag of bullets in the *pochette* on the other side.

The performer comes forward with the pistol in one hand and the ramrod in the other, and having a small charge of gunpowder, screwed up in a bit of soft paper, concealed between the second and third fingers of his right hand. He hands the pistol and ramrod for inspection. While they are under examination, he asks, " Can any lady or gentleman oblige me with a little gunpowder ? " Nobody answers, and he continues, addressing some mild elderly gentleman, " Perhaps you can accommodate me, sir ? " The elderly gentleman naturally replies that he is not in the habit of carrying gunpowder about with him. " Excuse me," says the performer, " but I fancy you have a small packet of powder under your coat-collar. Permit me ! " and drawing his hand gently down beneath the collar, he produces the little packet. This he hands to the person who is holding the pistol, with a request that he will load it. While he puts in the powder, the performer drops his left hand to the *pochette,* and palms the little bag of bullets, which he forthwith produces from a gentleman's hat, or a lady's muff.* From among the bullets he requests the person who put in the powder to select and mark one. While this is done, he himself takes the pistol in his left hand, holding it muzzle upwards, and in the act of transferring it with apparent carelessness to the other hand, secretly drops into it the little tube, the open end upwards. The spectator having chosen and marked the bullet, is requested, for greater certainty, to place it in the pistol himself. A very minute portion of paper is added by way of wad, and the performer then takes the pistol, and rams it down. The bullet, of course, has fallen into the little tube, and as the ramrod fits tightly within the latter, it naturally, when withdrawn, brings out tube and ball with it. The tube and ramrod are made to match (generally black, but sometimes of brass or silver-plated) ; and therefore the tube, when on the rod, even if exposed, would not be likely to attract attention. The performer, however, prevents the possibility of its doing so, by holding the rod by that end, thereby concealing the tube with his hand. He now hands the pistol to a spectator, requesting him, for fear of accidents, to hold it muzzle upwards until the word to fire is given. The performer now takes up his position at the

---

* A muff, being open at each end, is an excellent thing whence to produce any small article—*e.g.*, a borrowed watch, a ball, etc. For this purpose the performer should take hold of one end of the muff with the hand in which is palmed the article in question, which is immediately allowed to slide gently through the muff, and is stopped by the other hand. If this is neatly done, the keenest eye cannot detect the deception.

furthest part of the stage, and during his short journey gains possession of the bullet. This is effected by sharply drawing away the
ramrod with the left hand, thereby leaving the tube open in the right,
and allowing the ball to roll out into the palm. The tube, having
served its purpose, is got rid of into the *profonde*, and the ball is either
slipped into the mouth or retained in the hand, according to the mode
in which it is intended to be produced.

Some performers use several small bullets. In our own opinion,
a single ball of tolerable size is not only more manageable, but more
effective. The mode of producing the bullet also varies. Some, instead of producing it in the mouth, hold up a china plate by way of
target, the bullet being held under the two first fingers against the
front of the plate. When the pistol is fired, the plate is turned horizontally, and the bullet released from the fingers. This plan is sometimes to be preferred, inasmuch as it creates an excuse for leaving the
stage for a moment to fetch the plate, an opportunity which is valuable in the event, which sometimes happens, of the ball, from an
excess of wadding or any other cause, not dropping readily from the
tube into the hand. To meet this possible difficulty, some tubes
have (to use an Irishism) a small hole through the *closed* end, so that
the performer, on leaving the stage, can, by pushing a piece of wire
through the hole, instantly force out the bullet.

THE BIRTH OF FLOWERS.—There are two or three different
tricks which go by this name. Of one of them we may dispose in a
very few words. It is purely a mechanical trick, having neither
ingenuity of construction nor dexterity of manipulation to recommend it. The apparatus consists of a cover *a* (*see* Fig. 246), a
base *c*, and an intermediate portion *b*, connected with *a* by means
of a bayonet-catch; *c* is beforehand partially filled with earth, and in
b, the top of which is perforated with small holes, is inserted a natural or artificial plant, or bouquet of flowers. The cover *a* is placed
over *b*, and the apparatus is ready. The performer, drawing attention
to *c*, pretends to sow some magic seed therein. He then places *a*
over it, and pretending to warm it with his hands, commands the
seeds to germinate. Releasing the bayonet-catch, he removes the
cover, and shows the flowers apparently just springing from the earth

in *c*. In some of the smaller sizes of this apparatus the bayonet-catch is dispensed with, the mere pressure of the fingers on the sides of *a* being sufficient to lift off *b* with it.

The trick which we are about to describe under the same title is one of a composite nature, and one which, proceeding from marvel to marvel, produces in good hands a great effect. It is divided into three portions—first, the production of a single flower, then of a

handsome bouquet, and lastly, of a large basket of flowers. The performer comes forward with his wand in one hand, and in the other a little box, in reality quite empty, but containing, as he asserts, magic seeds, capable of producing on the instant the choicest flowers. "I will first show you, ladies and gentlemen, their effect in the simplest

FIG. 246.

form. In the hurry of coming here this evening, I omitted to provide a flower for my button-hole. You will see how easily, by the aid of the magic seed, I can supply the deficiency. What shall it be? Clematis, rose, geranium? Suppose we say a rose. I take a single seed from my box—ah, here is a rose-seed—and place it in my button-hole." (He applies the supposed seed to the button-hole.) "I breathe on it to supply the necessary warmth. I wave my wand—Once! twice! thrice! The seed has blossomed, you see, into a handsome rose."

The explanation of this pretty little trick is exceedingly simple. The preliminary preparation is made as follows:—Through the centre of an artificial rose, without stalk, a short piece (about ten inches) of thin black elastic is passed, and secured by a knot on the inside of the flower. The other end is passed through the button-hole (from the outside), and thence through an eyelet-hole made for the purpose in the breast of the coat, immediately under the buttonhole. The extreme end is looped over a button sewn on the waistcoat about the region of the waistband. The tension of the elastic naturally draws the flower close against the button-hole, while yet allowing it, when necessary, to be drawn away from it to a distance of several inches. The performer, before coming forward to perform the trick, draws the rose away from the button-hole, and places it under the left armpit, whence, so long as the arm is kept close to the side, it cannot escape. When he waves his wand, with the words, "Once, twice, thrice!" he makes the first motion facing to the right, the second fronting the audience, and the third facing slightly to the left, at the same time striking the button-hole with the wand, and throwing up the left arm, when the flower, released, instantly springs to the button-hole, the slight turn to the left completely covering the manner of its appearance.

But the trick is not yet over. "You see, ladies and gentlemen, that I am not dependent on Covent Garden for a rose for my button-hole; but you will naturally say, 'Ah! the magic seed may be all very well for a single flower, but what if you wanted a complete bouquet?' I hasten to show you that this is equally within my power. Will some one oblige me with the loan of a hat by way of hothouse? Thank you. Here, you observe, is an ordinary drinking-glass" (this has, meanwhile, been placed on the table by the assistant), "in which I will drop, haphazard, a pinch of the magic seed." This he does with the left hand, the right being occupied with the hat, and then, with the glass in the left hand

FIG. 247.

and the hat in the right, comes forward to the audience, requesting a lady spectator to breathe upon the glass, which he immediately afterwards covers with the hat. He now requests the same or another spectator to count ten, to allow the mesmeric influence time to operate, and then, removing the hat, shows a handsome bouquet (natural or artificial) in the glass. Returning the hat, and handing the glass and flowers for inspection, he borrows a silk pocket-handkerchief, or in default of procuring one from the audience, uses one of his own, brought forward by the assistant. Drawing it ropewise through his hands to show that it is empty, he spreads it before him, holding it by two of its corners. Having exhibited one side of it, he spreads the other, when the shape of something solid is seen to define itself beneath it, and the handkerchief being removed, a large round basket of flowers (*see* Fig. 247), ten or more inches in diameter by two deep, is revealed.

The reader, with his present knowledge, will probably have already conjectured the mode in which the bouquet is brought into the glass. It is beforehand placed at the left hand corner of the *servante*, the stem slanting upwards at an angle of about 45°. When the performer, standing at the left hand side of the table, drops the imaginary seed into the glass with his left hand, his right, holding the hat, drops for a moment to the level of the table, and clips between the second and third fingers the stem of the bouquet, when, by simply bending the fingers, the bouquet is brought into the hat after the manner of the cannon-ball. (*See* page 305.) When the hat is placed over the glass, the bouquet is naturally brought into the latter.

We may here mention that there are bouquets of a special and rather ingenious construction, enabling the performer, in the act of producing the bouquet from a hat in the above or any similar trick, to cause it suddenly to expand to three or four times its original size. The bouquet is in this case made of artificial flowers, stitched on a framework forming a kind of miniature parasol, with a very short handle. The bouquet, when introduced into the hat, has a slightly conical shape, but the performer in withdrawing it puts up the parasol, so to speak, thereby spreading it to twelve or fourteen inches' diameter.

The production of the basket of flowers from the handkerchief is produced by wholly different means, and will require a somewhat minute explanation. In the first place, the flowers are secured to the sides of the baskets by silk or wires, so that they cannot fall out, in whatever position the basket is placed. To the basket are attached two black silk threads. The one (which we will call *a*) is about eighteen inches in length, and is attached to a button on the per-

former's waistband, immediately above the front of the left thigh.
Obviously, therefore, the basket, if fas-
tened by this thread alone, would hang
down loosely in front of the performer's
left knee. The second thread (which
we will call *b*, and which is attached
to the edge of the basket at a few
inches' distance from the first) is only
three or four inches in length, and
serves to suspend the basket behind the
back of the performer (concealed by his
coat) until the proper moment for its
appearance. For this purpose it has a
small loop or ring at the loose end, and
this is attached by means of a strong
short needle, after the manner shown
in Figs. 248 and 249 (the latter representing a slightly enlarged view of the
attachment), to the waistband of the
performer. The needle carries a third

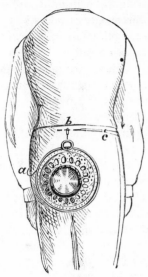

FIG. 248.

thread *c*, which, passing through the cloth of the trousers, is brought
round and attached to the centre button of the waistband, being concealed by the edge of the
waistcoat. The *modus
operandi* will now be easily understood. The bas-
ket is in the first instance
suspended by the thread
b. The performer, while
spreading the handker-
chief before him, osten-
sibly to show that it is
empty, crooks the little
finger under the edge of
his waistcoat, and pulls *c*,
thereby withdrawing the

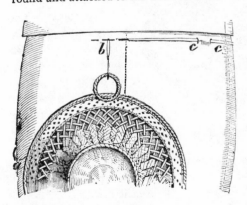

FIG. 249.

needle, and detaching *b*. The basket, being no longer held back by *b*, falls, but is compelled by *a* to swing round in front of the performer, who, while lifting it, still covered by the handkerchief, breaks *a*, and thus altogether releases it. The object of passing the needle through the cloth of the trousers is that it may not fall forward and be seen when *c* is pulled.

The contrivance last above described is the invention of Robert-Houdin, slightly simplified, however, inasmuch as he employed, in place of the needle, a little wire bolt working on a metal plate attached to the back of the waistcoat; but the principle in either case is precisely the same.

THE MYSTERIOUS SALVER.—This is a tin tray (*see* Fig. 250), ornamentally japanned, and of about twelve inches in diameter. There is a space of about three quarters of an inch between the upper and under surfaces of the tray, at one side of which, under cover of the curled rim, is an opening of about three inches in width. Within

FIG. 250.

this opening, so placed as to be within easy reach of the fingers of any person holding the tray, are two wire hooks, marked *a* and *b* in the figure. On gently pulling hook *a*, a little hammer *c* rises up at right angles to the surface of the tray, again falling back by the action of a spring as soon as the pull is relaxed. On pulling *b*, a similar movement is communicated to a sort of ladle *d*, sunk in the surface of the tray, and rising up in a direction parallel to that of the little hammer already mentioned. This ladle has a flat tin cover, hinged very loosely upon its outer edge (so as to open of its own accord when the ladle passes the perpendicular position), and japanned in such manner as to represent one of a circle of medallions forming part of the pattern of the tray, and therefore little likely to attract attention. If any small article be beforehand placed in the ladle, and *b* be pulled, the article will naturally be flung out upon the surface of the tray. In practice, however, the salver is always used in conjunction with a little glass tumbler, about three inches in height, which, being placed upon the medallion opposite to that which forms the cover of the ladle, the contents of the latter fall into the glass instead of upon the tray.

The salver is generally used somewhat after the following fashion :—A little round brass box, say an inch and a half in diameter and an inch deep, is handed to the audience, with a request that they will place any small article (such as a coin, a ring, a watch-key) in it. All necessary precautions are taken to prevent the performer knowing what the articles in question are, and the box is, for still greater security on this point, wrapped by the performer in a handkerchief, and handed to one of the audience to hold. The reader, with his present knowledge of the little faith that is to be put in the acts of magicians, however apparently straightforward, will readily conjecture that at this point there is a substitution. The performer, apparently wrapping up the box which has just been handed to him, really substitutes another of similar appearance, sewn in one corner of the handkerchief. This latter, which contains two or three metal buttons, or other objects adapted to cause a rattling when shaken, is so arranged that when the lid is pushed home a piece of cork within is pressed down upon the buttons, and they are made silent; but if the lid be raised ever so little, and the box shaken, they rattle. This latter is the condition in which the box is wrapped in the handkerchief.

The performer, leaving the dummy box, wrapped up as above, with the spectator, retires for a moment in order to fetch the salver. This gives him the opportunity to take the articles out of the box, to note what they are (we will suppose a ring, a florin, and a locket), and place them in the "ladle" of the salver. The empty box he places in one of his *pochettes*. He now brings forward the glass and salver, together with a paper lamp-shade (similar to those placed over the lights of a billiard table), wherewith to cover the salver while the supposed flight of the objects takes place. He first shows that there is nothing in his hands, on the salver, or in the glass, and then places the latter in its proper position, and covers the whole with the paper shade. His assistant holds the salver, using both hands, with his right in such a position as to have control of the hooks *a* and *b*. The performer requests the person holding the box to shake it, in order to show that the articles are still there. He then addresses the company to the following effect :—" Ladies and gentlemen, allow me to remind you of the position of affairs. Some articles, unknown to me, have been placed by yourselves in a box. That box has not been in my possession, even for a moment, but has remained ever since in the hands of the gentleman who is now holding it. Here, as you see, is a little glass " (he raises the shade with the left hand), " perfectly empty. I shall now, by virtue of my magic power, order the articles in the box, whatever they may be, to leave the box, and fall into this little glass, and I will tell you by the sound of each as it falls what the article is. Let us try the experiment. First article, pass ! " The assistant pulls *a*, and the little hammer *c* forthwith strikes the glass, simulating to some extent the sound of a small article falling therein. " That, by the sound, should be a coin, I should say a florin. Hold tight, sir, please. Second article, pass ! " Again the assistant causes the hammer to strike the glass. " That, ladies and gentlemen, is a ring. You must hold tighter yet, sir, if you mean to defy my power. Third article, pass ! " This time the assistant pulls *b*, causing the ladle *d* to rise, and to shoot out the three articles together into the glass. " That, I should say, was a lady's locket. Fourth article, pass ! " (This is a mere blind, and elicits no response.) " Ladies and gentlemen, there were three articles placed in the box, a ring, a florin, and a locket, and you will find that they have now all passed into the glass." (He removes the shade, and shows that they have done so.) " May I trouble you once more to shake the box ? " The repeated injunctions to hold tighter have naturally caused the holder to press the lid home, and the box is therefore silent, corroborating the assertion that the articles have departed. " Now, ladies and gentlemen, having conjured away the contents, I shall now proceed to conjure away the box ; but this time, by way of variety, I will do it visibly. Attention ! " He takes one corner of the handkerchief with his right hand.

"Now, sir, when I say 'Three,' will you please drop the handker-chief. One, two, *three !*" The performer shakes the handkerchief and pulls it rapidly through his hands till the corner containing the box comes into the left hand, the box having apparently vanished. "The box has gone, you see, but where ? that is the question. Pardon me, sir, you have it in your pocket, I think," addressing some elderly gentleman of innocent aspect. With the handkerchief still dangling from his left hand, the performer thrusts the other hand into the waistcoat or breast pocket of the individual in question, and produces from thence the missing box, which he has a moment previously palmed from the *pochette*.

The weak point of the trick, as above performed, is the sound of the hammer on the glass, which is but a poor imitation of that of coins, or the like, falling into it. In some trays the hammer is altogether dispensed with, the performer himself holding the tray, and the necessary sound being produced by the assistant actually dropping a coin into a glass behind the scenes, as near the standing place of the performer as possible. This latter plan is much to be preferred.

A further improvement consists in the use, in place of the salver, of a small round table, or *guéridon*, made on the same principle (without the hammer), and worked by pulling a string from behind the scenes. With a little dexterity, the articles may be introduced into the "ladle," while in the act of placing the glass upon the table, or of moving the latter to the front of the stage, though it is more usual to do this behind the scenes, and then to bring the table forward, as described in the case of the salver.

The trick may be varied by borrowing four half-crowns or florins, duly marked, which, being exchanged, and their substitutes placed in the half-crown casket (*see* page 202), are thence made to pass one by one into the glass.

THE VANISHING DIE.—The effect of this trick, in its simplest shape, is merely to make a die, some three inches square, pass through the crown of a hat, and be found inside. The trick in this form is but a poor and transparent affair, but it is sometimes useful as affording a pretext for borrowing a hat which you design to make use of for some other purpose; and it furnishes the germ of two or three really effective illusions. The apparatus consists of three portions—a solid wooden die, generally painted black with white spots, a tin counterpart thereof,—fitting loosely over it, and exactly similar in appearance, but with one side open,—and an ornamental cover of thin pasteboard (sometimes this also is of tin), fitting in like manner over the hollow die. The trick is worked very much after the manner of the "cone," recently described. The performer comes forward, having the solid die in the one hand, and the cover, with the tin counterpart within it, in the other. Placing these on the table, he borrows two hats, which he likewise places on the table, mouth upwards. "Ladies and gentlemen," he commences, "I have here a block of wood" (he lets it fall on the floor, the sound sufficiently indicating its solidity, and again picks it up), "and a cover of simple pasteboard." He places the cover over it, as if merely suiting the action to the word, and in again removing it, leaves the tin die over the solid one. "If any one would like to examine it, he is perfectly welcome to do so. I have here also two hats, borrowed haphazard from the audience, and, as you can all see, perfectly empty, and not prepared in any way. "Now I propose to make this solid die" (he tosses it carelessly into one of the hats, and again apparently takes it out, but really takes out the hollow shell only) "pass right through the crown of one of these hats, and fall into the other." He places the hats one upon the other, mouth to mouth, and the tin shell, with the opening downwards, upon the uppermost. "Here is the die, which I cover, thus. Now, at my command it shall pass downwards through the hat. One, two, three! Pass! See, the cover is empty" (taking it up with gentle pressure, so as to lift the shell with it, and placing both on the end of his wand, proving, apparently, that the cover is empty), "and here, in the lower hat, is the die. Let us try the experiment again. I will replace the die in the lower hat. One, two, three! Pass!" He lifts the cover, without pressure, leaving the hollow die on the upper hat. "It has obeyed, you see. Once more. One, two, three! Pass!" Again the cover is empty, and again the die has passed into the lower hat.

THE DIE DISSOLVING IN A POCKET HANDKERCHIEF.—The trick

last described has two drawbacks—first, that it is very generally known, and, second, that the principle is rather too obvious, the secret being very easily guessed, even by persons not endowed with special sagacity. There is, however, an improved form of the same trick, in which an additional element is introduced, whereby these disadvantages are, to a great extent, removed.

The apparatus used is the same as in the last case, with the addition of a coloured handkerchief, prepared as follows: Five square pieces of stout pasteboard, each a shade larger than one side of the solid die, are joined together with hinges of tape or cloth, in the form shown by the dotted lines in Fig. 251. The centre piece, *a*, is attached to the middle of the handkerchief, the others being allowed to hang loose

FIG. 251.

upon their respective hinges. A second handkerchief of similar pattern is then laid upon the first, and the edges of the two are stitched together all round.

The performer having exhibited the solid die and cover, as already explained, and having removed the latter (with the hollow die within it), places it upon the table. Spreading the prepared handkerchief beside it, he places the solid die upon the centre of the handkerchief, and gathering up the four corners of the latter, lifts it, bag-fashion, with his left hand, the four loose flaps of pasteboard naturally folding themselves up around the die. He now takes it with his right hand, clipping the solid die within the pasteboard, and turns the whole over as in Fig. 252, thus bringing the die uppermost, with the folds of the handkerchief hanging down around it. He next takes in the left hand a borrowed hat, holding it up for a moment, to show that it is empty. Then, turning it mouth upwards, he remarks, " I will place the die here in the hat." Suiting the action to the word, he lowers his hand into the hat, but, as if suddenly bethinking himself, he says, " No! I won't use the hat at all. Perhaps some one will kindly hold the die." In withdrawing his hand, however, he relaxes the pressure of his fingers, thereby leaving the solid die in the hat, though as the folded pasteboard retains its cubical shape, the handkerchief still

FIG. 252.

appears to contain the die. Grasping it immediately below the folded shape, he gives the handkerchief in charge to one of the spectators, who is directed to hold it in like manner. The hat he places carelessly upon the table. He now once more lifts the cover with the hollow die, rattling his wand within it to show that it is empty. Again replacing it, he commands the die to pass from the handkerchief under the cover. The person holding the handkerchief is asked if he felt it depart, but he naturally maintains that it is still in the handkerchief. "You are mistaken," says the professor; "what you see is merely the ghost of the die still clinging to the handkerchief. Allow me!" and taking one corner he requests the owner to drop the handkerchief, which he then shakes out, exhibiting both sides to show that the die has vanished. He then lifts the cover, and shows the hollow die, which the spectators take to be the genuine one, and concludes the trick by finally commanding the die thus shown to pass into the hat; which, on being turned over, is found to contain the solid die, while the hollow die is again raised with the cover, and the latter shown apparently empty.

THE DIE AND ORANGE.—The die in this instance is about three and a half inches square. It has the usual ornamental tin or pasteboard cover, but there is an additional item of apparatus employed, a square wooden box, with hinged lid, and of such a size as just to contain the die. The effect of the trick is as follows:—The die is brought forward in the box, the performer holding the square cover in his other hand. The die being then taken out of the box, and placed on the table, the box is shown empty, and the cover placed over the die. The performer, having mysteriously procured an orange from the hair or whiskers of a spectator, drops it into the box, which is then closed. He now asks the spectators, in order to impress the facts on their memory, where they suppose the two articles to be. They naturally answer that they are where they have just seen them placed ; or, if they venture to question this, the performer raises the cover and opens the box, and shows that die and orange both remain *in statu quo*. He now commands the two articles to change places. Lifting the cover, the die is found to have disappeared, the orange having taken its place, and, on opening the box, it is seen to contain the die, which is taken out, and exhibited on all sides to the company. The die and orange, being again covered over, at command change places as often as the company please.

The reader will doubtless have conjectured that there are in reality two dice and two oranges. The box when first brought forward contains in reality *two* hollow dice, one within the other. The smaller and innermost (the one which is afterwards taken out and placed under the cover) is placed in the box with its open side towards the hinges, and contains an orange. The performer takes it out, taking care, of course, that the orange does not fall out, and places it (open side downwards) upon the table. The cover is now placed over it, and, if lifted with pressure, lifts the hollow die with it, and reveals the orange ; but if lifted by the button on top, so that the sides are not pressed, it leaves the die covering the orange.

We now return to the box. This contains a second hollow die, so placed that the open side is upwards, and the box therefore appears to be empty. The lid, however, contains a sixth side, exactly fitting the open space, and thus making the die complete. This moveable side is alternately made to form a lining to the lid or to form part of the die, according as a little button on the lid is moved in one or another direction. Both the true lid and this moveable portion of it are lined with looking-glass, so as to show no difference of appearance, whether the box is exhibited empty or as containing the die. When the sixth side is made to form part of the die, the latter may be completely removed from the box, and shown on all its sides without betraying the secret, the orange for the time being remaining enclosed within it.

It is a good plan to have a solid die matching those used in the trick, to be, if necessary, substituted and handed round for inspection. If the performer uses a trap-table, it has a very good effect to conclude the trick by causing the orange under the cover to fall through the trap, and then, lifting the cover and hollow die together, to show by rattling the wand within, that both die and orange have altogether vanished.

THE VANISHING CANARY BIRD AND CAGE.—This is another favourite die trick. The performer exhibits a canary bird in a little

FIG. 253.

oblong brass cage, measuring six inches by four. He next exhibits a die three inches square, showing all sides to prove that it is solid. This he places upon a tray, which is held by the assistant, and covers it with a fancy cover as already described. He now throws a handkerchief over the cage. Bringing it forward thus covered to the company, he orders the cage to vanish, the die to pass into a borrowed hat, and the bird to appear upon the tray in place of the die. No sooner said than done; he waves the handkerchief, which is seen to be empty, and on raising the cover the bird is found under it; while, on turning over the hat, out falls the die.

The disappearance of the cage, which is of the form shown in Fig. 253, will be readily understood by any reader who has followed the description of the "flying glass of water" described at page 367. The handkerchief used is double, and contains in its centre, stitched between the two surfaces, an oblong wire frame, in size and shape exactly corresponding with the top of the cage. When the performer throws the handkerchief over the cage on the table, he takes care to bring this wire shape immediately over the cage. When he apparently lifts the cage under the handkerchief, which he does standing behind his table, he really lifts the hand-

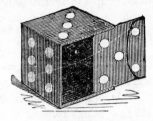

FIG. 254.

kerchief only, distended by the hidden wire, and with the other hand he gently lowers the cage out of sight upon the *servante.*

So much for the disappearance of the cage; but it yet remains to be explained how the bird

FIG. 255.

comes to be found under the cover in place of the die. This is effected as follows:—There are two dice, the one solid, the other of hollow tin, and having one side wanting, but capable of being closed at pleasure by means of a sliding lid, also of tin, which supplies the missing side, and is painted accordingly. The outer edge of this lid is folded over outwards in a semicircular form.

FIG. 256.

(*See* Fig. 254). The tray used (*see* Fig. 255) is of tin, japanned, and of ordinary appearance, but has a square piece of tin, of the same size as one of the sides of the die, soldered upon its centre at about one-sixteenth of an inch above the surface. Three of its sides are soldered to the tray, the fourth being left open. The centre of the tray is ornamentally japanned, in such manner as to conceal this special arrangement.

A duplicate bird is beforehand placed in the hollow die, which is then closed, and placed either upon the *servante* or in one of the secret pockets of the performer, who, having borrowed a hat, secretly slips the hollow die into it, and places it on the table mouth upwards. He now brings forward and offers for inspection the solid die, the cover, and the birdcage, placing the latter when returned upon his table, rather towards the hinder edge. "The die," he carelessly remarks, " I will place in this hat" (suiting the action to the word) ; "or, better still, I will place it upon this tray, so that you may be able to keep sight of it throughout the trick." So saying, he again takes out apparently the same, but really the hollow die, and places it on the tray with the moveable side downwards, in such manner as to hook the turned-over portion of that side into the open edge of the corresponding square upon the tray, and places the cover over it. Handing the tray to his assistant, he proceeds to cause the disappearance of the birdcage from the handkerchief, as already described. This done, he advances to the tray, and lifts the cover with the hollow die within it, first, however, sliding away cover and die together towards the opposite end of the tray (*see* Fig. 256), and thereby leaving behind upon the centre of the tray the moveable slide, the interior of which is japanned so as to correspond with the centre pattern of the tray, and thus does not attract any attention.

The solid die, having remained in the hat, may readily be produced when required.

THE DECANTER AND THE CRYSTAL BALLS.—The routine of this trick, as practised by different performers, varies a good deal. We propose to describe it in two forms, the first being as nearly as possible that which was adopted by Robert-Houdin.

First Method.—The apparatus in this case consists of four glass balls (two of plain glass an inch and a half in diameter, one of ruby-coloured glass of the same size, and one of plain glass, three-quarters of an inch in diameter) and a decanter of clear glass, with a hollow or "kick" underneath it just large enough to admit one of the larger balls. The decanter is two-thirds filled with port or claret, and is brought forward with the red ball beneath it, in the hollow we have mentioned, and is placed on the performer's table. The remaining balls are disposed as follows : the two large balls in the performer's left *pochette,* and the small one in the *pochette* on the other side. Thus provided, the performer comes forward, wand in hand. Taking the wand carelessly in his right hand, he says, "Ladies and gentlemen, I have already given you some proofs of the singular powers of this wand, but I do not know whether I have drawn your attention to one remarkable faculty which it possesses, viz., that if I strike anything with it, at the same time mentally calling for any object, that object is instantly produced from the article touched. Let us put it to the test." (He pulls back his coat-sleeves, showing indirectly, by a careless gesture, that his hands are empty.) "For the purpose of the trick I am about to show you, I require a crystal ball. Now, observe, I give but one gentle touch, not here upon the table" (he raps the table with his wand), "where you might suspect some mechanism or preparation, but here in my empty hand, and instantly, you see, a ball appears at my bidding." As he touches the table with the wand, thereby drawing the eyes of the spectators in that direction, he carelessly drops his left hand to his side, and takes from the *pochette* and palms one of the plain glass balls, which as soon as the wand reaches his hand he produces at the finger-tips. "The ball, as you see, ladies and gentlemen, is of solid crystal, without crack or flaw" (he takes it in the right hand, tosses it up, and catches it again). "The hardest steel would fail to chip it, and yet, by my magic power, I am able instantly to divide it into two equal portions, each round and true as the original." At the moment of tossing the ball in the air, all eyes are naturally attracted to it, and the performer has ample opportunity to again drop the left hand to his side, and palm the second ball. Keeping this in the palm of the left hand, he transfers the first ball to the finger-tips of the same hand. Drawing the wand across it, he allows it to drop into the palm, and to strike against the ball already there. Rubbing his palms together, as if to mould the divided ball into shape, he shows the two balls, professedly the divided portions of the first. Taking one in each hand, he continues, "I undertook to make the divided portions exactly equal, but I have not succeeded so well as usual. It seems to me that this one is rather the larger, what say you, ladies and gentlemen?" He places the two balls on the table, side by side, as if for comparison, and carelessly dropping the right hand to his side, palms between the second and third fingers (*see* page 273), the small ball. "Yes, this one is certainly the larger, but I can easily rectify the mistake by pinching a little piece off." Taking the ball in the left hand, he pretends to pinch off a portion from it with the right, at the same time letting the little ball fall to the finger-tips of the latter. He replaces the large ball on the table, rolling the little ball between the fingers, as though to give it roundness. "No, that one is still the biggest, I haven't taken quite enough yet. I must take a little more; or, better still, I will add this little piece to the smaller one." Taking the supposed smaller ball in the left hand, he pretends to squeeze the little one into it, presently letting the latter fall behind it into the palm of the left hand, and replacing the two larger balls side by side on the table, dropping the little ball at the first opportunity into the *pochette*. He continues, "I think they are now about right. The reason why I have been so particular about it is that I am about to pass one of these balls into the other, which I could not have done unless they had been of exactly the same size. Now which of them shall I pass into the other? It is for you to decide." He has meanwhile moved so as to be behind his table, standing sideways, with his right side to the table. Whichever ball the company decides is to be passed into the other, he takes in his right hand, immediately afterwards taking the other in the left hand, which he holds aloft, following it with his eyes. Stretching back the right arm, as though to give an impetus to the ball, he drops it into a padded box, or basket, placed upon the *servante* to receive it, immediately afterwards bringing the right hand with a semicircular sweep upon the left, and rolling the ball the latter contains between the palms, as though to press the one ball into the other; and presently showing that the hands now contain one ball only.

The same effect may be produced without the aid of the table, as follows:—Taking both the balls in his right hand, as in Fig. 257, the performer covers them with the left hand, retaining as he does so ball *a* with the thumb, but allowing ball *b* to roll down the left sleeve, which, with a little practice, will be found by no means difficult. He now rubs the palms together, as if rubbing the one ball into the other, and then separating them shows that the two balls have become transformed into one only. This he exhibits in the right hand, and while the eyes of the company are attracted to the ball, lowers the left arm, allowing the ball to run down the sleeve into the hand, whence it is immediately dropped into the *pochette* on that side.

FIG. 257.

The next step is the supposed colouring of the ball. The per-former continues, "Ladies and gentlemen, having proved to you my perfect control over the ball in respect of size, I propose to show you that I have equal mastery over it in respect of colour. This I shall do by passing it into this bottle of wine, which being red, the ball will become red also. Had the bottle contained a blue liquid, you would have found the ball become blue, and so on. The ball" (he takes it in his left hand, and apparently transfers it to his right by the *tourniquet*, keeping the right hand closed as if containing it, and dropping it from the left into the *pochette* on that side) "is consider-ably larger than the neck of the bottle. This, in a natural way, would be rather a difficulty, but to a magician it will give very little trouble. I have only to squeeze the ball a little" (he lifts the bottle with the left hand, at the same time slipping the little finger underneath it, to pre-vent the red ball beneath it falling, and holding the right hand an inch or two above it, works the hand as if compressing the ball), "and it gradually becomes smaller and smaller, till it melts completely into the bottle." He opens the right hand, and shows it empty, imme-diately afterwards shaking the bottle, and allowing the ball beneath to rattle slightly. "The ball is now in the bottle, as you see; the next step is to get it out, and it is rather difficult to do this without at the same time allowing the wine to escape. However, we will try. I have no doubt that by a strong effort of will I shall be able to manage it." He now takes the bottle between his hands, holding it so that the two little fingers are beneath, and after a little shaking, allows the ball to drop, as if through the bottle. This may be varied by holding the bottle with the left hand only, and striking the mouth with the palm of the other, allowing the ball to drop at the third stroke, professedly expelled by the compression of the air.

Second Method.—The balls used in this instance are five in number, two large, one of each colour; two small, one of each colour, and one (a trifle larger than these latter), of which one half is red, and one half white. The decanter is replaced by an ordinary wine bottle (*see* Fig. 258), prepared as follows:—A tin tube, *a*, three inches in length, closed at the bottom, but open

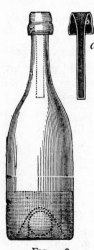

FIG. 258.

at the top, is made to fit within the neck (just so tightly, that it cannot fall out of its own accord), its upper edge being turned over all round, and japanned black, so that when placed in the bottle it may be undistinguishable from the actual neck. The cavity at the bottom of the bottle is filled with a resinous cement, in such manner as only to leave room for one of the larger balls. The tube is beforehand filled with port or claret, and placed in the neck. The bottle itself, which, if not naturally opaque, must be rendered so by an interior coating of black japan, should be nearly filled with water. Thus prepared, it is brought forward and placed on the table. The balls are disposed as follows: the two white ones in the left *pochette* of the performer, the two red ones and the parti-coloured ball in the *pochette* on the other side.

Coming forward to the audience, the performer produces the large white ball, either as described in the first form of the trick, or from his wand in manner described at page 276. While showing it in his left hand, he drops the right hand to his side, and palms the large red ball. Laying the white ball on his table, he remarks, " I have here a bottle of wine. We will begin by testing its genuineness." He lifts the bottle by the neck with the left hand, immediately transferring it to the right (which grasps it round the bottom), and introduces beneath it the red ball, which is thenceforth kept in position by the little finger. Taking in the other hand a wine-glass (which should be of such a size as just to contain the contents of the tube), he fills it with wine, and hands it to one of the company. In returning to his table, he secretly withdraws the tube. (This is easily done by grasping the bottle round the neck with the left hand, and gently drawing it downwards with the right, the turned over portion of the tube being clipped by the finger and thumb of the left hand, in which it naturally remains.) As the performer passes behind the table, he gets rid of the tube by dropping it on the *servante*. In placing the bottle on the table, he is of course careful not to expose the red ball underneath it. Taking the white ball in his left hand, he proposes to turn it red, and for that purpose to pass it into the bottle. Pretending to transfer it to the right hand by the *tourniquet*, he drops it from the left hand into the padded tray on the *servante*, and then apparently passes it into the bottle, as above. The routine of getting it out of the bottle again is the same as above described in relation to the first method.

We may, however, here note a variation in practice. Some performers, instead of introducing the red ball under the bottle at the outset of the trick, as above described, make no attempt to bring it under the bottle until after the white ball is supposed to have been passed into the wine, when the performer, raising the bottle with the left hand, transfers it to the right, and brings the ball under it, retaining it there with the little finger until he thinks fit to allow it to drop, pretending to squeeze the bottom of the bottle as if to force it out.

After having produced the red ball, the performer remarks, " Perhaps, ladies and gentlemen, you imagine that I have not really passed the ball through the bottle, and that the effect is, in reality, produced by the substitution of a different coloured ball. Let me assure you that so truly is the wine in the bottle, and nothing else, the cause of the change of colour, that you will find on examination that every particle of colour has left the wine, its whole virtue having been absorbed by the ball. Supposing for a moment that I could have exchanged the ball, you will hardly imagine that I could exchange the liquid in the bottle, which has been proved to be good old wine. Will the same gentleman who tried it before be good enough to taste it now?" Taking another glass, he fills it from the bottle, which is now found to contain nothing but water.

The performer, meanwhile, has again palmed the white ball, which he next produces, as being a new one, from his wand. Comparing the red and the white together, he pretends to discover that the red is the largest, and therefore pinches from it a small portion (the small red ball). He now discovers that he has taken too much, and that the red ball is now the smaller. He therefore pinches a second piece (the small white ball) from the white one, and finally rolls the two little balls thus obtained into one, producing the parti-coloured ball. The mode of producing these last effects will present no difficulty to any one who has attentively studied the description of the first form of the trick.

THE FLAGS OF ALL NATIONS.—This is, in good hands, a very pretty and effective trick, but requires considerable neatness of manipulation. Its effect is as follows :—The performer comes forward with a couple of miniature silk flags, measuring, say, three inches by two. Taking one in each hand, he brings the hands together, and begins to wave them backwards and forwards, when the flags are seen to multiply, the two being suddenly transformed into a dozen, quickly increasing to a still larger number. Not only do the flags increase in number, but in size also, until perhaps a couple of hundred have been produced, ranging in dimensions from one or two inches square to a foot or even larger, and of six or eight different colours.

This seeming marvel rests on a very slight foundation. The flags to be produced are of coloured tissue-paper, with flagstaffs made of wire, or of the "bass" of which scrubbing-brooms are made, so as to occupy very little space. These are rolled up together in little parcels, like with like, according to size. Thus arranged, they are placed, the smaller ones in the sleeve of the performer, and the larger ones about his person, with the ends just inside the breast of his waist-coat. While waving the first two flags backwards and forwards, he gets one of the parcels from the sleeve into his hands, immediately unrolling and developing it, when the two flags appear to have multiplied into fifty. Under cover of these, he draws down from the sleeve another parcel, which he develops in like manner, and after the sleeves are exhausted has recourse to the fresh store within the waistcoat. He all along takes care to retain in his hands a large and widespread bundle of the flags, which, being kept moving backwards and forwards, materially aids in covering the mode of production of the remainder.

THE UMBRELLA TRICK.—The performer comes forward with an umbrella, which may be either the common-place article of every-day life, or a brilliant fancy production, akin to Joseph's coat of many colours. This he hands for inspection, and meanwhile borrows a lady's handkerchief. The latter, for safe keeping, he places in an empty vase, which is left in full view of the company. The umbrella, duly examined, he places in a case, which may be either the ordinary glazed oilskin case, or a special apparatus prepared for the purpose. Whichever it be, the result is the same. On again uncovering the vase, the handkerchief has vanished, and in its place is found the silk covering of the umbrella. On removing the umbrella from its case, it is found to have lost its covering; but the handkerchief, torn in several pieces, is found fastened to its naked ribs, one piece to each. These are removed. Again the vase is covered, and the umbrella restored to the case. The torn fragments of the handkerchief are burnt, and their ashes invisibly passed into the vase; and on a new examination the two articles are found uninjured as at first.

With reference to the transformation of the handkerchief in the vase, it will be only necessary to state that the vase employed is either the burning globe (*see* page 246), or the "pea vase" described at page 351. In either case a duplicate umbrella cover is placed in the second compartment, and thus the vase may be shown to contain either the handkerchief or the umbrella cover at pleasure.

With regard to the umbrella, the reader will readily conjecture that an exchange is effected, but the mode of effecting it varies. If the ordinary glazed case is used, the umbrella is exchanged bodily for another, similarly encased, placed beforehand on the *servante.* This, however, requires some little dexterity, as an umbrella, from its length, is an awkward article to exchange; and this has led to the employment of cases specially constructed to effect the change. That most frequently used is an upright pillar of zinc or tin, oval in form, and open at the top, and so constructed as to stand upright without support (*see* Fig. 259). It is divided vertically into two compartments, in one of which is placed beforehand the second umbrella. Of course no

one can be permitted to examine or even look into the case, which is a serious drawback to the effect of the trick. There is, however, another form of case sometimes employed, which is a trifle less objectionable. This is a wooden tube, about three feet long, and three and a half inches square. (*See* Fig. 260.) Like the case already described, it is closed at the bottom and open at the top, and divided vertically into two compartments, *a* and *b*. One or other of these, however, is always closed by the flap *c*, which by virtue of a spring is normally compelled to take the position shown in the figure, thus closing compartment *b*. When required for use, the second umbrella is placed in compartment *a*, and the flap *c* drawn back (as shown by the dotted line) so as to close *a*, in which position it is held by a little catch. The

FIG. 259.

FIG. 260.

performer hands the genuine umbrella for inspection to one of the spectators, with a request that he will himself place it in the case. As soon as he has done so, the performer by a movement of his forefinger draws back the catch, and releases *c*, which flying back to the opposite position, shuts in the genuine umbrella, and reveals the substitute. When this apparatus is employed, the supposed restoration of the umbrella is omitted.

Some performers dispense with the use of the vase, and vanish and reproduce the borrowed handkerchief by sleight-of-hand, after one or other of the modes described in relation to handkerchief tricks.

The " Passe-Passe " Trick.—The trick which is specially designated by this name (which would appear to be equally applicable to about three parts of the tricks we have described) is as follows :—

The performer brings forward a bottle and a small tumbler, which he places side by side upon the table. Producing a couple of tin or pasteboard covers, ornamentally japanned, of a size to just go over the bottle, he places one of them over the bottle, and another over the glass. He now commands the two articles to change places, and on again removing the covers the glass and bottle are found to be transposed. Again he covers them, and again the change takes place; and this he repeats as often as he pleases, occasionally pouring out wine or other liquor, to show that the bottle is a genuine one, and not a mere make-believe.

The reader will already have anticipated that there are in reality two bottles and two glasses. The bottles are of tin, japanned to resemble the ordinary black bottle, but with the bottom only about a couple of inches below the neck, leaving an open space beneath for the reception of the glass. Each bottle has near the bottom, at the side which is kept away from the audience, an oval opening oi finger-hole, measuring about an inch and a half by one inch. When it is desired to lift the glass with the bottle, the middle finger is made to press on the glass through this opening, thereby lifting both together with perfect safety. The outer cover just fits easily over the bottles, and if lifted lightly leaves the bottle on the table, but if grasped with some little pressure, carries the bottle with it.

The mode of working the trick will now be readily understood. The bottle which is brought forward h is a second glass concealed within it, kept in position, while the bottle is brought in, by the pressure of the finger. The cover which is placed over this bottle is empty. The other cover, which is placed over the glass, contains the second bottle, which, being hollow below, enables the performer to rattle his wand within it, and thus (apparently) to prove the cover empty. Having covered the glass and bottle, he raises the cover of the first very lightly, leaving the glass concealed by the second bottle, but lifts the other with pressure, so carrying the bottle with it, and revealing the glass which has hitherto been concealed within it. By reversing the process, the bottle and glass are again made to appear, each under its original cover. Where it is desired to pour wine from either bottle, the performer takes care, in lifting it, to press the glass through the finger-hole, and thus lifts both together. For obvious reasons the glass into which the wine is poured should be a third glass, and **not** either of the two which play the principal part in the trick.

CHAPTER XVII.

Stage Tricks.

The present Chapter will be devoted to such tricks as by reason of the cumbrousness or costliness of the apparatus required for them, are, as a rule, exhibited only upon the public stage. The stage performer may, if he pleases, avail himself of the aid of mechanical tables, electrical appliances, etc., which enable him to execute a class of tricks which are beyond the scope of an ordinary drawing-room performance, though the wealthy amateur will find no difficulty in converting his own drawing-room into a quasi-stage, and qualifying it for the presentation of the most elaborate illusions.

The leading items of apparatus in stage magic are mechanical tables. These are of various kinds, many being specially designed to assist in the performance of some one particular trick. Putting aside these, which will be separately noticed, stage tables may be broadly divided into three classes—trap tables, piston tables, and electrical tables. In practice, these classes are somewhat intermingled, for it is rather the rule than the exception for a stage table to be fitted with both traps and pistons, while either or both of these may be found in conjunction with electrical appliances.

Trap tables are such as are provided with one or more "traps," their object being, at the will of the operator, to cause the disappearance of a given article into the interior of the table, or sometimes to produce or apparently change an article. The traps most generally used may be described as follows :—

1. *The Plain Trap.*—This consists of a thin plate of metal, generally zinc, screwed down flush with the top of the table. In this, which we will call the surface plate, is cut a hole, generally circular, and from two to four inches in diameter, closed by a flap or door,

which by the action of a spring hinge is pressed up level with the rest of the trap, though it instantly yields to pressure from above, again rising as soon as such pressure is removed. Figs. 261 and 262 represent the trap as seen detached from the table, Fig. 261 exhibiting its under side. *a* is the circular flap, *b b* the spring hinge,

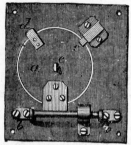

Fig. 261.

c a little bolt by means of which the trap may be fastened at pleasure, and which is worked by a pin projecting upwards through a slot in the surface plate, and through the cloth which covers the table; *d* is a small flat piece of metal, screwed to the under side of the flap *a*, and acting as a "stop" to prevent the flap being forced by the action of the spring above the level of the surface-plate. The "mount-ings" of the trap are generally brass, and attached to the zinc by screws. A brass eyelet, *e*, is sometimes soldered to the centre of the under side of the flap. To this is attached a cord, which may hang down ready to the performer's hand at the back of the table, or may be carried down a groove in one of the hinder legs, and either terminate in a pedal (to be pressed by the foot of the performer), or be continued behind the scenes within reach of the hand of the assistant.

The mode of working the trap is as follows :—Any small article, being placed on it, is covered over (either with an ornamental cover or with a simple handkerchief). The cord being gently pulled by either of the means above mentioned, the trap opens, and the article falls into the body of the table. As soon as the pull is relaxed, the flap

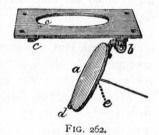

Fig. 262.

again rises and closes the opening. Where a cord is not used, the performer gets rid of the article by direct pressure on the trap, or the article upon it, with the one hand, while with the other he veils the opening in the table.

2. *The "Wrist" or "Pressure" Trap.*—With this form of trap the

use of a cord is unnecessary, the trap being worked from the surface of the table, by pressure upon a particular spot. The manner of its con-

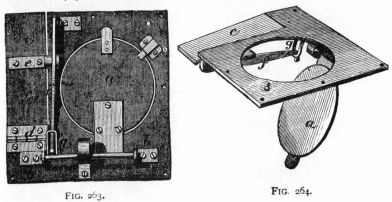

FIG. 263.   FIG. 264.

struction will become clear upon an inspection of Figs. 263, 264. Fig. 263 represents the under side of the trap; *a* is the flap, working

FIG. 265.

upon a spring hinge *b b*, as already explained in the case of the plain trap; *c c* is an oblong piece of metal, cut out of and lying flush with the surface-plate, and working upon an ordinary hinge at *d*. When *c* is pressed down, the crosspiece *e*, which is soldered to it, presses down the lever *f*, and this in turn acting upon the shorter lever *g*, which

is fixed at right angles to the rod upon which the flap *a* is hinged, causes the latter to open.

The mode of using the wrist trap is as follows :— The performer has occasion, we will suppose, to cause the disappearance of an orange, as for instance, in the "Bran and Orange" trick, described at page 335. Placing the orange upon the flap *a*, he places both hands round it as though to pick

FIG. 266.

it up between them. (*See* Fig. 265.) In this position the under side of the hand furthest from the audience (*see* Fig. 266, showing the right hand removed), is just over *c*, and pressing gently upon it, causes the flap to open, and the orange to fall through ; the position of the

hands completely veiling the operation. The operator now leaves the table, still holding his hands as though having the orange between them, and after a due interval, brings them closer and closer together, at last showing that it has vanished.

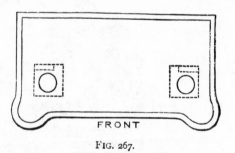

FRONT

FIG. 267.

The wrist trap is generally worked by the performer standing at the side of the table, and the traps are therefore made right-handed and left-handed, according to the end at which they are intended to be placed, the rule being that *c* must be so placed with reference to *a*, as to be when in use under the hand furthest from the spectators.

Fig. 267 illustrates this difference of make, to suit the one or the other end of the table.

3. *The "Rabbit" or "Dove" Trap.*—This, as its name indicates, is a trap for causing the disappearance of a rabbit or pigeon. The opening is in this case oval, measuring about eight inches by six, and closed by a double flap, divided down the middle (*see* Fig. 268, representing the under side of the trap.) It has no string, the animal being simply pushed down through the trap under cover either of a second rabbit, or of a piece of paper in which the victim is supposed to be wrapped. As the rabbit trap requires considerable space, and, moreover, involves the necessity of some sort of an inclosure within the table to prevent an unexpected reappear-ance of the animal, it is a convenient plan to de-vote to it a small special table. This should be circular; about thirty-two inches in height, and sixteen to eighteen in diameter. The upper part of the table must form a circular wooden box, about eight inches in depth, with an open-ing behind to get out the

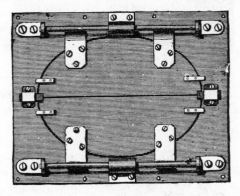

FIG. 268.

rabbit. The table may, like the principal table, have a *servante* behind it, which will greatly increase its utility. The depth of the upper part may be concealed by a hanging fringe; the general appearance of the table (seen from the back) being as shown in Fig. 269. A table of this class makes a very pretty side table, and may be balanced on the opposite side of the stage by another of similar appearance, but designed for some different purpose.

The interior of the table should be well padded with wadding or hay, that the animal may not be hurt by its sudden descent.

Each of the traps above-mentioned should be so made as to be capable of being secured, when necessary, by a bolt, or there would be considerable risk of a trap giving way unexpectedly under any article carelessly placed on it. The mode of bolting, however, varies considerably. Some traps are fastened by little bolts on the under side, which, being only get-at-able from the inside of the table, must be bolted or unbolted for good before the curtain rises, occasioning considerable embarrassment in the case of a slip of the memory. Others again are secured by means of long bolts, or wire rods extending across the under surface of the top of the table, each terminating in a hook at the back, within reach of the performer's hand. A third, and, we think, the best, plan is to have the bolt (as shown in Figs. 261 and

262, and therein marked *c*) worked backwards and forwards by means of a little pin projecting upwards through the surface plate and the cloth of the table. By the adoption of this plan the performer is enabled to draw back the bolt with the finger-tip in the very act of placing the article upon the trap. It will readily suggest itself to the reader that some provision must be made within the table for making the various articles drop noiselessly through the traps. The best plan of effecting this is to use what is called a "railway." This is a wooden frame just large enough to lie within the table, with a piece of black serge or alpaca stretched all over its under side. This is so placed within the table, as to slope gently down to the level of the

FIG. 269.

servante, with a fall of three or four inches. Any article dropped through a trap will not only fall noiselessly upon the surface of the stretched alpaca, but will immediately roll down the incline towards the *servante*, so that it is instantly get-at-able, should the performer have occasion to reproduce the same article at a later stage of the trick.

4. *" Changing"* *Traps.*—The traps which we have hitherto discussed have only had the faculty of causing the *disappearance* of a given article. Those which we are about to describe will not only do this, but will, moreover, produce an article on the surface of the table

where a moment previously there was nothing, or will replace a given object by another.

The trap for this purpose is a somewhat complicated arrangement, of the appearance shown in Figs. 270 and 271. The surface-plate *a a a a*, is oblong, measuring about twelve inches by six, with a circular open ing *b b* in the centre. Below it are fixed vertically two brass cylinders *c* and *d*, which are so arranged as to work backwards

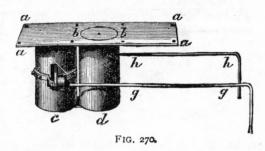

FIG. 270.

and forwards on a kind of railway *e f e f*, in the direction of the length of the surface-plate, just so far in either direction as to bring *c* or *d* in turn immediately under *b*. The two cylinders are soldered together, so that the one cannot move without the other. If, therefore, the cylinders are drawn back to the utmost by means of one of the bent iron rods or handles *g h*, the cylinder *c* will be below the opening *b*, as in Fig.

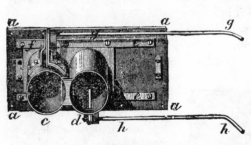

FIG. 271.

272. If, on the contrary, they be pushed forward, *d* will in turn be below the opening, as in Fig. 273. Each cylinder contains a brass piston, faced with zinc on its upper surface, and moved up and down by a lever attached at right angles to one or other of the iron handles *g h* already mentioned, and working through a vertical slot in the side of the cylinder. A piece of clock-spring, attached to the iron handle at the point of junction, gives the piston a gentle upward tendency, which is so regulated, that if either of the cylinders be brought under the opening *b*, the piston belonging to that cylinder is made to rise into

the opening, its upper surface resting just flush with that of *a a a a.*
The piston of the forward cylinder *c* is made to work very easily
within it, so as to rise spontaneously by the action of the spring; but
that of the hinder cylinder, *d*, for a reason which will presently appear,

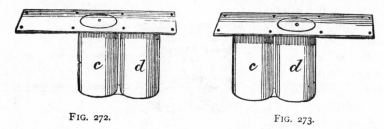

Fig. 272.　　　　　　　　　　Fig. 273.

works a lit le more stiffly, so as to require a little assistance from the
lever to make it rise into its proper position. The action of the
handles *g h* is outwards, in the direction of the arrows in Fig. 274,
the movement of either handle in the direction so indicated drawing
down the piston to which it belongs.

The handles further serve, as already mentioned, to move the cylinders backwards and forwards as may be required. It should, however, be noted that no backward or forward movement can take place

Fig. 274.

so long as either of the pistons
stops the opening *b;* but as
soon as the piston is, by turning the proper handle, depressed ever so little below the
level of the surface-plate, it no
longer forms any obstacle to
the movement. The trap is
fixed in the table in such manner that the handles *g h* shall
be just within the opening at
the back of the table (*see* Fig.
274), and thus be within easy
reach of the performer's hands
when standing behind it. We will suppose, for the sake of illustration, that the performer desires to change an empty tumbler (of

small size) to a full one. The trap is beforehand prepared by bringing the foremost cylinder *c* under the opening *b*. The full glass is then placed on the top of the piston, which is then lowered gently downwards by means of the proper handle, the glass sinking into the cylinder. The cylinders are now pushed forward, so that *d* in turn comes under *b*, the piston being then moved up into its proper place, and so closing the opening. This is, of course, arranged before the curtain rises.

When the performer desires to perform the trick, he places the empty glass upon *b*, and conceals it with a cover of any kind. Standing carelessly behind the table, and keeping the attention of the audience occupied by any observations he may deem most appropriate for that purpose, he takes hold with his right hand of the handle *h*, and turns it outward, thereby lowering the empty glass into *d*. As soon as he feels that it will sink no further, he shifts his hand to the handle *a*, and therewith draws the cylinders back so as to bring *c* under *b*, and then, by turning *g*, gently raises the full glass of water up through *b* to the surface of the table. The reader will now perceive the reason why, as already mentioned, the piston in *d* is made a little tight, so as to require the assistance of the handle to raise it into its position. It is necessary that this piston, when once depressed with the object to be changed, shall remain down while the hand is shifted from handle *h* to handle *g*. If it were not made to work somewhat stiffly, the moment the handle *h* was released the piston would instantly fly up again with the object upon it, thus neutralizing what had been already done. The cylinder *c*, which is to produce the substitute object, is not brought under *b* until the hand of the performer is already on the handle belonging to it, and can thereby check its upward ascent as may be necessary.

It is obvious that the changing trap will be equally available to produce an object under an empty cover. The object to be produced will be placed in *c* as above, the piston in *d* going down empty, and that in *c* rising with the object upon it.

The above are the traps in most frequent use, but there are others designed for special purposes. Thus there is a trap for causing the disappearance of six or eight half-crowns (as, for instance, in the well-known trick of the "crystal cash-box," which will be described in the course of the present chapter). Of course the coins could be made to disappear through an ordinary trap, but they would cause a suggestive "chink" in their fall. The trap to which we are now referring (*see* Figs. 275 and 276) is designed to prevent this tell-tale sound, and to cause the half-crowns to disappear in perfect silence. The opening in the surface plate is an inch and three-quarters in diameter, and

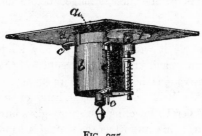

FIG 275.

is closed by a circular piston of brass or zinc, *a*, working up and down in a small brass cylinder *b*, and so arranged as to drop by its own weight to the bottom of the cylinder, save when kept up by a little lever catch at the side of the cylinder. A short pin *d* attached to this catch projects upwards through a slot in the surface plate, and stands up very slightly above the cloth of the table. The disc *a* being raised level with the surface plate, and secured by means of the catch, six or eight half-crowns or florins are placed on *a*. The performer, in making the motion of picking up the coins (with one hand), with the tip of the third finger pulls the pin *d* towards him. This withdraws the catch, and *a* instantly drops down to the bottom of the cylinder, carrying the coins with it. As soon as *a* reaches its lowest point, it draws down the pin *e*, thereby releasing a similar disc *f*, which, working laterally on a spring pivot at

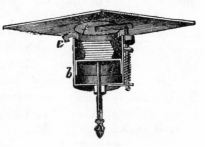

FIG. 276.

the edge of the opening, describes a semicircle, and assumes the position previously occupied by *a*, a portion of one side of the cylinder, at the top, being cut away to allow of its passage. Fig. 275 shows the trap in its first, and Fig. 276 in its second condition, the latter being, for greater clearness, drawn in section. The apparatus is rather complicated, and it is almost hopeless to endeavour to render it clearly intelligible by description only. In the absence of this special trap, the same object may be nearly as well effected with an ordinary trap by using half-crowns (be it remembered that it is always *substitute* coins which are made to disappear in this manner) which have been beeswaxed on both sides. A very slight pressure will cause a number of coins thus prepared to adhere together, and form for the time being a solid mass, which will fall through the trap without causing any "clink."

We next come to—

Pistons.—These are appliances for working pieces of mechanical apparatus—as, for example, the Watch Target, the Card Star, the Demon's Head, etc., etc. A piston (*see* Figs. 277, 278) consists of a brass tube *a*, about five inches in length by five-eighths of an inch in

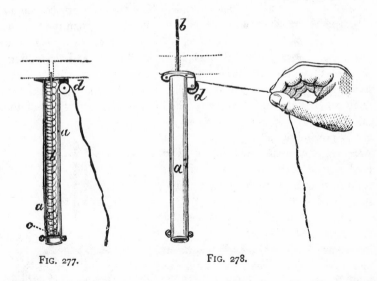

FIG. 277.   FIG. 278.

diameter, with a collar at one end pierced with screw-holes for affixing it to the under surface of the table. Within this tube works a wire rod, *b*, three-sixteenths of an inch thick, and terminating in a small round disc of brass *c*, just large enough to work freely up and down the tube. A spiral spring, also of brass, keeps the rod down, unless when forced upwards by pulling a piece of whipcord, which is attached to the disc *c,* and thence passes up the tube, and over a small

pulley *d,* which is soldered to the collar already mentioned. When this cord is pulled, *b* is forced to rise, which it does to the extent of about two inches above the surface of the table (*see* Fig. 278), again sinking under the pressure of the spring, as soon as the pull is relaxed. Each piston is screwed to the under surface of the top of the table, in which a small hole is bored, in order to allow of the upward passage of the piston rod. Where complicated mechanical pieces have to be worked, three, four, or more of these pistons are placed side by side. The cords are carried behind the scenes, either directly from the back of the table, or down grooves in the legs, and through holes in the stage to the hiding-

FIG. 279.

place of the assistant. Where a single piston only is required, it may be made to work in the central pillar of a light *guéridon,* or fancy table, such as shown in Fig. 279, the lightness and simplicity of the table, and the thinness of its top, apparently precluding all possibility of the presence of concealed mechanism. The cord may be made to pass down the centre pillar, so as to be quite invisible to the audience.

The mechanical pieces worked by the agency of these pistons vary greatly in construction, but they are alike in one particular, viz., that they are set in motion by one or more vertical rods passing up the shaft or column on which they stand, and each terminating in a flat metal disc, or pedal, which receives the upward pressure of the

FIG. 280.

piston. Fig. 280 shows the arrangement of the foot of a mechanical piece worked by one such rod only. Another specimen will have been observed in the case of the pedestal for the animated money. (*See* page 186.) Where three or four pedals are necessary, they are generally enclosed in a square wooden base, as in the case of the "Demon's Head," described at page 458.

Before quitting the subject of the tables used upon the stage, we must not omit to say a few words as to what is called the "bellows" table, though it is now comparatively little used. It was formerly (say forty or fifty years ago) the fashion among conjurors to use tables with drapery hanging to within a few inches of the floor. The table being, say, two feet seven inches high, this gave room for a box-like arrangement, of two feet deep, or thereabouts, within the body of the table. In this box, which was open at the back, was hidden an assistant, who worked the pistons, managed the traps, effected necessary substitutions, etc., etc. Conjuring under such circumstances was very easy work. In 1845, however, Robert-Houdin gave his first public performance, and one of the earliest of his reforms in the magic art was the suppression of the too suggestive drapery, and the substitution of tables of light and elegant form, allowing no possible room for the concealment of an assistant. A reaction set in in favour of the new fashion, which has ever since maintained its ground. The "bellows' table combines the apparent simplicity of the undraped table with the internal capacity of the old-fashioned draped article. There is a trick, formerly very popular as the wind-up of an entertainment, which consists of the magical disappearance of a youthful assistant, male or female. The subject of the trick, generally dressed in a page's costume, is made to mount upon a table, and is covered by a wicker cone, which being almost instantly removed, he or she has vanished. The table in this case is draped to within a few inches of the ground, but to show that no hidden receptacle is thereby concealed, the performer before commencing the trick lifts up the table-cloth, and shows that the top of the table is at most not more than two or three inches in thickness. The drapery is then again allowed to fall into position, and the trick proceeds. The table used in this trick is a bellows table; *i.e.*, it has a double top, or rather two tops, one above the other. The upper one is a fixture, with a large wooden trap (opening upwards) in it, to allow of the passage of the person to be conjured away. The under top is moveable, being in its normal condition pressed against the upper one by the action of four spiral springs (one in each leg of the table), but sinking down to nearly the depth of the cover under the weight of a person stepping upon it, and thus affording the requisite hiding-place, in which the person remains until the fall of the curtain enables him or her to come forth with safety. Cloth is nailed round three sides of the upper and lower boards, folding between the two when closed, after the manner of the leather of a bellows; and from this circumstance the table derives its name.

Small round tables (for the disappearance of a rabbit, or the like) are sometimes made on the same principle. The following will be found a simple and convenient arrangement :—Let the table be of the form shown in Fig. 281, and two feet seven inches high. Let the uppermost eight inches of the pillar be a plain cylinder *a a*, an inch and a half in diameter. Below this the pillar may increase in size, and may be of an ornamental character. Take two circular boards of deal or mahogany, each eighteen to twenty inches in diameter, and five-eighths of an inch thick. In the centre of one of them, *b*, cut a circular hole an inch and three-quarters in diameter. This will form the under side of the " bellows," the object being to allow the board to slide freely up and down on *a a*. The other board, which we will call *c*, is screwed firmly on to the pillar, to form the top of the table. Next take a strip of black alpaca, ten inches in width, and nail its opposite edges round *b* and *c*, leaving a small space at one side to give access to the interior. Tie a piece of cord elastic round the centre of the alpaca, tightly enough to exercise a considerable degree of tension. Fix such traps as may be desired in *c*, and glue over it a fancy-patterned cloth, with a fringe or border hanging

FIG. 281.

down nine or ten inches round the sides. The performer, before executing any trick with this table, may pointedly draw attention to the fact that it contains no drawer or other place of concealment. In doing this (*see* Fig. 282) he with one hand raises the lower board level with the upper (the action of the elastic drawing in the alpaca between the two), while with the other hand he raises the fringe; and shows, apparently, that the top of the table is but a single board.

The top of every conjuring table should be covered with woollen cloth, not only to prevent the clatter which would be occasioned by the placing of objects upon the bare wood, but to conceal the presence of the traps and pistons. The cloth used should, for this latter reason, be of two colours, and of a tolerably intricate pattern, as the outline of the traps will be thereby rendered much less perceptible; indeed, if the pattern of the cloth be a favourable one for the purpose, the traps should be, by gas-light, absolutely invisible. The cloth should be glued over the top of the table after the manner of a card-table; the upper surface of the traps being first roughed slightly, to make the glue adhere to the metal. When the glue is thoroughly dry (but not until then) the cloth may be cut along the outline of the traps with a very sharp penknife, and small holes bored to allow of the upward passage of the piston rods. As it is necessary in placing a mechanical piece upon the table, to do so exactly over the pistons, it

FIG. 282.

is well to have a couple of wire points projecting upwards a quarter of an inch or so from the surface of the table, in such positions that if the piece of apparatus rests firmly against these (which the performer can tell instantly by feel) it must necessarily be in proper position.

Where " wrist" traps are used, the cloth need not be cut out round

the little oblong slab marked *c* in Figs. 263, 264, but the cloth should
be without glue over this particular spot, and for half an inch round
it on either side.   The cloth will by this arrangement be found,
without cutting, to stretch sufficiently over *c* to allow of the proper
working of the trap.

Assuming that our stage appliances are complete, we will proceed to—

THE RABBIT TRICK.—The performer comes forward to the
audience, and borrows a hat.   He asks whether it is empty, and is
answered that it is; but he, notwithstanding, finds something in
it, which the owner is requested to take out.   The article in question
proves to be an egg.   No sooner has this been removed, than the
performer discovers that there is still something in the hat, and
immediately produces therefrom a live rabbit, quickly followed by a
second.   Not knowing what other use to make of these, he proposes
to pass one of them into the other.   The audience decide which is to
be the victim, and the performer, placing them side by side on the
table, proceeds to roll them together, when one is found to have
vanished, nobody knows when or how; but the theory is that it has
been swallowed by the remaining rabbit, to the (imaginary) increased
fatness of which the performer draws special attention.

Having thus passed one rabbit into the other, the next step is to
get it out again.   To do this the performer calls for some bran, and
his assistant immediately brings forward, and places on a table or
chair, a huge glass goblet, twelve inches or thereabouts in height,
filled to the brim with that commodity.   The performer takes the
borrowed hat, and (after showing that it is empty) places it mouth
upwards upon another table, so as to be at some considerable distance
from the goblet of bran.   He then places a brass cover over the
glass, first, however, taking up and scattering a handful of the bran to
prove its genuineness.   Taking the surviving rabbit, and holding it by
the ears above the covered goblet, he orders the one swallowed to pass
from it into the glass, at the same time stroking it down with the
disengaged hand, as though to facilitate the process.   He remarks,
" You must excuse the comparative slowness of the operation, ladies
and gentlemen, but the fact is, the second rabbit passes downwards

in an impalpable powder, and, if I were not to take sufficient time, we might find that a leg or an ear had been omitted in the process, and the restored rabbit would be a cripple for life. I think we are pretty safe by this time, however. Thank you, Bunny; I need not trouble you any more." So saying, he releases the visible rabbit, and on taking off the cover the bran is found to have disappeared, and the missing rabbit to have taken its place in the goblet; while on turning over the borrowed hat the vanished bran pours from it.

The reader who has duly followed our descriptions of the appliances employed in the magic art will have little difficulty in solving the riddle of this trick. The performer first comes forward with an egg palmed in one hand, and with a small rabbit in an inner breast-pocket on each side of his coat (*see* page 9). The first step is the pretended finding of *something* (it is not stated what) in the hat. The owner is requested to take it out, and while all eyes are naturally turned to see what the article may prove to be, the performer, without apparent intention, presses the mouth of the hat with both hands to his breast, and tilts one of the rabbits into it. This is next produced, and in placing it on the ground at his feet, the performer brings the second rabbit in the same manner into the hat. When he undertakes to pass the one rabbit into the other, he places both upon the table which contains the rabbit-trap, and, standing sideways to the audience, pushes the hindmost, under cover of the other, through the trap. This particular rabbit is not again produced, the rabbit in the "bran glass," which has already been explained (*see* page 383), being another as much like it as possible. It only remains to explain how the bran comes into the borrowed hat. This is effected by having a black alpaca bag filled with bran in one of the *profondes* or under the waistcoat of the performer. This bag is introduced into the hat after the manner of the goblets (*see* page 308), and the bran having been allowed to run out, the bag is rolled up in the palm, and so removed, the bran remaining, to be produced in due course.

It is obvious that the trick may be varied in many ways. The following is an effective modification :—A rabbit having been produced by natural or supernatural means, is placed on the principal table (close to the hinder edge), and temporarily covered with a borrowed hat, while the performer goes in search of a sheet of paper, which when obtained, he spreads upon a small side table. Lifting the hat slightly, he takes out the rabbit, and walking with it to the side table, rolls it up in the paper, making a somewhat bulky parcel. Coming forward with this to the audience, he turns toward the principal table, and saying, "Now, ladies and gentlemen, if you watch me very closely, you will see the rabbit fly out of the paper, and back to the hat." He crushes the paper together between his hands, and tearing it, shows it empty, while on lifting the hat the rabbit is again found safely ensconced beneath it.

The ingenious reader will readily guess that duplicate rabbits are employed. One of them is placed under the hat, and remains there throughout the trick. A second, of similar appearance, is placed in a box or basket on the *servante,* immediately behind the hat. This box has no lid, but is pushed until wanted just within the interior of the table, the top of which prevents the rabbit making a premature appearance. The performer, slightly raising the hat, as though to take the rabbit from under it, lifts up this *second* rabbit, which the spectators naturally believe to be the same which they have already seen, and in apparently wrapping it in paper on the side table, presses it, under cover of the paper, through the rabbit trap, and screws up the ends of the paper (which should be rather stiff) in such manner as to make it appear that the animal is still inside it. The same trick may be performed with a pigeon with equally good effect, and considerably less difficulty.

THE FAIRY STAR.—This is one of the most telling of stage card tricks. The performer, coming forward with a pack of cards, allows six to be chosen. His assistant meanwhile brings forward and places on a table a handsome gilt "star" on a stand. The performer, collecting the chosen cards, places them in his pistol, and fires them at the star, when, at the moment of the explosion, they are seen to attach themselves one to each of its points, as in Fig. 283.

The principal point to be explained is the construction of the star. Behind each "ray" is a moveable arm, working on a spring hinge at about two inches' distance from the point, and carrying a spring clip at its outer end wherein to insert a card. (*See* Fig. 284, representing a back view of the apparatus.) A card being placed in each of the clips, the six

arms, with the cards attached to them, are folded down one by one behind the centre of the star, which is just large enough to conceal them.
Each card, as folded, holds down the one which has preceded it.   When
the last card is folded down, the free end of a moveable button or
lever at the top of the pillar on which the star rests is so turned as to

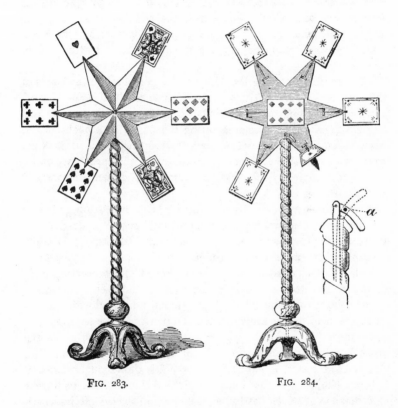

FIG. 283.   FIG. 284.

press upon the arm which holds the card last folded, and thus to keep
it and the five other cards preceding it in place.   This button, however, is so arranged as to be instantly withdrawn upon an upward
movement being communicated to a wire rod which passes up the
centre of the pillar, and terminates in a flat disc of metal at its foot.
The apparatus, thus prepared, is placed immediately over one of the

pistons of the table. At the moment of firing the pistol the cord of the piston is pulled. The piston rises, pressing up the disc and wire rod, the button is withdrawn, and the arms, being thereby released, revert to their natural position, exhibiting a card upon each point of the star.

There are many little differences of detail between the "stars" of rival manufacturers, but the foregoing may be taken to represent the general principle of all. Some have the addition of a rose in the centre, which opens simultaneously with the appearance of the cards, and discloses a watch, borrowed a moment previously from one of the spectators.

The mode of working the trick varies a good deal in the hands of different performers. The most legitimate method is to "force" cards corresponding to those already folded behind the star, and this method has the advantage of allowing the star to be brought in and placed upon the table before commencing the trick; and as it is not again touched by the performer or his assistant, the appearance on its points of (apparently) the identical cards just chosen seems really miraculous.

To be able, however, to force six cards in succession with ease and certainty, demands a more than average degree of dexterity on the part of the performer; and a "forcing pack" (*see* page 23) is hardly available where more than three, or at most four cards have to be forced. Various expedients have been adopted to get over this difficulty. Some professors simply collect, or allow their assistant to collect, the cards which have been drawn, and forthwith secretly exchange them for the same number of others. These latter are laid upon the table, and subsequently placed in the pistol, while the originals are carried off by the assistant behind the scenes, and there attached to the star, which is then for the first time brought forward. Others, again, use what are called "longs and shorts"—*i.e.*, two packs of cards, one of which has had a small portion shaved off its length or breadth. The performer offers the uncut pack for the company to draw from, letting each person retain his card, and then secretly exchanging the pack for the shortened pack, he requests each of the drawers (singly) to replace his card, and to shuffle freely. The substituted pack being a shade smaller than the returned card, the latter becomes a "long" card (*see* page 60); and therefore, however well the cards are shuffled, the performer is able, with absolute certainty, to cut at that particular card. " Here is your card," he remarks, " the knave of diamonds." As he names the card, the assistant, behind the scenes, takes the cue, and attaches a corresponding card to the star. The card named is removed from the pack and laid upon the table, in order to be subsequently placed in the pistol, and a second drawn card is returned and shuffled with the like result.

The star may, in the absence of a mechanical table, be placed on the hand, the disc being pushed up by the fingers. Some stars have a moveable stud at the side of the pillar, connected with the rod within, to facilitate this mode of working the trick.

The Card Bouquet.—This is a trick very similar in effect to that last described, though differing a little as to the manner of the appearance of the cards. Six cards are drawn, and placed in a pistol,

as in the last case. A vase (apparently of china, but really of tin, japanned), containing a handsome bouquet, is placed upon the table, and, at the instant of firing, the six cards appear ranged in a semicircle above the flowers in the bouquet. (*See* Fig. 285.) In this instance, the cards are attached to the branches of a sort of fan, so constructed as to open of its own accord, unless forcibly kept closed. The cards having been duly placed in position, this fan is shut, and pressed downwards through a narrow opening in the

FIG. 285.

lower part of the vase, the pressure of whose sides keeps it, for the time being, closed. When pressed upwards by the action of a piston, the fan rises above the level of the flowers, and at the same time opens and exhibits the six cards.

The vase is sometimes made with a second pedal, to produce a second series of six cards. In this case twelve cards are drawn ; six of these first appear, and then, at the command of the performer, these

six suddenly change to the other six. This is effected as follows :—
The twelve cards are pasted back to back in couples. Each of the
six arms which hold the cards is so arranged as to be capable of being
turned half round (after the manner of the centre of the "watch
target"), in which position it is retained by a catch, flying back however to its old position as soon as
the catch is released. The six
arms are each turned round in
this manner, bringing what are
naturally the hindmost cards
in front. The movement of
the first lever exhibits these
cards; that of the second lever
releases the six catches, when
the arms instantly fly round
and reveal the other six cards,
into which those first exhibited
appear to have changed.

THE DEMON'S HEAD.—
This is a large and effective
piece of apparatus, standing
about twenty-eight inches from
the table. It consists of a
grotesque *papier maché* head,
representing that of a demon
or satyr, and painted according
to taste. It is supported by
an ornamental brass column
about an inch in diameter,
springing from a velvet-covered
base, nine inches square and
four and a half high. (*See*
Fig. 286.) At the will of the
operator, the head rolls its eyes

FIG. 286.

and opens its mouth, and is sometimes made available in this way to
answer questions; the rolling of the eyes being taken to signify a

negative, and the open-
ing of the mouth an
affirmative. In addition
to these accomplish-
ments, the demon will
indicate chosen cards in
the following manner:
Five cards having been
selected, are returned to
the pack, which, after
being duly shuffled, is
placed in the demon's
mouth. The performer
now orders him to pro-
duce the chosen cards,
when two of them fly
from his mouth, and the
other two spring up be-
tween his horns.

The head owes its
movements to the action
of three different sets of
levers, each terminating
in a disc or pedal im-
mediately over a circular
hole in the under side of
the base. The apparatus
is so placed upon the
table that these openings
correspond in position
with the same number
of pistons. Fig. 287 is
a general view of the
internal mechanism, the
back of the head being
removed (as in fact it
may be in the original)
to give access thereto.

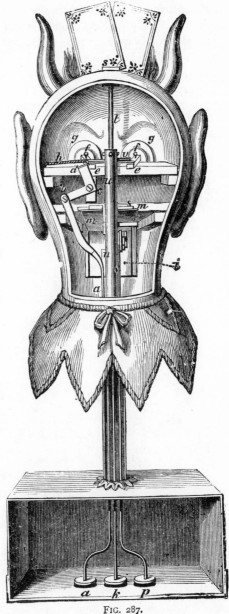

FIG. 287.

Fig. 288 exhibits (as seen from the rear) the action of the left-hand group of levers, producing the movement of the eyes. When an upward pressure is applied to the foot of the lever *a*, it causes the upper arm *c d* of the elbow piece *b c d* to describe an arc of about a quarter of an inch from left to right, thereby communicating a corresponding movement to the pair of levers *e e*, working on the pivots *f f*; and, as a necessary consequence, a reverse movement to the opposite ends

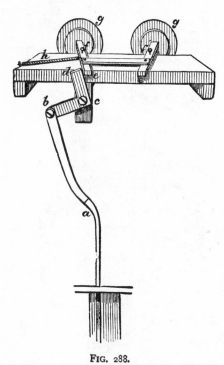

of such levers, on which are fixed the eyes *g g*. As soon as the upward pressure is removed, the spring *h*, a spiral coil of fine brass wire, draws back the levers *e e*, and with them the eyes, to their original position. To produce a continuous rolling, the pressure of the piston is applied and relaxed alternately, the effect to the spectator being as if the figure looked first to the left and then to the right, although as already explained, the active movement of the levers is in the one direction only, the normal position of the eyes being in the other direction.

Fig. 289 shows the action of the second or middle group of levers, serving to produce the opening of the mouth. The chin of the figure consists of a solid block of wood *i*, working on a pivot *j* in each cheek, and so counterweighted that its normal position is as in Fig. 289, thus keeping the mouth closed. When, however, the shaft *k* is raised by pressure from below, the lever *l* rises with it, and proportionately depresses the opposite end of the block *i*, thereby opening the

FIG. 288.

mouth. As soon as the pressure is removed, the block falls back into its original position, and the mouth closes.

The third or right-hand set of levers is a little more complex in its operation, inasmuch as it has to perform a double office, the expulsion of two cards from the mouth, and the elevation of two others at the top of the head. The cards to be shot from the mouth are placed beforehand (from the front) in the receptacle indicated in Fig. 289 by the letters m m, and a "plan" of which is given in Fig. 290, and a back view in Fig. 291. m m is a flat piece of tin, its edges folded over so as to form a receptacle or platform just capable of holding easily a couple of cards; n is a spring, which, when the cards are

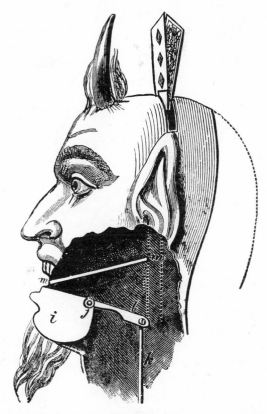

FIG. 289.

put in position, is "set" by being drawn back into the notch of the catch o. When an upward pressure is exerted by the shaft p p on the elbow-piece q q q, the latter pressing against r draws back this catch, and releases the spring, which forthwith shoots out the two cards from the mouth. The other two cards are inserted in the clip s

(*see* Fig. 291), consisting of two small pieces of sheet brass soldered to the end of the rod *t*, which works up and down piston-wise in the tube *u u.* Within the tube is a spiral spring which impels *s* upwards

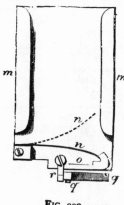

FIG. 290.

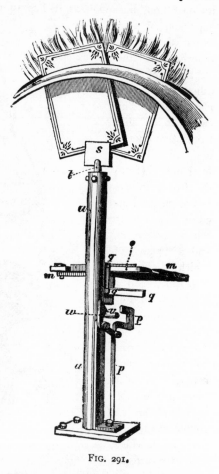

level with the top of the head, across which a slit or opening is made to allow of the passage of the cards. This portion of the apparatus is set by placing the two cards in the clip, and then drawing down the piston-rod by the cross-piece *v*, which is riveted thereto, and hitching such cross-piece under the catch *w*. The upward movement of the shaft *p*, at the same time that it draws back the catch

FIG. 291.

o, also draws back the catch *w*, thereby releasing *v*, and allowing the clip *s* and the two cards therein to spring upward, and appear at the top of the head.

It is hardly necessary to remark that the cards chosen by the audience are "forced" cards, of which duplicates have beforehand been placed in the head.

THE MAGIC PICTURE FRAME.—The performer, always borrowing, borrows this time a lady's handkerchief, and any small articles —say a watch and a glove. These latter he rolls up in the handkerchief, and places the ball or bundle thus made upon the table. He looks about in search of his magic pistol, which is immediately afterwards brought in by the assistant. The performer places the handkerchief, etc., in the pistol, the assistant meanwhile bringing forward and placing on the table a handsome picture-frame, mounted on a stand. It contains no picture, the space which the picture should occupy being filled by a board covered with black cloth. The performer, standing at the farthest available distance from the frame, takes aim at it, and fires,

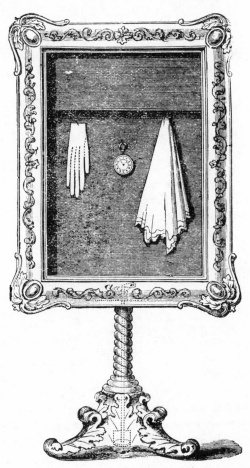

FIG. 292.

when the borrowed articles are seen instantly to attach themselves to the black background, whence, being removed, they are handed to the owners for identification.

The picture-frame, which is of the appearance shown in Fig. 292, and stands altogether about two feet high, is backed by a sort of wooden box, an inch and a half in depth, and a little smaller than the external measurement of the frame. The inside of this box is covered with black cloth, and in fact forms the true back of the frame; and it is upon this that the borrowed objects are fastened by means of small sharp hooks, the back opening on hinges to facilitate the doing so. An ordinary spring roller-blind, also of black cloth, works up and down just behind the opening of the frame. We have said an ordinary spring blind, but, in truth, the usual check at the side is wanting, and the blind therefore, if drawn down, instantly flies up again, unless held down from below. The blind terminates at bottom in a square lath, five-eighths of an inch in length by three-eighths in thickness, with a wire pin, half-an-inch in length, projecting at right angles from its hinder side. The ends of this lath, when the blind is drawn down, sink into two upright grooves, one at each side of the frame, thereby keeping the latter square, and the pin in a horizontal

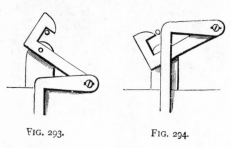

FIG. 293.　　　　　　FIG. 294.

position. The catch *a* (an enlarged view of which is shown in Figs. 293, 294) is now hooked over the pin, as in Fig. 293, thus holding the blind down. A wire rod, attached to this catch, passes down the column on which the frame stands, and terminates in the usual disc or pedal at bottom. When an upward pressure is applied to this, the catch assumes the position shown in Fig. 294, thereby releasing the pin, and allowing the blind to fly up. The blind is represented in Fig. 292 in the act of flying up, but, in truth, its rise is so rapid as to be practically invisible.

The sudden appearance of the articles in the frame is thus sufficiently accounted for, but it remains to be explained in what manner they were placed there, as they have (apparently) never been removed from the sight of the audience. It will be remembered that the smaller articles were rolled up in the handkerchief, which was then placed on the table. In truth, what is placed upon the table is a substitute handkerchief, similarly rolled up, while the original is dropped on the *servante*, and carried off by the assistant when he brings in the pistol. Having thus obtained possession of the articles, he quickly places them in the frame, and draws down and fastens the blind. This done, he closes the door at the back, and brings forward the frame, taking care to place it immediately over one of the pistons of the table. As the pistol is fired he pulls the cord, the blind flies up, and the articles are revealed.

THE FLYING WATCHES AND THE BROKEN PLATE.—This is a rather more elaborate form of the trick last described. The performer collects three or four watches from the company, the assistant, meanwhile, being sent to fetch a plate. On his return, the watches are laid one by one on the plate, and he is ordered to place them on the table. In attempting to do so he trips and falls, the watches being scattered in all directions, and the plate being smashed to pieces. The performer reprimands the offender for his carelessness, and picking up the watches, finds that they are injured in various ways. After a momentary hesitation, he hits on a way of repairing the damage. Calling for his pistol, he drops the battered watches and the fragments of the plate into it, keeping all down with a wad of newspaper. The assistant now brings in the picture-frame, as in the last trick, and the performer, taking good aim, fires at it. At the instant of firing, the plate is seen restored in the centre of the frame, with the borrowed watches encircling it. The performer advances to remove and return them to the owners, but is (or appears to be) thunderstruck at perceiving that the restoration is incomplete, a large piece being missing from the plate. (*See* Fig. 295.) After a moment's reflection, he discovers the cause of the defect, for, looking about upon the stage, he finds and picks up a fragment which he had overlooked when he put the rest in the pistol, and which consequently is wanting in the restored plate. He apologizes for the oversight, and proceeds to remedy it. Standing at the furthest portion of the stage, he makes the motion of throwing the recovered fragment towards the frame. It is seen to vanish from his hand, and the plate at the same moment appears whole as at first. The plate is removed, and with the restored watches handed to the audience for examination, when the closest inspection fails to discover any trace of fracture.

The first point to be explained is the mode in which the assistant obtains possession of the borrowed watches, in order to place them in the frame. The watches are collected by the performer in a changing apparatus (say one of the changing caddies described at page 348, or a drawer-box with a shallow inner drawer, as described at page 346). In this is placed beforehand a like number of dummy watches, and it is these latter which are placed on the plate, and meet the predestined downfall. The apparatus being left apparently empty, no suspicion is excited by the fact that the assistant, when sent to fetch the pistol or the frame, carries it off as no longer needed.

FIG. 295.

The sudden restoration of the piece apparently wanting in the plate, though marvellous to the uninitiated, is really effected by very simple means. The restored plate is throughout whole and untricken, but the effect of a piece wanting is produced by covering one portion of its outer rim with an angular piece of black velvet or alpaca, similar to that which covers the back of the frame. The illusive effect is perfect. The frame is provided with two pedals, the first releasing the black blind in front of the plate and watches, and the second serving to withdraw the angular piece of cloth already mentioned, and thus (apparently) effecting the complete restoration of the plate. The pretended disappearance of the broken piece from the hand at the moment of throwing is effected by taking it first in the left hand, and thence apparently transferring it to the right by the *tourniquet,* so that when the right hand is opened in the act of throwing, it is naturally found empty.

THE MAGIC PICTURE AND THE CHOSEN CARDS.—We notice this trick in this place as having a very close affinity, in effect, to the two last described. It is, however, wholly independent of stage appliances, and is equally well adapted for the drawing-room as for the platform. The performer, taking an ordinary pack of cards, allows three to be chosen. These are returned to the pack, and the pack shuffled. He then brings forward a small picture in a frame, and measuring, say, fourteen inches by twelve. Having exhibited both front and back, he entrusts the picture to a spectator to hold, and taking the pack of cards, throws them smartly against the glass, when in an instant the three chosen cards appear in front of the picture, but under the glass. The back of the frame is next taken out, and picture, back, frame, and glass are separately handed for inspection ; but the closest scrutiny of the audience cannot discover any mechanism or special arrangement to account for the effect above described.

The reader will already have anticipated that the three cards are "forced." The picture is on the principle of the frames last above described, with a slight variation. There are, in fact, two pictures exactly alike. One of these is pasted upon the wooden back of the frame, and upon this are fastened duplicates of the cards to be chosen. The second picture is mounted on cloth, and works on a spring roller artfully concealed in the upper part of the frame, taking, in fact, the place of the black blind in the other frames. This is kept down by a pin at the lower side of the frame, and is so arranged as to be released by the smallest pressure against the glass. The pack of cards, smartly thrown, supplies this pressure. The foremost picture flies up, and reveals apparently the same, but really a similar picture, with the chosen cards between it and the glass.

THE MAGIC PORTFOLIO.—The performer comes forward with a large portfolio, such as is used to contain engravings, and barely an inch in thickness. This he places sideways to the audience, upon a stand or trestle, thereby raising it to a convenient height, and at the same time negativing the possibility of its having any communication with the floor of the stage. Standing behind it, he proceeds to take from it a number of large engravings, then a couple of lady's bonnets of the latest fashion, and showing no sign of creasing or compression. These are followed by a large bird-cage, containing a number of living birds; and finally by three brass stew-pans, one containing haricot beans; a second, water; and a third, fire. Other articles are sometimes produced, but the above are those most generally used.

This really surprising trick is performed by the simplest possible means. The bonnets and the bird-cage are made to fold nearly flat, on the principle of the reticules and bird-cages described at pages 309 and 311. In this flattened condition they are placed in the portfolio, which being turned sideways to the audience, and the performer standing behind it, the side which is towards the spectators naturally forms a cover for the operator, and gives him every facility for developing the folded articles. The stew-pans, however, cannot be made thus compressible, and consequently a different plan is adopted in respect of them. These have india-rubber covers, after the manner of the bowls of gold-fish, and, like them, are concealed about the person of the performer, who, producing them under cover of the portfolio, appears to take them out of it. The pan for the fire contains a little spirits of wine, which the performer, still behind the portfolio, ignites with a wax match before producing this particular pan.

Where it is desired to produce a child, or other specially bulky object, the portfolio is for a moment placed on the table, behind which such object is placed. The object having been introduced into the portfolio, the latter is then transferred to the proper stand.

THE GLOVE COLUMN.—This is an ornamental column, sometimes of brass, sometimes of glass, on a massive foot and standing about two and a half feet high. It is surmounted by a metal cup, about an inch and a half in depth and two inches in diameter.

The mode of using the column is as follows:—Three or four rings are borrowed, also a white kid glove, and the whole are placed in the magic pistol. The column is then brought in, and placed upon the table. The magician takes aim at it, and fires. At the instant of his doing so, the glove, expanded as though containing a living hand, appears at the top of the pillar, with one of the borrowed rings on each of its fingers.

The glove and rings, as the reader will probably conjecture, are exchanged at an early period of the trick. There are plenty of ways of effecting this exchange. Perhaps, as regards the rings, the expedient of having them collected on the performer's wand by the assistant (*see* page 399) is as good as any. The assistant, having thus gained possession of the borrowed articles, arranges them as follows:—The glove is placed upon the end of a tube, which runs through the whole length of the column, terminating just within the cup at top, and is kept in position by an india-rubber ring slipped over it, and holding it tight to the tube. One of the borrowed rings is now placed over each of the fingers, and the glove thus prepared is pressed down into the cup, so as not to show above the rim. The column is now placed upon the table in such manner that the lower opening of the tube shall correspond with a small hole in the table, communicating by means of an india-rubber tube with a hollow ball of the same material, filled with air, and so placed as to be within reach of the hand or foot of the assistant. At the moment of firing a smart pressure is applied to the ball, thus causing a rush of air through the tube, and inflating the glove, which instantly springs up into a perpendicular position, with the rings upon it. The articles are now returned to the owners, and are identified as those which were borrowed.

Some columns have a large hollow black or gilt ball at the top, divided vertically into two parts, and so arranged as to fall apart at the moment of the inflation of the glove.

THE VANISHING POCKET HANDKERCHIEF, FOUND IN A CANDLE. —This was a favourite trick of Robert-Houdin, by whom, we believe, it was invented. The performer borrows a lady's handkerchief, drawing particular attention to the fact that he takes the first handkerchief which may be offered, and that it is wholly free from preparation. Fixing upon some gentleman among the audience, he asks him if he thinks he could set fire to the handkerchief. The person addressed naturally expresses his belief that he could. The performer ventures to doubt it, and at once fetches a lighted candle to enable him to try the experiment, meanwhile spreading the borrowed handkerchief over the top of a small round table, or *guéridon*, where it remains in full view of the spectators, showing clearly that it is not tampered with in any way. Returning with the candle, the performer hands it to the gentleman, and requests him to go and set fire to the handkerchief. Hardly, however, has he taken the first step to do so, when the handkerchief suddenly vanishes, its disappearance being so rapid that the spectators cannot even decide in which direction it travelled. The performer accuses the gentleman, who is still holding the candlestick, of having the handkerchief about him. This he naturally denies. The professor insists, and after keeping up the dispute as long as the audience are amused by it, offers to prove his assertion, and taking the candle from the candlestick, breaks it in half, and produces from it the borrowed handkerchief, which is immediately identified by the owner.

This capital trick requires the aid of a special table. The top is thin, and without fringe or ornament of any kind, allowing no apparent space for the concealment of even the smallest article. The centre pillar, however, is a hollow tube, and it is into this that the handkerchief is made to vanish. The first step in the trick is to exchange the handkerchief for a substitute. (*See* page 240.) This substitute is spread over the top of the table. The real handkerchief the performer carries with him when he leaves the stage under the pretence of fetching the candle, and utilizes his momentary absence in placing it inside the candle, which is hollow, and of the description mentioned at page 251. When the gentleman advances to set fire to the handkerchief, the pulling of a string by the assistant causes a clip to rise up in the centre of the table, and nip the middle of the hand-kerchief, which is instantly drawn down within the tube through a small trap at its upper extremity.

THE SPHINX.—Few tricks have of late years caused so great a sensation as this now well-known illusion, which was first introduced to the London public by the late Colonel Stodare, in 1865. We can-not better preface the explanation of the trick than by quoting a portion of the *Times* notice on the subject, of October 19, 1865 :—

"..... Most intricate is the problem proposed by Colonel Stodare, when, in addition to his admirable feats of ventriloquism and legerdemain, he presents to his patrons a novel illusion called the 'Sphinx.' Placing upon an uncovered table a chest similar in size to the cases commonly occupied by stuffed dogs or foxes, he removes the side facing the spectators, and reveals a head attired after the fashion of an Egyptian Sphinx. To avoid the suspicion of ventrilo-quism, he retires to a distance from the figure supposed to be too great for the practice of that art, taking his position on the border-line of the stalls and the area, while the chest is on the stage. Thus stationed, he calls upon the Sphinx to open its eyes, which it does—to smile, which it does also, though the habitual expression of its countenance is most melancholy, and to make a speech, which it does also, this being the miraculous part of the exhibition. Not only with perspicuity, but with something like eloquence, does it utter some twenty lines of verse ; and while its countenance is animated and expressive, the movement of the lips, in which there is nothing mechanical, exactly corresponds to the sounds articulated.

"This is certainly one of the most extraordinary illusions ever presented to the public. That the speech is spoken by a human voice there is no doubt · but how is a head to be contrived which, being detached from anything like a body, confined in a case, which it completely fills, and placed on a bare-legged table, will accompany a speech, that apparently proceeds from its lips, with a strictly appro-priate movement of the mouth, and a play of the countenance that is the reverse of mechanical? Eels, as we all know, can wriggle about after they have been chopped into half-a-dozen pieces; but a head that, like that of the Physician Douban, in the Arabian tales, pursues its eloquence after it has been severed from its body, scarcely comes within the reach of possibilities; unless, indeed, the old-fashioned assertion that ' King Charles walked and talked half-an-hour after his head was cut off,' is to be received, not as an illustration of defective punctuation, but as a positive historical statement.

"Davus might have solved the ' Anthropoglossus,' but Colonel Stodare presents us with a Sphinx that is really worthy of an Œdipus."

For the benefit of those who have never seen this illusion presented upon the stage, we will describe its effect a little more minutely. The Sphinx is always made a separate portion of the entertainment, as it is necessary to lower the curtain for a few moments before and after its appearance, in order to arrange and remove the necessary preparations. The curtain rises, and reveals a round or oval table, supported upon three slender legs, and utterly devoid of drapery. This stands in a curtained recess of ten or twelve feet square, open on the side towards the audience. The performer comes forward bearing a cloth-covered box, fifteen to twenty inches square, and places it upon the table already mentioned. He then unlocks the box, the front of which drops down, so as to give a perfect view of the interior, in which is seen a head of Egyptian fashion, and coloured in perfect imitation of life. (*See* Frontispiece.) The performer now retires to a position in the very midst of the audience, and raising his wand, says in a tone of command, " Sphinx, awake ! " The Sphinx slowly opens its eyes, looking first to the front with a strong gaze ; then, as if gradually gaining consciousness, to the one side and the other, the head moving slightly with the eyes. Questions are put by the performer to the head, and are answered by it, the play of the mouth and features being in perfect harmony with the sounds uttered. Finally, in answer to a query of the operator, the Sphinx declaims a neatly turned oracle in verse. This concludes the exhibition, and the performer closes the box. Should the audience call for an *encore*, the performer addresses them to the following or some similar effect :—
" Ladies and gentlemen, I am glad that the Sphinx has afforded you satisfaction, and I should be only too pleased to be able to indulge the

desire which you kindly testify of seeing it again. Unfortunately, this is not possible. The charm by which I am enabled, as you have seen, to revivify for a space the ashes of an ancient Egyptian, who lived and died some centuries ago, lasts but for fifteen minutes. That time has now expired, and the head which has astonished you with its mysterious eloquence has again returned to its original dust." As he speaks the last words, he again opens the box, and the head is found to have disappeared, leaving in its place a handful of ashes.

This singular illusion depends upon the well-known principle, common to optics as to mechanics, that "the angle of reflection is equal to the angle of incidence." Thus, if a person standing at the point *a*, in Fig. 296, look into a mirror placed in the position indi-

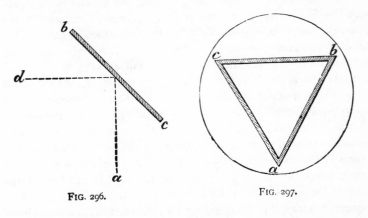

FIG. 296. FIG. 297.

cated by the line *b c*, he will see reflected, not himself, but whatever object may be placed at the point *d*. By an ingenious application of this principle a looking-glass may be used to conceal a given object behind it, while at the same time an image reflected in the glass may be made to represent what would be presumably seen if no glass were there, and thus prevent the presence of the mirror from being suspected. This is the secret of the Sphinx. The table, as already mentioned, has three legs, one in front, and one at each side. Between these legs the spectator sees apparently the curtains at the back of the recess, but really a reflection of the curtains at the sides. The space between the middle leg and that on either side is occupied by pieces of looking-glass (*see* Fig. 297, which represents a ground plan of the arrangement), extending from *a* to *b*, and *a* to *c*. The glass extends quite down to the floor, which is covered with cloth of the same material and colour as the surrounding curtains. The spectators, therefore, looking towards the table, see above it the curtains at the back, and below it the reflection of the curtains at the sides; which, however, if the relative angles are properly arranged, appears to be simply the continuation or lower portion of the curtains at the back. The illusion is perfect, and the spectator, from the position assigned to him, cannot possibly discover, by the evidence of his senses, that he is looking at any other than an ordinary bare-legged table, with the background visible in the usual way.

The rest is a very simple matter. The person who is to represent the Sphinx is beforehand placed, duly attired, underneath the table. There is a trap in the table through which he can pass his head at the proper moment. This trap is a round piece of wood, covered to match the surface of the table, and working on a hinge on the side nearest to the audience. It has no spring, but is kept closed by means of a button on the opposite side, and when released hangs down perpendicularly. It must be large enough to allow the passage of the somewhat elaborate headpiece of the Sphinx, and would therefore leave an open space visible round the neck. This difficulty is met by the expedient of having a wooden collar, whose upper surface is a facsimile in size and pattern of the trap, fastened round the neck of the representative of the Sphinx. When he lifts his head up through the trap, this collar exactly fills the opening, and thus shows no break in the surface of the table. The box is bottomless, and when brought forward by the performer is empty. A little caution has to be observed in placing it upon the table, for, if the performer were to approach the table *from the side*, his legs would be reflected in the glass, and would thereby betray the secret. He must therefore make his appearance from some quarter *outside* of the curtained recess, and advance to a position well in front of, and at some little distance from the table, when, by moving in a straight line from the audience towards the middle leg *a*, he prevents this inconvenient reflection. The placing the box upon the table, and the unlocking it, allow time for the representative of the Sphinx to get his head into position within it. This done, the box is opened, and the rest depends on the dramatic talent of the performer and his assistant. The performance being concluded, the box is again locked, and the head withdrawn, a handful of ashes b ing introduced on the trap in its stead.

The angle at which the two mirrors should be set cannot be determined absolutely, but will vary according to the distance and position of the surrounding drapery.

. Some performers use a shawl or a screen of cardboard in place of the box, but we doubt whether any method is more effective than that above described.

The ghastly illusion of the so-called "Decapitated Head," which drew crowds to the Polytechnic some few years since, was merely the "Sphinx" in a less pleasant form.

THE CABINET OF PROTEUS.—This is another adaptation of the principle on which the Sphinx illusion is founded. It is the joint invention of Messrs. Pepper and Tobin, by whom it was patented in 1865. The first steps towards a patent for the Sphinx were also taken in the same year, but the latter invention never proceeded be- yor provisional protection. The Cabinet of Proteus is a wooden closet, seven to eight feet in height by four or five feet square, supported on short legs, so as to exclude the idea of any communication with the floor. (*See* Fig 298.) It has folding doors, and an upright pillar extends from top to bottom of the interior, at about the centre

FIG. 298.

of the cabinet. At the top of this pillar, in front, is fixed a lamp, so that the whole of the interior is brightly illuminated.

The cabinet may be used in various ways. One of the most striking is as follows :—The folding doors are opened, disclosing the interior perfectly empty. (*See* Fig. 299.) The exhibitor directs his assistant to walk into the cabinet. He does so, and the doors are closed. Meanwhile, a couple of gentlemen, selected by the audience, are invited to stand behind or beside the cabinet, and see that no one obtains ingress or egress by any secret opening. Notwithstanding these precautions, when the doors are again opened, the assistant is

found to have vanished, and another person, different in dress, in stature, and in complexion, is found in his place. This person steps forth, makes his bow, and retires. Again the cabinet, now empty, is closed, and after an interval of a few moments, again opened. This time a human skeleton is found to occupy the vacant space. This ghastly object having been removed, and the door having been once more closed and opened, another person, say a lady, appears. This person having retired, the

FIG. 299.

doors are again closed; and when they are again opened, the person who first entered is once more found within. A committee from the audience are now invited to examine the cabinet within and without, but all their scrutiny cannot detect any hidden space, even sufficient to conceal a mouse.

An examination of Fig. 300, representing a ground plan of the cabinet, will make plain the seeming mystery. A moveable flap *a b*, working on hinges at *b*, extends from top to bottom of each side, resting when thrown open against the post *c* in the middle, and thus enclosing a triangular space at the back of the cabinet. The outer surfaces of these flaps (*i.e.*, the surfaces exposed when they are folded back against the sides of the cabinet) are, like the rest of the interior, covered with wall paper, of a crimson or other dark colour. The opposite sides of the flaps are of looking-glass, and when the flaps are folded back against the posts, reflect the surfaces against which

they previously rested, and which are covered with paper of the same pattern as the rest. The effect to the eye of the spectator is that of a perfectly empty chamber, though, as we have seen, there is in reality an enclosed triangular space behind the post. This is capable of containing two or three persons, and here it is that the persons and things intended to appear in succession are concealed. The assistant, entering in sight of the audience,

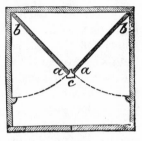

Fig. 300.

changes places, as soon as the door is closed, with one of the other persons. This person having retired, and the door being again closed, those who are still within place the skeleton in position in front of the post, and again retire to their hiding-place. When all the rest have appeared, the person who first entered presses the flaps against the sides of the cabinet, against which they are retained by a spring lock on each side, and the public may then safely be admitted, as their closest inspection cannot possibly discover the secret.

THE INDIAN BASKET TRICK.—This is another of the sensational feats identified with the name of Colonel Stodare, and is imitated from a similar illusion performed by the Indian conjurors. It is not a pleasant trick to witness, but, like the " Decapitated Head," it drew immense crowds, its fictitious horror being apparently its chief attraction. Its effect, as the trick was originally presented by Stodare, is as follows :—A large oblong basket, say five feet by two, and as deep as wide, is brought in, and placed on a low stand or bench, so as to be raised clear of the stage. The performer comes forward with a drawn sword in his right hand, and leading with the other hand a young lady, dressed in a closely-fitting robe of black velvet. Reproaching her upon some pretended ground of complaint, he declares that she must be punished, and forthwith begins to blindfold her eyes. She simulates terror, begging for mercy, and finally escaping from him, runs off the stage. He follows her, and instantly reappears, dragging her by the wrist. Regardless of her sobs and cries, he compels her to enter the basket, in which she lies down, and the lid is closed. Simulating an access of fury, he thrusts the sword through the basket (from the front) in various places. Piercing screams are heard from the interior, and the sword when withdrawn is seen to be red with blood. The screams gradually subside, and all is still. A thrill of horror runs through the audience, who are half inclined to call in the police, and hand over the professor to the nearest magistrate. For a moment there is a pause, and then the performer, calmly wiping the bloody sword on a white pocket-handkerchief, says. " Ladies and gentlemen, I fear you imagine that I have hurt the lady who was the subject of this experiment. Pray disabuse yourselves of such an idea. She had disobeyed me, and I therefore determined to punish her by giving her a little fright; but nothing more. The fact is, she had left the basket some time before I thrust the sword into it. You don't believe me, I see. Allow me to show you, in the first place, that the basket is empty." He turns over the basket accordingly, and shows that the lady has vanished. " Should you desire further proof, the lady will answer for herself." The lady at this moment comes forward from a different portion of the room, and having made her bow, retires.

This startling illusion is performed as follows :—To begin with, there are *two* ladies employed, in figure and general appearance as nearly alike as possible. Their dress is also exactly similar. The little dramatic scene with which the trick commences is designed to impress upon the audience the features of the lady who first appears. When she is blindfolded, she, as already mentioned, runs off the stage. The performer runs after her, and apparently bringing her back, really brings back in her place the second lady, who is standing in readiness, blindfolded in precisely the same way, behind the scenes. As the bandage covers the greater part of her features, there is little fear of the spectators detecting the substitution that has taken place. The substitute lady now enters the basket, where she lies, compressing herself into as small a compass as possible, along the back. Knowing the position which she occupies, it is not a very difficult matter for the operator so to direct the thrusts of the sword as to avoid any risk of injuring her. The chief thing to be attended to for this purpose is to thrust always in an *upward* direction. The appearance of blood on the sword may be produced either by the lady in the basket drawing along the blade, as it is withdrawn after each thrust, a

FIG. 301.

sponge saturated with some crimson fluid, or by a mechanical arrangement in the hilt, causing the supposed blood, on pressure, to trickle down the blade.

The only point that remains to be explained is the difficulty which will probably already have suggested itself to the reader, viz., " How does the performer manage to show the basket empty at the close of the trick ? " Simply by having the basket made on the principle of the "inexhaustible box," described at page 391. The performer takes care to tilt the basket over to the front *before* he raises the lid. This leaves the lady lying on the true bottom of the basket (*see* Fig. 302), while a moveable flap, fixed at right angles to the bottom, and lying in its normal position flat against the front of the basket, for the time being represents the bottom to the eyes of the audience. While the basket is thus shown apparently empty, the lady who first appeared in the trick comes forward, and is immediately recognized by the audience; and as they are fully persuaded that she was the person placed in the basket, the inference that she has escaped from it by some quasi-supernatural means seems inevitable.

The above is the form in which the trick was first introduced to the London public, but another *modus operandi* has since been adopted by some performers. The low table or bench on which the basket is placed is in this case constructed on the principle of the Sphinx-table, with looking-glass between the legs, and with a large trap in the top. The basket used is not made like the inexhaustible box, but the bottom is moveable, and hinged against the front, so as to lift up flat against it when required. One lady only is employed. When she is about to step into the basket, the bottom is pushed up from below, and she thus steps through the basket and the table, and thence passes, through a trap-door, beneath the stage. The basket is then closed, and the bottom allowed to fall back into its place. As the basket is left in this case empty, the performer may thrust into it in any direction at pleasure, the screams being uttered by the lady from her safe quarters below. At the proper moment the performer lifts the basket bodily off the table, and shows it really empty, while the lady, as in the former case, reappears in some other quarter.

ELECTRICAL TRICKS.—Some of the most mysterious of the stage tricks are performed by means of electricity, or, to speak more correctly, of electro-magnetism. In describing these, which are nearly all attributable to the inventive genius of Robert-Houdin, it may be desirable, in the first place, to explain in a few words what electro-magnetism is, and how it operates. Every school-boy is acquainted with the ordinary steel horse-shoe magnet, and knows that if the accompanying small iron bar, or "keeper," is placed within a short distance from its ends or " poles," it will be sharply attracted to them. In the case of the ordinary magnet this attractive force is permanent, but in that of the electro magnet it may be produced or destroyed at pleasure. The electro-magnet consists of a short piece of soft iron, (either straight, or bent into a horseshoe form), with copper wire (covered with silk or cotton) wound round and round it nearly to the ends. If a current of electricity from a galvanic battery is made to pass through this wire, the iron core becomes powerfully magnetic, the attractive force, however, ceasing as soon as the current is interrupted.

Almost any kind of battery may be used to produce the necessary current, but for magical purposes one of the most convenient is the Bichromate Bottle Battery, depicted in Fig. 302. This consists of a plate of zinc and a plate of carbon (or sometimes two plates of carbon) immersed in an exciting fluid, consisting of two ounces and a half of bichromate of potash dissolved in a pint of water, with the addition of one third of an ounce of sulphuric acid. The bottle is only filled to the top of the spherical portion, and the zinc is so arranged that it can be drawn up into the neck, and so out of the solution, when it is desired to suspend the action of the battery.

FIG. 302.

The wires for conducting the current should be of copper covered with silk or cotton, and one of them

FIG. 303.

must be connected with the zinc plate, and the other with the carbon plate of the battery, which has " binding screws" affixed for this purpose. For the purpose of instantly completing or disconnecting the electric circuit, the wires are affixed to the opposite sides of what is called a connecting stud (*see* Fig. 303),

being a circular disc of wood or porcelain, with a moveable stud or button in the centre. On pressing this stud with the finger, the ends of the two wires are brought in contact, and the circuit is completed; but as soon as the pressure is removed, the stud rises by the action of a spring, and the circuit is again broken.

Among the conjuring tricks depending upon the principle of electro-magnetic attraction, the simplest is that of

THE LIGHT AND HEAVY CHEST.—This is a small brass-bound box, with the ordinary handle at top. The performer shows that it is empty, and without mechanism or preparation. Having been duly inspected, it is placed upon a small pedestal fixed to the stage, when the performer requests that some gentleman of considerable personal strength will step forward. A volunteer having been found, the magician asks him whether he thinks he can lift the little box before him. He naturally answers that he can, and proves his assertion by lifting it accordingly, which, as the box only weighs a few pounds, it is not very difficult to do. "Wait a bit," says the professor, "you were able to lift it then, because it was my will and pleasure that you should do so. It now weighs" (say) "six pounds. I have only to breathe on it thus, and it will instantly weigh two tons. Try if you can lift it *now*." Again he tries, but the chest is as if glued to the pedestal, and the most violent efforts cannot dislodge it. Once more the performer breathes upon it, and it may be lifted with one finger.

The explanation may be given in half-a-dozen lines. The bottom of the box is an iron plate. The top of the pedestal is also an iron plate, and within it is contained a powerful electro-magnet, the poles being in contact with the plate, and the wires to convey the current passing beneath the stage to the hiding-place of the assistant. The latter, on receiving his cue from the expressions of the performer, presses the connecting stud and completes the circuit, thereby bringing the magnetic force into operation. Upon again receiving an agreed signal from the performer, he ceases to press the stud, the circuit is broken, and the iron ceases to possess any magnetic force. This may be repeated as often as desired.

The above trick is cited by Robert-Houdin in illustration of the great difference which there may be, in point of effect, between two modes of presenting the same illusion. The reader may possibly be aware that Robert-Houdin was employed by the French Government, at one period of his career, in a mission to Algeria, with the object of destroying, if possible, the popular belief in the pretended miracles of the Marabouts, whereby these latter had obtained an extraordinary ascendency over the minds of the ignorant Arabs. The plan adopted was to show, first, that a European could perform still greater marvels, and then to explain that these seeming mysteries were mere matters of science and dexterity, and wholly independent of supernatural assistance. The " Light and Heavy Chest " was one of the prominent features of the programme, but if presented under that name it would have produced but very little effect. The fact that the chest became immoveable at command would only have been attributed by the Arabs to some ingenious mechanical arrangement, beyond their comprehension, but exciting only a momentary wonder. With great tact, Robert-Houdin contrived to turn the attention of his audience from the object to the subject of the trick, professing, not to make the chest light or heavy, but to make the person who volunteered weak or strong at his pleasure. Thus presented, the trick had the appearance no longer of a mere achievement of mechanical or scientific skill, but of a manifestation of supernatural power. We will tell the rest of the story as nearly as possible in Robert-Houdin's own words, as related in the story of his life :—

" An Arab of middle stature, but well-knit, wiry, and muscular ; the very type of an Arab Hercules, came forward, with plenty of self-confidence, and stood by my side.

"' Are you *very* strong ? ' I inquired, eyeing him from head to foot.

"' Yes,' he replied, carelessly.

"' Are you sure that you will always remain so ? '

"' Perfectly.'

"' You are mistaken ; for in one moment I shall take away all your strength, and leave you as weak as a little child.'

" The Arab smiled scornfully, in token of disbelief.

"' Here,' I said, ' lift up this chest.'

" The Arab stooped, lifted the chest, and said disdainfully, ' Is that all ? '

"' Wait a bit,' I replied. Then, with the solemnity appropriate

to my assumed character, I made a gesture of command, and gravely
said—

" ' You are weaker than a woman. Try *now* to lift that box.'

" The strong man, perfectly indifferent about my magic spell, again
catches hold of the box by the handle, and gives a vigorous pull to
lift it ; this time, however, the chest resists, and in spite of the most
determined efforts, remains absolutely immoveable.

" The Arab wastes in vain over the unlucky chest an amount of
force which would have lifted an enormous weight ; till at last, exhausted, panting, and burning with shame, he ceases, looks dum-
foundered, and begins to appreciate the power of the magic art. He
has half a mind to give up the attempt; but to give up would be to
acknowledge himself conquered, and to admit his weakness; and
after having been famed for his muscular strength, to sink to the
level of a child. The bare idea makes him furious. Gathering
new strength from the encouragement which his friends offer
him by word and look, he casts towards them a glance which seems
to say, ' You shall see what the son of the desert can do.' Once
more he bends over the chest, his nervous hands grip the handle, and
his legs, planted one on each side of the chest like two columns of
bronze, serve as a fulcrum for the mighty effort which he is about to
make. It seems almost impossible but that under such a strain the
box must fly to pieces. Strange ! this Hercules, a moment ago so
strong and self-confident, now bends his head ; his arms, riveted to
the box, are drawn by a violent muscular contraction against his
chest; his legs quiver, and he falls on his knees with a cry of agony.

" An electric shock, produced by an induction coil, had just been
communicated, at a signal from me, from behind the scenes to the
handle of the chest. Thence the contortions of the unlucky Arab.
To prolong his agony would have been inhuman. I gave a second
signal, and the electric current was cut off. My athletic friend,
released from his terrible bondage, raised his hands above his head.
' Allah! Allah!' he cried, shaking with fright, then wrapping himself hastily in the folds of his burnous. as though to hide his disgrace,
he rushed through the spectators, and made his way to the door of
the hall."

To describe completely the " induction coil," above referred to, would be beyond the scope of the present treatise. It may, however, be summarily described as consisting of a coil of insulated copper wire, wound round a small bundle of straight iron wires, say five or six inches in length, and an inch in diameter. This is called the " primary " coil. Round this is again wound a quantity of much finer wire, also insulated. This constitutes the " secondary " coil. The ends of each coil are kept free. If a current of electricity be made to circulate through the wire of the primary coil, an independent current of great intensity is found to be thereby produced, by a mysterious process called induction, in the secondary coil. This current is strongest at the moment of first completing the circuit in the primary wire, and if a person is grasping the ends of the secondary wire, or any conducting substance in connection with it, at the moment when the circuit is completed, he will receive a very severe shock. A contrivance is attached to the coil, whereby the circuit is made and broken alternately with great rapidity, thereby producing a continuous shock, of such power that the victim loses for the time being the faculty of relaxing his muscles, and is compelled, after the manner of the unfortunate Arab, to grip, tighter and tighter, the cause of his pain, until released by the final severing of the circuit. Any reader who desires a more complete acquaintance with the induction coil, should purchase a little shilling manual, entitled, " Intensity Coils, How Made and How Used," by " Dyer " (Suter, Alexander, and Co., Cheapside), where he will find an excellent account of this interesting subject.

SPIRIT-RAPPING.—This deception is frequently performed by the aid of electro-magnetism, although the raps may be, and in most instances are, produced by much simpler methods. We will suppose that a table is to be the instrument of the raps. The top being removed, a hollow is made in the " frame " which supports it, and in the cavity thus made is fixed an electro-magnet, of the fashion shown in Figs. 304, 305. Upon one side of the horseshoe, at the centre of the curve, is screwed a brass spring *a*, to the opposite end of which is attached the keeper *b*. The effect of the spring is to hold the keeper about a quarter of an inch away from the poles of the magnet, save when a current of electricity is made to pass through the wire, when the horseshoe becoming magnetic, the keeper, in spite of the resistance of the spring, is brought down sharply into contact with the poles, and so remains until the circuit is again severed, when it flies back again to its former position. The little metal knob or hammer *c*, which is to produce the raps, is screwed to the under side of the keeper, and points between the two arms or poles of the magnet. If, therefore, the magnet be fastened to a piece of wood, or other hard surface, and an electric current be sent through the wire, the keeper is instantly drawn down to the poles of the magnet, and the hammer, moving with it, strikes the wood between the poles, and produces the rap. As soon as the

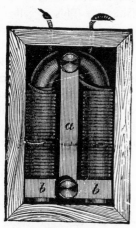

FIG. 304.

circuit is broken, the keeper and hammer are raised by the spring, in readiness for another rap ; and each time that connection with the battery is made, a rap is produced. The wires from the concealed magnet are made to pass down the leg of the table, and beneath the floor or carpet to the hiding-place of the assistant, who can thus summon spirits "from the vasty deep" or elsewhere, at his pleasure.

It will be found a very convenient arrangement to have the magnet enclosed in a little mahogany box,

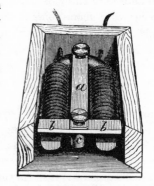

FIG. 305.

as shown in the diagrams, in which condition it can readily be fixed in any required position.

THE MAGIC BELL.—Precisely the same in principle, though differing somewhat in detail, is the magic bell. The bell, which is of glass, and of the form shown in Fig. 306, is hung up above the stage by two silk or woollen cords, and thus apparently placed wholly out of the reach of human influence. Nevertheless, at the command of the magician, it becomes endowed with seeming vitality. The hammer strikes any number of times at command, answers questions (with three raps for "yes," and one for "no," after the approved spiritualistic manner), indicates chosen cards, and generally displays a remarkable amount of intelligence.

The reader who has followed our description of the spirit-rapping magnet will hardly require an explanation of the magic bell. The brass cap from which the hammer projects, contains a small electro-magnet, the wire which carries the hammer being fixed to the keeper, and bringing the hammer down smartly on the glass whenever the electric circuit is made complete.

FIG. 306.

" But," says the sagacious reader, " how is the circuit made complete? In the former case there were hidden wires, passing through the legs of the table, to convey the electric current, but in this instance the bell is suspended in mid-air by a couple of ordinary cords. How can the electric fluid therefore be conveyed to the bell?" The answer lies in the fact that the cords are not quite *ordinary* cords. In appearance they are two pieces of common cord, with a brass hook at each end, for the purpose of first attaching them to corresponding hooks in the ceiling, and, secondly, attaching the bell to their opposite ends. But on a closer examination it will be found that a fine copper wire extends from hook to hook through the centre of the cord, making it a perfect conductor, while yet not diminishing in the least its perfect flexibility. The hooks in the ceiling communicate with hidden wires, and these with the electric battery behind the scenes.

THE CRYSTAL CASH-BOX.—This is a mahogany box with glass

top and bottom, the wooden portion of it being lined with velvet. (*See* Fig. 307.) In dimensions it is about eight inches long, by six wide, and three and a half deep, and it has a brass ring at either end.

The performer commences by borrowing (say) eight half-crowns, the owner of each being requested to mark it for the purpose of identification. With these the performer exhibits any trick whose leading feature is the passage of the coin from some one place to another. The trick having been performed, and the money identified, the operator still retaining it, returns to the stage, and placing the coins upon the table, addresses the audience to the following effect: " Ladies and gentlemen, I have given you a slight specimen of the certainty and speed with which I can make money travel. Who would go to the trouble and expense of Post-office orders when by simply taking the money in his hand, and saying, ' Pass,' he might make it fly direct into the pocket of his correspondent? But I will give you another and a still more surprising illustration." (Here the assistant brings in the crystal cash-box.) "Here

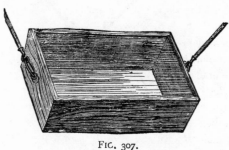

FIG. 307.

is a wooden box, closed on all sides, but with glass top and bottom, so that you may see for yourselves that there is no mechanism or preparation about it. Now I propose to pass these eight half-crowns, the identical half-crowns marked by yourselves, into this closed box. Where shall I place the box, so as to be at a distance from me, and at the same time in full view of all present? Perhaps the best thing I can do with it will be to fasten it to these two silk cords hanging from the ceiling. I will set the box swinging" (he does so), " so that you can all see that it is empty. Now I will take the money, and stand in any part of the room you like." (He walks to the chosen spot.) " Will some one oblige me by counting *three* in a distinct voice." One of the spectators does so, and the performer at the last word makes the motion of throwing the money towards the cash-box, in which it is instantly seen and heard to fall, his hand at the same moment appearing empty. The cash-box is taken down, and the money returned to the owners, who identify it as that which they had marked.

As the reader will doubtless have anticipated, the coins are already in the cash-box when the latter is hung to the cords. They are con-cealed by a moveable flap lying close against one of the wooden sides, in which position it is maintained by a spring, until an electric current is despatched along the cords. This brings into action an electro-magnet, hidden in the thickness of the box, thereby causing the flap to be momentarily lifted, and the coins to escape into the interior of the box.

When the performer, having exhibited the preliminary trick with the borrowed coins, places them apparently upon the table, he in reality exchanges them, and places the substitutes on the "money-trap" described at page 446, leaving the genuine coins within reach of his assistant, who forthwith carries them off behind the scenes, and places them in readiness under the flap of the cash-box. The performer having attached the box to the cords, and set it in motion, apparently picks up the heap of coins, which really sink into the table.* When the word "Three" is spoken, he opens the right hand, which is seen empty, and the assistant behind the scenes, taking the same word as a signal, presses the connecting stud, and completes the circuit. The flap is momentarily lifted, and the borrowed coins are heard and seen to fall within the box.

There is another box (the invention of Robert-Houdin) which goes by the same name, and with still better title, inasmuch as not only the top and bottom, but the sides and ends, are of glass, held together by a light metal framework. In appearance it is as shown in Fig. 308, and, being transparent throughout, it appears physically impossible that any object should be concealed in it; and yet, when

---

* If his table is not provided with the money-trap, the performer may really pick up the coins with his left hand, and thence, by the *tourniquet*, apparently take them in the right, keeping the right hand closed as if containing them. While the attention of the spectators is thus drawn to the right hand, the left may fall carelessly to the side, and deposit the coins in the *pochette*.

the box is suspended, and set swinging, the operator has only to take the (supposed) borrowed coins in his hand, and to pronounce the

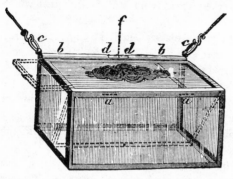

FIG. 308.

mystic "Pass," when the eight half-crowns are seen and heard to fall into the box, and may be taken from thence by the owners themselves, without even this near inspection of the apparatus revealing the secret of their appearance.

As in the trick we have just described, electricity is the motive agent; but in this instance it operates, not by its magnetic influence, but by another of its mysterious properties. If a tolerably powerful current be made to pass at some point in its circuit through a short length (say half an inch) of fine platinum wire, platinum being a bad conductor, the wire will, at the moment of completing the circuit, be heated to a white heat, or, if the current be very powerful, will even be fused altogether. A very few words will show how this simple scientific fact is made available to produce the desired result.

The box measures about ten inches in length, by five in breadth and five in depth, so that its back, front, top, and bottom are of exactly the same size. On the top, which slides out, in order to give access to the interior, is an ornamental design, measuring about four inches by three. This renders this particular portion of the top or lid opaque, and it is beneath this portion that the half-crowns are placed. Slips of glass are cemented to the

FIG. 309.

under side of the lid (*see* Fig. 309), so as to inclose a space just large enough to allow eight half-crowns to be placed, in two layers of four each, within it. The slips of glass serve to keep the coins in position laterally. Vertically, they are supported as follows :— The front of the box (*i.e.*, the side which, when the box is suspended, is nearest to the spectators) is made double. The outer portion is a fixture, but the inner is attached by hinges *a a* to the upper edge of the box, and may therefore be folded at pleasure against the top, though when released it falls back to its normal position against the front, in which position it is secured by a spring catch until again raised. It is upon this moveable side, thus folded up against the top, that the eight half-crowns are supported. The opposite edge of the top of the box is arranged as follows: *b b* is a metal tube, with an opening of about half-an-inch in length between *d d*; *c c* are two metal hooks or rings by which the apparatus is suspended, and through which the current passes. Each of these communicates with a piece of insulated copper wire, extending from *c* to *d*. The

space between *d d* is filled up by a round plug or pencil of wood (*see* enlarged view in Fig. 310), along which lies a small piece of very fine platinum wire *e e*, connecting the ends of the two copper wires. The moveable glass flap is held up

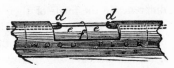

FIG. 310.

against the top by means of a little piece of black cotton *f*, which, passing through a minute hole in the outer edge of the flap, is made to pass round the wooden plug, and thus to cross the platinum wire at right angles, and in immediate contact with it. The practical application of the scientific principle to which we have alluded will now be obvious. At the moment of completing the circuit, the platinum, becoming red-hot, instantly severs the cotton, when down falls the flap, not altering in the least the general appearance of the box, but allowing the half-crowns to fall loose into its interior.

In order to prepare the apparatus for use, it is necessary first to remove the sliding lid, to place the moveable flap in position, and to fasten it with cotton as already described. The lid should then be turned upside down, and the half-crowns placed in position, after which the box also is turned upside down, and the lid allowed to slide gently into its place. The half-crowns are now secure, and the box may be brought forward and set swinging, without any danger of their making a premature appearance.

In some boxes the double flap is omitted, the front being single, but moveable, and working as already explained. In this case the box, when first brought forward, has the glass of the side towards the audience missing, but at a little distance its absence cannot be detected.

THE MAGIC DRUM.—This is in appearance an ordinary side-drum, but being hung up by cords from the ceiling, it will forth-with, without any visible drumsticks, give either a single rap or a roll, or keep time to any piece of music. It will further answer questions and tell fortunes, indicate chosen cards, etc., after the man-ner of the magic bell.

These mysterious effects are produced by two hammers or drum-sticks, fixed against one end of the drum on the inside. Each of these is attached to the keeper of an electro-magnet, but there is a difference in the mode of their working. One works after the man-ner of the bell, giving a single tap whenever contact is made, but thenceforward remaining silent until the circuit is again broken and again completed. In other words, each pressure of the connecting stud produces one rap, and no more. The second hammer is differ-ently arranged. By means of what is called a " contact-breaker," the movement of the keeper, when attracted by the magnet, of itself breaks the circuit. The circuit being broken, the iron is no longer magnetic, and the keeper flies back to its old position, thereby once more completing the circuit. As long as the pressure on the stud continues, therefore, the circuit is alternately made and broken in rapid succession, involving a corresponding movement of the keeper and hammer, and producing a " roll " of the drum. The use of the two hammers involves the necessity of two electrical circuits and two connecting studs, and of three cords to suspend the drum (one being common to both circuits). With a little practice in the management of the two studs, the single rapper may be made to beat time to a tune, while the other stud brings in the roll at appropriate intervals.

There are some drums (of an inferior character) made with one hammer only ; such hammer being arranged for the roll. Where it is desired to give a single rap, this may be effected by pressing and instantly releasing the stud with a light, quick touch; but some little dexterity is required.

In the case of all these appliances for magically answering questions, it is necessary that the assistant who has the control of the apparatus should be in such a position as to distinctly hear the questions asked. In fortune-telling matters the answer may generally be left to his own discretion; but for indicating what card is chosen, etc., it is necessary either that an agreed card be forced, or that a carefully arranged code of verbal signals should be employed, whereby the form of the question may itself indicate the proper answer.*
Considerable fun may be caused by the magician selecting an evidently "engaged" couple, and after asking how many months it will be before they are married, etc., inquiring, in a stage whisper, how many children they are destined to be blest with. The drum raps steadily up to (say) five, and this is accepted as the answer, when, after a moment's pause, two more raps are heard *in quick succession.* This alarming omen is received with general laughter, amid which the drum gives another rap, and then another, continuing until the performer, scandalized at its behaviour, unhooks it from the cords, and carries it, still rapping, off the stage. This last effect is wholly independent of electricity, being produced by the performer tapping with his fingers that end of the drum which for the time being is farthest from the audience.

There are some few other tricks performed by the aid of electricity, but any one who understands the principle of those above described may make a very shrewd guess at the working of the remainder. All tricks of this class, though ingenious and effective, are open to one or two serious objections. In the first place, the apparatus is very costly, and, secondly, they are unpleasantly liable, from the nicety of their mechanism and the absolute necessity of perfect electrical connection in all their parts, to hang fire at the critical

---

* This is the principle of the well-known "second-sight" trick, a detailed explanation of which we are compelled from considerations of space to omit, the system, as perfected by Robert-Houdin and others, being so elaborate, that an independent treatise would be needed to do it justice. An admirable account of the system, as applied to the French language, will be found in a work by F. A. Gandon, "*La seconde vue dévoilée,*" published in Paris in 1849.

moment, and leave the operator in a very embarrassing position. Imagine the feelings of a performer who, having just introduced his wonderful drum, which is to display unheard-of oracular powers, finds that the instrument remains as mute as the celebrated harp in Tara's halls, and refuses to bear out, in the smallest degree, his grandiloquent assertions. Yet this unpleasant result may occur at any time from the simple breaking of a wire, or some even slighter cause. This, it appears to us, is a serious drawback to electrical tricks, though where they are exhibited at their best no illusions are more beautiful, or have more of genuine magic about them.

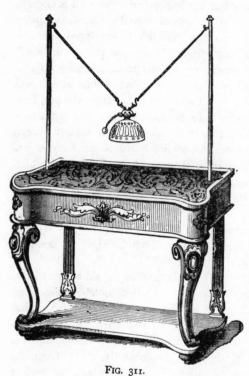

We should mention, before quitting the subject of these tricks, that in order to avoid the trouble and expense of fixing the necessary conducting wires in a building not specially appropriated to magical performances, an upright brass rod (which may be detached at pleasure) is

FIG. 311.

sometimes fitted on each side of the performer's table (*see* Fig. 311), and the apparatus in use (drum, bell, cash-box, etc.) is suspended by appropriate cords between these rods. The conducting wires are connected within the table with the lower ends of the brass uprights, and thence pass down its hinder legs to the battery behind the scenes. There are many considerations of convenience in favour of this arrangement, but the tricks performed are less effective than where the apparatus is hung fairly from the ceiling, and apparently out of all possible reach of mechanical influence.

THE AËRIAL SUSPENSION.—This is a very old trick, performed originally by the Indian jugglers, who kept the *modus operandi* a profound secret. The ingenuity, however, of Robert-Houdin penetrated the mystery, and in 1849 he made it a special feature of his *séances fantastiques.* At that time the public mind was much interested in the anæsthetic qualities of ether, which had then recently been discovered. Robert-Houdin manipulated this fact into a valuable advertisement. He gave out that he had discovered in the popular anæsthetic a still more marvellous property, viz., that when inhaled under certain conditions, it neutralized the attraction of gravitation in the person inhaling it, who became, for the time being, light as air. In proof of this, he brought forward his youngest son, then a child of ten or thereabouts, and after having made him smell at a small phial, really empty, but supposed to contain ether, caused him to recline in mid-air, with no other support than that afforded by, to all appearance, an ordinary walking-stick, placed in a vertical position under his right elbow. It is characteristic of Robert-Houdin's minute attention to the *mise en scène* of a trick, that while his son sniffed at the empty bottle, his assistant, behind the scenes, poured genuine ether upon a hot shovel, so that the fumes, reaching the nostrils of the audience, might prove, indirectly but convincingly, that ether was really employed. After the retirement of Robert-Houdin from the stage, the trick fell comparatively out of notice, till it was revived in a new form by the Fakir of Oolu (Professor Sylvester) in England, and contemporaneously by De Vere on the Continent. A full-grown young lady was in this case the subject of the illusion, and was made, while still suspended in air, to assume various costumes and characters. The illusion, in this new form, took the fancy of the public, and brought forth a host of imitators; but few have presented it with the same completeness as the two performers named. For a time it produced quite a marked sensation, equal crowds thronging to see Sylvester in London, and De Vere in Paris, St. Petersburg, Brussels, Pesth, Dresden, Strasburg, and other continental cities. Recent mechanical improvements, to which the last-named Professor has materially contributed, have greatly heightened the effect of the trick—the lady being made to rise spontaneously from the perpendicular to the horizontal position, and to continue to float in the air after her last ostensible support has been removed.

FIG. 312.

Apart from these special mysteries, which we are not at liberty to reveal, the trick is as follows :—The performer brings forward the girl or boy who is to be the subject of the illusion, and who is dressed ın some fancy costume. A low bench or table, say five feet in length by two in width, and on legs about six inches in height, is brought forward, and shown to be wholly disconnected from the floor or stage.

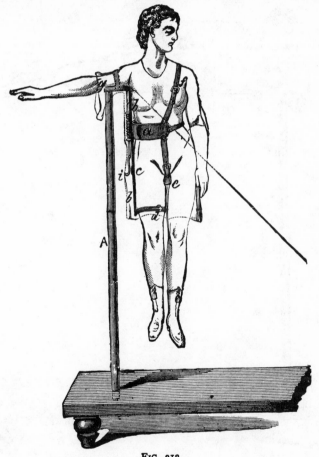

FIG. 313.

On this is placed a small stool, on which the subject of the experiment (whom, in the present instance, we will suppose to be a young lady) mounts. She extends her arms, and under each is placed a stout rod or pole of appropriate length. (*See* Fig. 312.) The performer makes pretended mesmeric passes over her, and in a minute or two her head is seen to droop, and after a few more passes her eyes close, and she is, to all external appearance, in a mesmeric sleep. The

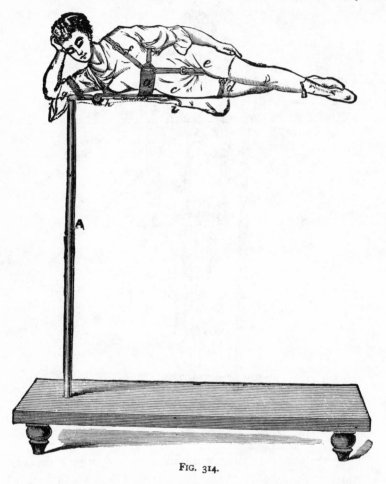

FIG. 314.

operator now takes the stool from under her feet, when she hangs suspended between the two rods. Again a few more passes, and the operator removes the rod that supports the left arm, and gently mesmerises the arm down to the side. Still the girl hangs motionless, with no other support than the single upright rod on which her right arm rests. (*See* Fig. 313.) The operator now drapes her in various costumes, still keeping up from time to time the supposed mesmeric passes. Bending her right arm so as to support her head, he next lifts her gently to an angle of 45° to the upright rod (as shown by the dotted line in Fig. 313), and finally raises her to a horizontal position, as in Fig. 314.

An inspection of the diagrams will already have furnished the clue to the mystery. Of the two upright rods, one (that placed under the

left arm) is wholly without prepara-tion, and may be freely handed for examination. The other, A, is either of iron throughout (this was the case with the pretended walking-stick used by Robert-Houdin) or of well-sea-soned wood with an iron core, and capable of bearing a very heavy weight. The lower end of this sinks into a socket in the low board or table already mentioned, and thus becomes, for the time being, a fix-ture. In the upper end is hollowed out a small space, about an inch in depth, for a purpose which will presently appear. The subject of the experiment wears, underneath her page's costume, a sort of iron corset, or framework, similar to that shown in Figs. 313 and 314, and more in detail in Fig. 315. An iron girdle, *a a*, passes nearly round the waist, the circle being completed by a

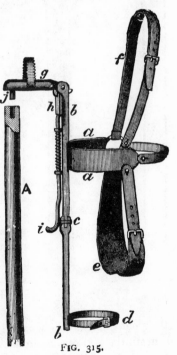

FIG. 315.

leather strap. At right angles to this, on the right side, is fixed an iron upright, *b b*, extending from just below the armpit nearly to the knee, but with a joint *c* (working backwards and forwards only) at the hip, a strap *d*, round the leg, keeping it in position, so as to allow

of bending the thigh.   From the back of the iron girdle, in the centre, proceeds a crutch *e,* also of iron, passing between the legs, and
connected by a strap to the front of the girdle.   A fourth strap *f,* connected with the girdle in front and rear, passes over the left shoulder,
and prevents any risk of the apparatus slipping downwards.   To the
upper part of the upright, *b b,* immediately below the armpit, is

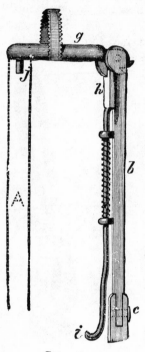

riveted a short flat piece of iron, *g,* working freely upon it.   The end of *g,* which
forms the joint shown enlarged in Fig. 316,
is welded into a semicircular ratchet, with
three teeth corresponding with a check *h,*
lying parallel with *b b,* and which, in its
normal position, is pressed up close into
the teeth of the ratchet by a spring, but
may be withdrawn by a downward pressure
on the hook *i.*   The opposite end of *g* has
projecting from its under side, at right
angles, an iron plug *j,* which just fits into
the cavity before mentioned in the top of
the rod A.   There is an opening in the
under part of the sleeve, to give passage to
this plug, which, when inserted in the
corresponding cavity of A, makes *g,* rela-
tively to it, a fixture.   The remainder of
the iron framework (and with it the lady)
remains moveable, to the extent that, by
means of the joint at *g,* it can be made to
describe an arc of 90° to the upright rod.
The mode of operation will now be
clear.   When the young lady mounts on

FIG. 316.

the stool, and extends her arms, the performer, in placing the upright
beneath them, takes care to let the lower end of A sink properly into
the socket, and to adapt the plug *j* to the cavity at top.   The apparatus is now in the position shown in Fig. 313, and when the stool
is removed, the lady is left apparently resting only on A, but in
reality comfortably seated in her iron cage, the different parts of
which are all carefully padded, so as to occasion her no discomfort.

Her legs and arms, being quite free, may be placed in any position that the performer chooses; and when presently he lifts her into a slanting position, as shown by the dotted line in Fig. 313, the check *h* drops into the second tooth of the ratchet, and thus maintains her in that position. After a short interval she is lifted into the horizontal position, as in Fig. 314, when the check drops into the third tooth of the ratchet, and so maintains her, apparently sleeping upon an aërial couch. As the support terminates above the right knee, the legs are kept extended by muscular power. This attitude is therefore very fatiguing, and for that reason cannot be continued more than a few moments. To replace the lady in the upright position, the performer places both hands under the recumbent figure, the left hand easily finding (through the tunic) and drawing down the hook *i*, thereby withdrawing the check, and allowing the lady to sink down gently to the perpendicular. The stool is again placed under her feet, and the second upright under her left arm, before the operator begins to demesmerise her, which he does after the orthodox fashion with reverse passes, the lady simulating as best she may the bewildered and half-scared expression of one newly awakened from a mesmeric trance.

CHAPTER XVIII.

Concluding Observations.

It now only remains to give the neophyte a few parting hints of general application. In getting up any trick, even the simplest, the first task of the student should be to carefully read and consider the instructions given, and to make quite certain that he perfectly comprehends their meaning. This being ascertained, the next point will be to see whether the trick involves any principle of sleight-of-hand in which he is not thoroughly proficient; and if it does, to set to work and practise diligently, till the difficulty is conquered. Having thus mastered the elements of the trick, he should next attack it as a whole, and in like manner practise, practise, practise, till from beginning to end he can work each successive step of the process with ease and finish. Having achieved thus much, he may perhaps consider that his task is at an end. By no means. Being perfect in the mechanical portion of the illusion, he must now devote himself to its dramatic element, which, as regards the effect upon the spectator, is by far the more important portion. The performer should always bear in mind that he fills the character of a person possessing supernatural powers, and should endeavour, in every word and gesture, to enter into the spirit of his part. As the true actor, playing Hamlet, will endeavour actually to *be* Hamlet for the time, so the *soi-disant* magician must, in the first place, learn to believe in himself. When he steps upon the stage he should, for the time being, persuade himself that his fictitious power is a reality, and that the wand he holds is not only the emblem, but the actual implement of his power. Every time he pronounces the mystic " Pass ! " or touches an object with his wand to effect some pretended transformation, he should force himself to forget the commonplace expedients by which the result is really attained, and to believe that the effect is produced by a genuine magical process. When he goes through the motion of passing a coin from the right hand to the left, he should have imagination enough to persuade himself, for the moment, that the coin has really been transferred as it appears to be. If a performer has sufficient imaginative faculty to do this—if he can so enter into the spirit of his part, as himself to believe in the marvels he professes, he will achieve an almost unlimited mastery over the imaginations of his audience.

As we have already intimated, each individual illusion should have its appropriate words and gestures—in technical language, its " patter," or " *boniment* "—carefully arranged and rehearsed, so as to produce the maximum of effect. These are, in truth, the very life of the trick. How much depends on *mise en scène* is forcibly illustrated by the account which we quoted in the last chapter from the life of Robert-Houdin, of his exhibition in Algeria of the " Light and Heavy Chest." We will borrow from the same high authority another illustration, purposely selecting one of the simplest of card tricks, the well-known feat of picking out a chosen card from the pack, placed in a person's pocket. The trick has already been described in outline, but we will recapitulate its effect in a few words.

The performer offers the pack to a spectator, and requests him to draw a card. (This card may or may not be " forced.") The card having been drawn and replaced in the pack, the performer makes the pass to bring it to the top, and palms it, immediately handing the pack to be shuffled. If the card was forced, he already knows it ; if not, he takes the opportunity to glance at it while the cards are being shuffled. The pack being returned, the drawn card is placed on the top, and the pack placed in the pocket of a second spectator. The performer now announces that he not only already knows the card, but that he is able to pick it out without seeing it from the remainder of the pack, which he does accordingly.

Presented in this barren form, the trick would attract only the most passing notice. We will now proceed to describe it, quoting again from Robert-Houdin, as it should actually be presented.

" Ladies and gentlemen, I shall commence my performance with an experiment which is wholly independent of dexterity. I propose simply to show you the extreme degree of sensibility which may be acquired by the sense of touch. We possess, as you all know, five senses—sight, hearing, smell, touch, and taste. In the ordinary way, each of these senses enjoys one faculty only; but when the mysterious influences of magic are brought to bear, the case is altered. All five of the senses may be exercised through the instrumentality of one— 'touch,' for example; so that we can not only touch, but hear, see, smell, and taste with the tips of the fingers. You smile, gentlemen, but I assure you that I am serious; and I venture to think that in a few minutes you will be fully convinced of the reality of the singular fact which I have mentioned.

"Here is a pack of cards. Madam, will you be kind enough to take whichever card you please; hold it for a moment between your hands, so as to impregnate it with the mesmeric influence of your touch, and then replace it in the middle of the pack.

"In order to exclude all possibility of sleight-of-hand, we will now thoroughly shuffle the cards; after which, for still greater certainty, I will show you that the card is neither at top nor bottom, whence you may be persuaded that it is placed just where chance has chosen to put it." (For the purpose of showing that the card is neither at top nor bottom, it may either be left second from the top after the shuffle, if executed by the performer himself, or being actually placed on the top, the second card may be drawn instead of the first by means of a *filage*.)

"Will some gentleman now have the kindness to empty his breast-pocket, and allow me to place the pack in it." (This is done.) "Now that the cards are placed in perfect darkness, I will endeavour, by virtue of that five-fold sensibility of touch which I have just mentioned, to discover, by the aid of my fingers only, the card which this lady drew. To make my task still more difficult, I will undertake to draw the card at such number as you yourselves may choose. What number shall it be?" (We will suppose that the reply is "Seventh.") "Seventh, be it so. Then six times in succession I must avoid taking the drawn card, and produce it on the seventh occasion only. One, two, three, four, five; six." (He exhibits six cards one by one, taking them from the bottom of the pack.) "Now to find the lady's card!

Yes, I think I have it. Before taking it out, I will read it with my little finger, which is the cleverest of the five. Yes! It is not a small card; it is not a club, nor a spade, nor yet a diamond. It is the king of ———— "' (He draws out the card, and places it face downwards.) " Will you be good enough, madam, to finish naming the card before I turn it over, and we shall see whether my little finger has been correct in its assertions." (The lady names the king of hearts, which the performer forthwith turns up.) " My little finger was right, you see. Will you be good enough, sir, to take the remainder of the cards out of your pocket, and testify that the experiment has really been performed exactly as I have stated."

The above example will show how, by the exercise of a little tact and ingenuity, a simple piece of parlour magic may be elevated to the dignity of a stage trick. The great secret is the directing of the minds of the audience into such a channel, that the *dénouement* for the moment seems to be a natural result of the causes artfully suggested by the performer. This may, to a considerable extent, be effected, as in the example above given, by the language and gesture of the performer in the individual trick ; but still more may be done by the artistic grouping of one trick with another, a comparatively simple feat being employed to prepare the minds of the spectators for the greater marvel to follow. Thus, in the recent performances of the Fakir of Oolu, the aërial suspension, which formed the staple of his programme, was pr eceded by the exhibition of a wooden rod or wand which (by means of certain projecting wire points, so minute as to be imperceptible at a very short distance), was made to defy the laws of gravity by clinging to his finger-tips in various positions without visible support. This minor illusion, being somewhat similar in effect (though wholly different as to the means employed), prepared the minds of the audience to receive the greater marvel of a living woman made to recline in mid-air. In like manner, the trick of the " Flying Money " (*see* page 172) forms an apt preparation for the introduction of the " Crystal Cash-box " (page 487). The series of tricks described under the title of the " Birth of Flowers " (page 411), affords another instance of the artistic combination of two or three different tricks in such manner as to enhance the effect of the whole; but, in truth, examples might be multiplied *ad infinitum*. In arranging an enter tainment, the performer should continually bear this principle in mind. The programme should consist not of a number of absolutely uncon-nected tricks, but of a series of ten or a dozen *groups* of tricks. As compared with each other, the groups should have as much diversity as possible; but, individually, each should consist of the same or a similar effect repeated in a more and more striking form (though pro-duced by different means), or else of a string of tricks united by some natural sequence, as in the case of the production of the two rabbits from the hat, followed by the rolling of the one into the other, and terminating with the reproduction of the vanished animal in another quarter. In order to make our meaning clearer, we subjoin a speci-men working programme, arranged on the principles we have stated.

PROGRAMME *(for performer's own use).*

1. Vanishing gloves (*page* 325). Transformed handkerchief (*page* 246). Handkerchief ultimately found in candle (*page* 249).

2. Borrowed half-crown, changed to penny, and back again (*page* 161); made to pass into centre of two oranges in succession (*page* 170). Three more half-crowns borrowed, and all four made to pass invisibly from performer's hand to goblet at a distance (*page* 200), and finally into crystal cash-box (*page* 487).

3. Shower of sweets produced from borrowed handkerchief (*page* 251), followed by bird-cages (*page* 311). Then bowls of gold-fish from shawl (*page* 371).

4. Eggs produced from mouth of assistant (*page* 329). Wizard's omelet (*page* 398). Dove wrapped in paper, and vanished (*page* 452).

5. Chosen card picked out of pack placed in a spectator's pocket (*page* 106). Chosen card caught on sword (*page* 121). The rising cards (*page* 125).

6. Borrowed watch, made to bend backwards and forwards (*page* 214). Made to strike the hour as a repeater (*page* 222). Placed in pistol, and fired at target (*page* 220).

7. The Chinese rings (*page* 401).

8. Rabbits produced from borrowed hat; one rolled into the other, and subsequently found in bran-glass (*page* 452). Multiplying balls and cannon-balls produced from hat (*page* 304).

9. Inexhaustible box (*page 391*), producing toys, reticules (*page 309*), and finally Chinese lanterns (*page 395*).

The above, with proper *mise en scène,* will be found an ample programme for a two hours' entertainment. It is hardly necessary to observe that the programme of the same entertainment for distribution among the audience would be of a very different character. This is always drawn up in the vaguest possible terms, so as not to reveal beforehand the actual effect of the different tricks. Thus the tricks in question would be described somewhat as follows ;—

PROGRAMME *(for distribution).*

1. The Enchanted Handkerchief.
2. The Flying Coins.
3. A Succession of Surprises.
4. The Fairy Omelet.
5. The Cabalistic Cards.
6. The Mesmerised Watch.
7. The Chinese Rings.
8. The Bewitched Hat.
9. The Feast of Lanterns.

Between each of the items above-mentioned, there should be an interval of one or two minutes (filled up by music), while the operator leaves the stage, and makes the necessary preparation for the next trick. It will further be found an advantage, where practicable, to divide the entertainment into two parts, with an interval of ten minutes or so between them, the curtain being let down during such interval. The few minutes' break is always acceptable to the audience (who are apt to become fatigued by too long protracted attention), and is especially valuable to the performer, as enabling him to re-arrange his *servante,* removing articles that have served their purpose, and replacing them by such as may be needed for the tricks to come. An overcrowded *servante* is a fertile source of annoyance and failure, as an article accidentally falling from it reveals the existence of a receptacle behind the table, and thereby deprives the performance of half its effect. When a re-arrangement of the *servante* between the parts of the performance is impracticable, it is well, if any tricks involving the production of articles from this quarter are included in the programme, to introduce such tricks as early as possible, so that the *servante* may be relieved of such articles, and left clear for its second use of getting rid of articles upon it. We have known a professor, performing the "flying glass of water" trick, and in placing the glass on the *servante,* knock down a cannon-ball, placed there to be introduced, later on, into a hat. That cannon-ball weighed on the professor's mind for the rest of the evening, and the performance was practically spoilt.

Having arranged his programme, and the appropriate " patter " for each group of tricks, the performer should conclude his practice by a series of three or four " dress rehearsals," with an intelligent friend to play the part of audience, and who should be invited to criticise with the utmost freedom. At these rehearsals there should be no " make believe," but each trick should be worked throughout with the same completeness in every particular with which it is afterwards to be exhibited in public. In the course of these final rehearsals the performer should tax his invention to see what amount of "incidents," or byplay, he can introduce in the course of the different tricks. Thus at the commencement of his entertainment, the trick of the " Flower in the Button-hole," or that of the " Vanishing Gloves " may be intro-duced—not professedly as an item of the programme, but as a little preliminary flourish. Again, if the performer has occasion for an egg or lemon in the course of a trick, it greatly enhances the effect, if instead of having the necessary article brought in by his assistant, he produces it himself from a lady's muff, or from the whiskers of a male spectator. These little matters, though small in themselves, tend to keep alive the attention of the audience, and to create a sort of magical atmos-phere, which will aid materially in disposing the spectators to receive with due respect the occult pretensions of the performer.

With respect to stage arrangements, the professional, performing evening after evening, with full provision of stage appliances, will quickly learn by experience how best to arrange those appliances for the purpose of his entertainment ; but the amateur, performing only occasionally, and in places not specially adapted for magical purposes, may be glad of some little practical counsel in this particular.

We will suppose, for instance, that he is called upon to give a
magical *séance* in a private drawing-room. The first point is to decide
which part of the room is to form the "stage." Having settled this,
the seats for the spectators should be arranged at the opposite end of the
room, leaving as wide a space between as can well be obtained, as many
"changes," etc., are effected during the journey from the audience
to the table, and the
longer this journey is,
the more time is avail-
able for the necessary
manipulations. At
the stage end, the
"table" will be the
principal feature, and
either behind or be-
side this, should be
placed a screen of not
less than six feet in
height, and four or
five wide, to serve as
"behind the scenes,"
and to afford the cover
necessary for the
various preparations.
Supposing a regular
screen is not avail-
able, one must be
extemporized. A large
clothes-horse, with a
curtain thrown over

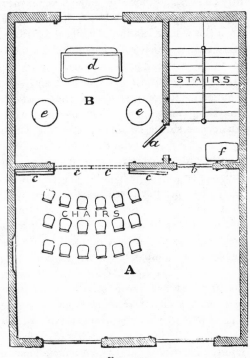

FIG. 317.

it, will answer the purpose very well. If, however, the drawing-room
be of the regular London fashion, *i.e.*, consisting of a large front and
a small back room, connected by folding doors, the screen may be
dispensed with, and the rooms arranged as in Fig. 317, which represents a ground-plan of two such rooms, with the adjoining staircase
and landing. The larger room, A, will form the auditorium, and the
smaller, B, the stage; *a* and *b* representing the doors leading to the

landing, and *c c* the folding doors between the two rooms. The folding doors (which act as curtain) being first closed, the spectators are marshalled into A, and requested to take their seats, and the door *b* is then closed, to remain so throughout the entertainment. The room B is arranged as follows :—The "table" *d* is placed in the centre, towards the back, with its *servante* properly arranged. This may either stand alone, or may be supplemented by a couple of side tables, *e e.* An ordinary table, *f,* should be placed outside the door, and upon this will be laid in due order the various pieces of apparatus and other articles which will be required in the course of the entertainment. A working programme should be kept on this table for the use of the performer and his assistant, with a note of the articles required for the purpose of each trick. This will enable them to have everything ready at the right moment, without delay or confusion. The door *a* should be kept open, so that the assistant, from his place by the table *f,* can instantly see and hear what is wanted.

When the performer has made his bow to his audience, there are still one or two little points that he will do well to bear in mind. They may be summarized as follows :—

1. *Don't be nervous.* (The reader may possibly consider that this is a matter in which he has no choice; but nothing could be a greater mistake.) A little diffidence is excusable on the first presentation of a new programme, but never afterwards.

2. *Take your time.* Deliver your *boniment* like an actor playing his part, and not like a school-boy repeating his lesson. Further, give your audience time to see and appreciate your movements. Young performers are very apt to exhibit the second phase of a transformation without having sufficiently indicated the first to the spectators. The change of, say, an orange to an apple, falls decidedly flat if nobody noticed that the article was an orange in the first instance.

3. *Don't make any parade of dexterity, and don't affect any unusual quickness in your movements.* If you are about to vanish a coin, don't play shuttlecock with it from hand to hand as a preliminary; but make the necessary "pass" as quietly and deliberately as you possibly can. Don't talk about "the quickness of the hand deceiving the eye," and still less do anything to support such an idea. The perfection of conjuring lies in the *ars artem celandi*—in sending

away the spectators persuaded that sleight-of-hand has not been employed at all, and unable to suggest *any* solution of the wonders they have seen.

4. *Don't force yourself to be funny.* If you are naturally humorous, so much the better ; but in any case perform in your natural character.

5. *Avoid personalities.* We except the case of the often recurring nuisance, the gentleman who professes to know how everything is done, and whose special endeavour it is to embarrass the performer. When you can make a person of this kind look like a fool (by no means a difficult task) by all means do so.

6. *Never plead guilty to a failure.* Keep your wits about you, and if anything goes wrong, try to save your credit by bringing the trick to some sort of a conclusion, even though it be a comparatively weak one. If you are so unfortunate as to experience a complete and unmistakeable break-down, smile cheerfully, and ascribe the *fiasco* to the moon being in a wrong quarter, to a little misunderstanding between two of your " controlling spirits," or any other burlesque reason, so long as it be sufficiently remote from the true one.

Bearing in mind these parting counsels, and thus armed against failure as well as prepared for success, you may safely ring up the curtain, and begin to " witch the world " with the marvels and mysteries of

MODERN MAGIC.

APPENDIX.

CONTAINING

EXPLANATIONS OF SOME OF THE BEST KNOWN SPECIALTIES
OF MESSRS. MASKELYNE AND COOKE.

BY

ARPREY VERE.

ANCIENT AND MODERN MAGIC.

CHAPTER I.

INTRODUCTION.

THE wonder excited by the marvellous automatons of Messrs. Maskelyne and Cooke has caused many inquiries into the art of mechanical conjuring. Although the productions of those gentleman at the Egyptian Hall have been thought by the general public to be unprecedented, we shall see that their marvels have been produced in ages long gone by, and that the art of conjuring, or producing apparently unaccountable and magical results by means of mechanism, was an art brought to great perfection hundreds of years ago, and long before '' Psycho'' astonished the metropolis.

My readers will perceive that the automatic figures of these caterers of wonders are neither original nor novel. I hope that, as the art of magic is so very popular, a brief exposition of the subject will be found interesting to many readers.

It is my intention in this and the following chapters to give a brief summary of the history of mechanical magic in ancient and modern times, and then to furnish a full explanation of how the apparently marvellous results of sleight of hand, second sight, and the mysterious movements of automata of the present day, are attained ; and my readers will no doubt reap a harvest of information on the subject, and will be able not only to perform many of the numerous tricks at which they have before been astonished, but will also be in a position to explain to the uninitiated '' How it is done.''

Passing over the ancient oracles which have been shown so frequently as being worked by the simple law of mechanics, I would merely mention that Plato and Aristotle both speak of certain statues made by Dædalus which could not only walk, but which it was necessary to bind in order to prevent them from moving.   The latter speaks of a wonderful Venus of this kind, and all we are told of the motive power is that Dædalus made it move by means of quicksilver.   Aulus Gellius mentions a wooden pigeon which possessed the power of flying, but the only fault of this piece of mechanism was that when the pigeon once settled, it could not renew its aërial flight.   Cassiodorus, who lived in the sixth century, gives a concise and graphic description of certain machines invented by Bœthius.   He says " the birds of Diomedes (a mechanician of that date) trumpet in brass, the brazen serpent hisses, counterfeit swallows chatter, and such as have no proper note send forth from brass harmonious music."   Accounts of the heads said to have been constructed by Roger Bacon and Albertus Magnus, are so mixed up with fables that we cannot rely upon their veracity ; and yet our experience has shown us that they could have been produced.   They are said not only to have moved, but spoken, and their heads were used as oracles.   Perhaps it will be remembered that some years ago a similar head, with the same power of imitating the human voice, was exhibited at the Egyptian Hall, London.

John Muller, known as Regiomontanus, was one of the cleverest mechanicians of the fifteenth century—that is, if we can rely on the testimony of Peter Ramus, who did not flourish until a hundred years afterward.   We must take Peter's account *cum grano salis.*   Regiomontanus is stated to have constructed an eagle which, upon the approach of the Emperor Maximilian to Numerberg, in June, 1470, perched upon the town gate, stretched forth its wings, and saluted him by an inclination of the body.   He is also said to have manufactured an iron fly.   At dinner one day, when surrounded by his friends, he produced it for their amusement, and caused the insect to fly from his hand, take a circle round the room, and return again to its maker. Charles V. after his abdication entered with zest into the study of mechanism.   He engaged the services of Torriano, said to be a very eminent artist, who accompanied him to the Monastery of Juste. Here they worked together.   Strada tells us that his Majesty frequently introduced puppets upon the table, some of which beat drums, some blew trumpets, others charged each other with couched spears, and with a ferocity almost human. He made wooden sparrows, which, by their flight, terrified and scared the superstitious monks, who thought him a magician and an accomplice of his infernal majesty. He is said to have made a mill which moved of itself, and which was so small that a monk could put it up his sleeve, and yet we are told that it was powerful enough to grind in a single day grain sufficient for the consumption of eight men !

Hans Bullman, a padlock-maker of Nuremberg, who lived in the middle of the sixteenth century, made figures of men and women which promenaded backward and forward, beat drums, and played upon the lute. The motive power in this case was known to be clockwork.

In the volume of " Mémoires de l'Académie des Sciences," of 1729, we find an account of a most extraordinary piece of mechanism invented by one Père Truchet, made solely for the amusement of Louis XIV. when a child. It consisted of a number of moving pictures, representing an opera in five acts, which the little figures enacted—of course, in pantomime.

Camus constructed with the same object a small carriage, drawn by two horses, which contained a little lady, with her coachman driving, and a footman and page holding on behind. When placed upon the floor of the table, the horses galloped along, and the coachman smacked his whip in quite a professional manner. When the carriage stopped, the page got down, opened the door, the lady stepped out, and with a curtsey bowed and presented a petition to the young king. She again bowed, entered the carriage, the page mounted, the coachman flogged his horses, the carriage glided on, while the footman ran behind, and at last jumped upon the box.

In 1738, there were exhibited in Paris, by M. Vaucanson, three automata, which have been reproduced in modern times : one represented a flute player in a sitting posture, which performed twelve distinct tunes ; the second was a standing figure, which discoursed harmony on a shepherd's flute, held in his left hand, while with his right he beat on a tabor ; the third was a life-size duck, which flapped its wings, quacked, drank water, ate corn, and even performed other functions of nature that made it more closely resemble its natural prototype.   Some idea may be formed of the *modus operandi* of the cornet player of Messrs. Maskelyne and Cooke, by the information afforded by Vaucanson himself, which was published in 1738, and which purports to give a full explanation of the method of working the automaton flute player.   The figure was five feet and a half high ; it was seated upon a rock, which was supported by a pedestal four feet high, by three and a half broad.   Within the pedestal were eight pair of bellows, which were set in motion by clockwork.   The wind was forced into these tubes, which ascended through its trunk, and terminated in a single reservoir connected with the cavity of the mouth. Another piece of clockwork within the pedestal was applied to execute the necessary motions of the fingers, lips, and tongue.   A revolving cylinder, with various pegs inserted in it, raised or depressed several levers, on the principle of a barrel organ ; and in this manner, it was said, music was produced very little inferior, if not equal, to the performance of a skilful flute player of flesh and blood.

One of the most ingenious inventors of mechanical figures was Mons. Maillardet, a Swiss.   He exhibited in London a beautiful figure which performed eighteen tunes on the piano, while imitating at the same time all the motions of the human player.   From a description given we learn that the bosom heaved, the eyes followed the motions of the fingers, and at the commencement and conclusion of an air the figure turned to the audience and made a graceful salute. Mons. Maillardet also constructed the figure of a boy kneeling that held in the right hand a pencil with which he executed some capital drawings and pieces of writing.

Another marvel produced by the Swiss was a magician, who answered any question put to him from twenty different medals.   The medal was placed in a drawer, and, after much cogitation and reference to his books, he, with a solemn wave of his wand, touched the drawer, which opened and displayed the required answer.

The celebrated automaton Chess Player will be well remembered. The history of this wonderful piece of mechanism is as follows : M. Wolfgang de Kempelen, a Hungarian gentleman, devoted himself from an early age to the study of mechanics.   In 1769 he paid a visit to Vienna on business of his office of Aulic Counsellor to the Royal Chamber of the domains of the Emperor of Germany in Hungary. He received an invitation from the Empress Maria Theresa to be present at certain magnetical experiments exhibited by a French gentleman of the name of Pelletier. While in conversation with the Empress during its exhibition, Mons. Kempelen asserted that he felt himself competent to construct a piece of mechanism far more surprising than those which they were witnessing. The Empress took him at his word, and bound him to keep or attempt to keep his promise. He kept it, and in six months he produced the famous Chess Player. When shown in Vienna, it caused the greatest excitement and admiration. It was the talk of society. The inventor, in spite of its success, persistently refused to exhibit it in public. He put it aside, and even took it to pieces, and for several years it was not used.

It was not until the visit of the Grand Duke Paul of Russia, and his consort, to the Court of Vienna, that the chess player was again brought to light, and exhibited by the wish of the Empress. The royal visitors were so delighted with its marvellous performance that they urged Kempelen to permit its public exhibition. He complied, and it was shown in various parts of Germany and France, and in 1785 it was brought to England. When Kempelen died, about 1803, the figure was sold by his son to Mons. Marlzel, and in 1819 that gentleman brought it again to the metropolis. That figure, exhibited some time ago in the Crystal Palace, was an improvement upon Kempelen's Chess Player.

The following is a description of the original Chess Player : The room in which it was exhibited had an inner apartment, within which appeared the figure of a Turk of the natural size, sitting behind a chest 3½ ft. 2 in. in breadth, and 2½ ft. in height. To this was attached the wooden shelf on which the figure sat. The chest was movable on casters, and could be moved to any part of the room. On its top, in the centre of the chest, was an immovable chessboard, upon which the eyes of the figure were always fixed. Its right hand and arm were extended on the chest, while the left, slightly raised, held a long pipe. Two doors in front and two doors in the back of the chest were opened, and a drawer in the bottom of it, containing the chess-men and a cushion whereon to place the arm of the automaton, was pulled out. Two smaller doors were also opened in the body of the figure, and a lighted candle was held within the openings thus displayed. This was repeated at the conclusion of the game, if the spectators so wished. The chest appeared divided by a partition into two unequal chambers, that on the right being the narrowest, and occupying one third of the whole. It was full of small wheels, and cylinders and levers. That to the left contained wheels, barrels with springs, and two quadrants placed horizontally. The door and drawer having been closed, the exhibitor wound up the works with a key inserted in a small opening in the side of the chest, placed a cushion beneath the arm of the figure, and then challenged any one of the company present to play a game with it. It was observed that in playing the automaton always selected the white pieces, and had the first move. Owing to a curious mistake of the inventor, the figure moved the men with his left hand. The error, when found out, could not afterward be rectified. Its hands and fingers opened, and then grasped a piece, which it conveyed to the proper square. In taking a piece, the same motion was made by the arm and hand as before ; it, however, conveyed the piece off the board, and then placed its own piece upon the vacant square. While and after his opponent made a move, the figure paused for a few moments as though contemplating its own. It intimated with a nod of the head when it gave check to the king. During the time the arm was in motion, a low sound of clockwork running down was distinctly heard. The works were wound up at intervals by the exhibitor, who otherwise did nothing but walk up and down the room. As we find that the automaton both lost and won—in Kempelen's time it very seldom lost—and that each game was different to the others, it necessarily follows that these phenomena are inconsistent with the sole effects of mechanism. Various conjectures have been offered as to the mode of communication between the figure and the intelligence which directed it. A plausible and probable explanation was given in 1821 in a pamphlet called, '' An Attempt to Analyze the Autom- aton Chess Player.'' In this brochure it is shown that in spite of the apparent display of the interior of the chest and the figure, there yet was ample space left unopened for the concealment of a person of ordinary size behind a false back to the narrowest division only. This is shown in the accompanying illustrations.

The basis for this elucidation of what was a profound mystery to the many was as follows :

The machinery was ostentatiously displayed when at rest ; but carefully secluded from view while in motion. By this means the spectator could not form any judgment as to whether the machinery was in any way connected with the automaton. There never was any variation in the method of opening the several doors. When winding up the clockwork, the key always made a certain number of revolutions, whether the motions of the figure, owing to the exigencies of the game, were more varied or protracted than usual. It was noticed that sixty-three moves were at one time made without the machinery being wound up, while at another time the machinery was wound up with the intervention of a single move. Whether or not the action of the automaton was produced by the agency of a concealed person I do not care to pronounce, but the illustration given proves clearly, I think, that it might have been so produced. Mons. Kempelen is said to have invented a still more extraordinary exhibition of his great mechanical genius—namely, a speaking automaton. How this figure became possessed of a voice, I will show in another chapter.

CHAPTER II.

KEMPELEN.

KEMPELEN'S Speaking Machine has been thus described.   It was of simple structure, and consisted only of five parts—viz., the reed, representing the human glottis ; an air-chest, with internal valves ; the bellows or lungs ; a mouth with its appurtenances, and nostrils formed to resemble those of the human body.   The reed was not cylindrical, but formed to imitate the reed of a bagpipe drone.   The hollow portion, however, was square, and the tongue of the reed, which vibrated, consisted of a thin ivory slip resting upon it horizontally.   This hollow tube was inserted into the chest, and the discharge of air occasioning a vibration of the ivory, the requisite sound was produced.   To soften its vibration, the part supporting the slip was covered with leather, and a movable spring shifting along the upper side of the slip brought the sound of the reed to the proper pitch.   The sound was more acute as the spring was moved forward to the outer extremity, because the vibrations then became quicker, and when shifted farther from the anterior extremity, the sound became more grave, as the vibrations were then slower.   A slight curvature of the ivory slip arose from the pressure of the spring, which was enough for the object desired.   One end of the air-chest, which was of an oblong figure, received this voice-pipe, containing the reed ; and into the opposite end was inserted the mouth of the bellows. Both the apertures were guarded by leather, to prevent unnecessary waste of air : two smaller air-chests were then put into it, each having a valve above closed by the pressure of a spring, and each having a round aperture adapted to receive through the side of the large air-chest a tin funnel, and a round wooden tube for producing hissing sounds—as *s, z, sch, j.* The voice-pipe was placed in the large air-chest, so as to be between the smaller air-chests. When all these parts were fitted to the air-chest, the operation of one lever raising the valve of the first smaller chest connected with the tin funnel produced the sound *s ;* while the operation of another, raising the valve of the second smaller chest connected with the wooden tube, produced the sound of *sch.* But it is proper further to explain that instead of being a simple funnel, it was, in fact, a tin box, with a square hole in the outer end, nearly covered by a slip of pasteboard ; and the wooden tube was merely the mouth- piece of a common flute, closed at the lower extremity, and with the air-hole modified and contracted : the letter *r* was produced by the rapid vibration of the ivory slip, owing to a strong discharge of air.

Mons. Kempelen's bellows, which were formed to supply the place of lungs, had no peculiarities. He found that his machine required six times the quantity of air used by a man in speaking. The muzzle, as I have observed, was inserted into the large air-chest, and the air which it discharged was also received by the small air-chest. With regard to the mouth, it consisted of a funnel, or rather bell-shaped piece of elastic gum, applied to the air-chest, and so adapted that the sound of the reed issued from it. Elastic gum was selected for this purpose as more nearly approaching to the natural softness and flexibility of the human organs. Independent of its communications with the reed producing the sound required, a tin tube connected it with the air-chest, by means of which it might be kept constantly full of air. This Mons. Kempelen considered a very essential, and even an indispensable part of the machine. Besides these there were small additional bellows, for the purpose of aiding the production of such sounds as *p, k, t,* which needed a greater emission of air. The nose consisted of two tin tubes, communicating with the mouth. When the mouth-piece was closed, and both tubes remained open, a perfect *m* was heard ; when one was closed, but the other open, *n* was sounded. By the combined means of all these contrivances Mons. Kempelen could make his figure repeat such sentences as *Vous êtes mon ami, Je vous aime,* etc. Upon Kempelen's machinery all succeeding talking figures have been based.

The most noted person who succeeded Kempelen in the art of magical automata was Robert Houdin.   He not only improved upon the production of his predecessors, but applied the basis of their materials to works comparatively original and unique.   His automata certainly place him in the highest rank of modern illusionists, and in giving in detail the principal of his inventions, I shall at the same time be affording a solution of the working of many surprising and ingenious automatic tricks, which have been exhibited in recent days.   One of his best productions was a Talking Figure, similar, but in many respects far superior, to that of Kempelen, the mechanism of which I have described above.

It has been asserted that Houdin first turned his attention to the construction of automata through the following trivial circumstance :

Being in company one day with a travelling showman, his assistance was asked to repair one of the figures the showman had accidentally broken.   Having seen the performance of the figure, which was none other than the well-known Dancing Harlequin, he was struck with the marvellous and apparently magical effects which could be produced by the simplest laws of mechanism.   He became so infatuated with the discovery the showman permitted him to make in the construction of the box and figure, that he, from that time, devoted all his thoughts and energies to the construction of automata.

The magic harlequin is worth description, not only because it takes so prominent a place among mechanical figures, but more because, in disclosing its mechanism, I shall be explaining the construction of a whole class of automata, which have been constructed on the same principle.   As will be seen by the illustration given above, a box was placed upon a table, and at word of command the box opened and a harlequin was discovered therein.   At a sign from the conjurer the figure leaped from the box, and then, apparently without being attached in any way to the box, it performed a variety of movements, imitating the action of the human pantomimist.   It further smoked a pipe or cigar, and blew a whistle.

Such was the figure which opened the eyes of Houdin to the marrels which the application of the simple laws of mechanics might produce ; and his great mechanical genius enabled him to succeed even better than he hoped when first he began his investigations of the automata that had already been exhibited.

The mechanism of the Magic Harlequin is extremely simple ; in fact, it will be found that the most marvellous and astounding effects are produced by the simplest contrivances. The box containing the figure was grooved in the back in nine places, each groove terminating in a hole pierced through the bottom of the box. Corresponding exactly with these holes were nine holes in the table upon which the figure performed. Below these holes at the back of the table, which

was always placed close up to the curtains at the back of the stage, and behind which the person who manœuvred the figure was concealed, were nine spring pistons worked by nine different strings passing over pulleys, each of which performed a different function, and were attached to that point in the figure which each was designed to move.

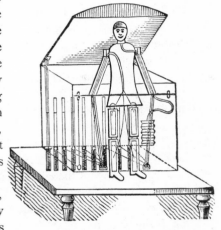

The figure of the harlequin, as the reader will perceive by the annexed illustration, was attached by means of two rods to a revolving bar fixed from side to side of the box, and so near the front that it was concealed from the eyes of the audience. When the harlequin was out of the box, the rods connecting it with the bar were hidden by the drapery of the figure. The first string worked the opening and shutting of the lid of the box. The second string, passing under a pulley immediately beneath the bar, passed over the shoulders of the figure, and by a sharp movement turned the bar and jerked the figure—which was reversed when in the box—out on to the table, the figure, of course, maintaining a standing posture, and being held up by means of the rods attached to the revolving bar. The shoulders were made to revolve on the two rods, so that the jerking motion would be easily produced. The third string passed through the body, and was attached to the legs, and produced a motion to imitate the stretching of the legs, known as the "splits." Another string closed the legs and simultaneously turned the head right and left. Another string lifted the legs and imitated the movements of a dance. Another string turned the figure back again into the box. In the corner of the box was a bellows, through the medium of which, and by means of a tube passing through the arm, and ending in the mouth, the concealed person, by manipulating the nine pistons which worked the bellows, was enabled to produce the effects of smoking and whistling.

It is upon this system of mechanism that very many modern tricks have been based—notably, the great rope acrobatic figure of Theodin. In this case, what was thought by the audience to be a rope was really a tube made to imitate a rope, and the strings passed through this tube and worked from the side of the stage, the rope serving the same purpose as the bar stretched across the box in the harlequin automaton.

Houdin was said to be the inventor of the well-known Magic Clock. This was a glass dial plate with hands, but with no visible works. This clever invention has within the last year or two been reproduced, and exhibited in many jewelers' windows. His chief automatic figures, besides the talking one I have already mentioned, were two performing French Clowns and the Cook of the Palais Royal. The clowns were shown one sitting on a chair, and the other standing beside it. At the request of the exhibitor, the standing clown raised the chair, with its occupant, above his head, while the latter went through a number of acrobatic performances that would have done honor to a living gymnast.

These capital figures were worked precisely on the same system as the Magic Harlequin, the strings, pistons, and machinery being necessarily of stronger make, and worked from beneath, instead of behind the stage. This was considered by the public, and Houdin himself looked upon it, as his *chef d'œuvre*, and a masterpiece in automatic figures it certainly was.

The Cook of the Palais Royal was a very amusing piece of mechanical application. It consisted of a faithful representation of a detached villa.   Houdin handed round a list of wines and liquors, requesting his audience to select **whic**h they liked best on the bill of

When one was mentioned, a figure of a young maid emerged from the doorway, descended the steps, and brought forward on a tray a glass of the desired wine.   When the person at whose order the wine was brought removed the glass from the tray, the figure turned and glided back into the house, again emerging with another glass of wine, and so on until the list was exhausted or the bibulous propensities of the audience were fully satisfied.

The same basis of machinery used in the Magic Harlequin was also employed in the Cook of the Palais Royal, each piston working a tap containing one kind of wine.   The operator at the back of the stage could hear the wine asked for, and thus knew which string to pull, and which tap to open, when the figure, which was made to pass under every tap, re-entered the house.

Houdin's Orange Tree was a capital trick, and, although exceedingly simple in its mechanism, produced the most startling effects. Houdin borrowed a handkerchief, which he burnt, or rather which he led the audience to think he burnt, at the sacrifice of a duplicate, in front of a plant placed in a box upon a table, which, at word of command, gradually began to bloom.   White blossoms were seen to emerge from four or five different shoots.   These disappeared, giving place to oranges, which Houdin removed from the tree and distributed among his audience, with the exception of one, which he left on.   This one opened, and out from it sprang two butterflies, and in the middle of the orange was found the burnt handkerchief.

In this trick also the spring pistons of the Magic Harlequin were used.   The real oranges were fixed on pins and hidden by the leaves.   A string or wire opened the leaves, gradually disclosing the oranges, which appeared at a distance to grow in size as the leaves spread wider.   Another set of wires, worked by another string, pushed the blossoms up fine tubes, and as the paper emerged from the tube the separate parts spread out, giving the appearance of growing blossoms.   As soon as the two halves of the sham orange in the centre were released, the butterflies, attached by wires to the stalk, and fixed upon delicate spiral springs, sprang out of their own accord, and presented the appearance of fluttering on the wing. The *bona fide* handkerchief was pushed into the halves of the orange through a hole in the back while Houdin was taking off the real oranges. A rose-tree, similar in its effects, was also exhibited by Houdin.

This clever mechanician was, I believe, the inventor of the Electric Bell, or, to be more precise, he produced it as a magical trick, long before the electric bell came into use.

The Magic Drum, swung from the ceiling by means of wires looking like cords, of which Houdin was the first exhibitor, was con-

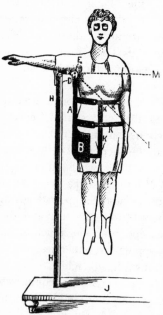

structed on precisely the same principles as the modern continuous electric bell, only worked with a much stronger battery and a more powerfully made electro-magnet.

Mr. Houdin was the first person to introduce the famous " Suspension in the Air" trick, centuries ago made so famous by the Fakir of Oolu, performed by the Hindoos. The lady selected for the trick is generally slight in figure. Previous to coming on the stage she binds close to her body a framework specially made to fit her. This frame consists of an iron bar, with front and back plate fitting on the hip by means of straps fastened round the body. The iron bar reaches as far as the armpit, where it is joined to another bar reaching from the armpit to the elbow by a movable circular plate indented in three places. At the end of the arm bar and immediately below the elbow is a pin of iron, which is made to fit into the hollow iron bar upon which the exhibitor rests the lady. At the top of the body bar is a spring stop, made to glide into the indentations of the movable circular hinge, and thus keep the whole framework in the position it is placed. The annexed illustration will more clearly show this single piece of machinery.

A is the iron bar, and B the hip plate. D is a spring stop fitting into the teeth of the joint F. F is the arm bar, and G is the pin fitting into the hollow tube H, which is fixed into a socket in the platform. The frame is fastened to the body by means of the leather straps K. When the body is raised to the position of L, the spring stop D slips into the middle indentation, and thus keeps the frame and the lady borne upon the frame in that position. When the body is raised to a horizontal position, M, the spring stop catches in the first indentation, and keeps the body perfectly straight. In commencing the trick the performer rests the figure upon two poles and then knocks one away. This is done to make the audience believe that the two poles are similar. I need scarcely say that the putting of the lady into a mesmeric trance is only a piece of acting ; it, however, adds very much to the effect of the trick, as the reader no doubt has thought up till now. It will be remembered, notably in the case of the Fakir of Oolu, that sometimes when the trick was performed *both* poles were taken away. What, then, you will ask, becomes of all my machinery ? The two poles were *seemingly* taken away. The poles used consisted of brass bars. The limelight beamed upon the figure of the sleeping lady, while the rest of the stage was comparatively dark. Thus, when the conjuror apparently took away the only support the figure had, the audience did not and could not perceive that he really took away the brass *case* of the second pole, leaving another, the actual pole on which the framework was fixed, and which was of the same color as the drapery of the stage. It was for the purpose of deceiving the eyes of the audience that the pole was encased in a *brass* shell in the first instance. He refixed the case before the stage was relit, and the lady woke up from her sham mesmeric trance.

CHAPTER III.

THEODIN.

CONTEMPORARY with Houdin were Theodin, Robin, Professor Anderson, and a whole host of minor stars, at whom I shall just take a passing glance, and then I will enter at once into the subject of modern automata, second sight or clairvoyance, optical illusions, and the other branches of the art of magic and conjuring. The principal production of Mons. Theodin was the rope acrobat, which I have fully explained in a preceding chapter. Mons. Robin also exhibited a very ingenious and interesting piece of automata, well known as the Magic Windmill. Upon a table a large-sized windmill was placed. The exhibitor tapped at the door, when the miller's head was seen at the window for a moment, as if he desired to know who was knocking, and then a few seconds after the door opened, and the miller appeared in full person, candle in hand and pipe in mouth.

Mons. Robin desired the miller to kindly grind a small sack of corn which he gave him ; the miller nodded assent, took the corn and entered the mill, the door closing upon him. Shortly afterward the sails of the mill went gaily round, and after a brief interval the miller opened his door and handed Mons. Robin the sack back, with the ground bran and corn mixed. This he was desired to separate, when he again entered the mill, and after a brief interval returned with the task duly performed. The door of the mill being closed, and the miller supposed to have retired to bed after his labors, Mons. Robin selected five cards, or, rather, made his audience believe *they* selected them ; he tore them up, and loaded a pistol with the pieces. He then fired at the windmill, when *lo ! presto !* one of the torn cards was perceived upon each sail of the mill, and one upon the door ! But this was not all. The firing of the pistol set the mill on fire, and the blaze was seen emerging from the top. I need scarcely say that Mons. Robin's Windmill was highly successful. The whole of the effects obtained by this clever conjuror from this one piece of automata was caused by precisely the same means as those of the magic Harlequin and the Cook of the Palais Royal. The same system of levers, valves, and pulleys was employed, and the whole was worked by a person off the stage.

The only automaton of Professor Anderson was, compared with that of his predecessors, extremely weak, and scarcely deserving of notice. It consisted of an old man, who nodded, shook his head, and raised his arm to ring a bell. The reader of these articles will know exactly how this was done. The head was worked beneath the stage ; one string causing the head to nod, another to turn from side to side, and a third raising its arm and letting its hand fall upon a bell. By these three simple movements it answered various questions put to it.

Before proceeding further, I may as well state that I have necessarily passed by a large number of automata which were exhibited by numerous other professors of the " black art " whom I have not even named. This was absolutely unavoidable, inasmuch as the space and time that would be required to give a full history of automatic conjuring is not at my disposal. But I have endeavored to give the principal wonders of mechanical art as applied to conjuring, those which I have omitted to mention being weak imitations of the great masterpieces, and therefore of no note. But, following up the sequence of events in the history of conjuring, I must make mention of Colonel Stodare's Living Head, especially as this will open up quite a new subject. Stodare placed upon a table, supported by legs, and beneath which the audience apparently saw the back of the stage, an empty box with folding doors in front. Having closed the doors of the box for a few minutes, he reopened them, when a living head, dressed to represent the head of a sphinx, was seen within the box. To all appearance there could not possibly be any connection of that head with a body. There was the head in a box of such a size as only to be capable of admitting a head. The audience saw that the body could not be placed beneath the table, for they perceived the curtains at the back of the stage, between the legs, while the table itself was at some distance from the curtains at the back, and the space between could plainly be seen.   The audience, however, could *not* see through the legs of the table, but what they saw was a reflection of the sides of the stage, which were made to correspond exactly with the back.   This was effected by means of two plate-glass mirrors, fixed so as to closely fit into the space between the three legs facing the audience.   The floor was covered with green baize, which was reflected in the glasses, and seemed to be a continuation of the floor.

The living body belonging to the animate head was in reality beneath the table, concealed from view by the mirrors.   The annexed illustration will show the position of the body during the performance.

In order that the reader may more clearly understand how this great optical illusion was produced, I will give a full explanation of an improvement upon this apparently wonderful phenomenon—the Fatima illusion— when the reader will more clearly comprehend the solution of what must have hitherto been to him or her a profound mystery.   But before doing so I may mention that simultaneously with the appearance of Colonel Stodare's Talking Head there was produced by Messrs. Pepper and Tobin an optical illusion founded upon precisely the same mechanical arrangement.   It was called "Proteus ; or, We're here and not here."   A cabinet 3 ft. 6 in. wide by 6 ft. high, standing upon four small feet so that the audience could see beneath it, was brought upon the stage.   It was then opened, and inside was seen a pillar in the centre from floor to top, on the point of which was hung a lamp. The cabinet was seen to be empty.   A person entered it, closing the door after him.   In a few seconds, when the door was reopened, it was found to be empty.   This was repeated with three different persons. A fourth went in, and on the door being opened the four persons were seen inside, and emerged from the cabinet. Of course, where these men concealed themselves was the cause of a great deal of surmise and conjecture ; but the reader who has seen this trick, after I have explained the mystery, will marvel at the ease with which he was deceived and hoodwinked.

From the preceding ground plan of the cabinet, it will at once be seen by the simple laws of optics how our very eyes may be made to cheat the other senses : A B, C D, is the floor plan of the cabinet. A B, B D, D C, and C A, representing the four sides. E is the pillar from floor to roof. Attached to the sides A C and B D, are two plate-glass sides fitting exactly, so as to form two sides to the cabinet, A E, B E, terminating in the pillar E. These plate glasses are movable on hinges in the direction indicated by the arrows, and could be moved close to the sides of the cabinet. The backs of the plate-glass doors are painted or papered to resemble exactly the sides of the cabinet, so that when closed the plate-glass sides appear to be *bona fide* sides of the cabinet. Thus, when a man stepped into the

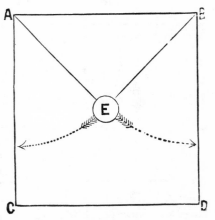

cabinet he merely opened the plate-glass sides, and stood behind them when the cabinet was opened. The glass reflecting the sides of the cabinet, which were exactly like the back, made it appear that the box was empty, the lamp being so placed that it was not reflected by the glass sides. From this it will be seen that as many persons as the space inclosed by the folding glass sides could hold, might easily enter the cabinet, and yet not seem to be in it.

This and the Living Head of Stodare were such good optical illusions, and so safe for the exhibitor to work upon, that succeeding conjurors have improved upon the trick, and produced one of the prettiest and most marvellous effects, that of a lady being seen on the table, without any lower limbs whatever, and yet able to talk and sing. No doubt many of my readers will remember to have seen Fatima when exhibited some little time ago in Lime Street, Liverpool. A description of this optical illusion, as seen by the public, will be scarcely necessary.

It will be remembered that to all appearance a half body was resting upon a small table standing on legs, which again rested upon a larger table likewise upon four legs, and that the space beneath the table was seen. In point of fact, the space beneath the table was *not* seen, for the remaining portion of the visible body actually stood in the space beneath the table. The table was really upon three legs placed at right angles. Between the middle and two other legs were two plate-glass mirrors, fitted closely to the legs and the top of the

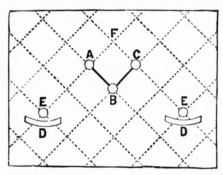

table. The pattern of the carpet was always of a square character, and the table was so placed that the reflection in the glass formed a continuation of the pattern, thus giving an appearance of space and a continuity of surroundings. The fourth leg of the table was produced by a very simple contrivance. A single leg, carved similarly to the legs of the table, was concealed behind each of the small screens which bore a lamp, and on each leg was a placard bearing the letters composing the name of Fatima, but written thus—AMITAF, so that, as seen in the glass, they appeared FATIMA. These legs were so placed that they threw their reflections in such a way as to continue and form one leg, the fourth leg of the table. The ground plan, as given here, will at once show the position of the table and the separate legs.

A B C are the three legs of table, A B and B C being the two plates of glass. D D are the two screens concealing the single legs E E. According to the laws of reflection the legs E E will be reflected in the point F, and thus present the appearance of four legs. Upon each of the legs is placed the placard bearing the name written backward, and the reflection so deceives the spectator that he fully believes he is looking at a fourth substantial leg. Of course the upper table upon which the visible portion of the body appears to rest is likewise made of three legs with looking-glass in between. The invisible portion of the body is concealed by the looking-glasses. The pattern of the floorcloth being of a cubic shape, the reflection in the glasses seems to be a continuation of the pattern. It was by these simple combinations of mechanics and optical contrivances that thousands upon thousands of persons were mystified and completely cheated of their senses.

CHAPTER IV.

AUTOMATA : PSYCHO.

WE now come to our own time, and to a description of the various automatic exhibitions of the present day. The most notable and successful, because the most original, exhibitors and inventors of automatic figures at the present day are Messrs. Maskelyne and Cooke, now located at that old "home of mystery," the Egyptian Hall, London.

Their first and, in my opinion, their best piece of mechanism was Psycho, the celebrated Whist Player, which they produced in 1865. A description of this interesting figure is scarcely needed. For years they contrived to keep the motive power and mechanical arrangements of this automaton an entire secret, while the public, the press, and the scientific world, saw, wondered, and were puzzled. Many and various were the solutions offered to account for the working of the Whist Player ; but the secret of the sinews and muscles, so to speak, of Psycho mystified every one. So thoroughly successful was the figure that, as a natural consequence, mechanicians set about producing something similar.

One of these imitations was exhibited under the name of Hankey. This was but a poor and clumsy representation of the original. It consisted of a rudely-constructed figure of a man seated on an octagonally shaped box, in which a boy was concealed, who worked the arms and head. The exhibitor was compelled to indicate the cards to be played by certain signs and motions, which often led to complications and mistakes. This revival of Psycho eventually came into the possession of Signor Boz, and was exhibited in Liverpool and various other towns under the new name of Yorick.

Professor Pepper likewise constructed an imitation of Psycho, under the *nom de théâtre* of Scynthia. This figure, though very ingeniously contrived, did not confessedly fulfil all the conditions of Psycho.

Cremer also introduced a whist player, which was a huge, complicated mass of wheels, levers, and elaborate mechanical contrivances, and necessitated a most careful supervision for a successful exhibition. It could never be relied on for a smooth and uninterrupted performance.

A French firm also constructed a whist player for Mr. Everett, and this eventually went to America. In this figure the boy was much better concealed than in the one I mentioned before.

One very ingenious solution of the construction of Psycho was offered in November, 1877. I partly reproduce it—not because it is a solution, but because it will enable the practical and ingenious reader to construct a figure something similar, although not at all equal, to the Whist Player of Messrs. Maskelyne and Cooke.

In Figs. 1*a* and 1*b* (elevation and plan), the wheels E and M have each a train of clock-

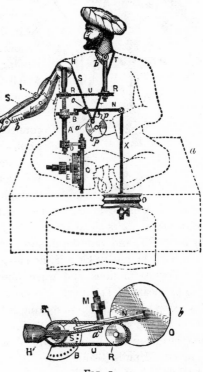

FIG. 1.

work (left out for the sake of clearness), which would cause them to spin round if unchecked. M, however, has two pins, *p p*, which catch on a projection on the lever, N. E is a crown-wheel escapement—like that in a bottle roasting-jack—which turns A alternately to the left and right, thus causing the hand to traverse the thirteen cards. A little higher up on A will be seen a quadrant, B (see plan), near the edge of which are set thirteen little pins. The end of the lever, N, drops between any two of them, thus causing the hand to stop at any desired card. The lever being pivoted at *c*, it is obvious that by depressing the end, N, B will be set at liberty, and the hand will move along the cards ; by slightly raising it this motion will be

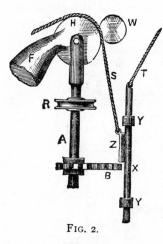

arrested ; by raising it still more the pin, *p*, is released, and M commences to revolve, and by again depressing N this wheel will, in its turn, be stopped. Near the bottom of the apparatus is a bellows, O, which contains a spring tending to keep the lever, N, with which it is connected by a rod, X, in the position shown. This is connected with the tubular support, which may be connected by a tube through leg of stool, and another tube beneath stage, with an assistant behind the scenes. By compressing or exhausting air through this tube it is obvious that the

FIG. 2.

lever, N, will be raised or depressed, and the clockwork set going accordingly. *a* is a crank-pin set in M, and connected with the head by catgut, T, and with the thumb by S. At R and R are two pulleys connected by gut. Thus if the hand moves round, the head appears to follow its motions, and when raised by pulling S, the head rises also by means of T. Further explanation seems almost unnecessary ; *l* is a stop to prevent elbow moving too far, and *b b* spiral springs, to keep thumb open and head forward respectively. When N is raised, M pulls T and S, the latter closing thumb, and then raising arm by pulley H. If the lever is allowed to drop, *p* will catch and keep arm up. On again raising N, the arm will descend.

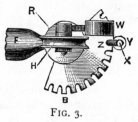

FIG. 3.

In addition to the above contrivance, we have in Figs. 2 and 3 another and simpler arrangement, in which only one train of clockwork is used. On the same axle as H is fixed a lever and weight, W, to balance the arm. A vertical rod, X, having a projection, Z, slides up and down in guides, Y Y, and carries the catgut, S and T. The quadrant, B, has cogs cut, between which Z slides and stops the motion of A, which is moved, as before, by clockwork. The lower part of X is connected direct with O. When X is slightly raised, as shown, A is free to move, but on exhausting air and drawing X down, Z enters the cogs and stops the hand over a card ; continuing to ex-

FIG. 4.

haust, the thumb closes and the card is lifted up. The details of the clockwork the origi- nator of this solution omits to give. He says there should be a fan on each train to regulate the speed. The figure should be so placed that an assistant can see the cards in the semi-circular rack Fig. 4.

The next remarkable automatic figure exhibited by the dual mysti- fiers at the Egyptian Hall is that called Zoe. It represents a female figure seated upon a stand. Before her is placed a semicircular drawing board, which is attached to the seat upon which the figure rests. Zoe writes figures and draws portraits of popular characters. To all appearance there is no motive power off the stage, and the exhibitor has no physical connection with the figure, whose movements and skill are apparently spontaneous. This is one of the most simple mechanical contrivances of the kind that has ever been produced. A thin steel rod runs through the seat in which the figure is fixed. The body and the arms of Zoe are above the stage, beneath which another arm and drawing-board are placed exactly in the same position as those above the platform. The mechanism is made to work so that the hand above is moved precisely as the hand below is guided by the artist. Thus, when Zoe is told to draw a portrait, say, of the Earl of Beaconsfield, the artist below guides the unseen

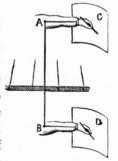

hand, while the hand above follows the movements of its guide below. The reader may see from the annexed plan at a glance the principles of the movement ; but it must be understood that this is not the only mechanism employed. It will, however, fully explain the principles of its motion.

It will be seen that whatever movement be given to the arm at B.

the arm at A must have the same movement simultaneously.   As the figure is brought on to the stage, and then fixed on to the seat, all suspicion of complicity with persons below the stage is removed ; but a rod is pushed through the pedestal and secured through the upper half while the exhibitor is seating the figure.

Another, and I think the latest production of note—no pun is here intended—brought before the public by Messrs. Maskelyne and Cooke is Fanfare, the cornet player.   This is the figure of a gentleman dressed in modern costume, holding in his hand a cornet, which he places to his mouth and plays in the most professional manner.   The whole performance of this mechanical marvel, however bewildering it may appear to the observer, consists of nothing more or less than remarkable clever "lipping" on the part of a living musician, who really plays the instrument in the lonely solitude of the regions beneath the stage.   The sound emitted from a brass instrument is altered in tone and pitch, according to the length and breadth of the tubes through which the wind is blown.   For a bass tone wide and long tubes must be used, while for a treble tone much shorter and narrower tubes must be employed.   The principles of construction are exactly similar in the cornet as in the euphonium and saxehorn, the difference of tone being produced merely by the different dimensions of the tubes.   The direction of the tubes—that is, whether they be twisted or straight, or in different folds—makes very slight, if any, difference in the tone of the instrument.   A cornet could be so constructed as to admit a much longer and straighter tube immediately in front of the piston tubes, and still have the tone of an ordinary cornet.   It must have been this principle which first suggested to the minds of Messrs. Maskelyne and Cooke the construction of an automaton cornet player.   The extra long tube of which I have made mention passes through the body of the figure into its mouth, where it meets the mouth of the cornet when it is placed against the lips.   This tube is passed through one of the legs of the chair on which the cornet player is seated, and thence beneath the stage, where a living cornet player manipulates the instrument in the hands of the figure by means of three strings or wires attached to the fingers of the figure.   Thus while he is blowing through the tube he has the string of the first piston on his forefinger, that of the middle piston on the middle finger, and that of the third piston on the third finger. As he mouths his instrument he moves his fingers in precisely the same manner as he would had he an instrument instead of only a tube to play upon ; and as he moves his fingers so he pulls the wires joined to the three fingers of the figure, and thus produces the change of notes which the exigencies of the tune require.

CHAPTER V.

MARIONETTES.

IN perusing these articles the reader must have observed, ere this, that a great deal of the success of mechanical, and, in fact, all kinds of conjuring,· consists as much in the credulity and ignorance of the audience as in the perfection of the trick itself.

It is not at all surprising that, centuries ago, the performer of a few juggling tricks, or the man slightly in advance of his age in science, should have been looked upon by the vulgar crowd as a person having dealings with another world, and that his Infernal Majesty himself should have been called in to father all his supernatural tricks and wonders. Happily we have reached an age when enlightenment has driven superstition almost entirely away ; and while we marvel and wonder at the cleverness of such men as Maskelyne and Cooke, Dr. Lynn, and many others, even the most ignorant of persons would never think that these gentlemen had any diabolical contract with such an uncanny gentleman as Mephistopheles. I make these remarks because the tricks I shall shortly describe have been performed, perhaps in a slightly different manner to what they are now, centuries ago, in the distant ages of Egyptian might, the earlier days of the Hindoos, and long before civilization had reached the west of Europe.

A venerable and oft-repeated magical delusion is that of dismembering a living person. Dr. Lynn relies upon this worn-out pantomime trick for the staple of his performance ; but it must be confessed that his method of manipulation and neatness of execution saves, what would be in a clumsy person's hand, a very sorry exhibition.

A man is brought upon the stage, and is told that his limbs are going to be amputated. The victim makes a rush behind the curtains, no doubt frightened that the threat would be duly executed, but is brought out and made to stand still while the exhibitor coolly cuts off an arm and then a leg. The frightened, trembling subject of the professor's carving operations is an assistant, who takes good care to be the first on the stage when a person among the audience is requested to step up and be carved. When he rushes off behind the curtains, it is to affix to one shoulder and thigh a dummy arm and leg, while his real limbs remain behind the curtains reclining upon rests. So quickly is this done that the audience cannot but believe that the arm and leg are the real flesh and blood contingents to the human frame. The professor carefully amputates the false arm and leg. Of course he can as readily replace the limbs by simply gliding the false limbs through the curtains, and releasing the *bona fide* leg and arm from their constrained and awkward position.

Another exhibition offered by Dr. Lynn to his patrons is that known as the Living Marionettes. This novel and amusing illusion was first introduced by a Frenchman, and was shown in the metropolis long before the British public had heard of Dr. Lynn, and before he brought it out as a novelty at the London Aquarium. On a small stage, a real living head, attached to a miniature body, sings, talks, and acts ; and it is plainly evident to the audience that while the head is really a human one, the manikin body is but a toy. Apparently the curious figures are not connected by any means with anybody, either at the back, sides, or beneath the stage. It will be noticed that the drapery is entirely of black, and that the eye is deceived, by the absence of any break in the color of the drapery, as to distance. The person appearing as the Living Marionette, fixes beneath his chin the framework of the body. The back drapery is so arranged that he brings on the stage with him the curtains forming the background to his head, while with wires fixed to the legs and arms, he produces a motion in the toy, giving it the appearance of walking on the stage ; so that while the Living Marionette is in the centre of the stage, the body of the man is behind it. Thus there are two backgrounds to the stage—one of black, fixed ; the other also of black brought on with the head ; but being black, is not seen by the audience, who imagine the head passes before the black curtain. Any number of heads can be shown, and two could perform at the same time by coming on the stage from each side, with each half a curtain or background fixed to their heads. The annexed illustration will show the head, to which is fixed a movable black frame, and the position of the real and the dummy body. There is sufficient space between the extremity of the stage and the fixed curtain at the back for the performer to stand and pass along. As I said before, the arms and legs of the toy are worked by means of wires passed through the counterfeit curtain. A very pleasing and startling entertainment may be obtained if the persons selected to perform are vocalists and comedians.

CHAPTER VI.

CLAIRVOYANCE.

IT is surprising with what avidity our forefathers, when they perceived some effect arising from an unknown cause, flew to the aid of *diablerie* and the supernatural for an elucidation of the mystery. Without seeking at once to work out a cause from the known laws of nature and natural phenomena, they stopped all pursuit in the paths of inquiry by at once bringing forward his Satanic Majesty as the cause of everything and every occurrence for the origin of which they could not give an immediate explanation.

We have happily reached an age which is distinguished for its matter of-fact treatment of all that appears mysterious and unusual. Thus we have, by our rigid inquiries into the truth, banished, or almost banished, those dread preventives of progress and civilization —superstition, and belief in the supernatural.

But even at the present day, with all its enlightenment and education, we find the weakness of our ancestors palpably predominating in the minds of the ignorant multitude, and spiritualism and magic looked upon by a certain number of persons as things existing and beyond the ken of men. Scientific inquiry — that broom that has swept away so many superstitions—has done its work well, and it cannot be long before the bigoted believers in the so-called " manifestation" of beings in another and unknown world will be looked upon, even by those whose belief in them is strongest, as the mechanical hanky-panky tricks of clever and astute conjurors, who feed upon the credulity and simplicity of their tools and followers.

Among the many subjects which were classed with the supernatural phenomena arising from the agency of unseen and spiritual powers, clairvoyance, or second sight, ranks conspicuous. It has been asserted, and by no mean authority, that second sight, or the belief in a secondary and unnatural sight, took its origin in the Scottish Highlands and Isles, where it was known by the name of *taisch*—a spectral or shadowy appearance ; but from the time when the Oracle at Delphi was sought by the populace, and when thousands were deluded by the mere mechanical tricks of a clever and crafty priesthood, even to this day, second sight has been looked upon as a spiritual visitation bestowed for some design upon persons who are made the instruments of Providence.

That at times men have had a prescience of what was to come cannot be denied, since murders and murderers have been undoubtedly discovered by means of visions which have been seen of the murderer, and the spot where the murder was committed.

Even Dr. Johnson, in his Journal in the Hebrides, where the belief in second sight prevailed to a great extent, hesitates whether to believe or deny ; and he asserts that he " came away at last only willing to believe." It is not my intention, nor have I the time or space, to enter fully into the subject of second sight of the past, but it is my intention to fully explain second sight, as it is understood now, and the reader will at once see how the old fabric of the superstitious ages melts into the most commonplace, and he will be perhaps vexed and annoyed to think that when witnessing a performance of second sight his mind misgave him, and he really was willing to believe.

The power, when blindfold, to discriminate things unseen, and promiscuously pick from a crowd of persons, and name miscellaneous and out-of-the-way articles, has been performed so cleverly that the greatest surprise and wonder has been created in the minds of even the most intelligent spectators. But like everything else to which the term magic has been and is applied, the wonderful and mysterious are only the simple and the commonplace, and the credulity of the audience leads to the merest trickery, to that marvel and wonder which surrounds a feat of legerdemain or clairvoyance ; but, as my readers will have already seen, as soon as second sight is explained, it will cause wonder no more.

There are always two persons engaged in an exhibition of clairvoyance—the person who asks what the article is and the person who answers. The whole secret of second sight lies in the method of asking what the article is. A sort of dictionary has to be learned by both, and this lesson is certainly not more difficult than that of the tragedian in learning his part ; but the audience are deceived by the simplicity of the questions asked. Although the words used by the questioner are nearly always the same, the position of the words is different. Hence, a different answer can be applied for every varying construction of the sentence.

When these different questions and their answers are thoroughly understood by the two accomplices, they can give an exhibition which to the uninitiated will appear marvellous and unaccountable. When the interrogator asks the question, '' Is this picture colored or plain ?'' the answer is '' Plain ;'' or if the question is, '' Is this picture plain or colored ?'' the answer is '' Colored.'' This is the whole ground-work of second sight, and in order more fully to illustrate this matter I will give a series of answers and questions which have been adopted by a number of English and American professors. In asking the color of an article, the question can be so differently constructed that each construction can bear the answer for every ordinary color.

What color is this ?   Black.
What is the color ?   Blue.
Tell me the color ?   Green.
Has it a color ?   White.
Any color ?   Orange, yellow.
Name the color ?   Brown.
Please name the color ?   Red.

These have only to be learned by two persons in combination, when they will be able to tell the color of any article. Should the exhibitor have an article of a mixed color, say, mauve, he first asks the question having red for the answer ; and then, before the reply can be given, again puts the query for blue. The clairvoyant thereby knowing it is a mixture of red and blue, he is able to know that mauve is the answer required. Again, in asking the nature of a stone set in a jewel the question may be thus arranged :

What is the stone ?   Topaz.
What stone is it ?   Jet.

Tell me the stone ?   Emerald.
Name the stone ?   Diamond.
Do you know the stone ?   Cornelian.
Any stone ?   Amethyst.

And so on *ad infinitum.*   In ascertaining the nature of a piece of
jewelry the questions may be put thus :

What is the metal ?   Gold.
What metal is it ?   Brass.
What metal ?   Silver.
Tell me the metal ?   Copper.
Name the metal ?   Iron ; steel.
Please name the metal ?   Bronze.
Can you tell me the metal ?   Tin.

The following questions, having replies for the usual articles found
upon persons assembled to witness a performance, may easily be
learned by a person gifted with a good memory, or by a person with
an ordinary memory by repeated application :

Name this ?   A pocket comb.
What have I here ?   A purse.
What is this ?   A toothpick.
This will puzzle you ?   Court plaster.
Speak loud ?   A letter.
Answer quickly ?   A handkerchief.
Has it a color ?   White.
Is it perfumed ?   Yes.
Tell me now ?   Keys.
Is this of any use ?   An almanac.
What is this for ?   To burn a cigar.
Do ladies use this ?   Yes ; a pincushion, needlecase.
Do you know this ?   A walking-stick.
Now, can you tell this ?   A pocket-book.
Would you like this ?   Yes ; a watch.
Do you admire this ?   A brooch.
Who gave me this ?   A lady—a bracelet.
What is in my hand ?   A pin.
Now, who gave me this ?   A gentleman—a chain.

What have I now ?   Money.

Now, what have I got ?   A sovereign.

Can you tell me again ?   A shilling.

Is this the same ?   Sixpence.

You say I have money ; but you don't say the kind ?   A florin.

You say I have money ; but you don't say its value ?   A half crown.

You say I have money ; but tell me its value ?   Ten shillings.

What is the value of the money ?   A penny.

I cannot hear you ?   A halfpenny.

I think I have given sufficient queries and answers to indicate the simplicity and the secret of second sight.   When all the particulars of the articles are required, although the questions may seem perplexing to the spectator, yet they are extremely simple to the person who knows each question and its reply by heart.

Here is an illustration of a complicated series of questions, and the reader will see at once that the answering is very simple :

What is in my hand ?   A pin.

What is the metal ?   Gold.

Any stone ?   Amethyst.

What have I now ?   Money.

You say I have money ; but you don't say the kind ?   A florin.

Can you tell me again ?   A shilling.

From the illustrations I have given above, the reader will perceive that, provided a large and well-selected assortment of questions, corresponding with replies, be agreed upon, and well known by the two confederates, almost any question may be answered and any article known, together with its properties, color, contents, etc.

Another exhibition of clairvoyance—the reading of writing sealed up and unopened—adds greatly to the mystery of the performance ; but how this is done can be easily explained.   Previous to going on the stage, a sentence is selected, and written in blacklead on a piece of paper.   During the performance similar pieces of paper are handed round to several of the audience, who are requested to write a sentence thereon.   These papers are sealed similarly to the prepared one, and placed in a hat.   The professor then pretends to select one at random, after having shaken up the papers ; but he really takes up the one he had already in his hand. The lady clairvoyant is then requested to read a sentence, which, of course, she can easily do. The paper is then handed to one of the audience and to their astonishment it is found to have been the actual sentence written. It will be understood that each writer of a sentence is ignorant of what another has written, and the given sentence is therefore thought to have been written by one of the audience. This suspicion may be heightened by the queer method of spelling, or the character of the caligraphy ; it may be made still more astounding by writing the sentence in a foreign language with a slight mistake in spelling, or grammar, upon which the clairvoyant can comment in her reply, and thus acquire a reputation for scholarly and linguistic attainments. The same means are resorted to in the adding up of a sum. The figures are all prepared behind the stage, and the *bona fide* sums given by the audience are never the ones answered by the clairvoyant. I think I have given, or I hope I have, a clear and full explanation of clairvoyance or second sight, and the reader may, by a little practice, become as perfect in this special branch of magic as the mysterious lady—Heller—Miss Anderson, Dr. Lynn, and a host of others, who have mystified and bewildered thousands of wondering spectators.

CHAPTER VII.

Spiritualism.

The belief in the materialization of spirits, and the visits of spiritual inhabitants of another world to the scene of their mortal sojourn for the sole object of giving specimens of their caligraphy on slates and ceilings, rapping and playing upon tambourines, sealed accordions, guitars, and so forth, affords another proof that there are no bounds to human credulity and stupidity.

A worthy doctor of philosophy, only recently deceased, said in my hearing, while speaking of the gross ignorance that prevailed among believers in spiritualism, that if a man stood in the middle of the road with a crowd of people round him, and asserted, with well-worded sentences and an apparent earnestness and belief on his own part, that two and two were five, he would find some among the crowd to believe him. Perhaps the doctor went a little too far in his observation, but it is, nevertheless, almost incredible that a large number of persons can be so bigoted and thick-headed as to persist in their belief in spiritualism when medium after medium has been most unequivocally found to be conjuror, trickster, and swindler. These conjurors and tricksters are not men who practise their art of deceiving on the stage in a legitimate manner, but they are men who pander to the credulity, bigotry, and fanaticism of the imbecile, obtuse, and weak-minded person who believe in spirit land, by claiming the power of recalling from that unknown region to which the soul is supposed to take its flight when it has shuffled off its mortal coil, those beings who have gone from earth never to return again, except by the agency of these mediums. In asserting their power of " calling up the spirits from the vasty deep," or from the sky, they offer as proof of their claim to be believed certain tests, which have been, and which I will show are, simply the hanky-panky tricks of the prestidigitateur and magician. The credulous followers of these mediums cannot or will not see the absurdity of bringing souls from the " world of spirits" merely to answer idiotic questions, and to perform such antics as even a wild and unrestrained boy would not be mad enough to do ; but they believe the assertions of the mediums simply because the tests which are applied to them consist of something more material and tangible than aërial nothings, and appear to be marvellous and beyond the power of the human mind to understand.

Have these spiritualists never witnessed the performance of a clever conjuror who confesses that all his tricks are worked by mechanical means and sleight of hand ? or have they never seen apparent wonders performed, the mystery of which they could not unravel ? They must have done so, and yet we have never once heard such men as Heller, Houdin, Professor Anderson, Maskelyne and Cooke, assert that their performances or manifestations were the works of materialized spirits.

One of the tests offered by the mediums is the rope-tying trick, made so famous by the Davenport Brothers. It has been clearly demonstrated that it was merely a trick. The medium has in his hand a coil of rope about twelve yards long. The lights are extinguished, and a few seconds afterward, when the gas is lighted, he is seen securely fastened to a chair, his hands tied, and the rope made fast between his wrists. One of the company is requested to examine the rope and seal the ends of the knot. The gas is again extinguished, and a tambourine is heard bounding about the room. A hand—and a very material hand—claps the faces of the nearest persons, hats are knocked off, a bell is rung, arms are pinched, and various other manifestations occur which fully convince the astonished devotees that some one—spirit or otherwise—is evidently giving free vent to a playful and mischievous disposition. The medium, of course, claims that these manifestations are performed by spirits summoned by him ; and he is believed, not because the spectators suppose that spirits could be so summoned and be made to manifest their presence, but that, because the medium is tied with a rope, the ends of which are so sealed as to prevent his getting free from the bondage into which the spirits have placed him, *he* cannot possibly be the one that played the tambourine, rung the bell, gave the blows, etc.—*ergo*, it must have been the spirits.

Now, had these faithful believers looked very carefully at the rope and the method of the tying, they would have discovered that the rope had previously been cut in halves, and then knotted with a fast knot in the middle. This knot is concealed by the medium before he binds himself, by holding it in his hand. The rope then, of course, looks like one continuous whole. When the gas is lowered, he places the two ends of the rope beneath him on the chair, and, in a manner which I can scarcely explain in writing or even by illustration, so binds himself, that by making a double running knot, and placing this double noose twice round his wrist, he can slip it, and thus free his hand at will. The knot may be concealed, because it is never touched or disturbed. When the room is again darkened, it is found to be a very easy matter for the medium to perform any of the usual manifestations.

Another test offered by a medium, and which was considered as convincing proof of the right of his claim of connection with the world of spirits, was the well-known sealed accordion test. The instrument was fast bound by tapes, and the tapes sealed at every note so as to prevent it being played in the ordinary way. As soon as the lights were out the accordion was heard to play, not too sweetly, but sufficiently well to show that the instrument was being manipulated. When the lights were again produced, the accordion was found just as it had been placed, fast bound by tapes, each note sealed, and the seals immaculate.

This trick may be performed by any of our readers without having the slightest introduction to the beings of another world. He has only to procure a small tube, place it in the valve-hole of the accordion, breath and blow into it alternately, and then by fingering the keys he will be able to produce precisely the same effect as our friends the mediums. In order to touch distant persons, or to make such things as guitars and tambourines play at different parts of the room, he has to conceal about him, or have hidden in some recess in the table or chair, a telescopic rod, extending several feet. To the end of this he fixes the tambourine or guitar, on the surface of which has been placed some phosphorus, and by waving the stick he makes it appear as if persons were floating over the heads of the company. The invisible hand is formed by a glove being fastened to the end of the tube. The glove is inflated or blown out through the tube, and when slapped on to the cheek of a person it has all the sensations of a cold hand striking the face. The glove covered with phosphorus and waved about is the mysterious hand, without any body, which caused so many to believe that a spirit was present.

At the end of this useful tube may also be fixed a reed trumpet or whistle, and by blowing through the tube sound can be evolved, and when the instrument is worked about in different directions a large but discordant band of spiritual musicians appear, to the materially and physically benighted listeners, to be in the room. To play the guitar, while floating in the air, seems a more difficult problem, but the reader will easily see how this is achieved. In the guitar is a musical box with a small piece of writing paper so placed as to touch the steel or vibrating tongues of the box, and this closely imitates the peculiar twang of the guitar.

When a medium, after having been caught in one or two of his performances, announces his intention of floating over the heads of the little world of spiritualists, they at once hold up their hands in silent admiration, and their belief in the invisible world becomes more vigorous. They then hasten to pay their guinea or two guineas to share in this manifestation of the spirit. The medium having called up the spirit from the "vasty deep," the room is darkened and a bull's-eye lantern is held at such a distance from the medium as to make his face appear vague and indistinct. He is then seen suddenly to rise, and in his aërial flight performs a beautiful curve. His face is sufficiently masked as to make the features indistinguishable ; but, at the same time, to make the audience fully assured that it is his face. The lantern is made to follow him, and in a moment the face is lost in darkness, but for one instant only, and then as the gas is lit the medium is seen with his toes just touching the platform, and his form descending to its ordinary upright position. Messrs. Maskelyne and Cooke and others have well shown that this floating in the air is one of the grossest deceptions ever offered to the most gullible of audiences. First, there is ready to hand a lay figure, got up to resemble the medium or professor. Hanging from the top of the stage are two cords, concealed from the audience. When the medium prepares for his flight the bull's-eye lantern is turned upon him, but the person holding the lantern, pretending that the focus is not altogether right, turns it away to arrange it, as it were. While this is being done, the medium quickly substitutes the lay figure. The ends of these cords are furnished with hooks, which are fastened on to the shoulders of the lay figure, and then the exhibitor by means of a pulley hauls the figure upward, the light being kept at such a distance as to just make the figure of the dummy visible, but totally unrecognizable. During one of the intervals of the lantern's wanderings the dummy is removed, and the medium is seen descending, by merely raising himself on his toes and lowering himself, and when the full light is upon him sinking on his knees.

In spite of the exposure of the tricks played by mediums, there are still persons to be found who really believe that the tambourines, accordions, guitars, etc., are played by spirit hands, and that beings from the invisible world make a special journey at every spiritual séance.

Messrs. Maskelyne and Cooke have, in their popular entertainment, done a great deal to destroy the belief in the spiritual world founded upon the tests offered by mediums, and have clearly shown that the tricks which the mediums assert can only be done by spiritual agency might be performed by any ingenious person.

Another trick which has been performed by Messrs. Maskelyne and Cooke is that known as the spiritual musical box. An oblong piece of glass is suspended by means of four cords hanging from the ceiling, and upon this glass is placed a musical box. At the word of command the box begins to play, and when desired by the exhibitor or one of the audience, it suddenly ceases. The effect is really marvellous, but the secret of the trick is very simple. In the box there is placed a balance lever, which, when the glass is in the slightest degree tilted, arrests the fly-fan, and thus prevents the machinery from moving. When the performer gives the word of command, the glass is made level, and, the fly fan being released, the machinery moves, and a tune is played. When commanded to stop, the cord on either side is slightly pulled, the balance lever drops, the fly fan is arrested, and the music ceases.

The writing by " spirits" on the ceiling is done in this way. The medium is bound, and when the room is lighted a written answer to a question asked is put upon the ceiling. The reader will have already guessed that this is performed by the medium by means of the telescopic tube, at the end of which he places a piece of chalk. He rubs the chalk on his head, to " show" that the spirits had raised him to the ceiling, as if he had performed the feat with his head. Another " crucial " test which these mediums offer is known as the

invisible writing. One of the company is asked to write a sentence or a number of figures upon a piece of paper. This paper is carefully folded, the lights are extinguished. In a few seconds they are again relighted, when the medium declares that the spirits have told him the contents of the paper, and he reads the sentences or tells the figures.

Again, the medium asks a gentleman to put the hands of a watch to any hour he chooses, and, when again the lights are lowered, he calls out the exact time to the exact minute. This all seems very mysterious and unaccountable, but I shall again show that we do not require spirit aid to perform these marvels. The medium has in his pocket a small phial containing phosphorus and oil ; and when this test is performed there is invariably a long cloth on the table. When the papers upon which the sentence or figures are written, or the watch, are placed on the table, the lights are lowered, and the performer stoops beneath the table, takes the paper or watch, opens the phial, from which a blue flame is emitted, and by this light he reads the sentence, or figures, or sees the time.

He replaces the articles, and can, of course, readily tell what he has read or seen.

The floating table has often been performed, but I have never attempted to do this spiritual manifestation. The medium generally has with him an accomplice, and they bind to their arms a flat iron rod, which terminates toward the wrist in a kind of hook concealed from the company by the cuffs of the shirt. The medium contrives to slip this hook under the edge of the table, as does also his confederate who sits opposite, while the dupe is sitting between. The annexed illustration will show the iron rod, and the method of fitting it beneath the table.

The reader will readily perceive that with the aid of these hooks the two persons can play all kinds of tricks with the table, making it go from side to side and glide from one part of the room to another.

There are other methods of tying besides those which I have already mentioned. Some mediums permit themselves to be tied by one of the audience. In this case the medium inflates his body and sits in such a position that all his muscles and limbs are distended. When he resumes his normal position the ropes become loose and he releases himself.

If there be any of my readers who have hitherto been inclined to believe in the professions of the medium, I hope that what I have said will open their eyes, and show them that the so-called materialization of spirits is purely and simply a myth, and that the mediums are nothing more nor less than clever but unprincipled conjurors.

CHAPTER VIII.

Parlor Magic.

The art of magic, as it is now understood, is no longer a secret and mystic profession ; it is a written art, and may be easily acquired by the clever mechanician, or any person having dexterous hands and a large amount of self-possession and impudence.   I say " impudence," because most of the best tricks are really so extremely simple that many persons of a timid or self-conscious disposition would feel ashamed to venture to perform them, in case of what they think must be inevitable detection and exposure.   But so blind is poor human nature that the clever conjuror can always select his man for " forcing a card upon him," even though he makes his dupe believe he has selected one at his own will and choice.   At the request of a large number of friends, I will conclude this volume by giving a few tricks which may be performed after a very little practice by anybody who will take a little trouble, and for the execution of which no, or very little, apparatus will be required—at any rate, only such as can be obtained either in any ordinary house, or at a very trifling expense. The task which I have set myself is not, as the reader might imagine, an easy one, for in endeavoring to give some tricks which have not before been already fully explained in books published on the subject, I find that there is scarcely a parlor trick which has not already been explained.   Therefore, to give some tricks that have never yet been exposed is really a very difficult and almost impossible task.   However, I have done my best, and the following little deceptions which the amateur conjuror may safely perform, will enable him to give a capital evening's entertainment to his friends or family circle.   I would just add one word before quitting the subject of magic and conjuring. My object in the foregoing chapters was to show the reader, first, that the art of magic is merely the art of a very clever illusionist, who, by swiftness of execution and a thorough knowledge of the laws of mechanics and optics, can make his audience *deceive themselves ;* secondly, to afford some entertainment to my readers ; and, thirdly, to set the ingenious at work to solve the mysteries of the art upon the basis I have given in these chapters. I venture to think, from the observations I have heard, that all these objects have been attained. And now for a few parlor tricks.

I. A SURPRISE.—You produce a bottle, which you ask a person to hold, inviting him to partake of a glass of the fluid contents. You give him a glass, and when he attempts to pour it out, lo ! he finds that in a few seconds the contents has frozen ! To perform this you must previously make a saturated solution of sulphate of soda and hot water, and fill therewith a clean white bottle, taking care to cork the bottle while the liquid is hot. The liquid remains in a fluid state so long as the bottle is corked. You show that the bottle contains a liquid, and in handing it to the person be careful to take out the cork. In order to give the preparation time to solidify, pretend to be looking about for a tumbler, and make some remarks about a sudden chill ; or you can feel the hand holding the glass, and suggest that it is very cold. In the meantime, the air acting upon the solution has caused it to become fixed and immovable, and when the person attempts to pour it out, he finds it impossible to do so.

II. INDIAN SAND TRICK.—This trick has been made famous by the Hindoos, who for many centuries contrived to retain the secret. It ᵔonsists of placing ordinary sand in a basin full of water, stirring the water and taking out the sand in handfuls, perfectly dry. It need scarcely be said that without previous preparation it is impossible to effect this. Take two pounds of fine silver sand, place it in a frying-fan, and heat well over a clear fire. When the sand is thoroughly heated place a small piece of grease—the composition of a paraffin candle preferred—among the sand, stirring it well up to get it thoroughly mixed. Then let the sand get cold. You place into a basin of cold water two or three handfuls, then stir the water well. It will be found that the sand repels the water, and can be drawn out perfectly dry. It is very important that only a small portion of grease be used, so that when you hand round the sand for examination its presence may not be observed.

III. The " Q " Trick.—This is a very simple and a very telling trick for the parlor. You take a number of coins or counters, and form them into a circle with a tail to represent a Q, as shown in the sketch annexed. You then ask a person to think of a number, and to count that number, commencing from the tail of the Q at B, and counting round the circle. When he has finished he is to count the number back again, but instead of counting the tail of the Q to go

round the circle, and you promise to tell him every time at which counter or coin he left off counting. In order that you shall not see him count, you leave the room while he does so. Supposing he selects the number 6 ; he commences to count from B, and leaves off at C ; he then counts again and leaves off at A. Now, while there are three counters in the tail of the Q, whatever number he thinks off, he will always stop at A ; so all you have to do is to count the number of counters or coins there are in the tail, and the same number in the circle will always be the coin last counted. You must be careful, when repeating the trick, to add one or two, or take one away from the tail, as always fixing upon the same counter would perhaps expose the trick.

IV. The Bleeding Thumb.—This is a very effective trick, but I am afraid, unless my pupil has some little self-sacrifice, and does not mind enduring a trifling pain in order to amuse his audience, this trick will never be performed. Previous to doing it, you puncture your thumb with a needle in one or two places, near the nail. You then assert that you will cut open your thumb and instantly heal it. You take a handkerchief and tightly bind the thumb therewith, keeping the thumb perfectly straight. You ask for a knife—the sharper the better—and, having obtained one, you pretend to cut the thumb, which you bend. This causes the blood to flow from the punctures. The blood spreads along the knife, which looks as though it had cut almost through the thumb. You then wipe the blood away, straightening the thumb, and show that there is no sign of wound or blood.

V. The Marked Florin in Oranges.—Previous to performing this trick, get two florins exactly alike, and mark them both similarly.

Then get two oranges and cut a slit in each. Place them on the table after you have put one of the marked florins inside one of them. Then borrow from the audience a florin, and request the owner of the florin to mark it. You then ask a person in another part of the room to hold it, but giving him *your* marked florin instead of the borrowed one. Then you go to the table and slip into the other orange the borrowed florin. You ask your audience in which orange they would like the marked coin to be found, remembering that as you face the audience it does not matter which they say—right or left—as your right is their left, and their left your right. Whichever orange they ask for, take the one containing *your* marked florin. You then ask the party holding the florin if he would be sure to know it again. Then give him the orange to hold on the point of the knife ; and in taking the florin from him conceal it in your hand, and say that you will cause it to pass into the orange which he holds. On cutting the orange open he, of course, finds your marked florin, which, on examination, he asserts to be the one held by him. Then say that it would have been totally indifferent which orange was selected ; and give the other orange to the person who lent the florin to hold. You then take *your* marked florin and say that you will cause it to pass in the orange he holds in his hand ; and request him to cut it open. He does so, and then perceives his own marked coin in the centre.

VI. The Chinese Pictures.—This is a very curious and surprising trick. You prepare a number of plain white sheets of paper, intermixed with which are several sheets on which are drawn various Chinese pictures. In showing these sheets to the audience, you take care not to draw out any of the pictures, but only the blank sheets. You then take a jug, having an even top, filled with water, placing the sheets on the top You then state that the water in the jug has the peculiar quality of drawing, but having been brought from China, can only draw Chinese sketches. You then dexterously reverse the jug, the sheets preventing the water from flowing out. After a few moments you draw out the sketches, and scattering them among the audience, you cause them to think that they have been drawn on the blank sheets. This is a very old trick of the Chinese, who first performed it. You can easily learn to tell which are blank sheets and which are the pictures by a simple mark placed on the top or in the corner of the latter.

VII. BAUTIER'S GREAT INK-AND-WATER TRICK.—This trick, first introduced by Bautier, at the Egyptian Hall, London, has, to the best of my belief, never before been explained. It is a remarkably clever deception, and, when dexterously performed, defies detection. It consists in showing a decanter filled with ink and another with water, and while each decanter is held by one of the audience, making the contents of each change places, the ink going into the one containing water, while the pure liquid is found in the one in which the ink was seen. Take two water bottles or decanters, and in one place a tassel of black fleecy wool, just long enough to touch the bottom of the bottle. The tassel must be tied by a knot at the top, and a small piece of string just hanging over the mouth of the bottle, attached to the knot. Then fill the glass with water. The bottle thus prepared looks at a short distance like a bottle of ink, and you have only to tell your audience that it is so to make them believe it. This, I am afraid, is inculcating in the mind of the reader the principle of false-hood—at least Mrs. Grundy might say so ; but a professor of magic is doing nothing but telling " crammers" from the commencement to the conclusion of his entertainment. Perhaps this is the reason why it is called the " black art," and was the cause of so much per-secution in the " good old days," when all was so pure and so virtu-ous, as the lovers of the *beaux temps* would have us believe. But pardon this digression. In the other bottle place a weak solution of the proto-sulphate of iron, about a half ounce to about a pint and a half of water. Have ready a bit of pyrogallic acid—about two thirds of a tea-spoonful, wrapped in a small piece of blotting-paper that has been blacked with ink. Having completed these arrangements, and asserted that you have on the table a bottle containing water and another ink, you borrow a handkerchief, with which you cover the bottle containing the clear solution, and in doing so you slip into it the pyrogallic acid ; and in handing the bottle to one of the audience to hold you give the contents a little imperceptible shaking. You then take another handkerchief and place it over the other bottle, which you hand to a person to hold. You then command the con-tents of each bottle to change places. Then, in removing the handkerchief from the ink bottle, you clutch the piece of string and quickly pull out the black wool and throw the handkerchief out of sight, showing the bottle to contain only water. You then ask the person holding the other bottle to remove the covering, when the fluid will be found to be " as black as night." This trick always causes the greatest astonishment.

VIII. CARRYING FIRE IN THE HANDS.—In performing this extremely simple trick, the audience must not be informed of what it is your intention to do, but it should be done when there is any delay in your other tricks, or some hitch occurs in getting anything you require, and which happens not to be at hand. For filling up a gap in a performance, it will be found extremely useful. In giving an entertainment of magic, always have on your table two burning candles ; they are both useful and ornamental, and serve to dispel any idea of the spectators that you cannot perform your tricks in a full light. You go to the table, having previously concealed a piece of paper in your hand between the two middle fingers, and place your hands around the flame, saying it is perfectly possible to retain the heat in the hand, and even carry the flame from one candle to another. You then blow out one of the candles, and quickly place your hands round the other, set fire to the paper in your hand, blow out the candle, quickly light the first and then the second, smothering the flame of the paper in your hand. This trick, when well done, causes great astonishment and surprise.

A CATALOGUE OF SELECTED DOVER BOOKS
IN ALL FIELDS OF INTEREST

A CATALOGUE OF SELECTED DOVER BOOKS
IN ALL FIELDS OF INTEREST

LEATHER TOOLING AND CARVING, Chris H. Groneman. One of few books concentrating on tooling and carving, with complete instructions and grid designs for 39 projects ranging from bookmarks to bags. 148 illustrations. 111pp. 7⅞ x 10.
23061-9 Pa. $2.50

THE CODEX NUTTALL, A PICTURE MANUSCRIPT FROM ANCIENT MEXICO, as first edited by Zelia Nuttall. Only inexpensive edition, in full color, of a pre-Columbian Mexican (Mixtec) book. 88 color plates show kings, gods, heroes, temples, sacrifices. New explanatory, historical introduction by Arthur G. Miller. 96pp. 11⅜ x 8½.
23168-2 Pa. $7.50

AMERICAN PRIMITIVE PAINTING, Jean Lipman. Classic collection of an enduring American tradition. 109 plates, 8 in full color—portraits, landscapes, Biblical and historical scenes, etc., showing family groups, farm life, and so on. 80pp. of lucid text. 8⅜ x 11¼.
22815-0 Pa. $4.00

WILL BRADLEY: HIS GRAPHIC ART, edited by Clarence P. Hornung. Striking collection of work by foremost practitioner of Art Nouveau in America: posters, cover designs, sample pages, advertisements, other illustrations. 97 plates, including 8 in full color and 19 in two colors. 97pp. 9⅜ x 12¼.
20701-3 Pa. $4.00
22120-2 Clothbd. $10.00

THE UNDERGROUND SKETCHBOOK OF JAN FAUST, Jan Faust. 101 bitter, horrifying, black-humorous, penetrating sketches on sex, war, greed, various liberations, etc. Sometimes sexual, but not pornographic. Not for prudish. 101pp. 6½ x 9¼.
22740-5 Pa. $1.50

THE GIBSON GIRL AND HER AMERICA, Charles Dana Gibson. 155 finest drawings of effervescent world of 1900-1910: the Gibson Girl and her loves, amusements, adventures, Mr. Pipp, etc. Selected by E. Gillon; introduction by Henry Pitz. 144pp. 8¼ x 11⅜.
21986-0 Pa. $3.50

STAINED GLASS CRAFT, J.A.F. Divine, G. Blachford. One of the very few books that tell the beginner exactly what he needs to know: planning cuts, making shapes, avoiding design weaknesses, fitting glass, etc. 93 illustrations. 115pp.
22812-6 Pa. $1.50

MANUAL OF THE TREES OF NORTH AMERICA, Charles S. Sargent. The basic survey of every native tree and tree-like shrub, 717 species in all. Extremely full descriptions, information on habitat, growth, locales, economics, etc. Necessary to every serious tree lover. Over 100 finding keys. 783 illustrations. Total of 986pp.
20277-1, 20278-X Pa., Two vol. set $9.00

BIRDS OF THE NEW YORK AREA, John Bull. Indispensable guide to more than 400 species within a hundred-mile radius of Manhattan. Information on range, status, breeding, migration, distribution trends, etc. Foreword by Roger Tory Peterson. 17 drawings; maps. 540pp.
23222-0 Pa. $6.00

THE SEA-BEACH AT EBB-TIDE, Augusta Foote Arnold. Identify hundreds of marine plants and animals: algae, seaweeds, squids, crabs, corals, etc. Descriptions cover food, life cycle, size, shape, habitat. Over 600 drawings. 490pp.
21949-6 Pa. $5.00

THE MOTH BOOK, William J. Holland. Identify more than 2,000 moths of North America. General information, precise species descriptions. 623 illustrations plus 48 color plates show almost all species, full size. 1968 edition. Still the basic book. Total of 551pp. 6½ x 9¼.
21948-8 Pa. $6.00

AN INTRODUCTION TO THE REPTILES AND AMPHIBIANS OF THE UNITED STATES, Percy A. Morris. All lizards, crocodiles, turtles, snakes, toads, frogs; life history, identification, habits, suitability as pets, etc. Non-technical, but sound and broad. 130 photos. 253pp.
22982-3 Pa. $3.00

OLD NEW YORK IN EARLY PHOTOGRAPHS, edited by Mary Black. Your only chance to see New York City as it was 1853-1906, through 196 wonderful photographs from N.Y. Historical Society. Great Blizzard, Lincoln's funeral procession, great buildings. 228pp. 9 x 12.
22907-6 Pa. $6.00

THE AMERICAN REVOLUTION, A PICTURE SOURCEBOOK, John Grafton. Wonderful Bicentennial picture source, with 411 illustrations (contemporary and 19th century) showing battles, personalities, maps, events, flags, posters, soldier's life, ships, etc. all captioned and explained. A wonderful browsing book, supplement to other historical reading. 160pp. 9 x 12.
23226-3 Pa. $4.00

PERSONAL NARRATIVE OF A PILGRIMAGE TO AL-MADINAH AND MECCAH, Richard Burton. Great travel classic by remarkably colorful personality. Burton, disguised as a Moroccan, visited sacred shrines of Islam, narrowly escaping death. Wonderful observations of Islamic life, customs, personalities. 47 illustrations. Total of 959pp.
21217-3, 21218-1 Pa., Two vol. set $10.00

INCIDENTS OF TRAVEL IN CENTRAL AMERICA, CHIAPAS, AND YUCATAN, John L. Stephens. Almost single-handed discovery of Maya culture; exploration of ruined cities, monuments, temples; customs of Indians. 115 drawings. 892pp.
22404-X, 22405-8 Pa., Two vol. set $8.00

THE MAGIC MOVING PICTURE BOOK, Bliss, Sands & Co. The pictures in this book move! Volcanoes erupt, a house burns, a serpentine dancer wiggles her way through a number. By using a specially ruled acetate screen provided, you can obtain these and 15 other startling effects. Originally "The Motograph Moving Picture Book." 32pp. 8¼ x 11.
23224-7 Pa. $1.75

STRING FIGURES AND HOW TO MAKE THEM, Caroline F. Jayne. Fullest, clearest instructions on string figures from around world: Eskimo, Navajo, Lapp, Europe, more. Cats cradle, moving spear, lightning, stars. Introduction by A.C. Haddon. 950 illustrations. 407pp.
20152-X Pa. $3.50

PAPER FOLDING FOR BEGINNERS, William D. Murray and Francis J. Rigney. Clearest book on market for making origami sail boats, roosters, frogs that move legs, cups, bonbon boxes. 40 projects. More than 275 illustrations. Photographs. 94pp.
20713-7 Pa. $1.25

INDIAN SIGN LANGUAGE, William Tomkins. Over 525 signs developed by Sioux, Blackfoot, Cheyenne, Arapahoe and other tribes. Written instructions and diagrams: how to make words, construct sentences. Also 290 pictographs of Sioux and Ojibway tribes. 111pp. 6⅛ x 9¼.
22029-X Pa. $1.50

BOOMERANGS: HOW TO MAKE AND THROW THEM, Bernard S. Mason. Easy to make and throw, dozens of designs: cross-stick, pinwheel, boomabird, tumblestick, Australian curved stick boomerang. Complete throwing instructions. All safe. 99pp.
23028-7 Pa. $1.75

25 KITES THAT FLY, Leslie Hunt. Full, easy to follow instructions for kites made from inexpensive materials. Many novelties. Reeling, raising, designing your own. 70 illustrations. 110pp.
22550-X Pa. $1.25

TRICKS AND GAMES ON THE POOL TABLE, Fred Herrmann. 79 tricks and games, some solitaires, some for 2 or more players, some competitive; mystifying shots and throws, unusual carom, tricks involving cork, coins, a hat, more. 77 figures. 95pp.
21814-7 Pa. $1.25

WOODCRAFT AND CAMPING, Bernard S. Mason. How to make a quick emergency shelter, select woods that will burn immediately, make do with limited supplies, etc. Also making many things out of wood, rawhide, bark, at camp. Formerly titled Woodcraft. 295 illustrations. 580pp.
21951-8 Pa. $4.00

AN INTRODUCTION TO CHESS MOVES AND TACTICS SIMPLY EXPLAINED, Leonard Barden. Informal intermediate introduction: reasons for moves, tactics, openings, traps, positional play, endgame. Isolates patterns. 102pp. USO 21210-6 Pa. $1.35

LASKER'S MANUAL OF CHESS, Dr. Emanuel Lasker. Great world champion offers very thorough coverage of all aspects of chess. Combinations, position play, openings, endgame, aesthetics of chess, philosophy of struggle, much more. Filled with analyzed games. 390pp.
20640-8 Pa. $4.00

HOUDINI ON MAGIC, Harold Houdini. Edited by Walter Gibson, Morris N. Young. How he escaped; exposés of fake spiritualists; instructions for eye-catching tricks; other fascinating material by and about greatest magician. 155 illustrations. 280pp.　　20384-0 Pa. $2.75

HANDBOOK OF THE NUTRITIONAL CONTENTS OF FOOD, U.S. Dept. of Agriculture. Largest, most detailed source of food nutrition information ever prepared. Two mammoth tables: one measuring nutrients in 100 grams of edible portion; the other, in edible portion of 1 pound as purchased. Originally titled Composition of Foods. 190pp. 9 x 12.　　21342-0 Pa. $4.00

COMPLETE GUIDE TO HOME CANNING, PRESERVING AND FREEZING, U.S. Dept. of Agriculture. Seven basic manuals with full instructions for jams and jellies; pickles and relishes; canning fruits, vegetables, meat; freezing anything. Really good recipes, exact instructions for optimal results. Save a fortune in food. 156 illustrations. 214pp. $6\frac{1}{8}$ x $9\frac{1}{4}$.　　22911-4 Pa. $2.50

THE BREAD TRAY, Louis P. De Gouy. Nearly every bread the cook could buy or make: bread sticks of Italy, fruit breads of Greece, glazed rolls of Vienna, everything from corn pone to croissants. Over 500 recipes altogether. including buns, rolls, muffins, scones, and more. 463pp.　　23000-7 Pa. $3.50

CREATIVE HAMBURGER COOKERY, Louis P. De Gouy. 182 unusual recipes for casseroles, meat loaves and hamburgers that turn inexpensive ground meat into memorable main dishes: Arizona chili burgers, burger tamale pie, burger stew, burger corn loaf, burger wine loaf, and more. 120pp.　　23001-5 Pa. $1.75

LONG ISLAND SEAFOOD COOKBOOK, J. George Frederick and Jean Joyce. Probably the best American seafood cookbook. Hundreds of recipes. 40 gourmet sauces, 123 recipes using oysters alone! All varieties of fish and seafood amply represented. 324pp.　　22677-8 Pa. $3.50

THE EPICUREAN: A COMPLETE TREATISE OF ANALYTICAL AND PRACTICAL STUDIES IN THE CULINARY ART, Charles Ranhofer. Great modern classic. 3,500 recipes from master chef of Delmonico's, turn-of-the-century America's best restaurant. Also explained, many techniques known only to professional chefs. 775 illustrations. 1183pp. $6\frac{5}{8}$ x 10.　　22680-8 Clothbd. $22.50

THE AMERICAN WINE COOK BOOK, Ted Hatch. Over 700 recipes: old favorites livened up with wine plus many more: Czech fish soup, quince soup, sauce Perigueux, shrimp shortcake, filets Stroganoff, cordon bleu goulash, jambonneau, wine fruit cake, more. 314pp.　　22796-0 Pa. $2.50

DELICIOUS VEGETARIAN COOKING, Ivan Baker. Close to 500 delicious and varied recipes: soups, main course dishes (pea, bean, lentil, çheese, vegetable, pasta, and egg dishes), savories, stews, whole-wheat breads and cakes, more. 168pp.　　USO 22834-7 Pa. $1.75

DECORATIVE ALPHABETS AND INITIALS, edited by Alexander Nesbitt. 91 complete alphabets (medieval to modern), 3924 decorative initials, including Victorian novelty and Art Nouveau. 192pp. 7¾ x 10¾. 20544-4 Pa. $4.00

CALLIGRAPHY, Arthur Baker. Over 100 original alphabets from the hand of our greatest living calligrapher: simple, bold, fine-line, richly ornamented, etc. —all strikingly original and different, a fusion of many influences and styles. 155pp. 11⅜ x 8¼. 22895-9 Pa. $4.50

MONOGRAMS AND ALPHABETIC DEVICES, edited by Hayward and Blanche Cirker. Over 2500 combinations, names, crests in very varied styles: script engraving, ornate Victorian, simple Roman, and many others. 226pp. 8⅛ x 11.

22330-2 Pa. $5.00

THE BOOK OF SIGNS, Rudolf Koch. Famed German type designer renders 493 symbols: religious, alchemical, imperial, runes, property marks, etc. Timeless. 104pp. 6⅛ x 9¼. 20162-7 Pa. $1.75

200 DECORATIVE TITLE PAGES, edited by Alexander Nesbitt. 1478 to late 1920's. Baskerville, Dürer, Beardsley, W. Morris, Pyle, many others in most varied techniques. For posters, programs, other uses. 222pp. 8⅜ x 11¼. 21264-5 Pa. **$5.00**

DICTIONARY OF AMERICAN PORTRAITS, edited by Hayward and Blanche Cirker. 4000 important Americans, earliest times to 1905, mostly in clear line. Politicians, writers, soldiers, scientists, inventors, industrialists, Indians, Blacks, women, outlaws, etc. Identificatory information. 756pp. 9¼ x 12¾. 21823-6 Clothbd. $30.00

ART FORMS IN NATURE, Ernst Haeckel. Multitude of strangely beautiful natural forms: Radiolaria, Foraminifera, jellyfishes, fungi, turtles, bats, etc. All 100 plates of the 19th century evolutionist's Kunstformen der Natur (1904). 100pp. 9⅜ x 12¼. 22987-4 Pa. $4.00

DECOUPAGE: THE BIG PICTURE SOURCEBOOK, Eleanor Rawlings. Make hundreds of beautiful objects, over 550 florals, animals, letters, shells, period costumes, frames, etc. selected by foremost practitioner. Printed on one side of page. 8 color plates. Instructions. 176pp. 9³⁄₁₆ x 12¼. 23182-8 Pa. $5.00

AMERICAN FOLK DECORATION, Jean Lipman, Eve Meulendyke. Thorough coverage of all aspects of wood, tin, leather, paper, cloth decoration — scapes, humans, trees, flowers, geometrics — and how to make them. Full instructions. 233 illustrations, 5 in color. 163pp. 8⅜ x 11¼. 22217-9 Pa. $3.95

WHITTLING AND WOODCARVING, E.J. Tangerman. Best book on market; clear, full. If you can cut a potato, you can carve toys, puzzles, chains, caricatures, masks, patterns, frames, decorate surfaces, etc. Also covers serious wood sculpture. Over 200 photos. 293pp. 20965-2 Pa. $3.00

SLEEPING BEAUTY, illustrated by Arthur Rackham. Perhaps the fullest, most delightful version ever, told by C.S. Evans. Rackham's best work. 49 illustrations. 110pp. 7⅞ x 10¾.   22756-1 Pa. $2.00

THE WONDERFUL WIZARD OF OZ, L. Frank Baum. Facsimile in full color of America's finest children's classic. Introduction by Martin Gardner. 143 illustrations by W.W. Denslow. 267pp.   20691-2 Pa. $3.00

GOOPS AND HOW TO BE THEM, Gelett Burgess. Classic tongue-in-cheek masquerading as etiquette book. 87 verses, 170 cartoons as Goops demonstrate virtues of table manners, neatness, courtesy, more. 88pp. 6½ x 9¼.
22233-0 Pa. $2.00

THE BROWNIES, THEIR BOOK, Palmer Cox. Small as mice, cunning as foxes, exuberant, mischievous, Brownies go to zoo, toy shop, seashore, circus, more. 24 verse adventures. 266 illustrations. 144pp. 6⅝ x 9¼.   21265-3 Pa. $2.50

BILLY WHISKERS: THE AUTOBIOGRAPHᴵ OF A GOAT, Frances Trego Montgomery. Escapades of that rambunctious goat. Favorite from turn of the century America. 24 illustrations. 259pp.   22345-0 Pa. $2.75

THE ROCKET BOOK, Peter Newell. Fritz, janitor's kid, sets off rocket in basement of apartment house; an ingenious hole punched through every page traces course of rocket. 22 duotone drawings, verses. 48pp. 6⅞ x 8⅜.   22044-3 Pa. $1.50

PECK'S BAD BOY AND HIS PA, George W. Peck. Complete double-volume of great American childhood classic. Hennery's ingenious pranks against outraged pomposity of pa and the grocery man. 97 illustrations. Introduction by E.F. Bleiler. 347pp.   20497-9 Pa. $2.50

THE TALE OF PETER RABBIT, Beatrix Potter. The inimitable Peter's terrifying adventure in Mr. McGregor's garden, with all 27 wonderful, full-color Potter illustrations. 55pp. 4¼ x 5½.   USO 22827-4 Pa. $1.00

THE TALE OF MRS. TIGGY-WINKLE, Beatrix Potter. Your child will love this story about a very special hedgehog and all 27 wonderful, full-color Potter illustrations. 57pp. 4¼ x 5½.   USO 20546-0 Pa. $1.00

THE TALE OF BENJAMIN BUNNY, Beatrix Potter. Peter Rabbit's cousin coaxes him back into Mr. McGregor's garden for a whole new set of adventures. A favorite with children. All 27 full-color illustrations. 59pp. 4¼ x 5½.
USO 21102-9 Pa. $1.00

THE MERRY ADVENTURES OF ROBIN HOOD, Howard Pyle. Facsimile of original (1883) edition, finest modern version of English outlaw's adventures. 23 illustrations by Pyle. 296pp. 6½ x 9¼.   22043-5 Pa. $4.00

TWO LITTLE SAVAGES, Ernest Thompson Seton. Adventures of two boys who lived as Indians; explaining Indian ways, woodlore, pioneer methods. 293 illustrations. 286pp.   20985-7 Pa. $3.00

JEWISH GREETING CARDS, Ed Sibbett, Jr. 16 cards to cut and color. Three say "Happy Chanukah," one "Happy New Year," others have no message, show stars of David, Torahs, wine cups, other traditional themes. 16 envelopes. 8¼ x 11.
23225-5 Pa. $2.00

AUBREY BEARDSLEY GREETING CARD BOOK, Aubrey Beardsley. Edited by Theodore Menten. 16 elegant yet inexpensive greeting cards let you combine your own sentiments with subtle Art Nouveau lines. 16 different Aubrey Beardsley designs that you can color or not, as you wish. 16 envelopes. 64pp. 8¼ x 11.
23173-9 Pa. $2.00

RECREATIONS IN THE THEORY OF NUMBERS, Albert Beiler. Number theory, an inexhaustible source of puzzles, recreations, for beginners and advanced. Divisors, perfect numbers. scales of notation, etc. 349pp.
21096-0 Pa. $4.00

AMUSEMENTS IN MATHEMATICS, Henry E. Dudeney. One of largest puzzle collections, based on algebra, arithmetic, permutations, probability, plane figure dissection, properties of numbers, by one of world's foremost puzzlists. Solutions. 450 illustrations. 258pp.
20473-1 Pa. $3.00

MATHEMATICS, MAGIC AND MYSTERY, Martin Gardner. Puzzle editor for Scientific American explains math behind: card tricks, stage mind reading, coin and match tricks, counting out games, geometric dissections. Probability, sets, theory of numbers, clearly explained. Plus more than 400 tricks, guaranteed to work. 135 illustrations. 176pp.
20335-2 Pa. $2.00

BEST MATHEMATICAL PUZZLES OF SAM LOYD, edited by Martin Gardner. Bizarre, original, whimsical puzzles by America's greatest puzzler. From fabulously rare Cyclopedia, including famous 14-15 puzzles, the Horse of a Different Color, 115 more. Elementary math. 150 illustrations. 167pp.
20498-7 Pa. $2.50

MATHEMATICAL PUZZLES FOR BEGINNERS AND ENTHUSIASTS, Geoffrey Mott-Smith. 189 puzzles from easy to difficult involving arithmetic, logic, algebra, properties of digits, probability. Explanation of math behind puzzles. 135 illustrations. 248pp.
20198-8 Pa. $2.75

BIG BOOK OF MAZES AND LABYRINTHS, Walter Shepherd. Classical, solid, and ripple mazes; short path and avoidance labyrinths; more — 50 mazes and labyrinths in all. 12 other figures. Full solutions. 112pp. 8⅛ x 11.
22951-3 Pa. $2.00

COIN GAMES AND PUZZLES, Maxey Brooke. 60 puzzles, games and stunts — from Japan, Korea, Africa and the ancient world, by Dudeney and the other great puzzlers, as well as Maxey Brooke's own creations. Full solutions. 67 illustrations. 94pp.
22893-2 Pa. $1.50

HAND SHADOWS TO BE THROWN UPON THE WALL, Henry Bursill. Wonderful Victorian novelty tells how to make flying birds, dog, goose, deer, and 14 others. 32pp. 6½ x 9¼.
21779-5 Pa. $1.25